The New Edinburgh History of Scotland

VOLUME I

From Caledonia to Pictland

The New Edinburgh History of Scotland

General editor: Roger Mason, *University of St Andrews*

Advisory editors: Dauvit Broun, *University of Glasgow*; Iain Hutchison, *University of Stirling*; Norman Macdougall, *University of St Andrews*; Nicholas Phillipson, *University of Edinburgh*

From Caledonia to Pictland
Scotland to 795

James E. Fraser

Edinburgh University Press

© James E. Fraser, 2009

Edinburgh University Press Ltd
22 George Square, Edinburgh
www.euppublishing.com

Reprinted 2009, 2010, 2012, 2014

Typeset in 11/13 Ehrhardt
by Servis Filmsetting Ltd, Stockport, Cheshire, and
printed and bound in Great Britain by
CPI Antony Rowe, Chippenham and Eastbourne

A CIP record for this book is available from the British Library

ISBN 978 0 7486 1231 4 (hardback)
ISBN 978 0 7486 1232 1 (paperback)

The right of James E. Fraser
to be identified as author of this work
has been asserted in accordance with
the Copyright, Designs and Patents Act 1988.

Published with the support of the Edinburgh University
Scholarly Publishing Initiatives Fund.

Publisher's acknowledgement
Edinburgh University Press thanks Mercat Press, publishers of
the *Edinburgh History of Scotland*, for permission to use *The New
Edinburgh History of Scotland* as the title for this ten-volume series.

Contents

Maps and Genealogical Tables

Acknowledgements

I am grateful to the series editors, and to Katherine Forsyth, for the opportunity to contribute to the New Edinburgh History. It arose in part from the successful completion of my doctoral dissertation, parts of which form the spines of Chapter 3 and Chapters 5–9; I was fortunate then, and remain so, to have benefited from the advice, encouragement and insights of my supervisors and examiners.

At a late stage, it was decided that, apart from its several maps and numerous genealogical tables, the book would not be furnished with illustrations. The period under investigation has been so comprehensively and wonderfully illustrated already in a number of recent publications, that any attempt here would have seemed perfunctory and redundant. Readers with limited access to these works will find many relevant illustrations on the Web.

The personal and professional journeys brought to an end by the completion of this book were made easier by the supreme collegiality of many colleagues. Dauvit Broun, Thomas Owen Clancy, Jonathan Davies, Nicholas Evans, Fraser Hunter, Ian Ralston and Alex Woolf provided advance sight of forthcoming research. Nick Evans's unpublished doctoral work has been indispensable in confirming and correcting my own deductions about the AD dating of events recorded in the Irish chronicles, as well as alerting me to others. It must be stressed, however, that his endorsement of my dates, some of which represent my own decisions, cannot be assumed. Alex Woolf provided advance proofs of the second volume of the present series, and read my own text while it was with the editors. Apart from some minor changes, where consistency seemed particularly desirable, whatever may be complementary between the two volumes is fortuitous rather than by design.

Having been widowed in the course of writing the book, my colleagues have been an indispensable support in many other, more profound ways. To a woman and man they rose to the occasion with great humanity, and I am grateful to them all. None of them is reduced in my esteem if I feel compelled to register especial thanks to Cordelia Beattie, Donald Bloxham, Steve Boardman, William Gillies, Gilbert Márkus, Donald Meek, Ian Ralston, Katie Stevenson, Christina Strauch, Simon Taylor and Alex Woolf. Of course, I appreciate the steadfast and ongoing support of my family and friends too numerous to mention. This book could not have been completed without them.

General Editor's Preface

The purpose of the New Edinburgh History of Scotland is to provide up-to-date and accessible narrative accounts of the Scottish past. Its authors will make full use of the explosion of scholarly research that has taken place over the last three decades, and do so in a way that is sensitive to Scotland's regional diversity as well as to the British, European and transoceanic worlds of which Scotland has always been an integral part.

Chronology is fundamental to understanding change over time and Scotland's political development will provide the backbone of the narrative and the focus of analysis and explanation. The New Edinburgh History will tell the story of Scotland as a political entity, but will be sensitive to broader social, cultural and religious change and informed by a richly textured understanding of the totality and diversity of the Scots' historical experience. Yet to talk of the Scots – or the Scottish nation – is often misleading. Local loyalty and regional diversity have more frequently characterised Scotland than any perceived sense of 'national' solidarity. Scottish identity has seldom been focused primarily, let alone exclusively, on the 'nation'. The modern discourse of nationhood offers what is often an inadequate and inappropriate vocabulary in which to couch Scotland's history. The authors in this series will show that there are other and more revealing ways of capturing the distinctiveness of Scottish experience.

It is fitting enough that the first volume in this series, dealing with the very earliest peoples who inhabited what was to become Scotland, should be graced on its cover by an image of Caledonia. Taken from William Hole's famous frieze in the Scottish National Portrait Gallery, the dominant figure of Caledonia is portrayed drawing back the curtain on the Scottish past, illuminating the grand processional pageant that unfolds round the walls of the gallery's ornate entrance hall. What follows in this volume, however, eschews the simple linearity of Scottish national development that informs Hole's frieze. Rather James Fraser's pioneering work, interrogating the available sources as never before, constructs a more complex story of the emergence of the Christian kingdoms of the early medieval centuries. Caledonia was the Roman name for North Britain and it is one of the most pioneering features of this volume that the Roman and post-Roman eras are treated as a single period. Such a broad chronological approach allows James Fraser to explore in far more detail than has hitherto been attempted how the Britons, Picts, Gaels and Northumbrians, and their polities, established themselves and interacted with one another in the shadowy centuries that preceded the crystallisation of the more recognisably 'modern' kingdoms of Scotland and England. The result is a remarkably innovative account of a complex period that challenges received wisdom about Scotland's 'national' origins by shifting the focus from the Dalriadic Scots to the emergence of a poly-ethnic and multicultural kingdom of the Picts. Wide-ranging and authoritative, this is a masterly study of the first eight centuries of North Britain's history that sheds a flood of light on the genesis of the medieval political landscape out of which the kingdom of the Scots subsequently emerged.

Introduction
Fabulousness, Obscurity and Difficulty: Narrative History to 795

This book is the herald of a revolution that has transformed early Insular history. Like all revolutions, it has known disturbing convulsions, its revolutionaries having sometimes been ungentle in their quest for radical change. What has been overthrown is a framework whose first rickety structure was in place 200 years ago, when George Chalmers published the first volume of *Caledonia* in 1807. The status at that time of the five centuries considered in the present book was lowly in Scotland. In 1756 the Society of Edinburgh for the Encouragement of Arts, Sciences and Manufactures had offered a gold medal for the best treatment of this period, yet, as Chalmers himself put it, 'the scholars of Scotland remained sluggish and silent'. Why did the glint of gold fail to slay this sluggishness for more than fifty years? Enlightenment Scotland had dismissed our period as a 'wild region of pure fable'. Gold medals or not, Chalmers had become convinced that there were 'veracious chronicles' containing 'the details of history', and he undertook to write an account of what are now termed Roman Iron Age Scotland and Early Historic Scotland, 'whatever might be [their] fabulousness, or obscurity, or [their] difficulties'.[1] These have remained the watchwords of this period ever since.

The nineteenth century saw Chalmers and a number of successors firm up a new framework for understanding these centuries. They were little less disruptive to the historical status quo of the time than the more recent convulsions heralded here. Their revolutionary methods involved

---

[1] Chalmers, *Caledonia*, v–vii; on Enlightenment attitudes see, for example, Devine, *Scottish Nation*, 64–72.

them in a quest to identify the 'genuine materials' of 'true History', and culminated in the masterly scholarship of William F. Skene, who wrote in 1876 of identifying 'the most reliable authorities' for Scotland's 'early civil history', and extracting from them 'the true facts'.[2] A 'solid foundation' having been laid down over seventy years, and a framework of 'true facts' having been erected upon it, Skene set about building an impressive edifice. Archie Duncan's landmark survey of our period a century later in the Edinburgh History of Scotland outlined some of the last renovations of Skene's weary structre. Nine years later, Alfred Smyth's controversial survey in the New History of Scotland provided a glimpse of a wobbly structure whose underlying framework was coming apart. It has since collapsed and brought the house down. This book attempts to emphasise this point – and to outline for non-specialists the new framework that has begun to be erected in its place.

In order to ensure understanding of something of the nature of the catastrophe, it will be necessary at various points, borrowing Marc Bloch's memorable metaphor, to 'open the door of the laboratory just a little'. Readers will be invited to look for themselves, not just upon the results of the labours of specialists, but also (to some extent) upon those labours themselves. To begin with, we may consider *Historia ecclesiastica gentis Anglorum*, the 'Ecclesiastical History of the English People', where Bede of Wearmouth-Jarrow wrote that the little Hebridean island of Iona was donated to the Irish missionary, Columba, by a Pictish king. For Cosmo Innes, in the middle of the nineteenth century, this piece of information was out of whack with 'our most settled notions of geography and history'. Iona lay outwith Pictish territory (it was thought), and *Vita sancti Columbae*, the 'Life of St Columba' written by Adomnán of Iona, offered a more plausible alternative: the island was donated by an Argyll king. Innes thus concluded that Bede was simply wrong. The 'true facts' and 'genuine materials' (and the falsehoods) had been established, and Innes could move on with his survey.[3]

The revolutionary scholarship of today cannot move on. Not yet. Specialists now advocate spending more time thinking about contradictory claims like these, even if they are false or fabulous. In this case, Bede got his information from a Pictish source. We want to know why the Picts who produced it were advancing the (possibly) invented claim that Iona was a Pictish island. Did they have something to gain from it? What does

[2]   Skene, *Celtic Scotland*, vol. 1, vii–viii; see also Innes, *Scotland in the Middle Ages*, v–vi.

[3]   Innes, *Scotland in the Middle Ages*, xii–xiii.

that agenda reveal about political and social attitudes? Again and again in this book, it will be argued that careful analysis of such claims – fabulous or not – can uncover more about the circumstances in which they were advanced than even exceptional scholars like Skene could appreciate. The techniques involved reflect fairly recent appreciations of the complexities surrounding authorship, often borrowed by historians from their colleagues in literary studies. By placing new insights of this kind alongside more conventional historical evidence – the type preferred by Chalmers and Skene – a fuller (but often rather different) picture of the past is sometimes possible.

HISTORY, PSEUDO-HISTORY AND THE PERIOD FROM 670 TO 740

In embracing the revolutionary methodology, this book will show that there is surprisingly much to be said and considered about the period roughly from 670 to 740, during which most of our textual evidence was penned. Most of these texts cast their attentions back to earlier times, which can hoodwink readers into focusing too much on those times, and too little on the crucial time of composition which shaped each author's work. That principle is central to today's textual scholarship, but can be difficult for non-specialists to understand fully.

The beginning of an explanation lies in an appreciation that Bede, Adomnán and the other monastic scholars who turned their hands to historiography (the writing of history) in Early Historic Britain were trained as bible scholars. Their own writings were accordingly influenced by their understanding of how biblical texts were written, and were supposed to be read. For example, in Matthew's gospel, Jesus, sitting on the Mount of Olives with his disciples, tells a story about a man who divided his property among three servants before a journey. Upon his return, he learned that two had made wise investments and that his wealth had grown in their care. Praising them, he said, 'Because you have been faithful with a little, I shall put you in charge of much'. But the third servant, who simply maintained what he had been given, was rebuked, and cast out 'into the darkness'.[4] No such man or servants ever existed: this fable is one of the many 'parables' related in the gospels – tales told by Jesus in order to teach important lessons. What bible scholars like Bede and Adomnán were faced with in these little stories were profound truths

---

[4] Mt 25:14–30.

lying below the surface. In this case, the parable teaches that whoever does not make the most of what they are given – by their master or by God – earns rebuke and damnation.

In the sublime *Monty Python's Life of Brian*, the title character attempts to relate a garbled version of this parable, and his audience fails utterly to grasp its subtle nature. As a result, he finds himself heckled by sceptical demands of proofs that the story is not a fiction. Until fairly recently, scholars of our period have been cut from a similar cloth. For them, as for the hecklers in the film, the tale could not be 'true' if the characters and situation were made up; and a 'false' tale was worthless for understanding 'true History'. Yet for Jesus – and for bible scholars like Bede and Adomnán – the truth of the parable lay in its lessons, which were unaffected by its fabulousness.

In *Vita Columbae*, Adomnán told a fable or parable of his own, adopting Jesus's method of marrying surface fiction to deeper truth. To some extent, however, he also addressed the kinds of concerns about 'truth' raised by the sceptical audience in *Monty Python's Life of Brian*. He wrote that a man chased down a girl in Leinster. Fleeing from him, she came upon Columba and his teacher – real historical figures in a real place. The girl hid beneath their robes, but the man was not daunted and killed her with his spear. Adomnán had recently formulated a law protecting non-combatants from the scourge of war. Columba's teacher in this parable, 'in great distress of mind' over the killing, represents the distress and sense of powerlessness of the whole Church prior to the introduction of Adomnán's Law. But Columba, who correctly pronounces that the killer will be struck down dead immediately by God, speaks with a different voice: that of the Church newly armed with that Law.[5]

As this book goes along, we shall see many other examples of such fables related by Adomnán, Bede and other monastic writers. Real figures and events will be found woven into partly fictional accounts – a kind of historical fiction that scholars call 'pseudo-history'. The purpose of early medieval pseudo-history was to relate profound parable-like truths, spiritual or political, while at the same time often seeking a measure of narrative truth. Adomnán's stories are set in the years of Columba's lifetime, but many of them are as fictional as this one, containing deeper truths that actually pertain to Adomnán's own age – in this case to his Law. One of the prime causes of the fall of the old framework is a tendency among the fine scholars who erected and renovated it to underestimate the extent to which their 'genuine materials' contained

---

[5] Adomnán, *V. s. Columbae*, ii.25.

pseudo-history – and indeed, the extent to which some of the 'fabulous-ness' they despised actually contained scraps of useful evidence about the fabulist and his times.

An important sub-category of pseudo-history in our sources sacrifices strict historical accuracy (as we might call it today) in the interests of more profound truths that were specifically historical, as monastic scholars understood the nature of history. Men like Bede and Adomnán were taught that the great historical books of the Old Testament were, as St Augustine of Hippo put it, 'more concerned, or at least not less so, to foretell things to come than to relate things past'.[6] On the back of such teaching, the study of historical events was encouraged because it might provide a scholar with insights into God's plans for humanity, just as the Old Testament was thought to prefigure the coming of Christ. As top scholars, Bede and Adomnán thus expected history primarily to shed light on the predestined present or future. It is no surprise that they sometimes 'discovered' that it did so (and occasionally even helped it to do so), reanalysing historical scenarios in order to identify the hand of God at work.

This literary technique of transposing a current scenario into an imaginary past setting – prefiguring the present with the benefit of hindsight – has been called 'historicising' the present by scholars.[7] To see it in action, we may turn once more to *Vita Columbae*, this time to Adomnán's story about a Pictish noble called Tarain, whom Columba assists after he is sent into exile. Did Columba really know a Pict with this name and these troubles? Maybe he did. On the other hand, Adomnán certainly did. Just as he was putting the finishing touches on his Law, a Pictish king called Tarain was cast out of his kingdom. He went in exile to Ireland, passing into obscurity. In Adomnán's story, Tarain the Pict too finds sanctuary among Gaels. Historicising of recent events by Adomnán may, therefore, be suspected here; in that event, the events as described almost certainly never happened.

Does the story's fabulousness render it useless? Not at all. Once we have caught him in the act, it becomes possible to learn more from Adomnán about the exile of King Tarain than any conventional source explicitly records. For example, Adomnán calls his character a mere *nobilis* or noble, not a *rex* or king – hinting that he accepted the validity of King Tarain's deposition. Moreover, that Columba helps Tarain the Pict to find sanctuary hints that Adomnán, abbot of Columba's monastery, was involved in

<hr>

[6] Augustine, *De Civ. Dei*, xvii.1.
[7] Dumville, 'Sub-Roman Britain'.

helping King Tarain. Adomnán's story ends with treachery: Tarain's host murders him 'by a cruel order', and Columba pronounces that divine punishment will see his treacherous killer descend 'to the infernal regions'.[8] The underlying message will have been as clear to Adomnán's contemporaries (assuming they were wise to his historicising) as it is to you: whoever tries to have King Tarain killed in exile 'by a cruel order' will earn a one-way trip 'to the infernal regions'. We shall see later that Bede's notion that Iona was a Pictish island, rejected by Innes as a falsehood, probably reflects this type of writing also.

Appreciating that these stories provide vital evidence – but relating to the period of authorship, not the lifetime of Columba – is the kind of recent thinking that doomed the old framework. Scholars today understand more and more about the years roughly from 670 to 740 as a result, because that is when Adomnán, Bede and others wrote about the past. In contrast, the eleven previous decades beginning roughly in 560 receive less attention in this book – despite the fact that most of our texts are set in these years. This paradoxical reduction in emphasis on the period before 670 – the period that will be best known to many readers, populated by some of the most famous figures in Scotland's early history – is the high, sometimes jarring price to be paid for our important insights into the period after that year. Put simply, the better scholars get at identifying historicising and pseudo-history in *Vita Columbae*, *Historia ecclesiastica* and other texts penned after 670, the less useful those works seem as reliable sources for the previous period.

In our examples here, Columba did not do or say the things that our authors maintain: they placed him in certain scenarios formulated in order to present the past in such a way as to inform the present, and even to influence it. It is a technique employed by many novelists and dramatists today. How consciously Bede and the rest did it is usually impossible to know. This book highlights many other examples, not confined to *Vita Columbae* and *Historia ecclesiastica*. As a result, it finds itself raising grave doubts about some of the best known features of the history that the old framework supported. Sometimes, those doubts come primarily from archaeology, or from another discipline which, like archaeology, has experienced its own comparable theoretical revolution and collapsing framework. For many readers, particularly those who peer but little into the specialists' laboratory, this aspect of the book will be difficult to accept. Revolutions have a habit of upsetting old orders in ways that even the revolutionaries do not expect or seek.

---

[8] Adomnán, *V. s. Columbae*, ii.23.

A DIFFERENT KIND OF NARRATIVE HISTORY

It was William Robertson, the Enlightenment's Scottish historian extraordinaire, who in 1759 declared our period 'the region of pure fable and conjecture' which 'ought to be totally neglected or abandoned to the industry and credulity of antiquaries'. In his considered opinion, the point at which Scots were to begin paying attention to their country's history was 1286 – part way through the fourth volume of the New Edinburgh History of Scotland. Robertson accepted that 'truth begins to dawn' in Scottish history a little earlier than this, but thought that 'the events which then happened . . . merit no particular or laborious inquiry'.[9] Chalmers rejected his arguments, and so does this series; yet Robertson had a point. It is only a few years since Leslie Alcock concluded that 'political and institutional history of conventional form' cannot be written for Early Historic Scotland, echoing the advice of Alan Anderson seventy years ago that writers of narrative histories 'avoid the early history of Scotland'.[10] These warnings bring us back to the fabulousness, obscurity and difficulties associated with our period that scholars have been trying to tackle since Chalmers's first attempt 200 years ago.

We must, of course, heed Anderson's words of warning, yet for all his eccentricities we ought not to leave unconsidered Thomas Lethbridge's strong reaction in 1954 against academic writing that is 'boring to the degree of tears for the sake of the imagined accuracy, which no history can ever possess'.[11] The demands of high scholarly standards, the pressures of formal 'research assessment' and an exponential growth in the notion that the search for knowledge begins and ends on-line conspire to ensure that the learned papers and articles which have shaped this book can be difficult for non-specialists worldwide to locate. Moreover, they often include features (such as dense prose, exhaustive footnotes, specialist jargon and untranslated original languages) which can seem intended to make our period even more obscure and difficult than it is already. This book seeks a compromise position between the justified and exacting demands of current scholarship and the justified demands of Lethbridge that scholars remain mindful of their wider obligations to engage, enthuse and educate non-specialists. The importance of the exercise may be thought to merit the attempt at something like a conventional narrative

[9] Quotations from Chalmers, *Caledonia*, vi–vii.
[10] Anderson, *Prospects of the Advancement of Knowledge*, 12; Alcock, *Kings and Warriors*, 1.
[11] Lethbridge, *The Painted Men*, 12–13.

history, lest the historical understandings of specialists and non-specialists continue to drift even further apart.

The compromise position requires me to proceed somewhat differently from other writers in this series. In part, my approach involves some unapologetic grappling with the difficulties surrounding the evidence most suitable for narrative history – opening the door of the laboratory in an attempt to explain how 'genuine materials' are currently being identified and used by specialists, or why other conventional materials have been sidelined. At these points, the narrative is unavoidably interrupted, and sometimes even undermined where there may be different but equally valid ways of interpreting the evidence. The work of generations of specialists has worked and re-worked through these materials – and, of course, through those other categories of evidence (often non-textual) which, though absolutely vital for understanding this period, are less useful for narrative history. A great deal has been uncovered about our period. Chalmers was right – it is worth the effort. Yet the number of sources suitable for weaving a continuous narrative has not grown much since Anderson pronounced the period unfit for such treatment. Indeed, the scholarly revolution that this book heralds was branded 'reductionism' by Alcock because it has slimmed even more Anderson's already slim pickings. There are plenty of useful sources – but collectively they allow only for a fairly superficial, episodic sort of narrative. Obscurity will be our constant companion in this book, as it was for Chalmers. That is why the present series can dispense with our 500-year epoch in a single volume.

My narrative, is therefore, inevitably full of gaps where suitable evidence eludes us, on top of those created by the asides in which the door to Bloch's laboratory is opened. I have been able to make use of the series' innovative format in accommodating some of those asides set off from the main text. The book says less about what was, than about what appears to have been. Its narrative spine encompasses the two centuries from the foundation of Iona in 563 until the death of Onuist son of Vurguist in 761, assembled from narrative sources and several other important texts. For the rest of the period, we lack the raw materials of narrative history – but not the materials for history itself. The Roman Iron Age can boast a wealth of archaeological evidence, but archaeologists now stress that their data tend to be very particular to individual sites and artefacts, and narrative history requires syntheses of 'big pictures'. I am fortunate that two magisterial archaeological syntheses, together spanning the whole of this period, have been published since 2003, and that two other syntheses published since 2001 provide equally definitive 'big pictures' relating to early medieval monumental art.[12] Other broad surveys have been published, targeted mainly at general audiences and copiously illustrated. What the narrative historian requires is not more of these – useful though they are – but specialist considerations of archaeological datasets surrounding any number of big-picture questions. Archaeology cannot (and should not) be directed by the needs of narrative history – neither indeed should textual studies. Yet recent examples, where scholars have been so inclined, shape the narrative of this book in parts and encourage optimism that still more narrative-friendly big-picture revelations can be expected from archaeology and other non-textual disciplines.[13]

In the Roman Iron Age particularly, as well as in the later eighth century, we can but 'imagine the whole as a picture in the fire'.[14] My fleeting perceptions through the flames will not all meet with acceptance. Increasingly detested in some archaeological circles, the writings of Tacitus, Dio, Ammianus and others provide the semblance of a narrative spine for this period – flashes that help to illuminate our non-textual data, at least where big pictures are concerned. Yet these flashes, like those provided by Northumbrian and Irish chronicles of the late eighth century, are mere stars in a constellation. They do not amount to detailed pictures. They provide a mere framework, which enables us to perceive general shapes against a dark background. Whether one sees a Great Bear, a Big Dipper, or a Plough – or no shape at all – depends on a variety of factors, and contributes to the richness of scholarly debate.

As an exercise in narrative history this book is, therefore, unlikely to satisfy all readers. Many non-specialists will share Lethbridge's wish for more narrative or more definitive statements about the period. Coverage of topics and areas of Scotland is as uneven as the evidence suitable for the task and will not satisfy everybody. Specialists in particular may feel that too many points of light have been joined up. An attempt has been made to strike a balance, between narrative and necessary discussion of important problems and themes, in the interests of outlining the new framework which specialists have been erecting from the wreckage of the old. If the book does its job, it will, at one and the same time, bring non-specialists up to date with the state of play among scholars, while stimulating specialists to debate and test different aspects of the framework that we have been assembling.

[12] Fisher, *Early Medieval Sculpture*; Alcock, *Kings and Warriors*; Harding, *The Iron Age in Northern Britain*; and Henderson and Henderson, *The Art of the Picts*.
[13] Woolliscroft and Hoffmann, *Rome's First Frontier*, 203–24; Hunter, *Beyond the Edge of the Empire*.
[14] Campbell *et al.*, *The Anglo-Saxons*, 20.

Certain aspects of the book may frustrate readers' expectations for reasons other than those outlined above. My treatment of ecclesiastical topics is superficial, being driven by the needs of the narrative and in anticipation of an imminent full and detailed study.[15] The very title *From Caledonia to Pictland*, which is not mine, I have embraced as highlighting both a convenient and a meaningful theme relevant to the whole of our period. Yet it invites a certain geographical focus, and one that, moreover, sits at odds with more gaelocentric conceptions of this phase of Scotland's past. When John Bannerman spoke of the Dalriadan Gaels of the period as 'our ancestors', and when Michael Newton wrote that 'it was, after all, the Gaels who forged the Scottish nation', they took up perspectives on these centuries very different from the one taken up here.[16] In this book, the Picts and their Caledonian ancestors hijack the centre-stage, as they did in Chalmers's survey. Moreover, the Bernician English are, from my perspective, not regarded as any less 'Scottish' than the Dalriadan Gaels, with whom they shared the fact of straddling the present confines of Scotland.[17] The validity of these potentially controversial features of the narrative, giving due consideration to the evidence as well as the polyethnic character of northern Britain in our period, may be judged from the pages of the book itself.

Like Duncan and Smyth, I have accepted the task of reflecting on Scotland's Roman Iron Age alongside its Early Historic centuries, which some archaeologists are in the habit of regarding as the 'Later Iron Age'. In the interests of coherence, I have focused on the bigger questions in the Roman Iron Age, as viewed in particular from a late Antique perspective. If the book has any single theme, it is that the Iron Age did not go gently into that good night. In Scotland, it was centuries old when, with the advent of Roman Britain in the south of the island, it became the Roman Iron Age. Over the next four centuries, the world of classical Antiquity developed seamlessly into the different 'late Antique' one, and by the end of late Antiquity the Latin West, including northern Britain, had become early medieval Europe. Any number of continuities and Roman legacies have been identified alongside the innovations involved in that momentous transformation.

We are interested in this book in a part of that grand process: the transformation of Iron Age Scotland into early medieval Scotland. Late

---

[15] Clancy, *The Making of Scottish Christianity*.

[16] Bannerman, *Dalriada*, v; Newton, *Gaelic in Scottish History*, 5, 28.

[17] For similar thinking, see Lowe, *Angels, Fools and Tyrants*; Harding, *The Iron Age in Northern Britain*, 5–6; Alcock, *Kings and Warriors*, xiii–xiv.

Antiquity was characterised by dynamic interaction between what had become of the world of classical Antiquity and its 'barbarian' neighbours.[18] Northern Britain, as presented here, was not divorced from it. The region experienced something along the same lines as others perched at the edge of the Roman Empire at the beginning of the fifth century. It is hoped that the book will help to encourage dialogue between specialists, for I believe that such intercourse is as important for understanding Scotland in our period as Romanists – classical and late Antique – take for granted in understanding what happened to Rome and her Empire. The book will have succeeded if it demonstrates the intellectual merit of such dialogue across a gulf that needs many more bridges.

[18] In scholarly writing 'barbarian' has transcended its narrow pejorative character; for discussion see, for example, Kulikowski, 'Nation versus Army', 69–70.

PART ONE

The Passing of Caledonia (69–597)

CHAPTER I

New Nations: Caledonia from Cerialis to Caracalla

On 4 February 211, L. Septimius Severus died at the city of Eboracum (modern York). The old Libyan usurper was the third ruling emperor of the Romans to set foot in their province of Britannia in southern Britain, and expired in the midst of his country's third major war in the north of the island. According to a History written some years later by Cassius Dio, a senator who had served in the emperor's advisory council during the war, Severus's enemies were two barbarian nations (*genoi*). One of these, the Calidones, had been known to the Romans for more than a century; first-century writers had made them synonymous with northern Britain, naming it *Caledonia*. Dio observed that in 197 the Calidones 'did not abide by their promises' to Rome, a pretext for war which reflected ongoing diplomatic contact stretching back for generations.[1] The relationships cultivated between the Romans and the various barbarian peoples of northern Britain over that time were complex and variable. They remained so after 211, but Severus's achievement in northern Britain represents a watershed of significance for the whole period examined in this book.

THE MAIATAI AND THE CALIDONES

In addition to treaty-breaking, Dio accused the Calidones of conspiring 'to aid the Maiatai', Severus's other foes in the north country. This nation is named in no other Roman text, and it is fortunate that Dio provided an indication of their location, 'next to the cross-wall that cuts the island in

---

[1] Dio, *Roman History*, lxxvi.8 [Cary, ed., *Dio*, 216]; from the text of excerpts, concerned with embassies (*de legationibus*) to and from the Romans, known as *Excerpta Ursiniana*, rather than from Xiphilinus's epitome of Dio.

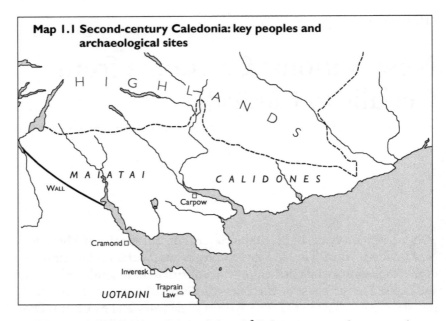

Map 1.1 Second-century Caledonia: key peoples and archaeological sites

half', with the Calidones 'beyond them'.[2] It is even more fortunate that a trace of them can still be found in the place-names of central Scotland, at Dumyat hill, where the Ochil Hills come nearest Stirling, and Myothill west of Falkirk above the Carron.[3] The two hills stand roughly at the edges of a district described in the twelfth century as stretching 'from the hill of the Britons [*mons Britannorum*] to the hill which is called Ochil [*Okhel*]', understood to be the Early Historic district of Manau.[4] Clackmannan is the most prominent of the places whose names still indicate that Manau encompassed the plain at the head of the Firth of Forth.[5]

Without assuming exact territorial continuity from the second century to the twelfth, the Maiatai appear roughly to have been a Manau people. Roman survey work a century before Severus had assigned the district to a different *civitas*, the Dumnonii. It is best not to translate *civitas* as 'tribe', which has a much narrower meaning than the Latin sense of a community sharing a civil identity. Another group of Dumnonii lent their name to the English county of Devon: did the River Devon in Clackmannanshire

[2] Dio, *Roman History*, lxxvii.12 [Cary, ed., *Dio*, 262]; from Xiphilinus's epitome of Dio.
[3] Watson, *Celtic Place-Names*, 24–5, 58–9; Rivet and Smith, *The Place-Names of Roman Britain*, 343–4, 404.
[4] Macquarrie, ed., *V. s. Servani*, 140; Clancy, 'Philosopher-King', 138–42.
[5] On Manau, see Watson, *Celtic Place-Names*, 103–5; Jackson, 'Northern British Section of Nennius', 30–1.

have particular significance for the Manau Dumnonii? First-century Dumnonia appears to have been rather larger than Manau, extending as far south as the Clyde (*Clota*), and as far north as Strathearn in the shadow of the Gask Ridge. Precise identifications of places named by the sources are debateable, but the place-names of Cardowan at Wishaw on the Clyde, and Dowanhill at Milngavie on the lower Clyde tend to reinforce the notion of the Clyde as the Dumnonian frontier, if they refer to the Dumnonii.[6] They were probably made up of smaller groups like most barbarian *civitates* in northern Europe: perhaps the Maiatai were one such Dumnonian group, dominating old Dumnonia as the second century came to a close.

They seem to have colluded against Rome after 197, but the Maiatai and the Calidones were apparently distinct nations. A century earlier, Cornelius Tacitus, now a much maligned commentator, had implied that the Roman conquest of the Dumnonii – he does not mention them, but rather the rivers Forth (*Bodotria*) and Tay (*Tauia*) – closed a significant phase in the subjugation of the north country.[7] Tacitus named his father-in-law, Cn. Julius Agricola, as the conqueror in *Agricola*, a laudatory synopsis of Agricola's career. He gave no dates, but his chronological indicators enable scholars to calculate that Dumnonia fell within a year of the death in 79 of T. Flavius Vespasianus, the usurper who founded the Flavian dynasty which held the Principate from 69 to 96. Tacitus went on to regard the conquest four years later of the 'peoples inhabiting Caledonia' (*Caledoniam incolentes populi*) as a distinct achievement, culminating in the battle of Mons Graupius.[8]

Tacitus's framework for understanding these Flavian conquests has been rejected by an important argument that the archaeology of the Flavian outposts of Scotland is difficult to reconcile with *Agricola*, and that these had instead been established more than a decade earlier than Tacitus claimed.[9] In the early 70s, Q. Petillius Cerialis was governor of Britannia and Agricola, later governor himself, was one of his legionary commanders. Together they fought a running and difficult war beyond the northern frontier. Tacitus names the Brigantes as their enemy, apparently a confederation, straddling the Pennines and the present Anglo-Scottish border, which had disintegrated into warring factions, pro-Roman and anti-Roman, after Rome began meddling in their affairs by supporting her Brigantian friends.[10] Tacitus's accounts of the politics

---

[6] Driscoll and Forsyth, 'The Late Iron Age', 4.

[7] Tacitus, *Agricola*, § 22; see also Rivet and Smith, *Place-Names of Roman Britain*, 470.

[8] Tacitus, *Agricola*, § 27; Smyth, *Warlords*, 42–3.

[9] Woolliscroft and Hoffmann, *Rome's First Frontier*, 178–90.

[10] Tacitus, *Agricola*, § 17; Tacitus, *Annoles*, xii.40; Tacitus, *Historiae*, iii.45.

behind this war are an object-lesson in Rome's capacity, intentionally or not, to affect her barbarian neighbours. Did this Brigantian war early in Vespasian's principate bring direct Roman authority as far north as the Scottish Highlands? The theory is particularly compelling in its stark reminder to scholars that *Agricola* is far vaguer and less committal about the war than the superstructure that scholarship has built around it. There is every reason (on Tacitus's own evidence) to keep an open mind about the northerly limits of Cerialis's campaigns.

Is the archaeological evidence, however, decisive against *Agricola*'s basic chronology? The debate between archaeologists has barely begun, and will no doubt continue for some time to come. In the meantime, the historian may be permitted a healthy scepticism. Certainly *Agricola* is open to the full range of critical authorial analysis that has so revolutionised our understanding of such Early Historic writers as Bede and Adomnán. Like them Tacitus cannot be understood as a commentator without extensive consideration of his own authorial circumstances. He did not write in a vacuum. Among his potential readers was Sex. Julius Frontinus. One of Rome's leading senators and generals when *Agricola* was published, Frontinus had also been Agricola's immediate predecessor, and Cerialis's immediate successor, in Britannia. He and his familiars knew exactly how far Roman control extended in Britannia when he had taken up the governorship and when he had demitted to Agricola a few years later. As a result, Tacitus ought to have handled this question with a full measure of his characteristic vagueness if he was planning a colossal fib. In fact, *Agricola* is surprisingly unambiguous: Roman control extended as far as the 'narrow space of land' (*angusto terrarium spatio*) formed by the Forth and Clyde estuaries, which Agricola 'made firm' with forts, so that 'the enemy [to the north] were pushed as if into another island' (*summotis velut in aliam insulam hostibus*).[11] Nowhere else in the text did Tacitus come close to this level of geographical precision. It is accordingly most unlikely that Frontinus had inherited and passed on a frontier a long way further north.

All of this was ancient history by the time that Severus came on the scene, and the Flavian occupation of the Maiatian and Calidonian homelands had been brief. Establishing this fact has been a remarkable achievement for archaeology, but it is too easy to equate briefness with insignificance. The point may be underlined by recognising that, as this book goes to press, the Flavian occupation was as long as the occupation of Iraq after the 2003 invasion. Dumnonia had seemingly been riddled with Roman installations in the course of conquest, frontier-building and

---

[11]   Tacitus, *Agricola*, § 23; Fraser, *Roman Conquest*, 50–3.

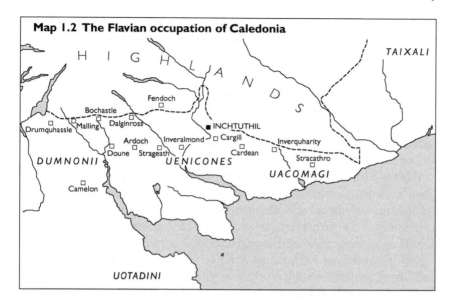

Map 1.2 The Flavian occupation of Caledonia

the establishment of a major route-way between the Forth and the Tay. It had also been wreathed by installations to the north and west, including towers on the Gask Ridge. Together with Tacitus's notion that the conquest of Dumnonia meant something, these fascinating towers, whatever their other functions, probably reflect a key Flavian political or ethnic distinction between the Dumnonii and their neighbours to the north, prefiguring the Severan cleavage between the Maiatai and the Calidones. Installations at the feet of the Highland glens above Strathearn and Menteith had established a Roman presence on the major routes linking Dumnonia with Atlantic Scotland and with Highland glens further north. Exactly what balance the Flavians had hoped to strike between containing and policing the Dumnonii, protecting their country from enemies and monitoring and controlling inward and outward movement overland will never be known.[12] It is no easier to know the extent to which such treatment at Flavian hands may have antagonised or mollified the Dumnonii, may have helped to lump their *civitas* together with neighbouring *civitates*, or may have galvanised them into the Maiatian *genos* encountered by Severus a hundred years later.

To the north of the Gask Ridge the Flavians had wreathed a more substantial country in forts, south and east of the Highlands. Here, too, the technique had involved outposts at the feet of Highland glens, which

[12] For discussion, see Woolliscroft and Hoffmann, *Rome's First Frontier*, 228–9.

would have both protected and contained, keeping watch on inward and outward movement to and from the Atlantic and the Moray firthlands. The barbarians further north and west may have factored as little in the Flavian wars as they had in the occupation. Another major route-way had been established between the Tay and the North Esk at the north end of Strathmore. At Inchtuthil, some five kilometres up the Tay from Cargill at the foot of Strathmore, construction of a twenty-two-hectare legionary fortress had begun at the nexus formed by the major route-ways of Strath Tay to the north and Strathmore to the east.

Within Strath Tay the place-name of Dunkeld (ninth-century *Dún Chaillden*), like Schiehallion in nearby Atholl, the Highland region of Perthshire, associates the Calidones with this northerly zone of Flavian occupation.[13] As with Dumyat and Myot Hill, place-names containing population-names are mainly suggestive of frontier status. Tacitus never explicitly named the vanquished *Britanni* of Agricola's last campaigns as Calidones, but the confederation (*conspiratio*) of *civitates* he defeated is likely to have consisted largely of communities encompassed by the occupation. It is possible to read the evidence from Flavian survey work as being in rough agreement, indicating that the Moray Firth and the Firth of Clyde between them encompassed the *Kaledonii*.[14] The country contained by Flavian installations had been rather smaller than this estuarine delineation of what may be called 'inner Caledonia', but included almost all of the farmland, and no doubt the vast majority of the barbarian population between the two estuaries, Dumnonian, Calidonian or otherwise.

By Severus's time a century later, the Calidones appear indeed to have been a nation based in inner Caledonia 'beyond' the Maiatai. We cannot know if they had constituted a self-conscious nation in Flavian times, rather than a mere *conspiratio*, and whether or not their identity was galvanised in part by interactions with the Romans over a hundred years. We know only that Dio says that, at the end of the second century, the Maiatai and the Calidones were 'the two principal British peoples (*gene*)', explaining that 'the names of the others have been merged in these two'.[15] A great deal turns on how this vague statement is interpreted. If it is not invention or carelessness, it suggests that something important had happened to barbarian identities in inner Caledonia between the Flavian and

---

[13] Watson, *Celtic Place-Names*, 21; Jackson, 'Two Early Scottish Names', 14–16.
[14] Watson, *Celtic Place-Names*, 19; Jackson, 'Two Early Scottish Names', 14–16; Rivet and Smith, *Place-Names of Roman Britain*, 387, 485–7; Hind, 'Caledonia', 373–5.
[15] Dio, *Roman History*, lxxvii.12 [Cary, ed., *Dio*, 262]; from Xiphilinus's epitome of Dio.

The location of Mons Graupius

Ever since Scotland's early antiquaries became aware of *Agricola*, scholars and enthusiasts have hunted for the battlefield of Mons Graupius. Nothing illustrates the vagueness of Tacitus's details better than the great variety of sites that have been identified. Most lay to the south of the Grampians, but the prevailing opinion was that Mons Graupius lay within them, on the assumption that the Calidones had thought and fought like modern Highlanders. A misreading of Tacitus's place-name as *Granpius* gave the Grampian Mountains their name.

With the advent of antiquarian and archaeological excavation, the favoured location shifted to the gap between the Grampians and the sea south of Aberdeen, Roman fortifications unearthed at Raedykes being identified as the camp where Agricola's legionaries watched the battle unfold. By the twentieth century, archaeology had identified different 'lines' of Roman sites which seemed to confirm the strategic significance of Raedykes.

It was the advent of aerial photography that toppled Raedykes from the top of the list of sites associated with Mons Graupius. Crop-marks revealed still more Roman sites north of the Grampians, invisible at ground-level, and so undisturbed by the spades of early antiquaries. The Pass of Grange became the foremost of the northern sites which now contended for the top of the list.

The more southerly option was not entirely abandoned, however. As early as 1926 Duncrub in Strathearn was associated with *Graupius*. A generation later it was confirmed that a Roman site lay at nearby Dunning, and in 1970 Richard Feachem proposed that a monument be raised at Duncrub to commemorate the battle. The fact that the Flavian surveys of northern Britain locate the place-name *Victoria*, victory, hereabouts strengthens Feachem's general case. No site yet identified satisfies the textual, archaeological and place-name evidence better than Dunning and its environs, Craig Rossie and the Gask Ridge being likelier candidates for the *mons* than Duncrub.

A new candidate forced itself to the top of the list later in the 1970s, despite doubts raised by scholars. Aerial photography had identified a new Roman site at Logie Durno, and its discoverer suggested that Bennachie south of it was Mons Graupius. As hills near Roman camps of Flavian date (or probable Flavian date) go, Bennachie is as good a candidate as any, but it is not obviously better than the others.

Severan horizons. Severus, supported by his son Antoninus 'Caracalla', waged his own northern war over much the same territory as the Flavians had done, his primary theatre confirming inner Caledonia as the homeland of the Calidonian nation. However, he made no attempt to occupy the Maiatian and Calidonian homelands. Indeed, the long-term outcomes of the two wars could not have been more different.

THE ELUSIVE FRONTIER

In the century following the Flavian conquests, northern Britain was a sink-hole of men and resources, barbarian and Roman alike. The fact may have been more apparent in hindsight, from the perspective of Severus, than it had ever been on the ground on a daily and yearly basis. The Flavian grip on the north country had been relaxed, either suddenly or gradually over more than thirty years. Then in 122, Hadrian, the second ruling emperor to set foot in Britain, had declared, in the words of the fourth-century *Historia Augusta*, that 'the Britons were incapable of being held under Roman authority', at least in the north country.[16] The imperial declaration had been literally set in stone by the erection of a new frontier line across the Tyne–Solway isthmus, including a great curtain wall, now famous, from sea to sea. For some unknown reason (which has attracted considerable speculation), the Hadrianic *limes* had been abandoned shortly after the emperor's death and a new one commissioned across the Forth–Clyde isthmus by Antoninus Pius, Hadrian's adoptive son and successor.[17]

In broad terms, it seems that the Hadrianic solution to the problem of the north country had failed. Twenty years later, there was a feeling somewhere that the barbarians to the south of the new Antonine frontier, in the zone which may be termed 'outer Brigantia', were governable after all, inviting the establishment of a more ambitious *limes*. It is not surprising that both the wall and the system of occupation behind it in outer Brigantia betray a sense of risk.[18] A commemorative *Britannia* coin issued *c.* 155 implies that a significant Roman victory had been secured by the governor,

---

[16] *Hist. Augusta, v. Hadriani*, § 5.2. For discussion, see Hanson and Maxwell, *Rome's North West Frontier*, 51–2.

[17] Breeze, *The Northern Frontiers*, 98–9, 102–12; Hanson and Maxwell, *Rome's North West Frontier*, 60–2, 75–99, 132–6. The emperor's lack of a military character was handled in different ways by the ancients; see, for example, *Hist. Augusta, v. Pii*, § 5.4–5; Pausanias, *Desc. of Greece*, viii.43.

[18] Breeze, *The Northern Frontiers*, 109–10.

Julius Verus, presumably north of the Antonine frontier in inner Caledonia. How fascinating that, as with Agricola's victory there seventy years before, Verus's success in a second Caledonian war had been followed by large-scale restructuring, including a loosening of the Roman grip on the north country.[19] Within ten years of the *Britannia* coin, in the early years of the troubled principate of the philosopher-emperor Marcus Aurelius, the Antonine Wall had been decommissioned and Hadrian's Wall reactivated. Can we conclude that outer Brigantia became less desirable – or more difficult – to control once the Romans had cowed the Calidones beyond it?

How much of this background was known to Severus will always be a mystery. In passing this activity had helped to define or reinforce outer Brigantia as a zone distinct from inner Caledonia. It had also created a divided island quite unlike anything that had gone before. Britannia in the south and *barbaricum* in the north continued on somewhat different paths through the Early Historic period and beyond. It took a century of doubt for the Romans to decide finally that, in political terms, outer Brigantia was to remain *barbaricum* as Hadrian had envisioned. Yet we shall see that the peoples of outer Brigantia themselves were not so sure about that, in ethnic terms at least. Indeed, the relative receptiveness of certain barbarian groups in the region to the idea of direct Roman control and their opposition to Hadrian's Wall cannot be dismissed as potential factors in explaining either the Antonine project or the generally unresolved frontier question that bedevilled the north country for over a hundred years.

Reaching Eboracum in 208, Septimius Severus may have been reasonably well informed about Britain. His murdered predecessor P. Helvius Pertinax, who had both fought in the north country and governed Britannia, had been his associate; and his own brother P. Septimius Geta had served there also.[20] In those years, the principal trouble-makers in *barbaricum* were almost certainly from outer Brigantia. In 182, in the early years of the principate of Commodus, invaders had breached Hadrian's Wall and, according to Dio, 'proceeded to do much mischief', including the annihilation of a body of Roman soldiers.[21] This incursion probably had not originated very far to the north. The striking siege-works – if that is what they are – at Burnswark Hill, outside Ecclefechan in lower Annandale, could be the work of Ulpius Marcellus, the governor who had 'ruthlessly put down' the mischievous barbarians. If so, such a siege

---

[19] For the evidence, see Hanson and Maxwell, *Rome's North West Frontier*, 137–43, 148–50.
[20] Birley, *Septimius Severus*, 39, 171–2.
[21] Dio, *Roman History*, lxxiii.8 [Cary, ed., *Dio*, 86]; from Xiphilinus's epitome of Dio.

might imply that the Anavionenses of Annandale, who in the 150s may also have destroyed Blatobulgium, the Roman fort at nearby Birrens, had been heavily involved in these major troubles.[22] Marcellus's operations had seemingly reached the Tay.[23] Such a major campaign in the north after the 160s was almost certainly very rare – a proportionate response to an extraordinary threat – and even so it reached only the fringe of inner Caledonia. There seems to be little reason to suppose that the Calidones beyond had been much involved in Rome's ongoing frontier troubles of the second century – unless Calidonian groups had been creating indirect difficulties for Rome by troubling her friends in outer Brigantia.

Among the known peoples of this zone, the Uotadini of the east coastal lowlands have long seemed to be the key to understanding the complex relationships between Romans and barbarians in northern Britain. The notion that their leaders were collaborative allies of Rome as early as the Flavian period is an old one, but a convincing alternative interpretation of the evidence has yet to appear. There is reason to suppose that the Roman road linking Eboracum to the Forth skirted Uotadinian territory further east, its installations forming a frontier of sorts behind which the Uotadini could be protected or contained. One outpost along this line, Trimontium at Newstead at the foot of Eildon Hill, has rendered up a particularly rich harvest of archaeological finds. Some twenty-five kilometres east of Inveresk, where the road north from Trimontium probably reached the Forth, lay the great acropolis of Traprain Law in East Lothian. Above all else, the flourishing of this old Bronze Age site in the Roman Iron Age, including extensive finds of material of Roman provenance, convinces scholars that the Uotadini were very friendly with Rome, flourishing in second-century outer Brigantia with her blessing and support.[24] Uotadinian attitudes towards the Calidones across the Firth of Forth, the Dumnonii (and later Maiatai) at the head of the estuary, and the Hadrianic *limes* may have played a key role in shaping Roman frontier policy in the second century, if Rome was keen to keep this *civitas* onside.

[22] Campbell, 'The Roman Siege of Burnswark'; Harding, *The Iron Age in Northern Britain*, 59–62; Ralston, *Celtic Fortifications*, 116–17; Rivet, 'The Brittones Anavionenses'; Birley, 'Anavionenses'; Hanson and Maxwell, *Rome's North West Frontier*, 145.

[23] Dio, *Roman History*, lxxiii.8 [Cary, ed., *Dio*, 88]; from Xiphilinus's epitome of Dio; Birley, *Septimius Severus*, 74–5; Woolliscroft and Hoffmann, *Rome's First Frontier*, 206. See also Hanson and Maxwell, *Rome's North West Frontier*, 199.

[24] Harding, *The Iron Age in Northern Britain*, 189–91; see also Breeze, The *Northern Frontiers*, 150–3; Macinnes, 'Brochs and the Roman Occupation', 243–4; Armit, *Celtic Scotland*, 103; Breeze, *Roman Scotland*, 114.

It has long been recognised that the principal purpose of the different *limites* of northern Britain was to control and monitor movement – military or otherwise – back and forth across them. The implications are that such movement was very common and that considerable contact was maintained to either side. It is thought that trade with *barbaricum* was generally prohibited by Roman frontier policy.[25] The importation of Roman material – of which there is a great deal from native sites across northern Britain – is therefore likely to have originated largely as sanctioned subsidies acquired in episodes of formal diplomatic exchange. The barbarian 'promises' mentioned by Dio at the end of the second century will have been made in episodes of this kind, with subsidies serving as deal-sweeteners. Detailed analysis shows that the main source of material was the army. If access to the Roman military supply system was coveted by barbarian leaders, a clear motive was created for attacking Roman installations which had nothing necessarily to do with patriotic resistance or resentment.[26] A pronounced regional variation in the distribution of material has been identified and has been taken as symptomatic of significant diversity in the shape of barbarian society from region to region in this early part of the Roman Iron Age.

Thus, it seems that Rome had maintained contact with the Maiatai and the Calidones in inner Caledonia, and with their forebears, throughout the second century. Both peoples had seemingly remained outwith Britannia even at its greatest extent during the Antonine project, but none the less, they remained a part of Roman Britain as Rome herself understood it. Thus, we find the historian Herodian, writing *c.* 250, describing Severus's troubles with the Maiatai and the Calidones as a rebellion.[27] In 195 Clodius Albinus, the Tunisian-born governor of Britannia, had relocated to Lugdunum (modern Lyon) to challenge Severus for the Principate, his Britannic legions in tow; the restlessness of the Maiatai and Calidones followed in 197. These were propitious times to seek to renegotiate promises made to the vulnerable and distracted Romans, and grudges may have resulted if the civil war had hindered the movement of diplomats and subsidies into the north country. They were equally propitious times, of course, to go plundering: Herodian speaks of the *barbaroi* of Britannia 'laying waste the countryside' at this time, 'carrying off plunder and wrecking almost everything'.[28]

[25] Breeze, *The Antonine Wall*, 153.
[26] Whitaker, 'Supplying the System', 71; Harding, *The Iron Age in Northern Britain*, 191.
[27] Herodian, *History*, iii.14.
[28] Herodian, *History*, iii.14.

Dio's account implies that the Maiatai were the trouble-makers, and that they took prisoners from the Romans or (more probably) from their outer Brigantian allies.

In general terms, the crisis was probably fairly typical of Rome's frontier troubles in Britain throughout the second century. The barbarians were motivated to make mischief not by a pathological hatred for Rome, but by specific grudges that we cannot identify. One group having taken decisive military action, other groups joined in. It was probably also typical that Severus's first attempts to resolve the situation were diplomatic rather than military, there being no incursion into Britannia itself to be punished. He seems immediately to have sent Virius Lupus to the province, who in 196 had successfully preserved his rule on the Rhine despite pressure from Albinus. Dio reports that Lupus 'was compelled to buy peace' from the Maiatai 'for a large sum'.[29] That this pay-off or subsidy successfully defused the situation is clear: it was a dozen years before Severus turned up himself. Meanwhile, Lupus strengthened the Hadrianic *limes*, and the emperor sent a procurator to Britannia who had earned his name as a military policeman (*speculator*) and intelligence officer. His main commission was probably to gather intelligence in both Britannia and *barbaricum* in the wake of the recent convulsions across the island.[30] No doubt Severus always intended, if possible, to come to Britain himself, for his campaigns there fit a clear pattern, following on from his efforts to secure the Parthian and Saharan frontiers of the Empire by initiating aggressive campaigns.

Although the barbarians had been happy enough to flex their military muscle when it was to their advantage, it was also typical, in all likelihood, that they showed no great stomach for fighting the substantial forces that Severus brought into the north country in March 208. The old emperor, now in his early sixties, was as hard-nosed as they came, an old hand at brutal punitive warfare and a commander who had made short work of formidable foes in Mesopotamia and the Sahara. Even excruciating gout (or arthritis) could not stay his hand. According to Herodian, barbarian ambassadors now came to him, but failed to dissuade him from war.[31] In their worst nightmares they had probably not envisioned that their violence eleven years earlier could have had such an end result.

The evidence relating to the war that followed is crying out for the kind of dedicated and detailed synthesis that has repeatedly favoured the Flavian

---

[29] Dio, *Roman History*, lxxvi.8 [Cary, ed., *Dio*, 216]; from *Excerpta Ursiniana*.

[30] Birley, *Septimius Severus*, 171.

[31] Herodian, *History*, iii.14.

evidence. A great base was established on the site of an old camp at Carpow on the right bank of the Tay, some two kilometres west of Newburgh at the foot of Strathearn. It probably stood at the margins of Maiatia and Calidonia, and is thought to have served as the main staging point and supply depot of the war. The Calidones, the emperor's first target, continued to show little desire for fighting save in the form of opportunistic hit-and-run strikes which, though bold, failed to prevent their lands becoming greatly despoiled. The die having been cast by Severus, they seem to have made a reasonably good account of themselves, but before the year was out the emperor had 'forced the Britons to come to terms, on the condition that they should forsake a large part of their territory'.[32]

As far as we can tell from archaeological evidence, no territorial concession ever took place which would justify Dio's language. In the treaty negotiations of 208 or 209, perhaps at the new installation at Carpow, Severus may have withdrawn that condition in the interests of a long-term resolution to Britain's frontier troubles. The barbarian across the table is named by Dio as Argentocoxos. His unnamed wife, according to a story that reached Dio, distinguished herself in a witty rejoinder while jesting with the empress Julia Domna, a Syrian, who accompanied her husband on all his campaigns. East can hardly have gone further to meet West in Antiquity. This tale about Scotland's earliest historically-attested woman smacks of literary convention, Dio implying that she knew about Julia's promiscuous reputation. The implication that Argentocoxos, like Severus, was accompanied by his wife is fascinating, however, and says a great deal about the tone of the negotiations and the respect shown towards Argentocoxos. Perhaps we should recall Caesar's presentation of one German leader in his memoir, *De bello Gallico*, as a capable negotiator who knew a thing or two about the currents of Roman politics.[33]

In the short term the negotiations failed and both sides returned to the field. We cannot greatly credit the implications of Dio and Herodian in hindsight that Caracalla, later reviled as emperor, spoiled things by actively undermining his father, even trying to murder him.[34] There had been no decisive victory, and the Calidones, perhaps with an eye towards Severus's crippling infirmity and divided entourage, may have elected finally to test Rome's staying-power – ever her greatest advantage in

---

[32] Dio, *Roman History*, lxxvii.13 [Cary, ed., *Dio*, 264–6]; from Xiphilinus's epitome of Dio; Herodian, *History*, iii.14; for a discussion of commemorative coins issued to mark the victorious campaign(s), see Reed, 'The Scottish Campaigns of Septimius Severus'.
[33] Julius Caesar, *De bello Gallico*, i.44.
[34] Dio, *Roman History*, lxxvii.14 [Cary, ed., *Dio*, 268]; from Xiphilinus's epitome of Dio; Herodian, *History*, iii.15.

barbarian conflicts. The Maiatai, moreover, had yet to enter the frame, doing so only after the breakdown of the peace talks, perhaps in the hope of tipping the scales more in favour of the barbarians at the inevitable next round of talks. Now, however, Severus pulled out all the stops and Caracalla subjected the Maiatai to a brutal campaign of retribution, characteristic of his father at his most ruthless. The young co-emperor may have proceeded as far north as the Moray firthlands, burning and pillaging the whole time.[35] Their initial rejection of Severus's terms might have backfired disastrously for the Calidones and their Maiatian allies had fortune not intervened with the emperor's death, which seriously undermined Caracalla's bargaining position. With much bigger fish to fry back in Rome, he could not deliberate long over the treaties arising from his strenuous efforts of the previous summer.

What is striking about the terms that Caracalla now agreed with the barbarians of northern Britain is their remarkable success in pacifying a frontier that had seen an effusion of blood for more than a century. We know nothing about the details; perhaps whatever terms had been negotiated between Argentocoxos and Severus in 209 were put back on the table and agreed. The old emperor has been seen in some quarters as a great failure, a view encouraged by Dio, who said of Britain that 'we hold a little less than one half', and that Severus accordingly wished 'to subjugate the whole of it'.[36] If that was really his aim, it is clear that the emperor's efforts after 208 failed. But Dio generally seems to have taken a certain pleasure in portraying Severus in hindsight as failing in his (alleged) military objectives, despite much huffing and puffing. The emperor's alleged desire to outdo the Flavian conquest of the north country runs rather contrary to Herodian's notion – and the flavour of the rest of Dio's own account – that the war was initiated to suppress and punish treacherous barbarians. In pursuing that objective, Severus was, so far as we can tell, a spectacular success.[37] There is positive evidence in his favour: a considerable amount of construction carried out by the governor Alfenus Senecio along the Hadrianic *limes* in the years prior to the war.[38] These efforts tell against major conquests anticipated to the north – and so the mothballing of this frontier system.

[35] Hanson and Maxwell, *Rome's North West Frontier*, 205; if Reed, 'The Scottish Campaigns of Septimius Severus', 98, is correct that there was a Severan campaign in outer Brigantia it is more likely to have been the last.

[36] Dio, *Roman History*, lxxvii.13 [Cary, ed., *Dio*, 264]; from Xiphilinus's epitome of Dio.

[37] For a survey of the evidence, see Esmonde Cleary, *The Ending of Roman Britain*, 56–61.

[38] Duncan, *Scotland*, 28; Salway, *Roman Britain*, 222; Hanson and Maxwell, *Rome's North West Frontier*, 207–8; Birley, *Septimius Severus*, 170–1, 173.

After 211 there seems to have been no further question in Britain of where Britannia ended and *barbaricum* began. A frontier system 'in depth' had bedded down, through which Rome endeavoured thereafter to monitor and facilitate contact with *barbaricum*. After Severus and Caracalla, spies (*exploratores*) were employed to keep it under surveillance, perhaps in a fairly formal manner rather than a clandestine one. Some *exploratores* were probably official observers, posted permanently to their own bases or even sustained at native safe houses.[39] Provincial and Continental officials, diplomats, agents and probably traders and slavers also maintained presences here and there in *barbaricum*. Severus may have envisioned permanent coastal footholds, monitoring and interacting with the barbarians beyond them, and there are suggestions that occupation at Carpow, Cramond and Inveresk continued for some time after 211.

From the time that over a million nails were buried at unfinished Inchtuthil on the Tay, Rome's primary objective in northern Britain was surely a decisive, long-term answer to the frontier question. For most of the individual years of the next twelve decades, the different *limites* established by Rome had remained fairly secure, as long as they were maintained. From a longer-term perspective, however, fundamental problems with the Britannic frontier refused to go away. That changed after Septimius Severus died at Eboracum. It is very unfortunate that we do not know why, and that we shall never know for certain. A final decision about the position and status of outer Brigantia, acceptable on both sides, was surely part of the solution. Senecio's work at Hadrian's Wall reveals what that decision was. Another, perhaps large, part of the solution may have been the fact that an emperor had come into northern Britain personally, seeking to make a long-term impact, if various governors of yesteryear had been more inclined towards short-termism in the interests of immediately making names for themselves and furthering their public careers. Whatever the explanation and complexities, Severus and Caracalla succeeded where Antoninus Pius and Marcus Aurelius had failed in bequeathing to their successors a stable frontier in Britain which remained secure for generations. When that security finally broke down, both the Roman Empire and the barbarians of Britain had undergone very substantial internal changes which Severus and his son cannot have anticipated.

[39] Richmond, 'Roman and Native', 114–15, 125.

ROMANISING AND THE PEOPLES OF NORTHERN BRITAIN

After their war against Severus and Caracalla, our knowledge of the natives of northern Britain passes into a dimmer state from which it never really emerges until the Early Historic period. Severus surely destabilised inner Caledonia through his campaigning, and we can only guess at its recovery time after pulverisation at the hands of the legionaries, but he did not destroy the Maiatai. We find them as late as the seventh century in their Early Historic guise of the Miathi of *Vita Columbae*.[40] The Calidones, too, have a part to play later in this book. What resemblance these nations may have borne to their first- and second-century forebears is difficult to ascertain. Change is to be expected, but the continuity of names is a significant fact.

Popular culture, not least on the Web, has embraced the uplifting idea of a free Caledonia, where native Celts manfully and womanfully preserved their independence and their beloved ancient ways untouched by the grasping talons of a Roman eagle bent on forcing them to speak Latin, to worship dead emperors, to dine lying down and to bathe in olive oil in rooms equipped with under-floor heating. It is an utter fairy tale – our own way of writing pseudo-history which reveals more about ourselves (especially our anxieties about imperialism and globalisation) than it does about the past. The peoples of outer Brigantia and inner Caledonia had been snug in bed with the Roman elephant long before Severus came to northern Britain, and so they remained for the rest of the Roman Iron Age. Neither was Atlantic Scotland preserved unchanged. Occasional Roman and native military campaigns, and episodes of Roman occupation and withdrawal, tell only a small part of this story. More important for understanding Rome's impact on the north country are the subsidies that the barbarians continued to receive from the Eternal City, the obligations that receipt of this material entailed and the ways in which native attitudes towards such relationships helped to shape ethnic identities in *barbaricum*.

At one level, of course, relations between Rome and the peoples of northern Britain could be violent. When Herodian writes of opportunistic (even rebellious) *barbaroi* 'laying waste the countryside, carrying off plunder and wrecking almost everything', it is too easy to forget that the people responsible almost certainly treated each other in much the same way sometimes. Violence of this kind was entirely typical of 'non-state'

---

[40] Adomnán, *V. s. Columbae*, i.8–9.

human societies throughout history – what may be termed 'fully civil' societies (in preference to 'tribal' ones).[41] To judge from conceptions still in place in the Early Historic period across Britain and Ireland, Iron Age farming households capable of subsisting self-sufficiently from their own lands and livestock, year after year, will have produced the full stakeholders in each *civitas*. These bodies of 'normal freemen' will have enjoyed the full range of public rights and entitlements, forming the fully civil basis of the sovereignty of each *civitas*. Their precise rights and the workings of that sovereignty will never be known. Yet as Bloch astutely said of the early Middle Ages, it was 'an age when every man of action had to be something of a lawyer'.[42] For normal freemen throughout our period, whose very freedom was at stake when their lands and other resources were threatened, infringement of their rights demanded a response, which could include the initiation of blood-feud or 'customary vengeance'.[43]

By the Early Historic period, when the fully civil nature of society was coming under threat from state formation, the principal tactic in warfare across Britain and Ireland was still raiding and plundering, as it had been for the second-century Maiatai. The overwhelming majority of fully civil societies globally waged total war, pillaging enemies of livestock, slaves and other resources and possessions, destroying houses and means of production like crops and woodlands and killing or capturing means of social reproduction – children and women.[44] Throughout our period, the ordinary women, men and children of northern Britain must have lived in pretty much constant fear of such horrors. Early Historic anecdotes show that the bleak character of society stemmed ultimately from a cultural acceptance, shared with fully civil societies all around the world, of the justice of taking vengeance as compensation for injury, resulting in endemic warfare.[45] Other motives – the desire to win prestige by acquiring and redistributing territory and resources like cattle and women, the desire to subjugate enemies or rivals, the subconscious drive to affirm or redefine socio-political realities – pale in comparison, and may in any case confuse effects with motives.

---

[41] 'Fully civil' here is inspired by Charles-Edwards, *Early Christian Ireland*, 80.

[42] Bloch, *Feudal Society*, 107.

[43] Pelteret, *Slavery*, 29; Miller, *Bloodtaking and Peacemaking*, 179–89; Halsall, 'Violence and Society', 22–6. For the purposes of this book, I have preferred 'feuding' to Halsall's 'customary vengeance'.

[44] Keeley, *War Before Civilization*, 48; see also Alcock, *Kings and Warriors*, 202.

[45] Adomnán, *V. s. Columbae*, i.42; ii.23; ii.37; ii.42; Bede, *Hist. eccl.*, iv.21; Keeley, *War Before Civilization*, 115–17, 179; Halsall, *Warfare and Society*, 16; Alcock, *Kings and Warriors*, 122.

As regards the Roman Iron Age in northern Britain, Early Historic anecdotes and broad anthropological models are admittedly no substitute for hard evidence of endemic warfare. The search for evidence is complicated by the need to beware biased Roman reporting on the subject of native savagery. Reliance on archaeology alone, on the other hand, is unlikely to result in a conclusive case one way or the other. Weapons and 'fortifications' can be seen by some archaeologists as the stuff of endemic warfare, but by others as symbols with no necessary practical function. Similarly, the characteristic 'isolated farms' and unenclosed settlements of inner Caledonia can be seen as indicative of little violence, but there are other ways to explain such tendencies, which arguably sit comfortably alongside Roman textual evidence suggesting that the principal response to warfare was flight.[46] Asking hard questions of our evidence and challenging assumptions are greatly to be encouraged on this and other subjects. Yet we ought not to forget one anthropologist's warning that denying societies their capacity for unthinkable violence (when we have Roman and Early Historic textual evidence to the contrary) patronises and even dehumanises them.[47]

Because the *civitates* of outer Brigantia and inner Caledonia lacked state structures, groups were encouraged to take the law into their own hands – the essence of the blood-feud. This is not to say that they were necessarily disorganised or lawless. It is a modern Western conceit – informed by aversion to war and outmoded notions of 'primitive' and 'advanced' societies – which suggests that a society must be unsophisticated if it is warlike. The word *civitas* implies that Iron Age northern Britain had developed systems of consensual law typical of fully civil societies – law in which civil authority arose from consensus among normal freemen. A key principal in such systems was that the intervention of a credibly impartial third party was society's main vehicle for averting blood-feud. Indeed, Early Historic anecdotes show the Church taking the opportunity of violent clashes to stamp its presence on society in the interests of peace and its own status. In the Roman Iron Age, Rome too desired peace among natives under its direct control, and the example of Severus's war in inner Caledonia shows that she desired it as well beyond the frontier. She also wished to assert her presence, authority and status. Third-party intervention in local disputes would surely have suggested itself as an important

---

[46] For different discussions, see Woolliscroft and Hoffmann, *Rome's First Frontier*, 210; Hanson and Maxwell, *Rome's North West Frontier*, 5–6, 13–15, 23–5.
[47] Keeley, *War Before Civilization*, 179.

means to that end. It therefore seems simplistic to see proliferations of Roman military installations entirely in terms of subjugation and suppression of hostile barbarian patriots, and naive to assume that the Roman presence brought no benefits whatsoever. In countless anecdotes from Roman writing, war and the fear of it occur repeatedly as a driving force sending native leaders to Roman ones, hoping for their intervention. Yet there has ever been a fine line between the peace-keeper and the oppressor, and the enforcement of *pax Romana* could often be brutal.

If Lupus purchased peace from the Maiatai after 197, archaeology indicates that he was not unique. For some twenty years before and after Severus's principate, native leaders in northern Britain, like counterparts elsewhere in *barbaricum*, seem regularly to have received subsidies from the Romans in the form of lump sums of silver coins.[48] To characterise such subsidies as 'bribes' is to misunderstand the nature of gift-giving in prestige economies, by giving it an inappropriate, capitalist face. In return for diplomatic gifts throughout Europe, North Africa and the Near East Rome expected peace, goodwill and a measure of cooperation, in the same way that receiving a gift or a favour today usually creates a sense of obligation to reciprocate somehow. Rome may also have sought ready access to slaves, hides, wool and furs in northern Britain, in addition to building materials and livestock on the hoof. State *negotiatores* working to supply the legions could range very widely, and were probably not an uncommon sight in the north country. It has been noted already that the army appears to have been the origin for most of the Roman goods found at native sites from the first and second centuries, some of which were no doubt exchanged for supplies sought by these *negotiatores*.

Across northern Britain, the native settlements that seem to have had easiest access to Roman material in the earlier Roman Iron Age were those which were most elaborate in structure and form, whose inhabitants were, therefore, probably distinguished by their wealth and prestige. In outer Brigantia, and in particular in the eastern part, a hierarchy has been observed in the distribution of Roman goods, with most native sites having very restricted access, a small number having rich access and a middle tier in between. A feature of this pattern is an association of such finds with brochs, Iron Age Scotland's elaborate settlement structure *par excellence*.[49] In inner Caledonia, however, the pattern is not so complex, with no clear middle tier; and in Atlantic Scotland the pattern is different

---

[48] Hunter, *Beyond the Edge of the Empire*, 24.
[49] Macinnes, 'Brochs and the Roman Occupation'; Macinnes, 'Baubles, Bangles and Beads', 112; Hunter, *Beyond the Edge of the Empire*, 18.

again, with little differentiation between sites at all. In the latter two cases, archaeologists are encouraged to conclude that the *civitates* of these lands were, for the most part, 'flatter' societies than others in outer Brigantia – 'self-governing farmer republics' in which there were few or no formal distinctions between normal freemen.[50] Such a broad distinction between the societies roughly north and south of the Forth may be reflected in settlement archaeology, the greater tendency for southern settlements to be enclosed (or fortified) therefore reflecting societies with greater contouring than further north. The third-century Roman geographer C. Julius Solinus, whose sources were mainly first- and second-century texts, wrote some tantalising things about society in the Hebrides and the Northern Isles in *De mirabilis mundi*, 'On the World's Wonders'. Men in the Northern Isles, he says, shared their women in common, while the Hebrides were ruled by a single king who possessed nothing, that he might 'learn justice through poverty', subsisting on the resources of others and even taking their wives.[51] Dio, too, makes some brief and comparable statements, but both he and Solinus include quite preposterous other details which greatly undermine the value of their ethnographic comments.

Such 'flat' societies as may have been present in northern Britain at this time ought still to be regarded as hierarchical, despite the tendencies of some scholars. Distinct from self-sufficient normal freemen would have been two other categories of person: the semi-free whose farms were not self-sufficient and who, therefore, 'sold' their labour and service in order to make ends meet; and the unfree, for whom survival with few means required them to 'sell' their very freedom. The public rights of the semi-free were probably restricted, while the unfree probably enjoyed few if any entitlements.[52] At the same time, variable capacities among normal freemen to 'buy' semi-free and unfree labour and service will have differentiated them. In the early Middle Ages, all across the West, it was a prime benchmark of elite status to provide patronage for numbers of dependants or clients, and the Iron Age is unlikely to have been very different in broad terms. The central question for scholars is whether or not the elites of Iron Age northern Britain enjoyed rights and

---

50 Hunter, *Beyond the Edge of the Empire*, 18, 49; see also Macinnes, 'Baubles, Bangles and Beads', 112; Hanson and Maxwell, *Rome's North West Frontier*, 13–15. On 'farmer republics', see Woolf, *From Pictland to Alba*, 50–1, 299–300.

51 Solinus, *De mirab. mundi*, § 23.

52 For discussion of these categories and their origins in Britain and Ireland, see Charles-Edwards, 'Kinship, Status and the Origins of the Hide'. See also Hines, 'Society', 79.

entitlements distinct from other freemen, like the *nemed* ('privileged') of Early Historic Ireland and other Early Historic nobilities.[53] The alternative is that distinctions were informal, self-made and not inheritable, and based on prestige and influence rather than special rights denied to other freemen – somewhat akin to those enjoyed today by leading gangsters. The distribution of Roman goods at native sites in the first and second centuries may tend to suggest that it was only among certain outer Brigantian peoples that the more 'contoured' social structure associated with formal elites was common. Such key social differences may help to explain why the Romans treated outer Brigantia so differently from inner Caledonia and Atlantic Scotland in the first and second centuries. That said, there are two curious clusters of brochs in inner Caledonia, one about the Firth of Tay and another, larger one in the Maiatian heartland about the Forth basin. If lowland broch-building was an elite reflex inspired by increasingly contoured societies, the Forth cluster may be regarded as additional evidence of the pre-eminence of Maiatian leaders in the second century.[54]

The introduction of Roman goods into the prestige economies of the north country can have exerted a powerful new influence with consequences for the shape of society across *barbaricum*. All across northern Europe, it seems that barbarian elites could derive considerable prestige by securing direct access to Roman material. An important question for many of these groups was whether (or when) to seek to acquire goods through cooperation or through plundering. This universal constant reveals something of the awe that Rome was capable of inspiring, even where she did not rule. Access to her goods through diplomatic exchange, trade and plunder contributed at various points to the formation of 'premier leagues' of elites set apart from others in their communities with less direct access. Something of this very general European phenomenon – leading time and again to the formalisation of noble classes – is probably reflected in the distribution patterns of northern Britain, particularly in outer Brigantia and inner Caledonia.[55] The establishment of the Hadrianic *limes* in the 120s, and its re-establishment in the 160s, ought to have made access to Roman goods a great deal more restricted in outer Brigantia than had been the case during Pius's principate. Was this economic factor, and its ramifications for prestige economics across the

---

[53] Kelly, *A Guide to Early Irish Law*, 7–12; Pelteret, *Slavery*, 29–30. See Halsall, *Warfare and Society*, 21, for a general discussion.
[54] Macinnes, 'Brochs and the Roman Occupation', 242.
[55] Macinnes, 'Baubles, Bangles and Beads'; Harding, *The Iron Age in Northern Britain*, 187–9.

region, a key one in the frontier troubles that Rome experienced in the last third of the second century?

In common with other areas in late Antiquity, it seems that northern Britain underwent something of a social revolution as a result, in part, of Roman influences. An illustrative parallel from more recent Scottish history might, very generally, be found in the last quarter of the eighteenth century, when the introduction of Improvement economics and ideologies brought social 'turmoil' across rural Scotland. The key forces involved included new economic opportunities and attitudes among elites in particular. Rural Scotland had been feeling their influences for generations, the time-honoured social structures showing themselves resilient enough to absorb the pressure they created. What finally tore the social fabric was an acute increase in pressure arising mainly from sudden and specific economic changes.[56] For the relevant parts of Roman Iron Age Scotland, as elsewhere in *barbaricum*, the comparable breaking point appears to have come in the third century.

In the meantime, the demands of the natives in exchange relationships with Rome were highly selective and, indeed, luxurious. In the main they included fine brooches and other jewellery, as well as up-market (especially Samian) tableware and bronze or glass vessels, rare even by Roman standards, along with the wine that was served in them. These imports begin to reveal something of the nature of prestige economics and culture in northern Britain in this period – it seems to have revolved around hospitality (and feasting in particular) and to have encouraged personal adornment.[57] Scholars now recognise that such changes in native material culture represent part of the same romanising cultural phenomenon which, within Britannia itself, was bringing about much more substantial transformations – 'romanisation' proper. It is important for understanding the legacy of Septimius Severus in Scotland and his settlement of the frontier question that the phenomenon of romanising manifested itself quite differently in outer Brigantia than it did in inner Caledonia, with the Maiatai in the middle.

Late Antiquity saw the advent across both outer Brigantia and inner Caledonia of a new dominant burial rite in each zone, something which northern Britain as a whole had lacked earlier in the Iron Age, when individual agricultural communities – or even families – seem (on present evidence) to have maintained their own, sometimes idiosyncratic customs. In outer Brigantia the new rite saw the body laid flat on its back, and

---

[56] Devine, *The Scottish Nation*, 170–2, 180, discusses these processes.
[57] Hunter, *Beyond the Edge of the Empire*, 15–16.

buried in a grave lined with stone slabs (a 'long cist'), usually on a west–east alignment and unfurnished with grave-goods. This rite was not at all confined to outer Brigantia – there are examples all over Scotland – but it was mainly observed, sometimes in substantial cemeteries, between the Tay and the Tyne, thus encapsulating the Maiatian homeland as well as outer Brigantia. Long linked with christianisation because of grave-orientation and lack of furnishings, the rite is in fact little more than a variation of the dominant one practised, by the fifth century, throughout most of Britain, Ireland, northern Gaul and the Low Countries – areas christianised earlier (or later).[58]

What is particularly important about this kind of burial is its identification of the inhabitants of outer Brigantia as romanisers – active participants along with Roman provincials in a key cultural phenomenon. Their taste for Roman goods continued throughout the Roman Iron Age, with Traprain Law, possibly a highly influential centre, overflowing with Roman imports. By the end of the period the Roman religion – Christianity – had become established across the region also. Indeed, the key evidence of their christianisation, inscribed funerary and proprietal markers erected in Galloway, Tweeddale, Lothian and Fife further display outer Brigantia's romanising tendencies, being another widespread cultural phenomenon shared with some north-western Roman provincials and the post-provincial Romano-British population. In 122 Hadrian had placed outer Brigantia firmly in *barbaricum*, but for the rest of the Roman Iron Age its peoples refused to sever their links with *romanitas*. It is probably the main reason that they emerged from the Roman Iron Age as *Britanni* in Latin, Britons, rather than as Picts. From this perspective, the real possibility that the frontier troubles of the second century reflected outer Brigantian resentment at being shut out by Hadrian's Wall deserves to be restated, with knock-on effects for understanding the Antonine project.

The picture in inner Caledonia north of the Tay is rather different. Here, too, a new dominant burial rite appeared in late Antiquity: an extended inhumation burial like the long-cist rite, but covered by a low mound defined by ditches. Comparable barrow burials took place in parts of Anglo-Saxon England, interpreted as self-conscious departures from

---

[58] Halsall, *Early Medieval Cemeteries*, 5–13, 18–20. On the link with Christianity, see, however, Thomas, 'The Evidence from North Britain'; Thomas, *Christianity in Roman Britain*, 230–6; Duncan, *Scotland*, 69; Smyth, *Warlords*, 34; Maxwell, 'Settlement in Southern Pictland', 34–5; Proudfoot, 'The Hallow Hill and Origins of Christianity'; Burt, 'Long-Cist Cemeteries'; Smith, 'The Origins and Development of Christianity', 28–9; Carver, *Surviving in Symbols*, 22–3.

the romanising norm.[59] Can the same be said of the inner Caledonian 'square barrow'? Certainly the flow of Roman goods into inner Caledonia dried up in late Antiquity, its christianisation appears to have been somewhat later than that of outer Brigantia and its inhabitants never went in for the funerary and proprietal markers of their romanising southern neighbours. If this cultural trajectory represents a rejection of *romanitas*, it can none the less still be seen as a by-product of the romanising phenomenon, further confirming the powerful influence of Rome. Scholars are learning to stop assuming that certain shared trends in material culture are characteristic of peoples like the Calidones of inner Caledonia, or the Picts who emerged there in the later Roman Iron Age. However, the noticeably different imprints made in these two zones by cultural interaction with Rome could certainly have reflected, as well as affirmed and exacerbated, different ethnic identities in the north country at the time of Severus and Caracalla. The situation may, indeed, be likened to that which obtained along the Rhine between the Franks, whose underlying material culture derived much from late Roman practices, and the neighbouring Alamanni, whose material culture was more recognisably barbarian.

As in these other matters, Roman Iron Age nation-building in northern Britain, and the role of romanising in the process, cannot be studied in isolation. Although it had its own particular distinctions, the country again seems to fit a broad first-millennium pattern, whereby large barbarian political entities commonly developed in regions somewhat removed from the frontiers of great empires, but not immediately next to them. Regions like outer Brigantia Rome tended to regard as lying within her orbit, interfering in them regularly as a matter of border security.[60] Does this tendency help to explain the so-called 'utter confusion' of the frontier zone in the second century?[61] Arguably we are glimpsing instead confirmation of something that scholars have increasingly accepted: that Rome never had a grand, carefully considered frontier plan for application here or anywhere else in the Empire, but rather did her best to realise fairly vague objectives through unstable, ever-changing circumstances.

Nation-building in the Maiatian and Calidonian homelands raises the thorny subject of the construction of ethnic identities – 'ethnogenesis' – about which scholars of late Antique and early medieval barbarians have

---

[59] Carver, 'Conversion and Politics'; Halsall, *Early Medieval Cemeteries*, 8–9.
[60] Heather, 'State Formation in Europe'; see also Whitaker, 'Supplying the System', 65, 69; James, 'The Origins of Barbarian Kingdoms', 44.
[61] Smyth, *Warlords*, 40.

written a great deal, often with considerable antagonism. There is very little common ground shared by the architects of the dominant theoretical model and those who have criticised it. Ethnic groups in our period regarded themselves pretty unambiguously as communities united by common descent – *gentes* in Latin and *gene* in Greek. Yet ethnicity can be shown to be highly adaptable, and relies on additional strategies in fostering consciousness of difference from other groups. Actual differences in cultural practices can inform ethnic identities – such as romanising tendencies in the Roman Iron Age – but so, too, can mere perceptions of differences, which may be only partially accurate reflections of reality. It is all but impossible, therefore, to ascertain ethnic consciousnesses which may have underpinned the fledgling nations identified by Dio. The extent to which the Maiatai and the Calidones recognised different social structures or romanising tendencies between themselves is not obvious: we have only Dio's testimony to suggest that they did so at all. On the other hand, the ethnogeneses of these two nations may represent just a new phase in the cultivation of a significant ethnic frontier round about the Tay basin, hints of which have already been noted for the Flavian period, and have also been identified in previous epochs.

Ethnogenesis

The transformation of western Roman provinces into barbarian kingdoms, and the rise of medieval nations, have long compelled scholars to explore how peoples form ('ethnogenesis'). Their work has been informed by the human sciences, where ethnicity has long been a subject of great interest.

Nowadays, people talk a great deal about ethnic groups, but few think much about what the concept means. The human sciences define ethnicity as 'identification with a broader group in opposition to others on the basis of perceived cultural differentiation and/or common descent'. The origins of ethnicity are controversial, with some scholars arguing that it arises primarily from 'the givens of birth' – territory, language, religion and culture – and others arguing that it arises primarily as a function of political and economic interests and is sufficiently dynamic to be altered in line with changes in those interests.[62]

According to the dominant model for understanding ethnic developments within the barbarian kingdoms of first-millennium Europe,

---

[62] Jones, *The Archaeology of Ethnicity*, 56–83.

Ethnogenesis (continued)

such peoples as Goths and Franks originated as hodge-podges of small tribal groups. Having formed a sort of confederation and successfully overrun a portion of the Roman Empire, these barbarians settled, and looked to a leading group to guide them in adopting a new ethnic identity. The architect of this hypothesis, Reinhard Wenskus, called this elite group at the heart of every new barbarian nation its *Traditionskern*, or 'kernel of tradition', and concluded that its own particular 'authentic' traditions, preserving stories and an identity of great antiquity, were transferred to the entire nation that adhered to it.[63]

This theory has been robustly criticised, even within the so-called Vienna School that did so much to popularise it.[64] Its followers have sometimes been accused of placing a fanciful and unnecessary theoretical construct ahead of the primary evidence, and relying on naive conceptions of early medieval writings as reliable repositories of fossilised ancient traditions.[65] No scholar of early Scotland can fail to be struck by the similarities between these scholarly camps and those that have debated the value of much later written evidence in studying sub-Roman Britain, or debated how much authentic ancient tradition lies within the prose tales of early medieval Ireland. That these critiques are so similar may be no accident: one of the principal contributors to Wenskus's thinking was Hector Chadwick, one of the most influential scholars and teachers of early Insular history and literature in the first half of the twentieth century.[66]

Like all nations, the Maiatai and the Calidones were surely ethnically and culturally diverse, conjuring up a sense of shared identity only as circumstances required, not least in times of war such as those in which we encounter them in the *History* of Dio. Roman military activity in the Flavian and subsequent periods would have disturbed and reconfigured

---

[63] Wenskus, *Stammesbildung und Verfassung*; Wolfram, *History of the Goths*; Geary, 'Ethnic Identity'; Brooks, *Bede and the English*; James, 'The Origins of Barbarian Kingdoms', 47–8; Heather, 'Disappearing and Reappearing Tribes', 104–9.

[64] See, for example, Pohl, 'Telling the Difference', 67; Pohl, 'Ethnicity, Theory, and Tradition'.

[65] Key assaults upon the *Traditionskern* and its associated ideas include Goffart, 'Two Notes', 19–30; Reynolds, 'Our Forefathers?', 35–6; Goffart, 'Does the Distant Past Impinge'; Bowlus, 'Ethnogenesis'.

[66] Murray, 'Reinhard Wenskus on "Ethnogenesis"', 53.

populations, economies and conventional territories to such an extent that reinterpretations of group identities occurred.[67] No doubt some overt symbols of identity were developed, possibly including aspects of dress, armament, hairstyle or adornment.[68] Tacitus believed that the first-century Calidones were distinguished by red hair, and Rome was aware of barbarian methods of dying hair that colour.[69] If this was a marker of free status among the Calidones, research shows that it could have become per-ceived as an ethnic marker by outsiders. The 'massive' metalwork of inner Caledonia, with its regional variations and suggestions of Roman cultural influences may also represent such a phenomenon.[70]

Where did the first-century Uotadini, later the Gododdin, fit into such nation-building? In broad terms they shared some key cultural traits with the Maiatai, including a fashion for broch-building, but this need say nothing about political and ethnic allegiances. Their romanising tenden-cies were arguably more pronounced than those of any other outer Brigantian people, and may have set the fashion for the whole region. The principal evidence comes from Traprain Law, whose opposite number may lie at Burnswark, one of Scotland's larger hill-forts, which has pro-duced a mix of Roman and native material, and is famous for being 'gripped as in a vice' by Roman siege-works apparently dating to the second half of the second century.[71] Roman relationships with different outer Brigantian peoples need hardly have been uniform or consistent over generations. A tradition of stone-built domestic buildings seems to have grown up among the Uotadini. If it post-dates Roman contact – about which there is debate – it may speak of romanising influences, but still more of the enrichment of Uotadinian leaders either through access to Roman goods, or through tribute taken from neighbouring peoples. The possibility is worth considering that the Uotadini were a Maiatian people in 197 – perhaps even the engine that powered the Maiatian ethno-genesis – since at that period they once again lay outwith Britannia. At present there is no obvious reason to favour such an hypothesis.

In the final analysis, it must be clear that scholars cannot measure the success or failure of Roman frontier policy from the single and simplis-tic criteria of territorial expansion and contraction. Northern Britain

---

[67] Skene, *Celtic Scotland*, vol. 1, 121; Duncan, *Scotland*, 25–6; Heather, 'State Formation in Europe'; Hummer, 'The Fluidity of Barbarian Identity', 6–7.

[68] Pohl, 'Telling the Difference'; Brooks, *Bede and the English*, 5.

[69] Tacitus, *Agricda*, § 11; Pohl, 'Telling the Difference', 54.

[70] Jones, *Archaeology of Ethnicity*, 112–27; Pohl, 'Telling the Difference', 40–1, 51–2; Piggott, 'The Archaeological Background', 63–4; Hunter, 'New Light', 148–50.

[71] Campbell, 'The Roman Siege of Burnswark'.

remained unconquered after 211, but, as far as Rome was concerned, remarkably subdued. Her hand was reaching deep into its material culture, and touching even on the very social and ethnic identities of the inhabitants of outer Brigantia and inner Caledonia at least. Her legions had brought about occasional economic and political instability and no small amount of human misery, which will have chastened some and enflamed others. It is important not to dismiss the dire consequences for fully civil societies of being reduced to famine, ruin and desperation. No doubt internal conflicts and convulsions resulted. All indications are that, by 211, people had had enough and were willing to back a settlement. By then their *civitates* or 'farmer republics' were also beginning to change. Romanising everywhere owed as much to the initiative and energy of native leaders as to any avowed Roman policies. As regards the finer points of detail in evaluating the relative importance of native and extraneous factors contributing to social developments anywhere in *barbaricum* in this period, however, it is immensely difficult to be certain of anything.

CHAPTER 2

The Later Roman Iron Age and the Origins of the Picts

By the beginning of the fourth century, the Severan settlement in northern Britain was in tatters, and in the middle third of the century Roman Britain was probably mortally wounded. In the sole surviving native account, *De excidio Britanniae*, 'On the Destruction of Britannia', written a century or so later by the sixth-century cleric Gildas, the end of Roman government in Britain is brought about in no small part 'by two exceedingly savage overseas peoples': *Scoti* or Gaels 'from the northwest', and *Picti* or Picts 'from the north'. A first devastating incursion was repulsed by a Roman army arriving from the Continent. When it withdrew from the island, however, the barbarians reappeared. A second army delivered Britain from them once again, putting them 'to flight across the sea', though by then they had 'greedily taken heaps of booty overseas'. Once again, after the Roman soldiers withdrew, 'there eagerly emerged from the coracles that carried them across the waves foul hordes of Gaels and Picts, like dark throngs of worms, which wriggle out of narrow fissures in a rock when the sun is high and the weather grows warm'.[1] Gildas had a rare gift for such talk.

Now at last, Gildas says, the terrible invaders 'seized the whole of the extreme north of the island from its inhabitants, right up to the Wall'. This, he believed, was how Gaels and Picts from overseas had come to dwell in northern Britain, which, he implies, had previously been in Roman hands. This migrationist myth is pseudo-historical. Not yet satisfied, the barbarians in Gildas's narrative proceeded to raid and pillage at will across Britain once more, with no further help coming from Rome. In the years which followed, the population recovered, but came to fear a fresh wave of depredations. Its leaders, therefore, decided 'that

---

[1] Gildas, *De excidio Brit.*, i.14–17.

the ferocious Saxons . . . should be let into the island – like wolves into
the fold – to beat back the peoples of the north'. The Saxons, however,
rebelled, beginning to seize Romano-British territory for themselves,
further afflicting their beleaguered hosts and administering the *coup de
grâce* to Roman civilisation and culture in Britain.[2]

This sixth-century reconstruction of the end of Roman jurisdiction
in Britannia is highly rhetorical, simplistic and melodramatic, and a poor
guide to that complex process. Its broad thrust is worthier of closer
attention than the minute details. Gildas's basic story maintains that a
Roman island began to experience Pictish and Gaelic depredations.
These attacks were manageable only as long as Roman armies were available to meet them, crossing to Britain from the Continent. Otherwise,
Britannia was in great peril. It is a reasonable overview of the situation
on the northern frontier a century earlier than that in which Gildas set
it, beginning with the peace of the Severan settlement, and ending with
the infamous Barbarian Conspiracy (*barbaric[a] conspiratio*) which
caused a sensation across the Roman Empire 180 years before *De excidio
Britanniae*.[3]

THE PAINTED MEN

Bede is explicit in *Historia ecclesiastica* that the southern limit of Pictland
lay at the Firth of Forth in the 730s, not at the Tay or the Ochil Hills. On
that evidence the Maiatai might have been regarded as a Pictish people as
early as the fourth century, except that *Vita Columbae* gives no hint that
the seventh-century Miathi were Picts rather than Britons. It is possible,
therefore, that the southern Pictish boundary known to Bede was a relatively new development: in fact, a case can be made that it dates only to
the years after 698.

The persistence of some Roman Iron Age identities into the Early
Historic centuries gives fair warning that the political landscape of inner
Caledonia remained complex after the coming of Pictishness. The Pictish
peoples (*populi*), nations (*gentes*), kingdoms (*prouinciae*) and districts
(*regiones*) mentioned in eighth-century Northumbrian texts confirm that.
It is important not to underestimate such diversity. Our capacity to locate
and name particular Pictish kingdoms or districts is unfortunately quite
limited. The Gaelic quatrain *Mórseiser do Chruithne claind*, 'Seven

---

[2] Gildas, *De excidio Brit.*, i.19, 23–6.
[3] Ammianus, *Res gestae*, xxvii.8.

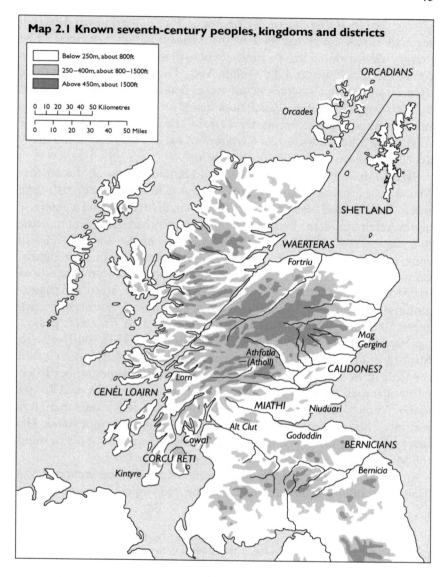

Map 2.1 Known seventh-century peoples, kingdoms and districts

Below 250m, about 800ft
250–400m, about 800–1500ft
Above 450m, about 1500ft

0 10 20 30 40 50 Kilometres
0 10   20   30   40   50 Miles

ORCADIANS

Orcades

SHETLAND

WAERTERAS
Fortriu

Mag
Gergind

Athfotla
—(Atholl)

CALIDONES?

Lorn

CENÉL LOAIRN

MIATHI   Niuduari

Alt Clut

Cowal   Gododdin

CORCU RÉTI   BERNICIANS

Kintyre   Bernicia

Children of Cruithne', probably dating from not much earlier than *c.* 850, seems to contain a glimpse of Pictish geography which has attracted generations of comment.[4] 'Seven children of Cruithne', says the poet

[4] The poem seems to belong to the same pseudo-historical milieu as the first section of the longer Pictish king-list, which appears to have been added to it during the reign of Causantín mac Cinaeda (862–76); see Broun, *Scottish Independence*, 55, 79.

(giving the Great Pict the name *Cruithne* or 'Pict'), 'partitioned Alba into seven divisions', such that 'each of them has his name on his land'. The literary device of giving territories eponymous ancient founders was common in Antiquity and the Middle Ages. The common idea that there were seven Pictish kingdoms or provinces from early times, encouraged by *Mórseiser do Chruithne claind*, thus stands on shaky ground. Even less valuable is the twelfth-century tract *De situ Albanie*, 'On the Situation of Alba', which like *Mórseiser do Chruithne claind* has factored in too many deliberations over early Pictish geography.[5]

By 730, it seems that the Miathi had become Picts – or at least that Manau had become a Pictish district (*regio*). The southern Pictish zone was to Bede's mind made up of such *regiones*, districts within a *prouincia* or sovereign kingdom. Pictland (*terra Pictorum*) had, in addition, come to consist of two or more sovereign kingdoms in the northern Pictish zone – the lands north of the Grampian Highlands.[6] It is an eighth-century Irish reference to a king of Picts *citra Monoth*, 'on this side of the Mounth', that indicates where Bede's more vague 'steep and rugged mountain ridges' lay, separating the northern and southern Pictish zones.[7] The district or feature known to the Welsh as *Bannauc*, 'peaky', has been identified with the Touch and Gargunnock Hills south-west of Stirling, drained by the famous Bannock Burn.[8] Yet in *Vita sancti Cadoci*, the 'Life of St Cadog' composed *c*. 1200, the Welsh hagiographer Lifris wrote that *mons Bannauc* 'is said to be situated in the midst of Alba' (*in medio Albanie*), Scotland north of the Forth.[9] If Lifris's information is accurate, the conventional identification of Bannauc cannot stand. His language, including his conception of Bannauc as a *mons*, calls to mind the Mounth instead, which is certainly 'peaky'.[10]

It seems that, by 730, the old march that had once separated the Maiatai from the Calidones had disappeared, unless it continued to

---

[5] *De situ Albanie*; Skene, *Celtic Scotland*, vol. 1, 280–1; Anderson, *Early Sources*, vol. 1, pp. cxv–cxix; Chadwick, *Early Scotland*, 38–42; Broun, 'Seven Kingdoms'; Woolf, 'The Verturian Hegemony', 107.

[6] Bede, *Hist. eccl.*, iii.4; iv.26. On Bede's use of *prouincia* and *regio*, see Campbell, *Bede's Reges and Principes*, 2–3.

[7] *Annals of Ulster* [*AU*] 782.1; Bede, *Hist. eccl.*, iii.4; v.9; Skene, *Celtic Scotland*, vol. 1, 130, 230–1.

[8] 'Aneirin', *Gododdin*. 'B-text', l, 255; Broun, 'Seven Kingdoms', 41n; Jackson, 'Britons in Southern Scotland', 81.

[9] Lifris, *V. s. Cadoci*, § 26; Davies, *Book of Llandaf*, 76, discusses the date of this text. I owe the reference to Alex Woolf.

[10] Bromwich, *Trioedd*, 278.

separate southern Pictish districts.[11] Northern Pictland, on the other hand, was understood by Bede to be home to sovereign kingdoms. This political distinction between unified south and disunited north is one important hint that Bede's informant was, as he tells us, southern Pictish.[12] It may be no coincidence that, when Bede wrote these words, Pictland was being dominated by a southern Pictish king. Discussing events set north of the Forth in the early 670s, Bede's contemporary Stephen, the hagiographer of *Vita sancti Wilfrithi*, the 'Life of St Wilfrith', known today as 'Wilfrid', similarly speaks of a political landscape consisting of distinct peoples (*populi*), even distinct nations or races (*gentes*).[13] Against this backdrop of Pictish political and ethnic complexity, Bede was even given to understand that the southern and northern Picts had divergent ecclesiastical histories. Thus, although Bede and his contemporaries regarded the *gens Pictorum* as a single nation, one ought not to push too far any suggestion of homogeneity or antiquity within this notion.

Whatever we make of the appearance of *Picti* in our sources in late Antiquity, then, we may feel assured that the term does not refer to a single political community or ethnic solidarity. There is no convincing evidence that it did so much before 700. The earliest surviving use of the term was regarded as self-explanatory. As far as Tacitus, Dio and Herodian were concerned, the peoples of northern Britain had been, collectively, *Britanni*. How did some of them become *Picti* in the century after the death of Severus? Gildas's notion of a great migration from overseas cannot be supported from other evidence. Disagreement persists among scholars about whether the term represents a latinisation of some native name, or whether it is entirely Roman, but the latter notion has always seemed most convincing.[14] The most common explanation is that *Picti* originated as Latin 'painteds', a Roman nickname arising from an actual tendency among the northern peoples to apply pigment to their skin. This conclusion seems broadly satisfactory, but may fail fully to appreciate the social context of the origins of *Picti*, and what it meant to Romans at a more fundamental level.

[11] Skene, *Celtic Scotland*, vol. 1, 231, had a convoluted sense of such a process.
[12] Chadwick, *Early Scotland*, 27–8, appreciated the Pictish provenance of Bede's information; see also Hughes, *Early Christianity in Pictland*, 1–2; Duncan, 'Bede, Iona, and the Picts', 20–1; Wallace-Hadrill, *Bede's Ecclesiastical History*, 92; Fraser, 'Adomnán, Cumméne Ailbe, and the Picts', 188–90.
[13] Stephen, *V. s. Wilfrithi*, § 19.
[14] Jackson, 'Pictish Language', 159–60, quietly rejecting Watson, *Celtic Place-Names*, 67–8. See also Nicolaisen, *Scottish Place-Names*, 150–1.

A consideration of parallel developments in Gaelic and British vernacular usage, evident by the Early Historic period, produces important
results. In medieval Welsh the word denoting Picts was *Prydyn*; in Old
Irish they were called *Cruithni*. When these two words were coined, they
denoted a native of Britain, just as *Britanni* did in Latin as late as *c.* 250
when Herodian wrote. *Cruithni* surely had that meaning when it was
applied in Ireland to a large population of 'Britons' in the north-east,
about whom more will be said later. Similarly *Alba*, the Gaelic name of
the Pictish kingdom by 900, seems originally to have meant 'Britain'
(Latin *Albion*), and a tenth-century source may imply that the British languages knew Pictland as *Albid*.[15] A parallel development is perceptible in
both Latin and the Insular vernacular languages, then, in which the old
term for 'a Briton' became deficient. The reason, it seems, was that it did
not allow one to differentiate at a general level between Roman Britons
and those who were not Romans. We have seen that the frontier question
remained unresolved in Britain until the early third century. By the end of
the third century, it had become possible, as never before, to differentiate
in Latin between a *Britto* – now specifically a Romano-British provincial
– and a *Pictus* – a Briton from *barbaricum*. The same facility also arose
within the Insular languages, although the dating is much less clear: both
came to borrow Latin *Brittones* (Old Irish *Breatain*; Old Welsh *Brython*)
for application to the Romano-British population.[16] Such linguistic
developments may be regarded as further confirmation of the
significance of the Severan settlement after 211.

What is surely instructive is that in all languages, the implication is that
the Britons called *Picti* in Latin were seen as those who remained barbarians.[17] *Picti* thus strikes one as something other than a mere nickname. Its
development as a way to differentiate between Roman and non-Roman
Britons reveals something important about identities in Britain in the
century after Severus. Latin shared the implication of the vernacular
Insular languages that it was inside Britannia – not among the Picts – that
Britishness had changed, creating the need for new ethnic terminology.
The undercurrent of disdain in *Picti* may not be unrelated to the diplo-
matic situation that seems to have developed between Rome and inner
Caledonia in the later Roman Iron Age, about which more will be
said later. The settlement archaeology suggests that it was never more

---

[15] For discussion, see Woolf, *From Pictland to Alba*, 178–80. See also Broun, *Scottish
Independence*, 79–80.

[16] Jackson, 'Two Early Scottish Names', 16–17.

[17] For another discussion of this nomenclature, not incompatible with mine, see Broun,
Scottish Independence, 81–3.

possible than in this period of 'abrupt disruption' in inner Caledonia for Romans to emphasise the barbarian character of its inhabitants.[18] Were these developments the end result of the Severan settlement? In any case, the Britons of inner Caledonia had become transformed in Roman eyes from *Brittones* into *Picti*, probably without realising it. Pictishness was thus an idea – a Roman idea – that arose without the necessity of a new, all-encompassing ethnic solidarity in inner Caledonia. It was probably a consequence of new ethnic consciousness in southern Britain – a sense of difference from the northern barbarians – that gave rise ultimately to the notion of Pictishness.

Neither in late Antiquity, then, nor in the Early Historic period, is there convincing evidence to suggest that Pictishness meant anything to the peoples of inner Caledonia before the end of the Roman Iron Age. Such evidence as we have suggests instead that the ethnic solidarities that were bedding down in 211 among the Maiatai and the Calidones persisted, possibly as late as the seventh century. What commentators like Bede and Stephen understood by *Picti* in the seventh and eighth centuries, when the term had clearly been adopted by the Picts themselves, need not bear much resemblance to what fourth-century historians and poets meant. Key questions for those interested in Pictish origins include, when and how the Pictish nations came to adopt the Latin label *Picti* as their own, and the ethnic implications surrounding this development. These questions speak in part of the Roman legacy in northern Britain and are considered in later chapters.

One of the earliest surviving references to *Picti* speaks of 'the Calidones and the other Picts', showing that this old nation at least was Pictish as late Antiquity understood it.[19] The territory assigned to it in the previous chapter went on to form the greater part of the southern Pictish zone known to Bede, with its various unnamed districts. Textual references to the Calidones are limited to the Roman Iron Age, save for indirect ones in Early Historic place-names like Dunkeld and 'the Calidonian forest' (*Coit Celidon*).[20] At present, our best guess at their fate is that the process of ethnogenesis that embraced self-conscious Pictishness involved the obsolescence of Calidonian identity in the southern Pictish zone. Thanks to the Romans, however, their name was destined for modern fame greater even than that of the Picts, and utterly dwarfing that of the Maiatai, all but forgotten today.

---

[18] Hunter, *Beyond the Edge of the Empire*, 49–50.
[19] *Pan. Latini*, vi.7.1.
[20] *Hist. Brit.*, § 56.

FORTRIU AND PICTISHNESS

Like the Calidones, the Verturiones who joined them in the Barbarian Conspiracy of the fourth century are unambiguously Pictish both in late Antique and in Early Historic times. Unlike the Calidones, however, this nation is unknown before the fourth century, and also detectable in Insular chronicles from the seventh century until the tenth. *Verturiones* passed into Gaelic as **Foirtrinn* (genitive *Fortrenn*, 'of **Fortriu*') from British, and into English as *Waerteras*. Scholars habitually use the Gaelic nomenclature, speaking of the Verturian kingdom as Fortriu, and so the English name might as well be used in reference to its people – the Waerteras.[21]

A comprehensive examination of the evidence shows that the Verturian homeland, long mis-identified with Strathearn, was in the northern Pictish zone, encompassing modern Forres and Inverness.[22] The nation seems, therefore, to have grown up at the margins of inner Caledonia and Atlantic Scotland. Both Agricola and Severus (or Caracalla) reached the Spey on their campaigns, beyond which Flavian surveyors had located the Decantae. There are strong suggestions at Birnie near Elgin that Rome maintained diplomatic contact with at least some leaders of this *civitas* through the second century.[23] As with the Dumnonii and the Maiatai, the relationship between the first-century Decantae and the fourth-century Verturiones is obscure. As the name of a kingdom (or province), *Moreb*, Moray, is not attested before the tenth century, but the name is probably Pictish, thus originating in our period.

It is clear that *c.* 700 Adomnán regarded the inhabitants of both the southern Pictish zone and Fortriu as Picts, as Bede did *c.* 731. At least some of their Pictish contemporaries shared in this view. Calidonian and Maiatian identity do not seem to have survived the implied Pictish ethnogenesis, but the Waerteras did, enduring beyond the end of our period and vanishing from the record along with Pictishness itself. The fact that their identity was spared obliteration is an important clue that the Waerteras played a key role indeed in embracing and promulgating self-conscious Pictishness. It points still further at the seventh century as a pivotal period in the rise of Pictish identity, the last quarter of which saw Verturian kings dominate both the northern and the southern Pictish zones.

---

[21] Watson, *Celtic Place-Names*, 68. The asterisk denotes a reconstructed nominative form which is not itself attested.
[22] Woolf, 'Dún Nechtain'.
[23] Hunter, *Beyond the Edge of the Empire*, 27–32.

We do not know if the Verturiones of the later Roman Iron Age grew up at the same time as the Maiatai and Calidones, or if they did so a little later. If there was a Verturian Traprain Law, it was probably in Moray at the multivallate coastal promontory fort at Burghead, home of the famous incised bull carvings. Of all the enclosed power centres identified from Early Historic Scotland, this stronghold is three times larger than any of the others, and the most elaborate in layout. Radiocarbon dates suggest that it may have been occupied in the fourth century, flourishing into the eighth and ninth centuries like the Waerteras themselves. Like many other strongholds of the period, Burghead was enclosed by walls constructed of stone and earth and laced with timbers held together with headless iron nails. When this kind of rampart was burned by a conquering enemy, the heat from the burning timbers could transform the interior rubble into a glassy 'vitrified' mess. It has been surmised of Burghead, given its size and position on the fine harbourage of Burghead Bay, 'that this was an important naval base for the Picts'.[24] It is a fair observation, but any suggestion of a 'Pictish navy' as a standing military force should be resisted. We ought probably to suppose instead that accessibility by sea for large numbers of vessels at a time was one of the features that particularly commended the Burghead promontory to its builders. Sea travel may indeed have been a key aspect of the peripatetic kingship of Moravian Verturian kings, and the principal means by which the Waerteras about the Moray Firth accessed their kings.

It is striking that in both fourth- and eighth-century sources Pictishness is envisioned as a product of a sense of common purpose among the peoples of inner Caledonia as far north as Moray. In the fourth century, in Roman eyes the link seems to be reflected in a shared lack of *romanitas*. Pictish attacks on Britannia may have been an important stage in the development of a sense of common purpose among leaders to either side of the Mounth, largely exclusive of other neighbouring peoples. There may have been a linguistic element to this process. Ethnic and place-names furnished by Classical texts have long been scrutinised for evidence pertaining to the language or languages spoken in northern Britain in the Roman Iron Age. More recently, the evidence of early medieval inscriptions and recorded place-names has become better understood and increasingly useful. The totality of the evidence demonstrates beyond reasonable doubt that a British dialect was spoken in

---

[24] Foster, 'Before Alba', 11; Carver, *Surviving in Symbols*, 29–31; Alcock, *Kings and Warriors*, 192–7. On the timber-lacing technique, see also Ralston, *The Hill-Forts of Pictland*, 28–9; Ralston, *Celtic Fortifications*, 48–57.

Pictland throughout our period. 'Scottish Gaelic' being our familiar way of denoting the Gaelic language that developed in northern Britain, it is reasonable to speak of 'Pictish British'.[25] It is true that Bede implies at one point in *Historia ecclesiastica* that British and Pictish were distinct languages, but the same chapter contains origin legends which take it for granted that Picts and Britons had entirely different racial origins. It is, therefore, not surprising that their languages were regarded, if mainly for political reasons, as distinct. It seems there were real idiosyncrasies in Pictish British, but these may have been comparatively minor.

The Pictish language

Bede's *lingua Pictorum* has been variously proposed to have been a Gaelic dialect (the ancestor of Scottish Gaelic), a British dialect, or some other language – perhaps a Germanic ancestor of Scots, or even a language surviving from Stone Age times. Not a single sentence written in this Pictish language has so far been identified. What survives in the main are various personal and place-names, as well as inscriptions whose readings can be uncertain and somewhat subjective.

In the 1880s W. F. Skene rejected the evidence that a British language was spoken by the Picts, asserting that the northern Picts were 'purely Gaelic in race and language', and that traces of British speech south of the Mounth spoke of British incursions.[26] Expert linguistic study of Scottish place-names in the next generation demonstrated, however, that a language that was British in character left traces of itself throughout the eastern lowland districts from Ross to Fife.[27] No subsequent study has dissented from this view.

H. M. Chadwick proposed, however, that this Pictish British language already co-existed with a Gaelic one as early as the Roman Iron Age, while Kenneth Jackson argued that, on the contrary, it co-existed with an ancient prehistoric tongue.[28] The Jackson thesis dominated the field for forty years, but has now been comprehensively undermined.[29] The same cannot be said for the Chadwick thesis, despite the fact that it relied to no small extent on archaeological theories that cannot stand contemporary scrutiny.

---

[25] I follow Woolf, *From Pictland to Alba*, 328, on this point.
[26] Skene, *Celtic Scotland*, vol. I, 231.
[27] Watson, *Celtic Place-Names*, 70–2, 339–424; Chadwick, *Early Scotland*, 52–5.
[28] Chadwick, *Early Scotland*, 50–80; Jackson, '*The* Pictish Language', 129–66.
[29] Smyth, *Warlords*, 46–52; Forsyth, *Language in Pictland*.

It is unnecessary to make room in Roman Iron Age Scotland for peoples who spoke any other language than variations on the Pictish British one. However, in the eighth century the sole 'Pictish' place-name related by Bede – *Peanfahel*, modern Kinneil on the Firth of Forth – appears to mix what linguists identify as British and Gaelic terminology. Considering their political position among the Picts, it seems likely that what Bede meant by *lingua Pictorum* was whatever tongue the ascendant Waerteras identified as their own. By the eighth century casual and official Verturian contact with Scottish and Irish Gaels had probably been happening for several centuries, and their language may have been known and spoken in a bilingual context in Pictish Moray for some time. On the evidence of *Peanfahel*, it seems possible that Bede's *lingua Pictorum*, our Pictish British, was a partially gaelicised (or otherwise hybrid) tongue spoken in Fortriu, which was also exerting reciprocal brittonicising influences on Scottish Gaelic.[30]

All indications are that the spectre of matrilineal inheritance among the Picts, rendering them unique in Britain and Ireland, can no longer be conjured up to support or undermine cultural or linguistic hypotheses. The well known matrilineal thesis was based on a naive over-reliance on Gaelic vernacular origin tales and the extant Pictish king-list, products of the first half of the ninth century (and later).[31] The king-list is very far indeed from an accurate record of kings succeeding to a single Pictish monarchic kingdom according to a single rule or custom of succession. Even the Merovingian royal dynasty in Francia, remarkably stable and tenacious by early medieval standards, maintained no consistent or predictable system of royal succession in the sixth century or later. Changes in royal dynasties over time, and in their conceptions of their kingships, routinely led to re-analysis of a kingdom's royal history. Sometimes the results were messy. The curiosities of the Pictish king-list can be explained without recourse to matriliny. Thus, it is no longer possible to mobilise them against Bede's information that matrilineal succession, far from being regular, surfaced in Pictish royal circles only 'where the matter came into doubt'.[32]

---

[30] On the relationship between Pictish British and Scottish Gaelic, see Woolf, *From Pictland to Alba*, 328–35.
[31] See, for example, Chadwick, *Early Scotland*, 89–98; Henderson, *The Picts*, 31–2; Anderson, *Kings and Kingship*, 165–72. On the date of the king-list, see Broun, *Scottish Independence*, 76.
[32] Bede, *Hist. eccl.*, i.1.

Bede made this point, along with the observation that 'the custom has been observed among the Picts to this day', because he was recording Pictish propaganda relating to the kings who ruled during the most active part of his career, who had claimed the kingdom through their mother's Pictish pedigree.[33] That these men made an issue of their maternal descent is not at all out of keeping with patrilineal succession. It played a part in Merovingian succession. Bede also says of the Bernician English king Oswald that he was the nephew of his predecessor Edwini 'through his sister Acha, and it was fitting that so great a predecessor should have so worthy a kinsman to inherit both his religion and his kingdom'.[34] Maternal ancestry was important in patrilineal societies. It may often have been useful in evaluating the royal pretensions of prospective kings with equally impressive paternal pedigrees.

If it was neither divergent succession customs nor separate languages, it may have been self-conscious Romano-British identity among the outer Brigantian peoples, as *cumbri* or 'fellow countrymen' of the provincials, perhaps encouraged by the burgeoning Church, that was mainly responsible for galvanising the notion that they were not *Picti* like nations to the north. Whatever interconnectivities crossed the Mounth between Verturiones and Calidones in the later Roman Iron Age, it is important that *Mórseiser do Chruithne claind* envisioned a Pictland of many parts beyond the end of our period. The Pictish discovery of the Latin concept of Pictishness probably led to attempts to blur sharp lines that differentiated Verturian, Calidonian and Maiatian Picts (and others?) – lines that these nations had sharpened in the course of Roman Iron Age ethnogeneses. By the end of the Roman Iron Age itself, however, the processes involved in forging Pictish nationhood in inner Caledonia had barely begun.

NEW FOES IN THE NORTH

The calamity of the Barbarian Conspiracy, involving the Calidones and the Verturiones, occurred some sixty years after the first Romano-Pictish war known to us, the details of which are obscure. It followed on from an invasion of the island by the emperor Flavius Constantius in 305, the senior emperor of the western provinces of the Empire, which had been

[33] Clancy, 'Philosopher-King', 146. Key prior studies challenging the matrilineal thesis include Smyth, *Warlords*, 57–75; Forsyth, *Language in Pictland*, 31; Ross, 'Pictish Matriliny'; and especially Woolf, 'Pictish Matriliny Reconsidered'. These works have successfully met the objections to Smyth's arguments raised by Sellar, 'Warlords', 35–41.
[34] Bede, *Hist. eccl.*, iii.6.

formally divided by Diocletian in 285. Since 286 the Britannic provinces had been arranged against the 'imperial college', led until 296 by the pretender Marcus Carausius, a disgraced Gallic general. Until his fall from grace, Carausius had been based at Bononia (modern Boulogne near Calais), with a commission to clear the North Sea of raiders, possibly including Pictish ones. After becoming senior Western emperor in May 305, Constantius, now ill, became the third ruling emperor to set foot in Britain. His agenda was no doubt broadly the same as Severus's had been a hundred years before: to satisfy himself of the fidelity of the fickle Britannic legions and of the northern barbarians.[35]

According to a panegyric poet at his court, Constantius 'so fully recovered' the island on this campaign 'that those nations . . . which cling to [its] extremities . . . obey your very nod'.[36] The poet was deliberately vague as to whether these barbarians were 'at peace either out of fear or subdued by arms or bound by gratitude', reflecting Rome's usual strategies for establishing her dominion.[37] It may be that the emperor launched only token military operations in *barbaricum*, his primary concern being to win over the Romano-British provincials who had propped up Carausius. Another poet, at the court of his son Flavius Constantinus, the famous Constantine, was similarly ambiguous about 'that final expedition of his', implying but never quite saying, in a famous phrase already quoted, that Constantine's father had reached 'the forests and swamps of the Calidones and the other *Picti*'. Constantius, the poet noted, did not think it particularly worthwhile to ravage northern Britain.[38] It may be that the Pictish peoples were eager to agree terms with Constantius after the disruptions to the status quo over the previous twenty years. The ailing emperor, who, like Severus, died at Eboracum in July 306, may have been just as eager to make a deal, and something of the former Severan settlement may have been renewed.

According to Ammianus Marcellinus, the Roman historian who described the events a generation later, the Barbarian Conspiracy that attacked Britannia in 367 included *Picti* from the north, 'divided into two nations (*gentes*)', Di-Calidones and Verturiones.[39] It also involved Gaels

[35] Barnes, *Constantine*, 6–7, 15–16, 27.
[36] *Pan. Latini*, viii.20.2–5.
[37] *Pan. Latini*, viii.20.2–5.
[38] *Pan. Latini*, vi.7.1–2.
[39] *Dicalydones* or 'double Calidones', suggests a fundamental division within Caledonian identity, perhaps highland/lowland, despite the second-century ethnogenesis; cf. Watson, *Celtic Place-Names*, 20; Rivet and Smith, *The Place-Names of Roman Britain*, 338.

(*Scotti*) from Ireland, Attacots (*Attacotti*), 'a warlike nation' whose origins were Insular but obscure to us, and Franks and Saxons from across the North Sea. The audacity of the conspirators seems to have been unparalleled. Their achievement implies levels of intercommunication across the Irish and North Seas that are not to be forgotten when confronted by evidence of similar links in Early Historic times. Fourth-century *barbaricum* was capable of producing grand alliances. So lasting was the impression left by the Conspiracy on the Romano-British psyche – as well as on subsequent generations of Picts perhaps – that two centuries later Gildas and his contemporaries saw the second half of the fourth century as the beginning of the end of Roman Britain.

By this time the Roman military had been completely restructured. The all-purpose legions of the prior age had disappeared and the fourth-century *limes* was manned by dedicated garrison troops, called *limitanei*, mere shadows of the flexible legionaries and auxiliaries who had built and manned the system in the second century. The story was the same across the Empire: the emperors preferred to focus their strained resources on mobile field armies which could back up the *limitanei* with decisive force when necessary, but boasted little of the old-school professionalism and discipline of the legionaries of bygone days – and nothing like their numbers. The Count (*comes*) of the Saxon Shore, Nectaridus, responsible for the *limitanei* who defended Britannia from Continental raiders and pirates, was slain in the onslaught of 367, presumably by Saxons or Franks. The Duke (*dux Britanniae*) in command of the northern *limes*, Fullofaudes, probably a general of barbarian origin, was meanwhile captured in an ambush.[40] His captors were presumably Picts. After the fall of the Count and the Duke, their forces vanquished, 'Britannia was brought into a state of extreme need', says Ammianus, and looked to the Continent for support. All the ingredients of the tradition related in *De excidio Britanniae* were now in place – Picts, Gaels and Saxons ravaging Britain and appeals to the Continent for help.

The reign of the new emperor Valentinian had begun three years earlier. Ammianus's account of his response to the crisis in Britain is vague, so that the Pictish contribution to the three-year struggle that followed is unknown.[41] That Fullofaudes was captured rather than killed – like the prisoners taken by the Maiatai in the 190s – implies that the

[40] On the origins of Fullofaudes, see Richmond, 'Roman and Native', 121.
[41] Ammianus, *Res gestae*, xxvii.8, describes the war; see also Tomlin, 'The Date of the "Barbarian Conspiracy"'.

Pictish invaders were intent mainly on booty (and ransom) rather than blood. At the time of the Conspiracy, Valentinian was on the Rhine dealing with an Alamannic invasion triggered, according to Ammianus, by complaints about what the emperor was prepared to pay the Alamanni by way of subsidy. The Alamanni, like the Picts, are first named in Roman writing *c.* 300, and arose just beyond the frontier in lands formerly held by Rome – in this case, around the upper Rhine and upper Danube. In northern Britain, as in Alamannia, it may have been Valentinian's perceived meanness with subsidies that had unsettled *barbaricum* with decisive results.

The provinces of Britannia had never before been overrun by barbarians, and had experienced nothing approaching the scale of the calamities of 367–70 in more than three centuries. Despite being consistently downplayed in many models, barbarian invasions, by devastating farms and settlements and taxing the Empire's military resources, contributed decisively to its collapse by exhausting the all important tax base and encouraging the disillusionment with Rome that saw different parts of the Western Empire break with the Eternal City. Within seventy years of the sack of Rome in 410, the Western Empire had collapsed entirely. Similarly, within fifty years of the Barbarian Conspiracy, Roman government had vanished from Britain. For the Romano-British provincials, that terrible assault probably had something of the same traumatic psychological effects as the sack of Rome was later to have on the whole Empire. Like areas overrun by German barbarians in the fifth century, Britannia in the grip of the Barbarian Conspiracy will have known predictable miseries: looting and destruction; the killing, capture and enslavement of free women, men and children; widespread rapine, not least at nunneries; encouragement of revolt among slaves and peasants. It is unfortunate that, at present, the archaeological evidence is too equivocal to confirm or disprove such a scenario.[42]

In a book that covers 700 years of history a three-year struggle can seem small, but this one may have been a watershed moment in British history. It seems the frontier system was never really restored to post-Severan degrees of effectiveness. Just six years after the war was concluded, a massive Gothic invasion across the Danube opened the floodgates of the barbarian incursions into the Empire which broke the Roman state in the West over the next hundred years. Did the Barbarian Conspiracy have a similar effect on the situation in Britain? If so, the Picts played a role, if an unquantifiable one, in encouraging the implosion and

---

[42] Esmonde Cleary, *The Ending of Roman Britain*, 45–6.

remilitarisation of Roman Britain. Gildas eventually blamed the melt-down on Magnus Maximus, a Roman officer who fought the conspirators in 367–70. Back in Britannia in 383, he was 'made emperor through a mutiny of the soldiers' and went to Gaul to establish himself.[43] Coin evidence suggests that he was forced to return in 384, probably to deal with a barbarian invasion, for the Gallic *Chronicle of 452* records that 'Maximus vigorously overcame invading *Picti* and *Scotti*'.[44]

The fourth-century Vettweiß-Friotzheim dice-tower, bearing the tri-umphalist inscription 'let us play with security: the *Picti* are defeated, the enemy annihilated', must commemorate campaigning in these years between 367 and 384.[45] Such chance contemporary testimony to the significance of the Pictish threat in this period is very precious. A further campaign, the third in thirty years, by the ubiquitous Romano-Vandal general Flavius Stilicho is alluded to *c.* 400 by the panegyricist Claudian at the imperial court of Honorius at Mediolanum (modern Milan).[46] Gildas believed that the Romans enjoyed some success against the invaders in this period of crisis. *Notitia dignitatum*, a 'register of offices' surviving from *c.* 400, duly records units of Attacots in the Roman army among the palatine auxiliaries stationed on the Danube frontier.

THE SHOE ON THE OTHER FOOT: PICTS ATTACK ROME

The Barbarian Conspiracy marks the first known incursion into Britannia by the denizens of Caledonia. Ammianus refers to two nations among these *Picti*: the Di-Calidones, 'double Calidones' and the Verturiones. The notion of a bipartite Calidonian nation implied by the prefix *di*-occurs as early as the Flavian survey, but we cannot know the nature of this division. What may have inspired these Picts to take the remarkable step of storming the frontiers of Roman Britain is ultimately unknown. Archaeology may provide a key clue. In inner Caledonia, a quite aston-ishing near dearth of coins and other Roman material at native sites after *c.* 250 has been observed. This phenomenon goes beyond the general reduction reflecting the bedding down of the Hadrianic *limes* as the per-manent frontier and the political and economic crises that gripped the Roman world in the third century.[47]

---

43 Prosper, *Chronicle*, §§ 1183, 1187, 1191; Gildas, *De excidio Brit.*, i.13.
44 *Chron. 452*, § 7.
45 Hunter, *Beyond the Edge of the Empire*, 4–5.
46 Miller, 'Stilicho's Pictish War', contains the relevant excerpts.
47 Macinnes, 'Baubles, Bangles and Beads', 113–14.

Concentrations of Roman 'small change' in the form of copper-alloy coins at various sites in outer Brigantia, on the other hand, show that Roman subsidy continued to reach its inhabitants in late Antiquity.[48] Throughout *barbaricum*, the main threat to Roman frontiers came mainly from the closest and most familiar barbarians with whom Rome had the most extensive contact. Not surprisingly, the archaeological evidence suggests that relations with outer Brigantia, perhaps delicate, went on being managed carefully and fairly successfully long after the dust had settled on the campaign trails of Severus and Caracalla. The famous late Antique Traprain Law silver hoard is generally regarded as a late example of subsidy. Low-value coins are most likely to reflect payments by the Roman state in return for various commodities. The Britannic economy became increasingly provincial as long-distance trade dwindled across the third-century Empire, and it seems that the administration looked to romanising outer Brigantia in its efforts to maintain a sound economic base.[49]

A consistent (if slight) level of interaction was also maintained with Atlantic Scotland into late Antiquity. That Pictland shows little sign of either formal or informal contact in this climate thus smacks of deliberate policy concerning the Calidones and Verturiones.[50] The comprehensiveness and continuity of the dearth of Roman material are more consistent with imposition by Rome than with native rejection. If they were committed to finding friends, the whole history of Roman imperialism tells us that the Romans would have identified and contacted pro-Roman factions, and supported them against anti-Roman ones. Did the new policy have something to do with changing attitudes towards peoples who were becoming tagged with the pejorative epithet *Picti*? How important in Roman policy-making were the population's inclinations not to romanise? By 235 the frontier had known a generation of unsurpassed peace and stability. Did successful reconciliation with the romanisers of outer Brigantia lead to a hardening of Rome's stance towards Caledonia during the 'third-century crisis' when money got tighter? We cannot answer such questions with any confidence. They are, and must remain, intriguing possibilities in which a number of different socio-economic considerations collide.

Another intriguing question is what happened when Rome cut off diplomatic relations after more than a hundred years. The Alamanni in the 360s

---

[48] Hunter, *Beyond the Edge of the Empire*, 34–6. See also Breeze, *The Northern Frontiers*, 139–40; Whitaker, 'Supplying the System', 67; Esmonde Cleary, *The Ending of Roman Britain*, 11–12.
[49] Esmonde Cleary, *The Ending of Roman Britain*, 73–4, 83–5.
[50] Hunter, *Beyond the Edge of the Empire*, 51–3.

attacked the Empire because they accused Valentinian's administration of meanness. Britain was one of the few provinces of the Empire that remained secure from foreign invasion in the third century, even in the most tumultuous years of the 'crisis'. Thus, there appears to have been no immediate military reprisal against Britannia itself, though we may speculate about whether the outer Brigantian peoples – with their own Roman imports – were as fortunate. The rebellion of Carausius in 286 may have presented the Pictish nations with their first real opportunity to strike at the Empire itself, but there is no evidence that his defection led to frontier trouble. The Conspiracy took place a good century after the diplomatic shift. Non-payment of anticipated subsidies may have soured the Calidones and the Verturiones against Rome, but it seems a weak explanation for the remarkable new-found aggression of the later fourth century.

Settlement archaeology offers another, more convincing, explanation. It seems that Roman subsidy was drying up in Pictland at a time when something very significant – perhaps dramatic – was happening to society. Apart from settlement evidence, obsolescence of other aspects of material culture which had persisted from the pre-Roman Iron Age point in the same direction.[51] The most obvious consequence was the creation of a Pictish military capacity, and a willingness, to threaten the Hadrianic *limes* beyond anything that the inner Caledonian peoples had shown in 300 years. The diplomatic capacity to treat with Irish and German peoples is also in evidence, and equally precocious by the earlier standards set by men like Argentocoxos. What had happened after 211?

We have already reflected on the parallel case of the social 'turmoil' experienced in late eighteenth-century Scotland, caused by a sudden intensification of comparatively gentle economic pressures and evolving elite attitudes, unleashing 'irresistible material and ideological forces'.[52] Ethnogenesis among the Maiatai and the Calidones – and perhaps the Verturiones too – had been an aspect of the changing cultural landscape for at least a generation prior to 211. Such shifting ethnic identities typically reflect (and shape) new social realities, but the processes were probably gradual. Did the cessation of the flow of Roman goods into inner Caledonia during the third century unleash comparable forces to those which struck Improvement Scotland, triggering social transformations that may have been fairly sudden and traumatic?

Social disruption is implied by the archaeology. The available evidence suggests that we may, therefore, turn to students of the aggressive Franks,

---

[51] Hunter, *Beyond the Edge of the Empire*, 45–50.
[52] Devine, *The Scottish Nation*, 172, 180.

Saxons and other Germans in this same period for our explanation. The establishment of substantial chiefdoms or even kingdoms where 'farmer republics' had formerly held sway, and the growing power of relatively few potentates in a district, encouraging disgruntled, displaced or dispossessed also-rans to seek their fortunes abroad, is thought to have been a leading factor in creating the barbarian pressures to which the Western Empire eventually succumbed.[53] The seemingly relentless Pictish threat to Britannia in the later fourth and fifth centuries probably reflects this same process in northern Britain.

ELITE CULTURE: *FAMILIARES* AND *COHORTES*

Can we test this conclusion that northern Britain developed in line with other parts of *barbaricum*? The Pictish invaders of Britannia in 367 enjoyed military success far to the south, some at least remaining in the field for a year or more. That kind of staying power implies that these armies were not predominantly made up of non-specialist fighters like the normal freemen of a 'farmer republic' – the forerunners of the 'common army' – who had set down their tools and taken up their spears. Rather, the implication is that Fullofaudes was ambushed and captured by a force consisting of warriors who were semi-permanently attached to their leaders, and whose only economic concern was to serve him. Such armies were certainly the norm in Early Historic times, but not obviously in the earlier Roman Iron Age. Parallel developments are known across Western Europe in late Antique and early medieval times, mainly as a result in each case of the rise of increasingly contoured societies.

All across the West a potentate's armed retinue – his 'war-band' or *comitatus* – consisted mainly of a core of seasoned warriors and a body of young men of suitable birth. Because they did not cultivate, such warriors superficially shared much in common with slaves, 'selling' their service to a potentate full-time in return for basic sustenance. However, these men were far from servile, specialising in fighting and enjoying great prestige. Adomnán calls this kind of retinue a *cohors* in *Vita Columbae*; other terms – *familia* (literally 'family'), *casus* (literally 'house'), and *muindter* – occur in reference to warfare in seventh- and eighth-century northern Britain.[54] The *cohors* of a fourth-century Pictish potentate will have been

---

[53] Halsall, *Warfare and Society*, 106–7. The potential for displacement arising from successful lordship is also discussed by Woolf, *From Pictland to Alba*, 21.
[54] Adomnán, *V. s. Columbae*, i.33, i.35 (*cohors*); *AU* 729.2 (*familia*); *V. s. Cuthberti anon.*, iii.6 (*casus*); *Annals of Tigernach* [*AT*] 638.1 (*muindter*).

just one part of his entire household. *Vita Columbae* tells the story of a Pictish *familia* consisting of a nuclear family and its adherents (*familiares*), who will have included a *cohors*, as well as other retainers.[55]

It was because they did not have to concern themselves with cultivating to survive – unlike normal freemen and their semi-free dependants – that the *cohors* could undertake long-distance campaigning with no danger of economic ruin at home. In return for this privilege, *familiares* obeyed their patron and provided service, the *cohors* undertaking to keep in practice, and to fight and even die to protect the patron from harm or shame. That, at least, was the idea, which may be derived by analogy. Lack of evidence means that we cannot speak intelligently about the details of such systems as they developed in northern Britain. Households of means, probably even as early as 367, will have included other specialist *familiares* – poets, advisers, craftsmen, builders – and after christianisation they probably also included a chaplain. Early Historic evidence suggests that the woman of the house was perfectly capable of maintaining her own retainers – including warriors – sustained by means provided by her kin or her dowry.

By analogy then, and particularly with consideration of the kind of society that emerged from the Roman Iron Age, the development of such retinues – or rather of the potentates who sustained them – is the likeliest explanation both of the unsettled archaeological record in inner Caledonia in late Antiquity and of Pictish long-distance aggression against Rome. The Severan settlement had successfully negotiated the choppy waters of the third-century crisis, but social transformation among the peoples beyond the Maiatai had moved the goalposts. The processes involved in the formalisation of previously informal elite status are too elusive and complex for conjecture to be much use. The famous suppression of the Roman Republic in a single century by a succession of military strongmen capable of exploiting patronage and elite faction to their personal advantage, may, in broad terms, be regarded as a useful parallel case. Those tyrant-princes made extensive use of terror and populism in securing their positions, all the while taking steps to make it seem that they were restoring and preserving the system they were overturning. The first formal potentates and chiefly or royal dynasties of Pictish Scotland may have become established in similar ways. The Picts who plagued fourth-century Britannia and negotiated with Irish, Attacot, Frankish and Saxon conspirators were probably a mix of tyrant-princes and men who had lost out in local contests for power, with little to lose in trying their luck in bold ventures against Rome.

---

[55] Adomnán, *V. s. Columbae*, ii.32.

A broad view of the archaeology suggests that the *cohortes* of northern Britain's potentates in our period rarely reached three figures. The Roman army in Britannia in the fourth century may have numbered as few as 12,000 soldiers, but achieving overwhelming force against them with followings of less than a hundred men must have involved several hundred warlords in the Barbarian Conspiracy. Back home, most wars will have been feuds fought primarily by farmers in warring kindreds, and a *cohors* of such a size, consisting of specialist fighters who knew and trained with each other and sported good equipment, represented considerable military force.

Even if the practical need lessened for lack of enemies or dangers, its symbolic function as an indicator of elite power and prestige (and a proving ground for young aristocrats) preserved the *cohors* as an institution. Away from the battlefield, potentates relied on their henchmen to perform any number of tasks. They might bear messages as ambassadors to the halls of other potentates, provide armed escorts to friends, or collect renders from 'base' clients (or tribute from subjects), acting in each respect almost as an extension of their patron's (or patroness's) person.[56]

As an aristocratic Northumbrian youth of the seventh century, St Wilfrid was sent by his father – a royal attendant – to serve in the royal household, and thence to a monastery to receive an education. Later, as a bishop, Wilfrid is said to have overseen the tutelage of similar youths, many of whom were destined for military rather than clerical careers.[57] We can only guess at how young warriors were educated more broadly before christianisation in fourth- and fifth-century northern Britain. At the end of their careers (or perhaps earlier), slowed down by injury or having reached a respectable age, such warriors could marry, settle down and enjoy the status their service and their inheritance had earned. No doubt they remained, however, very much within the fold of the potentate they had served. Wilfrid's father seems to have been such a man. He had served a king, and long after his retirement his son was received honourably at the royal court.

ELITE CULTURE: FUELLING THE PRESTIGE ECONOMY

With very few exceptions, all of the people who feature in this book, starting with the unknown Pictish leaders who fought in the Barbarian Conspiracy, were formal potentates, or were attached to them by kinship,

---

[56] See, for example, Adomnán, *V. s. Columbae*, ii.33.
[57] Stephen, *V. s. Wilfrithi*, §§ 2, 21.

marriage or service. They have been much studied in Early Historic times: archaeologists of their later Roman Iron Age counterparts have some catching up to do. Sustaining *familiares*, including a *cohors*, required elites to maintain access to considerable surpluses of resources, acquired through plundering campaigns, exchange, the collection of renders from clients among the tillers of the soil and the collection of tribute from subdued enemies. Informal elites will have behaved in much the same way in this and previous ages.

It has been noted already that the acquisition of luxury Mediterranean goods was a key factor in differentiating societies in *barbaricum*. Different parts of northern Britain may have acquired Mediterranean luxuries through different exchange networks. Both at the beginning and at the end of the Roman Iron Age, Atlantic Scotland can, for example, be shown to have interacted with Ireland, western Britain and western Gaul. Most commonly archaeologists find evidence at native sites in Scotland of Samian and other Mediterranean tableware and other objects related to conspicuous consumption.[58] Such finds are so common as to suggest wide redistribution. Until *c.* 600 elites continued to look to the Mediterranean basin, including (perhaps crucially) the Eastern (later 'Byzantine') Roman Empire, for exotic tableware and drinking vessels. Atlantic Scotland appears to have been linked with the Mediterranean directly by a long sea route, but Pictland's links may have relied on a separate, over-land route which brought goods into Anglo-Saxon England by way of the Rhine.[59] By the early seventh century, Merovingian Francia appears to have superseded the Mediterranean as the principal source of the fine tableware of northern Britain. It, therefore, seems possible that Merovingian links became as laden with symbolism as Roman links had once been. By 600 the Merovingian dynasty had become closely engaged with Britain and Ireland, supporting christianising initiatives and receiving the first generation of ecclesiastical *peregrini* discussed below.

To speak of 'trade' between northern British leaders, whether or not the Romans were involved, is misleading. It is unlikely that native society produced a mercantile class or markets in this period. All indications are that the civilian settlements (*vici*) which grew up around Roman military installations in northern Britain had little meaningful economic intercourse with native groups. The suggestion of the archaeological record is that instead, in outer Brigantia and later in Pictland, commodities passed through the courts of potentates rather than through marketplaces. Potentates thus

[58] Harding, *The Iron Age in Northern Britain*, 137, 192.
[59] Campbell, *Saints and Sea-Kings*, 43–6; Harris, *Byzantium, Britain and the West*, 143–88.

seem to have established and maintained themselves by controlling – 'protecting' they may have said – access to goods demanded throughout their dominions, and outdoing their rivals for such control on the war-path. By performing (and increasingly monopolising) the vital military role in a war-torn society, they and their war-bands will have enjoyed great prestige. Prudence could take a back seat to the demands and temptations of succeeding in the prestige economy, just as Roman aristocrats could flirt with bankruptcy in the hopes of getting ahead. Exchanging goods with Romans must surely have brought with it particular elements of both risk and reward, in the same way that exchange bound native to native.

ELITE CULTURE: CONSPICUOUS CONSUMPTION

In the final analysis, it seems justified to suppose that here, as in other matters like ethnogenesis, northern Britain was a fairly typical part of *barbaricum* in late Antiquity in experiencing social flux. The rise of the potentate (and the king) may explain another aspect of the archaeological record: the resurgence of votive deposition after an apparent hiatus since the Bronze Age. In fact, this pattern mirrors that for potentates. Known examples of the ritual in the Roman Iron Age routinely include objects of Roman and Romano-British provenance among the offerings, dominated on the whole by prestige goods. It has been suggested that votive deposition was reinvigorated as precocious nativism in the face of Roman influences.[60] As a classic example of conspicuous consumption, however, it is more likely to reflect emphasis on that fundamental aspect of prestige economics in contoured societies.

Northern Britain never developed the large shrine complexes, associated with state formation, of Celtic Gaul and classical Antiquity, but the evidence of ritual does suggest that its social landscape was changing as the Roman Iron Age progressed. The presence of Roman goods among the votive offerings confirms yet again the status which could be associated with their possession, helping to explain restlessness among barbarians – and especially potentates – deprived of them. Given the truism that christianisation cannot have brought about an instant revolution in the religiosity of anyone outside the social elites, it is particularly notable that deposition seems to stop abruptly at the christianisation horizon. We would have expected otherwise had votive deposition of the grander sort been driven by humbler religiosity.

[60] Harding, *The Iron Age in Northern Britain*, 81.

In other respects, consumption looks less conspicuous. The brooch was all but unknown in pre-Roman Iron Age Scotland, but elaborate examples seem to have been acquired from Rome with enthusiasm. This evidence may speak of innovative styles of dress associated with social differentiation and (as viewed from outside) ethnicity. By the eighth century the brooch had become intimately associated with status in Britain and Ireland.[61] Imported brooches were small and subtle rather than grandiose, implying that they performed their symbolic functions in settings that were interpersonal and intimate. Other indications that great spectacle may not have been made of Roman connections, and that people preferred to display them instead within intimate and restricted circles of friends and followers, include preferences for fine tableware and use of Roman coins.[62] There is no sign of lavish burial rites and other more 'public' expressions of status, save perhaps for votive deposition already discussed and, in the later Roman Iron Age in Pictland, settlement enclosure. This kind of evidence – or non-evidence – is consistent with the relatively small sizes of *cohortes* implied by the Early Historic settlement archaeology. However contoured their societies had become by the end of the Roman Iron Age, the potentates of northern Britain were clearly not enjoying the levels of grandiose opulence that some of their counterparts could enjoy in other areas of the West. There was only so much wealth that even the larger of northern Britain's populations could generate.

FROM 'FARMER REPUBLICS' TO KINGDOMS

Competition within new or existing formal elites for opportunities to exploit normal freemen and to extend one's influence to the regional level, will have seen many fall by the wayside. Where one man had a good thing going locally, men with regional pretensions probably sought to horn in on his racket. Those who lost out in these competitions may have been the driving force behind the frontier troubles that Rome experienced from within outer Brigantia in the Antonine period, and from the Picts in the fourth century. At various points here and there, formal elites became formal kings. The processes are, alas, lost to us. The Early Historic evidence enables us to be reasonably certain that kingship became a feature of society in Moray, Angus and Perthshire, Clydesdale, Lothian and the Borders, Argyll and Orkney. Other parts of northern Britain – areas like Fife, the north-east between the Dee and the Spey, the Highland glens,

---

[61] Etchingham and Swift, 'English and Pictish Terms', 44–8.
[62] Hunter, *Beyond the Edge of the Empire*, 16.

Sutherland, the north-west and the Western Isles, Shetland, Ayrshire and Galloway – cannot be shown to have developed kings. Some of these areas may have remained the preserve of 'farmer republics' as late as the Viking Age, while others are simply deficient in evidence.

The same sort social shift occurred (for very different reasons) among the Romano-Britons when Britannia re-militarised and native dynasties and kings asserted themselves upon the dismantling of Roman Britain. It also occurred among the Anglo-Saxons who settled and expanded in fifth-century southern Britain. The processes involved in all cases are mysterious. It is likely that certain districts never threw up kings of their own before they became subjugated by growing kingdoms nearby, or incorporated within them – a fate that in some cases may not have been visited upon them until after our period.

Analogous evidence informs us that kings in place in northern Britain at the end of the Roman Iron Age personified the sovereignty of the kingdoms that had thrown them up. Sovereignty itself, however, probably continued to be expressed by public assemblies and consensus among the normal freemen of these new kingdoms, just as in the days of 'farmer republics'. Kings in northern Britain are likely to have shared with Continental and Irish kings the right to summon the free to arms – and the opportunity to give them heavy doses of royal political doctrine at such hostings, which may or may not have coincided with the regular cycle of other assemblies. Sites like Traprain Law and Burghead, the latter so accessible by sea, may have been the foci of such activity.

We may feel certain that public rituals were devised whereby kings were inaugurated with the acclamation of the same freemen, even if they were actually selected to run the 'family business' by the members of a recognised royal dynasty, in consultation with leading potentates. *Vita Columbae* refers to such a ceremony.[63] As this story foreshadows, the Church would eventually persuade kings that royalty was a condition conferred by God. For most of our period, however, it was probably treated as a condition bestowed on kings by the free adult males of their kingdom, whose consensual acclamation was constitutionally crucial, even if it was largely automatic. That had been the way of things at Rome too, long after the sovereignty of Senate and *plebs* had become a fiction. Big social changes in the third and fourth centuries notwithstanding, the myth of 'government' by consensus died very hard in Britain and Ireland. It was still alive and well in Scotland at the end of the eighth century, despite the evident might of some of its eighth-century sovereigns.

---

[63] Adomnán, *V. s. Columbae*, iii. 5a.

CHAPTER 3

Uinniau, 'Ninian' and the Early Church in Scotland

Beginning in 542, as the Byzantine Roman eyewitness Procopius observed, 'there was a pestilence, by which the whole human race came near to annihilation'. It was the first recorded instance in Europe of bubonic plague, that most infamous of medieval pandemics. In Constantinople and its empire it killed most of the farmers, 'thus leaving a trail of desolation in its wake', but it did not remain confined to the Mediterranean basin. Rather, Procopius wrote, it 'embraced the entire world, and blighted the lives of all men . . . respecting neither sex nor age'.

Did the plague reach northern Britain? It was certainly part of an Irish Sea world which enjoyed significant interaction, some of it direct, with the Byzantine Romans in the fifth and sixth centuries. The terrible 'plague of Justinian' began to ravage Gildas's Britain and Ireland, according to native records, in the 540s and was still doing so in Ireland in the 550s. Far away, Procopius too noted this lingering persistence of the pandemic. This episode of plague, and another one about a century later, may have had profound effects on the populations of Britain and Ireland. For the moment there is precious little evidence.

In approximately 550, according to Irish chronicles, the pestilential terror claimed Ciarán, the young abbot of Clonmacnoise (*Cluain Moccu Nóis*) on the River Shannon in Offaly, a monastery he had founded in the previous year.[1] Ciarán was thirty-three when *Yersinia pestis* took him. No doubt throughout Britain and Ireland, as throughout the Roman world of Procopius, it seemed that 'afterwards confusion and disorder everywhere became complete'. The plague may have inspired Gildas to write, in *De excidio Britanniae*, that God's first warning to his forefathers to repent

---

[1] *AU* 549.1; *Chronicon Scotorum* [*CS*] 544.4; *Ann. Camb.* (Faral) 544.1.

their wickedness had come in the form of 'a deadly plague' which 'without a sword, laid low so many that the living could not bury all the dead'.[2]

A MAN CALLED CRIMTHANN

In the year of Ciarán's death the young St Columba, some five years younger than the stricken abbot, was studying the scriptures in Ireland. His name, according to later tradition, was Crimthann. His tutelage, according to the account of his life penned a century after his death, had begun at a tender age when his parents placed him in to fosterage in the care of a priest.[3] Bede wrote of his own early life in *Historia ecclesiastica* that he was seven years old when his kin placed him in the care of the monastery where he spent the rest of his life.[4] Crimthann may have been of a similar age when he began his study of the scriptures and philosophy. At that stage it was probably uncertain that he would remain a cleric.

Bede was made a deacon at nineteen and a priest at thirty. Crimthann was in this same intermediate period of his own development in the pestilential 540s, during which time he studied in Leinster, as well as under the moral theologian Uinniau, whose name was gaelicised as *Finniau* (later misread as *Finnian*).[5] No doubt his masters shared the view of Procopius of the pandemic that, 'it is quite impossible either to express in words or to conceive in thought any explanation, except indeed to refer it to God'. Those like Crimthann and Uinniau who survived its ravages can have regarded themselves as chosen recipients of divine protection. Did it spur some on to remarkable careers?

Uinniau, a bishop, may have trained Crimthann at the monastery of Moville (*Mag mBili*) on Strangford Lough in Down.[6] He had come to Ireland as a *peregrinus* (voluntary exile) from his native Britain,

---

[2] Gildas, *De excidio Brit.*, i.21–2.
[3] Adomnán, *V. s. Columbae*, iii.2, *praef. secund.* Adomnán names Columba's father and mother, but does not name Columba as Crimthann, maintaining that he was known as *columba* 'from the days of his infancy'.
[4] Bede, *Hist. eccl.*, v.24.
[5] For Columba's tutelage under Uinniau, see Adomnán, *V. s. Columbae*, i.1, ii.1, iii.4. That 'Findbarr' of Movilla and 'Finnian' of Clonard were in fact the same historical individual was proposed by Ó Riain, 'St Finnbarr', 72–5. For discussions of the name *Uinniau*, see Dumville, 'Gildas and Uinniau', 209–10; Clancy, 'The Real St Ninian', 13–14. For his tutelage in Leinster, see Adomnán, *V. s. Columbae*, ii.25.
[6] On the likelihood that Uinniau was associated with Movilla rather than Clonard, see Ó Riain, 'St Finnban' 65; Dumville, 'Gildas and Uinniau', 213; Charles-Edwards, *Early Christian Ireland*, 291–3; Clancy, 'The Real St Ninian', 14.

renouncing home and kin to serve God through the dissemination of the monastic life he had embraced.[7] It was a career path that some of his students – and theirs – also followed. The two most famous of these intellectual descendants both undertook their *peregrinationes* in their forties. If they emulated Uinniau in this he cannot have been born much later than *c.* 500, about a century after the last recorded Pictish incursion into Roman Britain. He seems to have been an exact contemporary of Gildas, with whom he corresponded about moral theology. Uinniau taught this British master to his disciples, and they did the same to theirs.

There is perhaps something of that arch-remonstrator of kings and ecclesiastical leaders in the acts of the Leinster-born Columbanus, who called himself *Columba*, a Latin term of endearment meaning 'dove' (in Gaelic he probably called himself *Colmán*). After studying under one of Uinniau's disciples, Columbanus entered the monastery of Bangor (*Bennchor*) on Belfast Lough, not far from Moville in Down, founded in the 550s. Here he studied under the founder Comgall son of Setna, whom Columbanus's hagiographer described as 'renowned for his virtues' and 'an outstanding father to his monks' who was 'famous for his religious studies and rules of discipline'.[8] Columbanus became a teacher and theologian. His pupils were probably a mix of those whose parents had committed them to Bangor and others who, later in life, had decided to embrace monastic life there.

About 591 Columbanus left his academic post to become a *peregrinus* on the Continent, where like Uinniau he founded monasteries governed by rules of his own devising, drawing from the ascetic teachings of that British master (*auctor*). One perceives something of the same kind of courage in Columbanus that Gildas exhibited, in feeling it was his duty to castigate kings and clerics in a manner 'well intentioned towards all of Christ's noble soldiers'.[9] Columbanus shows himself in his writings to have known *De excidio Britanniae*.[10] It became an infamous episode in his career that he refused to bless the illegitimate sons of the Merovingian king Theuderic II. He even presumed to write a letter to Gregory the Great, pope from 590 to 604, 'to subjoin the matter of my grief' on the subject of Easter reform.[11] About 605 the mission sent by Gregory to Britain to evangelise among the Anglo-Saxons wrote to 'our most beloved brethren, the bishops and abbots throughout the whole of Ireland',

---

[7] On Uinniau's British origins, see Dumville, 'Gildas and Uinniau', 209; Clancy, 'The Real St Ninian', 14–16.

[8] *AU* 555.3; *AT* 555.2; *Annals of Inisfallen* [*AI*] 558.1; Jonas, *V. s. Columbani*, §§ 3–4.

[9] Gildas, *De excidio. Brit.*, i.1.

[10] For discussion see Sharpe, 'Gildas as Father', 196–7.

[11] Jonas, *V. s. Columbani*, § 19; Columbanus, *Epist.* i.2.

professing knowledge of Columbanus in Gaul.[12] Church leaders of the early seventh century in the Latin West inhabited a small pool, and pebbles dropped by Uinniau could send ripples over long distances.

Crimthann, some twenty years Columbanus's senior, also came to be known as *Columba* in Latin, *Colum* in Gaelic. The name may have had a

---

St Ninian and Whithorn

The nature of 'minuscule' handwriting made misreadings of the letter *u* in manuscripts as *n* common in the Middle Ages. Such mistakes transformed *uinniau* into Finnian (that is, *vinnian*), and also created *Iona* out of *ioua*. A different transformation of *uiniau* into *niniau* makes surprisingly good sense of the surviving evidence of veneration of St Uinniau in south-west Scotland.[13]

In the eighth century a Life of a saint called *nyniau* was written at the Northumbrian monastery at Whithorn, or somewhere associated with it. The saint was cast in this lost work as a reformist British forerunner to the apostolicist Northumbrian Church in Galloway. He was also portrayed as extending his influence north of the Forth, as the Northumbrians had done in the prior two generations. Towards the end of the eighth century, this lost Life was roughly rendered into verse in *Miracula Nynie Episcopi*, 'the Miracles of Bishop Nyniau'.

Half a century earlier Bede wrote in *Historia ecclesiastica* that the southern Picts, 'as they testify', had received Christianity from Nyniau 'a long time before' the northern Picts. Bede's southern Pictish source was obviously aware of the lost Life. Its claim that southern Pictish Christianity was both older than northern Pictish Christianity and introduced by an orthodox bishop was probably formulated in the 710s, when ecclesiastical reforms were successfully introduced across Pictavia.

By the twelfth century, yet another misreading of *u* had transformed Nyniau into the more familiar *Ninian*. That the famous St Ninian is to be regarded as an unhistorical doppelganger of Uinniau (whose historical existence is irrefutable) can be a bitter pill to swallow. Yet this kind of fragmentation of the cult of early medieval saints, losing all cognisance of common origins, was far from uncommon in Britain and Ireland.

---

[12] Bede, *Hist. eccl.*, ii.4.
[13] Clancy, 'The Real St Ninian', 17–20, 23–6.

special meaning among those schooled in the Uinnianic tradition. Columbanus was about twenty years old, and had perhaps just come to Bangor, when Columba, aged forty-one, left Ireland as a *peregrinus* in the 560s. *Vita Columbae* maintains that Columba was wrongly excommunicated at a synod at Teltown on the River Blackwater in Meath just prior to his *peregrinatio*, and was later restored to communion.[14] Controversy may have fuelled his desire for pilgrimage.

Like both his younger namesake and his old master, over a span of thirty-four years Columba founded a number of monasteries in voluntary exile. He presumably formulated rules for monastic living that differed little from theirs. Our earliest textual evidence pertaining to his life and achievement, *Amra Choluimb Chille*, 'Elegy of Colum Cille' (as Columba came to be known), speaks of him as 'guardian of a hundred churches'. Adomnán calls him 'father and founder of monasteries'.[15] One of these foundations lay on the little Hebridean island of Í, known today as Iona, a late misreading of its Latin name *Ioua*.

COLUMBA THE SCHOLAR

A century after the foundation of Iona, according to later Northumbrian sources, Columba was cited by Bishop Colmán of Lindisfarne as his authority on the controversial matter of the calculation of the date of Easter. The tradition to which Colmán adhered came from his 'fathers and their predecessors', as *Vita Wilfrithi* states in a speech placed in the bishop's mouth, who were 'plainly inspired by the Holy Spirit, as was *Collumcillae*'.[16] Bede refers to Columba as a *doctor*, and says that 'some record of his life and words is said to have been recorded by his disciples'.[17] Such language implies that Columba was not cited at Whitby simply as an exemplary figure. Columbanus reckoned himself an authority on the same Easter *computus*, like Colmán rejecting others with vigour. It may be that Columba too wrote on the matter. *Amra Choluimb Chille* says that 'he set in motion seasons and calculations'.[18]

[14] Adomnán, *V. s. Columbae*, iii.3.
[15] Adomnán, *V. s. Columbae*, *praef. secund.* On *Amra Choluimb Chille*, see Herbert, *Iona, Kells, and Derry*, 9–10; Clancy and Márkus, *Iona*, 96; Charles-Edwards, *Early Christian Ireland*, 285.
[16] Stephen, *V. s. Wilfrithi*, § 10; Bede, *Hist. eccl.*, iii.25.
[17] Bede, *Hist. eccl.*, iii.4; v.9.
[18] *Amra Chol. Chille*, v.9.

This poem and *Vita Columbae* reinforce what Bede knew only from hearsay, that the founder of Iona was an energetic scholar and writer, just as one expects of a pupil of Uinniau. For his part, Columbanus composed Latin verse, wrote several sermons, rules for monastic living, as well as *De penitentia*, an influential penitential modelled on Uinniau's own. Some of his writings and thoughts were controversial in Francia. Does this fact help us to understand the alleged excommunication of Columba? Something of Columba's scholarship emerges from *Amra Choluimb Chille*, apparently composed soon after his death. Columba is called 'learning's pillar' by the poet, and cast as a teacher 'who would explain the true word', who 'made glosses clear by his wisdom', and who 'read mysteries and distributed the scriptures among the schools'.

Adomnán implies that *c.* 700 Iona possessed many books written by Columba's hand,[19] and he was more than a mere copyist. He wrote, according to Adomnán, with a reed (*cum calamo*) and ink held in a horn, in a small scriptorium supported on planks, where other monks occasionally studied alongside him. Adomnán, in his day, probably wrote his own great works in the same small cell. It is a rustic, simple image that too easily invites assumptions that these were uncultivated, simple men. The sixth and seventh centuries were something of a golden philosophical age in the Irish Sea basin. Columba was almost certainly an intellectual of rare ability, and Adomnán has few peers in northern Britain in all the centuries since his death. *Amra Choluimb Chille* implies that Columba wrote two songs, and medieval commentators thought these were *Altus Prosator*, 'The High Creator', and *Adiutor laborantium*, 'Helper of Labourers'. These hymns reveal a writer with profound biblical familiarity, as well as patristic and poetic learning and some understanding of Greek, a language that Columba knew.[20]

Columba's scholarship, like Columbanus's, probably included study of, and reflection on, moral theology Uinniau's pet subject. *Altus Prosator* shows familiarity with the seminal monastic theology of John Cassian of Lérins, who died in 433, and *Amra Choluimb Chille* indicates that Columba studied him, as well as the great monastic theologian Basil of Caesarea, who died in 379.[21] The main theological achievements of his immediate intellectual forebears lay in the particular subject of penitential scholarship. *De excidio Britanniae* is a *tour de force* in the importance of repentance. Its author Gildas also composed *De poenitentia*, a

[19] Adomnán, *V. s. Columbae*, ii.8–9, ii.44–5, iii.23.
[20] *Amra Chol. Chille*, viii.14.
[21] Clancy and Márkus, *Iona*, 55–7; *Amra Chol. Chille*, iv.10–11; v.5–7.

penitential listing transgressions and the penance to be prescribed in each case, varying according to the sin and the circumstances of the sinner. Not surprisingly, Gildas included here that 'for good kings we ought to offer the sacrifice' of the eucharist, 'but for bad ones, on no account'.[22]

Uinniau's *Penitentialis* proved more influential than Gildas's *De poenitentia*. 'Sins', Uinniau wrote, 'can be absolved in secret, we say, by penance and by very diligent devotion of heart and body'.[23] This notion of the absolution of sins through an ongoing programme of penance (rather than a single cleansing act of penance prior to death) was quite innovative in the sixth century. *Penitentialis Vinniani* contemplates the gravity of sins of thought as well as sins of deed. It teaches that the guilt of a sinful layperson, a 'man of this world', is 'lighter in this world' than that of a cleric, but that 'his reward is less in the world to come'.[24] Uinniau emphasised the importance of confession and penance. Even where he was unsure that grave sins could be expiated by penitential behaviour, he argued that 'it is better to do penance and not despair, for great is the mercy of God'.[25] He was particularly interested in sins pertaining to strife between individuals and in sexual indiscretions, but he also dealt tantalisingly with the practise of magic (*maleficus*). Columbanus's *De penitentia* borrows very heavily from *Penitentialis Vinniani*, and the two texts together became central to Western penitential thought in the early Middle Ages. Indeed, it has been said that the penitential theology of Gildas, Uinniau and Columbanus represents a distinctive contribution to mainstream medieval theology.[26]

Columba was a part of this important Irish Sea philosophical movement and without doubt he studied such material. Did he draw up a penitential? In several episodes of *Vita Columbae*, the saint is depicted assigning penance to sinners, and some of his thinking is in line with *Penitentialis Vinniani*. In one episode, he castigates a penitent for refusing relaxation of his penance by Columba and his deputy, his cousin Baíthéne.[27] In others, the saint repeatedly places penitents under his cousin's supervision. The implication here may be that Iona's penitential tradition was formulated by Baíthéne. Adomnán relates a story in which the truth of the scriptural mysteries was revealed to Columba, but went unrecorded because Baíthéne was not there to set them down, as if his

---

22   Gildas, *Praef. Gildae de Poenit.*, § 23–4.
23   *Penit. Vinniani*, § 10.
24   *Penit. Vinniani*, § 7.
25   *Penit. Vinniani*, § 22.
26   O'Loughlin, *Celtic Theology*, 48–56.
27   Adomnán, *V. s. Columbae*, i.21.

writings were later regarded as speaking with Columba's voice.[28] For the sins of fratricide and incest, Columba assigns twelve years' penance in *Vita Columbae*, longer than the seven-year period envisioned by Uinniau and Columbanus for capital sins like murder.[29] Columba's harshness here surely reflects the victimisation of kin, a particular detail that neither Uinniau nor Columbanus considered in their more general statements about murder and sexual aberrance.

For a layman wishing to enter monastic life, on the other hand, Columba assigns seven years' penance, in line with *Penitentialis Vinniani*. Like his old master, who emphasised the importance of confession, Columba objects when he attends a mass performed by a priest with unconfessed sins.[30] He also enjoins a reluctant wife to share her husband's bed, just as Uinniau had taught. Furthermore, Columba is depicted excommunicating 'persecutors of churches', and *Penitentialis Vinniani* too says that unrepentant despoilers of churches and monasteries were to be excommunicated.[31] On the whole, the impression given by *Vita Columbae* is that Iona's penitential tradition drew heavily from the teachings of Uinniau, and was probably similar to that enunciated by Columbanus in Francia. Here, as elsewhere, the evidence suggests that Columba's understanding of himself as a cleric was heavily influenced by his teachers.

COLUMBAN MONASTICISM

Columba is not famous for his scholarship, however impressive it was. Neither is he particularly famous for his achievements as a monastic leader. Columbanus composed the monastic rules *Regula monachorum*, the 'Rule of Monks', and *Regula coenobialis*, the 'Rule of Communal Life'. No such writings survive from Columba's pen, but *Vita Columbae* provides vivid impressions of the rules and rhythms of monastic and communal life in a Columban monastery as envisioned by his seventh-century successors, whose rules were widespread in northern Britain. As an idealised monk, Columba is said to have been unable to go an hour without prayer or study, and to have maintained a glad heart, despite relentless meagreness of diet and lack of sleep 'beyond the strength of man'. *Penitentialis Vinniani* observes that a cleric who was ill-tempered

---

[28] Adomnán, *V. s. Columbae*, iii.18.
[29] Adomnán, *V. s. Columbae*, i.22.
[30] Adomnán, *V. s. Columbae*, i.40, ii.39.
[31] Adomnán, *V. s. Columbae*, ii.24, ii.41; *Penit. Vinniani*, §§ 30–1, 41–5.

was guilty of 'great and capital' sin, for such a state of mind would 'slay the soul and cast it down to the depths of hell'.[32]

There were obviously religious duties to be performed in any monastic environment. A bell summoned monks to the church at Iona. Adomnán mentions mass and the singing of psalms, implying that a monk should not sing with excessive exuberance. Columbanus's *Regula coenobialis* punishes monks for speaking loudly.[33] It is study, however, which dominates monastic life in *Vita Columbae*, because prayer and attendance at church services were less likely to be productive of the kinds of anecdotes preferred by hagiography. None the less, the prominence of scholarship in the Columban dossier is notable, if for no other reason than that it is easily forgotten. Baíthéne is said to have brought a psalter to Columba for his approval, implying that the saint was a stickler about accurate copying. Monks of the Ionan community are depicted in *Vita Columbae* going about their business while carrying books, and one takes notes on a tablet (*tabula*).[34]

Slates have been discovered by excavation at an early medieval monastic site in the island of Inchmarnock in the Firth of Clyde, upon which pupils scratched letters. The literate culture of a monastery had a material and resource dimension. A community needed a steady supply of calves whose hides could be prepared as the vellum upon which manuscripts were penned. A new gospel book consumed the hides of more than 100 calves, and a new bible some five times that number. Evidence of vellum preparation has been discovered at the Early Historic monastery at Portmahomack in Easter Ross. Some manuscripts were 'illuminated' with illustrations and decorative art, expressed in the Early Historic art style now called 'Insular', its principal themes broadly similar to those found throughout the West. The subtleties and complexities of illumination imagery, with multiple levels of expression of narrative and theological concepts, encapsulate the impressive intellectual milieu represented by an Early Historic Insular monastery. 'Handbooks' of motifs probably existed as points of reference for artists. Inks and paints were made from a range of natural products, ranging from soot to crushed apples.

The mobility of the monks of Iona can surprise those who assume that they lived utterly withdrawn and cloistered lives. Both Columbanus and Columba are said by their hagiographers to have shared a penchant for leaving their monasteries for brief solitary contemplation. Columbanus,

---

[32]   Adomnán, *V. s. Columbae, praef. secund.*; *Penit. Vinniani*, § 29.
[33]   Adomnán, *V. s. Columbae*, i.37, i.44; Columbanus, *Reg. Coenob.*, § 5.
[34]   Adomnán, *V. s. Columbae*, i.23–4, i.35.

'a lover of solitude', regularly took long walks, and occasionally spent longer spaces of time in caves. Columba too took solitary walks at Iona, and occasionally retreated to the unidentified island hermitage of Hinba, or separated himself from other monks while travelling.[35] The abbot seems to have travelled often, moving about Iona's extended estate (of which the island itself was only a part) and various monasteries under his charge, and making still other journeys to places like Lochaber (*stagnum Aporum*), Skye (*insula Scia*) and Ardnamurchan (*regio Artda Muirchol*).[36] Adomnán, a frequent traveller himself as abbot of Iona, probably made these same journeys. He may even have modelled Columba's movements largely on his own. Both he and (apparently) Columba made journeys to redeem or comfort captives. *Penitentialis Vinniani* says that 'we prescribe and urge contributing' for their redemption.[37]

Lesser Ionan brethren were also mobile. Adomnán relates stories involving them in transit between monasteries, but makes it clear that they were not to travel without their abbot's consent. Similarly Columbanus's *Regula monachorum* makes it plain that monks were to 'do nothing without counsel' and were 'to go nowhere with complete freedom'.[38] This was no individualist's idyll. Senior monks are said in *Vita Columbae* to have been given charge of different Ionan daughter monasteries in northern Britain, the Hebrides and Ireland. They moved about in that capacity, often back and forth from Iona itself. The deputy abbot Baíthéne was the leader (*praepositus*) at Mag Lunge in Tiree, the exact location of which is uncertain. As the man to whom Columba sent penitents, Baíthéne sometimes sends them in turn to Hinba, where Columba's uncle Ernán was *praepositus*.[39] In 597 Baíthéne, eleven years his cousin's junior, succeeded to Columba's abbatial office. His own successor a year later, Laisrán son of Feradach, the son of another cousin, was *praepositus* at Durrow on the River Brosna in Westmeath while Columba lived, a monastery which Bede believed was founded before Iona.[40]

---

[35] Jonas, *V. s. Columbani*, §§ 8–9, 11–12, 17; Adomnán, *V. s. Columbae*, i.21, i.30, ii.4, ii.26, iii.5, iii.8, iii.16, iii.18. For a discussion of Hinba, see Macquarrie, *Saints of Scotland*, 91–102.

[36] Adomnán, *V. s. Columbae*, i.12, i.33, ii.10, ii.20, ii.26.

[37] *Penit. Vinniani*, § 32.

[38] Adomnán, *V. s. Columbae*, i.2, i.6, i.12, i.18, i.19, i.31, ii.38; Columbanus, *Reg. Monach.*, § 9.

[39] Adomnán, *V. s. Columbae*, i.30, i.41, ii.15; iii.8; on Hinba, see i.21, i.45. On Tiree, see Fisher, *Early Medieval Sculpture*, 10.

[40] *AU* 598.1; *AT* 598.1; *CS* 598.1; *AI* 601.2; Adomnán, *V. s. Columbae*, i.29. On Baíthéne's death-year, see Herbert, *Iona, Kells, and Derry*, 38–9.

The abbot of Iona had a *minister* or attendant. Columba's *minister* Diarmait seems to have been his constant companion and confidante, but is never portrayed by Adomnán engaged in particularly monastic activity. When he travelled, the abbot was accompanied by companions who need not always have been 'fully' monastic. An abbot thus strikes one as analogous to a potentate in secular society. He is always in the company of attendants, is never depicted working fields himself, and has hands and head occupied by other matters. Bishops could be attended by warriors. Wilfrid in the 670s had a lieutenant (*praefectus*), whom he commissioned to abduct a boy whose mother had promised him to the Church, but changed her mind.[41]

Given the capacity of warriors to victimise churches, it is no surprise that clergy could rationalise maintaining bodyguards, encouraged by prevailing social attitudes which expected men of great status to have a *cohors*. On the Continent, monasteries seem fairly routinely to have made gifts of horses and even weapons to those who donated land, or to have received such things as gifts to be redistributed in this way. Adomnán depicts Columba engaged in just such an exchange, sending a decorated sword to a lord whose retainer wished to join the Iona community.[42] Bede fretted that bishops were too easily seduced by what he called 'the soft life' (*vita remissioris*), maintaining courts like a potentate's, given over to merriment, feasting, and story-telling.[43]

Monks, on the other hand, could often be found in the barley fields of Iona or raising monastic buildings, and Adomnán refers to such vital tasks as grain-threshing, fence-building, fruit-gathering, milking, lumbering in Ardnamurchan and sealing on Mull. A senior monk was the *operum dispensator*, the 'allocator of work' on the Iona estate.[44] These elders were probably analogous to leading members of a lordly household. Columba's most trusted deputies were his cousins and kin, just as potentates included kin in their retinues. The daily and seasonal chores of maintaining a monastery as a living community must surely much resembled those undertaken by farmsteads great and small throughout northern Britain.

A monk's life could be as hard as that of any agricultural labourer. Adomnán speaks of the grief and 'the hard and heavy discipline of monastic life', which Columba was able to alleviate at Iona. In his *Regula*

---

[41]   Stephen, *V. s. Wilfrithi*, § 18; see Halsall, *Warfare and Society*, 48 for Continental parallels.

[42]   Adomnán, *V. s. Columbae*, ii.39; Halsall, *Warfare and Society*, 77–80, 88, 96, 101.

[43]   Bede, *Ep. ad Ecgbertum*, § 4; McClure and Collins, *Bede*, 344–5 (trans.).

[44]   Adomnán, *V. s. Columbae*, i.37.

monachorum, Columbanus wrote of the perfect monk, 'let him come to his bed weary, and sleep walking, and let him be forced to rise while his sleep is not yet finished'.[45] Two pilgrims arriving at Iona in *Vita Columbae* are told that they cannot remain there for a year, as they desire, unless they take monastic vows to uphold rules such as this one. Perhaps it is not surprising that the abandonment of vows by new monks was apparently a fairly common occurrence. Adomnán calls lapsed monks 'sons of perdition' (*filii perditionis*), a common phrase among monastic writers. In his time, such men could include kings who had retired to monastic life, only to return to their kingdoms at a later date.

Monastic life at a Columban monastery thus consisted of a mix of mundane and laborious tasks, study and church observances. The *Regula monachorum* of Columbanus says 'we must eat daily, for the reason that we must go forward daily, pray daily, toil daily, and read daily'. On the matter of diet, Columbanus wrote, 'let monks' food be poor' and governed by temperance, such that 'we must fast daily, just as we must feed daily'.[46] It was customary at Iona, according to *Vita Columbae*, to fast on Wednesdays. The monasteries founded by Columbanus were also expected to fast on Wednesdays and Fridays, until the ninth hour of the day.[47]

Some monks sought even greater hardship than could be found at a monastery like Iona. *Vita Columbae* speaks of such anchorites living at Hinba and Durrow. Other monks hunted for a hermitage for themselves in the Hebrides, and one made several unsuccessful attempts to find one. He can hardly have failed to find islands: we are to suppose instead that he could find none that were both unoccupied and suitable to sustain a hermit. The failure of prospective anchorites to find hermitages in *Vita Columbae* suggests that Adomnán was hesitant to advocate eremitic quests, even if he was not inclined to condemn them. Columbanus wrote that 'monks must everywhere beware of a proud independence', and also that 'if temperance exceeds measure, it will be a vice and not a virtue'.[48] It seems that Adomnán, perhaps following a *Regula* laid down by Columba, shared such anxieties.

Prospective hermits arriving at Iona were accommodated in a guest-house, where visitors could include monks, emissaries, pilgrims, abbots, potentates, exiles and ordinary men, both familiar and unfamiliar. Several

---

[45] Adomnán, *V. s. Columbae*, i.37, ii.39; Columbanus, *Reg. Monach.*, § 10.
[46] Columbanus, *Reg. Monach.*, § 3.
[47] Adomnán, *V. s. Columbae*, i.26; Columbanus, *Reg. Coenob.*, § 13.
[48] Columbanus, *Reg. Monach.*, §§ 3, 9.

exiles described in *Vita Columbae* are warriors whose flight from the world of feasting halls and battlefields was not sincere. Visitors could be given hospitality for as long as three days and three nights, depending on their familiarity, before receiving an audience with the abbot or his deputy. Secular poets sometimes performed at monasteries, even in the refectory – a monastery's equivalent of the feasting hall. 'Pilgrims', *Penitentialis Vinniani* enjoins, 'are to be received into our houses'.[49]

IONA AND 'THE CELTIC CHURCH'

That *Vita Columbae* so often reflects the injunctions of *Penitentialis Vinniani* in its depiction of monastic life, as well as Columbanus's two *Regulae*, suggests that these writings by men with whom Columba shared close intellectual connections ought to be reasonable guides to the substance of any *Regulae* that the founder of Iona may have formulated. It also seems reasonable to suppose that his thinking about the whole nature of his *peregrinatio* was shaped by the philosophical movement to which he belonged. No scholar of the period would now refer to that movement as 'the Celtic Church': like Thomism and the other -isms of later medieval Christian philosophy, its distinctiveness from other modes of thought, and its occasional clashes with them, must not be confused with alienation from the wider Church.

The establishment of the Gregorian mission to the Anglo-Saxons in 597, the year of Columba's death, introduced controversy into Insular Christianity. Columbanus had already encountered it on the Continent. The mission brought various relatively innovative teachings current in Rome, and believed that the bishop of Rome, heir to the apostle Peter, was invested with the authority to require bishops to bring their dioceses into conformity with his. Across the Latin West, advocates of such 'apostolicist' thinking, as we shall call it here, encountered resistance from 'traditionalist' bishops who believed that local ecclesiastical tradition had too much authority of its own to be cast aside lightly in favour of new-fangled ideas.

Vita Columbae observes that Columba once prophesied 'concerning the great dispute that after many days arose among the churches of Ireland over diversity in the time of the Easter festival', one of the key matters of issue between the apostolicists and the Insular traditionalists.[50]

---

[49] *Penit. Vinniani*, § 33.
[50] Adomnán, *V. s. Columbae*, i.3.

Bede's *Historia ecclesiastica* quotes a letter sent to Ireland by pope-elect John IV, shortly before his consecration in December 640, which included Ségéne (*Segenus*), the fifth abbot of Iona, among its addressees. He was another kinsman of Columba, Báithéne and Laisrán. Another addressee was probably Ernéne (*Ernianus*) son of Crasén, the principal subject of Columba's Easter prophecy. Ernéne and Ségéne were enjoined by the pope-elect to forsake their traditional Easter calculation, as well as other teachings they had sent to Rome for comment.[51] It was surely with reference to John's letter that Adomnán – or rather his main source – included Iona's thoughts on Easter.

Resistance to apostolicist reforms from traditionalist British and Irish clerics, who preferred not to abandon customary observances, is one of the best known features of Early Historic Insular history. At several points in the past it has suited commentators to make much of such tensions between these 'Celtic' traditionalists and the apostolicist reformers, who advocated conformity to an orthodoxy governed by the apostolic authority of the Church at Rome. This situation superficially seems to prefigure clashes between Protestants and Catholics, but it is most extravagant to liken philosophical debates of the seventh century to those of the Reformation. No traditionalist was more vehement in his rejection of the reformist case for modifying the Easter calculation than Columbanus, who wrote to the pope himself to complain. Yet he also described the *ecclesia Romanae*, the Roman Church, as 'the most honoured flower of all Europe', led by 'the fairest flower' of that Church.[52]

Columbanus would not have thanked anyone who described him as un- or anti-Roman, or (particularly) as unorthodox. The Insular Churches of the sixth and seventh centuries ought to be understood as sharing with the Scottish Church of the eleventh century orthodoxy 'in all essentials', resisting conformity 'on the fringe rather than at the heart of doctrine', not least on matters of observance and jurisdiction.[53] The calculation of the date of the important Easter festival, celebrating the resurrection of Christ, was inconsistent across Christendom at this time, with no less than three systems in operation. Britain and Ireland were not unique in their minor philosophical divergences from the increasingly influential modes of thought advocated by the bishop of Rome.

---

[51] Bede, *Hist. eccl.*, ii.19; Adomnán, *V. s. Columbae*, i.3.
[52] Columbanus, *Epist*. i.1.
[53] Barrow, *Kingship and Unity*, 70–1.

The Easter controversy

Like the Jewish Passover from which it was adapted, Easter occurs in the third week of Nisan, the first lunar month whose full moon occurs on or after the spring equinox. Long before the sixth century, Easter had been decoupled from Passover so that it would fall exclusively on a Sunday. But which Sunday?

By the seventh century Rome had adopted the Dionysiac formula, which dated the equinox to 21 March. The scheme also regarded it as self-evident that the third week of a lunar month could not contain a full moon (the mid-point of the month). Since a full moon occurs 14.76 days after a new one, the Dionysiac formula defined the third week as beginning with its fifteenth day and ending with its twenty-first. Whichever of those seven days was Sunday was Easter.

This formula replaced an ambiguous earlier scheme, but a different formula again was in place in Britain and Ireland. This one dated the equinox to 25 March, and, reckoning a lunar month as beginning with a new moon, had the third week beginning with the fourteenth day. If that day was Sunday, Easter was held before the full moon in this scheme – unthinkable in Dionysiac thinking.

In the course of the seventh and eighth centuries, the Dionysiac formula eventually displaced the earlier scheme, whose adherents strenuously defended it. In the meantime, the two systems often produced an identical Easter – when a full moon did not occur in the gap between 21 and 24 March (which delayed the Easter month in the Insular reckoning by another lunar cycle), and when Sunday fell between the fifteenth and twentieth days of the month inclusive (a six-in-eight chance). Thus, the Easter controversy could fortuitously fail to attract attention to itself for long stretches of years.

All of these calculations based on lunar months created an astronomical problem, in that the 'year' of twelve lunar months (29.53 days each) is almost eleven days shorter than the 365.24-day solar orbit of the earth. In order to synchronise these two different astronomical periods while preserving the integrity of the lunar month (abandoned in the modern calendar) it was necessary to insert the occasional extra lunar month, in its entirety. The Dionysiac and Insular systems differed in their approach to this problem, and the prospects of revolutionising the calendar may well have been a major source of resistance and conservatism.[54]

---

[54] The intricacies of the controversy are admirably addressed by Charles-Edwards, *Early Christian Ireland*, 391–405; see also Rollason, *Northumbria*, 141–2.

Bede famously refers to the 'irregular' subordination of bishops within the Ionan *familia*, the monastic federation under its rule, as if the abbot exercised something like metropolitan authority over a 'province' consisting of Iona and its daughter houses. The long-held convention arising from Bede's information, that subordination of episcopal authority and non-territorial episcopates were key features of a 'Celtic Church', has been largely given up by scholars.[55] The ways in which the spiritual and temporal responsibilities and authority of the Church in Ireland were apportioned to bishops and powerful abbots in different areas at different times could be eclectic. In Iona's case, the possibility exists that Columba developed a model inspired by a concept of overlordship among his royal kin.

The successive generations of monastic commentators who provide our primary evidence of the Churches of Early Historic Britain and Ireland probably make episcopal roles, functions and behaviour seem rather less central and overarching than they were in fact.[56] *Vita Columbae* shows Columba deferring to a bishop at mass, having discovered him to be a bishop, and notes that the superior of a monastery in Tiree summoned a bishop for the ordination of a new priest.[57] Adomnán thus does not seem to have questioned the spiritual authority of bishops. In maintaining that bishops in Ionan monasteries were subject to the authority (*ius*) of the abbot of Iona, Bede may have been thinking of a monk's obligation – even if he happened to be a bishop – to be obedient to his abbot on matters of monastic life. The situation may have been analogous to that of thirteenth-century kings of Scots who held lands from the English king. In that context they were dutiful subjects, but in Scotland they were sovereign lords, a distinction that could be difficult to maintain at all times.

CHRISTIANITY BEFORE COLUMBA

It is difficult to establish from archaeological evidence alone how deeply Christianity had penetrated into Romano-British society before official links with Rome were severed some forty years after the Barbarian

---

[55] Most recently and comprehensively by Etchingham, *Church Organisation*; see in particular 12–46 for discussion of the paradigm. See also Herbert, *Iona, Kells, and Derry*, 34.

[56] For discussion in an Anglo-Saxon context, see Coates, 'The Role of Bishops', especially 194–5.

[57] Adomnán, *V. s. Columbae*, i.36, i.44.

Conspiracy. It appears to have become established at least by the third century. The Roman establishment did not finally embrace the religion, to the exclusion of ancestral pagan practices and more recent cults, until about a generation before Rome lost or surrendered control of her Britannic provinces. By standards established throughout the Empire, Roman Britain may have been relatively lacking in Christianity. Yet there is no doubt that it had become entrenched in the island by the beginning of the fourth century.

Pagan observances, native and foreign in origin, had by no means been obliterated even by the end of that century. Yet the spread of Christianity across the Irish Sea and beyond the northern frontier by *c.* 400 is testimony to the success and vitality of some at least of the four (or five) Britannic provincial Churches of the fourth century. One of these produced the controversial but accomplished lawyer and moral theologian Pelagius, whose writings gave rise to the Pelagian school of thought, declared heretical in 418, which in various forms remained influential for centuries thereafter, not least among British and Irish theologians.

The previous chapters have examined economic, diplomatic and military intercourse between the Romano-British provincials and the barbarians of northern Britain during the Roman Iron Age. We may be fairly certain that there were occasionally Christians north of the frontier in the fourth century, especially in outer Brigantia. Seventh- and eighth-century textual evidence, along with the famous example of St Patrick in Ireland, can condition us to envision christianisation as a process involving organised missionary activity and apostolic saints. Neither was strictly necessary. Christian activity of a more prosaic kind, in other contexts, was very important in paving the way for the chiefly or royal conversions that are likely to have been crucial in christianising fully civil communities like those in northern Britain. Serving in the Roman army, everyday contact with Christian merchants and even interaction with Christian Roman hostages or captives were all recognised by the fifth-century Gallo-Roman historian Prosper of Aquitaine as exerting christianising influences on barbarian peoples.[58]

The human sciences understand that the intellectual framework of societies like those in fifth-century northern Britain could become oriented towards Christian cultural and cosmological concepts through what may be called 'bottom-up' pressure, arising from casual interaction with ordinary Christians. It seems particularly true where perceptible social or cul-

[58] Charles-Edwards, *Early Christian Ireland*, 210; Fletcher, *The Barbarian Conversion*, 80–1; Cusack, *Conversion*, 39, 65.

tural innovations had taken place which were regarded (rightly or wrongly) as reflecting the influences of a macrocosm like the Roman Empire or Latin Christendom. The effect of this phenomenon of perceived romanising, where it took place, was not to christianise outright communities in contact with Christian macrocosms. It was rather to familiarise them with Christianity and to establish receptiveness regarding Christians and their ideas. In fully civil societies, political and legal frameworks were governed by consensus. Christians or pro-Christians among the normal freemen had regular formal opportunities to make their voices heard. Within such environments, the conversion of individual potentates, whether by missionary effort or through some other process, became a real possibility. So too, of course, did martyrdom, if an assembly was hostile.

Scholars once took it for granted that christianisation reflected the essential truth of the religion and the power of its God. Even where this point was not put forward in devotional terms, it was imagined that Christianity conveyed messages about life, humanity and death that pagan theologies simply could not match. Yet societies devise religious systems that satisfy their social and spiritual requirements, and one must look elsewhere to understand the appeal of Christianity. Work on the subject by social scientists has shown that christianisation is likely to have been primarily a two-step process in an environment like fifth-century northern Britain. The first of these processes was the individual conversions of potentates, with all the ramifications for their retinues and clients. The second was communal conversion of the kind envisioned by Adomnán, who wrote in *Vita Columbae* of crowds of heathen Picts having 'magnified' or 'glorified the God of the Christians'.[59] Similarly, Bede wrote in *Historia ecclesiastica* of mass baptisms of Deirans and Bernicians after the conversion of their king in the 620s.

Modern missionary ethics reject the validity of such 'conversions'. There is abundant evidence to show that in general this was not the case in late Antiquity and the early Middle Ages. Here the social forces that bound fully civil communities together exerted such a powerful influence on individuals that communal consensus at a feasting hall or assembly – or mass baptism – was probably thought to be binding on everyone, regardless of whether or not each normal freeman had experienced the deeply personal phenomenon of conversion, or had even been present. Opting out of such collective undertakings was tantamount to opting out of the community as a whole. Such courageous non-conformity was probably very rare.

[59] Adomnán, *V. s. Columbae*, ii.27; ii.32.

Christianisation and consensus: the example of Edwini's Deira

The description below by Bede of the decisive moment in the christian-isation of the Northumbrians during the reign of Edwini son of Alle (616–33) is very famous. It is likely to be mainly the product of the imagination of its author, rather than an account of real events. The expectation that Christianity was embraced because pagan priests knew secretly that their divinities were worthless and powerless, and because it offered certainty in the place of doubt, is Christian prejudice. None the less, this story reveals a great deal about the general role of discussion and consensus in royal decision-making, and so the potential for Christian sympathisers to have influenced royal decision-making prior to christianisation.

> When the king had heard his words, he answered that he was both willing and bound to accept the faith that Paulinus taught. He said, however, that he would confer about this with his loyal chief men and his counsellors . . . A meeting of his council was held, and each one was asked in turn what he thought . . .
>
> Coifi, the chief of the priests, answered at once . . . 'I frankly admit that, for my part, I have found that the religion which we have hith-erto held has no virtue nor profit in it. None of your followers has devoted himself more earnestly than I to the worship of our gods . . .; if [they] had any power, they would have helped me more readily . . . so it follows that if, on examination, these new doctrines now explained to us are found to be better and more effectual, let us accept them at once without any delay.'
>
> Another of the king's chief men agreed . . . and then added, 'This is how the present life of man on earth, King, appears to me . . . A sparrow flies swiftly through the hall: it enters in at one door and quickly flies out through the other. For the few moments it is inside, storm and wintry tempest cannot touch it; but after the briefest moment of calm, it flits from your sight . . . So this life of man appears . . . ; what follows or indeed what went before, we know not at all. If this new doctrine brings us more certain information, it seems right that we should accept it.'
>
> Other elders and counsellors of the king continued in the same manner . . . Why need I say more? The king publicly accepted the gospel which Paulinus preached, renounced idolatry, and confessed his faith in Christ.[60]

---

[60] Bede, *Hist. eccl.*, ii.13.

A mass shift in religious orientation cannot, at the outset, have much influenced the daily lives and spirituality of these new Christians. The process of taking the teachings of the Christian religion to the people, and providing spiritual guidance and pastoral care, was infinitely more complex and challenging. This phase of christianisation occupied bishops and secular priests right through the Middle Ages. We get only fleeting glimpses in our sources of the 'secular clergy' charged with the task in our period. The situation reflects lack of interest in such men on the part of monastic authors, and is poor evidence of any real dearth of priests and bishops. Like Gildas, Columbanus denounced worldly clerics, and *Vita Columbae* ridicules one such churchman, 'a wealthy man respected among the people', whom Columba disdains for travelling in a carriage, retaining stray cattle in his enclosure and keeping the company of prostitutes.[61] Bede too tended to presume the worst about secular clerics. Monastic writers could regard them as their spiritual inferiors for remaining fully engaged with the world outside the cloister, and especially for being complicit in the luxurious and self-indulgent (and sinful) lifestyles of formal and informal elites.

Apart from bishops, the most prominent priests in early Christian Britain and Ireland were probably chaplains attached to royal and noble households. Bede mentions them on two occasions, both members of queenly retinues.[62] Kings probably relied on their chaplains in formulating explanations (or justifications) of their violent and other political activities in line with Christian morality and justice, thus making chaplains vulnerable to the monastic accusations above. In the Roman Iron Age, leaders probably relied on pagan priests to identify and interpret omens and portents to help them in taking decisions. The tendency may have transcended the christianisation horizon. Bede's allegation that the bishop of Hexham warned his king against invading Pictland in 685 could be read in this way. Archaeology suggests that churches were sometimes built in or near to Early Historic power centres. There is such evidence of a chapel within the great Verturian fort at Burghead by the eighth century. Bede mentions a church at the Bernician royal power centre at Bebbanburg, now Bamburgh on the Northumberland coast, where relics of St Oswald (once king there) were kept and venerated.[63]

---

[61] Adomnán, *V. s. Columbae*, i.38; on this theme in the Gildasian tradition, see Sharpe, 'Gildas as Father', 199.

[62] Bede, *Hist. eccl.*, ii.9, iii.25.

[63] Bede, *Hist. eccl.*, iii.6; Ralston, *Hill-Forts of Pictland*, 31.

Although his mission field was in Ireland, the writings of the fifth-century Romano-British missionary Patricius, the famous St Patrick, allow us valuable insights into the activities of secular clerics and aspects of the expansion of Christianity from Britannia into neighbouring regions. Patrick's inspiration to undertake missionary work was spontaneous, arising from perpenal experience of the mission field. His missionary activities were mostly self-directed and reasonably successful, showing that christianisation in fifth-century northern Britain required no particular planning or direction on the part of ecclesiastical authorities. It was more likely to be spontaneous, driven by personalities and local circumstances. In Patrick's case it seems to have been some time before bishops back in Britain attempted to assert their authority over his successful efforts.

Apart from the pseudo-historical Ninianic hagiography of the eighth century, we can point to no dedicated mission to christianise the peoples of outer Brigantia, which in Early Historic times we shall term 'the North British zone'. A northward expansion of Christianity before and during the lifetime of Patrick is, none the less, a fact. Whithorn, so intimately associated with Ninian, was home to a Christian community in the fifth century when Patrick was treading the mission field of northern Ireland. The evidence consists of the 'Latinus stone', an inscribed fifth-century funerary monument that is unambiguously Christian. Of similar date is the 'Cat Stane', another funerary monument standing now within the confines of Edinburgh Airport.

These stones are the earliest examples of a corpus of a dozen inscribed monuments in the North British zone bearing Christian iconography, dating from the fifth, sixth and seventh centuries. They form a northerly extension of a greater corpus, with examples in Wales, south-west England, Man and Brittany, inspired by late Antique Romano-British monumental practice.[64] A comparable pattern is observable in these same regions as regards participation in a network of exchange which saw ceramics (and their contents) and coins of Byzantine Roman provenance arriving directly from the eastern Mediterranean.[65] Similarities in burial rites in this period have already been noted and linked with romanising tendencies. Only some of these monuments were established within an ecclesiastical milieu. The rest show that some North British elites in this period could speak and read British Latin, and expected this Romance language to be understood by some passers-by. There can be little doubt

---

[64] Forsyth, '*Hic Memoria Perpetua*', is the most recent examination of these stones.
[65] Harris, *Britain, Byzantium and the West*, 143–61.

that many could now regard themselves as Romano-British Christians, where it suited them, whatever that may have meant to them in real terms. We shall see that Patrick's writings show it to be true.

Without any sense of how representative a sample of this class of evidence survives, it is unwise to rely on the relative dates of individual monuments to seek to trace the progress of Christianity from region to region. The two earliest monuments come from opposite ends of the zone in Lothian and Galloway. Christian Britannia was visible from the coast at Whithorn. Lothian was more distant, but the archaeological evidence of prolonged and intensive interaction between the Uotadini and Rome has already been discussed.

The christianisation of Roman provinces came about largely through imperial and episcopal initiatives which raised the status and appeal of the religion in the eyes of elites. It is conceivable that North British potentates too, whose ancestors had so many romanising tendencies, were similarly willing to accept baptism. A conversion that pleased Romano-British elites to the south may have seemed politic in some cases. From *c.* 450 Christianity may also have come increasingly into vogue across the Romano-British zone as an aspect of solidarity in the face of incursions and expansion by aggressive Anglo-Saxon pagans.

The route followed by Christianity into Galloway may have passed through the *civitas* of Luguvalium (modern Carlisle) in the Solway basin, but it may also have passed through Ireland or Man. There are archaeological indications of increasingly strong late Antique links between Ireland and the North British zone, typical of the period for the 'highland' Romano-British zone.[66] There are also indications of British (Cruithnian) settlement in north-east Ireland and Irish settlement in Wales. Accordingly, the corpus of inscribed early Christian Insular monuments reflects cultural interaction between Britain and Ireland.[67]

Patrick's enraged letter to the warriors of Coroticos, apparently based at the stronghold at Clyde (now Dumbarton) Rock on the lower Clyde, shows them to have been Christians with Irish links and, to Patrick's mind, his fellow citizens. The important 'citadel fort' atop Clyde Rock (*Alt Clut*) seems to have been established towards the end of the Roman Iron Age, and was probably not very old when Coroticos held it.[68] Patrick's experiences are thus important additional evidence of interaction between Christians in Ireland and south-west Scotland in the

[66] Woolf, 'The Britons', 363.
[67] Forsyth, '*Hic Memoria Perpetua*', 121–2.
[68] Alcock, *Kings and Warriors*, 42–3; Foster, 'Before Alba', 15.

fifth century, perhaps paving the way for the movements of Uinniau a generation or two later.

The letter to the warriors of Coroticos is evidence too that Christianity was widespread across the North British zone, at least at the elite level, by the end of the fifth century. Throughout the Roman Iron Age its inhabitants exhibited a measure of cultural solidarity, not least in their romanising tendencies, and by the fifth century long-cist funerary rites, inscribed monuments and christianisation show the extent to which North British culture had homogenised. The same thing happened to the Alamanni of inner Germania over the same period of time.[69] Might we, therefore, envision fairly rapid christianisation across the North British zone? It does seem to have been something of a zone-wide phenomenon.

Here we surely have the context for the long-cist (and almost certainly monastic) cemetery on the Isle of May, which places Christians in the Firth of Forth in the fifth century.[70] The presence of fifth-century monks within sight of Fife is obviously significant, in the light of the eighth-century Pictish testimony that the southern Picts became Christians long before the middle of the sixth century. Yet Fife Christians may plausibly be regarded as northerly and peripheral outliers of a North British cultural phenomenon which remained largely distinct from southern Pictish culture in Early Historic times. This is not to say, however, that fifth-century christianisation in Fife could not have been written into Pictish history once the peninsula had become a Pictish district.

Dead Christians were thus being buried and commemorated in Galloway, Clydesdale, Lothian and Fife at the time when Patrick was appearing before Irish potentates. Where such princes could be convinced by missionaries – or by pro-Christian elements among their own people – that the Christian God was already at work in their communities, successfully challenging traditional divinities, their conversion could readily follow. It is a theme of early royal conversions, however, that kings required to be convinced that adoption of the new religion would bring military success, glory and riches. The demands of elite culture had to be met by Christianity.

As the personification of his people, the chief or king was the keystone in bringing about christianisation. Where they had any real choice in the matter, the decision to accept or reject baptism cannot have been easy.

---

[69]   Brather, 'Ethnic Identities', 159.
[70]   Yeoman, 'Pilgrims to St Ethernan'.

The taking of great care and considerable time in contemplating conversion is a recurring feature of such conversions as described in early medieval texts. In the case of northern Britain, hesitation may have been encouraged and cultivated by a priestly or druidic order, as Adomnán implies of the northern Picts.

Patrick wrote of pagan Irish potentates accepting gifts but then seizing and robbing him, freeing him and his belongings after a time 'for God's sake and the sake of the close friends whom we previously acquired'.[71] It was thus not only Patrick himself, nor the nature and substance of his message, which affected how he was treated at court. The quality and nature of his gifts were important considerations too, as were the identities and connections of the men in his entourage. Patrick was apparently supported by powerful men.

That secular clerics had to play the prestige games of gift exchange and name-dropping in order to maximise their influence helps us further to understand monastic attitudes towards them. It probably did not help if secular clerics routinely accompanied potentates and their warriors on campaign, supporting and ministering to them. With the establishment of a fully-fledged system of pastoral care, whenever that took place in different parts of northern Britain it is likely that secular priests operated from small chapels within clearly defined communities. Here they ought to have baptised and offered the eucharist, while training acolytes and maintaining the chapel building, its furniture and the local poor as best as they could with the renders that were due them.[72] Bede, perhaps unfairly, implies in an exasperated letter written to bishop Ecgberct of York in 734 that not much of this sort of activity was happening in eighth-century Northumbria.[73] It seems likely that levels of pastoral care were always highly variable.

The local character of native pagan cults reinforced and defined local and small-scale identities. It has been theorised that powerful princes who wished to exert authority over such communities ought to have been particularly amenable to the idea of conversion. Unlike pagan religion, Christianity furnished the convert chief with the revolutionary idea that the objects of local cultic veneration were false divinities. As a result, the shrines devoted to them could be destroyed with impunity – even zeal – and their cults suppressed. Christianisation may, therefore,

---

[71] Patricius, *Conf.*, § 52.
[72] This is at least attested in Irish legal texts; see Clancy, 'Annat in Scotland', 96–100, for discussion and bibliography.
[73] Bede, *Ep. ad Ecgbertum*, §§ 4–5; McClure and Collins, *Bede*, 345 (trans.).

have seemed an effective weapon with which chiefs might undermine the solidarity of neighbouring communities, while at the same time exploiting the centralist tendencies of Church authority and organisation.[74] It is an attractive theory, but its relevance for northern Britain cannot be established without more information about princes and native cults.

The decision on the part of kings and public assemblies to welcome or resist conversion must have been informed by a range of different concerns. Few of these were primarily spiritual or theological in character, yet contemporaries are unlikely to have made clear distinctions between spiritual and practical considerations. The personal charisma of individual clerics must have had a part to play in persuading people to convert. Some princes would have been baptised as an expression of loyalty towards, or friendship with, a Christian neighbour. For others it would have been an act of submission. Similarly, refusal to be baptised will have been rooted at least as often in defiance of particular political developments, and in antagonisms between kindreds or kingdoms, as in nostalgia for traditional religious practices or intellectual rejection of the Christian message.

Immediately it had become established in a new kingdom or 'farmer republic', the Church, with its centralist tendencies, almost certainly began exerting a centripetal influence on it. If interaction with Rome was a major factor exerting centripetal forces among outer Brigantian and inner Caledonian peoples in the Roman Iron Age, nativisation of Christianity may have continued to exert such forces in Early Historic times. *Synodus episcoporum*, the 'Synod of the Bishops', a list of canons applied by British missionary bishops to the fledgling Irish Church, indicates that they were inclined to coerce people into bringing their disputes to churchmen rather than to the courts of consensual law. Over time, where the Church was successful in this enterprise, the end result will have been greater standardisation, and the undermining of distinct customary institutions at the local level. This phenomenon could be exploited by kings who envisioned the domination or suppression of lesser princes, as many of Columba's contemporaries did.

However the leaders of the North British peoples converted, and for whatever reasons, convert they did. At the Isle of May, and no doubt elsewhere, they even furnished lands upon which men of Uinniau's disposition could found Scotland's first monasteries. They did so many years

[74] Higham, *The Convert Kings*, 26–7.

before Columba or even Uinniau were born. Did the religion remain confined to the North British zone in the century between Patrick's arrival in Ireland and Columba's in northern Britain? That question is crucial to understanding how the Christian religion reached the rest of Scotland, and is the subject of the next chapter.

CHAPTER 4

Word and Example: Columba in Northern Britain

It seems that Columba was an exceptional scholar and teacher, and so far as we know he was an able leader of monks. Scottish history has all but ignored these achievements, focusing instead on one riddled with problems. According to the simplified version of events recorded, probably *c.* 640, in the lost seventh-century Iona Chronicle, Conall son of Comgall, an Argyll king, was in about the fifth year of his sixteen-year reign when his court was visited in the second half of 563 by Crimthann son of Fedlimid.[1] The visitor may have presented himself as the *peregrinus* Columba (or Colum). Can Conall have overlooked the fact that he was a cousin of Ainmere of Cenél Conaill, overlord of the northern Uí Néill? These 'descendants of Níall' constituted five major dynasties whose dominions, even as early as Columba's lifetime, were spread through central and north-west Ireland. Ainmere dominated the two northern kindreds, their symbolic seat at Ailech near Derry, and his family, Cenél Conaill in Donegal, dominated Ailech in the late sixth century. The small entourage that accompanied the princely *peregrinus* to Argyll contained still other Cenél Conaill cousins of Ainmere. One of them, Baíthéne son of Brénand, we have already encountered. It must have seemed to Conall a particularly impressive assemblage of exiles, worthy of considerable hospitality.

The medieval Irish chronicles, which when carefully examined provide us with our insight into the text of the lost Iona Chronicle, record that, in the year of Conall's succession, there had been a 'flight' (*fuga*) or 'migration' (*immirge*) of Gaels 'before the son of Mailcon', evidently the Verturian Pict Bridei son of Mailcon.[2] Eighty years later when this part

---

[1] Adomnán, *V. s. Columbae*, i.9.

[2] *AU* 558.2, 560.2; *AT* 559.3; *CS* 560.3; *Annals of Clonmacnoise* 563.5. Bede, *Hist. eccl.*, iii.4, renders the name *Mailcon* as *Meilochon*.

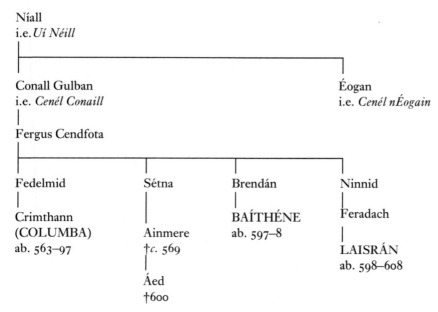

Table 4.1 Cenél Conaill and Iona (563–608)

of the Iona Chronicle was probably compiled, this event was envisioned as a great dislocation. We cannot know anything more about it on the available evidence. The record might even belong to the second phase of the Chronicle compiled *c.* 700. Close connections had grown up between Iona and Fortriu by then, and the fact that the Iona Chronicle contained the idea that a Verturian king was involved in Argyll affairs even before Columba's arrival is a little suspicious.

   Lorn and the kingdom of Cenél Loairn lay at the opposite end of the Great Glen from Fortriu *c.* 700, and the dominion of the kings of Picts may have been extending into this region by then. Bridei's alleged pursuit of Gaels in the middle of the sixth century may, therefore, represent seventh- and eighth-century wishful thinking in Fortriu, and little more. If, however, we accept that Conall was feeling vulnerable to Pictish pressure, he ought to have been particularly interested in establishing an amicable relationship with cousins of the king of Ailech, recently victorious over his southern Uí Néill counterpart at the battle of Cúil Dreimne.[3]

---

[3]   *AU* 561.1; *AT* 561.1; *CS* 561.1; *AI* 561.1. Ainmere backed one southern Uí Néill faction against another at Cúil Dreimne. For speculation on possible links between this battle and Columba's *peregrinatio*, see Smyth, *Warlords*, 94–8; Herbert, *Iona, Kells, and Derry*, 27–8.

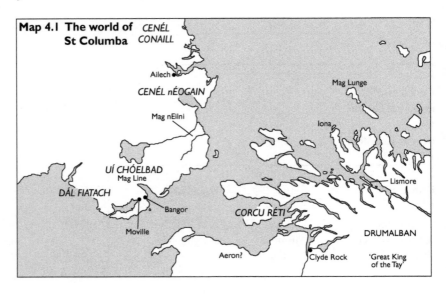

In the year of the foundation of Iona there was a great battle between as many as seven kings of the Cruithnian nations in the counties of Antrim, Londonderry, and Down. Victory here fell to a faction backed by Ailech. Northern Uí Néill interest in Cruithnian politics at this time may help to explain why a cousin of Ainmere chose Argyll as the destination of his *peregrinatio*.[4] Two years later Áed Dub, king of (probably) the Uí Chóelbad, the dominant Cruithnian kingdom in the seventh century, killed the king of the southern Uí Néill in Mag Line in southern Antrim, the Uí Chóelbad heartland.[5] Ainmere is unlikely to have shed many tears. None the less, the killing came to be regarded in hindsight at Iona as a heinous crime. If Conall and his people in Argyll were not already involved in the affairs of the Cruithni, they were destined shortly to become so. The story is taken up in the next chapter.

Vita Columbae's view, more than a century later, was that Columba was a *peregrinus* who went into voluntary exile after being unfairly excommunicated.[6] This information is to be preferred to Bede's notion, from a southern Pictish source, that Columba came to northern Britain specifically to evangelise among the northern Picts. Neither this primary

[4] *AU* 563.1; *AT* 563.2; *CS* 563.2. Smyth, *Warlords*, 100 dates the foundation of Iona to 574, but the 'close reading of Adomnán' involved eludes me.

[5] *AU* 565.1; *AT* 565.4; *CS* 565.1; *AI* 564.1. On Mag Line, see Charles-Edwards, *After Rome*, 13–15.

[6] Adomnán, *V. s. Columbae*, iii.3.

evangelical agenda, nor the further claim that the monastery of Iona was established through a Pictish donation, is supported by its own matter presented in the chronicles and *Vita Columbae*. Instead, Iona credited Conall with the Iona donation, and may have done so as early as the 640s.[7] According to one Irish chronicle, the *Annals of Ulster*, Conall was active among the Inner Hebrides (*Iardoman*) c. 570, perhaps including Iona.[8] This is no guarantee, however, that we are not here dealing with pseudo-history surrounding the donation, rivalling the Pictish tradition.

By 576, when Conall died, Columba and his monks had been established in the Hebrides for more than a decade. During the intervening period Columba's cousin Ainmere had been killed, and the kingship of Cenél Conaill, as well as dominion over the northern Uí Néill, had passed into the hands of more distant relatives. A degree of obsolescence may accordingly have been introduced into the relationship between Columba and Conall in the last years of the king's life.[9] From his perspective, the Iona abbot may have become yesterday's man.

COLUMBA'S PICTISH 'MISSION': THE EARLY IONA EVIDENCE

'God,' wrote Gildas in *De excidio Britanniae*, 'wishes for all men to be saved'. That being said, this rough contemporary of Columba cannot be shown to have advocated British evangelisation of Anglo-Saxons. We have little evidence, either, to suggest that Uinniau undertook missionary activity. Columbanus did some evangelising on the Continent in the immediate vicinity of some of his monastic foundations, but his enthusiasm for missionary work was never great, and soon left him entirely. It is, of course conventional to believe that Columba was very different, with a pronounced evangelising bent not found in his master or his fellow intellectual descendant of Uinniau and Gildas. Was he different? As already discussed, it would be something of a surprise if he was so.

In order to assess Columba's famous apostolic reputation and his significance for Scottish history, it is necessary to open the door of the historian's laboratory. In 713, a scant five months after taking up his office, Dorbbéne, the third recorded bishop of Iona, died.[10] The Stadtbibliothek

---

7 *AU* 574.2; *AT* 574.1; *CS* 574.1; *Ann. Clon.* 569.14.
8 *AU* 568.1; Watson, *Celtic Place-Names*, 40–1.
9 *AU* 569.1, 570.1; *AT* 569.1, 570.1; *CS* 569.1, 570.1; *AI* 569.1.
10 *AU* 713.5; *AT* 713.6; on *kathedra*, see Etchingham, *Church Organisation*, 92.

of Schaffhausen in Switzerland is home to a manuscript copy of Adomnán's *Vita Columbae* which concludes with its scribe's own words: 'whoever may read these books of the miraculous powers of Columba, let him pray for me, Dorbbéne, that after death I may possess eternal life'. It is conventional to identify the future bishop, who died nine years after Adomnán, as this scribe. That identification dates the manuscript to before 713, and is consistent with the handwriting.

In the course of his work, the scribe decided at one point to insert into the author's text a fragment of another book. Dorbbéne called it *liber de uirtutibus sancti Columbae*, the 'book about the powers of St Columba', and attributed it to Cumméne Find, abbot of Iona from 656 until his death in 668 or 669.[11] This chance interpolation is utterly priceless. It is the sole surviving fragment of the first book known to have been written in Scotland. It contains enough hints to show, on careful analysis, that Cumméne composed his book *c.* 640 – probably soon after 642 in fact. Its handling of the Easter controversy, linked to a papal letter of 640, has already been identified as Adomnán's source on the subject. There are several other instances where *Vita Columbae* is best understood as reflecting concerns from the 640s rather than the 690s, indicating that Adomnán borrowed extensively from this sixty-year-old collection of Columban stories in compiling his own Life.[12]

The text's treatment of Columba's missionary work among the Picts is a case in point. Here *Vita Columbae* splits into two groups of stories scattered through the text. In one group Columba travels *trans dorsum Brittanniae*, across Drumalban, to a land whose inhabitants are given no ethnic designation, *Picti* or otherwise. He forces an arrogant king to meet with him and, on his travels, performs a few understated miracles, encountering natives presented in fairly neutral ways. In the other group of stories, the saint goes into *prouincia Pictorum*, the Pictish district. Here he encounters dim-witted Pictish heathens and their hostile magicians – hardly neutral presentations – and he performs a series of 'miracles of power' of the highest order, raising the dead and changing the weather.

Analysis shows that the first set of stories is probably material taken by Adomnán from *De uirtutibus sancti Columbae*.[13] These early narratives are striking in their vagueness about who Columba encountered 'across Drumalban', and whether or not they were Christian. Does this vague-

---

[11] *AU* 669.1; *AT* 669.1; *CS* 669.1; *Ann. Clon.* 665.1.

[12] Herbert, *Iona, Kells, and Derry*, 13–26; see also Smyth, *Warlords*, 86; Fraser, 'St Columba', 322–7.

[13] Fraser, 'Adomnán, Cumméne Ailbe, and the Picts', 183–8.

ness reflect Cumméne's work? Adomnán may have muddied stories that had contained uncomfortable ethnic or historical details. The very placement of the saint's activities 'across Drumalban' is also striking. It is a poor description of Fortriu in northern Pictland from Iona's perspective in the Lorn basin. Did the story of Columba's activities among the Picts undergo marked changes between the 640s and the 690s?

Earlier even than *De uirtutibus sancti Columbae* is *Amra Choluimb Chille*. According to the poet, Columba was 'the teacher who would teach the peoples of the Tay'.[14] That river certainly lies across Drumalban from Iona. Does this evidence not imply that, until at least 640, it was thought at Iona that Columba's Pictish sojourn had taken him south of the Mounth, into a zone that boasts Christian burials dating from the fifth century at its southernmost fringes?

Amra Choluimb Chille reiterates this geography in another line, crediting the saint with having 'subdued with a blessing' the 'arrogant ones who surrounded the great king of the Tay'.[15] Here is another intersection with a story related in *Vita Columbae*, probably borrowed from Cumméne. Columba, we are told, arriving at the stronghold of the Pictish king Bruide, and finding the gates locked to him, forces them open after making the sign of the cross and thereby convinces the arrogant king and his household to treat him with respect.

As things stand in *Vita Columbae*, with the stories mixed together, the implication of Adomnán is, famously, that these arrogant Picts with their great king, whom Columba subdued, inhabited some stronghold in the northern Pictish zone near Inverness. The vitrified fort at Craig Phadraig at the western edge of Inverness, some two kilometres from the River Ness itself, is often identified as the stronghold (*munitio*) where Columba met Bruide – Bridei son of Mailcon. Indeed, in the stories which may be attributed to him rather than to Cumméne, Adomnán seems to insist through repetition that Columba went to northern Pictland, and went there as an evangelist. Why is his geography different from the earlier sources?

The explanation probably lies in the Pictish information that shaped Bede's understanding thirty years later. He wrote that:

> a priest and abbot . . . Columba by name, came from Ireland to Britain to preach the word of God to the kingdoms (*prouinciae*) of the northern Picts, which are those that are separated from their southern districts (*regiones*) by steep and rugged mountain ridges.

---

[14] *Amra Chol. Chille*, i. l. 15.
[15] *Amra Chol. Chille*, viii. ll. 5–6.

> For these southern Picts, who have their settlements within the
> same mountains, had a long time before, so they relate, received
> the faith of truth . . . [when] the Word was preached to them by
> Nyniau, a most reverend bishop and holy man of the British
> nation (*natio*), who had been regularly instructed at Rome . . .
> Columba came to Britain in the ninth year of the reign of a most
> powerful king, Bridei (*Bridius*) son of *Meilochon*, and he turned
> that people (*gens*) to the faith of Christ by his word and example;
> and so he received the aforesaid island [i.e. Iona] from them in
> order to establish a monastery.[16]

Bede's monastery had contacts at the Pictish royal court in the 710s, and
he probably related an historical doctrine embraced by the southern
Pictish king who dominated Pictland after 729. The immediate purpose
of the southern Pictish source seems to have been to stress the ancient and
orthodox origins of southern Pictish Christianity, in part by identifying
Columba as the apostle of the northern Picts. Such a claim surely dates
from the 710s, when apostolicist reform was introduced across Pictland,
despite the traditionalist opposition of so-called *Columbienses*.

Despite drawing the necessary distinction between north and south,
however, Bede goes on to imply that Columba converted all the Picts ('that
gens') to Christianity. Indeed, elsewhere he describes Iona as supervising
'all the Pictish monasteries'.[17] Why is his account inconsistent? By stressing Columba's links with the northern Picts, and transforming him into a
Patrick-like evangelist, Adomnán reveals that the Columban part of
Bede's understanding was older than the 710s. He wrote when Pictland
was being dominated by Verturian kings, not a southern one. It seems that
this encouraged Adomnán to alter earlier Ionan sources in order to keep
up with a north-centred and Iona-centred historical orthodoxy surrounding the christianisation of the *gens Pictorum*. These claims are fascinating
evidence, but they tell us next to nothing about Columba and his times.

DID COLUMBA VISIT SOUTHERN PICTS?

Is, however, the implication of the early Iona sources that Columba met
Bridei on the Tay really possible? That would seem to require a situation in which later kings based in Fortriu in the northern Pictish zone

---

[16] Bede, *Hist. eccl.*, iii.4.
[17] Bede, *Hist. eccl.*, iii.3.

could none the less consider a Columban visit to the Tay to be a visit to 'us'. By Adomnán's time a number of kingdoms in northern Britain and north-east Ireland were diphyletic – consisting of a territory containing two dominant kingdoms – with two 'communities of the realm' sharing and contending with each other for power.[18] We cannot doubt that Bridei was regarded as having been *rex Fortrenn*, king of Fortriu, by the early eighth century. If that realm was diphyletic in Adomnán's day, and if one 'half' of it touched the Tay, we might have a solution to our problem.

Alongside their many references to the kingdom of Fortriu, reflecting Iona's particular interest in that kingdom, the Irish chronicles name just one other Pictish kingdom – Atholl (*Athfotla*), an area of the Highlands through which the Tay and its tributaries flow and form the principal thoroughfares. The chronicles do name a third Pictish district (*terra*), Circhind, but they never acknowledge it as a kingdom (though it may have been one). Might Atholl, by 700, have been the second part of a diphyletic kingdom of Fortriu?

The name of Atholl

The earliest surviving reference to Atholl occurs in an eighth-century reference to a king there (*rex Athfoitle*) in the *Annals of Ulster*. *Mórseiser do Chruithne claind* associates it with the eponymous prince Fotla, a name conventionally interpreted as Gaelic *Fótla*, a poetic name for Ireland. The Gaelic prefix *ath-* is akin to English *re-* (as in 'replay'), and so Atholl has been understood as 'another Ireland', a region characterised by early Gaelic settlement.[19]

The longer Pictish king-list (*Floclaid*) and the *Chronicle of the Kings of Alba* (*co Achcochlam*; *satrapas Athochlach*), however, provide name-forms in *–oc(h)l-*.[20] The letters *t* and *c* were particularly prone to mutual confusion in Insular minuscule writing (note *Ach-* and *Ath-* in the previous sentence). Such *-oc(h)l-* spellings thus allow for the possibility that *-otl-* in the *Annals of Ulster* is a mistake for *-ocl-*.

---

[18] Brooks, 'The Formation of the Mercian Kingdom', 161; Byrne, *Irish Kings and High Kings*, 108.

[19] Watson, *Celtic Place-Names*, 228–9.

[20] The *Chronicle of the Kings of Alba* is the the the chronicle known variously as 'The Old Scottish Chronicle', 'The Pictish Chronicle', etc., renamed and discussed by Dumville, 'Chronicle of the Kings of Alba', 73; see also Dumville, *The Churches of North Britain*, 36n. See now Woolf, *From Pictland to Alba*, 88–93.

The name of Atholl (*continued*)

Gaelic *fochla* denotes 'north', a very common element in place-names (unlike *Fótla*). The Welsh cognate *gogledd* occurs in the well-known phrase *gwyr y gogledd*, 'North (British) men'. Another very common Gaelic place-name element is *áth*, a 'ford'. The Welsh cognate *adwy*, however, denotes a breach or pass (indeed, *áth* could also be an open space between objects). The root idea was apparently a place allowing for movement across or through something.

An hypothetical Gaelic **Áth Fochla*, Neo-Brittonic **Atui Guocled*, then, would have meant 'north pass' or 'north way'. It happens that Alan Anderson in 1922 referred to Atholl as 'the doorway of Moray', a fortuitous description that is entirely in line with this hypothetical place-name.[21] It is fairly clear that *Athfotla* became the normal form of the place-name in Scottish Gaelic, but the name-forms in the *Chronicle of the Kings of Alba*, along with the striking suitability of the name, suggest that *Áthfochla* could more correctly translate the Pictish British name of Atholl.

Bede's conception of the north–south division of Pictland was that the southern Picts 'have their seats within' the mountains separating the two Pictish zones. This too could be a reference to Atholl, confirming its prominence in this period. Elsewhere in his History, Bede shows that he did not regard the southern Picts as being confined to the Highlands. The idea of 'seats' (*sedes*) in the mountains probably, therefore, indicates that Highland Atholl had pride of place among the southern Pictish *regiones*, at least from the political perspective of Bede's Pictish sources. Was this because it was a part of the realm of Fortriu?

In the third Part of this book we will see evidence underlying the plausibility of the hypothesis that the Verturian kings of Picts held Atholl firmly in their grip by the eighth century – raising its stature in the eyes of Bede and the Iona chroniclers – as their key foothold in the southern Pictish zone. If they regarded it as part of their core territory by then, we would have the makings of a situation in which Columban activity in Atholl in the sixth century could have been regarded as activity 'in our kingdom' by the early eighth century. The proposition remains hypothetical, and has ramifications for the seventh century as well as for the sixth. It commends itself by seeming to solve our problem regarding the changing geographical emphasis in the Columban dossier. As we shall see,

---

[21] Anderson, *Early Sources*, I, 214.

it may further commend itself by solving later problems, but such things are no substitute for proof.

Even if the proposition is accepted, how are we to understand the position of Bridei son of Mailcon? One possibility is that he was in fact an Atholl king, the 'great king of the Tay' in *Amra Choluimb Chille*. Another is that he was a Moravian king, and was made in the hagiography to supplant some other 'great king of the Tay' whom Columba actually visited – just as Atholl may have been incorporated into the Verturian kingdom. Here the sources come to our aid. An obit in the Irish chronicles names a Pictish king during Bridei's reign called *Cennalath*, who appears as Galam Cennaleph in the Pictish king-list, said there to have reigned jointly with Bridei.[22] Was Galam the 'great king of the Tay' whose arrogance Columba dispelled?

COLUMBA THE MISSIONARY

The idea that Columba came to northern Britain as an evangelist is no less problematic than locating his 'mission'. At first glance *Amra Choluimb Chille*'s statement that he was 'the teacher who would teach the peoples of the Tay' seems to be a vague reference to missionary work. The preceding line of the poem, however, says that Columba 'would explain the true word' to Christians. Pastoral work among Christian 'peoples' in Atholl is a possible reading of the verse. The poem is panegyric, after all. Certainly Columbanus and Uinniau were committed teachers of other Christians, especially on aspects of monastic asceticism. Columbanus believed that the Church in Francia was in urgent need of instruction. It would be most remarkable if Columba did not feel the same way about any established Church in Pictland.

Like the other men with whom he shared so much else, Columba represented a vibrant reformist philosophical movement, bent on the reinvigoration of monasticism. Like Columbanus at Luxeuil, he was surely sufficiently motivated to evangelise in the immediate vicinity of his Pictish foundations. Such activity would not require the relevant Pictish areas to be any less Christian than Burgundy, but could have provided the kernel from which Columba's apostolic reputation grew. It has been noted already that *Vita Columbae*'s stories taken from *De uirtutibus sancti Columbae* are vague and inconclusive about Christianity – in marked contrast with the stories that Adomnán penned himself. Yet even Adomnán,

---

[22] *AU* 580.3; *AT* 580.2; *Ann. Clon.* 580.6; Chadwick, *Early Scotland*, 13–14; Anderson, *Kings and Kingship*, 248.

though he wished to give the impression that Columba had been an apostolic figure in northern Pictland, argued that the Picts owed him great respect because he was honoured by many Pictish monasteries, and as a result had extended his saintly patronage to the Picts.[23] His failure to say anything here about debts owing for christianisation may provide another glimpse of the earlier Ionan historical tradition which Adomnán was otherwise moulding to suit more recent pseudo-history.

Adomnán's implication that Columba principally made an impact on Pictish monasticism chimes entirely with the achievements of Columbanus and Uinniau and the school of thought they embraced and shaped.[24] Two Gaelic poems in praise of Columba, probably composed by Beccán of Rhum a generation before Adomnán became abbot of Iona, give no impression that the poet admired the saint for missionary work. Instead, Columba is celebrated by Beccán as a model monk and abbot, and a powerful patron saint. One of his poems, *Fo réir Choluimb*, 'Bound to Columba', says that the saint 'shattered lusts', fought 'wise battles with the flesh' and 'read pure learning', becoming 'a sage across seas'.[25] The other poem, *To-fed andes*, 'He Brings Northward', praises Columba for being a 'shepherd of monks' and a 'judge of clerics', as well as 'counsellor of the people'.[26] Here, in the poetry of a contemporary of Cumméne Find, the saint is cloaked in all the trappings of a monk of Uinniau's mould.

Bede's southern Pictish source material alone, the latest of our sources, explicitly claimed that Columba was the apostle of the northern Picts. It alleged moreover that he had come to Britain for that purpose. To judge from how it juxtaposed the achievements of Columba and Nyniau, its eagerness in expounding this claim was to stress the ancient and ortho-dox credentials of southern Pictish Christianity, and so its superiority over northern Pictish Christianity. Its apostolic claim regarding Columba may have been Verturian in origin, but it was not trumpeted by Columba's own monastery before Adomnán's abbacy, suggesting that its historicity is dubious. Other aspects of Bede's Pictish source material were even contradicted outright by Adomnán himself, and have accord-ingly been dismissed by scholars. For example, Bede was informed that Columba founded Durrow before becoming a *peregrinus*, but *Vita Columbae* says that it was founded while he was spending a few months in Ireland.[27] Why should the apostolic claim of whoever was responsible for

---

[23]   Adomnán, *V. s. Columbae*, ii.46.
[24]   Sharpe, 'Gildas as a Father', 199.
[25]   *Fo réir Choluimb*, §§ 12–13.
[26]   *To-fed andes*, §§ 10, 13.
[27]   Adomnán, *V. s. Columbae*, i.3.

composing Bede's Pictish source material about Columba be spared dismissal along with this and other claims?

The story of Columba and the Picts is, therefore, nothing like as straightforward as conventional narratives have long held. Its place in Scottish history requires careful rethinking. A fine scholar, a committed advocate of a certain kind of monastic life and a close relative of mighty kings, Columba may have visited Moray. He may have founded monasteries there. He may have evangelised in their neighbourhoods. On balance, however, the thin evidence is rather better that Columba went to Atholl and that he behaved there much as Columbanus did in Burgundy. There can be no doubt that he consorted with kings, and that he did have a strong message for Pictish ears, if monastic ones. Again, he may have founded monasteries and he may have evangelised round about them. Must his stature shrink as a result of such a reappraisal? It is as well to remember how great is Columbanus's place in Frankish ecclesiastical history, despite his having converted almost no one.

CONTEXTUALISING COLUMBA

Columba died on 9 June 597 at the age of seventy-six, more than thirty-five years after he first appeared in Argyll.[28] Comgall of Bangor, under whom Columbanus had studied, died in May 604 at the age of ninety, having led the community he founded for more than fifty years. The Iona Chronicle, for some reason, kept track of the fortunes of Bangor and its abbots in the sixth and seventh centuries. We ought probably to allow for the possibility that Columba regarded Comgall as his superior in life, a deference that need not have disappeared quickly after 597. Intriguingly, the earliest phase of the chronicle seems also to have paid close attention to the monastery of Lismore (*Les Mór*) in the island of that name in the Firth of Lorn. It recorded the death of Mo-Luóc in 594, apparently a fellow countryman of Comgall. It is a safe bet that he was abbot of Lismore, which may therefore have been a Bangor daughter house.[29] With records of the deaths of the abbots Neman in 613 and Eochaid in 637, the chronicles probably provide a complete list of the abbots of Lismore prior to 640.[30]

There is no reason to suspect Mo-Luóc and his successors of having been Columban monks, nor Lismore of having been an Ionan daughter

---

[28] *AU* 595.1; *AT* 595.1; *CS* 595.1; *AI* 597.1.
[29] *AU* 592.1; *AT* 592.1; *CS* 591.2; *Ann. Clon.* 590.2; MacDonald, 'Iona's Style of Government', 184–5. Mo-Luóc's real name was Lugaid.
[30] *AU* 635.7; *AT* 611.5, 635.4.

house. Adomnán ignores the place in *Vita Columbae*. In the 590s, Mo-Luóc may have been senior to Columba in terms of regional and ecclesiastical status and connections. His monastery was probably closely connected not just with Bangor, but also with one or more of the powerful kindreds about the Firth of Lorn which came to be encompassed in the kingdom of Cenél Loairn. After all, in Macdonald's memorable phrase, Lismore lies 'in the cockpit of the territory of Lorn', about whose inhabitants our sources are otherwise utterly silent until the last quarter of the seventh century – the next time an abbot of Lismore appears in the chronicles.[31]

In marked contrast to other parts of northern Britain, next to no attention has been paid to the christianisation of Argyll or the rest of Atlantic Scotland. The explanation lies in the tyranny of a paradigm. It has been accepted either that the first migrants to the area from Ireland post-dated the Patrician period (and so came as ready-made Christians), or else that Argyll adopted Christianity whenever (and however) 'Irish Dál Riata' did. The explosion of the migrationist model, yet to be discussed, demands fresh research into the christianisation of Argyll and the Hebrides. Perhaps attention will be drawn to the Gallo-Roman parallels of the double-armed cross on the Kilmory Oib stone at the head of Loch Sween, or the cave carvings at Eilean Mor at the mouth of the sea loch.[32] After all, fifth-century Gallo-Roman missionaries were at work among the Gaels a generation before the Irish mission of Patrick.

If we take seriously Iona's failure to trumpet the Pictish claim that Columba converted Bridei son of Mailcon to Christianity, it is particularly significant that the Verturian Church in Adomnán's time was, none the less, claiming Columba as its apostle. The Bernician Church in Bede's time claimed Aidan of the Ionan daughter house at Lindisfarne as its apostle, but a competing tradition – that christianisation had actually begun in the previous generation – required Bede to manipulate his narrative very carefully. We have only vague hints at what kinds of competing traditions may have been current in Pictland. We may be reasonably certain that some Ionan daughter house in northern Pictland achieved paramountcy over the Verturian Church through a Lindisfarne-like programme of vigorous ecclesiastical activity and royal patronage, and with the same capacity to suppress (almost) other historical claims.

It is becoming increasingly likely that we can even identify this Lindisfarne of the north as the monastery whose remains were discovered

---

[31] Macdonald, 'Two Major Early Monasteries', 47–9.
[32] For discussion, see Alcock, *Kings and Warriors*, 368–70. The stone may be associated with a well; see Fisher, *Early Medieval Sculpture*, 8.

at Portmahomack on the Tarbat peninsula in Easter Ross in the 1990s. Tarbat boasts several of Pictland's most impressive examples of monumental ecclesiastical sculpture. They are much later in date than the lifetime of Columba, testifying to Portmahomack's eventual emergence as a focus of the highest-level elite patronage in the eighth century and later, when a Pictish version of Columba's achievements was being promulgated. By then the monastery was old. Burial and burning had begun there by at least the middle of the sixth century, important evidence that its foundation probably pre-dates Columba. The monastery may have possessed the whole Tarbat peninsula as its estate, the massive cross-slabs at Nigg, Shandwick, Hilton of Cadboll and Portmahomack itself perhaps having been set up eventually as visible statements of ownership.[33] Holy Island is intervisible with much of the Bernician coast to the north and south, and Tarbat Ness too is intervisible with much of the Sutherland and Moray coastlands opposite. Similarly, just as the monastery at Lindisfarne lay opposite the Bernician royal stronghold at Bamburgh, Portmahomack lies opposite Burghead – albeit at more than twice the sailing distance.

It is instructive of the relationship between archaeology and text-based historical study that Portmahomack goes unnoticed – or at least unidentified as yet – in the textual record. The Irish chronicles do twice mention a monastery called *Nér* in the seventh century, now associated with the possession of Fetternear, 'the *fother* of Nér', seven kilometres southwest of Inverurie on the Don in Aberdeenshire. The interest of the chronicles is intermittent. The toponymic element *fother*, common across that part of Scotland that was formerly Pictish-British-speaking, has all the appearance of a recognised administrative term referring to land. Both Uineus abbot of Nér, who died in 625, and Nechtan of Nér, who died in 678, bear Pictish British names in form or character.[34] It is a good bet that both were Pictish clerics who trained in whole or in part at Iona, before being appointed to the abbatial office of Nér. Most of the work involved in spreading the Columbanian monastic tradition in Francia was done by Franks, not by Gaels. It is entirely likely that the monastery at Portmahomack was home to Pictish monks, as well (perhaps) as Gaelic ones.

It is unlikely that Nér was the monastery at Portmahomack, even though possession of a *fother* in the Garioch does not require Nér to have been located there. Yet that is the most likely conclusion, and the

[33] Carver *et al.*, Bulletins and Reports; Carver, 'An Iona of the East'; Carver, 'Sculpture in Action', 19–29.

[34] *AU* 623.1, 679.4; *AT* 679.4; *CS* 679.4. Skene, *Celtic Scotland*, 1, 284, seems to have believed that, even as late as 720, all of Pictland's clergy were either of Gaelic or of English extraction.

medieval church at Abersnethock in the Garioch, just three kilometres further up the Don from Fetternear, commemorated in different ways two saints with names remarkably like Uineus (Finan) and Nechtan (Mo Nethoc). On balance, it is likely that Nér lay here in the shadow of Bennachie.[35] The medieval cults of St 'Finan' and St Nechtan were robust in the rugged foothills of the Grampians.

The medieval church at Banchory on the Dee, twenty kilometres south of Abersnethock, commemorated St Ternan (*Terenanus*), venerated at eighth-century Iona as Taranan *ab Bendchair*, abbot of Bennchor, surely a monastery at Banchory.[36] There were many monasteries called *Bennchor* at this time in Ireland and Wales, some of which were very famous. The fact that the one at Banchory on the Dee was 'the' Bennchor, from Iona's perspective, indicates that the monks of Taranan's monastery were – or became at some point – brethren of the Columban *familia*. Like Uineus and Nechtan at Nér, Taranan bore a Pictish-looking name. The situation is complicated by Itarnan, whose death 'among the Picts' (*apud Pictores*) in 668 or 669 is recorded in the Irish chronicles.[37] The ogham inscription EDDAR-RNONN on a Pictish stone from Scoonie at the mouth of the River Leven in Fife probably commemorates the same Itarnan, better known today as St Ethernan, whose medieval cult included a commemoration in the Isle of May ('St Adrian'). Although their names bear a passing resemblance, Itarnan and Taranan are unlikely to have been the same person. Along with his Fife associations of uncertain date, Itarnan was culted in Aberdeenshire.

It is a leap of faith to conclude from such scattered notices that Nér and Banchory were Columban monasteries in seventh-century Pictland. Among the seventh-century clergy of Britain and Ireland were many highly mobile individuals, including monks who seem to have sought edification in part through occasional changes of scenery. The reasons may have been very similar to those underlying the potential mobility of present-day students progressing from primary and secondary education through the undergraduate and postgraduate ranks. Some up-and-coming monastic scholars may have been lured from one monastery to another by its academic reputation, the reputations of one or more of its teachers, its perceived status and interconnections within the wider world, and so on. In the seventh century Continental, Anglo-Saxon and British clerics took opportunities to study at monasteries in the Gaelic

---

[35] On Nér and its associations (and disassociation from Old Deer), see Clancy, 'Deer', (forthcoming).

[36] *Mart. Tallaght*, 12 June; Watson, *Celtic Place-Names*, 300. On the provenance of *Mart. Tallaght*, see Ó Riain, *Anglo-Saxon Ireland*, 11–13.

[37] *AU* 669.2; *AT* 669.2; *CS* 669.2.

world. Uineus and Nechtan of Nér, Taranan of Banchory and Itarnan may have been Pictish participants in this widespread phenomenon.

It is very likely that these monks established strong ties with Iona, but it must remain uncertain as to how 'Columban' they may have been as a result. There can be little doubt that each of them drank from the well-spring of Iona's consummate learning, not least on the subject of monastic life, as did many monks from all parts of Britain and Ireland in the seventh century.[38] It is a strange quirk of Pictish studies that evidence of such behaviour should be readily understood in terms of Columban (or even more generally Gaelic) dominion over Pictish intellectual and ecclesiastical developments – even in terms of colonisation by Gaelic ecclesiastical (and secular) personnel. In no other context are scholars so willing to regard foreign monks who respected the educational opportunities available among the Gaels as instruments of Gaelic expansionism. With the benefit of hindsight relating to their fate, students of the Picts can reach too quickly for such interpretations when others will do.

It is undeniable that over the long term Pictish ecclesiastics drew more extensively on Gaelic ecclesiastical culture than most other foreigners. The reasons for this are, however, more likely to lie in aspects of the Pictish worldview than in any Gaelic drive to subsume the Picts within the Gaelic ecclesiastical world. It has arguably been truer for the ecclesiastical sphere than any other that Picts have for too long been cast as passive, rather than active participants in their own history.

Monks at Nér and Banchory with Ionan connections may, then, tell us much less about the expansion of Ionan authority or Gaelic influences in seventh-century Pictland than we might like. It is interesting that both houses lay north of the Mounth, in fact along its eastern margins in Mar. They probably lay in the district known in *Mórseiser do Chruithne claind* as *Cé*, apparently named in the titles of two lost Gaelic sagas, *Orgain Maige Cé la Galo mac Febail*, 'The Ravaging of the Plain of Cé by Galo son of Febal', and *Orgain Benne Cé*, 'The Ravaging of Bennachie'.[39] The 'plain of Cé' (*mag Cé*) probably denotes the watershed of the Urie, within which Nér was situated. Cé may be regarded as something of a frontier region between the northern and southern Pictish zones. We know nothing about the district's politics – we have seen that this part of Scotland may have retained 'farmer republics' throughout our period.

Our textual evidence may, therefore, be telling us that the earliest Columban monasteries in the northern Pictish zone, whose leaders may

---

[38] Smyth, *Warlords*, 79.
[39] Dobbs, 'Cé'.

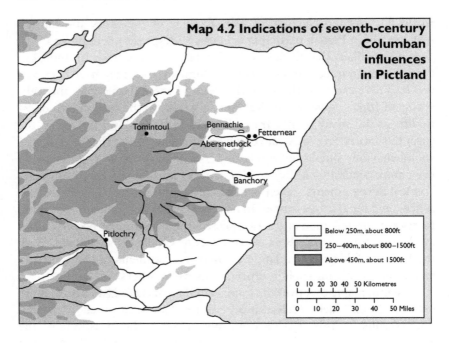

Map 4.2 Indications of seventh-century Columban influences in Pictland

have been taught at Iona, but were not necessarily under its authority, lay here in Mar, in the Pictish marcher district of Cé, rather than at Portmahomack. It is thus an important point that the district shows a preference for a different style of cross-marked stone than predominated at Iona. The same situation occurs at Lindisfarne, which was - certainly Ionan. Despite attempts to see in the distribution patterns of cross styles imprints of different monastic or missionary movements, a consideration of a region's cross-marked stones alongside other aspects of its material culture is more likely to explain these patterns.

The earliest abbot of Iona (other than Columba himself) for whom veneration is attested in north-east Scotland is Virgno (Gaelic *Fergnae*), the fourth holder of the office. This contemporary of Uineus of Nér is commemorated at a well near Tomintoul on the River Avon in Banffshire, and at another well at Pitlochry in Atholl, a region possibly visited by Columba himself.[40] Virgno's commemorations thus provide the kind of link between the Tay and possible Columban houses in Cé – via Strathspey – that tends to confirm our suspicions above about Columba's own travels. On the River Fiddich, which like the Avon empties into the

---

[40] Taylor, 'Seventh-Century Abbots', 53–4.

Spey, lies Mortlach in Dufftown, which has produced Pictish sculpture. It was dedicated to St Mo-Luóc of Lismore, but we cannot date any of these commemorations very easily. Virgno died in 625. According to Adomnán, he lived as an anchorite at *Muirbulc Mór*, the 'great sea-bay' on the island of Hinba. He was remembered in tradition as a Briton.[41] Was he actually a native of Pictland, whose 'Britishness' reflects the relative lateness of a Pictish ethnogenesis drawing stark lines between Briton and Pict?

A LAND OF NO APOSTLES?

However much the discussion in this chapter enables us to interpret the career of Columba, it sheds very little light on how Christianity became established in Pictland. The poorly understood christianisations represented by fifth-century evidence from southern Scotland have been relatively uncontroversial as compared with the even less well understood christianisations of the Pictish peoples. As Pictland was being defined in the eighth century, its earliest Christian communities were apparently those that had become established in outer Brigantia or the North British zone in the fifth century, including Fife. The binding together of the southern Pictish zone known to Bede, including Atholl within the mountains, is unlikely, however, to have taken place until many generations after the first Christians were buried at the Hallow Hill in St Andrews and in the Isle of May.

There are no easy solutions to the problems we face. There are no inscribed fifth-century funerary monuments in either of the Pictish zones like those in Lothian and Galloway. There are plenty of other cross-marked stones thought to be from the earliest phase of christianisation, but without inscriptions these are difficult to date with any confidence. *Vita sancti Germani*, a Gallic text of the late fifth century, takes it for granted that a Gallic bishop visiting Britain *c.* 430 would have encountered pagan Picts and Saxons. The presumption is significant, but there is little reason to believe that the story is historical. Patrick's references to Pictish *apostatae*, 'apostates', in his letter to the warriors of Coroticos towards the end of the century are controversial, but decent evidence that Christianity had reached some Picts, and not necessarily southern ones, by the end of the fifth century.

---

[41] *AU* 623.1; *AT* 623.2; *CS* 623.1; *AI* 624.2; Adomnán, *V. s. Columbae*, iii.23; Herbert, *Iona, Kells, and Derry*, 39–40.

St Patrick's *Picti apostatae*

In his withering remonstrance to the warriors of Coroticos, Patrick angrily characterised as *apostatae* an indeterminate group of Picts who had enslaved Irish Christians he had himself baptised.[42] What did Patrick mean by *apostatae*?

Latin *apostata* was borrowed from Greek αποστάτης, meaning 'deserter' or 'turncoat', and in ecclesiastical Latin came specifically to denote one who forsakes Christianity. If Patrick used the term with this meaning, his accusation of apostasy provides proof that some Picts were Christians in the last years of the fifth century. Such a reading of Patrick's evidence is conventional, and has normally been regarded as proof of the missionary efforts of St Ninian.

Instances in the Vulgate Bible where *apostata* simply denotes a wicked person allow for the possibility that Patrick did not regard these Picts as turncoat Christians,[43] but the etymology of the word implies that its primary meaning was always 'apostate', forsaker of Christianity. It seems that *apostata* became capable of denoting more general wickedness, but the warriors of Coroticos ought to have understood Patrick's terminology as accusing the Picts in question of being wicked Christians (like themselves) for having enslaved his neophytes. After characteristically careful analysis, Professor Dumville has concluded that Patrick implicates the Picts in question in the crimes of the Christian warriors of Coroticos, 'rebels against Christ' for having sold fellow Christians into slavery.[44]

These Picts, whoever they were, can only have been so implicated if they, like Coroticos and his men, were Christians. If they were not, their enslavement of Patrick's charges will have been no offence at all. Indeed, the intensity of his vitriol tends to give the game away: Patrick demonstrates nothing like this level of judgemental fervour in discussing heathens. Thus, it seems likely that *Picti apostatae* represents the same rhetorical streak in this letter which Patrick employed to denigrate Christians who had enslaved fellow Christians. As such, the term does not require these Picts to have been genuine apostates, any more than Patrick's words require us to believe that the warriors of Coroticos were genuine *rebellatores Christi*.

---

[42] Patricius, *Ep.*, §§ 2, 15.
[43] Macquarrie, *Saints of Scotland*, 58–9.
[44] Dumville *et al.*, *Saint Patrick*, 129–31.

How did this happen? It seems to have been through the medium of the British language that southern Pictish Christians first encountered some fundamental terminology of their religion. The evidence comes from a corpus of place-names containing variations on *ecles*, a term evidently borrowed into British from Latin or Romance *ecclesia*. It may have been the most common term for 'church' among both the North British and the southern Pictish peoples. There is no sign of it in the northern Pictish zone. The place-name evidence provides a measure of confirmation of the broad thrust of a Pictish historical understanding, imbedded in our surviving sources, that the roots of southern Pictish Christianity lay in the North British zone, unlike northern Pictish Christianity. Of themselves, however, these place-names do not date 'the childhood of Scottish Christianity' with any precision.[45]

The progress of Christianity into Pictland thus can just about be detected as a fifth-century phenomenon and attributed to a movement from the North British zone, but beyond that it remains little understood. Any or all of the general factors that led to the initial expansion of Christianity across Hadrian's Wall and the Irish Sea could have contributed to its continued expansion. The main missionary activity (such as it existed) may have been conducted, not by Romano-British clergy, but by clergy from the North British zone. Inner Caledonia maintained distinctions from outer Brigantia throughout the Roman Iron Age and there is, therefore, no particular reason to expect evidence characteristic of Romano-British or North British Christian behaviour to be found among the Picts. The earliest Pictish – and Argyll – churches are likely to have adopted nativised organisational and other formal practices, if not entirely distinctive terminology. Further nativisation could have occurred *in situ*. It may have been important for the religion's progress in these areas that, in the course of the fifth century, it had become a 'native' Insular religion, rather than the particularly 'Roman' one it had been in the fourth century.[46] Such a conceptual shift may be our best explanation for any lag time between the christianisation of the North British zone, with its romanising tendencies, and that of the rest of northern Britain.

It has been argued that the standing symbol-stones of Pictland were conceived as precocious expressions of religious, and specifically anti-Christian sentiment. The observed correspondence of the distribution pattern of these famous stones with that of square-barrow and related

[45] Taylor, 'Early Church in Scotland', 4–7; Clancy, 'The Real St Ninian', 10–11. The seminal study is Barrow, 'The Childhood of Scottish Christianity'.
[46] Charles-Edwards, *After Rome*, 1.

cemeteries may be taken as indicating that the stones, like the cemeteries, reflect instead the persistence of cultural tendencies that developed in inner Caledonia in the later Roman Iron Age, resisting romanising traits embraced in outer Brigantia. As already discussed, even resistance to romanising may be regarded as symptomatic of Rome's powerful influence. The monuments are conspicuously rare south of the Ochil Hills, where instead we find inscribed funerary and proprietary markers with their links with *romanitas*.

In fact, the prevailing art-historical argument maintains that the symbol-stones significantly post-date christianisation, even if the symbols themselves arguably developed earlier.[47] As such, they speak of the persistence of cultural traits of a certain kind in southern Pictland, from the Roman Iron Age through the Early Historic period. There is no reason to link them with pagan religiosity. Ogham writing seems to have been inspired in south-west Ireland by a desire to emulate the Roman fashion for erecting lithic commemorations, on the one hand, but also by a desire for a writing system other than the Latin alphabet. Were Pictish symbols developed for similar reasons?[48] If so, they represent still more evidence of the reach of Rome.

Was Christianity adopted quickly or gradually in Pictland? We have no answers as yet. The 'international' scale of the Barbarian Conspiracy makes a nonsense of any attempt to see the participation of both Di-Calidones and Verturiones as proof of self-conscious unity. We must resist any thought of a single 'Pictish Church' in the fifth or even the sixth centuries. Southern Pictish notions from the 710s, relating to the christianisation of the Picts, take for granted a pronounced distinctiveness north and south of the Mounth. Christianisation and exposure to Latin learning eventually furnished Pictish readers with examples, such as Gildas's writings, of their forefathers being cast *en masse* as *Picti*, hostile enemies of Rome. The adoption of symbolic art may reflect a self-conscious and overt strain of nativism among Christian Pictish elites which took its inspiration in part from the way in which the *Picti* were portrayed in Latin sources.

Post-colonial guilt can lead to presumptions that native communities always resisted and resented macrocosmic influences. There is plenty of

---

[47] Alcock, *Kings and Warriors*, 372; Henderson and Henderson, *The Art of the Picts*, 168–72; for a different view of the origins of the symbol-stones, see Smyth, *Warlords*, 78–9.

[48] Forsyth, *Language in Pictland*, 32; Forsyth, 'Literacy in Pictland', 54–5; Henderson and Henderson, *The Art of the Picts*, 59–60, 65.

evidence to the contrary in Antiquity, whether we examine romanising or christianising phenomena. Some peoples even actively petitioned their Christian neighbours to evangelise them, in order to acquire greater status, security, favour, or influence in their transactions with others. About those Christian women and men responsible for bringing their religion northwards, securing and presiding over the first native baptisms, we know little or nothing anywhere in northern Britain. As in other contexts, the figures and cults of great apostolic saints were destined to capture the popular and pseudo-historical imagination. Their stories drove the real activities of more prosaic missionaries from the historical memory, or else transformed them into more typologically mainstream saints whose stories could be reconciled with hagiography that had already realised widespread fame.

The question of the roots of Christianity in Scotland has been of immense importance to Scottish Christians since the Middle Ages. In most periods it has given rise to bitter debate. At the heart of the matter lies a fairly straightforward question: did the christianisation of Roman Britain during the course of the fourth century lead to the expansion of the religion into northern Britain, or did Christianity find its way north by some other (later) process? Bede's *Historia ecclesiastica* has understandably been tremendously influential. Scholars now recognise, however, that this eighth-century synthesis is taken at face value at our peril. It cannot really be regarded as decisive evidence regarding events and processes which took place generations before the lifetime of Bede. The same is true of the views put forward in the seventh and eighth centuries by Ionan monks. In recognising this, we recognise that we still have a great deal of sensitive work to do before we can begin to understand how the peoples of northern Britain became Christian peoples.

Postscript
'The Roman Interlude'

The phrase 'Roman interlude' has been appearing in our scholarship for some time now, as a short-hand way of taking a minimalist view of the Roman impact on northern Britain. Did anything of significance take place during the Roman Iron Age? If so, all thought of an 'interlude' must be given up.

In this Part of the book it has been given up with enthusiasm. The Roman Iron Age was surely a full act in the drama of Scottish history, not an interlude. Substantial social, cultural and ethnic change took place in outer Brigantia, inner Caledonia and parts of Atlantic Scotland, which gave shape to the Early Historic period. In fact, despite scholars' inclination to see the advent of native written sources as the end of one epoch and the beginning of another, it is not at all clear that this horizon marks much of a watershed in northern Britain. We shall see that a reasonable case is there for the making that the period *c.* 250 to *c.* 650 is more coherent in social, cultural and ethnic terms than either of the two classic periods under investigation in this book.

The Romans played a key role in bringing about the transformations in question. Factors besides their policies and the effects of 'sleeping with an elephant' were, of course, also important. Social and cultural processes do not have single causes, nor single points of origin in time or space, and they defy simple explanations. There has been no attempt here to deny native peoples a key role in their own transformation. A case has been set out instead that they did not emerge from the Roman Iron Age, as Smyth argued they did, 'untouched by even the thinnest veneer of Romanization'.[1] It has been supported by the collapse of the convention that 'romanization' can be understood only as 'the progressive adoption

[1] Smyth, *Warlords*, 18.

of Roman culture by indigenous populations', as well as Roman identity, as a result of imposition by Romans.[2] That certainly did not happen anywhere in northern Britain. It is now appreciated that romanising – whether outwith the Empire or inside it – involved indigenous elites, as a function of cultural interaction, in seeking to exploit Roman patron–client relationships to their own advantage. Obviously Rome was often willing (and occasionally eager) to oblige in pursuit of her own perceived interests and glory. The primary elements of her role were providing access to her material culture and exporting her particular idealised concepts for elite living. Conquest obviously changed the process, but the differences for conquered and unconquered romanising populations were mainly differences of degree, not of kind.[3]

Where the Romans conquered and colonised, as in southern Britain, access to their material and prestige cultures was pronounced and they exerted particularly strong influence. The extent to which Rome had much control over native adoptions of aspects of her culture is debateable in such areas. Instead, the prime movers were such native human traits as 'snobbery, eagerness to conform, ambition, or desire for amenity'.[4] As a result, even among Roman provincials like those of Britannia, tremendous variation was possible in romanisation.

Seeking to exploit Roman patron–client relationships and pursuing Roman material culture were not enterprises, however, that remained confined to elites under direct Roman jurisdiction. In northern Britain, as in the rest of *barbaricum*, developments in the shape of society, in material culture, in senses of identity and in religious allegiances were all affected by political and cultural interactions with Rome and Roman provincials. These effects were local reflexes of the same general romanising process experienced further south, and indeed across western temperate Europe. Native agency was not just involved, but decisive. Both Roman and native sought to take maximum advantage of one another in pursuit of their own interests.

Students of *barbaricum* have not hesitated in recognising that romanisation, defined in such sophisticated terms, developed from the human sciences, routinely reached hundreds of kilometres beyond the Empire's borders. The onus must lie with proponents of the 'Roman interlude' to prove that the experience of northern Britain was as unique within *barbaricum* as their model requires.

[2] Jones, *The Archaeology of Ethnicity*, 33.
[3] See, for example, Millett, *The Romanization of Britain*; see also Jones, *The Archaeology of Ethnicity*, 33–9.
[4] Levick, *Vespasian*, 142.

PART TWO

The Age of the Kings of Bamburgh (576–692)

CHAPTER 5

High Lords of Princes: Áedán, Urbgen and Aeðilfrith (576–616)

The first king in Scotland whose career is attested well enough in the sources to permit piecing together into a frail narrative is Áedán son of Gabrán. He was about forty when he became king in 576. His kingdom lay in southern Argyll, with districts in northern Antrim across the North Channel in Ireland as well, among a people known (a century later) as *Corcu Réti*. By 700, these 'descendants of Réta' were one of a number of Gaelic-speaking peoples lumped together under the well known name *Dál Riata*, but this coalescence had probably not yet taken place in Áedán's lifetime.

According to *Vita Columbae*, Áedán went to Iona in order to be ordained king by Columba. The famous story is unlikely to describe a real event. It dates to almost seventy years after Áedán became king, and some thirty-five after his death. By then he had become a figure of key genealogical importance: every subsequent king of Cenél nGabráin, the descendants of Gabrán, was apparently descended from him. In the early Middle Ages, such prominent ancestral figures were prone to attracting tall tales, told to honour (or humiliate) their living descendants.

In Áedán's case, the idea that he sought the blessings of Columba, who was at first reluctant to agree, but eventually relented, is exactly this kind of tale. It was penned at a time when Iona was trying to understand the disastrous kingship of Áedán's grandson Domnall Brecc, slain in 642. It is the kind of imaginary pseudo-history that early medieval writers were inclined to construct to pass judgement on current events, in line with what was perceived as divine judgement. *Vita Columbae* contains other pseudo-historical stories attached to Áedán which are not to be trusted. As a result, we can say rather less about his career than has sometimes been attempted.

ÁEDÁN SECURES HIS KINGSHIP

Áedán's succession in 576 was evidently challenged in 578. The occasion was a battle fought at Teloch, an unidentified place in Kintyre, which was apparently the home district of the descendants of Gabrán. Here fell Donnchad, a son of Áedán's predecessor Conall, 'and many others fell of the retinue of the sons of Gabrán'.[1] This encounter is probably to be understood as a clash between the families and followers of Áedán and Conall over the right to dominate Kintyre (seventh-century *Cenn Tíre*) and Cowal (medieval *Comhghall*), the two principal districts of the (diphyletic) Corcu Réti kingdom. Áedán's warriors presumably contained men from Kintyre, including his kin, and Donnchad probably died at the head of an army of Cowal men. This first battle in what amounts to a litany of six, comprising just about everything we know about Áedán, looks like it settled the issue of the kingship of the Corcu Réti. In the hindsight of the chronicle that recorded it, the battle of Teloch may have been regarded as foreshadowing the segmentation of the Corcu Réti into the rival *cenéla* that had emerged by the middle of the seventh century – Cenél nGabráin in Kintyre and Cenél Comgaill in Cowal.

As was to be the case again in Áedán's long and vigorous reign, victory came at a cost. He must have been able to call on an extensive reserve of men and resources in building up his *cohors*, reaching beyond the confines of Kintyre. Leaving *Vita Columbae* aside, considered later in this chapter, historians are almost entirely dependent on what Iona chroniclers, *c.* 640 and later, chose to record about Áedán, and their hindsight was selective. A twelfth-century Gaelic poem locates his birthplace on the Forth, but has little claim to historical reliability. Similarly late Welsh stories, giving the king a British mother, are preposterous in their other details. On the other hand, Áedán's sons Artúr and Conaing bore names of British and English derivation, respectively – perhaps their mother was indeed a North Briton whose family had English connections.[2]

In assessing appearances by Áedán in later stories and poetry, it is important to remember that the king was made famous by *Vita Columbae*, and also that every Scottish king after *c.* 1000 traced his ancestry through him. Similar caution is necessary in handling the Irish genealogy that alleges that the king met Báetán of Dál Fiatach at Island Magee in southern Antrim, and there recognised his paramountcy sometime before

---

[1] *AU* 576.1 (*bellum Telocho*), 576.3; *AT* 576.1 (*cath Delgon*).
[2] For optimistic summaries of the evidence, see, for example, Bromwich, *Trioedd*, 264–5; Ziegler, 'Artúr'.

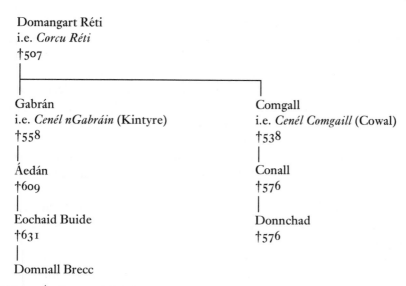

Table 5.1 Áedán son of Gabrán: some key relationships

Báetán's death in 583.[3] Dál Fiatach dominated the Ulaid, a powerful nation of the eastern half of Down across Belfast Lough from Island Magee, which gave its name to Ulster. About the time of Báetán's death, some six or seven years into his reign, Áedán launched his first recorded expedition, an extremely precocious sea-raid on Orkney (*Orc*).[4] The coincidence of his first expansionist efforts and the death of Báetán may be no coincidence at all. Perhaps the Ultonian king had indeed dominated north-east Ireland and Argyll prior to his death.

According to the chronicles, Áedán's predecessor had joined forces with the southern Uí Néill king Colmán Bec in 570, undertaking an expedition to the Inner Hebrides (*Iardoman*), one of which was already occupied by Columba's monastery in Iona.[5] Was it only now that Conall had brought the monastery under his protection, leading in later years to the notion that he was the donor of the island? This sea-borne campaign helps to contextualise Áedán's Orcadian voyage a dozen years later. *Vita Columbae* takes it for granted that Gaels undertook journeys throughout Atlantic Scotland, including the Northern Isles, in the sixth century. The voyages took their vessels along a coastline, and among Hebrides, which must have been fairly familiar, but which the historian finds wreathed in shadow.

---

[3] Anderson, *Early Sources*, vol. 1, 88; Byrne, *Irish Kings and High-Kings*, 110.
[4] *AU* 580.2, 581.3.
[5] *AU* 568.1; Watson, *Celtic Place-Names*, 40–1.

All indications are that the Outer Hebrides and the north-west seaboard were 'quite poor and politically and culturally insignificant', in relative terms when they became a Scandinavian playground in the ninth century.[6] Our best guess at an explanation must be that they did not much participate in the social and economic transformations that affected other parts of northern Britain in the later Roman Iron Age. Instead, society here may have remained quite flat, its leadership characterised by informal elites and 'farmer republics' rather than the kinds of formal potentates and kingdoms that attracted the attention of chroniclers. In fact, the region may have been regarded in Argyll and Fortriu as backward or barbaric, and so prime slave-hunting ground.

Áedán's memorable voyage through the region may have been a campaign directed at Orkney as the annals imply. It is as likely, however, that it involved a series of raids and general mayhem progressing as far along the coast as Áedán dared to venture. The idea would have been to enrich his *cohors*, and to confirm its faith in his leadership, as well as gaining booty and prestige for himself. Orkney could have been remembered simply because it was the furthest point reached by the expedition, underlining its scale and success. Sea-raiding was apparently quite common in Atlantic Scotland in this period, and earlier periods are unlikely to have been much different.

URBGEN AND THE STRUGGLE FOR THE NORTH BRITISH ZONE

These early years of Áedán's reign roughly correspond to the age of the vernacular British panegyric poetry addressed to Urbgen son of Cinmarch (*Urien* in modern Welsh) – if any of it is genuine, that is. These poems, along with the *Gododdin* elegies, take for granted a sphere of political influence for mighty North British kings stretching northwards from Yorkshire across the North British zone to 'beyond the Firth of Forth' (*tra merin Iodeo*).[7] Urbgen and his contemporary Guallauc son of Laenauc, whose principal bases seem to have lain in the southern districts of the zone, were praised for campaigning in Manau and in Gododdin, the Early Historic kingdom of the Uotadini. Another target was *Aeron*, perhaps Ayrshire, but alternatively Airedale in West Yorkshire. Early Welsh poetry is not easy to evaluate as historical evidence. Considering the extensive

---

[6] Woolf, *From Pictland to Alba*, 276–7, 299–300.
[7] 'Aneirin', *Gododin* 'B-text', l. 1209.

reach of the Bernician English kings across the North British zone in the seventh century – and Áedán's activities there in the 580s and 590s – the poetic notion that British kings ranged across it is at least plausible.

Aneirin, Taliesin and early Welsh poetry

Aneirin (*Neirin*) and Taliesin (*Taliessin*), named by *Historia Brittonum* as two early poets 'famed in British poetry', are credited in medieval manuscripts with the composition of a number of Welsh poems.[8] They are notoriously problematic as historical sources. They survive only in late manuscripts, and some of them are manifestly late. Indeed, the Welsh of Aneirin's *Gododdin* elegies and several Taliesin poems belongs to the early Middle Ages, but few linguists place it as early as the sixth century.

Conventionally, it has been maintained that these works remained in oral circulation for more than two centuries before finally being committed to writing in 'updated' Welsh. More recently, this hypothesis has been challenged. Some scholars argue instead that a sixth-century horizon cannot be proven, and that the poetry should be understood as a product of poets of the late first millennium, composing in a poetic voice assigned to an earlier period of history. Another view is that painstaking analysis *does* prove that the poetry was first composed, even penned back in that period.

The historian who is not also an expert in Welsh linguistics or in poetics can contribute very little to this debate. As a result, prudence requires us to place little reliance on early Welsh poetry as a guide to events. Yet historians may be permitted to raise some points of interest. For example, it is remarkable that Urbgen, as he is portrayed in *Historia Brittonum*, is a fairly one-dimensional British king notable for wars against the English, whereas in Taliesin's poems he is praised as often for his wars with other Britons as with the English. Is this a hint that the poetry predates the ninth-century History's Anglo-centric depiction? Also, while it is true that *Historia Brittonum* derives the royal dynasty of Gwynedd from a Gododdin prince, it places his journey to Wales almost 150 years prior to the lifetimes of Anerin and Taliesin, and the *Gododdin* elegies make no explicit play on this origin myth, and indeed do not allude to it at all. This too could be seen as favouring a relatively early date of composition. Certainly historians in Wales cannot otherwise be shown to have maintained a detailed interest in Gododdin that would help us to contextualise a relatively late pseudo-historical *Gododdin*.[9]

---

[8] *Hist. Brit.*, § 62.
[9] Charles-Edwards, 'The Authenticity of the *Gododdin*', 54–5.

Historia Brittonum, the 'History of the Britons', is a complex work of synchronising history first compiled in ninth-century Gwynedd in north Wales. The compiling scholar, the artist formerly known as 'Nennius', attempted to synchronise a range of sources in order to construct a narrative of British history, including North British and Northumbrian chronicles, royal pedigrees and king-lists which were probably all eighth-century works.[10] The North British chronicle has not survived, but was primarily interested in the achievements of two families, the descendants of Gurgust – including Urbgen – and the descendants of Ceneu – including Guallauc. It is an interesting correlation with the panegyric poetry addressed to these two kings and attributed to Taliesin.

Historia Brittonum maintains that four British kings fought against the father and uncles of Áedán's Bernician contemporary, Aeðilfrith son of Aeðilric, naming these kings as Urbgen, Riderch, Guallauc and Morcant.[11] The statement is open to interpretation: does it represent a sequential list of kings? a grand alliance of four kings? In either case its accuracy is questionable. Even more doubtful are the indications of later genealogies that these four men were all akin. The conclusions reached by the *Historia Brittonum* historian tended to arise from his knowledge of famous stories and poems, rather than contemporary documents.

Unlike Urbgen or Guallauc, Riderch appears in *Vita Columbae* as Roderc son of Tóthal, an 'afflicted' king of Clyde Rock, of whom the saint prophesies that he 'will never be delivered into the hands of his enemies'.[12] His father Tutagual may have been *Tuduael*, a king whom the eighth-century hagiographer of Nyniau associated with 'St Ninian'. The association may be pseudo-historical, and in any case there are other candidates. Riderch's father need not have been a king at all. We may conclude from the testimony of *Historia Brittonum* that Riderch became famous for fighting Bernician enemies, perhaps after the death of Urbgen, whom he follows in the list of kings. Adomnán's evidence confirms that by 700 Riderch (and so Urbgen) was thought to have been a rough contemporary of Áedán.

It was Aeðilfrith's uncle Theodoric (*Deodric*), according to *Historia Brittonum*, flourishing some twenty years before his famous nephew, who

---

[10] For discussion, see Dumville, 'Chronology of the *Historia Brittonum*', 439–40; Dumville, ' "Nennius" '; Dumville, 'On the North British Section'; Dumville, 'Sub-Roman Britain', 176–7; Dumville, 'The Anglian Collection of Royal Genealogies', 45; Dumville, 'Historical Value', 5–7; Jackson, 'Northern British Section in Nennius', 22–7, 44–54, 56–62.

[11] *Hist. Brit.*, § 63.

[12] Adomnán, *V. s. Columbae*, i.15.

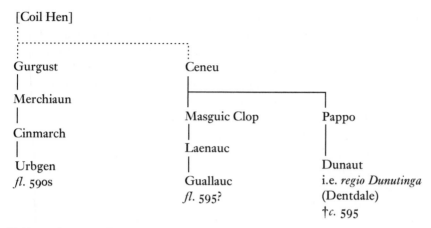

Table 5.2 Ancestry of Urbgen and Guallauc

'fought strongly against Urbgen and his sons'.[13] The poetry addressed to Urbgen calls his principal English enemy *Flamdwyn*, 'flame-bearer' – a nickname.[14] The *Historia Brittonum* historian calculated on the basis of his Bernician king-list that this foe was Theodoric. His synchronisation of the Gregorian mission to Canterbury with the reign of Theodoric's successor implies, however, that the historian believed that Urbgen flourished in the 590s, not the 570s.[15]

In that event, this famous North British king will have fought, not against Theodoric, but against Aeðilfrith, whose reign began *c.* 592. A point in favour of this conclusion is that Aeðilfrith's sons flourished at the same time as Urbgen's son Run, said by North British sources to have been active in the 620s. Bede, who makes Aeðilfrith an arch-enemy of his British neighbours, may therefore be telling the same story, from the other side, as *Historia Brittonum* with its four British kings.

Urbgen's background is very hazy. The tenth-century Cambro-Latin chronicle *Annales Cambriae* consists for this period of excerpts from a lost eighth-century chronicle from the North British zone.[16] It records a battle at *Armterid* in 573, probably Arthuret on the River Esk, some seven

---

[13] *Hist. Brit.*, § 63.

[14] Jackson, 'Northern British Section in Nennius', 47.

[15] Hunter Blair, 'The Bernicians', 151–2; Dumville, 'On the North British Section', 351–3; Dumville, 'Historical Value', 23; see also Dumville, 'Chronology of the *Historia Brittonum*', Dumville, 'Sub-Roman Britain', 189–90 and Dumville, 'Historical Value', 15–16, for further examples of errors of synchronisation in this text.

[16] Hughes, 'The Welsh Latin Chronicles', 235–7; Dumville, 'The Welsh Latin Annals', 462; Dumville, 'Historical Value', 15; Dumville, *Annales Cambriae*, v, ix–x.

kilometres north of Longtown in Liddesdale.[17] Medieval Welsh literature claimed a great deal about this battle, associating it with fictional and historical characters (including Áedán and Merlin), but provides little useful evidence. The brothers who apparently won the battle of Arthuret were cousins of Urbgen's father Cinmarch, their deaths recorded in 580.[18] It may, therefore, be that Urbgen succeeded one or both of them as king, and flourished into the 590s as *Historia Brittonum* envisions.

Urbgen is said in *Historia Brittonum* to have 'penned up' his Bernician foe (possibly Aeðilfrith) 'for three days and three nights in the island of Medcaut'.[19] This was the tidal island now known as Holy Island off the Northumberland coast. In later years the monastery of Lindisfarne was built here, within sight of Aeðilfrith's principal stronghold at Bamburgh. Bede referred to this fortress as the chief royal centre (*urbs regium*) of his people.[20] A note in the Northumbrian *Chronicle of 802* says that eighth-century Bamburgh was 'exceedingly well fortified (*munitissima*) but by no means large, containing about the space of two or three fields, and having one hollowed entrance ascending in a wonderful manner by steps'.[21]

Urbgen's allies in this war may have included Riderch of Clyde Rock and Guallauc, descendant of Ceneu. It would not be surprising if they included the Deiran king Aelle, the earliest known to Bede, whose daughter Acha Aeðilfrith took as one of his wives.[22] We shall encounter many alliances in this and later chapters. They were tricky things, and rarely brought allies together on the same battlefield, where there were many opportunities for theoretical equals to offend one another with disastrous consequences. Most armies of 'mixed' origin would have been conglomerations of unequals within which the lines of authority were clear.[23] The siege of Medcaut seems to have been a case in point regarding the volatility of alliances. According to *Historia Brittonum*, Urbgen met his nemesis here. He was assassinated 'out of envy, at the instigation of Morcant,

[17] Skene, 'Site of the Battle of Ardderyd', 95–6.

[18] *Ann. Camb.* (Faral) 573.1; 580.1; for discussion see Anderson, *Early Sources*, vol. 1, 74; Jackson, 'The Britons in Southern Scotland', 83. The genealogy of these men is contained in Harl. MS 3859, § 12.

[19] *Hist. Brit.*, § 63. The Harleian text has *insula Metcaud* here, but *insula Medcaut* elsewhere (§ 65); on preferring the latter form, see Jackson, 'Northern British Section in Nennius', 31–2.

[20] Bede, *Hist. eccl.*, iii.6.

[21] *Chron. 802*, s. a. 774. I follow Woolf, 'Onuist', in referring to the 'continuation of Bede' within *Historia regum Anglorum* as the *Chronicle of 802*.

[22] Bede, *Hist. eccl.*, iii.6.

[23] Halsall, *Warfare and Society*, 115–16.

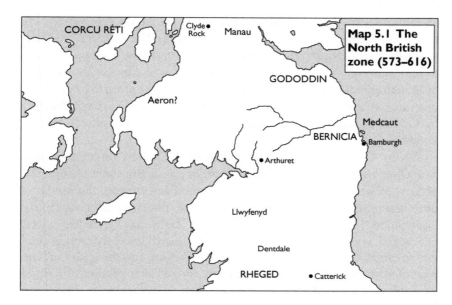

Map 5.1 The North British zone (573–616)

because his military skill and leadership surpassed that of all other kings'.[24] Whatever we make of this story, the future of hegemony north of the Humber belonged to the English Deirans and (especially) Bernicians.

How did the North British zone become the focus of so much military activity by the end of the sixth century? Occupation at Traprain Law appears to have subsided, perhaps dramatically, in the fifth century. The christianisation of the North Britons was already underway. Towards the beginning of the century Traprain's famous hoard of broken-up Roman silver plate was deposited, including examples with Christian iconography and inscription. At the end of the sixth century, Áedán was undertaking campaigns from Argyll into the North British zone, and Aeðilfrith was embroiled in wars with British kings whose grasp may have reached as far as Manau. A dramatic decline in the fortunes of the romanising North British leaders of late Antiquity after the ending of Roman Britain would seem to be implied by this evidence. Such a collapse might in turn explain the power struggles emerging from our evidence in the late sixth century.

Urbgen's career is difficult to evaluate, in view of the uncertain value of the corpus of poetry addressed to him. *Historia Brittonum* says of him, and the others who fought the Bernicians, that 'sometimes the [English]

[24] *Hist. Brit.*, § 63.

enemy and sometimes the [British] countrymen would gain victory'. It is another vague statement. The historian shared in Gildas's idealised vision of Anglo-British ethnic warfare. According to the poetry addressed to him, however, Urbgen's great military successes came at the expense of British enemies as well as English ones. Here he appears to be cut from the same pragmatist cloth as the southern British kings condemned by Gildas. It seems realistic enough a picture of sixth-century British kingship.

Where was Urbgen's kingdom? It is probably best understood as a 'successor kingdom' of an old Brigantian *civitas* of Britannia, though the process by which such kingdoms remilitarised and asserted themselves – or re-asserted themselves – in the fifth and sixth centuries is not clearly understood. In one poem addressed to him, Urbgen, as *glyw Reget*, lord of Rheged, is said to have led 'the men of Catraeth' into battle. He is elsewhere called *Reget diffreidyat*, defender of Rheged, and the leader of 'the men of Rheged' both at war and at court, as well as the father of a *Reget ud*, lord of Rheged.[25] If the poems are vaguely authentic, it seems that Rheged was Urbgen's kingdom, a land that surely contained Rochdale in southern Lancashire.[26] He is also called *vd Yrechwyd*, lord of Yrechwyd, in one panegyric and *Uryen yrechwyd*, Urbgen of Yrechwyd, in another.[27] At a guess, *Yrechwyd* may have been the name of the home district of the House of Gurgust, akin to Áedán's Kintyre, located somewhere in the greater realm of Rheged.

Urbgen is called *lyw Catraeth* as well, seemingly ruler of Catterick, at or near Roman Cataractonum, where Dere Street, the main Roman road north from York, crosses the Swale in North Yorkshire.[28] Catterick is one of the most often-mentioned sites in British and Northumbrian sources relating to our period. Nestled in the Yorkshire Gap, its strategic position became further emphasised when the Tees, twelve kilometres to the north, became the frontier between the English realms of Deira and Bernicia. Half that distance to the north of Catterick along the Roman road lies Gilling, where Bernician and Deiran forces clashed in 651. Catterick is named by Bede as the place where, a generation after Urbgen's time, Paulinus of York performed mass baptisms in the Swale,

[25] 'Taliesin', *Arwyre gwyr Katraeth*, ll. 1, 6, 27; *Uryen Yrechwyd*, l. 14; *Ardwyre Reget*, *passim*; *Eneit Owein ap Vryen*, l. 3; Clancy, ed., *The Triumph Tree*, 89–90 (trans.).
[26] Chadwick, *Early Scotland*, 144. Rochdale was *Recedham* in Domesday Book. See Rollason, *Northumbria*, 87–8, for a recent survey of the evidence.
[27] 'Taliesin', *E bore duw Sadwrn kat uawr a uu*, l. 13; Clancy, ed., *Triumph Tree*, 85 (trans.); *Uryen Yrechwyd*, ll. 1, 18–19.
[28] 'Taliesin', *Eg gwrhyt gogyueirch yn trafferth*, l. 9.

and where his deacon preserved an enclave of the York mission during the years of Lindisfarne's primacy.[29] A century later, the same church was being used for royal weddings.

Catterick was thus a major Northumbrian centre. The panegyrics addressed to Urbgen seem authentic in so far as they take for granted that Catraeth was no less significant a royal centre under British suzerainty. Archaeology at Cataractonum itself has been unable to verify this. It has been shown, moreover, that the Roman site probably passed into English hands well before Urbgen's time.[30] This discovery has been a boon to doubters of the historicity of the panegyric poetry. However, even assuming that material culture and ethnicity can be readily equated, there is no reason other than our own prejudices to presume that English possession of Catraeth and British dominion there cannot have coincided.

The place was in Deiran hands when, according to the *Gododdin* elegies, Catraeth was assaulted by a Gododdin force which was all but annihilated. The fact that these verses do not mention the English Bernicians has been taken as evidence that the campaign – if it ever happened – took place before the foundation of the Bernician kingdom.[31] However, the Bernician royal dynasty was scattered by its Deiran enemies in 616. Any Gododdin campaign conducted in the period 616–27 need, therefore, have taken little account of Bernicians. One reading of the *Gododdin* elegies even suggests that Catraeth was attacked by Gododdin warriors in alliance with Bernicians, perhaps led by the son of an Englishman![32] That Bede does not mention a campaign against Deiran Catterick during the reign of Edwini proves little. That king evidently fought many campaigns in establishing widespread hegemony, but Bede appears to have known very few details. It is difficult to think of another period when the denizens of Edinburgh are likely to have been under threat from Deiran enemies. The position of Catraeth in the surviving British poetry suggests that its final loss to English power was regarded by contemporaries as a particularly significant development. Was praising Urbgen as *lyw Catraeth* emblematic of his having acquired it?

---

[29] Bede, *Hist. eccl.*, ii.14, ii.20.

[30] Alcock, *King and Warriors*, 142–4.

[31] Dumville, 'Early Welsh Poetry', 2–3; Dumville, 'The Origins of Northumbria', 216; see also Hunter Blair, 'The Origins of Northumbria', 48–9, 50; Hunter Blair, 'The Bernicians', 146; Jackson, 'Edinburgh', 35–6.

[32] Koch, *Gododdin*, xxxix–xli, xlvii–xlviii. That the Catraeth expedition can have happened as late as 616–27 is discussed by Charles-Edwards, 'The Authenticity of the *Gododdin*', 63–4.

Urbgen's poetic associations with Rochdale and Catterick link the House of Gurgust with districts in the orbit of the Deiran English. His descendants have similar links in *Historia Brittonum*. The panegyrics suggest that, as *arbenhic teyrned*, 'high lord of princes', Urbgen exercised particular power over *Goddau*, whose men he sometimes led in battle, and *Llwyfenyd*, where he waged war and whence he received entreaties and access to wealth.[33] The river Lyvennet in Cumberland, emptying into the Eden, seems a firm pointer in the direction of the location of Llwyfenyd.[34] Urbgen is also found harrying English victims in the panegyrics, of course, as well as Manau and Gododdin, among more obscure peoples and territories. The impression created is that, before the rise of Aeðilfrith *c.* 600, while Áedán was establishing himself in Atlantic Scotland, Urbgen became the paramount prince in much of the North British zone, conquering some territories and harrying others into submission.

A similar impression is created of Guallauc, the third king in *Historia Brittonum*'s list of four enemies of the Bernicians. If this list is sequential, Guallauc will have flourished after Riderch, whose death is not recorded anywhere. Guallauc probably flourished after 595, the year in which, according to *Annales Cambriae*, his father's cousin Dunaut died.[35] That king's historicity is bolstered by a seventh-century donation to the Deiran church of Ripon in Yorkshire of a British district called *regio Dunutinga*, thought to be Dentdale in Cumbria.[36] Guallauc was probably Dunaut's successor, and the most prominent North British king after the death or eclipse of Riderch.[37]

The barest sketch of developments may be obtained from these sources. After the dismantling of Roman imperial power in northern Britain, Uotadinian power declined in the North British zone, aided perhaps by ongoing pressure from a restless Pictland. At the same time, as part of a wider trend across Britannia, Romano-British royal dynasties were emerging in Britannia Secunda, the northernmost province, at least two of which came to enjoy influence among the North British peoples.

---

[33] 'Taliesin', *Uryen Yrechwyd*, l. 26; *E bore duw Sadwrn kat uawr a uu*, l. 4; *Ardwyre Reget*, l. 44; *Eg gwrhyt gogyueirch yn trafferth*, l. 27; *Lleuuyd echassaf*, l. 10; Clancy ed., *Triumph Tree*, 88–9 (trans.).

[34] Jackson, 'The Britons in Southern Scotland', 82.

[35] *Ann. Camb.* (Faral) 595.2. The genealogies of these men are contained in Harl. MS 3859, §§ 9–11.

[36] Stephen, *V. s. Wilfrithi*, § 17; Chadwick, *Early Scotland*, 143; Bromwich, *Trioedd*, 334.

[37] Jackson, 'On the Northern British Section in Nennius', 31, raises doubts about the conventional placement of Guallauc in Elmet.

These peoples had probably been maintaining close contact with the Romano-British population for generations – domination of the region by the likes of Urbgen and Guallauc may have seemed perfectly natural. The subsequent rivalry for paramountcy north of the Humber between Deiran and Bernician dynasties, based east of the Pennines to either side of Hadrian's Wall, is given an historical context by this sketch of the underlying British politics. A reasonable possibility exists that this English power struggle represents continuity from older British competitions for paramountcy.

ÁEDÁN AND THE STRUGGLE FOR MANAU

Aeðilfrith, Urbgen and Riderch were not the only kings jockeying for position in the North British zone at the end of the sixth century. Some two years after his Orcadian adventure, Áedán launched a victorious campaign into Manau in 584 or 585. Some have hesitated to locate this *bellum Manonn* in Manau, because Gaelic gave the same name to the Isle of Man. Yet Man is twice called *Eumania*, not *Manau*, in the chronicles just a few years earlier, indicating that the two were different places.[38] We have seen that Urbgen may have become king in 580, and Rheged or Bernician pressure may have made Manau vulnerable to attack.

It has been suggested through a process of elimination that the next and most obscure of Áedán's known battles, *bellum Leithreid* of 592, relates to a campaign against Clyde Rock, attributed to Áedán in a Welsh 'triad', *Teir drut heirua ynys Brydein*, 'Three Unrestrained Squanderings of the Island of Britain'.[39] However, *Teir drut heirua* does not refer to military campaigns, but to gross abuses of hospitality, including Riderch's hospitality by Áedán 'the Wily' (*Aydan Vradawc*), who 'left neither food nor drink nor beast alive' at Clyde Rock.[40] If there is anything historical about this story, it suggests that Áedán held Riderch in submission at some point. It seems that the defences at Clyde Rock were modified *c.* 600 to include new ramparts.[41]

---

[38] *AU* 577.5, 578.2; *AT* 577.5, 578.2; *CS* 577.3, 578.2 (*Emain*). *Ann. Clon.* 580.8 translated its Gaelic source as 'Isle of Man'; Mageoghagan seems not to have recognised *Eumania* at *Ann. Clon.* 580.2.
[39] *AU* 590.2; *AT* 590.2; *Ann. Clon.* 589.2; Jackson, 'The Britons in Southern Scotland', 83; Macquarrie, 'The Kings of Strathclyde', 8; Macquarrie, *The Saints of Scotland*, 108–9.
[40] Bromwich, *Trioedd* § 54; Woolf, 'Early Historic Scotland'.
[41] Lowe, *Angels, Fools and Tyrants*, 17–18; Alcock, *Kings and Warriors*, 39.

Áedán thus apparently maintained a keen and sometimes active interest in North British affairs during his reign, possibly taking opportunistic advantage of troubles caused by Bernician and Rheged aggression. His enemies at Clyde Rock and in Manau in this period are difficult to perceive. They may have included 'Necton', the 'descendant (*nepos*) of Irb' (or Uerb), the only king named in the Pictish king-list between 563 and 724 who is absent from the Irish chronicles.[42] He is probably to be associated with two kings from much earlier in the list, Necton son of 'Erp' (or 'Wirp') and his brother Drest. The list credits the earlier Necton with the foundation of the monastery at Abernethy (*Aburnethige*), ten kilometres south-east of Perth.[43]

It is a peculiar reflex of this association that some copies of the list seem to have confused the two Nectons. One list goes as far as dating the foundation of Abernethy, with some confidence, to 225 years and eleven months prior to the founding of Dunkeld by the Pictish king Constantín between 807 and 818.[44] In the shorter king-lists, the foundation of Abernethy is attributed in one list to the later Necton, whose reign roughly spanned the years *c.* 601–*c.* 621, and in others to his immediate predecessor. These attributions surely arose from counting backwards (almost) 226 years from the reign of Constantín. If we feel compelled to reconcile the king-list evidence, we may propose that Necton 'descendant of Irb' was the real founder of Abernethy, the longer king-lists reflecting a pseudo-historical attempt to push the foundation further back in time.

In any case, this southern connection suggests that the descendants of Irb were not a Verturian kindred, but a southern Pictish one. That might explain why Necton does not appear in the Irish chronicles. Ciniod son of Lutrin, the Pictish king who died *c.* 633, is given a reign of nineteen years in the king-list and would, therefore, appear to have been the Verturian Pictish king during much of the reign of Necton further south.[45] Another 'descendant of Irb' (*moccu Irp*), a certain Elphin, seems to have flourished during the reign of the Verturian king Bridei son of Beli, whose ancestry links him with North Britons. Indeed, Bridei's

[42] Anderson, *Kings and Kingship*, 248.
[43] Anderson, *Kings and Kingship*, 246–7; Anderson, *Early Sources*, vol. 1, cxix–cxxi. Drest's death is recorded in *Ann. Clon.* 449.2; he was probably, however, a literary character akin to various Irish examples: see Chadwick, *Early Scotland*, vol. 1, xvi.
[44] Anderson, *Kings and Kingship*, 287.
[45] *AU* 631.1; *AT* 631.2; *CS* 631.1; *AI* 633.2; *Ann. Clon.* 632.1; Anderson, *Kings and Kingship*, 248. See Skene, *Celtic Scotland*, 1, 239, for the notion that the reigns of Necton and Ciniod overlapped.

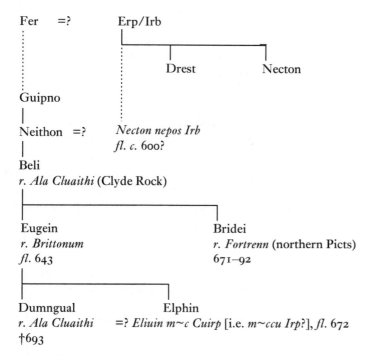

Table 5.3 Paternal ancestry of Bridei son of Beli

grandfather Neithon son of Guipno, whose legacy (*forba*) that king is said by the poem *Iniu feras Bruide cath*, 'Today Bridei Fights a Battle', to have claimed in 685, is thought to have been none other than Irb's descendant 'Necton'.[46] It is certainly easy to appreciate how a grandfather of Bridei son of Beli could have been inserted into a version of the Pictish king-list, even if it consisted largely of Verturian kings.

Returning to the age of Áedán and Urbgen, if later Welsh genealogists can be trusted, Bridei's family, the House of Guipno, were kinsmen of Riderch of Clyde Rock and his family, the House of Clinoch. We ought probably to be sceptical. If Neithon son of Guipno was 'Necton', however, that would mean that, in the early seventh century, descendants of Guipno laid claim to Clyde Rock as well as a kingdom which included Strathearn. The hypothesis is not preposterous. The Dumnonii of Flavian times seem to have occupied a territory that stretched from Clydesdale to Strathearn. We have taken it already that the Maiatian heartland was broadly the same – Clyde Rock lies just north of the western terminus of the Antonine Wall – and the Maiatai (*Miathi*) are,

---

[46] *Iniu feras Bruide cath*, ll. 1–2; Smyth, *Warlords*, 65.

after all, named in *Vita Columbae*. That the House of Guipno is associated with two regions that probably lay within Maiatian territory may
simply represent a degree of continuity in this zone as late 600, matching
the continuity of Maiatai/Miathi. In fact, *Guipno* itself looks like the
anticipated early Welsh form of UEPOGENOS, 'Fife-born'.[47]

Where does this trawl through bitty and complicated evidence leave
us? We seem to be faced with a reasonable possibility that, in the late sixth
and early seventh centuries, the kingdom which contained Clyde Rock –
we shall call it Alt Clut – was a 'lineal successor' of a Roman Iron Age district which included the plain of Manau and Strathearn. Certainly, and
despite the tendency of some scholars to equate the kingdom of Alt Clut
with the much later kingdom of Strathclyde, there is no evidence that the
heartland of Alt Clut lay in Clydesdale. The earliest contemporary
mention of anyone called 'king of Clyde Rock' (*rex Alo Cluaithe*) is as late
as 657, when two generations of Bernician expansion may have altered
dramatically the political landscape known to Áedán, Riderch and their
contemporaries. By then, all that remained of Riderch's kingdom may
have been a rump focused on Clyde Rock, control of Manau and
Strathearn having passed into Bernician or Pictish hands.

It was in Manau where Áedán won his battle in the mid-580s, and
where Urbgen, in roughly the same period, is said to have raided. Riderch
of Alt Clut, who may have maintained royal centres in Manau and
Strathearn, was also facing war with the Bernicians in this period as an
ally or successor of Urbgen, and *Vita Columbae* refers to him as 'afflicted'
by death anxiety. With a reign beginning *c.* 601, Neithon son of Guipno
could have been Riderch's successor in this putative Miathian kingdom.
By then Urbgen had been murdered and Aeðilfrith was reaching the
zenith of his power in the North British zone.

The Bernician king's subjugation of the Deirans is conventionally dated
c. 604, the year in which his son Oswald was born to the Deiran princess
Acha. Neithon was apparently an older contemporary of Acha's brother
Edwini, who went into exile *c.* 604. In 616 Edwini was restored to Deira after
the killing of Aeðilfrith, and established himself across much of his enemy's
northern hegemony. It has been determined that Edwini married one of his
daughters to Neithon's son Beli. The marriage encourages the idea that
Neithon linked himself with the Deiran enemies of his aggressive Bernician
neighbours, against whom Riderch – possibly his predecessor – had made

---

[47] Discussion with Alex Woolf has encouraged me to accept the MS reading *Guipno*
over the suggested emendation *GuiÞno*. The name may also occur in 'Aneirin', *Gododin*.
'B-text', l. 1267 (*Cipno mab Guengat*).

war. On this model, to judge from *Vita Columbae*, the Houses of Guipno and Clinoch were regarded as Miathi at Iona. It is uncertain how their wars with Áedán, and possibly with Urbgen, may have affected them. The sixth century was proving a difficult period for the North British dynasties, with the rise of powerful warlords beyond their borders.

About 598, as Aeðilfrith was on the rise in Bernicia, two of Áedán's sons were killed. One of their deaths 'in a rout of battle *in Saxonia*' is noted in a Columban prophecy in *Vita Columbae*, in an episode attributable to Cumméne Find.[48] In 603 Áedán himself campaigned against English enemies, but he need not have had much to do with the involvement of his sons in the events that led to their deaths, either fighting alongside or against English forces.

One group of Irish chronicles mistakenly attached notice of a different battle to their record of the killings of Áedán's sons. This distinct conflict claimed the lives of two other sons of Áedán, and is described in *Vita Columbae* as a battle against the Miathi.[49] Here it is said that 303 men were slain in Áedán's service, which must have represented a substantial proportion of his fighting strength.[50] The point of the hagiographical story about this battle was probably to emphasise *c.* 640 the (former) efficacy of Columba's patronage and protection of the family of Domnall Brecc, Áedán's grandson. None the less, that a precise number of casualties was remembered suggests that the battle was famous and widely known to have been very bloody. Columba's hagiographer probably chose it from the list of Áedán's several battles because a narrow victory illustrated his point best.

The battle has been linked with Áedán's victorious Manau campaign of the mid-580s, but the chronicles call it the battle of Circhind (*cath Chirchind*), where Áedán was defeated.[51] The subtext of the *Vita Columbae* story is that the king was very nearly vanquished, victory having been pulled from the jaws of defeat only by Columba's intercession. A more pessimistic appraisal of the outcome from an independent source need not surprise us. Perhaps Áedán and his *cohors* performed rather better in the battle than the rest of his army.

[48] *AU* 596.3; *AT* 596.2; Adomnán, *V. s. Columbae*, i.9.

[49] *AT* 596.2; *Ann. Clon.* 590.8 ('battle of Kirkynn in Scotland'); Adomnán, *V. s. Columbae*, i.8–9. On the conflation, see Anderson, *Early Sources*, vol. 1, 118–19; Anderson, *Kings and Kingship*, 36–7, 146; Broun, 'The Seven Kingdoms', 40–1.

[50] Adomnán, *V. s. Columbae*, i.8; Aitchison, *The Picts and the Scots at War*, 150–1.

[51] Chadwick, *Early Scotland*, 124, 139, linked *cath Chirchind* with the *bellum Miathorum*; he has been followed by Smyth, *Warlords*, 42; Broun, 'The Seven Kingdoms', 40–1.

The combined testimony of the hagiography and the chronicles indicates that Circhind, wherever it was, lay in Miathian territory. It was evidently the same place as *Círech*, one of the seven 'names on the land' mentioned in *Mórseiser do Chruithne claind*. Both its name-form and its Miathian associations imply that Circhind was a separate locale from Mag Gergind, a plain which, according to Irish sources, contained Fordoun in the Howe of the Mearns.[52] We shall see that there is reason to believe that a pro-Ionan Verturian hegemon conquered Manau and its satellite regions in 698, and Pictish readers a year or two later ought to have enjoyed *Vita Columbae*'s reference to the Miathi as *barbari*, overcome in battle with the help of Columba's prayers.

The mistaken insertion of the record of the battle of Circhind into the chronicles that describe it *c.* 598 means that we cannot isolate its correct date. There is some suggestion, perhaps, in Adomnán's ordering of the two battles, that Circhind was fought prior to the deaths of Áedán's sons among the English and, of course, *Vita Columbae* maintains that Columba, who died in 597, was still alive when the battle of Circhind was joined.

ÁEDÁN LOOKS TO IRELAND

With three victories in seven years, including at least two long campaigns, Áedán must have been feeling strong. In 586, a year or two after his Manau adventure, the Verturian king Bridei died after thirty years in power.[53] There is no evidence that Áedán ever tried his luck against him, even if his Orcadian raid afflicted communities within the Verturian orbit. His death may have emboldened the king of the Corcu Réti in his dealings with the northern Picts, even as Iona was forging relationships in Pictland. By 592 Áedán had consolidated his position, exhibited considerable martial prowess, brought glory to his *cohors* and apparently achieved sufficient security at home to spend protracted periods of time away from Kintyre and Cowal.

It was about this time, it has been suggested, that the king attended 'the great convention of Druimm Cete' in north-east Ireland, 'at which were present Colum Cille and Áed son of Ainmere'.[54] The latter king, the son

---

[52] *Éogan Már trá óenmac leis*, ll. 25–32; Watson, *Celtic Place-Names*, 109; Broun, 'The Seven Kingdoms', 31–2.

[53] *AU* 584.3; *AT* 584.1; *AI* 584.1; *Ann. Clon.* 584.1.

[54] *AU* 575.1; the misdating of the convention is discussed by Sharpe, *Adomnán*, 313, whose conclusions have been backed up by Meckler, '*The Annals of Ulster*', 45–9, and Fraser, 'St Columba', 331.

of Columba's cousin Ainmere, had become king of Ailech in the 580s, killing even his southern rival Colmán Bec, with whom Áedán's predecessor Conall had once ravaged the Inner Hebrides.[55] It seems that Áed and Áedán had it in mind to reach an Uí Néill-Corcu Réti accommodation of their own. The ulterior motives that colour *Vita Columbae*'s discussion of their summit in hindsight make it difficult to evaluate it as a source of reliable information. A later pseudo-historical claim that the kings discussed the Irish obligations of Argyll kings has been unduly influential.[56]

At this time, according to the Ultonian king-list, both the Ulaid and the Cruithni, north-east Ireland's two principal peoples made up of several nations each, were being dominated by the Cruithnian king Fíachnae Longshanks (*Lurgan*), king of the Uí Chóelbad in Antrim, who also had a claim on the great kingship of Tara monopolised by the Uí Néill. Fíachnae had assumed dominion over the north-east in 590 after the killing of his predecessor Áed Dub, opponent of the southern Uí Néill.[57] It may have been the slaying of Áed, who is reviled in *Vita Columbae*, and the rise of Fíachnae that paved the way for *détente* between the kings of Ailech and the Corcu Réti at Druimm Cete c. 592 – the other two main powers with interests in north-east Ireland.

It is even possible that Áedán fancied himself something of a Cruithnian king, and met with Áed in order to strengthen his position as a potential challenger to the mighty Fíachnae. His territories in Antrim east of the Bush were separated from the Uí Néill kingdoms further west by Mag nEilni, a Cruithnian district which, eventually, formed the northern 'half' of the (diphyletic) Uí Chóelbad kingdom. Was it debateable land in 590–2?

The presentation of Druimm Cete in *Vita Columbae* suggests that the summit established a three-way peace between Ailech, the Corcu Réti and the Uí Chóelbad. It also includes an episode in which Columba, on his way home to Iona from the summit, was welcomed by the bishop of Coleraine in Mag nEilni, and presented with 'almost innumerable gifts' collected from the inhabitants.[58] We must, therefore, allow for the possibility that, with Ailech backing, Áedán preserved a claim to Mag nEilni at Druimm Cete, either extending or safeguarding his influence west of the Bush. Fíachnae may have recognised this claim as the price of a peaceful frontier with the Corcu Réti.

---

[55] *AU* 580.1, 586.1, 587.1; *AT* 580.1, 586.1, 587.1; *CS* 580.1, 586.2, 587.1; *AI* 581.1.
[56] Fraser, 'St Columba', 318–21.
[57] *AU* 588.4; *AT* 588.5; *CS* 588.1.
[58] Adomnán, *V. s. Columbae*, i.50.

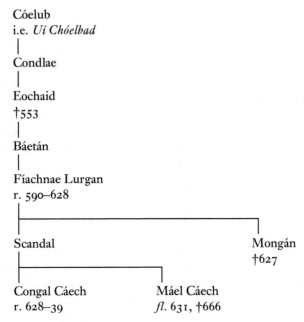

Cóelub
i.e. *Uí Chóelbad*
|
Condlae
|
Eochaid
†553
|
Báetán
|
Fíachnae Lurgan
r. 590–628

Scandal   Mongán
                                             †627

Congal Cáech   Máel Cáech
r. 628–39   *fl.* 631, †666

Table 5.4 Fíachnae Lurgan: some key relationships

After Druimm Cete, Fíachnae enjoyed tremendous success in central Ireland, pressing his Tara credentials. Meanwhile, Áedán's attentions were again drawn eastwards. His movements in the North British zone in the 590s, including two or possibly three wars, have already been discussed. They allow for the suggestion that, having reached an accommodation with his Irish neighbours at Druimm Cete, he succeeded over several years in softening up the Miathi. As a result, he set his sights on still more distant prizes.

Although his glorious reputation must have been tarnished to some extent by the close-run battle of Circhind, Áedán managed at least to extricate himself from that bloody field and to claim a victory. It is surely a testament of sorts to his royal qualities, and the grip he maintained on Kintyre and Cowal, and perhaps as well on Mag nEilni in Ireland and parts of Miathian territory. A similar episode would be played out in 603, when Áedán suffered another significant defeat in an invasion of the North British zone, this time venturing into the orbit of the vigorous Bernician king Aeðilfrith, who vanquished him at Degsastan, possibly in Liddesdale or Lauderdale.[59]

---

[59]   Lowe, *Angels, Fools and Tyrants*, 16; Skene, *Celtic Scotland*, vol. 1, 162; Anderson, *Early Sources*, vol. 1, 123.

In the meantime Áed son of Ainmere, the Ailech triumvir of the Druimm Cete settlement, had been slain in 600. Four years later his son was driven off by Colmán Rímid, king of Cenél nEogain, who wrested Ailech away from his Cenél Conaill rival.[60] These developments probably marked the end of the settlement at Druimm Cete. The range of activity of the triumvirs afterwards is impressive. There is no hint that any of them came to blows. The establishment of this *détente* was later used by Columba's hagiographers to criticise wars in the north-east of Ireland in the 620s and 630s.

It seems that Colmán Rímid reached his own accommodation with Áedán after the fall of Áed. The evidence comes from Degsastan three years later, where Áedán was supported against Aeðilfrith by Colmán's brother Máel Umai.[61] This campaign against the Bernicians may have stemmed from Áedán's earlier Miathian wars. Both he and Aeðilfrith, their power-bases at opposite margins of the North British zone, may have been competing now for slices of a collapsed hegemony – perhaps an hegemony established by Urbgen in the 580s. If Áedán was married to a British woman, this too may have been a factor in his thinking in 603.

A year after Degsastan, the mighty Fíachnae vanquished his Ultonian namesake, Fíachnae son of Demmán, king of Dál Fiatach.[62] Had Áedán's difficulties abroad and Áed's death convinced the Dál Fiatach king to challenge the status quo in the north-east? It is notable that Áedán does not appear to have been attacked by Fíachnae Longshanks. Instead, the great Uí Chóelbad king faced challenges from among the Cruithni, and *c.* 609 he emerged intact from an internal war. This challenge may well have arisen upon the death of Áedán, probably on 17 April 609 after a reign of thirty-four years aged seventy-three, possibly affecting balances of power in north-east Ireland.[63]

---

[60] *AU* 598.2, 602.2, 604.1, 604.5; *AT* 598.2, 602.2, 604.1, 604.4; *CS* 598.2, 602.2, 604.1, 604.4; *AI* 601.1, 605.3.

[61] *AU* 600.1; *AT* 600.2; *Ann. Clon.* 603.1; Bannerman, *Dalriada*, 87–8.

[62] *AU* 602.3; *AT* 602.3; *CS* 602.3.

[63] *AU* 608.1; *AT* 608.2; *CS* 606.1; *AI* 609.1; *Ann. Clon.* 604.3. *Mart. Tallaght* commemorates Áedán mac Gabráin on 17 April. As Anderson, *Early Sources*, vol. 1, 75, deduced, it is almost certainly he ('a youth from the clan of his son will take the kingship of Alba by force of his strength') of whom the *Propechy of Berchán* says that his death occurred on a Thursday; *Prophecy of Berchán*, § 120. 17 April was a Thursday in 609.

PSEUDO-HISTORY AND THE REIGN OF ÁEDÁN

Cumméne Find was composing *De uirtutibus sancti Columbae* in the same decade in which Jonas of Bobbio, near Piacenza in northern Italy, completed his Life of Columba's younger contemporary Columbanus. In the 640s Cumméne recorded marvellous anecdotes about his kinsman Columba, and seems to have spoken with old men who had known him. At the same time, he was like most hagiographers in his willingness to sacrifice historical accuracy (as we would call it) in order to ensure that the saint's story was an example of what scholars term a 'usable past'.

The fragment of *De uirtutibus sancti Columbae* that survives intact and unrevised is unequivocal in showing that Cumméne 'used' episodes from Columba's life. Here Cumméne wrote passionately about what he perceived to have been the fall-out from a battle fought on the plain of Moira (*Mag Roth*) near Lough Neagh in north-east Ireland. There, according to the chronicles, in 639 a king of the Uí Chóelbad was defeated and killed by the forces of Domnall son of Áed, grandson of Columba's cousin Ainmere. Within ten years of Domnall's victory, Cumméne wrote that the Corcu Réti king Domnall Brecc, Áedán's grandson, had participated in this conflict, laying waste Cenél Conaill territory, seemingly as an ally of the Uí Chóelbad. Iona lay in the orbit of the Corcu Réti kings; none the less, both Cumméne and his abbot Ségéne were, like Columba himself, scions of Cenél Conaill. *De uirtutibus sancti Columbae* was used to record Iona's disgust with Domnall Brecc's 'baseless' hostility towards Columba's (and the author's) kin.

This aspect of Cumméne's book presents the scholar with problems when it comes to evaluating *Vita Columbae* as a source for sixth-century history. Some have already been noted while opening the doors of the laboratory in order to evaluate the text's stories about Pictish Christianity. Nowhere is our dilemma better illustrated than in the chapter, certainly borrowed from Cumméne, in which Adomnán wrote that Domnall Brecc's grandfather Áedán was ordained as king by Columba, because it had been God's will. Had the saint had his own way at this time, Adomnán says, he would have chosen Áedán's brother Éoganán, who seemed a better potential king. It was only when God punished him that Columba relented.

It is clear from the interpolated fragment of *De uirtutibus sancti Columbae* attached to this story in the Schaffhausen manuscript that we would be naive to accept these details as historical facts. The story was concocted to pass judgement on Domnall Brecc. Under him, Cumméne wrote, the descendants of Áedán in Kintyre 'are still held down by strangers', as they had been since the battle of Moira, 'which fills the breast with sighs of grief'. Cumméne envisioned these developments as divine punishment for the king's attack on Columba's kin. He framed this belief in the form of a prophecy, made by the saint at Áedán's ordination, to the effect that his descendants would be stripped of their kingship by God if they ever made war on Cenél Conaill. No such prophecy was ever uttered by Columba. It was fabricated to explain the ill turn in Domnall Brecc's fortunes after 639. In order to encapsulate his point, Cumméne introduced into his parable that Columba had to be whipped by an angel before he would ordain Áedán. This idea allowed the writer to say that Domnall Brecc's actions had redirected this divine wrath towards himself.

There is no good reason, then, to believe that in 576, Columba had reservations about Áedán, nor that he really favoured Éoganán in a succession dispute. Rather, these were devices used by Cumméne seventy years later to pretend that Columba had had an inkling, all those years before, that Áedán's line would produce an unsuitable king in Domnall Brecc. Did an ordination of Áedán in the kingship by Columba take place at all?[64]

Our ability to appreciate the extent to which events of the reign of Domnall Brecc influenced Cumméne's presentation of the king's grandfather in *De uirtutibus sancti Columbae* requires us to be cautious about accepting Áedán's appearances in *Vita Columbae* at face value. What the text actually implies is that a succession crisis arose within Cenél nGabráin after 639, the descendants of Gabrán's sons Áedán and Éoganán contesting the kingship of Kintyre. The Irish chronicles reveal that Áedán's family stabilised itself and returned to prominence later in the century. Had it dwindled into obscurity instead, Adomnán would probably not have bothered to retain Cumméne's stories about Áedán in *Vita Columbae*. As it was, Áedán's reign remained historically significant because he still had very powerful descendants in the last years of the seventh century.

Cenél nGabráin maintained strong links with Iona. That too is evident from Áedán's treatment in Adomnán's Life, which omitted Cumméne's earlier gloomy prophecy about the dynasty. Adomnán also called them 'the royal kindred of Gabrán' (*regium Gabrani genus*).[65] Links are perceptible too in the Iona Chronicle's sustained interest in Áedán's descendants, denied any other Argyll family. In (re)constructing the sixth

---

[64] For debate on this point see Enright, 'Royal Succession', 85–8; Meckler, 'Colum Cille's Ordination of Aedán', 139; Fraser, 'St Columba', 333.
[65] Adomnán, *V. s. Columbae*, ii.22.

and seventh centuries in Scotland we must always remain aware of the fact that, in relying mainly on Iona and its records for our information, we are being pressed to accept that monastery's estimation of which events, people and places were significant. At times, that biased estimation may be misleading.

It was standard medieval hagiographical practice to reflect upon current links between a saint's church and various kingdoms through parables linking the saint in life with the relevant royal contemporaries. Episodes of *Vita Columbae* in which Áedán appears seem to serve hagiographical purposes that match up closely with those revealed in the surviving fragment of Cumméne's *De uirtutibus sancti Columbae*. Columba is depicted quizzing Áedán on the matter of the succession. He prophesies that Eochaid Buide will succeed, and blesses the boy and his descendants.[66] This story is part of the same retrospective portrayal of Columba, by Cumméne, as patron saint and protector of the forefathers and family of Domnall Brecc (Eochaid's son), who squandered that patronage and protection. In contrast to his son, Eochaid offers the saint a child's unconditional supplication. It is implied that this is how a king ought to make himself known. The use of Áedán as a metaphor continues in *Vita Columbae* in its discussion of the royal summit at Druimm Cete, where he and Columba helped to establish peace across north-east Ireland, in contrast to the divisive courses of action followed by their descendants, leading to the bloody field of Moira.

Once we appreciate the ways in which Áedán was 'used' by Cumméne in the 640s, it becomes difficult to believe that *Vita Columbae* tells us very much about his reign. As already discussed, our knowledge of the career of Columba too is much patchier than we would like. Happily, we are compensated with somewhat richer information about the 640s and the 690s, the contexts within which Cumméne and Adomnán wrote, than might otherwise be obvious. We would know nothing about the challenge to the supremacy of the descendants of Áedán by the descendants of his brother Éoganán in the 640s, were it not for our ability to read *Vita Columbae* in the suggested manner.

PSEUDO-HISTORY AND GAELIC MIGRATION

While we have the door of the laboratory open, we may consider other problems arising from the pseudo-historical tendencies of our primary

---

[66] Adomnán, *V. s. Columbae*, i.9; Bannerman, *Dalriada*, 95, sees it as an historical event.

informants relating to the origins of the Argyll and Bernician peoples discussed in this chapter. The tradition related by Gildas in the sixth century maintained that northern Britain was settled simultaneously by Pictish and Irish migrants from across the sea, wresting it away from Romano-British control. Two centuries later, Bede related a very different tradition in *Historia ecclesiastica*. The first Irish settlers of northern Britain, he wrote, were led there 'under the leader Reuda and won among the Picts, either by league or by iron, the seats that they still possess; from this leader (*dux*) they are still called *Dalreudini*, for in their language *daal* signifies "a part"'.[67]

Like Gildas, Bede envisions a migration, but this origin myth openly makes the Picts the earliest settlers of northern Britain. That priority is an important point. Moreover, it explicitly refers to Argyll as Pictish territory – giving the Picts still more priority. Finally, it implies that the entitlement of the Gaels to their lands could theoretically be revoked by a combination of Pictish political enmity and warfare. These elements are strong indications that Bede received his information from some Pictish version of this origin myth. There may have been a somewhat different Gaelic version.

Even before Bede wrote his History, Gaelic chroniclers and genealogists had known about Reuda. They had linked together the Cenél nGabráin and Cenél Comgaill kindreds – the Corcu Réti – naming them as descendants of a certain Domangart Réti, 'Domangart of Kintyre' as one chronicle calls him.[68] The author of Bede's Dalriadan origin story was aware of this genealogical tradition. It represents what the great-great-grandsons of Gabrán and Comgall believed – or wished – was true about their ancestry. Whether or not they were really related in this way is impossible to know.

All that is certain about the two *cenéla* or descendants of Gabrán and Comgall is that, from the middle of the sixth century to the middle of the seventh, they shared in a (diphyletic) kingship which encompassed Kintyre and Cowal in southern Argyll, reaching into Antrim in northeast Ireland. In reference to the Firth of Clyde, Bede observes that 'it was to the northern part of this arm [of the sea] that the Gaels . . . made their homeland' upon arriving in northern Britain.[69] This is surely a reference to Cowal and Kintyre, the home districts of the Corcu Réti kingdom. The story thus implies that the first Scottish Gaels – the founders of Dál Riata – were the ancestors of the Corcu Réti of southern Argyll. It was presumably with their partisans that the tale originated, before

---

[67] Bede *Hist. eccl.*, i.1.

[68] *AI* 503.1 (*Domongairt Cind Tire*).

[69] Bede, *Hist. eccl.*, i.1.

apparently passing through Pictish hands and, finally, into Bede's under-standing.

Medieval origin stories and genealogies were steeped in political significance not 'historical accuracy'. Where political outlooks differed, there could be different ideas about origins. There was an eighth-century genealogical tradition on offer in Argyll which Bede did not know – or did not accept. It differed from the Corcu Réti story by placing much more subtle emphasis on them, and disagreed with the notion that Dalriadan identity stemmed solely from them. The tradition is spelled out in the Gaelic tractate *Cethri prímchenéla Dáil Riata*, 'the four principal kindreds of Dál Riata', and brings to prominence Cenél nEchdach, a kindred prob-ably based in Upper Lorn in northern Argyll. Along with two other Lorn kindreds, Cenél nEchdach shared in what was probably a distinct realm focused on the Firth of Lorn. They seem to have been distinct from the Corcu Réti, for *Cethri prímchenéla* traces their ancestry, not from Domangart Réti (Bede's *Reuda dux*), but from a certain Loarn the Great (*Mór*), whom the text makes Domangart's uncle. The descendants of both men, Domangart and Loarn, along with those of a third brother Óengus, are together called *Dál Riata* in this text.[70]

What is the significance of such disagreement? There was a time when this kind of contradiction, as to whether Dál Riata contained two, three or four principal kindreds, would have been regarded as having a simple explanation: one tradition (usually the one favoured on Iona) is correct, and the others are wrong. More recently scholars have recognised in con-trary traditions evidence of contrary political 'spin' advanced by different groups. The tradition put forward in *Cethri prímchenéla*, unlike the Corcu Réti tradition, takes for granted a sense of parity among 'the four princi-pal kindreds' who dominated Argyll and its islands when it was penned after 706. Adomnán's use of the phrase *Scoti Brittanniae*, 'the Gaels of Britain', in *Vita Columbae*, a work of very nearly the same date, refers to this same sense of a single Gaelic nation in Atlantic Scotland. Bede gave it the name *Dalreudini*; *Cethri prímchenéla* called it *Dál Riata*.

Dalriadan political unity and identity were not necessarily very old, however, at the end of the seventh century. At that time, the Dalriadan kingdoms were being dominated by a paramount king, the *rex Dáil Riata*, who was king of Cenél nEchdach in the kingdom of Lorn. It is no coin-cidence that Cenél nEchdach receives more detailed attention in *Cethri prímchenéla* at this time than Cenél Comgaill or Cenél nÓengusso.

---

[70] *Ceth. prím. Dáil Riata*, §§ 22–45; Anderson, *Early Sources*, vol. 1, clvi; Fraser, *'Dux Reuda'*, 6–8.

Certainly the idea of a single Gaelic realm was being projected into the sixth-century past at Adomnán's Iona, but can we trust this? The Argyll community envisioned by *Cethri prímchenéla* and by the Iona chroniclers was significantly fragmented below the surface. It is less likely that the situation had dissolved into such a state, as has been proposed, than that the halcyon Dalriadan unity of Columba's time was a wishful invention of later men. As with the Picts, one must not press Dalriadan unity too far in the seventh century, nor assume that it had much antiquity.

As in the case of traditions pertaining to christianisation, scholars are bound to recognise that our different seventh-century origin traditions provide us mainly with an insight into Corcu Réti and other perspectives on Argyll in the seventh and eighth centuries. We shall return to these in later chapters. The famous origin legend transmitted to Bede is thus unlikely to relate reliable historical information. Less ambitious than the Pictish legend that brought the Picts to northern Britain all the way from Scythia, its evidence is no better for being plausible. On the back of it, as a vestige of obsolete scholarship, Dál Riata, its culture and its Gaelic language are conventionally said to have come to Scotland from Ireland *c.* 500. Scholars are rapidly abandoning that model. Neither is the tradition known to Gildas particularly helpful, save in its implication that the *Scoti* seemed, *c.* 540, to have been as firmly established in northern Britain, with the same antiquity, as the *Picti*.

The problem of the origins of the Scottish Gael thus requires fresh investigation on the part, mainly, of archaeologists and linguists. A people do not have origins that can be pinpointed to a single moment in time or a single place. Rather, ethnic identities are constructed and re-constructed, imagined and re-imagined, through an ongoing process of interaction between cultural practices and cultural self-consciousness. Identity, culture and the Gaelic language in Atlantic Scotland would not have developed as a single package: each would have developed as a result of a multiplicity of factors and phenomena, at different times and for different reasons. The early medieval notion of a migration from Ireland can be questioned. Archaeologists have fired salvoes against this and other 'diffusionist' models for understanding cultural change.[71] There is no clear evidence that the Roman Iron Age saw the dedicated colonisation of Argyll by a single Irish people. Gradual, piecemeal movements of colonists across the North Channel in both directions, who can have 'gone native' in

[71] Campbell, *Saints and Sea-Kings*, 11–15; Campbell, 'Were the Scots Irish?'; see also Nieke and Duncan, 'Dalriada', 8–11; Hingley, 'Society in Scotland', 9–10, for the Iron Age.

material terms upon their arrival and settlement, are not unlikely. Such movements probably started in the Stone Age, and remained a feature of the region for millennia down to (and well beyond) our period.

Such textual evidence as exists from the Roman Iron Age is thin for Argyll and open to question. The Flavian surveys placed *Epidii* in Kintyre, 'horsemen' whose name is certainly British in character not Gaelic. The Flavian surveyors were engaged in the serious work of preparing military and diplomatic intelligence. *Epidii* may represent a British translation of a native Gaelic name, but one requires strong contrary evidence before impugning the survey's testimony in this way. It is striking that later Gaelic *réti*, and even later *ríata*, normally denotes a riding horse. The ultimate ancestor of the different Dalriadan kindreds is said both in *Cethri prímchenéla* and in *Míniugud senchasa fher nAlban*, the 'explanation of the genealogy of the men of Alba' of roughly the same period, to have borne the name Eochaid, the Gaelic cognate (in later form) of *Epidii*.

Equestrian continuity in the ethnic terminology of southern Argyll conspires with material cultural continuity to suggest that no great cultural disjuncture took place here between the Flavian period and the seventh century. Yet the linguistic evidence points to a shift from British to Gaelic speech in the region. Once common assumptions that language and material culture are so inextricably linked that linguistic shifts must be detectable by archaeologists are now recognised as perpetuating antiquated culture-historical thinking which dominated scholarship in much of the twentieth century. Changes in one need not coincide with changes in the other.

The key to understanding the gaelicisation of Argyll is unlikely to lie in archaeology. The early writings of Ireland may be a better guide. We have seen in discussing *Picti* that the Cruithni, whose high king Fíachnae Longshanks was a major figure in 590s Ireland, bore an ethnonym denoting 'Britons'. Alas, such a suggestion of British colonisation in north-east Ireland, even in our distant period, can attract considerable unwanted and unwelcome attention from partisans keen either to exaggerate or to explain it away, to further modern political ideologies surrounding the fate of Northern Ireland. Yet the presence of Gaelic-speaking 'Britons' in the north-east is surely crucial for understanding how Gaelic-speaking Britons appeared in the adjacent part of Britain and cannot be ignored.

The Cruithni may have been British incomers from various parts of the west of outer Brigantia, Argyll and the Hebrides. Later Gaelic ethnographers distinguished Dál Riata from the Cruithni in racial terms. If we set such pseudo-history aside, we are confronted by two neighbouring

Early Historic peoples, one based largely in Britain with a small presence in Antrim, and the other based in Ireland but known there as 'Britons'. Together they form the kind of link between Argyll and north-east Ireland that scholars require to explain Gaelic in Argyll. Contrary to the conventional model and early medieval origin mythology, however, the link probably arose from incursions into Ireland from Britain, and not the other way round. There is nothing at all unlikely about the proposition that the inhabitants of Argyll 'went Gaelic' along with the Cruithni in Ireland, even if precisely how, and moreover when, such a process could have taken place remains unclear.[72]

PSEUDO-HISTORY AND THE *ADVENTUS BERNICIORUM*

Scholars encounter similar problems with the origins of Aeðilfrith's Bernicians. *Historia Brittonum* records that Aeðilfrith's grandfather Ida held territories 'north of the Humber estuary, and he joined Bamburgh (*Din Guairoi*) to Bernicia', giving Bamburgh its British name.[73] In associating this fortress with Ida which, by Bede's time, was the chief royal centre, and with an *imperium* 'north of the Humber', the Northumbrian source that informed *Historia Brittonum* cast Aeðilfrith's grandfather in genealogical pole position in Northumbrian dynastic history. He occupies the same position that Domangart Réti occupies in the seventh-century Corcu Réti dynastic tradition.

Bede's own historical consciousness was rather different, though he was clearly aware of a story like this. Once again, it is important to note that genealogical manipulation was a strategy by which men without obvious royal heritage could advance royal aspirations, when they possessed other necessary elements of royal excellence. Indeed, there are indications in our sources that Ida assumed pole position in Northumbrian royal tradition at a relatively late date, and that his story in *Historia Brittonum* is pseudo-historical.

In the first place, it anticipates a united Northumbria, apparently a product of the seventh century. Ida's association with Bamburgh, symbolising his majesty, is also problematic. Bede knew Bamburgh as *Bebbanburg*, 'named after a queen called Bebba'.[74] According to genealogical tradition,

---

[72] Woolf, 'Ancient Kindred?'; Sharpe, 'The Thriving of Dalriada', 50.

[73] *Hist. Brit.*, § 61.

[74] Bede, *Hist. eccl.*, iii.6.

Bebba was not Ida's wife, but Aeðilfrith's, thus giving Áedán's contemporary his own symbolic connection with Bamburgh.[75] Did the notion that the Northumbrian kingdom was founded by Ida supplant an earlier tradition linked with Aeðilfrith?

Bede likens Áedán's contemporary to King Saul – the first king of Israel – introducing him to readers of *Historia ecclesiastica* as 'a king most mighty and most eager for glory, who, more so than any other English ruler, ravaged the British nation, so that he may be thought comparable with Saul, once king of the Israelite nation'.[76] This analogy looks exactly like the vestiges of a tradition in which Aeðilfrith, not his (alleged) grandfather, was the key royal genealogical figure and regarded as the first Bernician king – its own King Saul. *Historia Brittonum* contains a number of anecdotes relating to Aeðilfrith, whom it calls 'flexor' (*flesaur*) or 'schemer'. It seems to begin its northern history with his reign, just like Bede. In the body of *Historia ecclesiastica*, Bede provides no indication that he thought there was anything noteworthy about Bernician history before Aeðilfrith. The eighth-century Bernician king-list places several of Ida's sons in the kingship after him, but Bede mentions none of these. His single mention of Ida in the History, 'from whom the Northumbrian royal family take their origin', occurs as an afterthought in the summary chronicle of events, provided 'in order to assist the memory'.[77] It may only have been introduced into these annals after 729, the year in which the last king of Northumbria descended from Aeðilfrith was succeeded by a man of different descent. Bede sent a draft of his History to the new king.

Bede's use of Aeðilfrith as part of his 'usable past' seems further to confirm that pole pseudo-historical position was usurped by Ida, probably beginning in 716. Casting him as another Saul implied that harrying British territory was righteous because, like Saul's enemies in Canaan, the Britons opposed true religion. Bede makes plainer this conceptual link between subjugation of Britons and British wickedness at the end of his History. He makes a brief positive comment about the Picts and a neutral one about the Gaels, in both cases on the basis of the existence of peace between them and the Northumbrians. He then says about the Britons that 'for the most part they oppose English folk through their innate hatred, and the whole state of the catholic church by their incorrect Easter and their evil customs'. As a result, they are 'opposed by the power

[75] Bede, *Hist. eccl.*, i.34.
[76] Bede, *Hist. eccl.*, i.34.
[77] Bede, *Hist. eccl.*, v.24.

of God and man alike' such that, 'although they govern themselves in part, yet they have also been brought partly under English mastery'.[78]

The point of view assumed by Bede in his History is thus that British intransigence regarding Easter, beginning in the time of Aeðilfrith, set God against them and justified their subjugation down to his own time. That Bede and Stephen were both inclined to cast Britons in a negative light seems to reflect this general Northumbrian doctrine, vilifying their British neighbours – not least in the North British zone – as an aspect of rationalising their conquest. This aspect of Bernician imperialism helps to explain the ongoing topicality of the apostolicist reforms two generations after Whitby. Bede used the figure of Aeðilfrith – not Ida or anyone else – to personify this key aspect of his people's past. It is as suggestive as his allusion to King Saul that the progenitor of the Bernician royal dynasty was thought until recently to be Aeðilfrith.

Finally, the surviving genealogical information gives Ida many sons, including Aeðilric, Aeðilfrith's father. These sons may represent different ancestors from whom eighth-century Northumbrian families with royal pretensions claimed their descent and connections with royalty through the device of claiming Ida as their ancestor. Here again we find a parallel. The surviving genealogies also give Aeðilfrith a large number of sons. That descent from Ida was still a very new political idea is as good an explanation as any for Bede's failure to comment on the specific genealogical claims of the non-'Aeðilfrithing' king Ceolwulf, to whom he dedicated Historia ecclesiastica.

The actual origins of the Bernician English are no easier to pin down than those of the Scottish Gael. The tradition known to Gildas informed him that Anglo-Saxon warriors settled in Britain as a deliberate policy for the repulsion of Pictish and Irish invaders. Thereafter there had been rebellions and Anglo-Saxons had seized territories, although Gildas provides no dates. Continental parallels of this Britannic policy are many. They suggest that cessions of territory – or perhaps billetings of German 'federates' among existing communities – were probably intended to be as much as a check on local developments as to provide a shield against distant enemies. We ought not to trust Gildas's narrative so much that we disregard the possibility of considerable overlap between Gaelo-Pictish aggression in the fourth century and an establishment of German federates inside Britannia.

The heartland of the Bernician kingdom under the Aeðilfrithing dynasty seems to have been the coastal plain of the Tweed basin, straddling

---

[78] Bede, Hist. eccl., v.23.

the present Anglo-Scottish border, centred on Bamburgh.[79] The first Bernicians might have been ceded (or billeted in) this district by Uotadinian or Romano-British leaders as part of a strategy for increasing the region's military might. It is more likely that they were groups of settlers from all over the North Sea basin, who seized and colonised their homeland themselves during the shadowy Anglo-British wars of the second half of the fifth century, which ended *c.* 500 in the divided island described by Gildas. It seems the Anglo-Saxon zone of control then reached at least as far north as Eboracum, for that was probably the 'city of legions' (*urbs legionum*) whose martyrs' shrines, according to Gildas, were inaccessible behind enemy lines. It may have reached further north still.[80]

A more radical possibility is that the first Bernicians were Britons who became ethnic Anglo-Saxons. Many ethnic Bernicians probably originated in this way. As yet the archaeological record is inconclusive, but the notable cluster of inscribed sixth-century Christian monuments in upper Tweeddale publicises the power and authority of Christian proprietors in the region. Was this because of the settlement (or existence) of committed non-Christians further down the Tweed?[81] The English dynasty that had become established in the Bernician kingship by the end of the sixth century was not Christian, and neither was Aeðilfrith. This need not preclude at all, however, the continuing existence of Christianity in the Tweed basin. The pagan Mercian hegemon Penda need hardly have been unique. Bede says that he bore no particular grudge against Christians in his kingdom, and more than once campaigned with Christian British allies despite remaining steadfast in his own pagan religion.[82]

Outside Bamburgh, a long-cist cemetery seems, like so many others across the North British zone, to span the period from the late Roman Iron Age to the end of our period, despite the likelihood of ethnic discontinuity.[83] The name *Berneich*, Latin *Bernicii*, is apparently British in origin. As a population name, it seems to denote something like 'gap people'. Was the 'gap' in question the Tweed basin, defined by the Lammermuir and Cheviot uplands? Scholars have decreasing expectations of clear archaeological distinctions between Britons and Anglo-Saxon newcomers in those parts of Britannia that lay outwith the

---

[79] Bede, *Hist. eccl.*, iii.6, iii.16; Smyth, *Warlords*, 31–2; Rollason, *Northumbria*, 48–50.
[80] Gildas, *De excidio Brit.*, i.10; Field, 'Gildas and the City of the Legions'; Rollason, *Northumbria*, 65–109, outlines some possibilities.
[81] Woolf, 'The Britons', 356; Forsyth, '*Hic Memoria Perpetua*', 119–20.
[82] Bede, *Hist. eccl.*, iii.21.
[83] 'Anglo-British Cemetery at Bamburgh'.

'civil' lowland zone. Both before and after their christianisation the Bernicians have proven elusive to the archaeologist, their material culture all but indistinguishable from that of their British neighbours (and fore-bears?).[84] A late exception exists in the furnished graves of the sixth and seventh centuries discovered outside Milfield on the River Till. Milfield was probably the site of the seventh-century Bernician royal residence of Maelmin, erected to replace the disused and better known Yeavering (*Gefrin*) some three kilometres upriver.[85]

It has been supposed, and also argued above, that the kingdom of Alt Clut was the lineal successor of the Dumnonian (or Maiatian) nation, separated from the Bernicians by the Gododdin in Lothian, certainly lineal successors of the Uotadini. In the ninth century it was maintained in Gwynedd that the local royal dynasty was descended from a migrant from Manau called *Cunedag* (modern Cunedda), 'with his sons to the number of eight'.[86] His story may be regarded as yet more Early Historic dynastic pseudo-history (note the number of sons).[87] The *Gododdin* elegies may include reference to a fourth and more elusive major North British successor kingdom in the south-west, its heartland in Wigtownshire, encompassing Whithorn and its neighbourhood, perhaps even spanning the North Channel into Cruithnian territories in Ireland.[88]

Whatever their origins, the Bernician kings established themselves as paramount princes across the North British region, and especially in the east, just as the Uotadini may have done in the Roman Iron Age. The expansion, associated by Bede with Aeðilfrith and pursued by his descen-dants, was perhaps occasioned at first by appropriation of Gododdin lands, along with their former position *vis à vis* neighbouring peoples. Many North British power centres retained their British names in the wake of Bernician conquest, at least before *c.* 650, suggesting that the early Bernician hegemony was polyethnic in character. Bede's disgust with the Britons in the 730s tells us nothing about Aeðilfrith's estimation of them. Possible polyethnic echoes with Urbgen's dominions, as described in the poetry, have already been mentioned.

---

[84] Alcock, *Kings and Warriors*, 45, 62, 234–6; Woolf, 'The Britons', 361.
[85] Bede, *Hist. eccl.*, ii.14; Alcock, *Kings and Warriors*, 62–3.
[86] Bede, *Hist. Brit.*, § 62; see also Jackson, 'On the Northern British Section in Nennius', 30.
[87] Dumville, 'Sub-Roman Britain', 181–3; *pace* the credulous response of Gruffydd, 'Gododdin to Gwynedd'. For examples of what was once thought possible, see Hunter Blair, 'The Origins of Northumbria', 32–7; Richmond, 'Roman and Native', 129–30.
[88] Dumville, 'The Origins of Northumbria', 217; Koch, *Gododdin*, lxxii–lxxiii; Clancy, 'The Real St Ninian', 25.

The North British zone thus may have emerged from the later Roman Iron Age with a great deal of coherence, just as its romanising material culture may imply. Continuity from a period of thinly-evidenced British paramountcy over English and British polities, to one of better-evidenced English dominance, has not conventionally received emphasis. Throughout the Roman world, where incoming barbarian peoples seized the reins of power, they quickly exploited and adapted existing structures and institutions. Little of Roman Britain's institutions were preserved into Anglo-Saxon times, but that was because they had already become obsolete within Romano-British society. What may be reflected dimly in the careers of Urbgen and Aeðilfrith is what had become of the patterns of power in Britannia Secunda, and in the frontier zone beyond it. The poetry addressed to Urbgen and his contemporaries is problematic, and cannot support a great deal of weight as regards political history. On the other hand, it does not stand in isolation. There seems to be no reason to reject out of hand the expectations of Bede and the poets of Urbgen and Guallauc that the North British zone retained from late Antiquity the kind of cohesion they describe in the time of Áedán son of Gabrán and his contemporaries.

We cannot contextualise with precision the details we are given. Pseudo-history haunts our steps, and the career of Urbgen will never have a detailed chronological framework that can command confidence. Confining ourselves to broader contexts, on the other hand, and noting the broad reconcilability of the evidence, we may draw sketchy conclusions with a reasonable claim to validity as a working model. On the matter of the historical origins of Bernicia and Dál Riata, and the extent to which those origins represent continuities from earlier times, it seems best to keep an open mind. Epigraphic and archaeological evidence may be unearthed to provide additional glimpses of the historical kings of the relevant period, confirming, refuting or qualifying sketch-lines provided by the existing evidence.

CHAPTER 6

Sighs of Sorrow: Iona and the Kingdoms of Northern Britain (616–43)

Aeðilfrith son of Aeðilric, king of the Bernicians, emerged from the late sixth-century wars of the North British zone as the dominant figure in northern Britain, having cowed his British and Corcu Réti challengers. Having vanquished Áedán's forces in 603, he seems to have subdued his Deiran English neighbours, and he extended his paramountcy over such British territories as (probably) East Lothian and (apparently) former inner Brigantian *civitates*. Anglo-British ethnic hostility is a general feature of our Early Historic textual evidence. It is equally clear that the Mercian and West Saxon kingdoms were, none the less, created from Anglo-British hegemonies in which British participation could be pronounced.[1]

The battle of Chester (*Caer Legion*), where a British king was killed and a large number of clerics slaughtered, allegedly on Aeðilfrith's orders, was fought in 615.[2] By then he was indisputably the mightiest prince in northern Britain. Having lived by the sword, the Bernician king died by it at the battle of the River Idle in 616. In the aftermath, his son Oswald was conveyed at the age of twelve to Argyll, or perhaps to Antrim and given sanctuary among the Corcu Réti.

CONNAD CERR AND THE IRISH

Áedán's last years had less lustre than the earlier part of his reign. His North British wars after 584 were increasingly unsuccessful. Yet he was the only major king of his generation in north-east Ireland or the North British zone

---

[1] See, for example, Woolf, 'Apartheid', 127–8.
[2] *AU* 613.3; *AT* 613.5; *AI* 614.1.

to die in his bed, unless Riderch of Alt Clut had been a major king. This fate seems to have been regarded at Iona *c.* 640 as a sign of divine favour.[3]

The fourteenth-century Scottish chronicler John of Fordun says that he was buried at Kilkerran (*Kylcheran*) at the south end of Kintyre. Fordun's source was probably an annotated Dalriadan king-list.[4] His testimony, if accepted, is a strong hint that Áedán's principal royal fortress was the nearby coastal promontory fort at Dunaverty, named in chronicle evidence from Adomnán's time. Carved stone footprints at St Columba's Chapel at Keil Point along the machar from Dunaverty have been taken as suggesting that royal inaugurations took place there.[5] It may have been to the gates of Dunaverty that Oswald came in 616.

Our seventh-century Irish chronicle evidence, which seems quite reliable, suggests that Áedán was succeeded in the kingship of the Corcu Réti after 609 by Connad Cerr, called *rex Dáil Riata* in 629. Connad was a son of Áedán's predecessor Conall, who had hosted or supported Columba, and his instalment would have been in line with an alternating pattern of succession between the two main Corcu Réti lineages, hinted at by the chronicles. The Dalriadan king-list disagrees with the chronicles, however, by making Áedán's son Eochaid Buide his successor.[6] *Vita Columbae* agrees. If both sources are reliable, we must envision a scenario in which Eochaid succeeded his father, but was later toppled by Connad. It is intriguing that versions of the king-list give Eochaid a reign of fifteen or sixteen years, because the chronicles record in 617 (fourteen years prior to his death) an enigmatic battle at a place called *Fidnach* which was, according to the *Annals of Ulster*, *in riaddai*, seemingly Corcu Réti territory.[7] Did Eochaid and Connad lead the opposing forces at *Fidnach*, and did Connad emerge from the field as high king? His byname, *cerr*, 'left-handed' (Latin *sinister*), may have been given by hostile Kintyre observers.

We may feel confident that Eochaid became king of Kintyre in 609, and that Connad became king of Cowal. The two kings may have reached some kind of formal arrangement by which they partitioned Áedán's legacy between them. Whereas the chronicles speak of Connad as *rex Dáil Riata*, the *Annals of Ulster* intriguingly call Eochaid *rex Pictorum* in

---

[3] Charles-Edwards, *Early Christian Ireland*, 503–5.

[4] Fordun, *Chron. gent. Scot.*, iii.31. The *Prophecy of Berchán* is surely speaking of Áedán when it notes that the king died *hi cCinntíre*, 'in Kintyre', confirming that a king-list was probably Fordun's source; *Prophecy of Berchán*, § 120.

[5] Nieke and Duncan, 'Dalriada', 11–12, 16; Foster, 'Before Alba', 9, 27 n.29.

[6] For the texts, see Anderson, *Kings and Kingship*, 253–91; for a collation and translation, see Anderson, *Early Sources*, 1, vol. cxxix–cxxxvi.

[7] *AU* 615.3; *AT* 615.3; see also Anderson, *Early Sources*, 1, vol. 151.

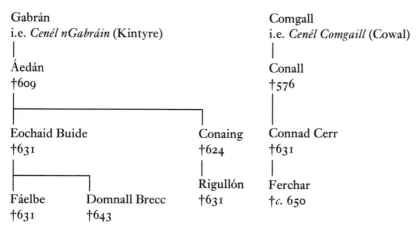

Table 6.1 Connad Cerr: some key relationships

his obit.[8] Much has been made of this designation as regards Gaelo-Pictish relations. Considering the evidence of Áedán's reign, however, a better explanation may be that it is a very rare mistranslation of *rí Cruithne*, king of the Cruithni.

The priority afforded to Eochaid in the king-list may, on the other hand, reflect Iona's partisanship, allowing for the possibility that Connad succeeded Áedán from the start. It may also reflect that fact that his descendants enjoyed a greater measure of royal power than Connad's in the middle decades of the seventh century, possibly shaping the hindsight of the king-list-makers. About his reign we can say little.

As in the case of Áedán, all we really know about Connad Cerr is his military record. It looks far less impressive. The Iona Chronicle may, however, have preserved less about him than he actually achieved, because he was not a descendant of Gabrán. There are indications from later in the century that the principal ecclesiastical links of Cenél Comgaill were not with Iona, but with Kingarth (*Cenn Garad*), now St Blane's in southern Bute in the Firth of Clyde, an island in their district.[9] Indeed, in seeking a chief royal centre for Cenél Comgaill, one could do worse than to suggest the Early Historic coastal hill-fort of Little Dunagoil, less than a kilometre from St Blane's. Connad and Iona may, therefore, have been pretty indifferent towards one another.

As a result of military setbacks and the rise of Aeðilfrith, Connad inherited from Áedán dwindling influence in the North British zone. The

[8]   *AU* 629.4.
[9]   Fraser, 'Strangers on the Clyde', 102–20.

king may also have inherited little of the Druimm Cete *détente* or its satellite political accommodations, making more challenging any ambitions he may have pursued in north-east Ireland. Whether as a result of Iona's lack of interest or genuine hesitancy, perhaps arising from unresolved issues in his relationship with Eochaid, we hear nothing of Connad in the chronicles for the first twenty years of his reign.

The affection towards Iona Oswald later exhibited suggests that his Corcu Réti hosts in exile after 616 were Kintyre Gaels. We are nowhere told that his host was a king, but it does seem likely. Both conclusions are encouraged by the political ascendancy enjoyed by Cenél nGabráin in Argyll during the reign of Oswald's brother Oswy (or Oswiu), who preserved his brother's policies regarding Iona for more than twenty years, long after he had become the most powerful king in Britain. It was thus a fateful day indeed for Iona when that delegation of heathen Bernician exiles which included the youthful Oswald fetched up at the court of Eochaid Buide in 616, a year before the enigmatic battle of Fidnach. We have before us a fascinating historical 'what if', if that battle marks a transfer of paramountcy from Eochaid to Connad. In that event, had Oswald arrived in Argyll a year later than he did, he might have gone to Cowal and aligned himself with Kingarth rather than Iona.

It seems that the Aeðilfrithings scattered after their father was killed, presumably seeking to protect the dynasty by putting its eggs in a number of different baskets. Some, Bede informs us, went north to Pictland. One of these exiles, Aeðilfrith's son Eanfrith, was probably the father of the Pictish king Talorcan son of 'Anfrith'. It thus appears that Eanfrith found shelter in Pictland, married a woman of a powerful Pictish royal dynasty and fathered at least one son, who became a king in Pictland in the 650s.

Can we identify his host? If Neithon son of Guipno was the same person as the Pictish king 'Necton', Irb's descendant, as discussed above, the evidence that his son Beli married a Deiran princess reduces the chances that Neithon's court previously played host to Eanfrith. On the foregoing model, that would rule out Manau and Strathearn. Yet Talorcan was active in Stirlingshire in the 650s, indicating that Eanfrith's host was probably a southern Pictish king. Was Talorcan's realm in Fife? We shall see that there is reason to believe that Bernicians established a foothold there in the second half of the seventh century.

During Oswald's time among the Corcu Réti, Connad Cerr became embroiled in the politics of north-east Ireland, just as Áedán had done before him. His predecessor may have staked claims in Ireland, not least to Mag nEilni, in the 590s, which Connad was keen to protect. After Áedán's death, the powerful Cruithnian king Fíachnae Longshanks of the Uí Chóelbad weathered an extended challenge to his position from within Antrim.[10] According to a Gaelic elegy, his son was killed in Islay by a British or Pictish warrior fighting in an army out of Kintyre, an episode dated in the chronicles to 627.[11]

At first glance the presence of Fíachnae's son in Islay has the appearance of an expansion of Uí Chóelbad interests into Argyll – a development with no clear parallel in the reign of Áedán. It is uncertain, however, that Islay was Corcu Réti territory as early as 627. At the end of the seventh century it was home to Cenél nÓengusso, a kindred identified by genealogical tractates of that era as distinct from the Corcu Réti. Was Eochaid Buide the aggressor from Kintyre in 627? If so, the killing of Fíachnae's son in Islay may represent the passing of the island from the Uí Chóelbad or even Dál Fiatach to Kintyre dominion.

Cenél nÓengusso and the Ulaid

The principal seventh-century kindred of the Ulaid nation were Dál Fiatach. Later tradition maintained that their king Báetán, who died in 583, subdued Áedán son of Gabrán, and Báetán's nephew Fíachnae fell in battle against Áedán's successor. These interactions reflect high levels of mutual interest among Corcu Réti and Dál Fiatach kings in this period, which may not have been confined to Ireland.

The evidence of Hebridean interests among Dál Fiatach relates to two later kindreds. One of these is the minor Dál Fiatach kindred Uí Ibdaig, whose key ancestor was Óengus Ibdach, 'Óengus the Hebridean'. The death of his son Fergnae c. 557 is recorded in the chronicles, which call him rí Ulad, king of Ulaid. No other Ultonian or Dál Fiatach king hailing from the Uí Ibdaig is on record; they seem to have been a very minor kindred in the great scheme of things in Ulster.[12]

The second kindred is Cenél nÓengusso, whose key ancestor was Óengus Mór, 'Óengus the Great'. Both Cethri prímchenéla Dáil Riata and Míniugud senchasa fher nAlban indicate that Cenél nÓengusso was a major Dalriadan kindred at the end of the seventh century, associated with Islay in Míniugud senchasa fher nAlban, but they go unmentioned in the surviving chronicle material. The principal lineages recorded in

---

[10] *AU* 608.1, 616.1; *AT* 608.1.

[11] *Is uar in gáeth dar Ile*, ll. 1–2; *AU* 625.2; *AT* 625.6 (*pretene*); *CS* 625.2 (*britone*); *AI* 626.3; *Ann. Clon.* 627.1 ('a Welshman').

[12] *AU* 557.1; *AT* 557.5; *CS* 557.1; *AI* 557.1; *Sench. Dáil Fiatach*, ll. 45–60. I am grateful to Alex Woolf for drawing my attention to Óengus Ibdach.

Cenél nOengusso and the Ulaid (*continued*)

these tractates descended from Óengus via Nadsluaig, called his grandson in *Cethri prímchenéla* and his son in *Míniugud senchasa fher nAlban*.
Crucially, the latter text also names a second son of Óengus and his
seven sons, whose descendants are not recorded. That second son was
a certain Fergnae, who thus shares his name with Fergnae son of
Óengus the Hebridean.[13]

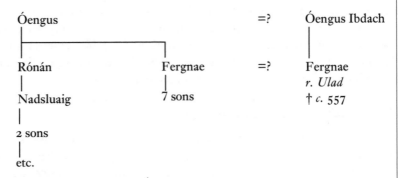

Table 6.2 Uí Ibdaig and Cenél nÓengusso

Thus, we seem to have two kindreds, both claiming descent from an
Óengus, called 'the Hebridean' in one genealogical tradition and linked
with Islay in the other, who had a significant son called Fergnae. The likelihood must be admitted that the two kindreds in fact represent a single
Dál Fiatach kindred, Fergnae's descendants in Ulster taking the name
Uí Ibdaig, and Nadsluaig's taking the name Cenél nÓengusso in Islay,
where 'descendants of the Hebridean' would have been nonsensical.

A year later Fíachnae was slain by the forces of the Dál Fiatach king
Fíachnae son of Demmán, whom he had defeated in 604.[14] Longshanks
had reigned for thirty-eight years, and for a time was the most powerful
king in Ireland. The chronicles record that he stormed and burned *Ráith
Guala* in 625, three years before his death. This record has been associated with a lost Irish tale crediting Fíachnae with an attack on Dún
Guaire, the Bernician stronghold at Bamburgh.[15] Bede says nothing

---

[13] *Ceth. prím. Dáil Riata*, §§ 59–70; *Mín. sench. fher nAlban*, §§ 21–2.
[14] *AU* 626.1; *AT* 626.1; *CS* 626.1.
[15] *AU* 623.3; *AT* 623.4; *CS* 623.3; *AI* 624.5. On Dún Guaire, see Byrne, *Irish Kings and
High-Kings*, 112; Jackson, 'Northern British Section in Nennius', 27–8.

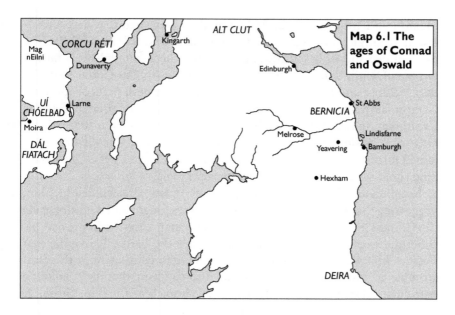

Map 6.1 The ages of Connad and Oswald

about a Cruithnian invasion during the reign of Edwini the Deiran, but Áedán's Degsastan campaign shows that such an invasion is far from impossible. Edwini's home territory was not Bernicia, and Bede does not seem to have known much Bernician history during Edwini's paramountcy between 616 and 633.

Even if the historicity of Fíachnae's Bernician campaign is rejected, it is not surprising that his death seems to have given rise to a power-struggle among the different kings of north-east Ireland. A year after his victory, Fíachnae son of Demmán met Connad in battle. The *Annals of Clonmacnoise* maintain that Connad came there in 629 to avenge the killing of Fíachnae Longshanks – another tantalising indication of Corcu Réti interests among the Cruithni. At the unidentified Ard Corand the Ultonian king was slain, and Connad emerged as the victor.[16] Áedán, for all his successes elsewhere, never won such a victory in Ireland, nor vanquished an army of Dál Fiatach, the most powerful of the Ultonian kingdoms in Down. Did Connad now lay claim to paramountcy in north-east Ireland as king of Ulster (*Ulaid*)? Was his Kintyre colleague Eochaid already dominating some Cruithnian districts?

Among other things, Connad's Ard Corand campaign may have given valuable experience to Oswald, now twenty-five years old, who may have

[16] *AU* 627.1; *AT* 627.1; *CS* 627.1; *Ann. Clon.* 627.4.

fought in a Kintyre *cohors* at Ard Corand. It happened that disaster followed triumph. Two years later, Connad was killed in battle at the unidentified Fid Euin ('Birdwood'). Among those who fell with him in 631 was Dicuill, king of Larne adjacent to the Antrim Corcu Réti district.[17] Larne and the Uí Chóelbad kingdom were both parts of the same Cruithnian nation, Dál nAraidi. Dicuill's presence further reflects the Cruithnian influence we have been attaching to the Corcu Réti princes after 592, arising from scraps of evidence like this. Dicuill may have joined forces with Connad only after Ard Corand, after which the Cowal king could have claimed overlordship over Larne.

Rigullón and Fáelbe, two grandsons of Áedán, also fell at Fid Euin, suggesting that Kintyre *cohortes* and potentates fought and died alongside the Cowal king on that grim day. The Dalriadan king-list has it that his colleague Eochaid died three months before the battle. It may be that Fáelbe, who was Eochaid's son, led the Kintyre contingent at the catastrophe of Fid Euin.[18] The casualty list suggests that they suffered particular calamity in Connad's army. One branch of the Irish chronicle tradition records that another casualty was a Saxon prince, Osric son of Aelfric (*Oisiric mac Albruit*). This, however, was the Deiran prince who succeeded Edwini as king of the Deirans in 633, slain in 634 – his name probably occurs here as an error.[19]

The leader of the forces that overcame and slew Connad was a brother of the new king of the Uí Chóelbad, Congal One-eye (*Cáech*). The brothers were grandsons of Fíachnae Longshanks. Congal went on to ally himself with Eochaid Buide's son Domnall Brecc before 639. Surely king of Ulster after Fid Euin, Congal had already killed the northern Uí Néill king of Cenél nEogain. Having thus overcome both the Corcu Réti beyond the Bush to the east of Mag nEilni, and Cenél nEogain to the west, Congal may have annexed that district in 631. Possibly Mag nEilni had been the prize at stake at Fid Euin.

Congal had bigger problems than Connad Cerr in 631, for he was defeated at the unidentified Dún Ceithirn by the new king of Ailech, Domnall son of Áed, whose father had treated with Áedán at Druimm Cete.[20] The battle features in *Vita Columbae*, in an episode in which

---

[17] *AU* 629.1, 629.3–4; *AT* 629.1; *CS* 629.1; *Ann. Clon.* 627.11. On Dicuill's origins, see Dumville, 'Cath Fedo Euin', 117–18, 120–1.

[18] Anderson, *Kings and Kingship*, 228–9; Anderson, *Early Sources*, vol. 1, cxxx.

[19] *AT* 629.1; *Ann. Clon.* 627.11. For this interpretation of *Albruit* (*pace* Moisl, 'Bernician Royal Dynasty'), see Anderson, *Early Sources*, vol. 1, vol. 153; see also Dumville, 'Cath Fedo Euin', 122–3.

[20] *AU* 629.2; *AT* 629.3; *CS* 629.3.

Columba of Cenél Conaill and Comgall of Bangor, a Cruithne, are said to have discussed it, saddened at the foreknowledge that their two peoples would fight a battle at Dún Ceithirn. It is possible that Connad and Domnall attacked the Uí Chóelbad in some concerted action, reminiscent of the *détente* of their forebears. This may at least be implied by the Life.

A joint military effort in two different theatres of war was typical allied behaviour in our period. In Connad's case, the objective may have been to protect the interests of Cruithnian subjects, including his own Kintyre kin, against an aggressive Uí Chóelbad king. At any rate, it is clear that, almost forty years after Druimm Cete, the Corcu Réti and the kinsmen of Columba continued to share the Uí Chóelbad as vexing rivals and enemies.

LOSING THE SCEPTRE: DOMNALL BRECC

Connad's conduct in Ireland seems to have been in line with that of his predecessors, who had established friendly relations with Ailech kings. With his death at Fid Euin, however, and the decimation of the Kintyre forces there, a significant realignment of the Corcu Réti took place under the ill-starred Domnall Brecc, grandson of Áedán. His father Eochaid had apparently died shortly before Fid Euin, and Domnall may have succeeded to the kingship only after his brother Fáelbe fell there with others of his near kin. Until then he may have been active mainly in central Ireland. A group of Irish chronicles places him in the host of the victor in a violent internal dispute within the southern Uí Néill kingdom of Meath in 624.[21]

It was presumably in part to preserve whatever interests remained to him in Ireland after Fid Euin – and not least to prevent further Uí Chóelbad incursions into his Irish districts – that Domnall manoeuvred the Corcu Réti into the camp of Congal One-eye in the 630s. A relatively late story that the two kings were related is interesting, but alas, cannot be trusted. The evidence is rather better that both had become involved in the affairs of Meath in the 620s, providing a possible context for their later concord.[22] The alliance was presumably sealed through marriage, though who may have married whom is an open and unanswerable question. Defeat at Fid Euin, with the loss of so many princes, must have left the Corcu Réti in a vulnerable and precarious position in Ireland, and perhaps in Argyll too. If in addition Domnall had been forced to cede Cruithnian districts to Congal – or else to Congal's new rival, Domnall

---

[21] *AT* 622.1; *CS* 622.1.
[22] *AT* 622.1, 628.3; *CS* 622.1, 628.3.

son of Áed, the northern Uí Néill victor at Dún Ceithirn – it ought to have been a blow to his family's fortunes.

Here then is the context within which Domnall took the fateful decision to back Congal in his struggles against the king of Ailech, which had begun in the year of Fid Euin. At Iona it was believed that the way forward for north-east Ireland, after the bloody wars of 628–31, was to restore the three-way peace represented (in Cumméne Find's mind) by the royal summit at Druimm Cete *c.* 592. Congal's grandfather Fíachnae Longshanks had been king of the Uí Chóelbad at that time, and seemingly complicit in the peace, which had disintegrated with very bloody consequences in the three years following his death. Domnall son of Áed had defeated Fíachnae's successor in 631, and the Corcu Réti had been badly battered that same year. No doubt the kin of the Cenél Conaill king at Iona were convinced that their kinsman had now emerged at the top of the pecking order in north-east Ireland, and that an alliance between him and Domnall Brecc would create a power bloc capable of holding Congal in check. In that way peace could be restored, all the more desirable because their Uí Néill kinsman would be in the ascendancy.

We can only speculate as to why neither the weight of such traditional alliances nor the influence of the Cenél Conaill abbot Ségéne at Iona proved successful in dissuading Domnall from his remarkable decision to side with the king whose forces had slain his predecessor, in order to make war on the king of Ailech. Fid Euin may have been such a terrible defeat that Domnall feared any arrangement that required him to confront Congal. Alternatively, the two kings may have agreed that, whatever enmities remained between them, it was in their mutual interests to check Ailech power in the north-east. There are other possibilities. One may conclude only that, for some reason or collection of reasons beyond recovery, alliance with Cenél Conaill struck Domnall as being less useful than alliance with Congal.

The consequences were dire. Congal was vanquished and slain at Moira in 639 by the northern Uí Néill, and paramountcy in north-east Ireland passed eastwards into the hands of the Dál Fiatach Ulaid, whose kings maintained it for most of the rest of the century.[23] Ferchar, the son of Domnall Brecc's predecessor Connad Cerr, seems to have become king of the Corcu Réti *c.* 638, and so about the time of Moira. Three years before that battle, it seems that Domnall had suffered a defeat in the district of Calathros, later the scene of fighting between armies out of Fortriu and Lorn, and so probably in the general vicinity of the Lorn

<hr />

[23] *AU* 637.1; *AT* 637.1; *CS* 637.1; *AI* 639.1.

basin.[24] His opponents in Calathros may, therefore, have been Lorn Gaels. In the year after the battle of Moira, he suffered further defeat by unnamed, possibly Cowal forces at a place called *Glend Mureson*.[25]

These successive defeats in Argyll may have left Domnall with very little power outside Kintyre. Cumméne Find wrote in *De uirtutibus sancti Columbae* that, since Moira, Domnall and the descendants of Áedán had been stripped of power (*sceptrum*) in the kingdom and subjugated by strangers (*extranei*). Although they claimed a common ancestor in Domangart Réti, both Domnall and Ferchar were his great-great-grandsons. By the 640s they and their sons were sufficiently far removed from Domangart to allow for segmentation into distinct kindreds, the familiar Cenél nGabráin, descended from Domangart's son Gabrán, and Cenél Comgaill, descended from his son Comgall. It is thus plausible that Cumméne referred to a Cenél Comgaill king of the Corcu Réti as an *extraneus*, especially given indications that, by Ferchar's time, the Cowal court was looking on Kingarth as its principal ecclesiastical associate.[26]

In a mere eight years, Domnall Brecc managed to undo the work of three generations of Corcu Réti kings and Ionan abbots in Argyll and Ireland, or at least failed to prevent the garment from unravelling. The achievement he had squandered is symbolised by Druimm Cete and the precocious policies of Columba, the saint's contemporaries Conall and Áedán and Conall's son Connad Cerr. Domnall thus has the dubious honour of being Scotland's first known 'bad king'. It may be a harsh judgement. Both Áedán and Connad seem to have overstretched themselves, suffering significant, even catastrophic defeats on battlefields in northern Britain and northern Ireland, respectively. Domnall had inherited inauspicious circumstances, and perhaps achieved as much as was feasible without a great deal of luck.

All the same, it is easy to appreciate how *De uirtutibus sancti Columbae* could cast the king as a man plagued by divine wrath, of whose dismal reign Columba had had sufficient foreknowledge to balk at ordaining his grandfather in 576. We know of no battles in which Domnall participated as king that he did not lose. It is an unfortunate epitaph.

---

[24] The mis-dated battle in *Calathros* (*bellum i Calathros*; *AU* 678.7; *AT* 678.6; *Ann. Clon.* 674.6) occurs eight years before an erroneous second obit of Domnall Brecc (*AU* 686.2; *AT* 686.3; *CS* 686.1, *Ann. Clon.* 681.1), and so is apparently to be dated to 634. Skene, *Celtic Scotland*, vol.1, 247, 291, mislocated Calathros.

[25] *AU* 638.1; *AT* 638.1; *CS* 638.1. For discussion of the place-name, see Skene, *Celtic Scotland*, vol. 1, 249; Anderson, *Early Sources*, vol. 1, 164.

[26] On Ferchar's dates, see Anderson, *Kings and Kingship*, 110-11. For discussion, see Anderson, *Early Sources*, vol. 1, 161; Fraser, 'Strangers on the Clyde', 111–12.

LINDISFARNE: A NEW DAWN FOR IONA

Having fallen under the shadow of Ferchar of Cowal, Domnall may have turned to an old friend for support and protection. Some three years after the Fid Euin disaster, the Bernician dynast Oswald had left the Gaelic world. A man of thirty, who had lived more than half his life among the Gael, Oswald returned a Christian to his homeland on the Tweed, and in 634 captured the Bernician kingship. Paramountcy over the Deirans seems to have followed swiftly on the heels of his victory. Adomnán says that Oswald went on to become *imperator totius Brittanniae*, emperor of the whole of *Britannia*. Bede says that he held in suzerainty (*imperium*) all the English and British inhabitants of *Britannia* save for those of Kent. Elsewhere, he adds that 'all the *nationes* and kingdoms of *Britannia*' accepted his word, 'British, Pictish, Gaelic and English'.[27]

Our source for Oswald's reign, Bede's *Historia ecclesiastica*, was composed almost exactly a century after Aeðilfrith's son and his army defeated and killed the British king Catguollaun at a burn outside Hexham.[28] Writing about thirty years before Bede, Adomnán recorded in *Vita Columbae* that Oswald once reported to Ségéne, Iona's Cenél Conaill abbot since 625, that, before fighting at Hexham, he had seen a vision of St Columba. The saint had encouraged him, and obtained from God that Catguollaun would be vanquished and Oswald made king.[29] Adomnán attributes the story to his predecessor Fáelbe, who had heard it told by the king. None the less, Cumméne Find's conception of how the patronage and protection of Columba had upheld Áedán and his descendants may have inspired the story in its final form.

Two centuries after the event, *Historia Brittonum* identified Catguollaun as a king of Gwynedd, the north Welsh kingdom in which that text was penned. A reasonable alternative case has been made, however, that he was actually Catguollaun Liu of the House of Ceneu, a kinsman of Aeðilfrith's contemporary Guallauc. If the identification is accepted, the 'rebellion' of Catguollaun Liu against Edwini, and the ensuing violence, takes on the appearance of a three-way struggle for paramountcy north of the Humber. It also involves the same Bernician, Deiran and North British dynasties that had clashed in the previous generation. Catguollaun may, therefore, have been reacting to Edwini's

---

[27] Bede, *Hist. eccl.*, ii.5; iii.6.
[28] Bede, *Hist. eccl.*, iii.1, names the burn as *Denisesburna*; *Hist. Brit.*, § 64 (*bellum Catscaul*); *Ann. Camb.* (Faral) 631.1 (*bellum Cantscaul*).
[29] Adomnán, *V. s. Columbae*, i.1.

suppression of the British kingdom of Elmet in south-west Yorkshire in the course of the 620s, whose last king Ceretic was probably Ceretic son of Guallauc.[30] A putative multi-ethnic list of Northumbrian hegemons may, therefore, be proposed in which Urbgen and perhaps even Guallauc might be inserted before Aeðilfrith and another British king, Catguollaun, might be inserted following Edwini's death in 633.

Catguollaun son of Catman or Catguollaun Liu?

In *Vita Columbae*, Adomnán related a story about the battle of Hexham, which allegedly came from the mouth of Oswald himself. The king reported that he had seen a vision of St Columba in his sleep, encouraging him and promising him victory over his foe, *Catlon Britonum rex fortissimus*, 'Catlon' the strongest British king. Thirty years later, Bede related more details – and different ones – in *Historia ecclesiastica*. He names *Catlon* as *Caedualla rex Brettonum*, who 'rebelled against' Edwini in 633.[31] The story of his rebellion became famous among the British-speaking peoples. He appears as a Pict (*Cathluan*) in king-lists and origin legends in Gaelic, where his father is called *Gub* or *Caitmind* (with variations). In *Historia Brittonum*, however, he appears as Catguollaun son of Catman, king of Gwynedd. But was this identification correct?[32]

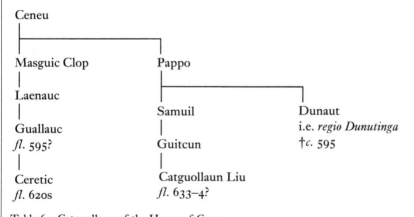

Table 6.3 Catguollaun of the House of Ceneu

---

[30] *Hist. Brit.*, § 63; *Ann. Camb.* (Faral) 616.1. Something along these lines is suggested by Koch, *Gododdin*, xxii–xxiii. On Elmet, see also Bromwich, *Trioedd*, 308, 375; Dumville, 'The Origins of Northumbria', 220–1.
[31] Adomnán, *V. s. Columbae*, praef.; Bede, *Hist. eccl.*, ii.20, iii.1. *Hist. Brit.*, § 61 and *Ann. Camb.* (Faral) 630.2 name the battle as *bellum Meicen*.
[32] Evans, 'Ideology, Literacy and Matriliny'; *Hist. Brit.*, § 61.

Catguollaun son of Catman or Catguollaun Liu? *(continued)*

The name Catguollaun was not particularly uncommon in the seventh century, and Cosmo Innes, who knew Bede but not, seemingly, *Historia Brittonum*, called *Caedualla* 'king of Cumbria'. After consideration of the evidence, Alex Woolf has indeed argued that Catguollaun was actually Catguollaun son of Guitcun of the House of Ceneu, a kinsman of Aeðilfrith's contemporary Guallauc.[33]

This man's late pedigree calls him 'the Plough' (*Liu*), a nickname with obvious military connotations. His family maintained the particular interest of the North British chronicle underlying *Annales Cambriae* and *Historia Brittonum* for two or three generations prior to the famous Catguollaun. It is also interesting that the father of *Cathluan* the Pict in the later Gaelic texts is sometimes called *Gub* (= Guitcun?). But there is no really decisive evidence. What may tip the balance of probabilities away from Catman's son is that a 'rebellion' in Gwynedd would come out of nowhere, whereas a rebellion in Elmet would fit seamlessly into Northumbrian history, which in the previous fifty years includes other episodes of Anglo-British conflict in which Britons managed to get the upper hand.

Both Adomnán and Bede wrote about Oswald long after his lifetime, in the full knowledge that a cult had grown up around him which regarded the king as a martyr and saint. When Bede calls him *rex Christianissimus*, it is because Oswald's revealed sanctity required that he be 'most Christian' in life. As Bede himself put it, 'his great faith in God and his devotion of heart were made clear after his death by certain miracles'.[34] Oswald is said to have set up a cross outside Hexham to mark his victory, about which stories were later told that bear only a passing resemblance to the king's own story about St Columba. This cross formed a focus of Oswald's later cult, and the influential church that grew up at Hexham took considerable advantage of its Oswald associations.

Whether or not Aeðilfrith's son in fact lived an exemplary Christian life is an unanswerable question. There is as much of the 'usable past' about Bede's treatment of Oswald's story in his History as there is about the treatment of Áedán in *Vita Columbae*. It is necessary to handle it with similar caution. For example, Irish chronicles record *c.* 639 'an alliance (*congregatio*) of Saxons against Oswald', and Bede's failure to mention

---

[33] Harl. MS 3859, §§ 9, 11, 19; Woolf, 'Caedualla *Rex Brettonum*', 21–2; Innes, *Scotland in the Middle Ages*, 102.
[34] Bede, *Hist. eccl.*, iii.9.

such convulsions is not good evidence that they did not happen.[35] It seems instead that Catguollaun was only the first of the men whom Oswald had to defeat in securing his grip on the Bernician kingship and establishing his paramountcy over his Deiran neighbours beyond the Tees. The *congregatio* may relate to the latter process.

As the dust was settling after his triumphant homecoming, Oswald proceeded in the kingship strong in the belief that his adoption of Christianity, probably in the Kintyre household of Eochaid Buide, had played a key role in maintaining his security as an exile and ensuring his ultimate return to his country. Thanksgiving was surely one of Oswald's motives in inviting Ségéne to provide him with a bishop to help him in the establishment of a Church.

'Up to that time', wrote Adomnán, 'all that part of *Saxonia* was shadowed by the darkness of heathenism and ignorance'. In fact, Bede knew that missionaries based at York in Deira had been working among the Bernicians for years prior to Oswald's victory at Hexham. At Yeavering, for example, Paulinus of York is said to have conducted mass baptisms in the River Glen over the course of six weeks.[36] Bede's attempt to acknowledge this bishop's achievement, as described in some of his sources, without compromising that of Oswald and the missionaries from Iona described in others, involved him in accusing the Bernicians (and the Deirans) of apostasy under the conquering Catguollaun. Yet the British king was himself a Christian, a fact which Bede tried to gloss over.

Oswald donated the tidal island of Medcaut, once apparently besieged by Urbgen, for the establishment of Lindisfarne, a new daughter house of Iona, in 634.[37] Other foundations followed in the Bernician heartland which are thought to date to the early years of the new mission. Thirty kilometres up the coast from Medcaut at St Abbs, the monastery of Coludaesburg was founded at 'the stronghold of Coludae', an obscure individual whose descendants gave their name to nearby Coldingham. The close connections between this monastery and the royal dynasty are clear: it became the destination of Bernician royal women in the second half of the seventh century.

The fortifications seem to have consisted of a double palisade before banks were dug to enclose the monastery. Double-palisading, a feature of the Early Historic enclosure works of both the Gododdin and the

---

[35] *AT* 635.2; *Ann. Clon.* 634.7.

[36] Bede, *Hist. eccl.*, ii.14.

[37] Bede, *Hist. eccl.*, iii.1–3. The Gaels appear to have known both the island and the monastery by a reflex of its old British name, *inis Medcaut* (*Hist. Brit.*, §§ 63, 65; *AU* 632.4; *AT* 632.3; *CS* 632.2).

Bernicians, had also been practised in the pre-Roman Iron Age in what became Uotadinian territory.[38] According to his surviving pedigree, Morcant, Urbgen's murderer at Medcaut, was the father of a certain Coledauc.[39] Was he the 'Coludae' of Coludaesburg and the donor of the site for the foundation of a monastery?

Fifty kilometres upriver from the mouth of the Tweed, just downriver from the old Roman fort of Trimontium at Newstead, the monastery of Melrose (*Mailros*) was founded at Old Melrose. This monastery bore a British name, and may have been a North British foundation pre-dating the Lindisfarne mission. There were Christians setting up inscribed stones only thirty kilometres further upstream in the sixth century. It was at Melrose that Cuthbert, the future saint, became a monk in the 650s.

The new mission was charged by Abbot Ségéne to Aidan (or Áedán), a bishop who set about the task of organising a new missionary Church. The job presumably involved assuming authority over any existing British churches, as well as churches founded by the York mission in the previous decade, in addition to establishing new ones. Bede's presentation of Aidan's episcopate makes him an exemplary bishop who was assiduous in his preaching, cared for the poor, admonished kings, built many churches and monasteries, redeemed slaves and recruited English children to be educated as clerics. He was also, at the same time, an exemplary monk like all bishops admired by Bede, whose abstinence, self-control, rejection of material wealth and studious habits were a model 'in great contrast to our modern slothfulness'.[40] Bede wrote his History towards the end of his life, when he was anxious about the state of the Northumbrian Church. He expressed this anxiety in his letter to Ecgberct of York. The correlations between his instructions to that bishop and his presentation of Aidan of Lindisfarne are striking. Such explicit use of the first Columban bishop of the Northumbrians as a foil for monks and bishops of his own time thus looks like yet more pseudo-history.

THE MOST CHRISTIAN KING: OSWALD SON OF AEÐILFRITH

As an exile among the Corcu Réti, Oswald had probably fought alongside Eochaid Buide, and possibly alongside Connad Cerr also. Did he fight at

---

[38] Alcock, *Kings and Warriors*, 183; Harding, *The Iron Age in Northern Britain*, 41.

[39] Harl. MS 3859, § 10. See also Bromwich, *Trioedd*, 466–7.

[40] Bede, *Hist. eccl.*, iii.3, iii.5. For discussion see, for example, Coates, 'The Role of Bishops', 179–82.

Ard Corand and Fid Euin? Now he was a great hegemon in his own right, far surpassing the power of his former hosts, even if our sources exaggerate his influence. The main thrust of Bernician expansion during the reign of his father Aeðilfrith seems to have been into Gododdin, across the Pennines and into Deiran Yorkshire. Afterwards Aeðilfrith's victorious rival Edwini seems to have built up a wide hegemony across much of southern Britain, which Oswald subsequently dominated in turn.

If Bede is to be believed, the Bernician, unlike Edwini, also subjugated Pictish and Gaelic districts. Of this we have precious little other evidence. In the same chapter in which he makes this claim, Bede also alleges that Oswald united the Bernicians and the Deirans into a single people. This we know from Stephen's *Vita Wilfrithi*, completed *c.* 716, to be spurious. The union was instead the achievement of Oswald's brother and successor Oswy (and Oswy's sons in turn), kings who also extended their paramountcy into Pictland and Argyll. The claim that Oswald ruled over Picts and Gaels, like the one that he united Northumbria may, therefore, represent historicising by later writers. The effect may have been to transform the reign of the saintly Oswald into a kind of template, embodying all that was expected of a good Northumbrian king.

If, on the other hand, there is something to Bede's, and indeed Adomnán's estimation of Oswald's power, the conventional attribution to him of a recorded siege of Edinburgh (*Eten*) in 640 may be justified.[41] There is certainly a sequence of annals relating to Northumbrian affairs in the Irish chronicles in these years. Archaeology has yet to establish conclusively Early Historic occupation on then Castle Rock at Edinburgh, allowing for the possibility that the stronghold of Din Etin stood elsewhere, perhaps on Arthur's Seat or Calton Hill. The siege probably marks at least the first stage in the final expansion of Bernician sovereignty into Etin, seemingly a district encompassing the coastlands of Mid- and West Lothian. That district was in Bernician hands by 655, when Oswy became holed up at the elusive stronghold of Iudeu, conventionally but very problematically identified as Stirling. The place is most likely to have been located in or around West Lothian, at a site allowing for the Firth of Forth to be called the 'sea of Iudeu' (*merin Iodeo*).[42] Whatever now remained of the sovereignty of Gododdin is unlikely to

[41] *AU* 638.1; *AT* 638.1; *CS* 638.1. For discussion see Jackson, 'Edinburgh', 35–42; Koch, *Gododdin*, lii.

[42] *Hist. Brit.*, §§ 64–5. The case for believing that *Iudeu* stood upon the Castle Rock at Stirling was put forward by Graham, 'Giudi'; it was reiterated by Jackson, 'Bede's *Urbs Giudi*'. Fraser, 'Bede', offers a critique.

have persisted much later than the fall of the strongholds at Edinburgh and Iudeu.

Expansion of Bernician suzerainty in Lothian in this period may have sought in part to control the preferred route-way between Iona and Lindisfarne. The Aeðilfrithing kings may also have sought more direct access to Frankish luxury tablewares, which in this period were being imported via the Irish Sea and redistributed by western potentates. The elites of Argyll and the Irish Sea basin imported wine, dyes, spices and fine wares directly from Aquitaine in south-west Francia, which were superseding Mediterranean goods on the tables of potentates in northern Britain. The main evidence consists of fragments of glass and pottery, and in particular a distinctive type of ceramic known as 'E-ware', recovered through archaeological excavation. The principal exports exchanged for these goods were probably precious metals and furs. Hunting dogs bred in northern Britain – well evidenced on Pictish monumental sculpture – were prized both by the Romans and by medieval Europeans.[43]

This shift in elite fashions and the prestige economy probably had political ramifications in the form of adjustment of power balances. The kings of the Corcu Réti may have controlled access to Frankish goods in much of northern Britain, their influence felt throughout a network of exchange reaching into the eastern lowlands. Yet E-ware may also have reached the lowlands through ports in Clydesdale, bringing prestige and power to the kings of Alt Clut, whose kingdom may have extended into Strathearn. The integrity of that kingdom may now have been threatened by Bernician expansion into Etin. There was, in addition, an east-coast exchange network through which glass vessels could have reached northern Britain via northern Francia.[44]

Domnall Brecc was apparently toppled from paramountcy by his Cowal rival soon after the battle of Moira in 639, the same year that Oswald fought his attested Saxon war. Having presumably already extended his protection to Iona, Oswald may c. 640 have done the same to Cenél nGabráin in Kintyre, possibly in exchange for tribute. The hypothesis would explain Iona's high estimation of the Bernician's power as voiced by Adomnán. Further circumstantial evidence in its favour arises from the subsequent reign of Oswy.

The payment of tribute in seventh-century northern Britain probably consisted in the main of a sum of cattle, or perhaps other livestock.

---

[43] Campbell, *Saints and Sea-Kings*, 45–7; Alcock, *Kings and Warriors*, 90–1, 416.
[44] Lowe, *Angels, Fools and Tyrants*, 18; Alcock, *Kings and Warriors*, 401.

Urbgen's poet celebrated his having taken 160 cattle as plunder from Manau. Tribute payments in cattle were probably a fraction of whatever a king expected to be able to take for himself in this direct way. The symbolic association between cattle taken in tribute and those taken as plunder would have made the necessary point that he who paid tribute was playing the role of a vanquished foe.[45]

The great double-palisaded enclosure at the Bernician royal centre at Yeavering, some three-quarters of a hectare in area, may have been a corral for animals taken on the hoof in tribute. Just downriver was Milfield, probably the royal centre of Maelmin. Here a similar enclosure has been detected by aerial photography, but the area within it is vast at ten hectares – larger by a factor of ten than enclosures at Yeavering and Sprouston. The expansion of Bernician hegemony continued into the middle third of the seventh century, and Oswy was taking tribute on the hoof not just from Argyll, but also from southern Pictland and British districts to the west. Was it at Milfield, some twenty-five kilometres inland from Bamburgh, that these great droves of cattle were collected, counted and evaluated?[46]

Bernician movements westward in Oswald's time may have contributed to another interlinkage. The dynasties of Cowal and Clyde Rock seem to have forged some kind of accommodation in the middle decades of the seventh century which had important political ramifications a generation later.[47] The relationship may have fortified Alt Clut against Aeðilfrithing pressure, while fortifying Ferchar of Cowal in his dealings with Cenél nGabráin. Domnall Brecc was killed in December 643 fighting Eugein son of Beli, a British king, in Strathcarron in the heart of the Forth–Clyde corridor.[48] It is one of the pieces of evidence pointing in the direction of collusion between Clyde Rock and Cowal. A grandson of Neithon son of Guipno, Eugein could be seen as settling a long-standing score, killing a grandson of Áedán, one-time hammer of the Miathi. In fact, it is worth pointing out that Eugein's association with Clyde Rock is inferred by scholars, and not explicit in any source. Did he rule in the same Miathian kingdom we have envisioned above stretching from Clyde Rock to Abernethy?

Eugein's victory, in addition to settling any family grudges, also rid Ferchar of his feckless main rival in southern Argyll. Domnall, coming

---

[45] 'Taliesin', *Ar vn blyned*, ll. 8–9. See Charles-Edwards, 'Early Medieval Kingships', 30–1.
[46] Lowe, *Angels, Fools and Tyrants*, 30; Alcock, *Kings and Warriors*, 255–6.
[47] Fraser, 'Strangers on the Clyde', 103–11.
[48] *AU* 642.1; *AT* 642.2; *CS* 642.1; *AI* 643.1; *Ann. Clon.* 681.1.

'from Kintyre', may have launched this expedition hoping to undermine Cenél Comgaill power by harrying their British backers.[49] Resentment that such support existed might have increased Cumméne's sense that Ferchar was an *extraneus*. Yet the situation may have been more complex. By the winter of 643 Oswald had been dead for over a year, slain in battle in August 642. It seems that he had been campaigning in Etin two years before at the margins of Eugein's kingdom. His death thus lifted pressure from Alt Clut, and, given all that we have seen, there is every likelihood that Domnall attacked in 643 as a pre-emptive strike, fearing what Eugein and Ferchar might do to Kintyre without the threat of the Bernician superpower to daunt them.

---

[49] *Gveleys y dull o Bentir a doyn*, ll. 966, 972; Clancy, *Triumph Tree*, 114 (trans.).

CHAPTER 7

Emperor of All Britain: Oswy and his Hegemony (642–70)

Oswy son of Aeðilfrith became king of the Bernician superpower after his brother Oswald was slain by the forces of the pagan Mercian king Penda on 5 August 642, at a place conventionally identified as Oswestry in Shropshire.[1] Like his brother, Oswy was thirty when the kingship passed to him. Unlike Oswald, he held it for more than twenty-seven years, dying peacefully at the age of just fifty-eight in February 670. Both the length of his reign and the non-violence of his death are remarkable for a seventh-century king of the Northumbrian English.

In fact Oswy, little known today, was one of the most successful kings in all of British history. It seems to have been he, and not his brother as Bede later wrote, who brought the four *nationes* of Britain under his sway in any meaningful sense. It was also he who established the Aeðilfrithing dynasty as permanent overlords of the Deirans, paving the way for the union of the *regnum Nordanhymbrorum*, the superpower kingdom of the Northumbrians. He must have been a man of great energy. His secret weapon was probably shrewdness in measures denied to Domnall Brecc of Kintyre or even his renowned brother. In addition to maintaining a successful military record, Oswy presided personally over the establishment of a single Northumbrian Church, and its reformation by the apostolicist model of ecclesiastical authority. Moreover, at the peak of his powers he overthrew Penda, the great villain of Bede's *Historia ecclesiastica*, avenging Oswald and christianising the pagan Mercians of the Midlands of England at the point of his bloody sword, an achievement that Bede surely hoped would be honoured by the superpower Mercian kings of his own day.

---

[1] Bede, *Hist. eccl.*, iii.9; *Hist. Brit.*, § 65; *AU* 639.3; *AT* 639.3; *Ann. Camb.* (Faral) 644.1.

It is a puzzle, then, that Oswy's success story was related in an equivo-cal manner by Bede. Whereas he twice characterised Oswald as *Christianissimus*, 'most Christian', the best superlative he could summon up for Oswy was *laboriosissimus*. Such a reference to 'hard work' was no com-pliment! Bede's Oswald is a paragon of virtue; Oswy is depicted warts and all. The reasons are probably many and varied. A desire to have Oswy pale in comparison to the martyr-saint Oswald, culted soon after his death, could be a factor. There had clearly been great tension too between Oswy and Wilfrid of York, whose committed partisans included Stephen his hagiog-rapher, and Acca, the bishop of Hexham who commissioned Stephen's work. They did not include Bede as such, but he worked in a monastery within Acca's see and was eager to please the controversial old bishop.

Another factor is that Bede finished writing his History under a king who was not descended from Oswy nor even from Aeðilfrith, being a member of the rival Ecgwulfing dynasty. Ecgwulf, whoever he was, seems to have been Oswy's contemporary. He may even have been Oswy's kinsman as eighth-century pedigrees claim. The eighth-century kings descended from him may have encouraged a certain critical treatment of Oswy's reign in the hope that it would tarnish the Aeðilfrithings. None of these factors can have been particularly good for Oswy's enduring rep-utation in the Northumbrian kingdom he had forged. It is another instance where the historian must be wary of problems relating to 'usable pasts'. Yet Oswy's flaws give him an air of humanity in the sources which prior kings in northern Britain lack.

THE FALL OF RHEGED

Oswy was four years old when his father was killed and he and his broth-ers went into exile. It is unlikely that he was Oswald's uterine brother, a son of the Deiran princess Acha: unlike him, Oswy never claimed the Deiran kingship himself. Was he an exile among the Corcu Réti? Bede reports that he was baptised among the Gaels and spoke their language, but that merely locates his exile somewhere in Argyll or Ireland.[2] His career prior to the death of Oswald is obscure, and he may have owed his realm in no small part to Penda, who had created the vacancy at Bamburgh.

In 642 Oswy was a father, his son Alchfrith and daughter Alchfled being of marriageable age within eleven years. Their mother was probably Rieinmelth. Her name (*Raegnmaeld*) is recorded in the ninth-century

---

[2] Bede, *Hist. eccl.*, iii.25.

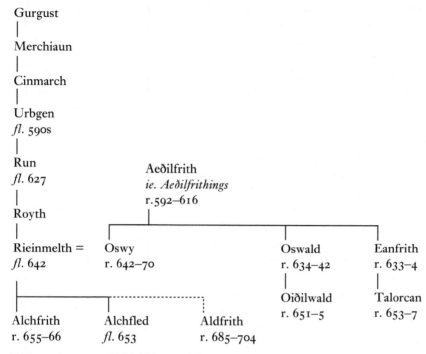

Table 7.1 Ancestry of Alchfrith son of Oswy

Liber vitae of Durham Cathedral, where it preserves names from a similar 'book of life' kept somewhere in seventh- and eighth-century Bernicia. An eighth-century Northumbrian genealogy in *Historia Brittonum* makes her Oswy's wife and queen, and says that Rieinmelth's father Royth was a grandson of the North British king Urbgen.[3] The possibility that Oswald's enemy Catguollaun was a scion of Guallauc's House of Ceneu has been mentioned. Clearly Urbgen's House of Gurgust also maintained a high political profile in greater Northumbria into the middle decades of the seventh century.

Penda's great hegemony of the same decades consisted of something of a hotchpotch of Anglo-Saxon and British polities. In 655 he faced Oswy in battle with the support of a substantial number of British potentates.[4] Oswy's connections by marriage with Rieinmelth's family may,

---

[3] *Hist. Brit.*, §§ 57, 63; see also Bede, *Hist. eccl.*, ii.14. On the date of the genealogical material, see Jackson, 'Northern British Section in Nennius', 22–7. On the name *Rieinmelth*, see Jackson, above, 41–2.

[4] *Hist. Brit.*, §§ 64–5.

therefore, have appealed to the great Mercian king while he was eyeing up potential successors to Oswald. Certainly Penda maintained a watchful eye over Northumbrian affairs in the aftermath of his decisive victory in 642.

Rieinmelth's grandfather Run son of Urbgen is said in *Historia Brittonum* to have been present at the baptism of Edwini in 627. Bede says nothing about Run: official doctrine maintained that the Britons made no effort to christianise the Anglo-Saxons, and also that British involvement tainted baptisms with the stain of unorthodoxy. That Edwini and Oswy cultivated links with the House of Gurgust is an indication that the poetry addressed to Urbgen need not greatly exaggerate his wide-ranging power and influence.

Possibly descent from Run and Urbgen were the bases upon which Oswy's son Alchfrith constructed his claim to Deira, where he became king in 655. By then, Edwini's realm had surely subdued or incorporated those ruled by the Houses of Ceneu and Gurgust, but Guallauc and Urbgen may, conversely, have dominated the Deirans in their time. Another possibility is that Rieinmelth's unknown mother was a woman of Deiran royal blood. In that event, Alchfrith would have been able to claim Deiran royal descent through a grandmother, as his predecessor Oiðilwald son of Oswald had done.

Vita Wilfrithi implies that, towards the end of his reign, Oswy annexed extensive British territories at least as far as the Ribble in Lancashire. Rochdale lies just over thirty kilometres further south of the Ribchester crossing of the Ribble. Oswy's conquests have accordingly been associated with the fall of Rheged, or at least the dispossession of its leading kindreds.[5] Alchfrith died or disappeared from Deira around 666, after he attacked his father,[6] and Oswegian campaigning in West Yorkshire and Lancashire in the late 660s would be consistent with punitive attacks on his son's British kin and their allies. Did they support Alchfrith against Oswy? If Oswy's son Aldfrith was another a son of Rieinmelth, which is far from certain, the 660s might mark his movement into monastic obscurity, whence he would return some twenty years later.

As they had nine years before – when the forces of Penda and Catguollaun slew Edwini – Bernicia and Deira were restored in 642 to their respective native royal dynasties. In Deira Oswini son of Osric, whose father had been killed by Catguollaun, took up the kingship. This settlement may have been sealed by marriage. Sometime before 645 Oswy

---

[5] Smyth, *Warlords*, 24–6.
[6] Bede, *Hist. eccl.*, iii.4.

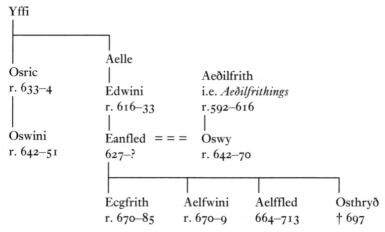

Table 7.2 Ancestry of Ecgfrith son of Oswy

married Oswini's kinswoman Eanfled, Edwini's daughter. At the same time, the Bernician king may have given a kinswoman in marriage to Oswini, whose marital situation we do not know. Irish chronicles record war between Oswy and British foes in 643.[7] Was bad blood stirred up by a repudiation of Rieinmelth for political reasons? Was the battle fought by Domnall Brecc of Kintyre and Eugein of Alt Clut, in December of that year, one theatre of Oswy's British war? Answers to such questions elude us.

THE FALL OF DEIRA

Having become established in Deira, Oswini seems to have made no attempt to restore the church at York to its former status as an episcopal seat. Paulinus, its missionary founder in the days of Edwini, died in exile in 644 having never returned. Instead, Bede maintains, the king culti-vated a close relationship with Bishop Aidan at Lindisfarne in Oswy's kingdom.[8] Despite the fall of Oswald and the restoration of Deiran sov-ereignty, it seems that Oswy continued to have 'many more allies' (*plures auxiliarii*) than his Deiran neighbour.[9] These *auxiliarii* may have included the king of Rheged, whose realm lay to the west of Deira proper. Oswini probably had no wish to antagonise Oswy, and every reason to court the

[7] *AU* 642.4; *AT* 642.4; *Ann. Clon.* 642.2.
[8] Bede, *Hist. eccl.*, iii.9; iii.14.
[9] Bede, *Hist. eccl.*, iii.14.

favour of his bishop if Aidan was disposed to discourage his king from aggression.

Yet at York, where parts of Roman Eboracum remained standing, the memory of Paulinus the metropolitan bishop was apparently retained, along with the rationale that had given rise to that status in the 620s, when Pope Honorius sent a pallium (the mantle of a metropolitan bishop) to York. This gesture had been in accordance with a plan for the ecclesiastical organisation of Britain enunciated by Pope Gregory the Great. That author of the mission to christianise the Anglo-Saxons in the 590s had written to Augustine, its leader at Canterbury, that 'to the city of York we wish you to send a bishop whom you shall decide to consecrate', once the mission had become established in the north. Such a bishop would then, according to the pope's plan, 'consecrate twelve bishops and enjoy honourable metropolitan rank'.[10] It was probably Paulinus's close relationship with Edwini, Aeðilfrith's enemy, that resulted in his exile during the reign of Oswald. Bede blames Catguollaun instead.

Eclipsed by the new Ionan daughter house at Lindisfarne, and deprived of its bishop, York was not forsaken by Paulinus's clergy. Neither were these men ever, so far as can be determined, brought fully enough under Aidan's jurisdiction to adopt his traditionalist practices regarding Easter and other matters, in preference to the apostolicist standard.[11] The conventional Lindisfarne-focused narrative for the period prior to 664 cannot quite obscure this continuity in the Deiran Church. Oswini's attitude towards Lindisfarne, however politic, was probably a disappointment at York. Did he take measures to mollify that church that are lost to history? If not, York's perspective on Oswini's grim ultimate fate may not have differed much from Iona's rationalisation of the fall of Domnall Brecc as divine punishment for spurning his proper ecclesiastical patrons.

No doubt Oswy was conscious throughout the 640s of the hegemonies established by his brother and father before him, *imperia* which had included Deira. Bede relates that he 'could not live at peace' with Oswini, despite the Deiran king's friendship with Lindisfarne. The result was apparently two years of strife before, in 651, Oswini was murdered, having been turned over to Oswy by a treacherous Deiran potentate after refusing battle. The episode took place at Gilling in the Yorkshire Gap near the Deiro-Bernician border, and left a mark on Oswy's reputation,

---

[10]   Hartmann, ed., *Gregorii I Papae Reg. Epist.*, xi.39; Bede, *Hist. eccl.*, i.29.
[11]   Bede, *Hist. eccl.*, ii.20; iii.25.

elevating Oswini to something like the status of a martyr.[12] Oswy's savvy queen Eanfled, whose marriage to him had probably been arranged by Oswini, is said by Bede to have pressed her husband successfully to make a public act of penance at Gilling through the establishment of a monastery there.

His public contrition notwithstanding, Oswy now contrived to place his nephew Oiðilwald, Oswald's son, in the kingship of the Deirans. Unless he was a child of Oswald's Gaelic exile, Oiðilwald cannot have been older than about sixteen in 651. Yet there is no positive evidence that Oswald enjoyed the support of Gaelic allies by marriage.[13] Had he, like Oswy, married a British princess? In any event, it seems likely that Oiðilwald's claim to Deira passed through his grandmother Acha, Edwini's sister and Eanfled's aunt. As already noted, one suspects that Oswy would have claimed the kingdom himself in 651 had he been Acha's son as is often assumed.

The new monastery at Gilling had Trumhere, a kinsman of Oswini and Eanfled, as its first abbot. If we could be sure that this scion of the Deiran royal house only now took the tonsure (the clerical haircut), it would hint at how the way was cleared for Oswy's nephew to emerge as the top candidate for the Deiran kingship. Trumhere may not have been the only dynast to cut his hair when the king of the Bernicians strode south of the Tees in 651.

Oswy's grip on Deira may have been looser than he had hoped. If he expected Oiðilwald to act as a dutiful nephew, he was to be disappointed. Oswald's son turned out for Penda against him four years later at Maes Gai: or maybe it was the other way round. Oiðilwald is described by Bede as actually 'leading the enemies of his own uncle and of his native land' on that occasion.[14] Moreover, there is nothing to suggest that Oiðilwald cultivated anything like the relationship with Finán of Lindisfarne that Oswini had maintained with his predecessor Aidan. That strategy had done Oswini little good in the end. Oiðilwald may instead have taken a lead, in both his ecclesiastical and his political policies, from the separatist inclinations of York.

---

[12] Bede, *Hist. eccl.*, iii.14. Unsurprisingly, Bede maintains that Oswy had 'far greater resources' than Oswini in this fateful confrontation between them.

[13] Ziegler, 'The Politics of Exile', explores some possibilities.

[14] Bede, *Hist. eccl.*, iii.24. Bede says that Oiðilwald 'ought to have helped them [Oswy and Alchfrith]' at *Campus Gai*, and unless this is an allusion only to Oiðilwald's kinship obligations, it would seem to refer to his subject status. On the rebellion of Oiðilwald see also Kirby, 'Northumbria in the Time of Wilfrid', 19 and Abels, 'The Council of Whitby', 7.

Preserving the close relationship of their predecessors, Oswy and Finán were together extending their power and influence far afield in this period. Lindisfarne's missionary work among the East Saxons presupposes that their kingdom, which marched with the Thames, had come within reach of Oswy's hegemony by the 650s. In 653, a year after the death of Ségéne of Iona, whose missionaries had established Lindisfarne, Oswy gave his daughter by Rieinmelth, Alchfled, in marriage to Peada son of Penda.[15] Peada's kingdom of the Middle Angles lay between the Humber and Essex. Penda gave his own daughter Cyneburg in marriage to Oswy's son Alchfrith. These interlinking marriages imply that the mighty Mercian hegemon was acknowledging that Oswy's *imperium* had grown to rival his own superpower after the fall of Oswini.

OSWY AND THE GAEL

A year or so before the murder at Gilling, the Cenél nGabráin dynast Conall Crandamnae, brother of the hapless Domnall Brecc, secured the kingship of the Corcu Réti after the death of the Cenél Comgaill king Ferchar son of Connad.[16] It seems that Ferchar had held Kintyre in subjection, probably since 639. There is no evidence that the Cowal king engaged in Cruithnian politics during his reign. Such silence may relate more to Ionan inattention than real inactivity, but, after the blood spilled at Fid Euin in 631 and at Moira in 639, the kings of the Corcu Réti may have retained few interests in north-east Ireland.

During Ferchar's reign the Uí Chóelbad king Scandal, kinsman of Congal One-eye, was dominating the Cruithni. He appears to have expanded his interests at the expense of Corcu Réti Antrim, even stripping lands and status from the episcopal church at Armoy.[17] Mag nEilni west of the Bush was probably well and truly in the hands of the Uí Chóelbad by 650, if its status had indeed been a prior point of dispute with the Corcu Réti as argued above. The record derived from Iona's seventh-century chronicle has little to say about Cruithnian affairs after the battle of Moira, even after the return to prominence of the descendants of Áedán. Had Corcu Réti interests in Antrim become completely suppressed? The situation is as likely to reflect the passage of Antrim

[15] *AU* 652.1; *AT* 652.1; *CS* 652.1; *AI* 652.1; *Ann. Clon.* 649.1; Bede, *Hist. eccl.*, iii.21.
[16] *AU* 694.5 = *AU* 650 on the basis of misdating of Domnall Brecc's death at *AU* 686.2; *cf.* Anderson, *Early Sources*, vol. 1, 167–8, 170; Anderson, *Kings and Kingship*, 30–1.
[17] Charles-Edwards, *Early Christian Ireland*, 59–61.

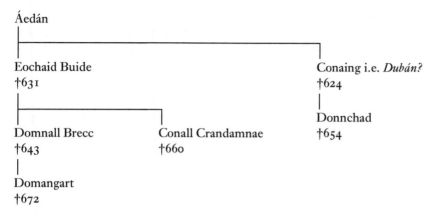

Table 7.3 Kings of Cenél nGabráin (643–72)

interests into other Corcu Réti hands than those of the Cenél nGabráin kings in Kintyre, ever the focus of Iona's interest among the Argyll Gaels.

It has been suggested above that Oswald took Kintyre under his protection after Ferchar's subjugation of Domnall *c.* 639, having previously done the same with Iona after the establishment of Lindisfarne. On that basis, it has also been suggested that Domnall fell in a pre-emptive attack on Alt Clut, fearing an attack after Oswald's death. Part of the reasoning leading to these conclusions was our foreknowledge that the 'subjected' Cenél nGabráin restored its grip on the Corcu Réti realm in 650, even as Oswy, friend of Iona, was reaching the zenith of his power. In fact, Cenél nGabráin suspiciously maintained its paramount position throughout the remainder of Oswy's reign.

Conall Crandamnae died in 659 or 660.[18] One version of the Dalriadan king-list names Donnchad son of Dubán as his colleague, whereas others name him as successor. There is no sign of anyone of this name in other sources. On record instead is Conall's cousin Donnchad, like him a grandson of Áedán, killed in 654 when an invasion of Stirlingshire came to grief in Strathyre (*Sráith Ethairt*) in the Highlands near Balquhidder.[19] *Dubán*, 'little dark one', looks like a nickname. Does it refer to Donnchad's father Conaing? If so, the chronicles would confirm that Donnchad had ruled jointly with Conall until he was slain.[20] We shall see that Donnchad's descendants certainly claimed the kingship successfully in and after Adomnán's time, lending force to such a reconstruction.

[18] *AU* 660.3; *AT* 660.4; *CS* 660.6; *AI* 659.1; *Ann. Clon.* 656.3.
[19] *AU* 654.5; *AT* 654.4; *CS* 654.4; Watson, *Scottish Place-Name Papers*, 91.
[20] Anderson, *Early Sources*, vol. 1, 177; Anderson, *Kings and Kingship*, 155–6; Fraser, 'The Iona Chronicle', 82–4.

Thus, Conall appears to have been succeeded directly in 660 by his nephew Domangart, a son of Domnall Brecc. Domangart's succession marks the first time on record, stretching back to Columba's time a century before, that kings of Kintyre held the Corcu Réti kingship successively. Was Oswy's influence as the mightiest king in Britain by 660 a key factor in this remarkable development? The possibility must be admitted that, as with the reign of Domangart's grandfather Eochaid Buide, the king-list reflects Cenél nGabráin partisanship on the part of its compilers. Domangart's reign lasted until he was killed in 672, two years after the death of Oswy.[21] Bede makes explicit reference to the tribute that Oswy took from the Argyll Gaels. If our sources can be trusted about stable Cenél nGabráin paramountcy during his reign, the good fortune of the Kintyre kings probably reflects the shadow Oswy cast over a realm whose kings shared his high estimation of Iona.

OSWY AND THE SOUTHERN PICTS

The victory in Stirlingshire over Donnchad of Kintyre in 654 was secured by Talorcan son of 'Anfrith', seemingly a son of Oswy's half-brother Eanfrith.[22] Talorcan had become established as a powerful Pictish king in 653, probably in the southern Pictish zone. We shall see reason to believe that his predecessors in the Pictish king-list, three sons of Vuid (or Wid) whom the list gives successive reigns from 631 until 653, were southern kings too.[23]

The anonymous *Vita sancti Cuthberti*, a Life of St Cuthbert penned *c.* 700, provides a clue that Northumbrian power in Pictland in Oswy's time may have been based in Fife, and so Talorcan's realm may also have lain there. It mentions *Niuduera regio*, a Pictish district visited by the saint.[24] The name is reminiscent of *Cantuara*, the ethnonym of the Anglo-Saxons of Kent, derived from the ethnonym *Cantii* borne by the Romano-British population of Kent. *Niud-*, linked with Newburn in Largo, probably preserves a native ethnonym borne by a Pictish people of

[21] *AU* 673.2; *AT* 673.2; *CS* 673.1; *Ann. Clon.* 669.2.
[22] *AU* 657.3; *AT* 657.4 for Talorcan's obit. He appears as *Talorce filius Enfret* in the Pictish king-list, Anderson, *Kings and Kingship*, 248. For an analysis of the circumstances surrounding his birth, see Miller, 'Eanfrith's Pictish Son'.
[23] *AU* 635.6, 641.2, 653.1; *AT* 641.2, 653.2; *CS* 641.1; *Ann. Clon.* 649.5; Anderson, *Kings and Kingship*, 248. Skene, *Celtic Scotland*, vol. 1, 246–7, wrongly places Gartnait in a battle in 635.
[24] *V. s. Cuthberti anon.*, ii.4; Bede, *V. s. Cuthberti*, § 11.

East Fife.[25] The Niuduari themselves, on the other hand, may have been Bernician settlers, like the Anglo-Saxon Cantuari. We have seen that Oswald may have been knocking at the doors of Manau as early as 640.

Bede speaks of Pictish tribute taken by Oswy. Is it a coincidence that one of his nephews (who may only have been a few years his junior) was becoming dominant in southern Pictland, even as another, Oiðilwald, was becoming established as king of the Deirans? It may be regarded instead as symptomatic of Oswy's imperial technique in districts adjacent to Bernicia. Its applicability in Deira demonstrates that there is no implication of matriliny in the Pictish example of this technique.

We know very little else about how Oswy managed to establish his remarkable *imperium*, not least among the Britons of the Pennines and the Cumberland and Lancashire coasts, several of whose districts were given over to English ecclesiastical possession shortly after Oswy's death.[26] His conquests here revolved around extensive and probably repeated harrying, and his subjugation of Deiran and southern Pictish districts was probably not bloodless. Repeated campaigns of devastation forced kings either to give face-saving battle – as with Oswini's abortive attempt in 651 – or to pay humiliating cattle-tribute in return for peace. It had probably been much the same for Argentocoxos in the Roman Iron Age.

Guret, the king of Clyde Rock who died in 657, is the earliest *rex Alo Cluaithe* on record whose title cannot have been applied retrospectively.[27] It has already been suggested that his kingdom by this date was the remaining rump of a larger Miathian realm which had included Manau and Strathearn prior to Oswald's reign. The surviving evidence does not explicitly attach Guret with the Houses of either Clinoch or Guipno. Instead, he seems to be 'Gwryat son of Guryan in the north' (*Gwryat vab Gvryan yn y Gogled*), one of the three men named in the Welsh 'triad' *Tri brenhin a vaunt o veibion eillion*, 'Three Kings Who Were Villein's Sons'.[28] Was Guret too Oswy's subject (*aillt*) and somehow dependent on him for his position at Clyde Rock?

In an incident that Bede dates to 655, *Historia ecclesiastica* says that Oswy offered to turn over to Penda, who had invaded Northumbria, 'an incalculable and incredible store of royal treasures and gifts as the price of peace'. According to *Historia Brittonum*, he made this offer because he

[25] Duncan, *Scotland*, 78.
[26] Stephen, *V. s. Wilfrithi*, § 17; for discussion see Smyth, *Warlords*, 24–5; Koch, *Gododdin*, cxvi–cxviii.
[27] *AU* 658.2.
[28] *Trioedd*, § 68.

had been cornered at Iudeu in the midst of the Firth of Forth, probably in or opposite West Lothian.[29] Penda's campaign thus coincided with an Oswegian sojourn in the north of his dominions, apparently aided by Deiran failure to offer much resistance. In an intriguing parallel, it seems as though Oswald too was campaigning in the Forth basin just prior to his final war with Penda. Bede goes on to say that Penda refused Oswy's 'price of peace', for only battle would satisfy him.

Historia Brittonum offers different details from its British perspective. According to the anonymous historian, Oswy 'gave back' all the riches with him at Iudeu, and Penda distributed them among his British allies. Oswy may have been in the process of taking tribute from North British and southern Pictish subjects when he was assailed at Iudeu – including subjects in Manau – and forced to restore it to them with Penda's involvement. Did Penda have North British allies? Was Oswald's attack on Etin in 640 the powder-keg that brought him against Penda in 642?

EMPEROR OF ALL BRITAIN: THE BATTLE OF MAES GAI

If any king in seventh-century Britain earned Adomnán's title *imperator totius Brittanniae* it was Oswy. At the height of his power in the 650s, he held sway from the Tay to the Thames, albeit with significant gaps here and there and varying degrees of sovereignty. Across this great empire, there were probably many areas held in nominal subjection, as well as a mix of kingdoms and 'farmer republics'. Pope Vitalian's decision, in correspondence with Oswy, to establish an *archiepiscopus Britanniae insulae* in the 660s, 'archbishop of the island of Britain', is independent corroboration of the reach of the great king's arm.[30] From an Insular perspective, such an *imperium* at this date might raise eyebrows, but there were kings on the Continent whose writ ranged as wide or wider. Although it is necessary to qualify what 'union' entails in this period, it is clear that the island came closer in Oswy's time to union under a single post-Roman regime than it would come for another three centuries.

As the Iudeu episode shows, prior to 655 Penda, the steadfast enemy of the Northumbrian hegemons, remained a major stumbling block in this imperial project. Bede speaks of a devastating invasion by him a few years after 651, reaching as far as the environs of Medcaut, the island

---

[29] *Hist. Brit.*, § 64–5.
[30] Bede, *Hist. eccl.*, iv.17.

home of Lindisfarne.[31] It is probably the same campaign as the one he dates to 655, and which *Historia Brittonum* brings to the Forth. The 'restitution of Iudeu' (*atbret Iudeu*) seems to have defused the situation, but Bede hints that Penda and Oswy agreed a time and place of battle. On 15 November 655, a Sunday, the superpowers met at Maes Gai on an unidentified river called *Winwaed* by Bede, in the district of Leeds (*Loidis*), probably in the orbit of the British kingdom of Rheged. Oiðilwald of Deira is said to have joined forces with Penda. The Mercian was slain, and his army, with another large British contingent, like that which had invested Iudeu earlier in the year, was destroyed in what British sources call a massacre (*strages*).[32]

Oswy's victory was complete. Maes Gai left him master of Britain. Almost twenty years passed before the superpowers crossed swords again. This major battle is, moreover, the last known occasion in which the Northumbrians faced a major British coalition. A year after Penda's death, according to *Annales Cambriae*, Oswy 'came and took plunder', probably from the lands of Penda's British allies.[33] The 'restitution' of Iudeu may thus have been paid back with interest within a year of Oswy's humiliation on the shores of the Firth of Forth.

The fate of Oiðilwald, who according to Bede withdrew and did not fight, is not known. Bede's sources may have over-egged his complicity with Penda. Caught between Bernicia and Mercia, the young king may have sat deliberately on the fence. If so, he miscalculated. He was replaced as king of the Deirans by Oswy's son Alchfrith, who had fought alongside his father at Maes Gai. By 655 Oswy had long since become Eanfled's husband, and Rieinmelth was dead or repudiated. Alchfrith may have faced his British maternal kin at Maes Gai, but his presence at Oswy's side may alternatively represent Rheged backing.

WHITBY: AN EMPEROR TURNS TO ROME

If Oiðilwald and York had been pursuing separatist policies prior to the battle of Maes Gai, it becomes all the more striking that Oswy, in the wake of his resounding victory, gave over to the Ionan *familia* six Deiran estates (and six Bernician ones) for the establishment of monasteries.[34] That he

---

[31] Bede, *Hist. eccl.*, iii.17.
[32] Bede, *Hist. eccl.*, iii.24; *Hist., Brit.*, § 64; *AU* 656.2; *AT* 656.2; *Ann. Camb.* (Faral) 656.1, 657.1.
[33] *Ann. Camb.* (Faral) 658.1.
[34] Bede, *Hist. eccl.*, iii.24.

presumed to do such a thing in a kingdom that was not his own shows that the Bernician king now possessed considerable Deiran estates. Were these lands seized from dispossessed adherents of Oswini and Oiðilwald?

Bede made much of Oswald's maternal heritage from Edwini's family to underline his suitability to rule the Deirans. Oswy must have been conscious that his sons by Eanfled, Edwini's daughter, would be able to make similar claims when they came of age. It is unfortunate that we can say little about significant women in our period. Eanfled is a rare exception. She seems now to have been one of the few members of her family outside clerical orders. Her support may have emboldened Oswy in annexing Deira, where he even presumed by 664 to sit in judgement over the kingdom's ecclesiastical establishment. Seventy years later Bede credited Oswald with uniting Bernicia and Deira, thanks to his Bernician paternity and Deiran maternity. Eanfled's sons possessed precisely the same parental pattern. Was it in their interests, later in the seventh century, that Northumbrian pseudo-historians first conceived of Oswald as founder of the kingdom? If so, it was an ideological position that tended to obscure the historical role of Oswy in pulling the *regnum Nordanhybrorum* together.

Queen Eanfled was apparently a consummate politician. She enjoyed significant influence with Oswy, successfully convincing him to found the monastery at Gilling, perhaps in 655, in penance for the murder of her kinsman Oswini in 651. It may have been an important gesture to the Deiran establishment: Eanfled was raised in Kent and only came north in the early 640s, where she may have had little contact with Oswini.

In the eight years after Maes Gai, Eanfled again fortified herself for a public confrontation with her formidable husband. By the 660s she and Alchfrith had forged a partnership of sorts, concerned with apostolicist reform and the ecclesiastical allegiances of the increasingly coherent *regnum Nordanhymbrorum*. At first glance, this important accommodation seems unlikely. Queenly machinations in favour of their own sons are something of a theme of early medieval history. The elder of Eanfled's sons, Ecgfrith, was ten years old in 655. He ought to have made Alchfrith uneasy and uncertain, since Eanfled's support would privilege her sons in the sweepstakes for Oswy's attention and favour. The son of a former wife, Alchfrith can hardly have forgotten that he had acquired Deira simply by being a handy alternative to the rebellious Oiðilwald. He could lose his kingdom as easily. Eanfled's sons were grandsons of Edwini, and could derive much prestige from that among the Deiran nobility. Years later one of these boys was killed in battle as a young man. When he was buried at York there was great lamentation, according to *Vita Wilfrithi*, befitting a scion of the Deiran royal kindred.[35] No doubt Alchfrith's British connections provided him with a measure of particular clout denied to his half-brothers. As Ecgfrith and his brother matured, however, Rieinmelth's son was in danger of becoming yesterday's man.

It may have been York that brought Alchfrith and Eanfled together. They were united apparently by a desire for ecclesiastical reform, and the apostolicists at York certainly shared that desire. For Eanfled, this goal may have been shaped in part by the wish to remove a potential sticking point in diplomacy between Oswy and her Kentish kin.

Oswy was actively interfering in the ecclesiastical status quo in Deira after the battle of Maes Gai, giving land to monasteries and taking decisive steps towards unifying the Northumbrian kingdoms. The separatists at York were probably becoming concerned. They may even have been indignant. Their church had, for a short time, been the ecclesiastical seat of the most powerful of the Anglo-Saxon kingdoms. Twenty-five years on, Deira had dwindled, and York faced eclipse by the Ionan daughter house at Lindisfarne. After Maes Gai, the Mercians, like the East Saxons, were granted their own bishop. In contrast, the Deirans were sharing the fates of the Middle Angles and the people of Lindsey, under the authority of extraneous bishops.[36] Such status may have been galling at York, where memories were retained of metropolitan prominence in the Gregorian plan.

James, the deacon who led the community at York, had come north from Kent like the Deiran heiress Eanfled. Despite the prevailing practices of the Ionan *familia*, Eanfled retained her allegiance to the tradition in which she had been raised. She was a natural ally of York. Bede implies as much when he notes that the ecclesiastical crisis resolved at the Synod of Whitby arose after Maes Gai 'by the encouragement of those who had come from Kent or from Gaul'. Indeed, Eanfled's leading role in the apostolicist reform party which forced Oswy's hand at Whitby emerges from a letter sent to him afterwards by Pope Vitalian. The pontiff made her a gift of 'a cross with a golden key, made from the holy fetters of the apostles St Peter and St Paul', a fitting symbol of the achievement of the apostolicists.[37]

As her party gathered its strength, it required a safe haven from Oswy and Lindisfarne. For this it seems to have turned to Alchfrith. The reformers may have seen recruiting him as crucial to attracting the

---

[35] Stephen, *V. s. Wilfrithi*, § 24.
[36] Bede, *Hist. eccl.*, iii.21; iii.24. Bede maintains that Lindsey and Middle Anglia were denied their own bishops because of 'a shortage of bishops', but it is more likely that the ecclesiastical subordination of these regions was deliberate.
[37] Bede, *Hist. eccl.*, iii.25; iii.29.

attention of Oswy and forcing him into action for political reasons. Perhaps they even hoped that Alchfrith's British connections would help the movement to spread among North British churches. If one were inclined to write an historical novel surrounding these events, the temptation would be strong to cast Eanfled as an arch-manipulator, bringing Alchfrith into play with the expectation that it would ultimately result in his removal, to the benefit of her own sons. The historian is not in a position to comment.

The story of the Synod of Whitby is famous. Bishop Finán died in 661. It was his successor Colmán who confronted apostolicism at Whitby on behalf of Iona. The bishop's adversary was a young priest, Wilfrid, whom the reformers put forward as their candidate for the episcopate at York after the Synod. There is reason to believe that Wilfrid was Deiran by birth, with connections to Eanfled's royal dynasty. In an overtly symbolic act, Alchfrith had previously placed the monastery of Ripon under Wilfrid's abbacy, before he was even old enough to be made a priest. The Bernician incumbent Eata had withdrawn north of the Tees to Melrose with his monks, including the young Cuthbert, like Wilfrid destined to be culted as a saint.

Deira and the origins of St Wilfrid

According to *Vita Wilfrithi*, Wilfrid was born in 634. His family was aristocratic with royal connections, his father's houseguests included 'companions of kings', and when he left home at fourteen, he had a mounted retinue, fully armed and suitably attired to appear at the royal court.[38]

Where Stephen is explicit, Wilfrid's Northumbrian linkages before 664 are all Deiran, and it is likely that he was a native of that kingdom. In the 660s he received royal support and patronage there. After 664, he was made a bishop by the Deiran king, in 'consultation with the counsellors of the realm'. Upon leaving his father's house *c.* 648, he went to the Bernician court, but it was to the queen, the Deiran princess Eanfled, that Wilfrid was presented by the *nobiles* who had known him as a boy.[39]

Queen Eanfled placed the young Wilfrid in the service of a nobleman, but 'after a circle of years', consulting with Wilfrid's father, she sent him to her cousin Eorconberht, king of Kent. From there, 'with the blessing of his kin', Wilfrid moved on to Lyon in southern France.[40] Stephen, of course, attributes these movements to spiritual motives – a desire to

---

[38] Stephen, *V. s. Wilfrithi*, § 2.
[39] Stephen, *V. s. Wilfrithi*, § § 2–3, 7–11, 22.
[40] Stephen, *V. s. Wilfrithi*, § § 2–3.

perfect his understanding of scripture – but they so conveniently set the stage for Wilfrid's adult career that their authenticity may be doubted.

Problems of authenticity with Wilfrid's adventures in Lyon have been known to historians of the Franks for some time.[41] Even his alleged pilgrimage to Rome from Lyon need not have taken place. Stephen himself observes that Wilfrid learned 'many things from the most learned teachers' in Lyon, and was tonsured there. Moreover, his adult career shows that the Frankish Church was perhaps the strongest single influence on his thinking.[42]

Can Wilfrid's journey from Northumbria to Lyon, a 'circle of years' after c. 648, be explained in secular terms? The likelihood that he belonged to an important Deiran family may be important. In August 651, the Deiran king, Eanfled's kinsman Oswini, was murdered. When the Deiran royal dynasty had last suffered a comparable calamity (in 633–4), Eanfled and her Kentish mother had found refuge in Kent, but her brothers were sent on to Francia for their protection.[43] Is it a coincidence that Wilfrid's movements 'a cycle of years' after c. 648 (and so possibly in 651) are so similar to those of these ill-fated Deiran aeðilings in 633–4?

According to Bede, Oswy opened the Synod with words befitting a king committed to unifying the Northumbrian kingdoms, and indeed the whole island. He invited Colmán to speak. The bishop asserted that Iona regarded its practices, including its Easter calculation, as authoritative because they had been passed down from the teachings of Columba, from a tradition stretching back to the apostle John. Wilfrid responded with the apostolicist belief that the bishop of Rome and the general consensus of Christendom carried the greater authority. He quoted from the Book of Matthew Jesus's pledge to St Peter that 'I will give you the keys of the kingdom of heaven'. The Columban clergy did not dispute Matthew's testimony. Oswy accordingly decided in favour of the apostolicists.[44]

Our sources focus on questions of Easter and the tonsure. They entirely ignore Oswy's presumption to make such an important decision

---

[41] See, for example, Nelson, 'Queens as Jezebels', 65; Foley, *Images of Sanctity*, 30; Wood, *The Merovingian Kingdoms*, 201.

[42] Stephen, *V. s. Wilfrithi*, § 6; Wood, *Merovingian Kingdoms*, 252–3. On the specific potential influences of Lyon churchmen on Wilfrid, see Foley, *Images of Sanctity*, 84–5, 100, 122.

[43] Bede, *Hist. eccl.*, ii.20.

[44] Bede, *Hist. eccl.*, iii.25; Stephen, *V. s. Wilfrithi*, § 10.

on behalf of the Deirans, as well as the Bernicians, Northumbrian unity under a single ruler having become natural by the early eighth century. They gloss over as well any political elements in his decision. His conception of his future relationships with Alchfrith in Deira, with southern Anglo-Saxon churches under the sway of Canterbury and with Continental leaders can all have influenced the imperial-minded Oswy in turning his back on Iona in favour of Rome.

Our sources also skirt the important fact that Whitby saw York supplant Lindisfarne as the chief church in Oswegian Northumbria, restoring the status quo envisioned by the Gregorian plan some sixty years before. The most telling evidence that this plan was indeed placed before the Synod comes from *Vita Wilfrithi*. Here Wilfrid is called metropolitan bishop of York at his accession in 669, and a quotation from a document produced by the papal curia in 679 recognises his responsibility for a province encompassing the whole of northern Britain. Bede's reaction against it has led to this testimony being dismissed by modern scholars, but a detailed consideration of that reaction shows it to be less convincing than Stephen's case.[45] Bede's suspicious failure to explain York's restoration, or to speak of Wilfrid as *metropolitanus*, is probably to be explained with reference to his own times. Writing seventy years after the Synod, Bede knew that Theodore, archbishop of Canterbury, had successfully overturned Whitby's elevation of York to metropolitan status, and that the issue had sputtered out in subsequent years.

Having lost the debate in 664, Colmán of Lindisfarne withdrew to Iona with many monks into the embrace of Cumméne Find. Three or four years later the bishop left Iona, founding a monastery in the island of Inishbofin off the Galway and Mayo coasts of Ireland, where he remained as superior until his death in 675.[46] Cumméne, who had written *De uirtutibus sancti Columbae* in the 640s, had become abbot in 656, and now watched his great monastic confederation become stripped of its influential Bernician province.[47] To judge from his impassioned condemnation of Domnall Brecc for turning his back on the patronage and protection of St Columba, Cumméne probably had choice words for Oswy. These events probably encouraged the nostalgia about Oswald

---

[45] Fraser, 'All the Northern Part of Britain'. See also Gibbs, 'Decrees of Agatho', *passim*; Charles-Edwards, *Early Christian Ireland*, 431–2. For a counter-argument, see Brooks, the *Early History of the Church of Canterbury*, 72.

[46] *AU* 668.3, 676.1; *AT* 668.1, 676.1; *CS* 668.1, 675.1.

[47] *AU* 657.1; AT 657.2; 657.2; *Ann. Clon.* 653.3.

detectable a generation later in *Vita Columbae*. Yet it was Oswy's son Ecgfrith, and not Oswy himself, who was destined to suffer Domnall's bloody fate.

THE STRUGGLE FOR YORK

The first bishop of York after Whitby was probably a certain Tuda. When he died of plague within months, Oswy chose Ceadda (St Chad) to be consecrated as his successor.[48] There is no suggestion that either Oswald or Oswy had ever participated in the selection of a bishop of Lindisfarne. That Oswy now felt entitled to nominate bishops probably reveals something of the reasoning that underlay his pro-York decision at Whitby. The Gregorian plan required the northern metropolitan at York to seek his consecration from his southern colleague and vice versa. Ceadda accordingly made his way south, but before he arrived the bishop of Canterbury too had died of plague.

York was in Deira not Bernicia. There Alchfrith had his own royal candidate for the episcopate in the young priest Wilfrid. *Vita Wilfrithi* maintains that Wilfrid was nominated by both Oswy and Alchfrith, but Bede disagrees. Alchfrith alone, Bede says, 'sent the priest Wilfrid to the Gallic king to be consecrated bishop for him and for his kingdom', after which Oswy nominated Ceadda, 'imitating the actions of his son'.[49] It is at this point in our sources that Alchfrith vanishes without trace or explanation, save for Bede's vague early observation that Oswy 'was attacked . . . by his own son Alchfrith'. Given his shadowy fate, we are bound to accept Bede's confrontational version of events. Oswy would seem to have eliminated Alchfrith shortly after his son's decision to interfere in the see of York. We have already noted the possibility that his (probably unpleasant) fate was followed up by Oswegian campaigning against Alchfrith's maternal kin in Rheged, who may have backed him.

Wilfrid was already abroad when Ceadda learned of the death of the bishop of Canterbury. Oswy's nominee to the northern province had little time to lose. He went now to the bishop of the West Saxons, and was duly consecrated with the support of British bishops within the Wessex orbit. The year seems to have been 666, three years before this consecration was overturned and Wilfrid placed in the see of York.[50]

---

[48] Bede, *Hist. eccl.*, iii.28.
[49] Stephen, *V. s. Wilfrithi*, §§ 11–14; Bede, *Hist. eccl.*, iii.28.
[50] Bede, *Hist. eccl.*, v.19; Stephen, *V. s. Wilfrithi*, § 14.

If there is anything historical about Stephen's description of the consecration of Wilfrid by twelve bishops at Compiègne in the Frankish kingdom of Neustria (one of whom was his old mentor Agilbert, now bishop of Paris), these prelates surely acted in expectation that this consecration would be controversial.[51] Agilbert had once been bishop of Dorchester. News may have reached him from Wessex of Ceadda's consecration there, requiring him to devise a plan for challenging that rite's validity. Was part of that plan to throw the great weight of Ebroin, the mayor of the Neustrian palace, behind Wilfrid's case?[52]

Despite formidable foreign support, Wilfrid's options after the obscure elimination of Alchfrith were limited. Stephen maintains that he returned to his abbatial office at Ripon in Deira, and abided there, 'except when frequently he was invited, out of sincere affection, by Wulfhere, king of the Mercians, to fulfil various episcopal functions in his realm'.[53] This may be a disingenuous admission that Wilfrid, *persona non grata* in Oswy's Northumbria, could not actually return there, and spent the first years after his consecration in Mercia under the protection of Wulfhere son of Penda effectively an exile. Certainly Bede is very vague about his return from Francia. These Mercian connections may have been damaging to Wilfrid in the 670s.

In March 668 Theodore of Tarsus became archbishop of Canterbury, receiving from Pope Vitalian supremacy over all the bishops of Britain. Archbishops were technically distinct from metropolitan ones, and superior to them, so that Theodore's commission need not be seen as invalidating Wilfrid's metropolitan primacy at York.[54] As already noted, this impressive commission was probably in line with one that Oswy, in conjunction with his wife's kinsman Egbert, king of Kent, had requested for their nominee Wigheard, who had died en route to Rome for consecration as bishop of Canterbury. In his return letter to the Bernician hegemon, the pope calls him *rex Saxonum*, king of the Saxons. Oswy had no doubt involved himself with Egbert in the nomination of Wigheard on the basis of such paramountcy, and Archbishop Theodore's even wider supremacy was no doubt envisioned by Vitalian as mirroring Oswy's own. Before settling on a replacement, the pope revealingly referred to the bishop of Canterbury as 'your bishop' in his letter to Oswy.[55]

[51]   Stephen, *V. s. Wilfrithi*, § 12.
[52]   Wood, 'Northumbrians and the Franks', 19.
[53]   Stephen, *V. s. Wilfrithi*, § 14.
[54]   Charles-Edwards, *Early Christian Ireland*, 417–21.
[55]   Bede, *Hist. eccl.*, iii.25; iii.29.

The great king had no hand in the appointment of Theodore. Despite his best efforts to secure control over both his own Northumbrian Church and the wider Anglo-Saxon one, Oswy had been foiled by the pope. Before too long he would be foiled again by Theodore. Perhaps it was around this time, with the thirtieth year of his reign looming, that the son of Aeðilfrith began to consider abdication and pilgrimage to Rome.[56]

Theodore arrived in Kent from Rome at the end of May 669. On his way he received hospitality from Bishop Agilbert in Paris, spending 'a long time' in the company of Wilfrid's former mentor. No doubt he sought to benefit from the experience of a bishop who had spent years in Ireland and Britain, and who had attended the Synod of Whitby.[57] Agilbert had also consecrated Wilfrid, and before that had been a familiar of the departed Alchfrith. Even before the new archbishop arrived in Britain, then, his meeting in Paris will have prepared him for dealing with Oswy.

Having reached Canterbury, Theodore toured the Anglo-Saxon kingdoms. Did he travel still further into other parts of Britain in line with his papal commission? In Northumbria he took a no-nonsense approach in his dealings with the *rex Saxonum*. The old Greek assessed the York situation, judged Ceadda's consecration irregular and installed Wilfrid in his see as the legitimate bishop of York. Theodore's strategic thinking is reasonably clear, for he promptly re-consecrated Ceadda and installed him as bishop of the Mercians.[58] As a result Wulfhere was provided with a bishop who was a favourite of Oswy, while at the same time Oswy was forced to accept in Wilfrid a bishop friendly with the Mercian king. These two appointments were probably intended to foster amity between the two superpowers. The state of Mercio-Northumbrian relations does seem to have been a particular concern of the archbishop during his twenty-year episcopate.

YORK AND THE ECCLESIASTICAL DIMENSION OF EMPIRE

Wilfrid genuinely believed, almost certainly, that he had been legitimately consecrated as metropolitan bishop of York, his authority outlined by Gregory the Great. Some of his more audacious moments outlined in

---

[56] Bede, *Hist. eccl.*, iv.5.
[57] Bede, *Hist. eccl.*, iv.1.
[58] Stephen, *V. s. Wilfrithi*, § 15; Bede, *Hist. eccl.*, iv.2–3.

Vita Wilfrithi become easier to understand once this is appreciated, not least because the southern limits of his perceived primacy were probably controversial. Stephen says that, in the last years of Oswy's reign, Wilfrid enjoyed jurisdiction over an ecclesiastical realm (*regnum ecclesiarum*) that 'increased to the south over the Saxons and to the north over the Britons, the Gaels and the Picts'.[59] Reflecting his disquiet, Bede was to qualify this claim, maintaining that the bishop's authority had extended only 'as far as King Oswy was able to extend *imperium*'.[60]

There is little to indicate that Wilfrid recognised Bede's limits. The text of a contemporary document, copied into Stephen's Life, records that the bishop, in Rome in 679, spoke in council 'for all the northern part of Britain, Ireland and the islands, which are inhabited by English and British peoples, as well as by Gaelic and Pictish peoples'.[61] It therefore seems that Wilfrid fancied the Pictish, Gaelic and British bishops of northern Britain, including the Hebrides ('the islands'), as his suffragans as metropolitan bishop. The claim would become familiar to medieval Scottish clerics, as would Canterbury's hostility to it.

As in those later times, the extent of York's effective power across the Bernician hegemony, much less beyond it, is open to considerable question. It is not impossible that Oswy looked upon his 'conversion' at Whitby as a springboard for demanding greater conformity to his rule across his dominions, couched in ecclesiastical terms.[62] The retention of traditional ecclesiastical observances and Easter calculations among the Picts and the Argyll Gaels, at odds with the decisions at Whitby, suggests that their Churches never acknowledged Wilfrid's metropolitan authority. Yet there is no hint in the anonymous *Vita Cuthberti* that Cuthbert's alleged journey from Melrose to a Pictish district apparently in Fife, during the Bernician dominion there, was anything but routine. Such journeys between Northumbrian and southern Pictish monasteries were probably relatively common.[63] We need not assume that clerics who crossed the Forth in either direction met with unreserved ethnic hostility.

The anonymous *Vita Cuthberti* implies that the Niuduari of that district, possibly Fife Picts dominated by Bernician settlers, were not particularly hospitable towards Cuthbert. The travelling Melrose monks, stranded by contrary winds, would have starved to death among them had

---

[59] Stephen, *V. s. Wilfrithi*, §§ 19–21.
[60] Stephen, *V. s. Wilfrithi*, § 21; Bede, *Hist. eccl.*, iv.3.
[61] Stephen, *V. s. Wilfrithi*, § 53.
[62] Charles-Edwards, 'Nations and Kingdoms', 42–3.
[63] *V. s. Cuthberti anon.*, ii.4; Bede, *V. s. Cuthberti*, § 11; Kirby, 'Bede and the Pictish Church', 10–11.

there not been a miraculous intervention.[64] Apparently there was no help to be had. The point ought not to be stressed, however, as the hagiographer can hardly have told the tale otherwise and made it a good miracle-story. We have casual references in contemporary or near-contemporary sources to the activities of Gaelic clergy among Picts and Anglo-Saxons, and of English and Pictish clergy among Gaels, with little trace of ethnic antagonism. Modern expectations rooted in ethnic nationalism have no place in our period. Frontiers between peoples presented little barrier to the mobility of churchmen and churchwomen. Much of this intercourse is likely to have been rooted in relationships between individual monasteries and ecclesiastical *familiae*. They need have had little to do with pretensions of supremacy between churches or peoples.

It would, therefore, not be surprising if a metropolitan bishop at York maintained active interests in ecclesiastical affairs and developments across northern Britain (and indeed beyond), even if only in scattered pockets. Reciprocal interest in York and its claims on the part of northern Church leaders outwith Northumbria is hardly unlikely. Some Pictish and other clerics in traditionalist areas may now have become adherents or advocates of apostolicist philosophical notions. Complex ecclesiastical interlinkages across Britain and Ireland both reflect and surely facilitated high levels of general cultural interaction at elite levels of society. The best evidence that northern Britain, including Pictland, was a full partner in that interaction is its participation in the Insular art-style already in flower by this period in manuscript illumination, metal-work and sculpture.[65]

Whatever tensions remained between York and Bamburgh in 669 when Wilfrid was forced on Oswy relaxed when the king died less than a year later on 15 February 670. Bede maintains that he had made his peace with Wilfrid before the end. According to him, the great king decided that if he survived what proved to be his final illness he would abdicate and go to Rome, and 'asked Bishop Wilfrid to act as his guide, promising him no small gift of money'.[66] Whether or not there is any truth to this story it is impossible to know.

The last and greatest of the sons of Aeðilfrith to rule the Bernicians was laid to rest in the burial ground of the monastery of Whitby. Here Eanfled his widow took up the abbacy, and Aelffled their daughter

---

[64] On the name *Niuduera/Niuduari*, see Hunter Blair, 'The Bernicians', 168n.
[65] Henderson and Henderson, *The Art of the Picts*, 11–12, 15–17, 28–9, 34–5, 74, 94–5, 172.
[66] Bede, *Hist. eccl.*, iv.5.

eventually succeeded her. In his fifty-eight years, Oswy had experienced war and peace, exile and dispossession, kingship and *imperium* and had participated in the christianisation of large areas of the Anglo-Saxon world. Made mindful of the Gregorian plan for the organisation of the Church in Britain, and throwing his weight behind it, Oswy had established and maintained an ongoing, if limited and particular, interest in the ecclesiastical and political activities of the whole island. The real impact of this interest, and the pretensions of the likes of Ceadda and Wilfrid in northern Britain, are matters that are difficult to evaluate within the bounds of the evidence.

Wilfrid may have regarded it as an auspicious beginning to his episcopate that Oswy perished so soon after his installation. The new king, Oswy's son Ecgfrith, at the age of twenty-five was some ten years Wilfrid's junior. Ecgfrith and his brother Aelfwini, apparently his subordinate king in their mother's native Deira, attended the dedication of a new church at the Deiran monastery of Ripon. They sent an unequivocal signal of their support by donating various lands to Wilfrid. They did so, in Stephen's words, 'with the consent and subscription of the bishops and all the foremost men (*principes*)'. These men also donated 'consecrated places in various districts which British clergy had deserted when fleeing from the hostile sword wielded by the hand of our own people', and substantial wealth 'for the adornment of the house of God'.[67] Wilfrid and the queen mother had a prior history of mutual support as apostolicists at Whitby. Ecgfrith's remarkable and ostentatious generosity towards his metropolitan bishop, with districts acquired by Oswy, may have owed much to the ongoing influence of his shrewd mother. The occasion may have marked the dawn of a sweeter deal for her countrymen in Deira within the Northumbrian project.

For those who followed ecclesiastical affairs, at least, it was apparent that the accession of Ecgfrith was bringing with it a new outlook. A grandson of both Edwini and Aeðilfrith, Ecgfrith had no need to fear any conjuring up of the memory of either glorious predecessor. It has already been suggested that it was probably during his reign that Bede's politically neutral notion of a Christian and united Northumbria, forged by the joint efforts of Edwini and Oswald, was first encouraged. There are suggestions in the evidence of attempts on Wilfrid's part to foster cults surrounding Edwini and Oswald, convert kings slain by a pagan and his British allies. Alongside these kings, whose holiness emerges larger than life from the pages of Bede's History, the memory and achievement of

[67] Stephen, *V. s. Wilfrithi*, § 17.

Oswy, tarnished here and there by the grim necessities of effective kingship, could not measure up. Perhaps Wilfrid in particular wanted it that
way.

For all that he had made Northumbrian unity a political reality, historical memory made Oswy something of a divisive figure. His death may
have come as something of a relief to those who had spent long years
wriggling under the weight of his thumb. As a man, he may have fallen
well short of heroism as we measure it today. Yet he had been a remarkably effective king and hegemon, the architect of the realities that the historians of Ecgfrith's time (and later) projected back into the past. He was,
without question, northern Britain's most important king of the seventh
century. English history has claimed him, but it should be clear from this
chapter that Scottish history also has a strong claim to Oswy.

CHAPTER 8

Bull of the North: Bridei son of Beli and the Fall of the Aeðilfrithings (671–92)

THE HUMBLING OF FORTRIU

It was not long after the death of the peerless Oswy before precocious neighbours challenged the great king's young heir to prove himself worthy of his father's extensive legacy. Ecgfrith's first challenge came from Pictland, where his kinsman Talorcan had been dead since 656.[1] If Oswy's claim to paramountcy among Picts began in Talorcan's reign, *Vita Wilfrithi* provides a hint as to what happened to it after his nephew's death.

Stephen makes special mention, in his account of Ecgfrith's Pictish war, of a certain 'brave *subregulus*' called Beornhaeth, a 'subject king' who fought for him. Beornhaeth's kingdom is not, however, named. This same subordinate appears among the potentates commemorated in the Durham *Liber vitae*. His son Berctred later fought for Ecgfrith too, and died fighting Picts. Another man of similar name, Berctfrith, is supposed to have been another kinsman: he too fought against Pictish foes.[2] *Vita Wilfrithi* was completed *c.* 716, but may have been largely written by 713 only a few years after this last battle, the first Northumbrian victory over Picts since Ecgfrith and Beornhaeth vanquished them in 671. Did the hagiographer make special mention of Beornhaeth in order to link Berctfrith's recent victory with that previous great triumph north of the border?

The Pictish dimension shared by these men suggests that Beornhaeth's kingdom, held in subjection to Ecgfrith, had pronounced

---

[1] *AU* 657.3; *AT* 657.4; *CS* 657.4; *Ann. Clon.* 653.4.
[2] *Lib. vit. eccl. Dunelm.*, fol. 12. On these men, see Hunter Blair, 'The Bernicians', 170–1; Charles-Edwards, 'Early Medieval Kingships', 31–2.

Pictish interests. Was it inside Pictland? As already observed, the district of Niuduera in Pictish Fife implies by its name that it was held by Bernician incomers. It is reasonable to suppose that Beornhaeth and his kin represent the royal dynasty of these Niuduari, their kingdom in Fife. Such a conclusion is supported by admittedly circumstantial evidence. Berctred's devastating invasion of Brega in 684, a southern Uí Néill kingdom in eastern Ireland, for some reason came to be regarded as a prelude to Ecgfrith's final Pictish war in 685. Does this association not become easier to understand if Berctred was a *subregulus* like his father, his homeland inside the southern Pictish zone?[3]

The *Annals of Clonmacnoise* maintain that Berctred attacked Brega in reaction to an alliance between Gaels and Britons. The kings of Alt Clut on the southern margins of Pictland apparently had Gaelic allies in Cowal in this period. If they had Brega allies too, that ought to have posed a threat to any Bernician *subregulus* in Fife. A further clue may lie in Stephen's description of Berctfrith as 'the leader second in rank to the king' (*secundus a rege princeps*) in Northumbria in 704, who upheld the Aeðilfrithing succession against an Ecgwulfing challenger.[4] Such details would suit a Niuduarian prince who could, in that case, have been a kinsman of Talorcan son of 'Anfrith', and so an Aeðilfrithing himself.

No source explicitly dates the Pictish 'rebellion' to 671. It has been inferred instead from circumstantial evidence surrounding a change in the Verturian kingship in that year. Events culminated in the battle of the Two Rivers: near a confluence, perhaps, of two Pictish streams, Ecgfrith and Beornhaeth won a decisive victory and confirmed Northumbrian suzerainty.[5] Does the 'rebellion' represent a disastrous attempt to subjugate or expel Beornhaeth after Oswy's death? If the expulsion of the Pictish king Drest son of Donuel from his kingdom in 671 has been correctly linked with these events, Drest was probably a ringleader and undermined by the calamity.[6] He continues to receive attention from the chronicles after his expulsion, indicating that he had been king of Fortriu in the northern Pictish zone, probably since 664,

---

[3] *AU* 685.2; *AT* 685.2; *CS* 685.2; *Ann. Clon.* 680.2; *Iniu feras Bruide cath*, ll. 11–12; Bede, *Hist. eccl.*, iv. 26. The translation of *roisaorbut Bruide bregha* as 'that Bridei would avenge Brega' is admittedly more satisfying historically than linguistically.

[4] Stephen, *V. s. Wilfrithi*, § 50.

[5] Fraser, *The Battle of Dunnichen*, 19–20.

[6] *AU* 672.6; *AT* 672.5; *Ann. Clon.* 668.3.

when the *Annals of Ulster* record fighting in Fortriu at a place called *Luith Feirn*.[7]

Drest's successor, Bridei son of Beli, is the earliest king explicitly called *rex Fortrenn*, 'king of Fortriu', in the chronicles. He is the first of four successive Pictish kings whose reigns collectively mark a turning point in Scottish history. He was Ecgfrith's cousin (*fratruelis*), and apparently the son of a Deiran half-sister of Eanfled.[8] He was also his cousin's nemesis, for on the afternoon of 20 May 685, a Saturday, Ecgfrith was killed in 'a battle against his *fratruelis*, who was a Pictish king called Bridei'.[9] Fourteen years earlier in 671, however, Bridei may have been the face of Ecgfrith's subjugation of the Waerteras in Fortriu.

On his father's side, Bridei was a grandson of Neithon son of Guipno, whose legacy (*forba*) is said by *Iniu feras Bruide cath* to have been at issue between Bridei and Ecgfrith.[10] Bridei appears by his famous victory to have wrested the southern Pictish zone from Northumbrian paramountcy, which has been taken already as evidence that Neithon was the Pictish king 'Necton', Irb's descendant, and evidence too, along with Abernethy associations, that the House of Guipno had formerly dominated a kingdom (we have been calling it *Alt Clut*) stretching from Strathearn to Clyde Rock. According to *Mór do ingantu do-gní*, 'Great the Wonders He Performs', a Gaelic elegy attributed to Adomnán, Bridei's father Beli had been a king of Clyde Rock.[11]

Bridei thus had decidedly southern origins. It is accordingly difficult to see how he could have been anything other than a 'new man' in the Verturian kingship, at best distantly related to his predecessors. The marriage of his parents represents some accommodation between Edwini and Neithon, whose two realms lay at the opposite margins of Bernicia. His brother Eugein – almost certainly a half-brother – flourished thirty years before him, and was evidently considerably older. He was the *rex Britonum* whose forces slew Domnall Brecc of Kintyre in Strathcarron in 643.

---

[7] *AU* 663.3, 664.3, 678.6; *AT* 663.3, 678.6; *CS* 663.3, 678.3; *Ann. Clon.* 659.1; 674.5. Drest's brother and predecessor had died in 663. There are Leitirfearn and Leitir Fearna ('alder-hillside') on the south side of Loch Oich in the Great Glen. Luith Feirn ('alder-gate') may have lain hereabouts.

[8] Woolf, 'Pictish Matriliny Reconsidered', 161–2.

[9] *Hist. Brit.*, § 57; *Birdei* is the spelling in 'the Harleian recension'.

[10] *Iniu feras Bruide cath*, ll. 1–2.

[11] *Mór do ingantu do-gní*, l. 8; see also Macquarrie, 'The Kings of Strathclyde', 9.

Did Oswy intervene in the search for a settlement of this conflict on his frontier, with the result that Bridei, Eugein's young half-brother, ended up at the Bernician court as a hostage? It is no more than a guess, arising from a guess – one scenario among many that would contextualise how this scion of the House of Guipno captured the Verturian kingship in an age of Bernician *imperium*. Oswy certainly assisted kinsmen into Deiran and (probably) Pictish kingships.[12] Did Ecgfrith do the same in Fortriu in 671? Oswy's household had, over the years, included at least three young men of Deiran royal maternal heritage. Bridei, whose brother and father had been kings in the Central Belt of Scotland, ought to have been valuable as a fourth one given Oswy's aspirations in the British west and the Pictish north.

Whatever the accuracy of these guesses, it seems that Bridei regarded himself as a subject of Ecgfrith after 671. He may have been subject to the authority of a southern overlord like Beornhaeth. That hypothesis would make sense of the *Annals of Inisfallen*, which state that the battle of Dún Nechtain, where Ecgfrith fell, was 'a great battle between Picts'.[13] Ten years after his installation, however, Beornhaeth may have been dead (his son flourished in the 680s and 690s), and Bridei was flexing his muscles north of the Mounth. Within a few years he moved into the southern Pictish zone, where an Anglo-Pictish province may have been in place, its chief kingdom in Fife and its chief episcopal seat, from 681, at Abercorn on the Forth. As Bede remembered it some fifty years later, after the fall of Ecgfrith in 685 'the hopes and strength of the English kingdom began to ebb and fall away, for the Picts recovered their own land which the English had held, and the Gaels who were in Britain (and some part of the Britons) recovered their liberty'.[14] The evidence from Argyll suggests that Bernician paramountcy there may have begun unravelling much earlier than 685.

BRIDEI, CENÉL ɴGARTNAIT AND THE GAEL

Domangart son of Domnall Brecc, king of the Corcu Réti since 659 or 660, was slain in 672, a year or so after Bridei took power in northern

---

[12] Woolf, 'Pictish Matriliny Reconsidered', 161–2; Woolf, 'The Verturian Hegemony', 108, although the context of the argument has been adjusted here to take account of a northern Fortriu. For a different view, see Smyth, *Warlords*, 63–7.

[13] *AI* 685.1 (*cath mór eter Cruithnechu*).

[14] Bede, *Hist. eccl.*, iv.26.

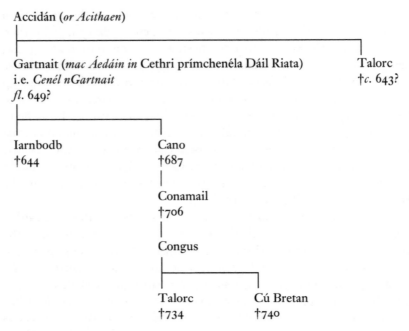

Table 8.1 Cenél nGartnait

Pictland. Bridei only steps into the light of history in 681, when he 'annihilated' the Orcadian islands.[15] Yet he may have made an earlier move into Atlantic Scotland. The *Annals of Ulster* record the capture of two men, probably in Argyll, in the same year as Domangart's killing. One of these, Elphin, has been identified as a 'descendant of Irb' like the Pictish king 'Necton'.[16] If that king was the same person as Neithon son of Guipno, Elphin was Bridei's kinsman. These linkages are clearly tenuous, but they receive a measure of support from other evidence.

Elphin was seized alongside Conamail son of Cano, whose son, according to a pedigree recorded in *Cethri prímchenéla Dáil Riata* after 706, was a member of a different branch of Cenél nGabráin than Domangart.[17] That kindred, Cenél nGartnait, first caught the attention of the Iona Chronicle in the late 660s, when it returned to Argyll from Ireland, having apparently sailed there three years earlier 'with the people of Skye'.[18] Its leader would seem to have been Cano son of Gartnait,

[15] *AU* 682.4; *AT* 682.5.

[16] Fraser, 'Picts in the West'; see also Smyth, *Warlords*, 64–5.

[17] *Ceth. prím. Dáil Riata*, §§ 14–21; Anderson, *Early Sources*, vol. 1, clvi.

[18] *AU* 668.3, 670.4; *AT* 668.1, 670.4; *CS* 668.1, 670.3; *Ann. Clon.* 666.1.

Conamail's father, later immortalised in the Gaelic story *Scéla Cano meic Gartnáin*, the 'Tale of Cano son of Gartnán'. The author of this unhistorical romance followed *Cethri prímchenéla* in making Conamail's grandfather Gartnait a son of Áedán son of Gabrán, Domangart's famous ancestor. However, the chronicles disagree. They name Gartnait's father as Accidán (rather than Áedán), even recording the death of his brother Talorc son of Accidán in 643.[19]

The chronicles also make Gartnait a contemporary of Áedán's grandsons. The alternative scenario makes him Áedán's son, and is harder to believe, for we know of no other grandson of Áedán who lived later than 660, and Gartnait's son Cano, not yet at the end of his natural life, was killed twenty-seven years after that. Another of Gartnait's sons seems to have been killed in a fire in 644, leaving his brother Cano at the head of the dynasty.[20] The internal consistency of these chronicle records is compelling in favour of their reliability.

The capture of Conamail son of Cano alongside Elphin is fascinating, because the names of their earliest forebears, along perhaps with their Skye connections, imply that Cenél nGartnait were a Pictish, or a Gaelo-Pictish kindred. By Cano's generation, they were operating comfortably within a Gaelic milieu stretching from Skye to Ireland. Their rise to prominence provides a rare opportunity to discuss northern Atlantic Scotland. It has already been noted that the region may have been home to peoples who seemed backward and barbaric from the perspective of places like Iona by the middle of the seventh century. If so, from the perspective of those responsible for our sources, Skye probably stood at the edge of civilisation – a sensible place to establish bases for exploiting the peoples beyond.

Upon their return to Skye, Cano and his family seem to have become embroiled in a generation of conflict with sons and grandsons of a certain Éoganán son of Túathalán, who died in 659 or 660 and may have been a grandson of Áedán, who had a son called *Túathal*.[21] An incursion into Skye at the height of the power of Cenél nGabráin by one branch of that kindred may therefore be posited. The descendants of Túathalán may have hoped that, through controlling Skye and extending their influence

[19] *AU* 686.2; *AT* 686.5; these annals belong to AD 643 like the death of Domnall Brecc, also recorded erroneously here; Anderson, *Early Sources*, vol. 1, 179–80, 194.
[20] *AU* 643.4; *AT* 643.4.
[21] *AU* 660.3, 668.3, 670.4; *AT* 660.5, 668.2, 670.4; Anderson, *Kings and Kingship*, 154–5; Fraser, 'The Iona Chronicle', 84–6.

northwards, they could reach the stature of the more established branches of Cenél nGabráin in Kintyre.

In any case, it seems likely that such an incursion was the cause of Cenél nGartnait's brief sojourn in Ireland. It may have been the death of Oswy, sending a shudder through Cenél nGabráin, which brought them back to Skye. Sons of Éoganán were slain in 676 and 679. Did Cano establish the upper hand against his foes in the 670s, only to be killed himself in 687?[22] Their prominence in *Cethri prímchenéla* suggests that Cenél nGartnait enjoyed considerable prominence *c*. 706. If his son Conamail was captured in 672 in the company of a kinsman of Bridei son of Beli, the possibility cannot be ruled out that Cano, and after him his Cenél nGartnait kin, flourished in this period with Verturian backing.

Conamail survived his capture, living until 706, when he too was slain some eighteen years after his father.[23] In the intervening period, a third son of Éoganán had been slain, as had two of his grandsons, in a fight in Skye (*imbairecc i Scii*).[24] This sad litany of killings and counter-killings set the stage for Cenél nGartnait's prominent place in *Cethri prímchenéla* after Conamail's death. They remained a prominent dynasty for another forty years, until they fell afoul of Pictish aggression.

What are we to read into links between Bridei and Cenél nGartnait in the year of the killing of Domangart of Kintyre? Along with evidence of strife between Cenél nGartnait and Cenél nGabráin, they allow for a circumstantial case for believing that Bridei and Cano were implicated in the king's death. Is *Cethri prímchenéla*'s controversial notion that Cenél nGartnait were a key segment of the powerful Cenél nGabráin *c*. 706 also to be explained as reflecting Verturian backing, enabling them to move to the centre of Argyll politics? Drest of Fortriu had been expelled from his realm only a year before Domangart died, and seems to have remained in the orbit of Iona until his death in 677. Elphin and Conamail may have been pursuing that cashiered king when they were seized.

That Picts, and quite possibly Waerteras, were involved in Argyll politics in the 670s is suggested by one other chronicle record. The *Annals of Ulster* record that in 675 'many Picts were drowned in the land of Awe' (*i Llaind Abae*), probably a mistake for 'in Loch Awe' (*i lind Abae*).[25] It is uncertain what business, foul or fair, brought these unfortunates

---

[22] *AU* 677.4, 680.6, 688.2; *AT* 688.2; *CS* 688.2.

[23] *AU* 705.4.

[24] *AU* 692.4, 701.7.

[25] *AU* 673.3, 676.3. For discussion of these annals, see Fraser, 'Picts in the West'.

into the heart of Argyll three years after the capture of Conamail and Elphin.

Domangart's successor was his cousin Máel Dúin son of Conall. The king of Cowal at this time was probably Finnguine Fota, a great-grandson of the sixth-century king Conall son of Comgall. His son Dargart has been identified as the father of two eighth-century Pictish kings, speaking of still more of interlinkages between Pictland and Argyll at this time. Cenél Comgaill, as previously mentioned, had long main-tained interlinkages with the kingdom of Alt Clut, where Bridei's nephew Dumngual son of Eugein was now king. Did he, Finnguine and Bridei form a three-way alliance after 671, reminiscent of the Druimm Cete tri-umvirate of *c*. 592, after Bridei became king of Fortriu?

In 677 Ferchar Fota, (probably) king of Cenél nEchdach, based (prob-ably) in Upper Lorn, was soundly defeated in battle by British forces.[26] Four years later Britons also invaded Mag Line, the Uí Chóelbad heart-land in Antrim, the royal centre of Ráith Mór (outside modern Antrim Town) being assaulted and the king slain.[27] Who were these Britons, winning stunning victories at the margins of the Corcu Réti kingdom? Were they the same forces who, a year after the fall of the Uí Chóelbad royal centre, laid siege to its counterpart, the stronghold of Dunadd (*Dún At*) in Mid-Argyll?

It is difficult to ignore the evidence that the dominant military power in Atlantic Scotland in the 670s and 680s was a British one, Alt Clut being foremost among the suspects. If this kingdom had been stripped of inter-ests in Strathearn and Manau by the Bernicians in the middle decades of the century, such a burst of activity in Atlantic Scotland could be seen as reflecting a major realignment of its interests. Links with Alt Clut and Fortriu, whose kings were near kin, may have enabled Finnguine of Cowal to enjoy considerable influence in Argyll. Such interlinkages, however shadowy, provide a context for the marital link between the royal dynasties of Fortriu and Cowal apparent *c*. 700, as well as for British and Pictish activity in Argyll.

Is it a coincidence that the British invasion of Mag Line took place in the same year as Bridei's devastating attack on Orkney? Is it a coincidence that the (possibly British) siege of Dunadd took place in the same year as the (probably Verturian) siege of Dundurn in southern Pictland? The evidence is admittedly thin – we are attempting to establish a story from a succession of blurry snapshots. None the less, the case is reasonable that

[26]   *AU* 678.3; *AT* 678.4.
[27]   *AU* 682.2; *AT* 682.3; *CS* 682.3; *Ann. Clon.* 677.1.

Bridei (Beli's son) and Dumngual (Beli's grandson) were both quite active in Argyll politics during their reigns, following on from the deaths of Oswy and Domangart. By *c.* 700 Pictish writers had developed a pronounced sense that Argyll was Pictish territory as recently as 563.

Whoever had slain Máel Dúin's royal cousin in 672, then, the result may have been an overturning of a regional status quo that had bedded down in Oswy's heyday, and under his distant supervision. Was it the first successful blow struck against Ecgfrith's suzerainty in northern Britain? Máel Dúin and his heirs fought a losing battle over the next twenty-five years for paramountcy in Argyll, not least it seems, against Pictish and British foes, or at least foes from Skye and Cowal backed by such foreign powers. If we have correctly deduced that Máel Dúin's predecessors had owed their own dominion to Bernician backing, the 670s may have seen Cenél nGabráin administered a bitter dose of their own medicine.

Ecgfrith had secured his position in Pictland in 671, but he may have lost it in Argyll over the next ten years. He faced stern challenges from beyond his southern borders, possibly encouraging Bridei and Dumngual to cast ambitious eyes towards the Atlantic. One is reminded of the joint Picto-Mercian pressures applied to the Northumbrian kings in the middle decades of the next century, but there is no comparable evidence that Bridei, Dumngual and the Pending kings of Mercia were conspiring against the Northumbrians in the 670s.

THE GLARE OF THE COMET

It was in 672 that Wulfhere son of Penda led 'all the southern kingdoms' to war against Ecgfrith, who was fresh from his overwhelming victory at the battle of the Two Rivers. Like Drest, the Mercian king was defeated, but he retained his kingdom until his death three years later. On the back of these impressive victories against Northumbria's mightiest neighbours, Wilfrid of York found himself presiding over a *regnum ecclesiarum* that extended across the North British zone into Argyll and Pictland. According to his hagiographer, Wilfrid was now ordaining priests and deacons 'in every part' of this great province.[28] He believed that he had the authority to speak 'for all the northern part of Britain, Ireland and the Isles'. These heady days were not to last.

In 678, less than a decade after Wilfrid's installation at York, as Bede reports it, 'there appeared during the month of August a star, known as a

---

[28] Stephen, *V. s. Wilfrithi,* § 21.

comet, which remained for three months'. In fact, as Irish chronicles record, this 'bright comet seen in the months of September and October' was visible not in 678, but in 676. Bede was well aware of it, having taken his description from *Liber pontificalis*, the 'Book of the Popes', where the correct year was clearly recorded.[29] This 'mistake' may have been intentional. Bede goes on to say that 'in the same year, there arose a dissension between King Ecgfrith and the most reverend Bishop Wilfrid', who was 'driven from the seat of his episcopate'.[30] Misdating the comet of 676 associated this ill omen not just with the tribulations of Wilfrid, but also with Ecgfrith, whom the bishop's supporters regarded in hindsight as doomed to suffer the ill fortune of a man punished by divine wrath.[31]

At the root of this remarkable change in Ecgfrith, once among Wilfrid's most public supporters, lay an ongoing dispute between York and Canterbury, to whose archbishop Wilfrid owed his episcopate. Theodore convened a council on the River Lee at Hertford, on the frontier between Essex and Mercia, in September 673. Wilfrid did not attend; he sent proxies instead. There he was designated *Nordanhymbrorum gentis episcopus*, 'bishop of the Northumbrian people'.[32] This title is rather different from *episcopus metropolitanus Eboracae civitatis*, 'metropolitan bishop of the city of York', the title given to Wilfrid in *Vita Wilfrithi*. The differences imply that Theodore was mounting a challenge against Wilfrid's so-called metropolitan authority, limiting his province to Northumbria, and did not recognise Wilfrid's claim to authority across all northern Britain.

Theodore had come to Canterbury as 'archbishop of the island of Britain', in parallel with the great power enjoyed by Oswy at the time of his papal appointment. Perhaps he had been prepared to look the other way while Oswy was paramount. By 673, three years after the great king's death and in the wake of Wulfhere's marshalling of the 'Southhumbrian' kingdoms against Ecgfrith, the archbishop was evidently moved to challenge the Synod of Whitby on the matter of York's metropolitan pretensions. Now that the frontiers between Northumbria and Mercia were hardening, Theodore may have resisted Wilfrid's metropolitan claim for fear of seeing himself relegated by the papacy to co-equal status as a mere metropolitan responsible only for southern Britain.

---

[29] Poole, 'The Chronology of Bede's *Historia Ecclesiastica*', 27–9; *AU* 677.1; *AT* 677.1; *CS* 677.1 (one of the key pieces of evidence showing that the Irish chronicles are a year out here).

[30] Bede, *Hist. eccl.*, iv.12.

[31] Stephen, *V. s. Wilfrithi*, § 24.

[32] Bede, *Hist. eccl.*, iv.5.

At Hertford, having made this challenge, Theodore outlined a code of good episcopal practice which, coincidentally or not, represented an indictment of the recent activities of the irrepressible bishop of York. It was agreed 'that no bishop intrude into the sphere (*paruchia*) of another', nor 'claim precedence over another out of ambition', and rather that a bishop 'should be content with the government of the people committed to his charge'. These standard precepts stand in contrast to Wilfrid's presumption to include under his jurisdiction bishops outside the *gens Nordanhymbrorum*. The Council also prohibited bishop's 'in any way to interfere with any monasteries dedicated to God, or take away forcibly any part of their property'. The bishop of York had only recently accepted donations from Ecgfrith of 'consecrated places', possibly including monasteries, 'in various parts' wrested from British hands by Oswy in Lancashire.[33]

With this Council, a Continental stamp was placed on the Anglo-Saxon Church, and Wilfrid's example was condemned. The writing was on the wall for him, for he believed his authority ran as far as the *imperium* of the Northumbrian hegemon, empowering him to interfere in the now obscure sees of British, Pictish, Gaelic and other English bishops.[34] Small wonder he failed to turn up at Hertford. It would be interesting to know whether or not Theodore had received complaints from prelates in northern Britain regarding Wilfrid's conduct.

The powder-keg of the last stage of the dispute was Lindsey, the subjection of which Ecgfrith secured through his victory over Wulfhere. Wilfrid's hagiographer included Lindsey in the see from which the bishop was expelled, but Bede did not. Instead, *Historia ecclesiastica* explicitly names someone other than Wilfrid as the predecessor of the bishop installed in 678.[35] We may infer that the disagreement of our sources reveals the nature of this particular dispute. Bede characteristically sided with Theodore. Lindsey, lying south of the Humber, clearly stood outwith Wilfrid's jurisdiction from Theodore's perspective of him as *Nordanhymbrorum gentis episcopus*. Having assumed jurisdiction, as if by right of conquest, Wilfrid had thus transgressed the code outlined a year later at the Council of Hertford. He had thereby invited the penalty established there for such a violation: to be 'excluded from exercising any priestly office and from our [episcopal] fellowship'. However, Paulinus, as

---

[33]   Bede, *Hist. eccl.*, iv.5.
[34]   Charles-Edwards, *Early Christian Ireland*, 432–3, has suggested that Wilfrid saw York as a 'new, orthodox Iona'.
[35]   Stephen, *V. s. Wilfrithi*, § 24; Bede, *Hist. eccl.*, iv.12.

metropolitan bishop of York, according to Bede had evangelised in Lindsey and built a church at Lincoln, where *c*. 627 he consecrated a new bishop of Canterbury.[36] No doubt Wilfrid accordingly regarded Lindsey as part of his metropolitan province at York.

The archbishop appears to have waited several years before executing this sanction. The delay was largely the result, no doubt, of the power and patronage of Ecgfrith. Oswy's son was now every bit the *imperator* his father had been, unless he had lost his influence in Argyll. It was when his patronage was revoked, as a result of the 'dissension' mentioned by Bede, that the bishop of York was finally stripped of his episcopal dignity by the archbishop. The circumstances surrounding his falling-out with the king are not clear. From the outset of his career, when he was given the abbacy of Ripon, Wilfrid had been a controversial figure. Stephen implies that he was the victim of a whispering campaign, and blames Ecgfrith's queen Eormenburh. Unconvinced scholars have suggested that Wilfrid's Mercian connections alienated Ecgfrith, and other sugges-tions are possible.[37]

When he became king in 670, Ecgfrith was already married to the East Anglian princess Aeðilthryð, but within a year or two she had become a nun at St Abbs (or Coludaesburg). Her story is presented in *Historia eccle-siastica* as a classic example of a royal woman opting for a monastic life in order to preserve her virginity.[38] Wilfrid played a part in this process, but it is unlikely that Ecgfrith resented him for it. Bede reveals that there were those who doubted the official version of events. After twelve years of childless wedlock, and having become the most powerful man in Britain, Ecgfrith may have been finding it inconvenient to be married to Aeðilthryð and eager for a new marriage and new political opportunities. Thus, the dissolution of the marriage by Wilfrid on the grounds of non-consummation is as likely to have been perceived by Ecgfrith as a bless-ing as a blight.

Stephen's association of Wilfrid's expulsion with Eormenburh is worthy of consideration. Her name suggests Kentish origins. The Kentish king Egbert, who died in 673, had taken counsel together with Oswy in 664. Eanfled's motives in pressing Oswy to reform the Northumbrian Church earlier that year may have stemmed in part from a desire to steer him diplomatically in the direction of Kent. Egbert's father was Eanfled's cousin, and Ecgfrith and Egbert's successor, his

---

[36] Bede, *Hist. eccl.*, ii.16, ii.18.
[37] John, 'Social and Political Problems', 51.
[38] Bede, *Hist. eccl.*, iv.19.

brother Hlothere, were kinsmen, as well as joint heirs to fruitful political links between their predecessors. Eormenburh probably came from a Kentish family to wed Ecgfrith through similar linkages between Canterbury and Bamburgh, the two new kings seeking to support one another. Was Eanfled maintaining an interest in that relationship as abbess at Whitby? Aeðilred, brother and successor of Wulfhere as king of the Mercians, undertook a devastating campaign across Kent in 676, leaving Ecgfrith and Hlothere facing a common enemy situated between their two kingdoms.[39]

The subtext of Stephen's accusations that Eormenburh was responsible for Ecgfrith's change of heart towards Wilfrid may, therefore, be that the king was moved to expel his bishop – who had once consorted with Wulfhere – as part of a blossoming pro-Kentish policy. Oswy had at least paved the way in the 660s for such a policy. Archbishop Theodore can certainly have encouraged it, and taken advantage of the circumstances to press for the excommunication of the wayward bishop of York.

ABERCORN AND THE FALL OF THE SOUTHERN PICTISH ZONE

With Wilfrid removed, Theodore partitioned his *regnum ecclesiarum* in line with ambitions set out at Hertford. He installed a monk from Eanfled's Whitby, Bosa, in a truncated see of York which had seemingly become, in effect, the province of the Deirans. For the first time since 635 Deira had a bishop of its own. Theodore also created a Bernician province, giving it to Eata, the ex-abbot of Ripon who had withdrawn to Melrose when Ripon was given to Wilfrid by Alchfrith. His seat was apparently established at Wilfrid's grand new church at Hexham.[40] The architect of the Council of Hertford cannot have supported any attempt on Eata's part, as bishop of Hexham, to interfere in any Pictish or Argyll see.

The memory of the pallium of Paulinus, conjured up by the York party at Whitby, had now been dispelled save in Wilfrid's eyes. He

---

[39] Gibbs, 'The Decrees of Agatho', 224; see Bede, *Hist. eccl.*, 111.29, iv.5, iv.12. The peculiar Kentishness of *Eormen-* is discussed by Brooks, 'Kingdom of Kent', 64.

[40] Stephen, *V. s. Wilfrithi*, § 24; Bede, *Hist. eccl.*, iv.12. Bede was unsure whether Hexham or Lindisfarne had been the seat of this see; within a few years both would be episcopal seats.

returned to Ecgfrith's court in 680, armed with a papal petition for his restoration, but was seized and imprisoned, latterly at the coastal strong-hold at Dunbar (*Dynbaer*), where archaeology has unearthed evidence of a substantial Early Historic settlement.[41] Only at Edinburgh further west, or at Iudeu further still, could the deposed bishop have been incar-cerated further away from his lost seat. In subsequent years, Wilfrid's expulsion and York's demotion exerted an appreciable effect on Northumbrian historiography, inspiring writers to obscure certain points and exaggerate others surrounding events and decisions made at Whitby. We are fortunate that they did so inconsistently, enabling schol-ars to peer through their different smoke-screens to observe something of the times.

The see of Bernicia as newly defined at Canterbury included some Pictish territory. A further subdivision was carried out in 681, establish-ing a Pictish province (*prouincia Pictorum*) with its episcopal seat at Abercorn.[42] The see was charged to Trumwini, perhaps another Whitby monk of Eanfled's like Bosa of York, and was probably near – and cer-tainly intervisible with – the stronghold of Iudeu. It is important that Theodore had come to Canterbury in 669 as 'archbishop of the island of Britain'. He was not an Anglo-Saxon himself, and his papal remit was not limited to the Anglo-Saxon kingdoms. There is little reason to believe that he went through the trouble of establishing the see of Abercorn, and installing a new bishop there, out of some unrealistic claim to jurisdiction in Pictland. No doubt the decision addressed as real a perceived need as the contemporaneous establishment of the newly-conceived and delim-ited bishoprics of York and Hexham.

We cannot assume that this perceived need was entirely a Northumbrian one. The demarcation and foundation of a new see at Abercorn fits rather comfortably alongside the suggestion above that the dominant king in the southern Pictish zone after the battle of the Two Rivers in 671 was Beornhaeth, possibly based in the Niuduarian district in Fife. Agitation by Beornhaeth, or by his son Berctred, is no less likely to explain Abercorn's elevation than naked Northumbrian or Cantuarian imperialism. Were there other, more ancient sees in southern Pictland whose prior superiority the elevation of Abercorn, with Cantuarian backing, was intended to undermine?

Further north, if Bridei had been extending his reach into Argyll by force and diplomacy in the 670s, he seems to have changed his priorities

---

[41] Stephen, *V. s. Wilfrithi*, §§ 34–9; Alcock, *Kings and Warriors*, 212–17.
[42] Bede, *Hist. eccl.*, iv.12.

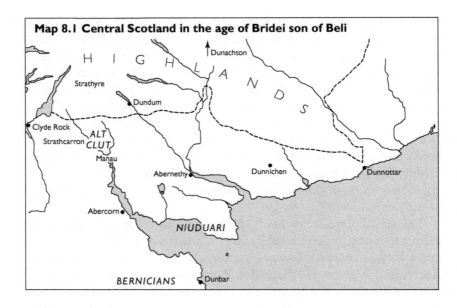

Map 8.1 Central Scotland in the age of Bridei son of Beli

rather dramatically in the 680s. The *Annals of Ulster* record a siege of Dunnottar (*Dún Foither*) in 680 and, in the year following Bridei's devastating Orcadian campaign, the siege of Dundurn (*Dún Duirn*) already mentioned.[43] The last two campaigns took place in the same years as known or suspected British aggression in the Atlantic zone. Dunnottar, of course, stood in the northern marches of the southern Pictish zone and Dundurn in its southern marches if the kingdom of Alt Clut extended as far north as Strathearn. The 'citadel fort' at Dundurn seems to have been established about 600, but its first timber palisade was later dismantled and new timber-laced stone walls were built using nails. These ramparts were eventually burned and replaced. Was the destruction of the palisade a result of the siege of 682?[44]

These engagements at Dunnottar and Dundurn imply a period of pronounced pressure across the southern Pictish zone, during a decade when Bridei was the only Pictish king whose military exploits can otherwise be shown to have interested the Iona chroniclers. He is thus the likeliest assailant, although none is named. This spate of warfare beyond the Mounth began almost to the year in the wake of Ecgfrith's apparently decisive defeat on the Trent in 679. There Aeðilred and the Mercians secured

---

[43] *AU* 681.5, 683.3.
[44] Foster, 'Before Alba', 14; Carver, *Surviving in Symbols*, 28; Ralston, *The Hill-Forts of Pictland*, 19.

a famous victory over the Northumbrians, and Ecgfrith's brother Aelfwini was slain.[45] Cenél nGabráin were already under pressure in Kintyre by this date, probably from foreign-backed kindreds in Cowal and Skye. Now the Mercian king was rolling back Ecgfrith's suzerainty south of the Humber.

The threat to southern Pictland came next, almost certainly at the hands of Bridei. By the middle of the 680s the great hegemony which Ecgfrith had inherited from his father was coming apart at the seams. On 20 May 685 the seams burst completely, and a Gaelic poet sang the praises of the Verturian king whose forces left Ecgfrith dead on the battlefield. The location of this important engagement on the shores of a lake called *Linn Garan*, remembered in Bernicia as *Nectanesmere*, was Dún Nechtain, the location of which is disputed. According to the poet, Bridei's prize in victory was his grandfather's legacy – seemingly entitlement to claim kingship between Dunnottar and Dundurn. In the shorter term, however, the *prouincia Pictorum* associated with Abercorn may have lain beyond his reach in Fife and Manau.

Bellum Dún Nechtain: Dunnichen or Dunachton

The conventional identification of Dún Nechtain with Dunnichen Hill five kilometres east of Forfar in Strathmore has been challenged in a stimulating article concerned principally with demonstrating – conclusively – that Fortriu lay north of the Mounth. That Dún Nechtain is to be identified with Dunachton seven kilometres north-east of Kingussie in Badenoch, rather than with Dunnichen, is a distinct argument – its acceptance or rejection has no great bearing on the matter of Fortriu's location.[46]

The argument revolves around Bede's placement of the battle *in angustias inaccessorum montium*, literally 'in defiles of unapproachable mountains'. Bede was not an eyewitness, and we do not know the source of his information. Dunachton fits his description admirably.

Does Bede's description rule out Dunnichen? No one thought so before 2006, but it required a measure of 'special pleading' that Dunachton does not. Proponents of Dunnichen could point out, for example, that it is uncertain how tall a hill must be before it deserves to be called a *mons* in Latin. The Pictish cognate *monid* was applied both

---

[45] Bede, *Hist. eccl.*, iv.21; Stephen, *V. s. Wilfrithi*, § 24; *AU* 680.4; *AT* 680.4. On the significance of this battle in the north, see Fraser, *Battle of Dunnichen*, 26–7.
[46] Woolf, 'Dún Nechtain'.

Bellum Dún Nechtain: Dunnichen or Dunachton (continued)

to the Mounth (mountains by anyone's estimation), and to humbler hills like Moncrieffe. Either location could have been difficult to approach (*inaccessus*), whether because of rugged or boggy terrain, and *angustiae*, literally 'narrow places', is similarly relative. Moreover, Stephen, in *Vita Wilfrithi*, observes of Wilfrid that God took care of him *in angustiis suis*, 'in his tight spots' ('dire straits' has the same meaning), so that Bede's *in angustias* could mean 'into distress'.[47]

Scholars have a satisfying aversion to such special pleading, but it is probably necessary to prevent Dunnichen from vanishing completely from the radar. After all, if Bridei was likely to be found fighting anywhere in the 680s, it was in the southern Pictish zone, where Dunnichen probably lay a long way inside his *imperium* by 685. That was precisely the region that was at stake in the fighting, if *Iniu feras Bruide cath* has been read correctly.

And then there is the cross-slab in Aberlemno kirkyard, seemingly of early type and influential, with its unique depiction of scenes from a battle.[48] Bede's text throws great weight behind the case for Dunachton, but it seems a remarkable coincidence that Pictland's only surviving carved battle-scene should stand within five kilometres of a different *Dún Nechtain* if it is not the site of the famous battle.

UP FROM THE ASHES: ALDFRITH SON OF OSWY

Thus ended the life of Ecgfrith son of Oswy, and with him died the hegemony of the Aeðilfrithing kings of Bamburgh, never to be resurrected. Gibbon's famous pronouncement, that the decay of Rome was 'the natural and inevitable effect of immoderate greatness', might explain the results at the River Trent and Dún Nechtain. Perhaps we ought to be less surprised that the *imperium* collapsed than that it endured for as long as it did.

Ecgfrith's successor Aldfrith, in Bede's words, 'ably recovered the destroyed state of the realm, albeit within narrower limits'.[49] The northern frontier that he preserved seems to have extended from the Forth in the east, or perhaps the Ochil Hills, to the Solway in the west, Whithorn and its environs still being encapsulated within the Northumbrian kingdom.

---

[47]   Stephen, *V. s. Wilfrithi*, § 9; Lewis and Short, *A Latin Dictionary*.
[48]   Cruickshank, 'The Battle of Dunnichen'; Henderson and Henderson, *The Art of the Picts*, 38–40, 67 (but see 134–5, 179, for resistance of links with any specific battle).
[49]   Bede, *Hist. eccl.*, iv.26.

We cannot as yet date the Bernician conquest of Galloway. Among Aeðilfrithings, only Oswy is credited with fighting wars against British enemies. A 'hall' unearthed in excavations at Lockerbie Academy, as well as the monastic site excavated at Hoddom ten kilometres further down the Annan, suggest that Annandale at least lay firmly inside Oswy's realm.[50]

The Gaelic wisdom-text *Bríathra Flainn Fína maic Ossu*, 'Sayings of Fland Fína son of Oswy', is attributed to Aldfrith. Irish genealogical tradition later maintained that he was the son of a certain Fína, daughter of Colmán Rímid, a contemporary of Áedán son of Gabrán.[51] That Cenél nÉogain king led the northern Uí Néill for two years until his killing in 606. His brother fought alongside Áedán against Aeðilfrith. The Cenél nÉogain maternity eventually assigned to Aldfrith by the Irish genealogists is not impossible, but neither is it altogether likely. It would require Colmán, killed six years before Oswy was born, to have fathered Fína very late indeed in his natural life, enabling her to be Oswy's contemporary.[52] More worryingly, his branch of the Cenél nÉogain dynasty was not in power when Oswy went into exile. How eligible a bachelor was Oswy anyway before 5 August 642? Who would have foreseen the chain of circumstances that brought him to power in Bernicia, much less his impressive royal career thereafter? On the face of it, a dynastic link between these two mighty houses is more likely to have been concocted by a pseudo-historian than to reflect Aldfrith's real heritage.

The starting point in the construction may have been the peculiar fact that this English king had a Gaelic persona as a well known Gaelic author. Aldfrith was called *sapiens*, 'wise', by the Iona chroniclers, *doctissimus* by Bede, 'most learned' and *sapientissimus*, 'most wise', by Stephen.[53] In the latter case, Aldfrith's wisdom was presumably thought to be in evidence when, under pressure from Archbishop Theodore and Oswy's daughter AelfflED, abbess of Whitby, the new king invited Wilfrid of York to return to Northumbria in 687. Stephen may have erred in stating that Wilfrid became bishop of Hexham, instead of Ripon, both being monasteries which he had founded.[54]

There are intriguing suggestions that AelfflED had been an instrumental force in securing a smooth succession after the shock of her brother's

---

[50] Richardson and Kirby, 'Lockerbie Academy'; Lowe, *Angels, Fools and Tyrants*, 46, 48–61.

[51] *Mín. sench. Síl Chuind*, 140a, ll. 39–40.

[52] Colmán's brother died in 612, seemingly of natural causes (*AU* 610.2; *AT* 610.3; *CS* 610.3; *AI* 612.2).

[53] *AU* 704.3 (*sapiens*); *AT* 704.4 (*ecnaid*); *Ann. Clon.* 700.2 ('prudent').

[54] Stephen, *V. s. Wilfrithi*, §§ 43–4; Poole, 'St Wilfrid', 14–15.

death at Dún Nechtain. The anonymous *Vita Cuthberti*, composed towards the end of Aldfrith's reign, maintains that she was called on to recognise his claim to be as much her brother as Ecgfrith. The point is thus made that Aldfrith's claim to rule was weak, being almost entirely dynastic in nature, without the usual support of a robust lordly reputation.

In his writings Bede acknowledged doubts about Aldfrith's parentage. These may not be as compelling as they first seem. The succession of his son Osred to the kingship was challenged in 704, and in 716 Osred was murdered and replaced. Bede wrote after these events, and his doubts about Aldfrith's descent from Oswy may simply reflect a posthumous charge of illegitimacy levelled at the king's descendants by their Ecgwulfing rivals.

There are Continental examples of men claiming to belong to royal kindreds, seeking confirmation from relevant women.[55] We ought not to allow the possible claims of his sons' rivals to influence us over much, and can accept Aelffled's verdict on Aldfrith's heritage. If he was not a son of Fína he may have been a son of Rieinmelth, Oswy's first known wife, and a brother of Alchfrith. In that event, he could have been sent into obscurity after Alchfrith's fall in the 660s, paving the way for Ecgfrith as heir-apparent.

The anonymous *Vita Cuthberti* provides an explanation for the king's learning, his Gaelic persona Fland Fína and his Gaelic literacy. Until Ecgfrith's death, he had been a monk at Iona. Not surprisingly, he cannot be shown ever to have taken to the field of battle. *Bríathra Flainn Fína* closes with a consideration of reasons that learning is better than 'the martial life' (*láechdacht*), described as 'a woeful occupation'.[56] The circumstances surrounding his abortive marriage to Cuthburh of the West Saxon royal dynasty beg the question whether Aldfrith endured sexual relations only as long as was necessary to ensure the continuity of the Aeðilfrithing dynasty. He was presumably involved in the decision to allow Cuthbert, the subject of the anonymous *Vita Cuthberti*, to switch his episcopal seat. Cuthbert had become bishop at Hexham in 684, but switched for Lindisfarne in the year of Wilfrid's restoration to episcopal orders.[57] Cuthbert had been extracted from Lindisfarne to take up the episcopate, circumstances to which the monk-made-king could obviously relate.

---

[55] Wood, 'Kings, Kingdoms and Consent', 15.
[56] *Bríathra Flainn Fína maic Ossu*, §§ 7.1–20.
[57] Bede, *Hist. eccl.*, iv.28.

It may be that Stephen's conception of Wilfrid's restoration was more grandiose thirty years later than had actually occurred at the time. The formidable old Archbishop Theodore died in 690, and shortly afterwards Wilfrid and Aldfrith fell out. Stephen implies that Theodore expressed remorse about his handling of Wilfrid's case, and that Wilfrid began to voice objections to the terms of his restoration. Bede's version of events suggests that his main complaint was that he had not been restored to York.[58] In any case, Wilfrid now withdrew once more to Mercia. He was received by Aeðilred, now indisputably the mightiest Anglo-Saxon king, whose queen Osthryð was another daughter of Oswy and Eanfled. Desperately unpopular among her husband's people, in part for advancing the cult of St Oswald, Osthryð was assassinated in 697, the third of Oswy's children to be slain in eighteen years.

SHIPS IN THE NIGHT: BEDE AND ADOMNÁN

The joint monastery of Wearmouth-Jarrow in Bernicia was the setting of a chance meeting in 688. For the historian of Early Historic Scotland, it is as fascinating an event as any war or battle, royal death, theological controversy, Christian mission or conversion. The occasion was the visit of Adomnán, a sixty-year-old Irish ambassador. Ten years previously he had become abbot of Iona, long associated with the Bernician Church through Lindisfarne. The abbot was shortly to set to work on *Vita Columbae*, a text which has furnished us with much evidence in this study.

In 664 the relationship between Iona and her *paruchia* – her sphere of jurisdiction – under the bishops of Lindisfarne had ended. In 688 the abbot of Iona was surely the kind of celebrity, none the less, whose visit to Wearmouth-Jarrow caused something of a sensation among the monks. Among them was Beda, a local teenager. He is now known to us as 'Bede', whose historical and hagiographical works later in life we have, again, already encountered at length. Since the age of seven, Bede had been living in the care of 'Benedict' Biscop, abbot and founder of Wearmouth and Jarrow. The young man was now studying to become a deacon, success coming four years later in 692.[59]

'He was a good and wise man,' Bede wrote of Adomnán years later, 'with an excellent knowledge of the scriptures' – high praise indeed

---

[58] Stephen, *V. s. Wilfrithi*, § 45.
[59] Bede, *Hist. eccl.*, v.24.

from one of the most highly regarded scriptural scholars of the age.[60] His estimation of Adomnán was rooted in part in the abbot's sympathies for the apostolicist reforms that Colmán of Lindisfarne had rejected at Whitby. It also stemmed in part from the abbot's recent book *De locis sanctis*, 'On the Holy Places', describing holy sites in Palestine – which had fallen under Islamic dominion in Adomnán's youth – as well as adjoining Byzantine and Coptic lands. The abbot of Iona presented the book to Aldfrith, and the ex-monk had it 'circulated for lesser folk to read'. One of these 'lesser folk' himself, Bede so appreciated *De locis sanctis* that he composed an abridged version in part (probably) as an aid to teaching.

Adomnán wrote some ten years later in *Vita Columbae* that it was in order to visit Aldfrith that he made this journey to Northumbria. As on a previous occasion two years before, the abbot treated with the king for the release of Irish captives.[61] No Cenél Conaill abbot of Iona was more closely related to the dominant royal line of the family than Adomnán, and he was probably entirely comfortable in a royal court. There can be little doubt that he was particularly comfortable in Aldfrith's presence. Until 685, the year before Adomnán's first embassy, the king had been a monk of the Ionan fraternity and so an adherent of traditionalist observances.

It may have been intended as a salve to Aldfrith's anxieties that his old abbot registered sympathy for the apostolicist reforms so eagerly recalled by Bede. *Historia ecclesiastica* maintains that Adomnán experienced a full-scale reformist conversion, and went on to reform nearly all the Irish churches 'who were not under the dominion of Iona', amounting to 'the greater part of the Gaels in Ireland' as well as 'some of the Britons in Britain'.[62] It is impossible to find corroboration of this claim in Irish sources or Adomnán's own writings. Instead, Bede seems here to make the abbot of Iona the personification of right-thinking Irish clerics.

But who were the 'Britons in Britain' who went over to apostolicism in the last quarter of the seventh century? It is interesting that Kingarth in the Firth of Clyde was not under the dominion of Iona at this time. Thus, it is possible that it was one of the Gaelic Churches which had reformed its practices by the 690s. In that event, was the Church of Alt Clut one of the British Churches which accepted reform at this time?[63]

---

[60] Bede, *Hist. eccl.*, v.15.

[61] Adomnán, *V. s. Columbae*, ii.46; *AU* 687.5; *AT* 687.5, 689.6; *Ann. Clon.* 682.1.

[62] Bede, *Hist. eccl.*, v.15.

[63] Bede, *Hist. eccl.*, v.15 and v.21, and Adomnán, *V. s. Columbae*, ii.46, relate to these events. See also *AU* 687.5; *AT* 687.5, 689.6; *CS* 687.5; *Ann. Clon.* 682.1.

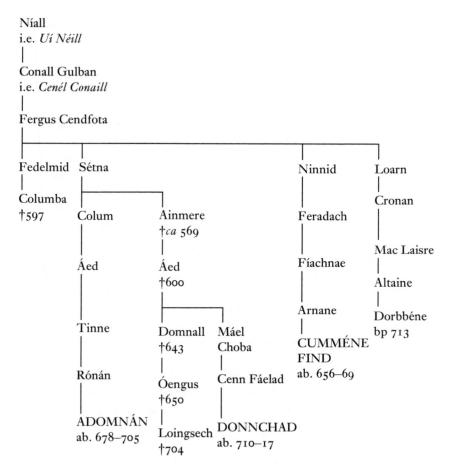

Table 8.2 Adomnán: some key relationships

The Northumbrians were struggling with the political and economic uncertainties of a collapsing superpower when Adomnán visited them. There had been successive military disasters and a stripping away of the Aeðilfrithing hegemony. The ominous misery of bubonic plague too had been afflicting Britain and Ireland since the 660s, when it had claimed the bishops of Canterbury and (probably) York. In *Vita Columbae*, Adomnán wrote that 'although we walked in the midst of this danger of plague', he and his entourage managed to avoid contracting it, 'through the prayers of our venerable patron on our behalf', namely Columba. The founder of his monastery had also provided the same patronage to the Picts to Adomnán's mind. By implication, however, he had withdrawn it from the plague-ridden Northumbrians, despite the twin facts that their

Christianity had its roots in Iona and that their king was a former Columban monk. Bede too was a plague survivor, seemingly alone among all the monks and monastic pupils at Jarrow, save for their leader Ceolfrith, who in 689 succeeded to the abbacy of the joint house.[64] Like the abbot of Iona, the young Bede can hardly have ascribed his fateful singling-out to anything other than divine providence.

Opening the door of the laboratory has shown that stories related by Adomnán and Bede in their respective writings often reveal a great deal more about the time during which they were penned – and about the world of the audience – than about the past events they purport to describe. Those things that *Vita Columbae* reveals about Adomnán's own times as abbot of Iona are invaluable testimony, just as has already been seen of what may be recovered of Cumméne Find's writings in the 640s. Adomnán completed *Vita Columbae c.* 700. To the core of stories about Columba, first related over fifty years earlier in Cumméne's *De uirtutibus sancti Columbae*, Adomnán seems to have added more miracle stories modelled primarily on aspects of such universally influential hagiographical works as the Lives of St Martin and St Germanus and the *Dialogues* of Gregory the Great. In this way, *Vita Columbae* universalised what seems formerly to have been an intimate, Iona-focused story of Columba and his sanctity.[65]

A somewhat later historical perspective is provided by Bede, who wrote in *Historia ecclesiastica* that Iona had formerly dominated the ecclesiastical affairs of Pictland. It has been conventional to conclude from Bede's testimony that Adomnán's monastery, having introduced the Picts to Christianity, proceeded to govern the Pictish Church for a century and a half. In the famous and influential estimation of Skene, the Pictish Church 'was in every respect a Scottish Church, with a Scottish clergy supplied from Ireland', consisting of Columban foundations 'spread all over the whole nation of the Picts', the members of which 'owed their civilisation to its influence, and intrusted [*sic*] the education of their children to its monastic schools'.[66] One gets this impression from no seventh-century source at Iona itself. The model rests entirely on Bede's testimony.

In *Vita Columbae*, thirty years before Bede finished his History, Adomnán complained instead that there were 'many foolish people' among the Picts 'who ungratefully fail to recognise that they have been

[64]   *V. s. Ceolfridi*, § 13–14, though Bede is not named as the *puerulus*; Webb and Farmer, *The Age of Bede*, 217–18 (trans.).

[65]   Herbert, *Iona, Kells, and Derry*, 138–42.

[66]   Skene, *Celtic Scotland*, vol. 1, 276.

protected from plague by the prayers of the saints', and, specifically, by the prayers of his great predecessor Columba. These are not the words of a man whose monastery stands at the pinnacle of Pictish Church life. As already mentioned, all contemporary indications are that in the seventh century Iona's principal interests in Pictland lay in Atholl and Mar. We are bound to conclude that Bede's maximalist estimation of Iona's importance among the Picts alludes to a situation that had only just begun to develop when he met Adomnán in his youth, as the dust was still settling on the battlefield of Dún Nechtain. Its development is discussed below, along with the development of the single Pictish nation (*gens Pictorum*) that Adomnán and Bede took for granted. Both are likely to have been elements of political and ecclesiastical programmes that gripped Pictland after the Verturian victory over Ecgfrith in the battle of Dún Nechtain.

Even against the backdrop of a particularly and demonstrably precocious monastic community at Iona, Adomnán was a remarkable figure of great character. His feelings of being 'daily beset from every quarter by laborious and almost unsustainable church business' were not idle.[67] He had to conduct his impressive scholarship alongside teaching, or at least overseeing the development of pupils, managing the extensive temporal affairs of his monastery and the Ionan *familia* and playing host to diverse visitors. He was also inclined to fight for causes. One of his particular passions was the ethical treatment of captives. In addition to his missions to Northumbria in the 680s to secure the release of Irish captives, Adomnán formulated an ambitious law for the protection of women, clerics and other non-combatants from violence. He promulgated this *Lex innocentium* at Birr in Offaly in Ireland in 696 or 697.[68]

It is difficult to believe that Adomnán's busy St Columba, with his diverse interests, was not crafted to some extent in his own image. Such contemporaries of the ninth abbot of Iona as Ceolfrith at Wearmouth-Jarrow and Cuthbert at Hexham bore similar burdens. No doubt it was the norm at the greater monasteries across northern Britain, both known and unknown to us. Yet it is difficult to believe that any abbot in Britain or Ireland could boast a burden as heavy as Adomnán's, given the sheer distances and logistics involved in overseeing the monasteries of the Ionan *familia*. His portrayal of Columba as an abbot constantly concerned for the welfare of the monks throughout those monasteries,

---

[67] Adomnán, *De loc. sanct.*, iii.6.

[68] *AU* 697.3; *AT* 697.3; *CS* 697.1; *AI* 696.1; Adomnán, *V. s. Columbae*, ii.25. *Lex innocentium* was subsequently known as *Cáin Adomnáin*, Adomnán's Law, but also, probably, as *Lex Coluim Chille*.

sending them benevolent prayers, comfort and protection 'by remote control', suggests that Adomnán was understandably concerned to assure the far-flung Columban brethren that they were always in the thoughts and prayers of their abbot, however remote he could appear.[69]

UP FROM THE ASHES: PICTAVIA

Bede regarded what has been described above as Verturian expansion into southern Pictland after Dún Nechtain as a *reconquista*, in which 'the Picts recovered their own land'. Such a view projects backwards concepts of a *prouincia Pictorum*, which saw both Adomnán and Bede recognise political coherence across the whole *gens Pictorum*, north and south. Bede's sources did the same thing with Northumbrian history, projecting into the early seventh century a political unity that had required the progressive efforts of Oswy and Ecgfrith to be realised. It was something like referring to 'Scotland' for convenience in our period when no such place existed. Various extraneous observers had been referring to *Picti* in northern Britain for centuries, as indeed they had been referring to *Scoti* in Ireland and *Saxones* in southern Britain. Such externally imposed nomenclature tells us little about the internal workings of politics and ethnicity among the peoples thus labelled.

The conventional tetrarchy of four kingdoms in Scotland, formed by Columba's time, is as unhelpful as the obsolete seven-kingdom heptarchy of Anglo-Saxon history. In the case of England, and for that matter Ireland, it would seem to have been only as the seventh century progressed that the ethnic labels *Saxones* (and subsequently *Angli*) and *Scoti* began to be politicised and associated with single realms ruled by a *rex Saxonum* or a *rex totius Scotiae*. These developments were shaped by the centripetal forces exerted by the Church, but also by war and conquest, not least on the parts of Aeðilfrithing and Uí Néill kings, respectively.

The suggestion that the Picts fit the same model hardly seems radical. By embracing the idea of a single Pictish *gens*, ruled collectively by a *rex Pictorum*, the architects of Pictishness bought into Roman terminology. They also fitted themselves into the grand historical narrative of classical Antiquity. A national myth locating Pictish origins in Scythia was a particular nod in this direction, typical of the ways in which learned people contributed to the constructions of ethnic identities in late Antiquity. The place of the *Picti* in the grand sweep of Roman history, as fierce

[69] Smyth, *Warlords*, 89.

enemies of the Eternal City, may have shaped what Pictishness was envisioned to be after 685.

Prior to the seventh century, it must be allowed that Verturian and (post-) Calidonian political, ethnic and other identities rooted in the later Roman Iron Age probably persisted in Pictland north and south of the Mounth. Hints of post-Maiatian ones in Alt Clut in the far south have been considered already. Coalescence of peoples in inner Caledonia had begun by the second century, but the process may have owed something latterly to Bernician expansion and conquest. It culminates in Bede's reference to a single Pictish *prouincia*, overseen by the bishop of Abercorn after 681, seemingly encompassing the *regiones* to the south of the Mounth.

Further north, the kingdom of Fortriu may have been diphyletic by 685, with rival colleague-kings in Atholl (*Athfotla*) and Moray (later *Moreb*). In the next generation, kinsmen of the Verturian kings were ruling in Atholl. In the 680s, south and north were falling together to such an extent that one king could style himself *rex Pictorum*, at least to his neighbours. The first compilation of the Pictish king-list, which reached its final form in the ninth century, dates to about this time, its first certainly contemporary 'entry' having been taken from a record made in 663. The king-list envisions the idea of joint kingship, presupposing the existence of a bipartite nation, just as one would have predicted.[70]

Bede was aware of Northumbrian king-lists in these same years which had been deliberately manipulated, including the subjection of awkward or embarrassing reigns to *damnatio memoriae*, erasure from history.[71] No doubt Pictish king-list-makers mobilised their hindsight in similar ways. The king-list famously makes no king the son of a previous one until the last half of the eighth century. The list of sixth- and seventh-century kings contains several instances where men of the same generation, or perhaps two generations, within a kindred maintained a grip on the kingship. Yet there were probably four significant shifts in the ruling dynasty between 671 and 789 inclusive. Such disruptions, including the supercession and destruction of royal houses, were common in early medieval kingship. As such, what the king-list reveals is difficulty in maintaining a grip on a kingdom for more than a generation or two.

Looking back on the Pictish kingdom, several generations after its disappearance, one Scottish chronicler called it *Pictavia*.[72] The union of the

---

[70] On the compilation, see Evans, 'Ideology, Literacy and Matriliny', forthcoming. On joint kingships, see Wood, 'Kings, Kingdoms and Consent', 17–20.

[71] Bede, *Hist. eccl.*, iii.1.

[72] *Chron. Kings of Alba*, § 1.

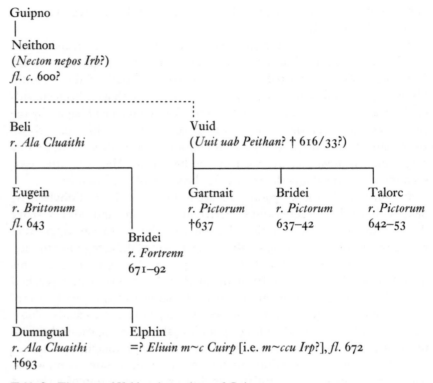

Guipno
|
Neithon
(*Necton nepos Irb?*)
fl. c. 600?

Beli
r. Ala Cluaithi

Vuid
(*Uuit uab Peithan?* † 616/33?)

Eugein
r. Brittonum
fl. 643

Gartnait
r. Pictorum
†637

Bridei
r. Pictorum
637–42

Talorc
r. Pictorum
642–53

Bridei
r. Fortrenn
671–92

Dumngual
r. Ala Cluaithi
†693

Elphin
=? *Eliuin m~c Cuirp* [i.e. *m~ccu Irp?*], *fl.* 672

Table 8.3 The sons of Vuid as descendants of Guipno

two main Pictish zones into Pictavia seems to have owed much to the military successes of Bridei son of Beli in the period 680–5. It has been supposed that 'Neithan' is the correct name of the father of 'Wit' son of 'Peithan', the subject of an 'A-text' *Gododdin* elegy, so that a link can be postulated between Bridei's grandfather Neithon son of Guipno and the historical sons of Vuid (or Wid), who reigned in Pictland successively from 633 until 653.[73]

It has already been observed that the campaign commemorated in the *Gododdin* elegies may have taken place during the reign of Edwini of Deira between 616 and 633. Gartnait son of Vuid died in 637, making it unproblematic for his father to have fallen in battle against Edwini. If Gartnait and his brothers were grandsons of Neithon son of Guipno, like Bridei, these links would imply that three cousins of Bridei, presumably southern Pictish kings, were included in the Pictish king-list. In that event, the king-list –

[73] 'Aneirin', *Gododin*. 'A-text', ll. 384–7; Clancy, *The Triumph Tree*, 47–67 (trans.). For discussion see Smyth, *Warlords*, 65; Koch, *Gododdin*, 207.

composed *c.* 664 and possibly during Bridei's reign as king of Fortriu – could be seen as placing emphasis on his royal credentials as a kinsman of southern Pictish kings. The possibility that the list thus presents a mixture of Verturian Waerteras and Bridei's own southern kin – and may do still more mixing of this kind in the earlier and more mythic section – undermines this source as evidence of succession practices among the Picts.

Natives of the two Pictish zones by the early eighth century would have been discouraged in various ways from cultivating consciousness of difference reinforcing ethnic divisions. The wave of the future was the idea of belonging to a single community of descent, the *gens Pictorum*, with a common history, common political and economic interests spanning the Mounth and common cultural traits. Bridei's own *cohors* – no doubt a substantial group of warriors cloaked in glory from their many victories from Orkney to Dundurn – was probably an important ideological force in this movement. A Pictish ecclesiastical history of some description was apparently formulated by the end of the seventh century. Adomnán was able to use it to shape the Columban dossier relating to Pictavia. There are strong indications, moreover, that the Pictish origin myth known to Bede was also composed in Pictland *c.* 700.

It is important to avoid the trap of excessive elitism, however, in seeking to understand ethnogenesis, even if we are unable to appreciate how elites and normal freemen negotiated the consciousness of pan-Pictish nationhood. We may expect that, like romanisation, the notion was embraced most eagerly by those who regarded it as a boon to their own interests, and that, again like romanisation, ethnogenesis could take on a life of its own. It may have been embraced particularly eagerly by the Church, which seems to have transmitted some of its key ideas.

The movements of Bridei, best considered among those of his immediate successors, in bringing the ecclesiastical landscapes of northern and southern Pictland into harmony are remarkable. In effect, what lay before the Waerteras after 685 was the task of bringing about what may be usefully called 'the Pictish Church'. That task would have required ecclesiastical leaders to consider how much diversity and how much unity was desirable in custom and practice across Pictavia.

Some of the groundwork may already have been laid by Northumbrian interference in Pictish ecclesiastical affairs. Both Beornhaeth in the far south and Bridei in Fortriu may have been under pressure to be apostolicist and consistent in their ecclesiastical activities, including how their respective Churches were organised. There is no hint in Bede's narrative that either region introduced apostolicist reforms in this period, only to back-slide after 685. Bede, for whom reform was a matter of particular specialist interest, would surely have mentioned such developments. None the less, the southern Pictish zone in particular, experiencing the successive primatial claims of York and Abercorn, may have developed a reformist and conformist underclass, much as Deira did in the middle third of the seventh century. It has already been pointed out that Bede's southern Pictish source relating to the christianisation of the Picts imagined that southern Pictish Christianity had apostolicist origins.

It is uncertain what happened to Abercorn in the wake of Dún Nechtain. We know that its English bishop withdrew from his see with his monks, but when? It may not have taken place until 698, six years after Bridei's death. Here, as elsewhere, Bridei's footprints in the ecclesiastical landscape of the southern Pictish zone are faint. The end of his southward trail is only really detectable from our slightly better ability to observe where the footprints of his immediate successors start. These imply that Bridei's remarkable conquests of the 680s were encompassed by the strongholds of Dunnottar and Dundurn, and probably did not reach further south than Strathearn.

Something of his mark may have been left at Abernethy, the foundation legend of which names as its donor a son of Erp. Some kind of kinship between the founder and Bridei has been contemplated already. The long and the short of the difficult and scrappy evidence may be that Bridei felt a special connection with this monastery. There are suggestions that Abernethy achieved primatial status during the Pictish period, both in the king-list and, for what it is worth, in Walter Bower's *Scotichronicon*. Bower, writing at Inchcolm in the Firth of Forth in the fifteenth century, noted that 'a certain chronicle of the church of Abernethy' maintained that, *per aliqua tempora*, 'for some period', it had been 'the principal royal and episcopal seat of the whole Pictish kingdom (*regnum Pictorum*)'.[74] A window of sorts exists for Abernethy to have played that role after 685 – at least between the Mounth and the Ochils – in a period when the paramount king in Pictland was probably a friend, and before the *regnum Pictorum* need have extended into Fife or Manau, the presumed immediate hinterland of Abercorn. It seems unlikely that our picture of Bridei's achievement in southern Pictland, or for that matter in Argyll, will ever get much clearer than these fleeting, semi-connected details. Evidence considered in the next chapter clarifies things a little more, but Bridei son of Beli will always be an enigma to us – a personification of the fabulousness, obscurity and difficulty which characterise our period.

---

[74] Bower, *Scotichronicon*, iv.12; see also Anderson, *Early Sources*, vol. i, cxx–cxxi.

Postscript
Scotland and the Aeðilfrithing
Legacy

By the end of the seventh century, northern Britain was in the midst of a transition from its late Antique period to its early medieval one. The status quo which had emerged by the end of the third century was becoming a thing of the past. The Maiatian and Uotadinian nations of outer Brigantia had become subsumed within the remarkable Aeðilfrithing *imperium*. The Calidonian nation had, perhaps, largely weathered that same storm, only to succumb to a new tempest from the Verturian north. A new breed of *imperator* had appeared, the greatest of whom – men like Áedán, Oswy and Bridei – could meddle in the affairs of communities as far afield as Orkney, Tweeddale and Ulster. A parallel development – expansive and provincialising tendencies – had also arisen at churches like Iona and York. The first rumblings of a future of political, military and economic dominion by great lords based in lowland Scotland were being felt, the Bernicians perhaps representing the last in a long line of dominant groups in the North British zone stretching back to the Roman Iron Age. That Age, already mortally wounded, was put to the sword on the battlefield of Dún Nechtain.

This Part of the book maintains that it is a gross error, rooted in conceptions of human diversity current during the rise of nationalism in the nineteenth century, to regard the legacy of the Aeðilfrithings as 'English' history distinct from 'Scottish' history. The so-called Migration Period saw Roman frontiers across western Europe inundated by barbarians and the development of new settled peoples. It was one of the most significant periods of recorded European history. Ostrogothic and Lombard incursions into Italy, their subsequent settlements and the relationships that Roman communities established with the newcomers, profoundly transformed both native and barbarian. Circumstances were comparable in Spain as a result of Vandal and Visigothic conquests, and in Gaul after the coming of the Franks and the Burgundians. They were comparable too in Britain as natives and newcomers endeavoured to cope with the advent of the Anglo–Saxon peoples.

In modern Scotland, nationalist sensitivities can react against emphasis on the importance of the Anglo–Saxons and the ripples their impact sent across the whole of Britain as well as Ireland. Yet if we recognise that the Roman status quo of the prior epoch was significant and far-reaching, its transformation, inevitably sending shockwaves throughout areas linked with Roman Britain, cannot be mere anglocentrism. Just as in other areas of Europe, Africa and the Near East, incursions by barbarians were important aspects of the transition from late Antiquity to the early Middle Ages. Just how important they were will always be controversial. In Britain, the late Antique status quo became disrupted at an earlier date than elsewhere, through a combination of barbarian pressure and changes in native Romano–British behaviour.

As a result of this early collapse of *romanitas*, the Anglo–Saxons retained far more of their former social and cultural character, for far longer, than was common elsewhere. At the same time, the Roman Britons developed uncommonly stark senses of alienation from them and hostility towards them. These peculiarities are not well understood. Without Roman institutions to exploit, a comparatively rapid and comprehensive conquest was impossible. It may have taken the better part of a century of conflict before the first Anglo–Saxon regimes were securely established. The comparatively slow pace of change arguably allowed for ethnic solidarity to be retained among both natives and newcomers, and for ethnicity to adapt to shifting circumstances in ways that were denied to many Continental peoples.[1]

Romano–British communities had the opportunity to develop robust new senses of themselves and consciousness of difference from Anglo–Saxons, which could resist easy assimilation. The result, by the seventh century, was the bedding down of regional identities into new 'national' ones, the retention of several vernacular languages and religious diversity. The nature of the Migration Period thus, as in other European contexts, created the stage and the backdrop for the playing-out of medieval, and indeed modern British history.

In both western and northern Britain, it seems to have been in the course of the seventh century that new native national and ethnic identities really firmed up alongside that (or those) which was (or were) also bedding down among the Anglo–Saxons. At the end of the fifth century,

---

[1] Woolf, 'The Britons', 353–5; Charles-Edwards, 'Nations and Kingdoms', 29–30.

the British missionary Patrick conceived of warriors based at Clyde Rock as 'my own people' (*mei*) and fellow countrymen, and also as 'fellow citizens of the holy Romans' (*cives sanctorum Romanorum*).[2] Some fifty years later, Gildas conceived of himself as a Briton and regarded the Romans as extraneous people.[3] For Patrick, the establishment of Anglo-Saxon regimes in Britain in the middle decades of the fifth century was not remarkable. For Gildas, a hundred years after the fact, they were the central and most deplorable aspect of recent politics and history. Something important had changed in Britain in the generation separating Patrick from Gildas, Uinniau and Columba.

Yet Gildas tells us himself that most British kings and clerics did not share his vision of things. It was probably because they did not perceive irreconcilable differences between themselves and their neighbours – English as well as British – that so many North British 'successor kingdoms' known to Urbgen and Aeðilfrith *c.* 590 became assimilated within the dominant British and English realms of the first half of the seventh century. The same thing happened in the Mercian sphere of influence. The 'givens of birth' may have marked certain peoples as Britons or Anglo-Saxons, but in an age of shifting territorial realities when many potentates may have spoken both British and Anglo-Saxon and may have had kin on both sides of the ethnic divide ethnic identities can still have been quite fluid. Patrick, in writing to a North British court, regarded himself as a fellow Briton and a fellow Roman; but, in addressing himself to his Irish converts in the very same letter, he accused their British enemies of believing that 'it is a disgrace that we are Irish' (*indignum est Hiberionaci sumus*), thus regarding himself as an *Hiberionacus* like them.[4]

Oswy died exactly a century after Gildas did, when starker lines of difference are perceptible on a par with Gildas's formerly eccentric views. Ethnic identities which survived into Oswy's period (and had not already become transformed by earlier conquests) proved less amenable to suppression or assimilation than had formerly been the case. Key evidence in this regard in northern Britain lies in the place-names of southern Scotland. The extensive evidence of English settlement-names of early character in East Lothian, Tweeddale and Northumberland, contrasts with a relative dearth of such names to the North British west and Pictish north.[5] It seems that seventh-century North Britons and southern Picts

---

2 Patricius, *Ep.*, §§ 2, 11.
3 Wood, 'End of Roman Britain', 22.
4 Patricius, *Ep.*, § 16.
5 Jackson, 'Britons in Southern Scotland', 84; Nicolaisen, *Scottish Place-Names*, 68–83.

were less likely than their Gododdin neighbours of a prior generation to become ethnic Bernicians after conquest.

Another language-related reflex of this phenomenon may have been the emergence of vernacular panegyric poetry like that attributed to Taliesin, supplanting an earlier ethos, lasting into Gildas's lifetime, in which the Romance language of Britain was supreme.[6] The flourishing of Insular art before the middle of the seventh century, blending traditional styles and workmanship from all across Britain and Ireland crucially seems to date from the age of more fluid ethnic mentalities.

What has this ethnic transition to do with the Aeðilfrithings or the history of Scotland? Oswy seems to have intended to push the *imperium* he had established by 655 to the ends of the island, building on the remarkable imperial successes of his father and his father-in-law. Within thirty years, that *imperium* had come apart at the seams and metropolitan and quasi-metropolitan pretensions of York and Iona were faltering. Changing Insular attitudes towards post-Roman identity may have been an important factor in explaining Ecgfrith's inability to emulate his predecessors as *imperator*. The end of the seventh century seems instead to have been a new dawn for the *gens Nordanhymbrorum*, the *gens Pictorum*, the *gens Brittonum* and the *Scoti Britanniae*, in which they became increasingly distinct from one another, but also increasingly coherent as political and ethnic groupings.

The hegemony of the Aeðilfrithing kings is of key importance in the story of this transition. In Pictland, the Bernician regime may have become established in the first instance as a function of ties of kinship. Perhaps at this time senses of identity were still somewhat more fluid than they became a generation later. Oswy seems to have set the wheels in motion for the process of counter-conquest and native ethnogenesis that encouraged the creation of Pictavia. In Argyll, the influence of the Northumbrian superpower may have provided Cenél nGabráin with the necessary clout to maintain a grip on the Corcu Réti, and perhaps to enjoy a measure of wider paramountcy as well. At the same time, the relationship between Bamburgh and Iona before the Synod of Whitby, and perhaps to some extent thereafter, can have done Iona little harm. Oswald was remembered with reverence in *Vita Columbae*.

In the British periphery of Aeðilfrithing Bernicia, Gododdin and Rheged would seem to have become assimilated within the Northumbrian project as a result of conquest. Alt Clut – or at least its rump focused on Clyde Rock – avoided their fate, seemingly along with North British folk

---

[6] Woolf, 'The Britons', 373–7.

further south. Here again ethnic solidarities seem to have firmed up which survived into the Viking Age. Left in an isolated position, the kings of Clyde Rock established interlinkages with the kings of Cowal and Fortriu. It may have been an active expression of a contra-Aeðilfrithing political mentality. The Mercian kingdom may have been forged around a similar contra-Aeðilfrithing bloc at the other end of the hegemony, involving Anglo-Saxon and British leaders alike.

The northern bloc seems to have capitalised energetically on the tribulations of Ecgfrith, bringing about decisive shifts in the balances of power in Pictland, Argyll and the Clyde estuary. These shifts, in turn, may reflect a northern manifestation of a wider phenomenon which saw native communities throughout the island finally embracing a post-Roman Britain which, for the first time in six hundred years, lacked, even rejected a single, dominant political idea. In Pictish northern Britain a new idea had emerged from the wreckage of the thinking of the late Antique epoch. From that seed, watered by the kings of Bamburgh, was to grow the flower of Scotland.

PART THREE

The Pictish Project (692–789)

CHAPTER 9

League and Iron: Bridei son of Der-Ilei, Iona and Argyll (692–707)

As late as the 640s, a range of evidence suggests that the Pictish 'principate' (*principatus*) of Iona was largely confined to monasteries in Mar, in the district of Cé, and in Atholl, perhaps linked via routes through Strathspey. Bede's information was that the Ionan *familia* extended its influence, 'for no short time' holding supremacy (*arx*) over 'all the Pictish monasteries'.[1] When did this expansion take place? In *Vita Columbae*, Adomnán accepted – as Bede later did from southern Pictish information – that Columba was an evangelist among the northern Picts, so that the natural assumption has long been that Ionan supremacy simply spread along with christianisation. But Adomnán's complaints that the Picts were giving Columba insufficient honour, despite the presence of Columban monasteries among them, is one of a number of indications already discussed that the Ionan primacy envisioned by Bede was, in fact, largely a development of the years after *c.* 700.

Where did the historical position originate, which informed Bede and seemingly influenced Adomnán? Indications that Bede's southern Pictish informants were relating Verturian history have already been noted. The position seems to reflect official thinking put forward after the Verturian conquest of the southern Pictish zone in the 680s and probably came ultimately from someone close to the Verturian court. Did Adomnán get his information from Portmahomack?

The implication of the evidence is that the victor of Dún Nechtain, Bridei son of Beli, singled out Iona and its *familia* for special favour. He may not have been the first Verturian king to do so; however, he may have turned to it additionally for help in binding north and south together. Yet an interesting element of confrontation runs through Adomnán's

---

[1] Bede, *Hist. eccl.*, iii.3.

portrayal of Columba and the northern Picts.[2] Was the ninth abbot of Iona uneasy about getting into bed with a Verturian establishment given to interfere aggressively in Argyll affairs?

FORTRIU AND THE STATUS OF ARGYLL

It is interesting to open the doors to the laboratory again, and to consider Bede's Pictish and Dalriadan origin legends alongside Adomnán's perspective on Gaelo-Pictish relations. Bede's myth about Dalriadan origins contains Picto-centric elements, as already discussed; as for the Pictish myth, he says that the Picts attested to it. The author of the latter story made use of Gaelic pseudo-history, but the belief that the myth was 'foisted on the Picts by the Irish' misunderstands the power dynamics of northern Britain *c.* 730 when Bede wrote.[3] The plundering of Gaelic pseudo-history is a clue to the circumstances surrounding the myths' composition. All Picts, the author wrote, were distinguished by Irish heritage, being descendants ultimately of Pictish immigrants who had married Irish women. Because of this ancient association it was in order for Picts, the myth states, to ask for Irish military support and perfectly legitimate, in a succession dispute, to claim kingship on the basis of maternal heritage.

Bede's Pictish and Dalriadan origin myths

To begin with the inhabitants of the island were all *Brettones*, from whom it receives its name. They sailed to Britannia, as it is said (*ut fertur*) from the land of Armorica [i.e. across the Channel], and appropriated to themselves the southern part of it.

After they had got possession of the greater part of the island, beginning from the south, the *gens Pictorum* sailed from Scythia, as they testify (*ut perhibent*), into the ocean in a few long-ships, and were carried by the wind beyond the furthest bounds of Britannia, reaching Hibernia and landing on its northern shores. There they found the *gens Scottorum*, and asked permission to settle among them, but their request was refused . . .

The Irish (*Scotti*) answered that the island would not hold them both; 'but we can give you some good advice as to what to do', they said.

---

[2] Márkus, 'Iona: monks, pastors and missionaries', 132–5.
[3] Bede, *Hist. eccl.*, i.1 (*ut perhibent*); Smyth, *Warlords*, 60–1.

'We know of another island not far from our own, in an easterly direction, which we often see in the distance on clear days. If you will go there, you can make a settlement for yourselves. But if anyone resists you, make use of our help' (nobis auxiliariis utimini). And so the Picts went to Britannia and proceeded to occupy the northern parts of the island, because the Britons had seized the southern regions. As the Picts had no wives, they asked them of the Irish, who consented to give them, but only on condition that, where the matter came into doubt (ubi res ueniret in dubium), they should elect their kings from the female royal line rather than the male. And it is well known that the custom has been observed among the *Picti* to this day.

In the course of time, after the Britons and the Picts, Britannia received a third, Irish, nation (natio Scottorum) into the Pictish part (in Pictorum parte), who with Reuda their leader came from Hibernia, and won the lands that they still possess by friendship or by iron (uel amicitia uel ferro).

This sequence of notions surrounding the Gaelo–Pictish relationship makes it virtually certain that the legend was composed *c.* 700, about the time that Adomnán was completing *Vita Columbae.* Why? The man who became king of Picts in 696 or 697, another Bridei, appears to have based his claim to the kingship on being the son of Der-Ilei his (almost certainly Pictish) mother, his father Dargart having probably been Dargart of Cenél Comgaill.[4] As a Pictish king who claimed the kingship through his mother's patrimony, Bridei's situation is made perfectly and suspiciously legitimate by the origin legend, right down to the case of doubt (*in dubium*) – the expulsion of his predecessor – required for the mobilisation of the matrilineal argument. He was also a man of Gaelo-Pictish heritage – the origin legend suspiciously normalises that by assigning such heritage to all Picts. It is, therefore, intriguing that the legend also normalises Pictish recourse to Gaelic support in looking to make new settlements in Britain. A possible manifestation in the reign of Bridei son of Der-Ilei is discussed below. Finally, the origin mythologist, who was probably close to the Verturian royal court, took for granted the essential homogeneity of the *gens Pictorum,* a political stance that was probably not much older than the 680s, when Bridei son of Beli was extending his arm south of the Mounth.

---

[4] That Der-Ilei was a woman has been established by Clancy, 'Philosopher-King', 128–31; that it was through her that her sons claimed kingship in Fortriu is discussed by Clancy, above, at 133, 135.

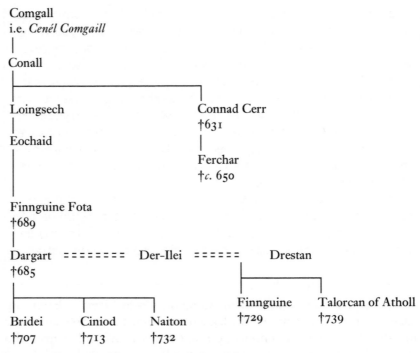

Table 9.1 Ancestry of the sons of Der-Ilei and Dargart

Such historicising of political realities through origin mythology is characteristic of early medieval 'ethnic ideology', which could contain many such symbolic abstractions. It is important that the myth envisions Pictishness as a partial product of Gaelic heritage. Moreover, by giving the Picts Scythian origins it was providing them with the same original homeland as Gaelic learning had established for Gaeldom, a link that may have been partly accidental and partly intentional. The myth might, therefore, be regarded as seeking to rationalise a single Gaelo-Pictish community of descent, in which the Picts enjoyed precedence but Gaels were not denied honour.

With this thought in mind, we may return to Bede's Dalriadan origin legend with its suspicious Picto-centric stances. Gaelic entitlement in Argyll post-dates Pictish entitlement here. It was obtained from the Picts 'by league and by iron', and so could theoretically be revoked if league of friendship (*amicitia*) failed and the Picts sought to re-assert their rights 'by iron'. This myth is thus consistent with the Pictish one, giving the Picts the upper hand in Gaelo-Pictish relations. Similarly consistent is another claim related by Bede – explicitly from a Pictish source – that the island of Iona was donated to Columba by Picts, implying, like the origin mythology, that Argyll was Pictish, in parts as late as the sixth century.

Taken together, this evidence from Pictish sources expresses a consistent political doctrine, developed *c.* 700, in which the Gaels of Argyll inhabit territory properly Pictish – with Pictish consent – and the Picts in turn are a people that had, long ago, happily intermarried with Gaels and had not forgotten it. This doctrine is likely to reflect contemporary realities, and must be added to the bitty evidence discussed in the previous chapter of Pictish movements in Argyll after 671.

What did the Argyll Gaels make of all this? Adomnán, also writing *c.* 700, espoused a very different doctrine. On the one hand, he wrote that Columba had acted as patron of the Argyll Gaels and the Picts during the plagues of 686 and 688. These disasters had mainly struck Northumbria in the wake of the battle of Dún Nechtain, from which time such an all-encompassing view of the Picts was particularly appropriate. In this respect, Adomnán may be regarded as taking up the same kind of Gaelo-Pictish perspective that is imbedded in Bede's Pictish material.

Yet Adomnán makes a point in this same chapter of *Vita Columbae* of stating that the Gaels and the Picts are divided from one another, using the verb *disterminare*, 'to delimit'. He even formulates an artful sentence likening the delimiting power of Drumalban by association with that of the Pyrenees. The significance of Drumalban as a barrier between Pict and Gael is also emphasised by repetition throughout the Life. Here we have a context for the confrontational element of *Vita Columbae* as regards the Picts.

Adomnán on plague, Picts and Gaels

This also I consider should not be reckoned among lesser miracles of power, in connection with the plague that, twice in our times, ravaged the greater part of the surface of the earth. Quite apart from the other wider regions of Europe – to wit, Italy and the city of Rome itself, and the provinces of Gaul on this side of the Alps, and the Spanish provinces, separated by the barrier of the Pyrenean mountain (*Pirinei montis interiectu disterminatis*) – the islands of the ocean, to wit Scotia and Britannia, were twice utterly ravaged by a terrible pestilence, save two peoples (*populi*) only: those were the Pictish population (*plebs Pictorum*) and the Gaels of Britain (*Scoti Brittanniae*), divided from one another by the mountains of Drumalban (*inter quos utrosque dorsi montes brittannici disterminant*). And, although neither people is without great sins, by which the eternal judge is often provoked to

---

Adomnán on plague, Picts and Gaels (*continued*)

wrath, none the less he has, until now, spared them both, enduring patiently.

To whom else can this favour, conferred by God, be attributed than St Columba, whose monasteries, placed within the boundaries of both peoples, are held in great honour by them both, down to the present time? Yet what we are now going to tell is, as we judge, not to be heard without sorrow: that there are, in both peoples, many great fools who (not knowing that they have been protected from disease by the prayers of the saints) ungratefully abuse God's patience. We, however, give frequent thanks to God, who, through the prayers of our venerable patron on our behalf, has protected us from the invasion of plagues, both in these our islands, and in Saxonia [England], when we visited our friend King Aldfrith, while the pestilence still continued, and devastated many villages on all sides.

If *Beatha Adamnáin* can be believed, a comparatively late 'Life of Adomnán' of questionable historical value, at his death in 692 Bridei son of Beli was buried at Iona, and Adomnán mourned him.[5] It is a suitable fate for a king who may have advanced the interests of Iona in Pictland for his own political and other purposes. Yet Adomnán's Pictish animals in *Vita Columbae* are portrayed as extremely aggressive and dangerous beasts, which Columba commanded to 'go no further' and sent 'in swift retreat, as if being pulled back by ropes'.[6] The question of how closely Iona should align itself with the Verturian court was apparently not easily answered.

THE RISE OF CENÉL NECHDACH

Having taken account of these big political ideas relating to the status of Argyll from a Verturian perspective, we are equipped to interpret the events on the ground in the period after Dún Nechtain. Máel Dúin, king of the Corcu Réti from 672 until his death in 688, seems to have been the last of the descendants of Áedán to inherit a share of the wide-ranging power cultivated by the Kintyre kings since *c.* 650. His position seems to have been under threat from the first, however, for his predecessor

---

[5] *AU* 693.1; *AT* 693.1; *AI* 691.1.
[6] Adomnán, *V. s. Columbae*, ii.26–7; on this, see Márkus, 'Iona: monks, pastors and missionaries', 116.

Domangart had been slain and a conspiracy between Cano of Cenél nGartnait and Bridei son of Beli may have been suspected of the killing.

By the tenth year of Máel Dúin's reign, a coalition may have formed between Bridei, his nephew Dumngual of Clyde Rock and Finnguine of Cowal, probably the grandfather of the Verturian king Bridei son of Der-Ilei. The military reach of this coalition may have extended from Lorn to Antrim in north-east Ireland, regions troubled by British incursions in these years, and it may also have been behind the sieges of Dunadd and Dundurn in 682. At the same time, Verturian backing may have contributed to the flourishing of Cenél nGartnait in northern Argyll, to be discussed below.

Vita Columbae refers to *caput regionis*, the 'chief place of the district' in Argyll, where vessels from Gaul might be encountered.[7] This *caput* is conventionally identified as Dunadd, but the famous stronghold on the River Add was probably not accessible to sea-going vessels.[8] In contrast, Dunollie on Oban Bay in Iona's neighbourhood is a promontory fort site wreathed by the sea. It is more frequently mentioned in the chronicles than any other Argyll stronghold, and once as an *arx*, a 'stronghold' word with connotations of paramountcy.[9] Dunollie is thus arguably as likely as Dunadd to be Adomnán's *caput regionis*.[10]

This is not to say that Dunadd, attacked in 682, was not by then a centre of particular significance. This inference, confirmed by archaeological investigation, makes good sense of the behaviour of the Pictish king Onuist son of Vurguist in 736. Although it has earlier occupation horizons extending back into prehistory, the establishment of a substantial 'nuclear' stronghold at Dunadd appears to date from the seventh century. Its ramparts had been raised by the time of Máel Dúin and the siege of 682. At the entrance to the inner citadel are famous carved-stone footprints, conventionally supposed to have been used in royal inaugurations. There are also archaeological suggestions that the site was repeatedly altered, at least in part to affect sight-lines to and from the citadel and the footprints.[11]

Máel Dúin was probably inaugurated at Dunadd in 672, and Domangart son of Domnall Brecc may have been inaugurated there before him in 659 or 660. The position of the stronghold in Mid-Argyll

---

[7] Adomnán, *V. s. Columbae*, i.28.
[8] Lane and Campbell, *Dunadd*, 3–4.
[9] *AU* 734.6.
[10] Alcock, 'The Activities of Potentates', 33; restated in Alcock, *Kings and Warriors*, 83.
[11] Campbell, *Saints and Sea-Kings*, 21, 24–5; Lane and Campbell, *Dunadd*, 90–3; see also Alcock, 'Activities of Potentates', 26.

seems particularly significant. It did not stand in the heartland of Cenél nGabráin, nor any of the 'principal kindreds' of Dál Riata, but rather in the midst of them as befits a focus of high kingship.[12] It is unfortunate that radiocarbon dating does not allow for the kind of precision necessary to establish whether the foundation of Dunadd occurred during the period before or after the rise of the Aeðilfrithing kings. That it took place in the seventh century, however, is an important factor for understanding the development of high kingship in Argyll – the making of the famous kingdom of Dál Riata.

How the siege of 682 affected Argyll politics is impossible to know for certain. Máel Dúin was king for another six years, but Finnguine of Cowal may have eclipsed him in the wake of the siege, backed by Alt Clut and Fortriu. By 684, Dumngual of Alt Clut may even have been allied with Fínsnechtae Fledach, king of Síl nÁedo Sláne, in the southern Uí Néill kingdom of Brega. That at least would be one way of contextualising the Northumbrian attack on Brega in that year, undertaken, according to the *Annals of Clonmacnoise*, because of a Gaelo-British alliance. Dargart son of Finnguine was killed in 685.[13] It was the same year as Bridei's great victory at Dún Nechtain – and Dargart's wife was a Pict – but suggestions that Ecgfrith was vanquished by a grand alliance are unnecessary. Within four years both Máel Dúin and Finnguine were also dead. The chronicles record a great Dalriadan campaign against the Cruithni and the Ulaid in 690, an impressive initiation, perhaps, of the new *rex Dáil Riata*, apparently Máel Dúin's brother Domnall Dond.[14]

Does this ambitious military venture presuppose relatively robust concord between the two great segments of the Corcu Réti under Domnall? The political momentum in Argyll seems in any case to have passed into the north in the 690s. It is conventional to speak of Cenél Loairn as a single people and, indeed, a single Lorn kingdom is likely to have existed by 690. Yet *Míniugud senchasa fher nAlban* clearly separates these 'descendants of Loarn' into 'three thirds', including Cenél nEchdach and Cenél Cathboth, each probably dominating a local realm. The Cenél nEchdach king Ferchar Fota died in 696 or 697 – unfortunately the chronology of the Irish chronicles in these years still requires untangling. His rise to prominence culminated in paramountcy in Argyll, established in 695 when Domnall Dond was killed.

[12]   Nieke and Duncan, 'Dalriada', 16–17.
[13]   *AU* 686.3; *AT* 686.7; *CS* 686.2 (*AT* and *CS* show that *AU* 693.6 is a late corruption).
[14]   *AU* 689.7, 690.3, 691.3; *AT* 690.3; *CS* 689.6, 690.3.

Cenél Loairn

Lorn today, as it was in the Middle Ages, is a region of three parts: Upper Lorn and Mid Lorn divided by Loch Etive, and the rugged country of Nether Lorn west of Loch Awe and north of Loch Melfort and Loch Avich. Similarly, although it is conventional to speak of Cenél Loairn as a single kindred, *Míniugud senchasa fher nAlban* separates them into 'three thirds': Cenél Salaich, Cenél Cathboth and Cenél nEchdach.[15] That these three *cenéla* were contemporary with Cenél nGabráin and Cenél Comgaill is confirmed by 'the slaughter of Cenél Cathboth' in 701. Can we locate them?

Cethri prímchenéla Dáil Riata records two segments of Cenél nEchdach to represent Cenél Loairn. The apical ancestor linking them is not the eponymous Eochaid, but his son Báetán. Place-name evidence suggests that Báetán became an eponym in his own right. An act of John Balliol locates 'Cenel Vadan' in Morvern, while Archattan parish, roughly co-terminous with Upper Lorn, was known as *Ballebhodan*.[16] There is, therefore, reason to believe that (as *Cethri prímchenéla Dáil Riata* implies) the descendants of Báetán son of Eochaid came to dominate Cenél nEchdach, and that the *cenél* occupied Upper Lorn or Benderloch, with possessions in Morvern on the other side of Loch Linnhe.

The chronicle record of 'the slaughter of Cenél Cathboth' comes hard on the heels of 'the destruction of Dunollie' by a Cenél nEchdach dynast. It is, therefore, reasonable to suppose that Dunollie was a Cenél Cathboth stronghold in 701.[17] The likelihood that it was in fact the symbolic royal centre of the Lorn kings, rather than the possession of a single kindred, means that we must proceed with caution. However, there is reason to place Cenél Cathboth here in Mid Lorn, separated from Cenél nEchdach by Loch Etive.

What of Cenél Salaich? Adomnán writes in *Vita Columbae* about setting off for Iona 'from the mouth of *flumen Sale*' by sea, but quickly becoming stranded on a nearby island until, thanks to Columba's intervention, a south-east (*ulturnus*) wind blew up.[18] This story implies that the river mouth in question lay south-east of Iona. Our attention is thus attracted to the island of Seil off the coast of Nether Lorn, *Saoil* in

---

[15] *Mín. sench. fher nAlban*, § 41; there are conflicting conceptions of how these segments related to Loarn Mór in §§ 39–40.

[16] Watson, *Celtic Place-Names*, 122; Grant, 'United Parishes', 1.

[17] *AU* 701.8–9.

[18] Adomnán, *V. s. Columbae*, ii.45.

Cenél Loairn (continued)

modern Gaelic and *Sóil* in the twelfth-century *Book of Leinster*.[19] If Cenél Salaich were based in Nether Lorn, it would be a neat fit with the foregoing evidence.

A year after Ferchar's death, his son Ainbcellach was driven from the kingship of Lorn, and in 701 or 702 another son, Selbach, seems to have brought about 'the slaughter of Cenél Cathboth'. Both Lorn events are linked in the *Annals of Ulster* with attacks on Dunollie, overlooking the Firth of Lorn, probably the principal royal stronghold of the Lorn high kings.[20] The first two phases of the stronghold, identified archaeologically, date to *c.* 700.[21] Dunollie was burnt in 685, perhaps marking the seizure of the kingship of Lorn by Ferchar, whose own realm was probably beyond Loch Etive in Upper Lorn, possibly including part of Morvern.[22] The fates of Ferchar's sons imply that Cenél Cathboth successfully challenged Ainbcellach's succession in 697 or 698, removing him to captivity in Ireland. Their own (unnamed) leader was, however, toppled in turn by Selbach son of Ferchar in 701 or 702.

A GAELO-PICTISH HEGEMON: BRIDEI SON OF DERILEI

Cethri prímchenéla Dáil Riata, apparently composed soon after these events in Lorn, ignores Cenél Cathboth, relating instead two Cenél nEchdach lineages. It also implies that Cenél Comgaill remained prominent further south in Argyll a generation after the death of Finnguine Fota, the kindred's last known dynast of any significance. Was their prominence aided by the fact that Finnguine's grandson Bridei happened to be the mightiest king in northern Britain? In 692 his great namesake, Bridei son of Beli, died; Dumngual of Alt Clut perished a year later.[23] After so much potential interest in Argyll over twenty years, did their deaths contribute to the unsettled state of the region between 695 and 702, which saw three Corcu Réti kings slain and two Cenél Loairn kings toppled?

---

[19] Watson, *Celtic Place-Names*, 41.
[20] *AU* 698.3–4, 701.8–9.
[21] Alcock, 'Activities of Potentates', 31–2.
[22] *AU* 686.1.
[23] *AU* 694.6; *AT* 694.2.

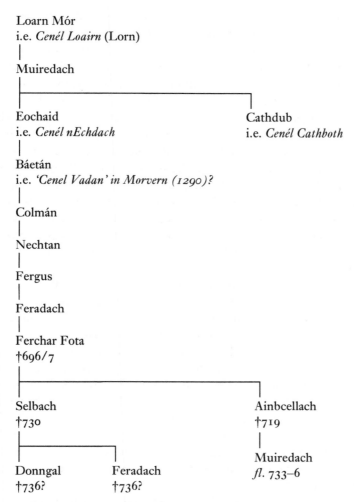

Loarn Mór
i.e. *Cenél Loairn* (Lorn)

Muiredach

Eochaid
i.e. *Cenél nEchdach*

Cathdub
i.e. *Cenél Cathboth*

Báetán
i.e. *'Cenel Vadan' in Morvern (1290)?*

Colmán

Nechtan

Fergus

Feradach

Ferchar Fota
†696/7

Selbach
†730

Ainbcellach
†719

Donngal
†736?

Feradach
†736?

Muiredach
fl. 733–6

Table 9.2 Kings of Cenél nEchdach (*c.* 695–736)

It may be significant that it was also an unsettled period in Verturian politics. Bridei's successor was Tarain, possibly the son of Ainbtech, whose killing in 692 would then suggest that his son's succession was messy.[24] Indeed, four years later Tarain was driven from the kingship and replaced by Bridei son of Der-Ilei.[25] A siege of Dunnottar in 693, apparently a key

[24] *AU* 693.5; Anderson, *Early Sources*, vol. 1, 201; Chadwick, *Early Scotland*, 17; Clancy, 'Philosopher-King', 135. The king's father's name as it appears in the king-list, *filius Enfidaig*, is unlikely to be in the nominative case.
[25] *AU* 697.1; *AT* 697.1.

centre at the margins of the southern and northern Pictish zones, could have been an episode in a protracted struggle between the two men.[26]

Despite his exile, Tarain continued to attract the attention of the chroniclers of Iona. In fact, *Vita Columbae*, written at this time, contains an episode in which the saint commits a certain exiled Pictish nobleman called Tarain to the protection of a Gael, who incurs the wrath of Columba for having the exile murdered.[27] Can this be a coincidence? Taken with the chronicle evidence, the tale may be read as implying that the historical Tarain, cast out of Fortriu, made his way to Iona after being cashiered. He may have received the protection of Adomnán before, as the chronicles inform us, he found final sanctuary in Ireland in 699 or 700. Here, as with the removal of Ainbcellach of Lorn in bonds to Ireland, we would like to know more than our sources reveal about such Irish destinations. The Tarain story in *Vita Columbae* ought to have served as a warning to Bridei that Iona would frown on attempts to have his exiled rival murdered.

Bridei's reign, having been established, was comparatively short. It seems none the less to have been highly significant as regards Gaelo-Pictish relations and the Ionan principate in Pictland. The political doctrines surrounding the former, put forward in origin mythology dating from his reign, smoothed over his particular personal circumstances as a usurper, downplaying his 'otherness' as the son of a Cowal Gael. Questioning Gaelic sovereignty in Argyll, however, and even Gaelic exclusion from Pictishness, probably reflected movements Bridei son of Beli had initiated in Atlantic Scotland in the previous generation. Such suggestion of continuity in Argyll policy from the reign of the elder Bridei into that of the younger provides a context for Adomnán's handling of Gaelo-Pictish relations in *Vita Columbae*, written in the middle of the younger Bridei's reign.

As both king of Fortriu and a descendant of Comgall, Bridei provided the Verturian kingship with realistic expectations of pushing its post-Dún-Nechtain hegemony across Drumalban. One apparent result was the growth of a Pictish presence in Ireland, exploited by Tarain in exile, not least because of Verturian links with Iona. In 696 or 697, having captured his kingdom from Tarain, Bridei became a guarantor of *Lex innocentium*, which Adomnán 'gave to the people' at Birr in 696 or 697.[28] The

---

[26] *AU* 694.4.

[27] *AU* 699.3; Adomnán, *V. s. Columbae*, ii.23.

[28] *AU* 696.1, 697.4; *AT* 696.1; *CS* 696.1. *Bruide mac Derilei rí Cruithintuathi* is guarantor § 91; see Ní Dhonnchadha, 'The Guarantor List', 181, 214.

ninth abbot of Iona, for his part, described his Tarain character in *Vita Columbae* as a man 'who belonged to a noble family'. Bridei and his court probably welcomed the fact that he was not described as an exiled king.

In Argyll itself, the period of the Verturian succession war had been bloody. In 695 Domnall Dond had been slain; a year or two later his kinsman Eochu too was killed, but not before being nominated by Adomnán as a guarantor of *Lex innocentium*.[29] Ferchar of Lorn may have been responsible for both killings. He too died before the end of 697, but seems to have held the kingship of Dál Riata for the better part of a year prior to his death, the first king outwith the Corcu Réti to appear in the king-list.

The successes of Ferchar and his sons in this period, and those of Bridei in Fortriu, explain the way in which Cenél nEchdach and Cenél Comgaill were treated by the *Cethri primchenéla* genealogist after 706. Do they also explain why he took an antagonistic line towards Cenél nGabráin? The Kintyre pedigree spelled out here is not from the family of Máel Dúin and Domnall Dond, which had dominated Argyll after 650, but rather from Cenél nGartnait, the Skye kindred that seems to have emerged victorious from some twenty-five years of war in the north a few years before the text was penned.

The tractate supports the claims – very probably spurious ones – of Congus son of Conamail of Cenél nGartnait to be a descendant of Gabrán, even identifying Cenél nGartnait as the principal segment of Cenél nGabráin. Evidently Congus was a man of great political significance *c.* 706, capable of getting away with such a claim. Two of his sons were prominent in Gaelo-Pictish relations in the 730s. More importantly, his father Conamail, killed in 706, was consorting with a possible kinsman of Bridei son of Beli in 672. Was the family history of Cenél nGartnait accepted in *Cethri primchenéla* because of the kindred's Verturian connections? How far did the kindred owe its rise to prominence to Verturian backing?

By making brothers of the founders of the four principal kindreds of Dál Riata, the genealogist was looking on these kindreds as constituting a single Dalriadan community of descent. The placement of the founding brothers on a co-equal genealogical footing recognised the distinctiveness of the four kindreds, but implied that they were co-equal in status. *Cethri primchenéla* thus takes direct issue, as already discussed, with the tradition known to Bede, which prioritised the Corcu Réti. That tradition, which Bede is likely to have acquired from Pictish informants, looks distinctly out of place in early eighth-century Argyll. Did its Corcu Réti

<hr>

[29] *Euchu ua Domnaill* is guarantor § 85; see Ní Dhonnchadha, 'The Guarantor list', 181, 212.

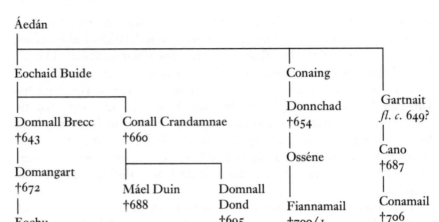

Table 9.3 Cenél nGabráin and Cenél nGartnait (672–706)

partisanship avoid obsolescence in Pictland because of the Corcu Réti paternity of the sons of Der-Ilei?

There is precious little evidence that kings of the Corcu Réti dominated the peoples of Lorn prior to 695, though the defeat of Domnall Brecc in Calathros in 636 may represent an attempt. It is, therefore, possible that in Argyll the forging of the familiar kingdom of Dál Riata from earlier distinct nations like the Corcu Réti and Cenél Loairn was a phenomenon mainly of the seventh century, in line with architectural developments at Dunadd. That there are comparable developments elsewhere in Britain and Ireland in the same half-century, including Pictland, has been discussed in the previous chapter.

The rise of Cenél nEchdach and the kingdom of Lorn, the principal church of which was probably at Lismore 'in the cockpit' of the realm, was presumably troubling at Iona. Lismore went unmentioned in *Vita Columbae*, where Adomnán made no mention at all of Cenél nEchdach or Cenél Loairn. Leaders of Cenél nGabráin had been killed in recent years and superseded by Lorn kings, a situation that smacks of the one that Cumméne Find had lamented in *De uirtutibus sancti Columbae*, when the descendants of Áedán had been subjugated by 'strangers'. Yet Adomnán did not reproduce this part of his predecessor's book. His contemporary Dorbbéne, the scribe of the Schaffhausen manuscript of *Vita Columbae*, believed, on the other hand, that it was worth resurrecting only a few years later.

Can we explain this varied treatment of Cumméne's text, which happily resulted in our being provided with Dorbbéne's precious excerpt

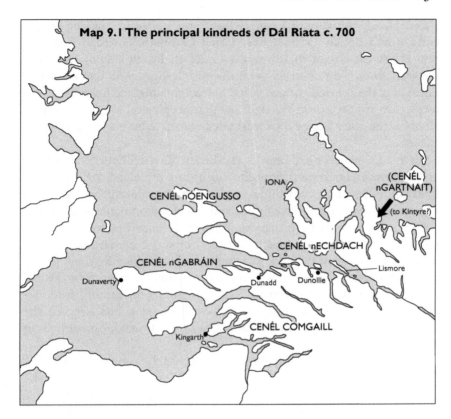

Map 9.1 The principal kindreds of Dál Riata c. 700

from it? With the death of Ferchar in 696 or 697 and the dispossession of his son a year or two later, paramountcy in Argyll seems to have returned briefly to the hands of Áedán's descendants, in the person of Fiannamail son of Osséne. This grandson of Áedán's grandson Donnchad son of Conaing was the second guarantor of *Lex innocentium* from Cenél nGabráin.[30] He had probably assumed the kingship of Kintyre after the killing of Eochu in 696 or 697, prior to capturing the kingship of Dál Riata. Was he dominant long enough after *c.* 698 for Adomnán to satisfy himself that the descendants of Áedán were secure in their (rightful) position as he was completing *Vita Columbae*?

As things panned out, Fiannamail was slain in 700 or 701, the third Cenél nGabráin king killed in just six years.[31] His nemesis may have been

---

[30] *Fiannamuild ua Dunchatai* is guarantor § 77; see Ní Dhonnchadha, 'Guarantor list', 181, 208–10. For discussion, see also Fraser, 'The Iona Chronicle', 82–4.

[31] *AU* 700.4 (*rex Dál Riati*); *AT* 700.3 (*rí Dal Araidhi*).

a Cenél Cathboth king of Lorn. Selbach son of Ferchar, having apparently won a decisive victory over Cenél Cathboth, emerged from the
remarkable carnage of these years as Cenél nEchdach king of Lorn and
rex Dáil Riata.[32] In contrast to all the Argyll kings who had risen and
fallen over the previous fifteen years, Selbach maintained his position for
more than twenty years. We shall see that keeping an eye on Verturian
affairs at the other end of the Great Glen may have been a key part of his
success.

In 672 a monastery had been established in the neighbourhood of Skye
at Applecross (*Aporcrosan*), opposite Raasay on the mainland. Possibly the
foundation had had something to do with the movements of Cenél
nGartnait, who had left Skye for Ireland *c*. 668 and returned to the island
c. 670. It has already been suggested that Skye in this period lay 'at the
edge of civilisation' as it was understood by our ecclesiastical sources.
The prize at stake in the long war fought and won there by Cano son of
Gartnait and his son may have been a controlling interest in 'civilising'
the island and its associated areas. The opportunity of running the ecclesiastical side of such a project may have been what had tempted the
founder of Applecross, Máel Rubai, to sail from Ireland, probably from
Bangor.[33]

Cenél nGartnait's principal foes were probably a minor segment of
Cenél nGabráin with Iona in their corner. Did Cano forge a similar relationship with Applecross? Mo-Luóc, the Lismore saint, had flourished
a century earlier, a man of Cruithnian extraction like the founder of
Bangor. It is far from certain that Lismore was a Bangor daughter house.
If that could be established, what would it imply about the further spread
of the Bangor *familia* to Applecross into the neighbourhood of a kindred
that as early as 672 may have been enjoying Verturian support? Would it
constitute a hint that a relationship was established between Fortriu and
Lismore? Would it suggest a link between Cenél nGartnait and Cenél
Loairn?

Máel Rubai was about forty when he came to Applecross, where he
remained abbot for fifty years, dying in 722. Apart from these barest of
details, his career is quite obscure. He and his monks may have ranged
widely in the shadowy north of Atlantic Scotland, or they may have
limited their activities to Skye or an even smaller region. They may or

---

[32] *AU* 701.8–9; the schema proposed by Hudson, *Kings of Celtic Scotland*, 20, takes no
account of Cenél Cathboth.
[33] *AU* 671.5, 673.5, 802.5; *AT* 671.5, 673.4; *CS* 671.5, 673.3; Mac Lean, 'Maelrubai',
173.

may not have enjoyed Verturian or Cenél Loairn support. Máel Rubai's cult as a saint had wide appeal in the medieval Hebrides and northern Scotland, but we know little about his life, his work, or his allegiances when the Skye kindred Cenél nGartnait was enjoying political prominence.

MAKING SETTLEMENTS: BRIDEI AND THE SOUTHERN PICTISH ZONE

The Pictish origin legend associated with Bridei son of Der-Ilei establishes that the king and his court were committed to the notion of a single *gens Pictorum*. Accordingly, it was not just across Argyll that the king cast his shadow. Der-Ilei's patrimony is obscure, but her sons were destined to play key roles in Pictish politics. It seems that, after the killing of Bridei's father, his mother was re-married to a certain Drestan. Their son, Talorcan, was king of Atholl (*rex Athfoitle*) by the 730s, the Ionan *familia*'s old foothold in the southern Pictish zone.[34] The chronological precedence of Der-Ilei's marriage to Dargart is suggested by the fact that their son Naiton had adult sons by 710, while Talorcan had not yet reached the end of his natural life in 739.

It has already been suggested that Bede's description of the southern Pictish zone implies that Verturian hegemony there depended on Atholl's incorporation into the greater realm of Fortriu. It seems that, after Dargart's killing in 685, Der-Ilei was wedded to an Atholl dynast in the southern Pictish zone conquered in the year that she was widowed. Bridei son of Beli must surely have been involved in choosing her marriage partners. Der-Ilei's marriage to Drestan was surely a key part of a strategy for pulling Atholl and Moray into the intimate embrace detectable during the adulthood of their sons. The Verturian strategy south of the Mounth may, therefore, have involved the expansion of the reach of the kingdom of Atholl across the Tay basin – the heart of the medieval district of Gowrie, later linked conceptually with Atholl.[35] By the 720s one son of Der-Ilei, Dargart's son, was king of Fortriu, while another, Drestan's son, was king of Atholl. We have already seen that making sense of Columba's movements among the Picts involves us in thinking about how ancient such ties between Moray and Atholl may have been *c*. 700.

---

[34] *AU* 713.7, 739.7; *AT* 713.8, 739.6. That Bridei and Talorcan were uterine half-brothers is established by Clancy, 'Philosopher-King', 133–4.

[35] See Woolf, *From Pictland to Alba*, 227, for discussion of Gowrie.

The younger Bridei's grip on the southern Pictish zone may have been tested and confirmed within twelve months of his seizure of Fortriu. In 698 a Pictish force won a resounding victory in battle over the Northumbrian *dux* Berctred. He and his father Beornhaeth probably maintained a personal interest in opposing Verturian expansion in the southern Pictish zone. The Northumbrian king Aldfrith did not fight in this battle in which Berctred fell.[36] The effect of this Pictish victory – over a man who may have regarded himself as entitled to dominate southern Picts – was probably to cement the Verturian grip on southern Pictland. Did it assure Adomnán that Columba had by now extended his patronage to all Picts?

An even more significant outcome of the war of 698 is possible. By Pictish standards there is good evidence that Bridei and Ionan primacy moved into Fife and Manau – districts we have been linking with Berctred and Beornhaeth as *subreguli* of the Bernician kings. In the twelfth-century *Vita sancti Servani*, the Life of St Seruan or 'Serf', Bridei *filius Dargart* and Adomnán are credited, respectively, with donating Culross in west Fife and St Serf's Isle in Loch Leven to St Serf. Adomnán is also said to have granted Fife and another district which probably approximated Early Historic Manau.[37]

The relative lateness of these details is cause for concern. The fact that the two men certainly cooperated in other matters, however, allows for a degree of optimism that Bridei and Adomnán did intervene together in the ecclesiastical constitution of Manau and Fife after 698.[38] That new Columban miracle-stories based in Pictland were added to the Columban dossier by Adomnán suggests that he acquired enough personal experience of the *prouincia Pictorum* to sustain the notion that he had new information about the saint's time among the Picts. It is important, however, that his stories focus in the main on events in Fortriu proper.

It may have been as late as 698, then, before the Ionan principate began to expand its interests south of the Mounth, on the back of significant Verturian and Atholl patronage. How did Iona establish supremacy (*arx*) over the *monasteria* of Pictavia? Monks could have been manoeuvred, with royal pressure, into various key abbatial offices and perhaps also into key episcopal seats. Perhaps it was only now that Portmahomack joined the *familia*, for even in Fortriu there was probably work to be done to

---

[36] *AU* 698.2; *AT* 698.2; *Ann. Clon.* 693.1; Bede, *Hist. eccl.*, v.24. *Lib. vit. eccl. Dunelm.*, fol. 12, records Berctred's name after his father's,

[37] Macquarrie, ed., *V. s. Servani*, 140.

[38] See Clancy, 'Philosopher-King', 138–42.

bring monastic houses into Iona's fold. Is it a coincidence that the chronicles begin to speak for the first time, in the early eighth century, of a see and bishop of Iona? Having been one player among many in the ecclesiastical history of Pictavia in the seventh century, influential perhaps, but not necessarily dominant even in the northern zone, Iona now established a principate encompassing both sides of the Mounth. The process had probably begun, but not finished, as Adomnán completed *Vita Columbae* c. 700. The Picts in the origin legend are told to call on Gaelic assistance in making settlements in northern Britain if anyone resists them.

This new ecclesiastical settlement is barely perceptible today. For instance, Bridei son of Beli may not have replaced Trumwini, Canterbury's bishop of Abercorn, with a candidate of his own choosing – his flight could have been as late as 698. *Vita Servani* speaks of St Serf founding the church at Culross, on the north shore of the Firth of Forth, during the younger Bridei's reign. He is said to have landed at Kinneil on the south side of the estuary, cast his staff over the water (an impressive six kilometres) and founded his church where the staff landed.[39] Nothing was more emblematic of a bishop and his authority than his crosier. The fact that this fanciful story envisions Serf's emblem coming to Culross from across the Forth is therefore arresting. After all, Kinneil lies only nine kilometres west of Abercorn (for Serf, a mere staff's throw). The two places were mentioned in the same breath by Bede.[40]

The possibility may, therefore, be entertained that Culross, home to early medieval sculpture, was chosen by Bridei son of Der-Ilei or his counsellors to supplant Abercorn across the Forth as the episcopal seat with jurisdiction over Manau and west Fife, captured in 698. It may have been only now, in other words, that the Antonine Wall came to form the frontier between Pictavia and Northumbria, as Bede implies by providing Pictish and English names for the wall's terminus on the Forth. Reorganisation of this ecclesiastical province may still be discernible through the main toponymic term denoting a church in the region: *bod*.[41] Was Serf the see's first Pictish bishop, flourishing c. 700? Perhaps not. *Seruan* is very rare in the corpus of Welsh names, but a son of Clinoch bears it in later genealogies. This Seruan was an uncle of Riderch of Clyde Rock, and ought to have flourished in the sixth century.

---

[39] Macquarrie, ed., *V. s. Servani*, 140.
[40] Bede, *Hist. eccl.*, i.12.
[41] Macquarrie, *The Saints of Scotland*, 151–2; Taylor, 'Early Church in Eastern Scotland', 95–101.

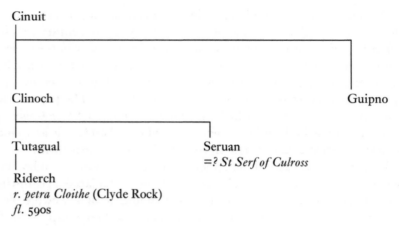

Table 9.4 Seruan of the House of Clinoch

That Clydesdale and Manau could have remained linked together under Miathian rule has been discussed at length. The further suggestion that Seruan son of Clinoch was the historical St Serf would fit that model quite comfortably. Certainly a Pictish king and an abbot of Iona *c.* 700 could have made donations 'to' St Serf in this district long after the man himself had died and been laid to rest (according to *Vita Servani*) at Culross. Manau and its environs were probably being ruled by ancestors and kinsmen of Bridei son of Beli when Seruan son of Clinoch flourished. If he was St Serf, his cult ought to have been an obvious choice for patronage when the region was conquered by the Verturian Picts in the late seventh century.

For the rest of the southern Pictish zone, the movements of the Ionan principate after the battle of Dún Nechtain are even more difficult to establish. Fife proper may not have passed into the Verturian hegemony until 698. The most common Gaelic term for a church, *cell*, seems to have been active as a toponymic element *c.* 700. The evidence consists mainly of two commemorations, within a cluster of *cell-* church-names, of Donnchad son of Cend Fáelad, who held the principate (*principatus*) of Iona from 707 or 708 until his death in 717.[42] The episcopal seat for this district was perhaps at Cennrígmonaid, the later St Andrews, the place-name alluding to a foundation on royal land. Cennrígmonaid is first attested in 747. Reason to believe that by then it had become the pre-eminent episcopal seat in southern Pictavia is discussed below.

---

[42] *AU* 707.9, 717.1; *AT* 707.5, 717.1; *CS* 717.1. Taylor, 'Early Church in Eastern Scotland', 98–101.

A little further north in Strathearn, Abernethy may have put forward that claim prior to the conquest of Fife and Manau, based, as already suggested, on a connection with the kin of Bridei son of Beli. If Culross too was a church linked through kinship with the victor of Dún Nechtain, privileging such establishments across the zone formerly ruled by Bridei's kin begins to look like a coherent strategy.

Further north still in Atholl, it is likely that the Ionan principate had become established at an early date, even in Columba's lifetime, whence his rules for monks and other teachings may have spread in a manner comparable to the spread of Columbanus's influence on the Continent, quite apart from any spread of Ionan primacy. If Verturian dominion south of the Mounth flowed from Atholl, a move may have been afoot to manoeuvre an Ionan cleric here into primatial position as *prím-epscop*, 'foremost bishop', in southern Pictland.[43] As Bede understood it, Adomnán and his successors would have maintained primacy over such a cleric as head of the *familia* to which he belonged. This, *de facto*, will have given Iona ultimate authority.

In fact, the chief bishop in southern Pictavia during the younger Bridei's reign was probably none other than Cóeti, the 'bishop of Iona' (*episcopus Iae*), possibly a monk of English extraction like Aldfrith had been. Like Bridei, this bishop was a guarantor of *Lex innocentium*; he died in 712 some five years after the king.[44] This man, like his contemporary Donnchad, was culted as a saint in Scotland. The cult was confined to Atholl, the chief church of which in the Middle Ages at Logierait bears his name (*Logie Mahedd*), where the Tummel meets the Tay.[45] At first glance, it seems far-fetched that a man styled *episcopus Iae* could have governed the Atholl Church, or indeed have been based there, perhaps at Logierait. Yet at late as the 1190s the bishopric of Dunkeld included Argyll, and there is nothing implausible about the idea that Cóeti's see encompassed that district along with Atholl. Indeed, the movements of the Atholl king Talorcan son of Drestan in the 720s and 730s add considerable strength to that conclusion.

The only other Scottish-based bishop attested in the guarantor-list of *Lex innocentium* is Curetán, bishop of Ross (*episcopus Ruis*), presumably *prím-epscop* in Fortriu, his seat probably at Rosemarkie in the Black Isle

---

[43]   Taylor, 'Early Church in Eastern Scotland', 101–2.
[44]   *AU* 712.1; *AT* 712.1. *Ceti epscop* is guarantor § 21; Ní Dhonnchadha, 'Guarantor list', 180, 191. For the suggestion that Cóeti was English, see Charles-Edwards, *Early Christian Ireland*, 308.
[45]   Watson, *Celtic Place-Names*, 314; Taylor, 'Early Church in Eastern Scotland', 101–2.

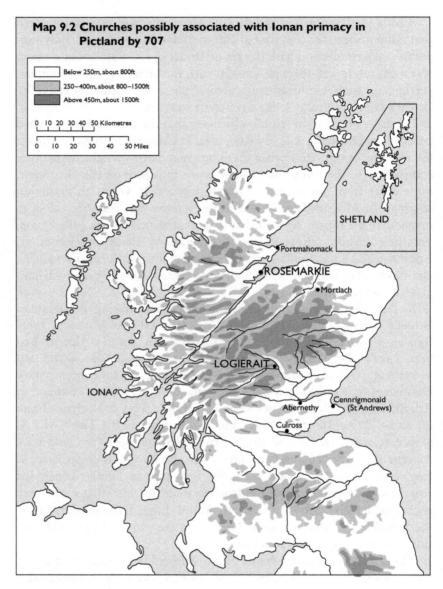

Map 9.2 Churches possibly associated with Ionan primacy in Pictland by 707

Below 250m, about 800ft
250–400m, about 800–1500ft
Above 450m, about 1500ft

0 10 20 30 40 50 Kilometres
0 10   20   30   40   50 Miles

SHETLAND

Portmahomack
ROSEMARKIE
Mortlach
LOGIERAIT
IONA
Cennrígmonaid (St Andrews)
Abernethy
Culross

where monumental sculpture survives.[46] Our evidence thus seems to locate one Pictish episcopal guarantor of Adomnán's Law north of the Mounth and one south of it in Atholl (and Iona), respecting Bede's

---

[46] *Curetan epscop* is guarantor § 22; Ní Dhonnchadha, 'Guarantor list', 180, 191; *Mart. Tallaght*, 16 March. On Curetán's connection with Rosemarkie, see Watson, *Celtic Place-Names*, 315; Fraser, 'Rochester, Hexham and Cennrígmonaid'.

principal division of Pictavia perfectly. Rosemarkie in Curetán's time may have been one of the chief engines driving the Pictish pseudo-historical orthodoxies discussed at length above, relating to the achievement of Columba, the origins of the Picts and the status of Argyll in the era of Verturian expansion. Here again there is place-name evidence relating to churches to suggest a flurry of Ionan activity *c.* 700, similar to that identified in Fife and Atholl. Curetán is likely to have been very close to the Verturian court. He may have been a Portmahomack monk in origin, but it is difficult to guess what relationship may have existed between Rosemarkie and Portmahomack in this period.

The district of Cé included Mar, where Ionan interest was attracted to at least one monastery throughout the seventh century. It may also have included Mortlach in Dufftown on the frontier between Moray and Banffshire, which by the sixteenth century was thought to have been the place where the see of Aberdeen had originated. If it was the episcopal seat of Cé in 700, about which there is much room for doubt, Mortlach would have resembled a number of seats of the time, including Abercorn (and possibly Abernethy), situated at the very edge of their see, at its frontier with the dominant regional kingdom that played an active part in their establishment.[47]

In the far north, it seems there was a Pictish bishop on Orkney in the early ninth century. Possibly an Orcadian see had been established by 700, but the presence of a bishop may be explained in other ways.[48] The silence of our sources makes it difficult to know how this and various other parts of Scotland may have been provided with bishops and ecclesiastical provinces at this time.

Different categories of evidence considered here confirm that the extension of Verturian hegemony across the southern Pictish zone by the two Brideis from 680 onwards brought with it the concept of a single Pictish Church, forged (and defined) by the Ionan principate. The younger Bridei's Argyll blood was probably of little importance in his decision to look to Iona to provide the engine for driving these developments. A more important factor was surely that Adomnán's monastery already held entrenched interests on both sides of Drumalban, and also on both sides of the Mounth. It may have been uniquely suited to the Verturian superpower's needs in this respect. Did the two Brideis also derive incentive to patronise Iona from the fact that their mighty neighbour and colleague in Northumbria after 685 had

[47] Woolf, *From Pictland to Alba*, 269–70.
[48] Woolf, *From Pictland to Alba*, 287–8.

formerly been a monk at Iona whom Adomnán could influence? Overt patronage of the Ionan *familia*, especially in his southernmost districts, must have given Bridei son of Der-Ilei a means of applying pressure to Aldfrith to discourage Northumbrian attempts to return in force to southern Pictland.

PRINCIPATUS: A JOB TOO BIG FOR ONE MAN?

The establishment of Ionan primacy in Pictavia towards the end of the abbacy of Adomnán was probably reflected by developments in the headship of the Iona community over the next generation. An eighth-century abbot-list indicates that Conamail son of Fáelbe, yet another guarantor of Adomnán's Law, succeeded Adomnán in September 705.[49] The chronicles record, however, that Donnchad son of Cend Fáelad, whose cult we have already encountered in Fife, obtained the principate (*principatus*) two or three years before Conamail's death in 710.[50] This division of the headship of Iona, separating the *principatus* from the abbot's office, has been interpreted conventionally as a schism. Viewed in the context of the foregoing discussion, however, another explanation is possible.

Is it likely to be a coincidence that this cleavage arose as Iona's Pictish interests became very greatly expanded? Adomnán made it a point to observe in *De locis sanctis* that the burdens of his office 'from every quarter' were 'laborious and almost unsustainable'. He made this statement many years before the burden he bequeathed to Conamail became even weightier, thanks to the pro-Ionan policy of the Verturian hegemons. In *Vita Columbae* owe find Adomnán reassuring his *familia* that St Columba, however busy or distant, never stopped thinking and worrying about his monks. The beneficiaries of his 'remote control' miracles are, moreover, almost always in Ireland. The works of the ninth abbot of Iona thus contain hints that the size and scope of the Ionan *familia* had become a problem. There is even suggestion that the Irish branch needed particular reassurance of their abbot's attentions.

Did the workload involved in managing the affairs of Iona become so onerous for a single man that, in 707 or 708, Donnchad was given responsibility for overseeing the monastery's *principatus* abroad, while Conamail

---

[49]   *AU* 704.2; *AT* 704.3; *CS* 704.2; *AI* 704.1; *Ann. Clon.* 700.1; Herbert, *Iona, Kells, and Derry*, 57. *Conamail mac Conain epscop* is guarantor § 23; Ní Dhonnchadha, 'Guarantor list', 180, 191–2.

[50]   *AU* 707.9, 710.1; *AT* 707.5, 710.1; *CS* 710.1.

continued to lead the Iona community itself? Did Conamail also give particular thought after this division of responsibilities to the monastery's
Irish daughter houses? Bede certainly uses the term *principatus* in reference to Iona's Pictish primacy. A hands-on link with Pictavia would
explain Donnchad's commemorations in Fife, just as has already been
suggested for Cóeti in Atholl. These conclusions are supported by the
fact that Curetán of Ross was certainly active in the region where the
place-name evidence mirrors that pertaining to his two contemporaries.

In 710 Donnchad appears to have taken up the abbatial office at Iona
at Conamail's death; their names are sequential in the abbot-list. His place
as primate in Pictland may have been taken up by Cóeti, the 'bishop of
Iona' associated with Logierait, perhaps with a northern colleague like
the obscure Brecc 'of Fortriu', who died in 725, possibly Curetán's successor.[51] A year after Cóeti's death, Dorbbéne, probably the scribe of the
Schaffhausen manuscript of *Vita Columbae*, seems to have succeeded him
in the *kathedra* or 'seat of Iona'.[52] To judge from Cóeti's festal day, he died
on 24 October 712, and it was the new year before Dorbbéne was
appointed. The new bishop died in turn after a scant five months on 28
October, showing that he was not appointed until late May 713.[53]

Dorbbéne follows Donnchad in the abbot-list, however, suggesting
that the division of responsibilities between the two men was adjusted,
the management of Iona passing to Dorbbéne. Did Donnchad return to
Pictavia and the Ionan principate there? It would be another three years
before Fáelchú son of Dorbbéne, aged seventy-four, was chosen to
occupy the *kathedra* of Iona.[54] In the meantime, the Pictish Church
underwent apostolicist reform, the run-up to which may have seen royal
interference in this episcopal succession. When Donnchad died in 717,
Fáelchú would seem to have taken up the abbatial office, just as Ionan
expulsions from Pictavia were greatly lightening the workload involved in
managing monastery and principate.

The details of such a reconstruction are clearly open to question. What
is striking is that these complexities in Iona's leadership structure arose
during the reign of Bridei son of Der-Ilei, a time of primacy in Pictavia,
and seem to have resolved themselves after that principate was brought to
an end. It is true that in 722 Fáelchú, then eighty years old, surrendered

[51] *AU* 725.7.

[52] *AU* 713.5; *AT* 713.6.

[53] *AU* 713.5; *AT* 713.6; see also *Mart. Tallaght*, 24 October, 28 October (a Saturday in
713, as the chronicles record).

[54] *AU* 716.5; *AT* 716.4; *Ann. Clon.* 713.2.

the principate to another monk, but the idea here may simply have been to provide support to an aged abbot, no doubt calling on the experience of previously dividing the leadership.[55] Upon Fáelchú's death in 724, the headship of the monastery appears to have reverted once more to a single incumbent, Cilléne Fota, succeeded at his death two years later by his namesake, Cilléne Droichtech.[56]

A NEW STATUS QUO

With Bridei son of Der-Ilei we catch our first glimpses 'on the ground' of a powerful king in northern Britain whose suzerainty, if not his direct authority, is likely to have stretched from the Northern Isles to the Forth and from Buchan to Argyll. His realm remained an empire of many units, far removed from a single, centralised kingdom. There may only have been a handful of major kingdoms involved, along with a large number of smaller autonomous units, including 'farmer republics'. The kingdom of Alba of the period after ours is not so clearly prefigured in any earlier reign by a Pictish or Argyll king.

The regime Bridei inherited in 696 or 697 probably owed much to the examples and achievements of the Aeðilfrithings in the previous two generations. Certainly parallels can be drawn between Bridei's situation and those of these English kings. It may be compared with that of Oswald in particular. That king had spent his formative years in Argyll, but became king elsewhere, and thereafter worked assiduously to bring Ionan clerics into his dominions and to privilege them. Indeed, the parallel may be taken further. In Bede's conception of the past, Oswald made a great deal of his mother's patrimony in consolidating his royal position, something that has been suspected above of reflecting Ecgfrith's propaganda rather than Oswald's.[57] Bridei son of Der-Ilei did the same in Fortriu a decade after Ecgfrith's death.

It has been suggested that the early Verturian hegemons borrowed the 'mechanisms of over-lordship' devised by the Bernician kings as Northumbrian hegemons,[58] at least in the southern Pictish zone where they had once held sway. In this their links with Iona can have been of service. Mutual affection for the monastery may have seen Bridei and

[55] Herbert, *Iona, Kells, and Derry*, 60.
[56] *AU* 722.6, 724.1; *AT* 722.5, 724.1, 726.2.
[57] Bede, *Hist. eccl.*, iii.6.
[58] Woolf, 'Onuist', 36.

Aldfrith open their courts to one another after the war of 698. Afterwards they seem to have lived in peace, no doubt with a degree of help from the good offices of the Columban clergy and their leader Adomnán, a man known personally to both kings.

CHAPTER 10

Nations Reformed: Northumbria and Pictavia (704–24)

Towards the end of the reign of Aldfrith in Northumbria, Berhtwald, archbishop of Canterbury, convened a Council. Bishops duly gathered at Austerfield, south-west of Doncaster on the frontier between Mercia and Northumbria. Aldfrith and Wilfrid, the oft-exiled ex-bishop of York, were present at this assembly, probably convened in 702, so that Wilfrid's case could be heard.[1] Stephen took the opportunity here of placing in Wilfrid's mouth a speech enumerating his many achievements in restoring the Church to health and apostolicist orthodoxy after Whitby and introducing key aspects of Mediterranean ecclesiastical culture, including the monastic Rule of St Benedict. Bede would later take issue with *Vita Wilfrithi*'s notion that these achievements amounted to a one-man show. Advised that the Council of Austerfield did not recognise his claims to York, nor to the temporalities of any monastery he had founded, save for Ripon, Wilfrid characteristically refused to accept its decisions.

Now on the cusp of seventy, Wilfrid once more took his case to the papal curia.[2] The old bishop was again excommunicated. The problems that Ecgfrith and Aldfrith experienced with the stubborn Wilfrid, whose refusal to accept their ecclesiastical interventions took him repeatedly to Rome to secure counter-interventions, may have been factors in the failure of Bridei son of Beli or his younger namesake to embrace apostolicist reform. The pressure applied to the Northumbrian kings by Canterbury may have been an additional factor.

---

[1] For discussion of the date, see Poole, 'St. Wilfrid', 18; Kirby, 'Bede, Eddius Stephanus and the "Life of Wilfrid" ', 113.
[2] Stephen, *V. s. Wilfrithi*, §§ 46–7.

THE BOY WHO WOULD BE KING

Aldfrith died at Driffield, thirty kilometres north of Hull in the heart of Deira, on 14 December 704.[3] Bede does not provide these details. His reticence is symptomatic of his suppression of the fact that, as Stephen informs us, the king's successor was Eadwulf, commemorated in the Durham *Liber vitae*. His reign lasted a matter of weeks into the new year before he was driven from the kingdom by supporters of Aldfrith's son Osred, who was only eight years old.[4] Consecutive chapters of *Vita Wilfrithi* reflect this succession dispute, disagreeing about whether Aldfrith named Osred his heir, or whether he was uncertain on his deathbed about who should succeed him.[5] It seems that Eadwulf went into exile somewhere in the orbit of Iona – possibly Pictavia – for his death in 717 is recorded in the Irish chronicles, as is the killing of his son Earnwini in 740.[6] These chronicles call him Eadwulf son of Ecgwulf (*Etulb mac Ecuilb*), and his son Ecgwulf's grandson (*Ernan nepotis Ecuilp*) – unique witness to their Ecgwulfing heritage. Stephen's inconsistency about whether or not Aldfrith had named Osred his heir is one of his Life's key hints that it was completed *c.* 716, the year in which Osred was replaced by a kinsman of Eadwulf.

As she had done after the battle of Dún Nechtain, Aldfrith's sister Aelffled of Whitby acted to preserve her Aeðilfrithing dynasty, supporting the boy Osred in his sensational bid for the kingship. It is in her mouth that Stephen places the allegation that Aldfrith had intended Osred to succeed him, whereas the king's uncertainty about the succession is placed in his own. Readers of *Vita Wilfrithi* were thus invited to conclude that Aelffled, who died in 713, had borne false witness, another indication that the Life was completed after Osred's murder in 716. Stephen implies that he was placed in the wardship of Berctfrith, 'the leader second in rank to the king'. We have encountered this prince already, accepting the supposition that he was a kinsman of Berctred and Beornhaeth and supposing that he could have derived his prominence in 705 from kinship

---

[3] *AU* 704.3; *AT* 704.4; *AI* 705.1; *Ann. Clon.* 700.2; Dumville, *Ann. Camb.* 704.1; *Ang.-Sax. Chron. E*, s. a. 705. That the correct year was 704 was established by Poole, 'St. Wilfrid', 22–3.

[4] Bede, *Hist. eccl.*, v.18; Stephen, *V. s. Wilfrithi*, § 49; *Lib. vit. eccl. Dunelm.*, fol. 12.

[5] *V. s. Wilfrithi*, §§ 59–60; Kirby, 'Bede, Eddius Stephanus and the "Life of Wilfrid"', 107.

[6] *AU* 717.2 (*Etulb m. Ecuilb*), 741.7 (*Ernan nepotis Ecuilp*); *AT* 717.2 (*Etulb mac Eouilb*); *Chron.* 766, s.a. 740. I follow Woolf, 'Onuist', in referring to the 'continuation of Bede' as the *Chronicle of 766*.

with a Pictish king who had been a grandson of Aeðilfrith. Stephen refers
to a siege of Bamburgh in which Osred, in Berctfrith's custody, held out
against his enemies, presumably led by Eadwulf.[7]

According to Stephen, Aelffled also supported Wilfrid, now suffering
the effects of a stroke. The boy-king's influential aunt maintained that her
late brother had repented of his opposition to Wilfrid on his death-bed,
as their father is said to have done by Bede.[8] Another Council was convened. Despite resistance from Northumbrian bishops, Berctfrith and
Aelffled convinced them to allow Wilfrid to take up the episcopate of
Hexham and the temporalities of Ripon. According to Stephen, the old
prelate sent a quarter of Ripon's wealth to Rome and divided the rest
evenly. Did Wilfrid wish to demonstrate by this grand gesture that it had
been out of principle, and not for gain, that he had fought his cause for so
long?

Although the succession of minors would become familiar in later
medieval Scotland, nothing of the kind is attested in northern Britain at
any earlier point than this. That a boy could be taken seriously as king in
Northumbria in 705 is testimony to the extent to which kingship had
developed as an institution there in the course of the seventh century.
Clearly many of its principal elements, including even generalship in war,
could now be delegated to lieutenants of different ranks without necessarily dishonouring the king. It would have been unthinkable in the world
of Urbgen and Aeðilfrith a hundred years earlier. No doubt Osred's
way had been paved somewhat by his father's reign. As a former monk
Aldfrith had already challenged traditional notions of kingship. Was the
succession of a boy made less intolerable as a result?

Osred's position was not strong. His custodians seem to have been sensitive about alienating people, exemplified at the Council on the River
Nidd which finally restored Wilfrid to Hexham, evidently under Mercian
pressure. The controversial old bishop was buried at Ripon on his death
in 709.[9] The appointment of one of his favourite disciples Acca as his successor at Hexham suggests an ongoing desire to placate his supporters,
not least Ceolred son of Aeðilred, king of the Mercians. Acca, along with
Wilfrid's kinsman Tatberct, abbot of Ripon, soon commissioned Stephen
to compose *Vita Wilfrithi*. The partisan treatment of Northumbrian
history in this text may have been the ultimate inspiration for Bede, a
priest at Jarrow since 703, to turn his hand to historical writing towards

---

[7] Stephen, *V. s. Wilfrithi*, § 50.
[8] Stephen, *V. s. Wilfrithi*, § 49.
[9] Bede, *Hist. eccl.*, v.19.

the end of his career.[10] If so, we owe a great debt to Acca. He was still in office twenty years later when Bede was completing *Historia ecclesiastica*, and provided Bede with information.

Despite policies of reconciliation, Osred had no personal credibility, depending entirely on his Aeðilfrithing heritage for his personal excellence. His father had done the same. In such circumstances, the accusation of illegitimacy against Aldfrith, already discussed, would have been particularly damaging. Perhaps it made him impetuous for personal glory. In 716 Osred was killed in Mercia, aged just nineteen. The circumstances of his death are surrounded in mystery. Not for another four and a half centuries would a boy be king in northern Britain, so far as we are aware.

NEW BLOOD: THE ECGWULFINGS

The assassination of Osred, like the strife at the time of his succession, reflects shifts among the Bernician nobility as regards the kingship of the *regnum Nordanhymbrorum*. Since the death of Aeðilfrith, exactly one hundred years before, every Bernician king had been descended from him. It was for precisely this reason that Aeðilfrith was so famous. His grandson Ecgfrith had fallen without progeny. A successor had been chosen on the basis that he too was a grandson. Aldfrith's lineage had proven decisive: he had none of the other royal credentials that court poets were in the habit of praising. The succession of his son Osred is equally remarkable. In neither case had succession been straightforward. Aeðilfrith's granddaughter Aelffled had become involved as an unimpeachable representative of the dynasty. The Irish chronicles record her death in 713.[11] Three years later, when Osred was slain, the dynasty may have sorely missed the astute woman who had been its champion for almost thirty years. *Vita Wilfrithi* implies at one point that she was still alive when it was penned, but indications have already been noted which suggest that Stephen revised the text *c.* 716 after the dynastic change of that year.[12]

For Coenred son of Cuthwini, Osred's successor, was no descendant of Aeðilfrith.[13] According to genealogical information preserved in *Historia Brittonum*, the *Chronicle of 766* and the *Chronicle of 802* – all three

---

[10] Goffart, *The Narrators of Barbarian History*, 235–328.

[11] *AU* 713.3; *AT* 713.4 (*filia Ossu in monasterio Ild moritur*).

[12] *V. s. Wilfrithi*, § 59; Kirby, 'Bede, Eddius Stephanus and the "Life of Wilfrid"', 106–10, dated the revision too late.

[13] *AU* 718.1 (*filius Cuidine*); *AT* 718.1 (*mac Cuitin*).

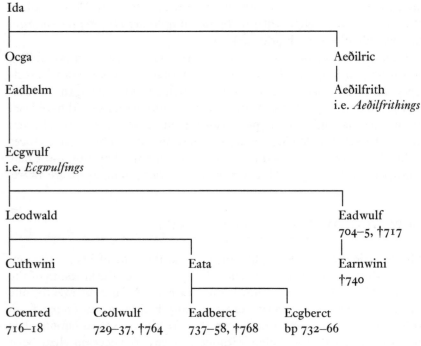

Ida

Ocga

Eadhelm

Ecgwulf
i.e. *Ecgwulfings*

Aeðilric

Aeðilfrith
i.e. *Aeðilfrithings*

Leodwald

Cuthwini

Eata

Eadwulf
704–5, †717

Earnwini
†740

Coenred
716–18

Ceolwulf
729–37, †764

Eadberct
737–58, †768

Ecgberct
bp 732–66

Table 10.1 The Ecgwulfing kings of Northumbria (716–39)

relying on one or more eighth-century Northumbrian source[14] – Coenred was instead a great-grandson of Ecgwulf, whose father Eadhelm is said to have been Aeðilfrith's cousin.[15] The same Ecgwulf was the father of the pretender Eadwulf, who had failed to deny the kingship to Osred in the winter of 704–5.

It may be inferred that these Ecgwulfings founded their claim to the kingdom on two genealogical precepts. The first of these was that Aldfrith had not really been Oswy's son. The second was their own claim of descent from Ida, said in the eighth century to have been the great-grandfather of both Oswy and Ecgwulf. It has already been noted that we cannot place much faith in either of these precepts. What they indicate more generally is a desire in certain circles to break the Aeðilfrithing

---

[14] For discussion of the Northumbrian material, see Forsyth, 'Evidence of a Lost Pictish Source', 20–1.

[15] The pedigree of Coenred's brother Ceolwulf is preserved in an English text from *c.* 796; Dumville, 'The Anglian Collection', especially 30–7. The genealogy of Eadberct and Ecgberct in *Hist. Brit.*, § 61, however, shows that *Ecguald* in this pedigree should be *Ecgulf*; the error may have been to repeat the *-uald* of *Lioduald* in the previous line.

monopoly on the kingship after the battle of Dún Nechtain. Bede's conviction that the ills he perceived in the Northumbrian Church all dated from Osred's reign may be read in a similar light.[16]

Ida may have been an obscure ancestor in the Aeðilfrithing lineage before the Ecgwulfings claimed ancestry from him. As already discussed, it is unlikely that he had any significance in Bernicia until the Ecgwulfings established themselves in the kingship and laid out the genealogical basis on which they built their claim to it. There are traces of both the Aeðilfrith-centred and the Ida-centred outlooks in Bede's History, suggesting that the security and future of the Ecgwulfing dynastic revolution remained uncertain as late as the 730s when Bede wrote in the (unstable) reign of Coenred's brother Ceolwulf.

PROBLEMS AT THE PERIPHERIES: ORKNEY, COWAL AND MANAU

In the three years following on from the death of Aldfrith, both Adomnán of Iona and Bridei of Pictavia died, the last in 707. Bridei was succeeded by his brother Naiton (Gaelic *Nechtan*). He is known to posterity primarily because of the reform (*correctio*) he initiated in the Pictish Church and his expulsion (*expulsio*) of Iona clergy from his kingdom.

The traditional dating of the *correctio* places it *c.* 710, solely from the context into which Bede (who provides no date) inserts the relevant chapter into *Historia ecclesiastica*. The first time during Naiton's reign that the different *computus* tables produced divergent dates for the Easter festival was in 712. It has been proposed that it ought not to have been until this divergence took place that the apostolicist reforms became a subject of anxiety, attention and discord.[17] The Irish chronicles record that Iona, now intimately connected with the Pictish Church, adopted the reformed calculation of Easter in 716.[18] Does this record also mark the more general Pictish *correctio*?

Bede knew this date, reporting that the English *peregrinus* Ecgberct, whom he understood to have been a key figure in Iona's reformation, arrived at that monastery in 716, 'not long after' the Pictish *correctio* (*nec multo post illi*).[19] Elsewhere, he reports that the traditionalist reckoning of

---

[16] Bede, *Ep. ad Ecgbertum*, § 13; McClure and Collins, *Bede*, 352 (trans.).
[17] Duncan, 'Bede', 26–7.
[18] *AU* 716.4; *AT* 716.3.
[19] Bede, *Hist. eccl.*, v.22.

Easter was given up by Iona in 715. This alternative date occurs in the chapter in which Bede outlines Pictish ecclesiastical history from Pictish information. Does his dating discrepancy relate to two reformations in consecutive years, one (Naiton's *correctio*) in 715 and the other (reformation at Iona) in 716?[20]

Ecgberct and the Pictish *correctio*

It has long been suspected that Ecgberct, the English monk who, according to Bede, abandoned the idea of evangelising on the Continent in favour of reforming the Columban *familia*, was a pivotal figure in the Pictish *correctio*. It has even been argued that he left Ireland, where he had trained, and travelled to Pictavia advocating reform, becoming a reformist voice at Naiton's court.[21]

These speculative arguments cannot be sustained. Bede, our main source of information about Ecgberct, reports that as a young pupil in Ireland he was stricken with plague and vowed to God that, in return for his life, he would 'live in exile and never return to the island of his birth, to wit, Britain'. So fond was Bede of this anecdote that he mentioned it twice.[22] He greatly admired Ecgberct, whose reformist successes among the Columban clergy Bede regarded as the final repayment of the debt his people owed to Iona for their christianisation. He would never have mentioned Ecgberct's oath had he harboured the slightest suspicion that he had broken it in order to join Naiton's court.

We can conclude only that Ecgberct's exile among Gaels and Picts never saw him violate his oath that he would not return to the shores of Britain. Can he have lived and worked among Picts anywhere other than Britain? The key to understanding this problem is the fact that Ecgberct went to Iona in 715 and remained there until his death in 729. Although the great monastery tends today to be regarded as an 'Irish' house, there were Picts among its monks. More importantly, as we have seen, by 700 Iona was being regarded in Pictland as a Pictish monastery and part of the Pictish Church. Thus, the fact of living at Iona in Atlantic Scotland is sufficient to place Ecgberct 'among Gaels and Picts', while continuing to honour his vow never to return to Britain. As such, his

---

[20] Bede, *Hist. eccl.*, iii.4.
[21] Kirby, 'Bede and the Pictish Church', 18–19; Duncan, 'Bede', 22–41; Lamb, 'Pictland'.
[22] Bede, *Hist. eccl.*, iii.27; iv.3.

> role in the reformist movement is unlikely to have been much greater than Bede sets out in *Historia ecclesiastica*; in fact, Bede probably exaggerates it in order to make his point about repaying a spiritual debt to Iona.

The decision to reform the Pictish Church, including Iona, may have been made in 715, with Easter 716 being Iona's first reformed observance of the festival. Bede's reason for distinguishing Naiton's *correctio* from Iona's Easter reform may have been a desire to introduce Ecgberct into the story. He implies that he, like Adomnán, began pressing the Columban *familia* to reform in the 690s. One reading of the evidence would, therefore, be that Ecgberct was invited or permitted by Adomnán to work in the interests of reform among his monasteries in Ireland. Did their relationship anticipate the partition of the headship of Iona that followed Adomnán's death?

An apparent hiatus in the see (*kathedra*) of Iona after October 713 could be a related development. From that date Naiton may have used his influence to interrupt the episcopal succession in order to press Iona to agree to a council addressing reform. A new incumbent was finally appointed on 29 August 716 – after the first reformed Easter at Iona. The chronicles tell us that the new bishop Fáelchú was seventy-four when he received this office.[23] We are given the age of no other abbot, bishop or *princeps* of Iona at his accession. Did Fáelchú's age have some bearing on his appointment? Did it seem particularly desirable to lay the responsibility of supervising the *correctio* at the feet of a senior member of the Iona community? If Fáelchú had entered a Columban monastery in his childhood, he would have known men who had known Columba himself.

So long as it was accepted by scholars that the entire Pictish Church was governed by Ionan primates from an early date, it was logical to regard the apostolicist reformation of Naiton as a major turning point. It has accordingly attracted a great deal of comment. Such a model may suit parts of the northern Pictish zone, but for much of Pictavia the *correctio* would seem rather to represent the abandonment of an ecclesiastical policy no more than a generation old. For Naiton, it represents a change of heart regarding ecclesiastical allegiances which demands as much explanation as may be uncovered from the thin evidence. That evidence points to a number of challenges arising in the first decade of his reign.

---

[23] *AU* 716.5; *AT* 716.4. 29 August was indeed a Saturday in 716, as the chronicles record.

In 707 or 708 Bécc grandson of Donnchad was killed, seemingly a kinsman of Fiannamail, the Cenél nGabráin king of Dál Riata slain seven years before. The killings of these grandsons of Donnchad son of Conaing hint at convulsions in Kintyre, interestingly at a time when the Cowal dynast Bridei son of Der-Ilei was dominating much of northern Britain.[24] Then, in 710, two sons of 'Nectan son of Dargart', the new Pictish king Naiton son of Der-Ilei, were slain in 'a conflict within Cenél Comgaill'.[25] Was this ongoing bloodshed among the Corcu Réti princes related somehow to Verturian interference? The last of these episodes suggests a parting of the ways between Naiton and his paternal kin in Cowal. Had his sons been dominating Cowal – even the Corcu Réti – on their father's behalf? This personal tragedy within Naiton's household was presumably more or less directly responsible for the succession crisis that followed his abdication.

If Naiton was losing influence in Argyll after 710, still more trouble was on the horizon in his other more peripheral dominions. Does the battle in Orkney recorded in the *Annals of Ulster* in 709 or 710 relate to a challenge to Verturian dominion there?[26] In 711 the young Osred's guardian and lieutenant (*praefectus*) Berctfrith led an English army into Manau at the frontier between Pictavia and Northumbria. According to the 'northern recension' of the *Anglo-Saxon Chronicle*, incorporating an eighth-century Northumbrian text, he brought about 'a slaughter of the Picts' at a place between the Avon and the Carron (*betwix Haefe 7 Caere*), round about modern Falkirk on the Antonine Wall.[27]

Anglo-Saxon *praefecti* were rather more kingly than a translation like 'lieutenant' implies.[28] If he was a kinsman of Beornhaeth, and if his family had a claim to southern Pictish districts, Berctfrith's victory over Pictish forces could have sorely tested Naiton's grip on those territories. The chronicles name a single Pictish casualty, Finnguine son of Deileroith, who has been identified as the father of Vurad (or Wrad) son of Finnguine, apparently part of the inner circle of the kings of Atholl in 729. The death of Gartnait, another son of Deileroith, is recorded in 716, confirming this family's prominence during Naiton's reign.[29] Finnguine and Gartnait may, therefore, have ruled successively as kings of Atholl,

[24] *AU* 697.4, 707.3.
[25] *AU* 710.4. For discussion of this evidence, see Clancy, 'Philosopher-King', 132–3.
[26] *AU* 709.4.
[27] *AU* 711.3; *AT* 711.3; *Ang.-Sax. Chron. E*, s. a. 710; Bede, *Hist. eccl.*, v.24, s.a. 711.
[28] James, 'The Origins of Barbarian Kingdoms', 42–3.
[29] *AU* 716.2; Clancy, 'Philosopher-King', 136–7

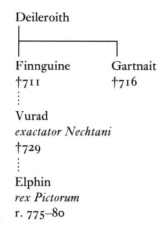

Deileroith

Finnguine   Gartnait
†711   †716
⋮
Vurad
exactator Nechtani
†729
⋮
Elphin
rex Pictorum
r. 775–80

Table 10.2 Finnguine son of Deileroith and his possible descendants

dominating southern Pictland as Verturian subjects in the early eighth century.

In the same year as Berctfrith's triumph, a Dalriadan host, probably led by the Cenél nEchdach king of Dál Riata, Selbach son of Ferchar, defeated a British army at the unidentified Lorg Ecclet.[30] A Dalriadan force had been massacred by a British one as recently as 705 in Glen Leven (*i nGlenn Lemnae*). The topographical terminology is difficult to link with the Lennox Leven, but the armies may have met in the environs of Inverarnan at the northern tip of Loch Lomond.[31] The battle of Glen Leven was the last of a handful encounters since 677 in which British forces excelled themselves against Gaelic opposition in and around Atlantic Scotland. The turning of the tables in 711, following on from the Cenél Comgaill in-fighting of the previous year, may signal the final collapse of the Alt Clut–Cowal–Fortriu coalition that has been discussed above. The convulsions in the royal dynasties of the Corcu Réti in the three years after the death of Bridei son of Der-Ilei may have been symptomatic of a new period of Lorn ascendancy – or they may have paved the way for it.

A year after the British defeat at Lorg Ecclet, Tarbert (*Tairpert Boiter*) in the middle of the Kintyre peninsula was burnt and Dunaverty (*Aberte*) at the southern tip, probably the royal seat, was besieged by Selbach.[32]

---

[30] *AU* 711.5; *AT* 711.5.
[31] *AU* 704.1; *AT* 704.2; *CS* 704.1 (*AU*'s Latin shows that *ic Linn Leven* is incorrect).
[32] *AU* 712.5; Anderson, *Early Sources*, vol. 1, 213–14.

These events must denote a major invasion of Kintyre in 712 and a crushing blow against Cenél nGabráin, only a year after Cowal too may have fallen as Selbach made his way to Lorg Ecclet. It was a decisive affirmation by Selbach of his paramountcy over the Corcu Réti. Is it a coincidence that it followed in the wake of Naiton's troubles in Cowal and Manau? Artbran son of Máel Dúin, who died in 716, may have been the son of Máel Dúin son of Conall and king at Dunaverty during this calamitous period.[33]

In Pictavia, the king's uterine brother Ciniod was slain in 713, two years after the disaster in Manau. Now Naiton 'tied up' his half-brother Talorcan son of Drestan, a tantalising detail. Was Talorcan implicated in Ciniod's death?[34] If so, had Ciniod been dominating the southern Pictish zone on his brother's behalf? Or was Ciniod killed by Naiton himself, and Talorcan seized, as co-conspirators in some plot against the *rex Pictorum*? We do not have the information to decide between these and other possibilities. Talorcan was probably only now coming of age, and the real culprit in any shenanigans linked with him was probably his father Drestan, Der-Ilei's husband. It was probably in 729, twenty-five years later, that Talorcan became king of Atholl – a year in which Vurad son of Finnguine, possibly a son of the man slain fighting Berctfrith in Manau, was killed alongside Talorcan's kin. It has already been suggested on this basis that Finnguine was king of Atholl. Was his brother Gartnait, who died in 716, a co-conspirator against (or alongside) Ciniod son of Der-Ilei?[35]

We have frustratingly few and vague details, but can catch glimpses of a period of strain for Naiton in his dealings with both his paternal and his maternal kin, on both sides of Drumalban, in the years leading up to the *correctio* for which he is famous. His tribulations only strengthen the case, laid out in the previous chapter, that his brother Bridei too, and before him Bridei son of Beli, had extended the Verturian hegemony across Drumalban. Naiton, however, would seem to have been a rather less effective hegemon than his predecessors, especially at the edges of his *imperium*. Bede perhaps supplies us with something of an 'apology': Naiton was as much a philosopher as a king.[36] Now in its third decade, the Verturian expansion may simply have been running out of steam.

---

[33]   *AU* 716.8; *AT* 716.7.
[34]   *AU* 712.4, 713.4, 713.7; *AT* 713.5, 713.8; *Ann. Clon.* 710.4; see also Clancy, 'Philosopher-King', 134–6.
[35]   Clancy, 'Philosopher-King', 135–6.
[36]   Bede, *Hist. eccl.*, v.21; Clancy, 'Philosopher-King', 125–6.

THE PICTISH REFORMATION

It does not necessarily follow that Naiton's regime became severely weakened by these difficulties. After all, the great Oswy had his share of troubles in Deira and along the Mercian frontier in the 650s, but remained a very powerful prince, in part through successful problem-solving. It seems very unlikely that Naiton's change of heart regarding Ionan primacy in Pictavia was unrelated to his difficulties, but does it represent a strong and decisive stroke, or weak grasping at straws?[37] The Synod of Whitby in 664 probably came about in part because of opposition to Oswy's regime, but its resolution shows a king at the peak of his powers. Its outcome was greatly influenced by politics, and in particular questions surrounding the sovereignty of the Deiran kingdom and Church. Suggestions that Naiton reformed his Church essentially as an act of international diplomacy, seeking to bring it into closer alignment with Northumbria, are not particularly satisfying. We have no indications that he made approaches to the boy-king of Northumbria. We have instead good evidence of internal tensions within Northumbria, and convulsions in – even a contraction of – the Verturian hegemony, which together can explain the apparent cessation of large-scale campaigning across the Forth for some time after 711.

The *correctio* took place, according to Bede, as a result of proceedings held at a council (*consessus*) attended both by 'many learned men' versed in Latin and by 'nobles' (*optimates*).[38] The parallels with Whitby are obvious. We do not know where Naiton's Council met. If recent troubles had tested Naiton's grip on southern Pictavia – the jewel in the crown of the Verturian hegemony – his dissatisfaction with the Ionan status quo would have a particularly strong flavour of Whitby about it. Indeed, the southern Pictish source that informed Bede about christianisation in Pictavia implies tension between southern and northern Picts, with the former stressing that their Church was older and their apostle an apostolicist. Reform and the abolition of Ionan primacy had been embraced by Oswy as part of a settlement with the Deirans, who could (and seemingly did in part) make exactly the same argument. As a result he, in no uncertain terms, took control of the kingdom, but York was given control of the Church, perhaps as a kind of consolation prize. The apparent hiatus in the episcopal succession at Iona after October 713 has already been taken as a hint that Naiton was planning his Council by the end of that difficult year.

---

[37] Herbert, 'The Legacy of Columba', 4.
[38] Bede, *Hist. eccl.*, v.21.

Was Naiton's strategy in embracing apostolicist reforms much the same as Oswy's? There are Continental parallels also. The great Merovingian king Clovis, for example, seems to have brought Gallo-Roman bishops into his council even before his conversion as a way of strengthening his grip on the Gallo-Roman parts of his *imperium*.[39] There is no particular reason to doubt that Aeðilfrithing dominion had encouraged the development of a significant apostolicist underclass among the southern Picts. *Correctio*, coupled with the removal of Ionan primacy, may have appealed as a way to reconcile disaffected southern Pictish clerics with their place in Verturian Pictavia.

Naiton himself has always figured prominently in analyses of the *correctio*, but it seems unlikely that the impetus towards reform lay entirely with him. Bede implies that the Ionan *familia* was itself of divided opinion. The English monk Ecgberct had apparently been an advocate of apostolicism within the *familia* for some years prior to 716. It has been suggested that Donnchad too, now abbot of Iona, was an advocate.[40] Bede provides vague hints about such a reformist party. He informs us that Naiton had become well-versed in the arguments involved in the Easter debate, and possessed the reformed Easter *computus*.

However it transpired, Bede makes it clear that, prior to his Council, Naiton had already made up his mind about what was to happen. The king thus pledged, before the fact, that the Picts 'would always follow the customs of the holy Roman and apostolic Church, so much as they might learn them'. This pledge included the promise that, with assistance, the *rex Pictorum* would build a stone church 'after the fashion of the Romans' and dedicate it to St Peter, the apostle and first pope.

'After the fashion of the Romans' (*more Romanorum*) here probably refers to the use of mortar, rather than the dry-stone method of architecture ubiquitous across the north country since the Iron Age (and indeed earlier). It would have been quite ridiculous for Bede to claim that peoples who had built Clyde Rock or Clatchard Craig, not to mention Burghead, did not build in stone. In fact, the *more Romanorum* in question was Frankish. In 675, a year after the foundation of his monastery at Wearmouth, Benedict Biscop recruited masons from Francia to build his church *iuxta more Romanorum*, dedicated to St Peter.[41] The Pictish king's promises were thus as much about flattering Wearmouth-Jarrow as about romanising, though it is likely that they also reflect an appreciation of a

[39]   Wood, 'Kings, Kingdoms and Consent', 24–5.
[40]   Taylor, 'Early Church in Eastern Scotland', 100; see also Smyth, *Warlords*, 137.
[41]   Bede, *Hist. Abbatum*, § 5; Webb and Farmer, *The Age of Bede*, 191 (trans.).

pattern of church dedication which Northumbria had previously embraced, a matter discussed later.

The king's words are known to us because Naiton sent an embassy to Ceolfrith, abbot of Bede's monastery of Wearmouth-Jarrow. The abbot was asked to compose an explanation of the 'catholic observance of holy Easter', by which the king 'might carry through [reform] easily and with greater authority', and 'would be able to confute more convincingly' the traditionalists.[42] It has long been suspected that Bede's access to sources of Pictish provenance, consulted in the composition of *Historia ecclesiastica*, reflects this connection at this time. The king of Picts was by now hostile towards the particularisms of Iona, if largely for political reasons. A certain amount of historical information may have been included in his missives to Ceolfrith – perhaps at the abbot's request – in order to give him some grounding in the particular context of the dispute and the arguments he was being enlisted to confute.[43] Were the speeches composed by Bede and placed in the mouth of Colmán at Whitby based on Ionan arguments from *c.* 715?

Because of this appeal for assistance, scholars have sometimes suspected the *correctio* of being part of a wider political accommodation between Naiton and Bamburgh. He enlisted the expertise of Northumbrian stonemasons to build his stone church. Yet these gestures need reflect little more than connections between Pictish and Northumbrian Churches grown from seeds planted during the age of Aeðilfrithing hegemony. Such relationships may have been cultivated still more, among alienated southern Picts, after the rise of Ionan primacy.

Wearmouth-Jarrow was a logical place to seek authoritative and convincing help. It had a reformist past, but unlike Abercorn, Hexham, Lindisfarne and York that past did not include primacy in Pictland. Its abbot could, therefore, be cast at a Pictish Council as a disinterested observer of ecclesiastical developments, whose views on reform were devoid of political agenda. Surely pro-reform arguments put forward within Pictavia could not be divorced from politics so easily, especially if they were symptomatic of a north–south divide. Ceolfrith could, moreover, consult an expert in *computus* in his community in order to produce an authoritative document. This master was none other than Bede himself, who had completed *De temporibus*, 'On Times', a dozen years earlier.

[42] Bede, *Hist. eccl.*, v.21.
[43] Duncan, 'Bede', 20–36, though we need not presume that a single letter was involved.

If he played a personal part in the drama, it may be no coincidence that Bede's account of the *correctio* is the longest chapter of *Historia ecclesiastica*. Ceolfrith's letter was probably written in consultation with him. It leaves us in little doubt as to the real objects of the Naiton's concern at the Council, and hints that the meeting was held at a Columban monastery. There seems little reason to suppose that the Ionan *familia* was alone among the traditionalist clerics of Pictavia, north and south. However, the final section of Wearmouth-Jarrow's missive, following a detailed enunciation of Easter *computus* and the proper tonsure, indicates that it was the intended audience of the argument:

> Do not suppose me to have pursued the argument thus far as one who holds wearers of this tonsure as contemptible, who have upheld catholic unity by faith and works. On the contrary! I assert confidently that many of them were holy men, and worthy in the sight of God, among whom was Adomnán, renowned abbot and priest of the *Columbienses*, who was sent with a mission from his people to King Aldfrith . . . None the less he could not bring to better ways the monks of Iona, over whom he presided as lawful leader. Had his influence been sufficient, he would have made it his business to correct their tonsure also.[44]

Bede tells us that Naiton had Ceolfrith's letter read aloud at the Council, and translated into Pictish British. There can be little doubt why he did. It explicitly condemns Iona – music to the ears of any who resented that monastery's primacy.

At the same time, however, the letter very clearly upholds and honours the memory of Adomnán. It had been in concert with him that Naiton's predecessors had developed Ionan primacy in Pictavia. As such Ceolfrith provided the king with the ability to pass negative judgement against Iona without simultaneously disparaging the policies of his brother – not to mention whatever Columban allegiances he may have exhibited himself in those years. For all we know, the philosopher-king may have been a lapsed Columban monk. Instead, Wearmouth-Jarrow's authoritative response enabled the *rex Pictorum* to portray his condemnation of the traditionalists of the Ionan *familia* as, in effect, a continuation of the work begun by Adomnán and Bridei. This was no doubt exactly the kind of help Naiton had hoped to receive. No wonder, as Bede relates, that the king was 'delighted' (*gauisus*) by the letter.

---

[44]   Bede, *Hist. eccl.*, v.21.

The decision to reform was announced, and was enforced throughout Naiton's dominions 'by royal authority throughout all the Pictish kingdoms (*prouinciae*)' – or should that be 'dioceses'? – seemingly without significant difficulty. Bede thus implies that Naiton still enjoyed considerable influence among the Picts, as well as a strong brand of royal power. The latter impression is confirmed in his brother's reign by Adomnán's Law. Law-making in early medieval times was an exercise in consensus-building. This fact is reflected in *Lex innocentium*, in its anticipation that promulgation in Ireland under the auspices of the 'king of Ireland' (*rí Erenn*) – Adomnán's Cenél Conaill kinsman Loingsech son of Óengus – required the abbot to marshal the consent of dozens of kings and bishops. For promulgation in Pictavia, on the other hand, the law required the consent of just three men: the *rex Pictorum* and the bishops of Rosemarkie and Iona.

Was the Pictish promulgation of *Lex innocentium*, therefore, a token gesture? Naiton's *correctio*, brought about as an act of royal will through a Council, suggests otherwise. Bridei could have promulgated Adomnán's Law in the same way, at a *consessus* of his own. These are very precious hints that eighth-century Pictish kingship more closely resembled a Northumbrian-style regime than Irish 'incremental' high kingship. It may be a related point that, as far as we can tell, in Pictland, as in England, kingdoms did not bear the dynastic names of their dominant family as they did in Ireland.[45] It is also important to remember that Pictavia, in terms of its arable land and likely population base, was not a particularly large kingdom by Irish or English standards.

THE END OF IONAN PRIMACY

It has been suggested above that, as a result of the *correctio*, the elderly Fáelchú was placed in the *kathedra* of Iona in August 716 in order to reform the Ionan *familia* in Pictavia. In the following year, the chronicles record 'the expulsion by King Nechtan of the *familia* of Iona beyond Drumalban'.[46] Inevitably, it has long been suspected that this *expulsio* must extend in some way from the *correctio*. Certainly both singled out *Columbienses* for discredit – and in particular the *familia* of Iona itself. It has been conventional to suppose that Columban intransigence in Pictavia in the face of reform was responsible for the expulsion, but there

---

[45] Charles-Edwards, 'Early Medieval Kingships', 33, 37–9.
[46] *AU* 717.4; *AT* 717.3; *CS* 717.2.

is no hint of such trouble in Bede's History. More importantly, such stub-bornness seems unlikely after reform had been accepted at Iona itself, especially if the idea of an abbatial schism is rejected.

The key to understanding the expulsion is the notion of the *familia* of Iona (*familia Iae*). The phrase was used in Irish sources to denote the community of Iona itself, rather than the otherwise attested *familia* of Columba (*familia Columbae Cille*), encompassing the whole network of Columban clergy in Britain and Ireland.[47] Significantly, Ceolfrith's letter to Naiton explicitly condemned the monks of Iona (*in Hii insula*), not what he called the *Columbienses* as a whole. These distinctions are impor-tant. The implications of the terminology are that it was not the Columbans *en masse*, but rather those clergymen, like Fáelchú, who belonged specifically to the Iona community, who were expelled across Drumalban in 717.

The effect of this *expulsio*, then, must have been the dismantling of Ionan primacy over the monasteries of Pictavia, in the south where it had only recently been established, and in the north where, in parts, it may well have been more than a century old. It did not necessarily leave Pictavia entirely bereft of *Columbienses*, nor extinguish the cult(s) of their patron saint(s). The monastic rules favoured (and possibly written) by Columba, for example, may have endured at various Pictish monasteries. Nor is there any reason to believe that Gaelic clergy from Argyll or Ireland, outwith the *familia Iae*, were any less welcome in Pictavia after 717 than they had been before.

The situation may be likened to the transfer of power and authority that took place at reformed Lindisfarne in 664. Here some members of the *familia* chose to retreat to Iona with their intransigent leaders, no doubt regarding themselves as men expelled by Oswy.[48] Others, however, chose to stay behind in conformity with the new order. We cannot assume that the likes of Cuthbert repudiated St Columba or their own patron, St Aidan, nor abandoned their writings and teachings. Some Pictish examples may have been similar to the rather different situation described by Bede at reformed Ripon. Here the suggestion is that most or all of the community, including Cuthbert, forsook the monastery in a show of sol-idarity with their leaders.[49] On the whole, it seems likely that the Pictish Church included prominent clergy after 717 who had been dutiful

---

[47] Etchingham, *Church Organisation*, 126–7.
[48] Bede, *Hist. eccl.*, iii.26; see also Charles-Edwards, *Early Christian Ireland*, 320–1, 336–43.
[49] Bede, *V. s. Cuthberti*, § 8; *Hist. eccl.*, v.19.

Columbienses until then. Such people may even have continued to think of themselves as *Columbienses*. Adomnán has been envisioned as having taken the opportunity of composing *Vita Columbae* to affirm for his community that embracing apostolicism made him no less a partisan of St Columba.[50]

Current thinking regarding the Synod of Whitby stresses continuity. We must guard against assumptions that the reformation of Naiton resulted in drastic upheaval, though no doubt there were local disruptions. Does disturbance of its principate lie behind the two-year delay between the Easter reform on Iona in 716 and the reform of the tonsure there?[51] It is perfectly possible that *Columbienses* and their churches continued to receive high-level patronage in Pictavia, and continued to flourish under new ecclesiastical bosses. The example of Whitby suggests that a significant amount of change in personnel is to be expected in the highest offices.

Perhaps more than anything else, the *explusio* represents a 'repatriation' of sorts of Columban monasteries across Pictavia and their realignment under the authority of local bishops, some of whom may have been *Columbienses*. Presumably informed by correspondence originating in Naiton's court, Bede reports that the *correctio* was put into effect 'through all the Pictish *prouinciae*'. The plural usage here perhaps reflects such a putative break-up of the monolithic Ionan primacy (as Bede perceived it) into a plurality of provinces.

If the sum total of the evidence suggests that the primacy of Iona obtained at a relatively late date in many areas of Pictavia, and for a relatively restricted period, it is important not to exaggerate the importance the Columban *familia* in Pictland prior to the abbacy of Adomnán. This is not to say that the Columban monastic rules and other teachings cannot have been influential at monasteries outwith Iona's principate. It is no more desirable, on the other hand, to overestimate the immediate ramifications of the *correctio* and *expulsio*. The Iona Chronicle remained interested in, even infatuated by Pictish affairs for a generation afterwards. It would not be surprising to discover that the cult of St Columba was more widespread in Pictavia in the 720s – and that more Picts were prepared to acknowledge him as a patron or to follow his teachings – than had been the case in the 690s when Adomnán registered his dismay that so many Picts refused to give the saint his due. From the standpoint of this exhortation, the period of Ionan primacy in Pictavia, however

---

[50] Herbert, *Iona, Kells and Derry*, 142–3.
[51] *AT* 718.6; *CS* 718.3.

brief, could have been a success. Yet Columba's successors soon lost their authority over the Pictish daughter houses of his monastery. They would never re-establish it. Subsequent centuries demonstrate that this severance did the cult of St Columba little long-term harm east of Drumalban.

SELBACH SON OF FERCHAR: THE OTHER NORTHERN HEGEMON

After his military successes against the Corcu Réti and the Alt Clut Britons during the most difficult years of Naiton's reign, Selbach son of Ferchar rebuilt Dunollie, destroyed by him in 701 or 702, seemingly in the course of crushing Lorn rivals.[52] Perhaps he now felt a keen need for a royal centre to match his greatness. If the treatments of Cenél Comgaill and Cenél nGartnait in *Cethri prímchenéla Dáil Riata* after 706 reflect an era of Verturian power and influence in Argyll, Selbach's burst of aggression after Naiton ran into difficulties probably reflects it too, if in a very different way.

Selbach had defeated Britons in 711, crushed Cenél nGabráin in Kintyre in 712 and had surely subdued the Corcu Réti by 714, seemingly including Cenél nGartnait, whose claim of descent from Áedán was recorded in *Cethri prímchenéla*. Did a subsequent Dalriadan victory over more (or the same) British enemies at the obscure 'stone that is called *Minuirc*' in 717 enable Selbach to subjugate Beli son of Elphin, king of Clyde Rock?[53] Such a feat had not been equalled since the heady days when Áedán son of Gabrán had been at the peak of his power, more than a hundred years before.

Beli was the nephew and successor of Dumngual son of Eugein, understood in previous chapters to have been a very robust and influential actor in Atlantic politics in the late seventh century, in association with his uncle Bridei son of Beli and the Cowal kin of Naiton. For Beli, as for Naiton, the political situation had changed a great deal by the end of his reign. The Alt Clut king, who died in 722, seems only to have suffered defeats, latterly at Minuirc, twice losing the field to Dalriadan enemies probably led by Selbach.[54]

---

[52]   *AU* 701.8–9, 714.2; *AT* 714.2.
[53]   *AU* 717.5; *AT* 717.4; *CS* 717.3.
[54]   *AU* 722.3; *AT* 722.3; *Ann. Camb.* (Dumville) 722.1. Macquarrie, 'The Kings of Strathclyde', 10, seems to mistake the Harleian 'Strathclyde' pedigree for a king-list, and unnecessarily makes Beli's father a king of Clyde Rock.

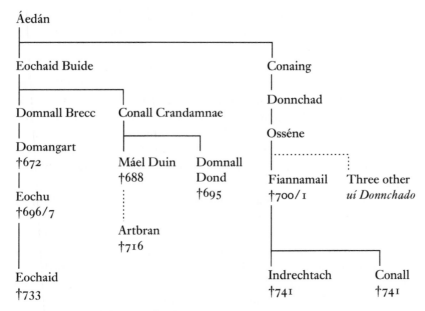

Table 10.3 Cenél nGabráin (706–41)

In 719 a grandson of Donnchad son of Conaing was slain, the third whose killing is recorded in the chronicles. The chronicle interest implies that Donnchad's descendants were sharing in the Cenél nGabráin kingship in this period of Lorn domination. The first grandson, Fiannamail son of Osséne, had been a guarantor of *Lex innocentium* along with a descendant of Eochaid Buide. The next, slain in 707 or 708, may have been succeeded in the kingship by a son of Máel Duin son of Conall, another descendant of Eochaid. Some five generations now separated these men from Gabrán son of Domangart, and the kindred identified with this obscure ancestor was probably coming to the end of its natural life. Gaelic kindreds appear to have disintegrated between four and six generations after the apical ancestor, with new lineages forming up who traced their descent from more recent dynasts.

In this case, it seems that Gabrán's son Áedán became the key apical figure in the eyes of Gabrán's descendants, the most illustrious of whom were Áedán's descendants too. By the early eighth century, however, Áedán's own sons Eochaid and Conaing had begun to supplant him. The segment descended from Eochaid had dominated Cenél nGabráin in the seventh century, but a series of killings in the 690s seems to have made room alongside them for Conaing's descendants, grandsons of his son Donnchad. It is fascinating that, in the reign of Máel Coluim (II) son of

Cinaed (1005–34), Alpínid genealogists had texts to hand in which two notable branches of Áedán's descendants were acknowledged, descended from Eochaid and from Conaing.[55]

It is impossible to determine whether the violent deaths of most of the Cenél nGabráin dynasts on record in this period reflect Lorn aggression or internal hostility, or some mix of the two. The king of Cenél nGabráin in the latter years of Selbach's regime – the chronicles call him *rex Cind Tire*, king of Kintyre – was Donnchad Becc, possibly yet another grandson of Donnchad son of Conaing. In 719 he led Cenél nGabráin to war against Selbach, fighting a *bellum maritimum* or sea-battle against him on 6 October.[56]

Only a month before, Selbach had fought another battle at Finglen (*Findglen*) against his brother Ainbcellach, who was defeated and killed there in the glen of Allt Braglenmore, between Loch Scamadale and Loch na Speinge on the rugged southern frontier of Lorn.[57] The king would seem to have been left vulnerable to an opportunistic Donnchad, who vanquished him in a fascinating but obscure naval encounter. Naiton's greatest troubles in this decade seem to have come from within his own paternal and maternal kindreds. Now Selbach experienced a similar challenge to his paramountcy from a kinsman.

Donnchad of Kintyre died in 721, possibly signalling to Selbach that the time was ripe for abdication to a monastery. He cut his hair in 723, making way for Donngal his son to succeed him.[58] Like Aeðilred of Mercia twenty years before, however, Selbach may have remained vigilant in retirement of the affairs of his son. Four years later he became a 'son of perdition', as Adomnán would have called him, abandoning the monastery and returning to the world to fight at Ros Foichnae, perhaps another sea-battle. Possibly, like the abdicant East Anglian king Sigeberht, he did so because of the irresistible imprecations of his former *cohors*, warriors who 'would be less afraid and less ready to flee', Bede relates of Sigeberht, 'if they had with them one who was once their most vigorous and distinguished leader'.[59] Selbach's foes were the Kintyre

---

[55]   Woolf, *From Pictland to Alba*, 226–7.

[56]   *AU* 719.7; *AT* 719.5. 6 October was a Friday in 719; *AU* (*die .ui. feriae*) has the correct day, and a chronicle related to *AT* was used to correct the month.

[57]   *AU* 719.6; *AT* 719.4. Both chronicles give the date as Thursday, 13 September, but 13 September was a Wednesday in 719. Probably Thursday, 14 September is correct, but possibly the battle took place in April or July, when the thirteenth day of the month was a Thursday.

[58]   *AU* 721.1, 723.4, *AT* 721.1, 723.4.

[59]   Bede, *Hist. eccl.*, iii.18.

war-band (*familia*) of Eochaid son of Eochu, a descendant of Eochaid Buide whose father had been a guarantor of Adomnán's Law. The battle of Ros Foichnae may have been indecisive, and in 730 Selbach died.[60]

ABDICATION: TO WIN AN EVERLASTING KINGDOM

Naiton too chose the path of abdication, cutting his hair in 724, a year after Selbach.[61] His ecclesiastical interventions bear the marks of a remarkable political gesture made towards nobles and church leaders – perhaps mainly in southern Pictavia – who were resentful of, or disaffected by, the status quo built up by his predecessors. Such sentiment could have reflected more general dissatisfactions with the Verturian regime. It would seem that the ground was shifting under Naiton's feet, and that decisive, even radical action was required to cure the regime's ills. The likelihood that the *correctio* represents some kind of concession, along with the questionable notion that Naiton was removed from power in 724, have led to the thesis that his reformation was an act of a king whose position was crumbling under pressure from rivals and enemies.[62]

Was Naiton driven from the kingship? By this time, he had left the darkest years of his reign ten years behind him. He had reformed the Pictish Church, including Iona and the Columban *familia*, and expelled Ionan clerics from Pictavia. After such shows of his considerable strength, the king of Picts does not seem to have experienced undue difficulty in his regime, testifying to the effectiveness of whatever political settlement accompanied the reformation.

His abdication might have been the reluctant flight of a frightened man, but it should not be considered in isolation. Coenred of Mercia gave up his kingdom in this period 'for the sake of the Lord', as Bede put it with regard to yet another king, 'and to win an everlasting kingdom'.[63] Coenred's father, Ecgfrith's opponent Aeðilred, had abdicated in 704, becoming abbot of the monastery at Bardney in Lindsey, a district wrested from Ecgfrith in 679. None the less, the old king summoned Coenred a few years later to advise his son on the matter of Wilfrid's restoration – a situation that might have been familiar to Donngal son of Selbach after 623. *Vita Columbae* names several kings and warriors who

---

[60] *AU* 727.3, 730.4; see also *AT* 726.9.
[61] *AT* 724.2; *Ann. Clon.* 722.2.
[62] Smyth, *Warlords*, 73–5.
[63] Bede, *Hist. eccl.*, v.7; for a parallel discussion, see de Jong, 'Monastic Prisoners'.

came to Iona and other monasteries as fugitives from the secular world, and implies that such exiles often lacked sincerity when they took their vows.

Naiton's successor as king of Fortriu was apparently a certain Drest, who eventually forced him back into public life. Drest's co-conspirators – 'the *exactatores* of Nechtan' – included the old king's half-brother Finnguine, whose brother Talorcan Naiton had bound in 713. The possibility that the same faction, associated with Atholl, included the sons of Deileroith and acted against Naiton on both occasions has already been raised. The conventional translation of *exactatores* as 'tax-gatherers' here has had to be given up.[64] Drestan, the father of Finnguine and Talorcan was probably not the same person as King Drest.

The new king's rough treatment of his predecessor allows for the suggestion that the abdication was not voluntary. Yet the king cannot have been younger than forty in 724, by which time he had outlived his brother by almost twenty years, and he was probably nearer sixty, having had adult sons who fell in 710. In addition, Bede implies that the old king was a genuine scholar – a philosopher-king. For all these reasons it seems likely that Naiton's abdication was sincere. Indeed, the way in which he would be wielded as a political weapon by rivals for his abandoned kingship is another indication that disgrace and forced abdication were not involved. Like Selbach and Aeðilred, however, it was not given to Naiton to enjoy a peaceful and obscure retirement.

[64] *AU* 729.2; Woolf, 'AU 729.2', 133–4.

CHAPTER 11

'When Óengus took Alba': Despot, Butcher and King (728–61)

'Good the day', wrote Gruibne, a (legendary) Gaelic poet, 'when Óengus took Alba, hilly Alba with its strong princes; he brought battle to seats, with boards, with feet and hands, and with broad shields'.[1] The remarkable man apparently commemorated in this quatrain, *Fó sén dia ngaib Óengus Albain*, dominated northern Britain in the middle third of the eighth century like no king before him. To Gaelic observers he was Óengus son of Fergus, the Pictish king responsible for 'smiting' Dál Riata, to which the quatrain probably refers. Like the sons of Der-Ilei, he cultivated interests in Argyll. His military and other interventions among the Gaels were none the less unprecedented, and unparalleled in (recorded) Pictish history. He seems to have negotiated successfully with the paramount king in Ireland and may even have invaded that country, a feat not matched until the fourteenth century.

In some English records he was Unust, and in the *Chronicle of 766* 'a despotic butcher who stained the beginning of his reign with criminal blood, and continued likewise right up to the end'.[2] He is the first Pictish king known to have invaded Northumbria, but he also established a peace treaty with his English neighbours. He is the first Pictish king known to have invaded Clydesdale too, ushering in a new age of royal ambition south of the Antonine Wall that culminated in the Scottish annexations of Lothian and Strathclyde in the tenth and eleventh centuries. No other king of Picts attracted the sustained interest of English or Irish chroniclers. He was an ally of Aeðilbald of Mercia, the greatest English king of the age, and the first king of Picts to be commemorated in the source of the Durham *Liber vitae*.

---

[1] *Fó sén dia ngaib Óengus Albain*; Clancy, *Triumph Tree*, 144 (trans.).
[2] *Chron. 766*, s.a. 761. The translation is based on Charles-Edwards, 'The Continuation of Bede', 139.

His own Pictish British name was Onuist son of Vurguist (or Wrguist).[3] It was 150 years before so impressively precocious a king reigned again in northern Britain. It is a matter of particular regret that we can recover so few details about him.

THE WINNING OF THE SOUTH

Onuist burst suddenly and decisively into the lens of the Iona chronicler in 728, when he and his *cohors* – or rather *familia* – overwhelmed the forces of a Pictish king, Elphin, at the hill of Moncrieffe (*Monid Chroib*) outside Perth, killing one of his sons and many of his men.[4] As a power centre, the Pictish stronghold at Moncrieffe, in the crook of the Tay and the Earn, is intriguing. It is only eight kilometres downriver from Forteviot, site of the (presumably) later 'palace' (*palacium Fothuirtabaicht*), and lies even closer to Abernethy and also to Scone, site of the (presumably) later monastery (*ciuitas Scoan*) symbolic of kingship in Alba. Was Moncrieffe, therefore, a key royal centre in the southern Pictish zone by 728, whose status passed to Forteviot or Scone?

Onuist's victory may have secured him access to a substantial royal treasury. Elphin meanwhile withdrew with what remained of his men to another stronghold called *Castellum Credi*. This otherwise unidentified place may have been the 'hill of confidence' (*collis credulitatis*) of nearby Scone. There was a second engagement, and the Iona chronicler described Elphin's defeat as lamentable (*lacrimabilis*), something of a partisan comment implying perhaps that the hapless southern king enjoyed the sympathies of the Columban clergy in 728, and that Onuist did not.[5]

Elphin was the colleague of Drest, both kings having succeeded the abdicant Naiton son of Der-Ilei in 724. Neither king is given a patronymic in the sources, making it impossible to know much about their backgrounds. A partition of Pictavia between them seems to have taken place as part of the succession accommodation arising from the abdication. Anglo-Saxon kingdoms could be partitioned among a dead king's heirs, and subdivisions also took place within the great kingdom of the Merovingian Franks. There is no evidence that Elphin and Drest ever came to blows.

[3] Forsyth, 'Evidence of a Lost Pictish Source', 24–5, anticipates that *Oniust* is the correct Pictish British name-form, but the attested form *Onuist* is used here.

[4] *AU* 728.4; *AT* 728.4; *Ann. Clon.* 725.1.

[5] *AU* 728.4; *AT* 728.5; *Ann. Clon.* 725.2; Skene, *Celtic Scotland*, vol. 1, 288; Anderson, *Early Sources*, vol. 1, 224.

The chronicles' apparent partisanship towards him suggests that Elphin was a Verturian prince, who apparently controlled the important southern stronghold of Moncrieffe. Before 728 he was probably king of Atholl, a realm now closely linked with Fortriu through the kinship of their ruling dynasties, and probably dominating the whole Tay basin. He may have acquired that kingship as early as 716. Now he was 'deprived of all his territories and people'.[6] The *Annals of Clonmacnoise* include the curious information that 'Eolbeck the son of Moydan and the rest of the nobles and people of the Picts turned their backs to Elphin'.[7] It is unfortunate that this statement is unique to this difficult chronicle.

Naiton's successor Drest *rex Pictorum* was presumably king of Fortriu after 724. Was he related to Naiton's half-brothers, with whom the chronicles link him in 729? Someone had taken the new king's son Simul captive in 725. A year later, Drest took a more notable captive in the person of Naiton, forcibly extracted from his monastic retirement after two years. The king must have been under pressure. Presumably the seizure of the old ruler was perpetrated in the expectation that his custody would infuse Drest's kingship with an extra degree of credibility in the face of some internal or external challenge.

The enigmatic Onuist, having crushed Elphin and taken power (*nert*), turned his attentions northwards.[8] Vanquished and disgraced, Elphin meanwhile fled into parts unknown to us, disappearing into obscurity even as his new foe was emerging from it. Was this royal Pictish exile the same man as Elpin of Glasnevin, a monastery in County Dublin, whose death in 758 is recorded in the Irish chronicles which form our main source for Onuist's reign?[9]

Who was this scourge of the southern Pictish king? Our main clues regarding Onuist's origins come from *Éogan Már trá óenmac leis*, 'Éogan Mór Had a Single Son', a Munster genealogical tractate of early medieval date. The genealogist made Onuist a descendant of a certain Cairpre Cruithnecháin, 'from whom [descend] the Éoganachta of Mag Gergind in Alba'.[10] It has already been noted that this plain (*mag*) was distinct from Circhind, where Áedán son of Gabrán once fought Miathian foes. Indeed, Mag Gergind lay at the opposite margins of the southern Pictish zone from the Miathi according to Irish sources containing Fordoun in

[6] *AT* 728.5; *Ann. Clon.* 725.2.
[7] *Ann. Clon.* 725.2.
[8] *AT* 728.4 (*rogab Aengus nert*).
[9] *AU* 758.1; *AT* 758.1; *Ann. Clon.* 754.2.
[10] *Éogan Már trá óenmac leis*, ll. 25–32; see also Chadwick, *Early Scotland*, 41.

the Howe of the Mearns.[11] The stronghold of Dunnottar in the Mearns was attacked in 693, possibly an episode in the succession struggle between Tarain and Bridei son of Der-Ilei. It was also attacked in 680, probably by Bridei son of Beli, and that year may mark the conquest of Mag Gergind by the Waerteras of Fortriu.

Onuist thus seems to have been a native of the Mearns, possibly born into a Verturian kindred established there after 680. That *Éogan Már trá óenmac leis* could envision his kin as 'Éoganachta' suggests that Onuist was the descendant of an obscure Vuen (or Wen), the Pictish British cognate of Gaelic Éogan. Onuist's great successes would seem to have brought lasting fame and status to his home district. *Genelach Dáil Araidi*, a ninth-century pseudo-historical tractate, envisions the Pictish colonisation of northern Britain as a conquest of 'the plain of Fortriu in the first place' (*mag Fortrenn primo*), confirming that kingdom's primacy, and then a conquest of Mag Gergind (*mag Cergin*), thus giving Onuist's homeland pride of place among the districts of southern Pictavia.[12] Moreover, the name *an Mhaoirne*, the Mearns, first attested in a tenth-century context in the *Chronicle of the Kings of Alba*, denotes the base of operations of a maer or steward.[13] Does the fact that the Mearns was 'the' stewartry (among many) imply that the district enjoyed special status in the eyes of the royal dynasty?

It is a happy intersection with such suggestions of southern origins that Onuist first appears on record at Moncrieffe. His brother and eventual successor Bridei is called *rex Fortrenn* in the chronicles, and another brother Talorcan led the Waerteras into battle in 736. These Verturian connections may, however, speak more of the totality of Onuist's capture of the *regnum Pictorum*, and his use of his brothers as his deputies beyond the Mounth, than of Verturian origins. He himself is never called *rex Fortrenn* in any source.

What may have brought this Mearnsman to challenge Elphin in 728 on the banks of the Tay and the Earn must remain obscure, but it is likely that they were rivals for dominion in the southern Pictish zone. Onuist's Mearns origins lend strength to the suggestion above that Elphin was Atholl-based. Was Onuist, in the first instance, seeking to wrest control of Gowrie and Atholl away from the Verturian hegemons?

Having a son, Bridei, who in 731 was capable of leading an army, Onuist can hardly have been much younger than about forty when he moved

---

[11]   Watson, *Celtic Place-Names*, 109; Broun, 'The Seven Kingdoms', 31–2.
[12]   *Gen. Dáil Araidi*, 64; Skene, *Chron. Picts and Scots*, 318–21; Calise, *Pictish Sourcebook*, 22–36.
[13]   *Chron. Kings of Alba*, § 39; Watson, *Celtic Place-Names*, 110–11.

against Elphin. He must have been born during the reign of Bridei son of
Beli, and was probably in his seventies or even his eighties when he died.
Onuist may, therefore, be seen as the first *rex Pictorum* born and raised in
the new Pictavia, shaped by the achievements of the Verturian hegemons
who had been unabashed in courting the leading clerics of northern Britain.
Perhaps this background offers some explanation for his unwillingness to
be constrained by the frontiers of the hegemony he inherited from his predecessors. Yet his precocious reign may also have been driven by the spectre
of illegitimacy, one salve for which could be success on the campaign trail.

THE WINNING OF THE NORTH

Having destroyed Elphin, Onuist pressed on. His retinue (*familia*), mentioned specifically by the chronicles in 729, may have been forcing his
hand.[14] It is just possible to detect from the terse chronicle data how he
portrayed himself in this new campaign. At the unidentified Monid
Carno beside (probably) Loch Lochy (*Loch Loogdae*) in the Great Glen,
Onuist triumphed over 'the enemy (*hostis*) of Nechtan'. The loaded
phrase surely refers to Drest, Naiton's captor since 726. More loaded
language records that a number of 'the oppressors (*exactatores*) of
Nechtan' were killed by Onuist's men, including Naiton's half-brother
Finnguine.[15] As already mentioned in relation to the tantalizing events of
713, Finnguine's family were connected with Atholl: his brother Talorcan
seems to have become king of that realm about this time, and Elphin
may have been their kinsman (even their brother). Is there just
enough passing similarity between the names to allow 'Eolbeck' son of
'Moydan' in the *Annals of Clonmacnoise* to be the same person as
Biceot son of Moneit, killed with his son at Monid Carno? If so, Biceot,
like Finnguine, could be seen as having rallied round Drest in Fortriu
after spurning Elphin in 728, no doubt along with other Atholl men.

  The language of the chronicles suggests that Onuist, now surely king
of the southern Picts, cast himself as the avenger and liberator of Naiton,
whose captors and hostile kinsmen in the north were (he could argue)
denying the old king his well-earned retirement in the service of God.
Patristic writings, and especially those of St Augustine of Hippo, had
long since established the Christian morality of wars undertaken to
protect the peace of the Church. Had Drest not violated that peace?

[14] Woolf, 'Onuist', 36.
[15] *AU* 729.2; *Ann. Camb.* (Dumville) 728.1. My reading of *hostis* here as 'enemy' rather
than 'army' has now been confirmed as preferable by Woolf, 'AU 729.2', 132–3.

Both Onuist and Drest, then, sought to use the figure of Naiton to their political advantage as they struggled to maintain and justify their positions and actions in the late 720s. Drest probably did so to emphasise closeness and continuity with his predecessor, a position also aided by the support of the old king's Atholl kin. Onuist seems to have used Naiton to justify hostility towards Drest and Finnguine. Their competing strategies have been taken already as evidence that Naiton was no discredited figure, chased from his kingship in 724.

Like Elphin at Moncrieffe, Drest managed to elude Onuist in their first encounter at Monid Carno, possibly Carn a' Ghrianain above the River Gloy on the south side of Loch Lochy, the only place in this area currently containing an element like *Carno*. The relentless Onuist again went in pursuit, and Drest was killed by his foe's warriors at the unidentified Druimm Derg Blathuug on 12 August 729, a Friday, perhaps not long after their prior encounter.[16] Druimm Derg ('Red Ridge') is, unfortunately, a common place-name in Scotland. Talorcan son of Drestan, whose brother Finnguine had fallen at Monid Carno, remained at large. In fact, it seems he emerged from the events of 728–9 as king of Atholl. As if to confirm the evidence, already discussed, linking Cóeti bishop of Iona with Atholl, as if his see straddled Drumalban, Talorcan played out the last acts of his life in Argyll. His presence there may be thought to represent the prelude to a remarkable new phase in Onuist's rise to power. It involved a sequence of events that is of great significance for understanding the gradual shaping of the kingdom of Alba.

Within the space of a year or two, Onuist had managed to rise from relative obscurity in the Mearns to dominate Pictavia. He had slain or ruined the men who had emerged as joint kings in 724, captured the powerful realm of Fortriu and restored Pictavia to the dominion of a single high king. Yet Pictavia remained a composite realm still, as Bede's conception of a bipartite nation in the 730s reflects.

Onuist had also succeeded, it seems, in delivering the old king from his captors; Naiton died three years later.[17] What did he make of his vigorous southern liberator? Did he even know him? It seems that the reformer was not restored to his monastery. If Onuist enjoyed a reign of thirty years, as attested in the king-list, he cannot have assumed the high kingship until about the time of Naiton's death in 732.[18] It therefore seems that Naiton, doubtless with the southerner's encouragement,

[16]   *AU* 729.3; *AT* 729.4; *Ann. Clon.* 726.3.

[17]   *AT* 732.7; *Ann. Clon.* 729.7.

[18]   Anderson, *Early Sources*, vol. i, cxxv; Woolf, 'AU 729.2', 134.

re-grew his hair and returned to power among the Waerteras. In the process of restoring him to the kingship, Onuist and his men killed a number of the king's uterine kinsmen, and thus paved the bloody way for his own succession. In the Mearns, Onuist was presumably counting on Naiton to ease his eventual acquisition of the *regnum Pictorum*.

ONUIST AND THE GAEL

Having regained his liberty sometime after 713, Talorcan son of Drestan, Naiton's half-brother, was now king of Atholl. He seems to have set up his court in Argyll. Talorcan's movements and Onuist's reaction to them surely reflect the altogether more shadowy Pictish movements into Argyll, outlined above, during the reigns of the previous Verturian hegemons stretching back to the early 670s. Like the hapless Drest, Donngal son of Selbach, king of Cenél nEchdach in Lorn, had been challenged after his father's retirement. It had actually been the old king Selbach himself who had faced this threat in battle. The chronicles are vague about the outcome of this clash in 727 between Selbach and the retinue (*familia*) of Eochaid of Cenél nGabráin. It is clear that, in any event, Cenél nEchdach eventually gained the upper hand in the struggle. Selbach, it seems, had not become a 'son of perdition' for nothing.

In 731, the year after Selbach's death, Bede completed *Historia ecclesiastica*, and Eochaid son of Eochu, faced by a collapsing cause, followed a now familiar path, entered a monastery and died there in 733.[19] Four generations and a hundred years now separated Eochaid from his namesake Eochaid Buide, the son of Áedán whom Columba earmarked for kingship. Cenél nGabráin was probably on the verge of its inevitable segmentation. It was the better part of three centuries before scholars in the time of Causantín son of Cuilén (995–7), a grandson of one grandson of Cinaed son of Alpín, identified Eochaid Buide as Cinaed's ancestor, artificially linking the Alpínids to the royal dynasty favoured by St Columba in *Vita Columbae*.[20] In fact, it seems that this lineage had nothing whatever to do with the House of Alpín.

Eochaid's successor in the kingship of Kintyre was probably Talorc son of Congus, whose father was named a scion of Cenél nGabráin in

---

[19] *AU* 731.2; *AT* 731.2, 733.5.
[20] Skene, *Celtic Scotland*, vol. 1, 321–2, recognised the artificiality of the Dalriadan pedigree assigned to Cinaed; Broun, *The Irish Identity*, 146–53, comprehensively undermines the objections of Chadwick, *Early Scotland*, 131–2. 'Alpínids' is a term coined by Woolf, *From Pictland to Alba*.

Cethri prímchenéla Dáil Riata after 706. In the 670s, as we have seen, Talorc's grandfather Conamail had been captured in the company of a man who has been identified as a kinsman of Bridei son of Beli. On that basis, the possibility has been raised that his kindred Cenél nGartnait rose to prominence in the late seventh century with Verturian backing. In year of Talorc's accession, he fought and lost a battle against Onuist's son Bridei and fled the battlefield.[21] In that same year, Donngal burned the stronghold of Tairpert Boitir, which presumably guarded the strategic carrying-place across the middle of the Kintyre peninsula at Loch Tarbert, and may have occupied the site of Tarbert Castle.[22] What had brought both Pictish and Lorn forces against Kintyre in 731? It is tempting to suppose that Talorcan of Atholl was being harboured by Talorc, a man whose family may have had sympathies with a Verturian establishment now under pressure from Onuist. Bridei was presumably acting as a royal lieutenant on this campaign; possibly his father was lining him up to wrest the kingship of Atholl from Talorcan. Did he come to some arrangement with Donngal? The Lorn king may simply have been acting as a supreme opportunist when he attacked Tairpert Boitir. It was presumably he, as *rex Dáil Riata*, who spearheaded the successful Dalriadan seaborne offensive into north-east Ireland, also recorded in 731.[23] His ships may have diverted to the Kintyre coast before or after this impressive raid on Antrim, after the king caught wind of Talorc's tribulations.

Such a reconstruction of the relationships between Onuist, Donngal, Talorcan and Talorc is speculative. However, the eventual fates shared by Talorc and Talorcan show that in his eyes Onuist did regard them as equally guilty of whatever offence justified their destruction. Indeed, the circumstances surrounding Talorc's reign are remarkable for what they imply about how Onuist conceived of Pictavia. His Verturian predecessors the sons of Der-Ilei maintained personal and political interests in Argyll as descendants of Comgall, and not least as precocious patrons of Iona. Their personal circumstances had apparently fostered some of the political doctrines detectable in Bede's Pictish material in which Argyll was regarded as Pictish. Before these kings, Bridei son of Beli had apparently pursued an active Argyll policy, and was probably also a patron of Iona. There may even have been Pictish invasions of Argyll in 675 and 710.

We do not know how Onuist may have been related, if at all, to these powerful predecessors in the kingship of Pictavia, nor what interests in

---

[21] *AU* 731.6; *AT* 731.6; *Ann. Clon.* 728.2.
[22] *AU* 731.4.
[23] *AU* 731.5; *AT* 731.3; *Ann. Clon.* 728.1.

Argyll he may have felt he possessed. It seems most likely that his son's principal aim in 731 was to locate and arrest Talorcan of Atholl. His family knew how to make trouble: they had been a thorn in Naiton's side, on and off, for almost twenty years. On top of that, they may also have been regarded by Onuist's family as their principal rivals for paramountcy in the southern Pictish zone. If Talorc's kindred had indeed been linked with the Verturian establishment that Onuist had recently overthrown in Fortriu and Atholl, his court should have been attractive to Talorcan. As an Atholl dynast, Talorcan is likely to have been much more familiar with Argyll politics than Onuist, but he was up against a truly remarkable opponent.

Onuist's strategy in dealing with Talorc became more direct after he had succeeded Naiton as *rex Pictorum* in 732. The events of 733 set the stage for some remarkable movements in 734, but are difficult to untangle. In that year Flaithbertach son of Loingsech, king of Cenél Conaill, led a Dalriadan fleet (*classis Dál Riata*) to war against Cenél nÉogain, the other great kindred of the northern Uí Néill. The result of this reinvigoration of the old Donegal–Argyll axis, much vaunted by Cumméne Find a hundred years earlier, was decisive defeat on the River Bann, at the county border between Antrim and Londonderry.[24] Within about twelve months, Flaithbertach had abdicated, the last Cenél Conaill king to dominate the northern Uí Néill. It was an important moment in Irish history, for Cenél nÉogain preferred the cult of St Patrick at Armagh to that of St Columba, scion of their rivals in Donegal.

A piece of precious information recorded in one chronicle indicates that Flaithbertach got his fleet *a Fortreanoibh*, 'from Fortriu'.[25] Two years earlier Donngal of Lorn and Bridei son of Onuist had attacked Kintyre, seemingly in a joint venture against Talorc son of Congus, if not one undertaken by friends. Do the inconsistencies relating to the origins of Flaithbertach's fleet reveal that the Bann campaign was a second joint venture involving Donngal and Bridei, who may have succeeded Naiton as king of Fortriu a year earlier? Confirmation of a kind seems to be provided by the chronicles: Donngal also raided the unidentified island of Inis Cuirenrigi in 633, and, crucially, he 'dishonoured Tory Island (*Torach*)', an Ionan monastery off the Donegal coast, 'dragging (*traxit*) Bridei from there'.[26]

The capture of Bridei son of Onuist was outrageous, exhibiting all the signs of a desperate act. It presumably took place after the catastrophe on

[24] *AT* 733.4; *Ann. Clon.* 730.1; Anderson, *Early Sources*, vol. 1, 229–30.
[25] Radner, ed., *Fragmentary Annals*, § 221.
[26] *AU* 733.1; *AT* 733.1.

the Bann. Did the fleets of Dál Riata and Fortriu convey the battered remnants of Flaithbertach's forces back along the coast to Donegal? If they had gone to war as allies of a kind in 731 and 733, why did Donngal now betray Bridei? Had they simply had their fill of one another? A better explanation may relate to trouble back home in Lorn. In this same year, the chronicles record, Muiredach son of Ainbcellach 'assumed (*assumit*) the kingdom of Cenél Loairn'.[27] Ainbcellach had been king of Lorn before being deposed in 698 or 699, and his brother Selbach had later vanquished and killed him during Naiton's reign. Did his son seize the kingship in 733 after hearing the news from the Bann? If so, Donngal could have captured Bridei in order to encourage Onuist in Pictavia to support him in recovering Lorn. Another possibility, however, is that Donngal seized Onuist's son because he felt betrayed himself, suspecting Onuist of helping his cousin to snatch his kingdom.

If Onuist's predecessors had been casting their shadows across Argyll, the fact that Ireland now lay within his own reach may speak of an increasingly strong Pictish presence in the west Highlands. *Éogan Már trá óenmac leis* makes Onuist both a native of the Mearns and a descendant of the ancestors of the Éoganacht kindreds that, between them, controlled the kingdom of Cashel in Munster. This tractate thus hints at the forging of an alliance between Onuist and an Éoganacht king, as such alliances commonly led to the 'discovery' of a genealogical link between the allies.[28]

The king of Cashel and paramount king of Munster in the early 730s was Cathal son of Finnguine of the Éoganacht Glendamnach, who appears as a literary character, afflicted by a tapeworm, in the fanciful *Aislinge Meic Con Glinne*, 'the Vision of Mac Con Glinne'. In 721, Cathal had devastated Brega, the kingdom of the Síl nÁedo Sláne of the southern Uí Néill, in alliance with the king of Leinster.[29] According to the Munster-based *Annals of Inisfallen*, the Uí Néill king of Tara had now submitted to him, leaving the Éoganacht king of Cashel paramount king of the Irish. Cathal had remained active, and in 735 he got the better of the king of Leinster in battle, an outcome viewed differently in different chronicles.[30] However, in 737 he met the new king of Tara at the

---

[27] *AU* 733.2; *AT* 733.2.

[28] Dumville, 'Kingship, Genealogies and Regnal Lists', 77, 79–81.

[29] *AU* 721.6; *AT* 721.3; *AI* 721.2. The Cathal who attacked the southern Uí Néill in 733 (*AU* 733.7) is unlikely to be the Éoganacht king; the Munster-based *Annals of Inisfallen* say nothing about it. See Charles-Edwards, *Early Christian Ireland*, 477–9.

[30] *AI* 735.1; Cathal's 'victory' here is an 'escape' in *AU* 735.3; *AT* 735.3.

monastery of Terryglass in Tipperary, the frontier setting connoting equality of status.[31]

Catait, a word later identified as Pictish (*Cruithnech*) and denoting a type of brooch, appears in *Bretha nemed toísech*, a legal tract thought to date from the reign of Cathal son of Finnguine. An alliance of convenience between Onuist in Pictavia and this king of Cashel – made distant kinsmen by *Éogan Már trá óenmac leis* – can have been agreed at any point between Onuist's accession in 732 and Cathal's death in 742.[32] By becoming a guarantor of *Lex innocentium* in 696 or 697, Bridei son of Der-Ilei had linked himself with Irish kings and the monastery at Birr in Offaly, not far from Terryglass. He may have blazed the trail along which Onuist was moving forty years later. In October 727, Adomnán's relics had been taken to Ireland for the first renewal of *Lex innocentium*, an initiative of Cilléne Droichtech, who had become abbot of Iona in the previous year.[33] Cilléne's byname *droichtech*, like Latin *pontifex*, literally means 'bridge-builder', and suggests that Cilléne was a bishop before becoming abbot.[34] The chronicles do not mention a Pictish promulgation of Adomnán's Law at this time, but they did not do so in 696 or 697 either, when we know Bridei had promulgated it.

Onuist had not been king in 727, the thirtieth anniversary of Birr, but he had become the future of Pictish kingship by the time of the return of Adomnán's relics to Iona in 730.[35] If Naiton was now invited by Cilléne to renew Adomnán's Law, the occasion may have familiarised Onuist with the Irish political landscape. Onuist was no less ambitious in his royal alliances in Britain. Indeed, he took paramount kingship in northern Britain to levels of activity throughout Britain and Ireland that, if they were not unprecedented, may only have been realised previously in the days of the Barbarian Conspiracy almost four hundred years earlier. Perhaps Onuist turned to Cashel only after his son had been captured, part of events that may reveal flirtation with an alliance with Cenél Conaill before the battle of the Bann.

---

[31] *AU* 737.9; Herbert, *Iona, Kells, and Derry*, 63; Charles-Edwards, *Early Christian Ireland*, 280.

[32] Etchingham and Swift, 'English and Pictish Terms', 32; *AU* 742.3; *AT* 742.3; *AI* 742.1.

[33] *AU* 727.5, 730.3, 752.1; *AT* 726.2, 727.5, 730.1; *Ann. Clon.* 727.1. On the evidence of Cilléne's involvement, see Herbert, *Iona, Kells, and Derry*, 61.

[34] Bourke, 'Cillíne Pontifex'.

[35] *AU* 730.3; *AT* 730.1.

THE SMITING OF CENÉL nECHDACH

Donngal, who may have remained in Donegal after losing Lorn, was not the only Dalriadan king to lose his kingdom at this time. In 734, Talorc of Kintyre, who may have been harbouring Talorcan of Atholl, 'was overcome by his brother, passed into the grasp of Picts, and drowned by them'. His unscrupulous sibling was probably Cú Bretan son of Congus, who died in 740.[36] Three years earlier, Talorc had been vanquished by Bridei. Now it seems that Onuist destroyed him. It appears that he did so, however, at a distance, for the chronicles do not say that the Pictish king invaded Argyll in 734. He worked instead through a local agent, Talorc's brother Cú Bretan.

A similar fate awaited Talorcan of Atholl, who was 'completely bound' (*conprehensus alligatur*) in the same year near Dunollie, a stronghold presumably held by the usurper Muiredach, now king of Lorn. Was he as complicit in Talorcan's apprehension beside his fortress as Cú Bretan had been in Kintyre? It would be five more years before Talorcan too would be drowned by Onuist.[37] These drownings were probably public and highly visible executions. The possibility that Muiredach in Lorn, who avoided coming to harm, was complicit in these seizures of enemies of Onuist, both delivered into Pictish custody, hints that Onuist had previously backed his seizure of Donngal's kingship. By now he and Onuist certainly shared a common enemy in Donngal. Selbach's son too was in Argyll in 734, but he was wounded in an attack on the unidentified Dún Leithfinn, and fled to Ireland 'from the power (*a potestate*) of Onuist', leaving the stronghold to be destroyed.[38] His destination may have been Donegal.

That the *potestas* or power of Onuist was so very tangible in Argyll in 734, resulting in the capture of two of his opponents and the flight of a third, is very striking. The apparent ritual element in the executions of Talorc and (eventually) Talorcan by drowning speaks of political sensitivities and legal uncertainties surrounding their deaths.[39] The chronicles make Talorcan's family conspirators who oppressed Naiton. Was his execution justified as the elimination of a disturber of the peace of the Church? For his part, Donngal had 'dishonoured' a Columban monastery. Onuist was behaving as though he regarded Argyll as a region

---

[36] *AU* 734.5, 740.5; *AT* 734.4 (reverses the positions of Talorc and his brother); *Ann. Clon.* 731.1; Anderson, *Early Sources*, vol. 1, 236.

[37] *AU* 734.6, 739.7; *AT* 739.6.

[38] *AU* 734.7.

[39] Halsall, 'Violence and Society', 32–3.

of his own realm, within which he felt entitled to protect or seize people and interests and even to order their deaths. In an interesting parallel, a Brega king was 'drowned in a pool' by his southern Uí Néill overlord in 851.[40]

In broad terms, Onuist may be seen as putting into practice in 734 the political doctrines espoused in the Pictish writings known to Bede by 731, reflecting the outlooks of his Verturian predecessors. We have seen that the likelihood is strong that by now the Pictish establishment regarded the realm of Atholl as encapsulating both that district and Argyll. The events of 734 seem almost to be ostentatious demonstrations of Onuist's perceived *potestas* west of Drumalban. Executing and dispossessing troublemakers were audacious expressions of royal authority. Even for Merovingian kings, it was often not worth risking the disquiet such acts normally roused. The Carolingian period was dawning in Francia during Onuist's reign, in which Frankish kings mainly reserved the death penalty for pagans and those who broke faith with the king. The execution of the Deiran king Oswini by agents of Oswy in 651 had resulted in the foundation of a monastery as a public expression of remorse. It may also have been the execution of Oswy's brother Eanfrith that stigmatised the British king Catguollaun in the eyes of posterity as 'a barbarian even more cruel than a heathen'.[41]

Viewed in this light, it becomes easier to understand why Onuist was called 'a despotic butcher' in one notice of his death. The payback for having endangered his reputation in this way was the toppling of men who had probably harboured Talorcan of Atholl, and the elimination of Talorcan himself. It had taken six years, but the succession wars sparked by Naiton's abdication were finally over. They had resulted in the establishment of a new man in the kingship of Pictavia and the eclipsing of Fortriu after some fifty years of paramountcy in northern Britain.

In the process, Onuist had also established a pretty firm grip on Argyll, stamping his perceived authority over it in league with the likes of Muiredach and Cú Bretan. Having put the finishing touches on his seizure of Pictavia, and having established his *potestas* in both Atholl and Argyll, Onuist may none the less have remained distracted by the Gaelic world. Unlike the less fortunate Talorc and Talorcan, the dispossessed and wounded Donngal remained at large, and Bridei remained his captive. In 735 Cathal son of Finnguine fought his decisive war against Leinster, and it may have been about now that he became Onuist's ally, a

---

[40] *AU* 851.2.
[41] Bede, *Hist. eccl.*, ii.20, iii.14.

diplomatic situation that could have been a factor in the meeting between Cathal and his Tara counterpart at Terryglass in 737.

In 736 Donngal returned to Argyll. He does not emerge from the sources as a particularly attractive figure, but perhaps it simply highlights the rare gifts of his impressive father. He displayed little of Selbach's panache for survival, and squandered the *imperium* that his father twice placed in his unreliable grip. Yet there can be little doubting his determination and energy. Despite successive setbacks, and an undisclosed wound sustained at Dún Leithfinn, Donngal was back in Argyll two years after his prior disgrace. Onuist's reaction to the news was decisive. It was a turning point in Scottish history.

Striking westwards – at a guess down Glen Lochy from Perthshire – the Mearns hegemon personally conducted a devastating assault on Argyll which probably carried him down the length of Loch Awe, laying waste to the region in a brutal campaign of destruction (*uastatio*) typical of the age.[42] As far as we know, no prior Pictish invasion of Argyll was on a par with this one. It is the first time since the battle of Dún Nechtain that we can be certain that a *rex Pictorum* personally led his own men on campaign against foreign enemies. Onuist may have felt that his planned assault on Dunadd required his personal involvement. Yet the earliest Carolingians, Onuist's contemporaries in Francia, seem to have compensated for their lack of security as a usurping dynasty by breaking from Merovingian custom in order to lead Frankish armies in person. If there are suggestions that the sons of Der-Ilei emulated Merovingian and Northumbrian models, secure enough in their position to entrust wars to deputies, the fact that Onuist fought his own battle in 736 might speak of a king less secure than his predecessor.

If Muiredach of Lorn had received Pictish support in capturing the kingdom – and Talorcan's capture outside Dunollie is a nod in this direction – the relationship soured. In the same year as Onuist's Argyll campaign, at a place called *Cnoc Coirpri* located 'between lakes' (*Etar Linddu*), in the district of Calathros, Talorcan son of Vurguist, Onuist's brother, led the Waerteras of Fortriu to victory over Muiredach and the host of Dál Riata, 'in which encounter many nobles fell'.[43] The battle may have taken place in Benderloch, the 'hill between two lochs' (*beinn eadar dá loch*) between Loch Etive and Loch Creran.[44] That would place it in Upper Lorn, probably the very heartland of Cenél nEchdach. The

[42] *AU* 736.1; *AT* 736.1; *Ann. Clon.* 733.1.
[43] *AU* 736.2.
[44] Anderson, *Early Sources*, vol. 1, 233; Watson, *Celtic Place-Names*, 241.

chronicles seem to envision a clash of 'national' armies. Talorcan led the men of Fortriu there, suggesting that Onuist had placed his brother in the Verturian kingship as a subject after Naiton's death, or more likely after his son Bridei had been captured, who may have led a Verturian fleet to Ireland in 733. In the notice of his death in *Annales Cambriae* Talorcan is made a king, and the later Pictish king Drest son of Talorcan was probably his son.

Vanquished, Muiredach fled with his army into obscurity. Meanwhile – and it does look as though it was a two-pronged campaign – Onuist reached Dunadd. The *rex Pictorum* now 'took hold' (*obtenuit*) of the place and set fire to *Creic*, possibly simply indicating 'the rock' of Dunadd, burning it to the ground. Archaeological excavation at Dunadd has established a significant disjuncture in the eighth century involving programmes of dismantling and expansion of walls and ramparts.[45] Unfortunately, it is impossible to establish whether such work was undertaken during the ascendancy of the Cenél nEchdach kings after 702, or after the capture of Dunadd by Onuist in 736. The burning down of a hill-fort probably involved dismantling its timber inner buildings, palisading and revetments, heaping the wood upon the stone walls along with brushwood and burning the material for several days. The heat built up in this way not only sometimes melted or 'vitrified' timber-laced stone walls (Dunadd did not have these), but may even have made the stone glow. It must have been quite a spectacle, symbolising utter defeat.[46]

If it happened at Dunadd in 736, it surely symbolised much. The stronghold is not mentioned again in the increasingly deficient chronicles, or anywhere else, and there is little archaeological indication of high-level occupation as late as 800. The major expansion in the eighth century was probably a Cenél nEchdach initiative, reflecting the rise of the Lorn kings. The site may not have persisted in its major functions after its fall to Onuist. He had a keen eye for the value of ritualised brutality.

It seems to have been here at Dunadd that the great king finally captured not just the hapless Donngal, but also his brother, both of whom he bound in chains (*catenis alligauit*).[47] They pass into oblivion, their ultimate fate unknown to us, if perhaps predictable in the light of the known drownings of Talorc and Talorcan. Disgraced on two fronts, Cenél nEchdach returns to the obscurity from which it first emerged in the late

[45] Lane and Campbell, *Dunadd*, 93–5.
[46] Harding, *The Iron Age in Northern Britain*, 91; Alcock, *Kings and Warriors*, 182–3; Ralston, *Celtic Fortifications*, 143–63.
[47] *AU* 736.1; *AT* 736.1; *Ann. Clon.* 733.1.

seventh century. The news was not all good for Onuist, however: after three years as Donngal's captive, Bridei died a short time after his captor's destruction, leaving us to speculate as to the circumstances of his passing.[48]

It was probably to the events of 736, and later those of 741, that the poet referred when he spoke of 'the day when Óengus took Alba' with its 'strong princes'. The subjugation of the Gaelic peoples of Argyll by the kings of Picts seems to have been visible on the horizon to those responsible for the Pictish origin myth which is so inclusive of Gaelic heritage. It may also be regarded as prefigured by Ionan primacy over the Pictish Church, and the personal interests on both sides of Drumalban that the sons of Der-Ilei brought with them to the Verturian kingship. It can only have been aided by interlinkages beneath the surface of our textual record.

The free rein Onuist enjoyed at a distance in Argyll in 734, and the capture and possible decommission of Dunadd in 736, however, represent something of a different order from the activities of his Verturian predecessors. His Argyll campaign is reminiscent of the devastating incursions conducted across Northumbria by Catguollaun in 633 and by Penda in 651 and 655. At these times Northumbrian kings had become holed up in Bamburgh and other royal strongholds, and had either purchased their liberty or, in the case of Catguollaun's enemies, had suffered execution or death in desperate battle.[49]

CENÉL NGABRÁIN: TO SMITE OR NOT TO SMITE

Despite some thirty years of relative obscurity in the shadow of Cenél nEchdach, Cenél nGabráin enjoys something of a surprise resurgence in the chronicle record in the wake of Onuist's final victories over the Lorn kings. Although he destroyed Talorc son of Congus, from the Cenél nGartnait pseudo-segment of the descendants of Gabrán, there is no record that Onuist attacked Dunaverty in 736, probably the royal centre in Kintyre. By playing ball with the Mearns hegemon and giving up his brother two years before, Cú Bretan son of Congus may have ensured that Kintyre would be spared the worst ravages of Onuist's malice.

---

[48] *AU* 736.1; *AT* 736.1; *Ann. Clon.* 733.1. See also *Ann. Camb.* (Dumville) 736.1, where Bridei may be masquerading as *Ougen rex Pictorum*.
[49] Bede, *Hist. eccl.*, iii.1, iii.16, iii.24.

Cú Bretan lived until 740, and Onuist returned to Argyll in force in 741. The two events may have been related. The object of the campaign would seem to have been Indrechtach son of Fiannamail, a descendant of Áedán whose father had been slain in 700 or 701. Indrechtach and his brother fell at the unidentified Forboros.[50] The *Annals of Ulster* record a second battle 'against Indrechtach' in this year at Druimm Cathmail, fought 'between the Cruithni and Dál Riata', as well as 'the smiting (*percutio*) of Dál Riata by Óengus son of Forgus'.[51] It, therefore, seems very likely that *Cruithni* here, unusually, refers to Pictish forces (*Cruithintúath* in Gaelic) rather than to the Cruithni of Ireland. Does that suggest that the *coup de grâce* visited on Indrechtach involved a Pictish seaborne incursion against him in Ireland?[52] Certainly the movements of Onuist's unfortunate son indicate that his reach could extend across the North Channel.

The battles of Druimm Cathmail and Forboros may represent, then, yet another extensive campaign launched by Onuist or his lieutenants into Argyll. Was it occasioned by the death of Cú Bretan and Onuist's rejection of the man who was chosen to succeed him? The phrase *percutio Dáil Riata*, 'the smiting of Dál Riata', is vague, but probably indicates destruction or annihilation. The Irish chronicles now contain a thirty-year gap before referring again to Dál Riata, namely to Áed Find son of Eochaid, called *rex Dáil Riata* at his death in 778.[53] His father was probably Eochaid son of Eochu, who had given up the kingship of Kintyre in 731. Áed's brother Fergus, who died three years after him in 781, is similarly called *rí Dáil Riata* in his obit.[54]

Percutio Dáil Riatai la hÓengus mac Forgusso

The phrase *percutio Dáil Riata* is unique in the Irish chronicles from our period, so that a good translation becomes problematic. Generally speaking, *percutio* signifies 'striking' (hence English *percussion*). In order to understand the *percutio* of a people, however, we must consider how *percutio* is used in the Vulgate Bible, the influential text of which was crucial in shaping the Latin vocabularies of monastic writers in this period. Out of 554 occurrences, about a third (30.51 per cent) signify some kind of killing strike inflicted upon individuals. Apart from this very specific usage, most (28.52 per cent) 'smitings' in the Vulgate are simple strikings of individuals

---

[50] *AU* 741.6.
[51] *AU* 741.10.
[52] Anderson, *Early Sources*, vol. 1, 237.
[53] *AU* 778.7; *Ann. Clon.* 769.4.
[54] *AU* 781.3; *Ann. Clon.* 778.4.

Percutio Dáil Riatai la hÓengus mac Forgusso (continued)

or objects – various 'hittings', 'beatings', etc. The tendency for the term to signify, above all else, a killing strike is, however, notable.

There are seventy-four instances (13.36 per cent) in the Vulgate of peoples or cities experiencing *percutio*, in contexts where the best translation is usually 'destruction', 'conquest' or 'annihilation'. This is the second most common specific usage. Such episodes are particularly common in the Old Testament, where God and the Israelites often smite their foes. There are about as many additional instances (11.55 per cent) where *percutio* means 'destruction' of things other than a community. This meaning is certainly to be applied to *percussio Demeticae regionis*, a 'smiting' of the district of Dyfed, recorded in *Annales Cambriae*.[55] Rather less commonly (11.19 per cent), but not infrequently, *percutio* is used in the Vulgate to signify 'affliction' – a withering strike against an individual or population 'struck' (usually) by disease or plague.[56]

If it emerges from this analysis that *percutio Dáil Riata* almost certainly refers to something pretty disastrous for Dál Riata, it is well to remember that the term is uniquely applied to this event. The Irish chronicles tend to use other words – *uastatio* and *deletae* in particular – to signify the kind of devastation or destruction of a district that we find in the 'smiting' of Dyfed in *Annales Cambriae*. On the whole, 'conquest' or 'annihilation' are the most likely concepts that *percutio* is trying to get across in this passage – a withering strike against a people rather than a place. Unfortunately, such a conclusion hardly answers all of our questions about what on earth was happening in Argyll in 741.

Pseudo-historians at work in the time of the Alpínid kings of Alba, perhaps beginning with Domnall (II) son of Causantín (889–900), constructed a Dalriadan historical context for the dynasty which included an ingenious fusing of its family tree to Áed's pedigree.[57] As a result, Áed Find has been regarded conventionally as the king who saved Dál Riata from obliteration, preserving the Gaels until the day when his descendants would conquer the Picts. It is striking that his particular segment of Cenél nGabráin, which alone among the chief kindreds of mainland

---

[55] *Ann. Camb.* (Faral) 645.1
[56] This analysis was facilitated by the online texts of the Vulgate at: http://www.perseus.tufts.edu and http://www.latinvulgate.com.
[57] Broun, *The Irish Identity*, 146–53; Woolf, *From Pictland to Alba*, 96–9, 119–25, 220–1.

Argyll cannot be shown to have clashed with Onuist, should have emerged from the 'smiting' with the kingship in hand. But what was the nature of that kingship? All indications from contemporary evidence are that Argyll was decisively annexed by 741, *percutio Dáil Riata* referring to the collapse of several of its leading dynasties. Such a development is reflected by *Fó sén dia ngaib Óengus Albain*, the quatrain which celebrated the conquest. The archaeological evidence from Dunadd is not inconsistent with such a proposition.

One is reminded of Frankish purges of the royal families of neighbouring peoples or, closer to home, the extinguishing of the relatives of Edwini of Deira after the conquest of his kingdom by the Aeðilfrithings. It is too easily imagined, with the benefit of hindsight, that the fortunes of Dál Riata must somehow have recovered sufficiently to allow for a Gaelic conquest of the Picts. To do so is to misunderstand the nature of the historicising efforts of the pseudo-historians who set to work after the descendants of Cinaed son of Alpín had secured exclusive access to the Pictish kingship in the tenth century. The notion that any kind of conquest of the Picts took place at all seems to have arisen in the minds of Scottish historians no earlier than the reign of Alexander II (1214–49).[58] There is thus no reason whatsoever for surprise that we do not find this infamous myth corroborated in the evidence from our period.

Something like the smiting had been envisioned by earlier generations of Pictish hegemons. There had been no less than three significant Pictish invasions of Argyll in the space of ten years, with five notable battles, three kings toppled, two strongholds breached and destroyed and untold damage arising from the brutality of the typical *uastatio*. That kind of sustained military pressure had proven too much. Like several North British kingdoms south of the Forth which fell foul of Bernician expansion in the seventh century, Dál Riata appears to have crumbled beneath the relentless weight of Pictish domination. What effects (if any) this development may have had on the ordinary Gaels of Argyll are unknown, and probably unknowable.

THE LAST GASP OF THE AEÐILFRITHINGS

For all that Gaeldom absorbed him, Onuist did not lose sight of the Northumbrians. Bede provides disappointingly little explicit information in his works about the years of his own adulthood. There are occasional,

---

[58] Broun, *Scottish Independence*, 72–3.

very important allusions. He appended a brief chronicle to the end of his History, occasionally noting events not discussed in the text. Those who copied it had a tendency to continue his little chronicle. One reliable continuation was the ultimate source of two surviving texts: the *Chronicle of 766* (often called 'the continuation of Bede') and the *Chronicle of 802* (imbedded in the eleventh-century *Historia regum Anglorum* attributed to Symeon of Durham). These chronicles shed invaluable fragmentary light on the middle decades of the eighth century, including the reign of Onuist.

The murder of the young king Osred in 716 had brought a new dynasty into the Northumbrian kingship. Bede makes no comment on the morality or circumstances of the killing. The supporters of the Ecgwulfing pretender Coenred ought to have taken great pains to emphasise how just the assassination had been. The fact that Bede is so reticent suggests that the great scholar received such justifications with little enthusiasm. It is also important that he omits any mention of the brief kingship of Eadwulf son of Ecgwulf after the death of Aldfrith. Yet Bede was not prepared to question the justice of Osred's murder either. After all, Coenred's brother Ceolwulf was king of Northumbria when Bede completed his History, a draft of which he sent to this 'most glorious king', to whom he even dedicated it.

Coenred reigned only until 718. Bede was so uninterested in him that we do not know whether he died or was killed, abdicated or was driven from the kingdom. His successor Osric son of Aldfrith, Osred's brother, reigned until his death on 9 May 729.[59] Osred had only been about nineteen when he was murdered. His brother can hardly have been any older, and so must have been younger than thirty when he died. It seems that in the course of his reign Galloway was brought directly under Osric's authority, resulting in Bernician settlement in the region. The monastery at Whithorn, appropriated by the Northumbrian Church, was given to Pecthelm as an episcopal seat, ushering in a new phase of development at the site.[60] In these years a lost Life of Ninian (*Nyniau*) was composed, owing something to existing traditions surrounding Uinniau.

During Osric's reign, Coenred's two-year kingship before it may have been branded officially as a usurpation. Bede says of Osric's successor, Coenred's brother Ceolwulf, that 'the beginning and course of his reign have been filled with so many and such serious commotions and setbacks, that it is as yet impossible to know what to say about them'.[61] It is just

---

[59] Bede, *Hist. eccl.*, v.22–3. The name of Osric's father, *Alfrith*, is recorded in a twelfth-century Durham text.
[60] Bede, *Hist. eccl.*, iii.4, v.23; Alcock, *Kings and Warriors*, 219–20.
[61] Bede, *Hist. eccl.*, v.23.

possible to read this passage, referring to the 'beginning' of the reign, as indicating that Osric's death and Ceolwulf's succession were tumultuous. Would the Aeðilfrithings challenge Ceolwulf's succession? Uncertainty presumably explains Bede's refusal to discuss Osred's murder, or the reigns of Coenred and Osric. It could have tainted his History had he adopted the partisan historical viewpoint of the losing side in a quarrel not yet ended. Aeðilfrith is much more prominent in *Historia ecclesiastica* than Ida, included as an afterthought. Eadwulf is not mentioned at all. These facets of the History probably reflect the fact that it was largely written in the last years of a young Aeðilfrithing king whom Bede could hardly have expected to die as early as 729. Had the Ecgwulfings managed to monopolise the kingship after 716, the relative places of Aeðilfrith and Ida in his History may have been quite different.

Bede noted in the year of Osric's death, putting the finishing touches on the first draft of his History, that 'two comets appeared around the sun . . . in the month of January and remained for almost a fortnight', to much general alarm.[62] In that ominous year Onuist killed Drest in Pictavia, and, in Northumbria, Osric died young – a king for each comet. Of these last years of his life, Bede spoke of 'these favourable times of peace and prosperity'. In fact, he recorded that 'at this time the *natio Pictorum* have a treaty of peace (*foedus pacis*) with the *gens Anglorum*'.[63] The contrast between Stephen's hostile and dehumanizing characterisations of Picts as beasts (*populi bestiales*) and ants (*greges formicarum*), written in the last decade of Naiton's reign, and Bede's much more friendly tone suggests that the Anglo-Pictish peace treaty was not concluded until after the rise of Onuist in 728. The conventional idea that peace broke out in a fit of anglophilia by Naiton a decade earlier is thus unlikely. The temptation to attribute Northumbrian artistic and technological influences in Pictland after *c.* 650 to Naiton's alleged 'admiration for all things Northumbrian' is also to be resisted.[64]

As a southern Pictish king with the Northumbrians at his doorstep, Onuist may have regarded good diplomatic relations with Ceolwulf as an essential prerequisite in his planning for war in Argyll. The peace had clearly failed by 740. Briefly deposed and tonsured in 731, Ceolwulf was restored, but in 737 he cut his hair again and returned to monastic life. His abdication may have been an important factor in the breakdown of

[62] Bede, *Hist. eccl.*, v.23.
[63] Bede, *Hist. eccl.*, v.23.
[64] Henderson, *The Picts*, 132; Henderson and Henderson, *The Art of the Picts*, 176–7, assumes a suitably more cautious position.

relations between Northumbria and Pictavia. By then, Onuist had crushed his rivals for paramountcy in Atholl and Fortriu, and smashed his enemies in Argyll, and the idea of trying his luck against a new Northumbrian king may have become appealing to him. Casting himself as the indignant avenger of a betrayed royal colleague had, after all, worked once before.

AGAINST AEÐILBALD AND ONUIST: EADBERCT SON OF EATA

Ceolwulf's successor was no Aeðilfrithing, but another great-grandson of Ecgwulf, his cousin Eadberct son of Eata.[65] For the first time in three attempts, the kingship had successfully passed between two Ecgwulfing kings. No doubt their success reflects considerable efforts behind the scenes over a generation, all unnoticed by our sources. According to the *Chronicle of 802*, probably compiled at Hexham (or within its orbit), Ceolwulf retired to Lindisfarne, where he remained for twenty-seven years until his death.[66] Eadberct may have wanted his cousin kept within reach of Bamburgh.

Eadberct proved a highly effective king, more so perhaps than anyone since Ecgfrith had fallen on the field of Dún Nechtain fifty years before, and certainly more so than any of his successors down to the end of our period. His brother Ecgberct was the bishop of York, to whom Bede had written an impassioned letter in 734. Two years before Eadberct was made king, Ecgberct received a pallium from Rome and the rank of metropolitan bishop, to which Wilfrid of York had clung in vain after being deposed by Theodore of Canterbury.[67] It is unlikely to be a coincidence that this generation saw the production of a Northumbrian Life of Ninian, cast as an orthodox British bishop who converted Picts, and whose shrine was an object of Anglo-Saxon pilgrimage. This is exactly the kind of ethnically inclusive imagery one expects of an age in which metropolitan status over northern Britain was restored at York. Bede does not hesitate to suggest that British bishops should defer to the bishop of Canterbury. No doubt he would have felt the same way about York and the Pictish, Gaelic and

---

[65] *Chron. 766*, s. a. 731, 737; *Chron. 802*, s. a. 732, 737.

[66] *Chron. 766*, s. a. 737; *Chron. 802*, s. a. 737, 764. On the Hexham dimension of the *Chronicle of 802*, see Woolf, 'Onuist', 37–8. Ceolwulf is not among the *reges vel duces* in the *Lib. vit. eccl. Dunelm.*, fol. 12; there is a Ceolwulf among the *presbyteri* on fol. 19b, but this might not be him.

[67] *Chron. 766*, s. a. 735; *Chron. 802*, s. a. 735.

British bishops of northern Britain had he lived to see its metropolitan status restored.

Ecgberct's elevation had been foreseen by Bede, who advised him on the matter before his death in 735. It must have been galling to Acca, Wilfrid's disciple, the bishop of Hexham in deference to whom Bede was arguably more kindly towards Wilfrid in *Historia ecclesiastica* than he might otherwise have been. In 731 Acca was expelled from his see for unknown reasons, after more than twenty years in place. It is reasonable to suspect that he had been sympathetic to whomever forced Ceolwulf from the kingship in that year.[68] Indeed, there are strong hints, in *Vita Wilfrithi*'s references to Acca 'of blessed memory' (*beatae memoriae*) c. 716, that he had been expelled from Hexham the last time an Ecgwulfing king had acquired the kingship.[69]

Acca was never restored, dying in October 737.[70] The possibility has been entertained that he found refuge at Onuist's court, and successfully persuaded the king to plant the cult of St Andrew, patron saint of Hexham, at Cennrígmonaid (now St Andrews).[71] Opening the Pictish court to an exiled Northumbrian bishop – especially if he had conspired against Ceolwulf – ought to have been provocative, however, at a time when a *foedus pacis* had recently been agreed. Onuist was focused on the Gaelic west at this time, and is unlikely to have courted trouble on his southern frontier. In addition, Acca's mentor Wilfrid was remarkably consistent, in his many periods of exile, in seeking sanctuary at the Mercian court. Acca may have followed his example.

The king of the Mercians, Aeðilbald, had been king since 716. Bede acknowledged his paramountcy over the southern English kingdoms when he spoke of the year 731 as 'the fifteenth year of the reign of Aeðilbald', and observed that every kingdom 'right up to the Humber' was subject to him.[72] It is remarkable that, despite a violent traditional rivalry, as well as dynastic in-fighting in Northumbria, where several men with no battle experience held the kingship, there were no wars between the Northumbrian and Mercian superpowers for sixty years after the battle of the Trent in 679. The same structures that made it possible for

---

[68] *Chron. 766*, s. a. 731; *Chron. 802*, s. a. 732; Kirby, *The Earliest English Kings*, 124–5; Woolf, 'Onuist', 37.

[69] Kirby, 'Bede, Eddius Stephanus and the "Life of Wilfrid"', 107–8, missed this implication.

[70] *Chron. 802*, s. a. 740.

[71] Woolf, 'Onuist', 38; see also Skene, 'Early Ecclesiastical Settlements at St Andrew', 313–5 (modified in Skene, *Celtic Scotland*, vol. 2, 261–75, especially 272–4).

[72] Bede, *Hist. eccl.*, v.23, v.24.

kings like Aldfrith and Osred to assume the kingship – including prominent ministerial roles for attendants of proven military skill – may have
ensured that Northumbria did not appear vulnerable in this period
despite its troubles. This appearance of formidability seems to have subsided, however, after the abdication of Ceolwulf in 737.

A year or so earlier, Onuist had devastated Argyll, captured Dunadd
and eliminated Donngal of Lorn and his kin. The *Chronicle of 766*
records in 750 a West Saxon uprising 'against King Aeðilbald and
Óengus', evidently a reference to Onuist. This evidence implies that the
two most powerful rulers in Britain by 736 had forged some kind of
accommodation or alliance by 750, similar to the arrangement that Onuist
seems to have reached with Cathal of Cashel in the 730s. Thus, Aeðilbald
and Onuist probably acted in concert in 740, when Northumbria was
afflicted by war from both quarters.[73] The treaty of Anglo-Pictish peace
mentioned by Bede had not long outlasted him.

It is unclear whether the Northumbrians invaded Pictavia in 740, or
whether it was the other way round. The killing of Earnwini son of
Eadwulf in December 740, whose father had attempted to block the
succession of Osred, is recorded in both Northumbrian and Irish
chronicles.[74] Since Eadwulf may have gone into exile in Pictavia, it has
been suggested that the Picto-Northumbrian war of 740, in fact, related
to a failed attempt by Earnwini, backed by Onuist, to capture the
Northumbrian kingship from Eadberct.[75] In that event, we would have to
envision an invasion of Northumbria. Certainly Onuist has all the aggressive credentials for such a move, and he has been suspected here of having
done something like it with Muiredach of Lorn in 733.

After Eadberct mustered his strength and went north, becoming
'occupied against the Picts with his army', Aeðilbald crossed the Trent
from Mercia 'through impious treachery', his forces despoiling 'a
Northumbrian district'.[76] This record implies that Aeðilbald had broken
a peace treaty. The middle of the eighth century may seem a remarkably
early point in British history at which to find the inhabitants of the island
subject in the main to the domination of two paramount kings, the one
English, with a southern orbit, and the other Pictish, with a northern one.
At the same time, Onuist had apparently agreed a treaty with the king of
Cashel, enemy of the Uí Néill in Ireland.

[73] *Chron. 766*, s. a. 740, 750.
[74] *AU* 741.7; *Chron. 766*, s. a. 740; *Chron. 802*, s. a. 740 gives the date.
[75] Woolf, 'Onuist', 37.
[76] *Chron. 766*, s. a. 740.

These diplomatic efforts are quite remarkable. In many respects, from the perspective of our own century, these seem like quite primitive men, yet there was also a sophistication about them which foreshadows future developments in Insular kingship. The *Chronicle of 766* even implies in 750 that Aeðilbald and Onuist were casting themselves as joint high kings, though scholars have questioned the integrity of this record.[77] Earlier precursors can be put forward, for example, the period when Wulfhere was dominant south of the Humber and Ecgfrith north of it. Yet Britain's later medieval future as an island home to two principal monarchs may not be more clearly foreshadowed any earlier than in the age of Onuist and Aeðilbald.

It has been observed already that the abdication of Naiton had been in line with Mercian practice. Links between Onuist and Aeðilbald place beyond doubt the proposition that Pictish kings could be interested in and aware of developments in the Mercian court and probably vice versa. If there is reason to believe that the Verturian regime in Pictavia was established in part in emulation of Northumbrian imperial models, it may be proposed that contact with Aeðilbald's kingdom continued to provide Naiton and Onuist with access to Anglo-Saxon ideas. Interlinkage between Pictish and Mercian art probably reflects this contact.[78] Both the Mercians and the Northumbrians had extensive experience of *percutio*, as their British neighbours to the west could attest. For centuries to come, ambitious kings of Pictavia, and eventually of Alba, sought to extend their influence among the English inhabitants of Lothian and neighbouring regions. Onuist's ambitions in the 740s explored forward-looking potentials in foreign and military policy.

The year after their concerted assault on Northumbria saw Aeðilbald fighting against the West Saxons, while his Pictish colleague returned to the warpath in Argyll (and possibly Ireland) to 'smite' Dál Riata. The prospects of aggressive neighbours of the calibre and might of Aeðilbald and Onuist, working in tandem against him and prepared to eradicate neighbouring princes, must have unsettled Eadberct. In the event nothing of particular note seems immediately to have come of these developments. Both hegemons turned their attentions elsewhere.

Had Eadberct purchased security along his frontiers by paying cattle-tribute to the kings of Mercia and Pictavia? It is worth comparing his ability to weather these pressures to the 'smiting' of Dál Riata. Such a

---

[77] Charles-Edwards, 'The Continuation of Bede', 138. For discussion see Woolf, 'Onuist', 38.

[78] Henderson and Henderson, *The Art of the Picts*, 113.

comparison speaks of the respectability of the lingering strength of eighth-century Northumbria. Despite having long passed its zenith as a superpower, the kingdom built by the Aeðilfrithings still surpassed anything that could be amassed among the Argyll Gaels. This kind of wider perspective makes more stark the absurdity of the 'usable past' concocted by the Alpínids, in which a polity the size of Dál Riata managed a Pictish conquest quite beyond the reach of the Northumbrians, even at the high pinnacle of their strength.

Perhaps it was in this part of his reign, when his arm was reaching beyond the Forth, that Onuist made the kind of impression that would see him join the kings commemorated in source of the Durham *Liber vitae*.[79] Possibly we are to infer that the king of Picts actively patronised at least one prominent Bernician church – possibly one with historical links with southern Pictish Churches.

MUGDOCK: A SMITER SMITTEN

Further suggestion that Eadberct successfully purchased a respite from aggression in 740 emerges from subsequent events along the Forth frontier. In 744 'a battle (*proelium*) was fought between Picts and Britons'.[80] No prior Picto-British war is known to us. The sons of Der-Ilei were Cowal dynasts, and Alt Clut and Cowal seem to have had a history of cooperation. Bridei son of Beli is likely to have had good relations with his nephew Dumngual at Clyde Rock. The fact that they had been scions of the House of Guipno may have given Onuist a sense of entitlement to claim Alt Clut districts. As a southern Pict, he may even have been related to the House of Guipno or the House of Clinoch in some way.

The king of Clyde Rock at this time was Teudubr son of Beli, a distant kinsman of Bridei. The vagueness of our evidence makes it unclear once more who was the aggressor in this war. The Pictish king could have provoked Teudubr in any number of ways in his generally aggressive dealings with his neighbours. Given Onuist's track record, however, one may be forgiven suspicions that it was he who brought war to Alt Clut and not the other way round. The location and outcome of the battle are unknown, as is the position of Clyde Rock six years later when Teudubr died in 750.[81]

---

[79] *Lib. vit. eccl. Dunelm.*, fol. 12.

[80] *Chron. 802*, s. a. 744.

[81] *Chron. 766*, s. a. 750; *Ann. Camb.* (Dumville) 750.2. I take it that the equivalent record at *AT* 752.2 has somehow misplaced the event of Teudubr's death.

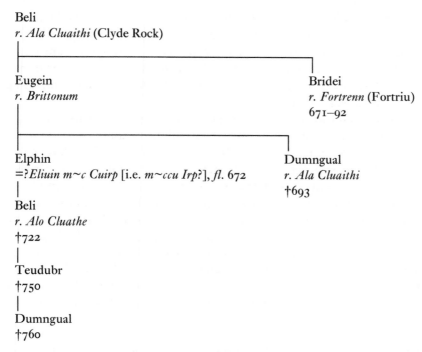

Table 11.1 Teudubr son of Beli: some key relationships

By that fateful year, Onuist and Eadberct had become allies. Before the year was out, Talorcan son of Vurguist, conqueror of Lorn and probably king of Fortriu under his brother, brought an army south of the Forth. At Mugdock (*Mocetauc*), two kilometres north of Milngavie and some sixteen kilometres from Clyde Rock, Talorcan fell, his warriors routed by a force of Alt Clut Britons.[82] Teudubr's predecessor Dumngual seems to have been a major player in the Atlantic power politics of the 670s and 680s, and there can be no doubting that his frustratingly obscure kingdom was capable, on its day, of considerable military clout.

If Talorcan was leading Waerteras from Fortriu into Lorn in 736, what was he doing so far south in 750? In that year the *Annals of Ulster* record, rather enigmatically, 'the end of the rule of Óengus' (*aithbe flatho Óengussa*). Had his brother replaced him in the kingship, by agreement or by violence? In the same year, that of Teudubr's death, the *Annals of Tigernach* record a battle 'between the Picts themselves' at Asreth in the district of Circhind (*terra Circin*). Was Talorcan the victor, and Bridei son

---

[82] *AU* 750.4 (*Catohic*); *AT* 750.3; *Ann. Clon.* 746.2 ('brother of K. Enos' here shows that *AT*'s reference to a brother of Talorcan is corrupt); *Ann. Camb.* (Dumville) 750.1.

of Mailcon, who fell there, a challenger to his succession?[83] Did Onuist's brother march from glory in Circhind, evidently an old Miathian district, to destruction at Mugdock? Had Bridei received support from Clyde Rock against Talorcan six years after the Britons had warred with Onuist? Did Talorcan's shattered forces come running back to Onuist entreating him to resume his reign?

This patchwork of sketchy evidence can be stitched together in a number of ways. The gaelocentric conventional reading of *aithbe flatho Óengussa*, as denoting the end of Onuist's domination of Argyll, is unnecessary. The most straightforward reading is that, voluntarily or otherwise, he gave up his kingship in 750 after more than twenty years in power, occasioning a struggle between his brother and Bridei. Both men having fallen within months, Onuist's abdication proved to be short-lived. By the end of the year he had been restored, his brother (yet another) Bridei – called *rex Fortrenn* in his obit – had presumably been installed in Fortriu and no interruption of Onuist's reign is recorded in the Pictish king-list. Had it not been for the record of the *aithbe* made by Gaelic observers (probably) hostile to Onuist, the episode would never have come to light.

END OF AN ERA: THE TREATY OF CLYDE ROCK

Mugdock and the teetering of Onuist's power in Pictavia probably shook northern Britain. For Teudubr, or if the battle was fought after his death for his son and (probable) successor Dumngual, the scale of the victory may have approached that of the battle of Dún Nechtain sixty-five years before, foiling the imperial designs of a neighbouring superpower. It is true that, with intestine war gripping the Picts, Eadberct of Northumbria opportunistically 'added the plain of Kyle (*Cyil*), with other districts (*regiones*), to his kingdom' in the year of Mugdock, possibly indicating a conquest of Ayrshire.[84] Yet rejection of the conventional tetrarchy of four kingdoms in northern Britain, one for each ethnic group, requires caution about assuming that Ayrshire was dominated by Clyde Rock because its inhabitants were British. There is no evidence that it was so.

[83] *AU* 750.11; *AT* 752.3. There were two Pictish kings called Onuist son of Vurguist in different centuries, so why not two kings called Bridei son of Mailcon? Adomnán, *V. s. Columbae*, ii.33, believed that the earlier and more famous Bridei had died of natural causes, not in a battle like Asreth.

[84] *Chron. 766*, s. a. 750; Skene, *Celtic Scotland*, vol. 1, 294–5. Macquarrie, 'The Kings of Strathclyde', 11, incorrectly names as Teudubr's successor *Rotri rex Brittonum* at *Ann. Camb.* (Dumville) 754.1, surely the so-called 'Rhodri Molwynog' of Gwynedd.

The Early Historic stronghold at Dundonald, seven kilometres south-west of Kilmarnock, may have been the key stronghold of Eadberct's British enemies in Ayrshire.[85] Northumbrian aggression there can hardly have been welcome at Dumngual's court, even if he did not claim Kyle as his own. For the first time in more than sixty years, a Northumbrian king was proving himself a credible warrior beyond his own frontiers. It may have been vitally important, as it proved to be for the Carolingians who supplanted the Merovingians in the Frankish kingship, for the Ecgwulfings to prove themselves, at last, as effective war leaders, unlike the last few Aeðilfrithing kings. Eadberct's success must have robbed Mugdock of some of its lustre at Clyde Rock, but Ayrshire may have seemed like an acceptable price to pay for a decisive victory against north-ern Britain's most formidable military machine in living memory.

The first Pictish military setback on record for some forty years, coupled with an interruption of Onuist's suzerainty, probably gave the hegemon an air of vulnerability after 750. Also in that year, according to the *Chronicle of 766*, Cuthred, the West Saxon king, 'rose up against King Aeðilbald and Oengus', a record we have already encountered.[86] The Mercian hegemon, now an old man, found himself faced with a faltering Pictish ally, an expan-sionist Northumbrian neighbour and an ambitious West Saxon one. Did anxiety about his northern frontier prevent Aeðilbald from tightening his grip on Wessex? In 752 he and his army were defeated by Cuthred, and five years later Aeðilbald was murdered by his *cohors*.[87] It was an ignominious end for a man who had dominated the Anglo-Saxons for over forty years, and the kind of grim fate that must have lurked at the backs of the minds of some ageing kings in our period who chose the tonsure. Onuist may have been one such king himself in 750.

Surely Eadberct, like Cuthred, felt a perceptible easing of pressure as the grip of the Picto–Mercian alliance relaxed. Had he and Cuthred con-spired together in 750? He had flexed his muscles and acquired Ayrshire as his reward. Also in that year, he took Coenwulf, bishop of Lindisfarne, into custody. This extraordinary development probably relates to the fact that, according to the *Chronicle of 802*, a harmless (*innocens*) son of Aldfrith called Offa had taken refuge at Lindisfarne, until, 'almost dead with hunger, he was dragged unarmed from the church'.[88] Thirty-five years after the assassination of Offa's teenaged brother Osred, and twenty

<hr>

[85] Driscoll and Forsyth, 'The Late Iron Age', 7, 11.

[86] *Chron. 766*, s. a. 750.

[87] *Ang.-Sax. Chron. E*, s. a. 752, 755; *AU* 757.2; *AT* 757.2; *Ann. Camb.* (Dumville) 757.1; *Chron. 766*, s. a. 757; *Chron. 802*, s. a. 757.

[88] *Chron. 802*, s. a. 750.

after their brother Osric died young, it seems that the Aeðilfrithing dynasty still had teeth to gnaw at the Ecgwulfings. The language of the *Chronicle of 802* suggests that its partisanship lay with Offa; the *Chronicle of 766* is silent.

It was probably because this Aeðilfrithing had been given sanctuary that the king 'led Bishop Coenwulf captive' to Bamburgh, 'and made him abide in the church of St Peter' there.[89] Eadberct's predecessor and kinsman Ceolwulf was still a Lindisfarne monk when Offa sought refuge there. We ought probably to keep an open mind as to whether his sympathies lay with Offa and the bishop, or with his kinsman at Bamburgh.

In the course of Eadberct's eventful reign, a robust silver coinage began to be minted in Northumbria. Aldfrith's reign had seen the first striking of coins anywhere in northern Britain, and Eadberct seems to have been the first of his successors to resume the practice. Northumbria alone struck coins in the eighth century, but these issues probably did not serve as money in the usual sense of currency within a monetary economy. The sum total of this and other evidence suggests that Eadberct experienced both a wave of confidence and an invigoration of his kingship after his earlier difficulties, and especially after the battle of Mugdock, just as Cuthred had done in Wessex. That these shifts in the balances of power across Britain in the middle of the eighth century occurred in the wake of convulsions in the *imperium* of Onuist may be coincidental. Yet it may be that his alliance with Aeðilbald was a prime prop supporting the status quo across Britain in the 740s. A decade's achievement can seem all too fleeting in the historian's hindsight.

It seems that Onuist was not yet finished with Clyde Rock. According to the *Chronicle of 802*, a Pictish army next appeared there some six years after Mugdock, led by the old king of Picts himself. The account is unique and oddly detailed.[90] It is the only time the chronicle gives the regnal year of Eadberct in relating information about him. It reports that on 1 August 756, a Monday, he and Onuist led forces to Clyde Rock, and 'on that account the Britons accepted terms (*conditiones*) there'. It is strange to be given so precise a date for such an event as this. It suggests particular significance about this gathering of kings, and in particular about the *conditiones* agreed by the Britons.

---

[89]   *Chron. 802*, s. a. 750 (on his succession to Lindisfarne, see s. a. 740). Bede, *Hist. eccl.*, iii.6, mentions in *Historia ecclesiastica* that there was a church of St Peter at Bamburgh in the eighth century; *Historia regum Anglorum*'s notion that Coenwulf's confinement was *in Lindisfarnea*, rather than at the royal stronghold to which he had been led, probably represents an erroneous deduction.

[90]   *Chron. 802*, s. a. 756.

What was involved in this treaty? Does it amount to a submission to the regimes that had been squeezing Alt Clut in a vice since 744? Such bloodless capitulations are not unheard of in the early medieval West. They usually involved much activity and negotiation on the part of envoys and clerics on either side, including bishops.[91] If something like this took place at Clyde Rock in August 756, bloodlessness represents something of a departure for Onuist son of Vurguist. It may reflect a new approach to foreign affairs at his court at Dunnottar after the battle of Mugdock.

The final stage of the proceedings would seem to have taken place at Govan (*Ouania*) on the Clyde, possibly at the edge of the Alt Clut kingdom. There follows a gap in our written evidence of this kingdom of more than a century, save for a record of a fire at Clyde Rock in January 780. The last comparable record in *Annales Cambriae* is in 777. Both traditions probably used a lost North British chronicle, which must have terminated *c.* 780.[92] When we next hear of Clydesdale, we find its affairs greatly entangled with those of Scandinavian and Alpínid kings in the late ninth and tenth centuries.[93] No doubt Alt Clut remained sovereign after the treaty of Clyde Rock, but it may have been forced to accept client status between the rock of Pictavia, with its Dalriadan conquests across the Clyde estuary from Clyde Rock, and the hard-place of Northumbria, with its recent conquests further down the coast.

The same difficult account in the *Chronicle of 802* goes on to say that the army that went to Clyde Rock subsequently marched from Govan to *Newanbirig*, an English stronghold whose identification is disputed, where on 10 August 'nearly the whole army perished'.[94] After receiving so much detail up to this point, it is jarring to encounter such vagueness at the climax of this episode. No clue is given as to who attacked the (presumably) Northumbrian army. It is a further oddity about this seemingly calamitous event that it went unrecorded in other Northumbrian and Irish chronicles. There is a hint of hostility towards Eadberct in the *Chronicle of 802*'s handling of his capture of Offa. Perhaps this attitude explains its unique record of the king's defeat.

Interest in Onuist was otherwise pronounced in the chronicles, suggesting that scholars have been correct in generally presuming that the vanquished army was Northumbrian, returning home from Clydesdale

---

[91] For discussion, see Nelson, 'Violence in the Carolingian World', 97–100.

[92] *AU* 780.1; *Ann. Camb.* (Dumville) 777.1; Hughes, 'The Welsh Latin Chronicles', 240; Dumville, 'The Welsh Latin Annals', 466.

[93] See now Woolf, *From Pictland to Alba*, 109–11, 152–7.

[94] For discussion of *Ouania* and *Newanbirig*, see Woolf, 'Onuist', 39 and bibliography.

or attempting an attack on Mercia, and not the joint force that had beset Clyde Rock. Awareness of a record like this one may, however, have inspired the writer of the earlier of two foundation legends of St Andrews (*c.* 1100) to place his Pictish king called *Hungus son of Urguist* in northern England, surrounded by a large English army, to win a great victory after having a vision of St Andrew. Onuist and Dumngual of Alt Clut have each been identified by scholars as Eadberct's assailant on his march from Govan. The general thrust of Northumbrian history in the second half of the eighth century suggests that an attack by a dynastic rival is at least as likely. Choosing seems impossible, although convulsion followed Eadberct's retirement only two years later.

Onuist son of Vurguist was an exceptional practitioner of the art of Early Historic kingship. The evidence lies not so much in the catalogue of his military successes, impressive though that is, as in his ability to weather adversity after 750. It was an age when a king's reign might rapidly unravel. Alone among his main contemporaries, who included very formidable kings, Onuist maintained himself in his kingdom almost without interruption until the end of his natural life. He avoided death in battle and assassination by a rival, or by his own retinue. However we understand the tangled events of 750, thereafter he was king for a further eleven years – as long as the whole reign of Bridei son of Der-Ilei.

Onuist died in 761, having reigned in Pictavia for some thirty years.[95] It was an extraordinary reign, characterised by a meteoric rise to prominence, relentless pursuit of rivals at home and foes abroad, the infiltration of his kin into the upper echelons of the Pictish elites and ambitious diplomatic enterprises. As a Mag Gergind king fully committed to Pictavia, Onuist brought the achievements of his Verturian predecessors full circle, putting the finishing touches on the *gens Pictorum* as a political idea. The list of his imperial activities is long, even in an age of thin evidence, and allows one to appreciate his neighbours' estimation of his vigour as 'despotic butchery' shedding 'criminal blood'.

It is unfortunate that we know nothing about the kind of king Onuist was at home, to balance against this external view of him as conqueror and despised *tyrannus*. He need not have been beloved, but he might have been. It has been proposed that the exquisite St Andrew's 'sarcophagus' housed his remains, perhaps a generation after his death. Such translations of royal remains seem in Britain, however, to have been reserved for kings regarded as 'royal martyrs', and Onuist is thus an unlikely

---

[95] *AU* 761.4; *AT* 761.3; *Ann. Clon.* 757.1.

candidate.[96] His son Bridei has more potential, his death in 736 having links with the impious crime of his capture.

At the outset of his reign, Onuist justified his seizure of power as an attempt to protect Naiton son of Der-Ilei from his captors (*exactatores*), who may not have thanked him for restoring him to power instead of the cloister. There are other indications that Onuist remained careful to adorn his activities with such justifications and to invest considerable resources in the Church. That Church, as the Carolingian Church did as a matter of custom, may have rallied around the king after the battle of Mugdock, helping to restore the credibility of his regime. Onuist was the devil they knew. At the time, no one younger than about forty would have had much memory of any prior *rex Pictorum*. When he died eleven years later, the reigns of Bridei son of Beli and the sons of Der-Ilei had all but slipped from living memory.

Like Oswy and Bridei, the conqueror of Argyll may be regarded as the towering figure and consummate political survivor of his age, whether one views him in a Pictish, a northern British, or even a wider pan-British context. He is arguably the Pictish king most deserving of a place in the Scottish popular consciousness. Yet one can get carried away in heaping accolades on this man. One ought to remain mindful as well of what his enemies thought of him. Onuist surely possessed an array of personal qualities in measures that place him among Scotland's most successful kings in any age. Like every other eighth-century king in northern Britain, however, his success and continuing viability stemmed as often as not from his sword-hand, with all the terrible rapine and pillage that entailed. The voices of those who acclaimed him deserve attention. So, too, do the chilling last gasps of those he drowned.

[96] Davies, *The Cult of St. Constantine.*

CHAPTER 12

Dragons in the Air: A Doubtful Generation (761–89)

The achievement represented by the tenacious reigns of Onuist and Eadberct is conveniently demonstrated by the convulsions experienced by their realms in the run-up to the Viking Age. Successful expansionist regimes of the early Middle Ages tended to experience difficulty maintaining themselves, once the possibility of further expansion waned. Since 685 the Northumbrians had become squeezed between Mercian and Pictish superpowers, and internal troubles afflicted every Northumbrian king after Aldfrith. Eadberct was no exception, but coped well enough to contemplate expanding his frontiers; yet there would be no Ecgwulfing hegemony.

AEÐILWALD MOLL AND THE RESURGENCE OF DEIRA

After resigning the kingdom to Oswulf his son in 758, Eadberct retired to the cloister, probably at York, where his brother was still archbishop and Alcuin (or Alchwini), the future luminary of the Carolingian court, was a leading monk. According to some versions of the *Chronicle of 802*, the old king was laid to rest there in August 768, having risen to the abbatial office.[1] He had maintained himself in the *regnum Nordanhymbrorum* for more than twenty years – the longest reign since Oswy – overcoming challenges from within and without. Oswulf, in contrast, was unable to hold his position for even twelve months. His own *cohors* turned against him and murdered him at a place called *Methel Wongtun* in July

---

[1] *Chron. 766*, s. a. 758; *Chron. 802*, s. a. 758, 768; *Lib. vit. eccl. Dunelm.*, fols 12, 17. Kirby, *The Earliest English Kings*, 126, reached the same conclusion. The archbishop himself died in November 766; *Chron. 802*, s. a. 766.

759.[2] The great Mercian hegemon Aeðilbald, Eadberct's foe, had suffered a similar fate two years before.

The assassination made way for a certain Moll, otherwise known as Aeðilwald, to be inaugurated as king within a fortnight.[3] His origins are not entirely obscure. The report of a papal legation at York in 786 noted that Oswulf's son, then king of Northumbria, 'was dwelling far to the north', as befits the Bernician origins of the Ecgwulfings.[4] In contrast, a papal letter received by Eadberct associates Moll with places in Deiran Yorkshire, indicating as well that he had been that king's leading courtier (*patricius*), to whom Eadberct had given monastic estates that the pope now wished to be restored to the Church.[5] One year after Eadberct cut his hair, Moll made good on whatever grudge may have lingered from being deprived of these lands. Some forty years of petty inter-dynastic strife followed, characterised by royal murders, humiliation, exile and disinheritance. The Aeðilfrithing dynasty had avoided these excesses of internal squabbling, perhaps, on the strength of its vast treasury, fed by its great *imperium*, enabling it to discourage rivals and reward loyalty. By the middle of the eighth century those days were long gone. Since 704 Eadberct alone had proven capable of coping with the new order.

The reasons for Oswulf's farcical failure to maintain the confidence and loyalty of his household are lost. Moll may or may not have encouraged it. One is reminded of the disintegration of the Pictish succession settlement established after the abdication of Naiton, and the Argyll one after the abdication of Selbach. In part, abdications may represent a strategy by which kings – and perhaps their inner circles in particular – attempted to ensure a smooth succession. Yet change ushered in periods of uncertainty, during which political communities took the measure of a king. The upheavals and 'turf wars' arising from the death or removal of a powerful modern gangster offer something of a parallel situation. Prudence may have demanded that nobles strive to be non-committal towards royal rivals. On the other hand, there were probably great rewards for committing oneself early to the successful cause of a new king.

Maintaining an enthused household and loyal lieutenants, not to mention a contented aristocracy, remained a challenge throughout a

---

[2] *Chron. 766*, s. a. 759; *Chron. 802*, s. a. 758. Oswulf is commemorated in the *Lib. vit. eccl. Dunelm.*, fol. 12.

[3] *Chron. 766*, s. a. 759; *Chron. 802*, s. a. 759.

[4] Whitelock, ed., *English Historical Documents*, 836–40.

[5] Whitelock, ed., *English Historical Documents*, 830–1.

king's reign. Even the highly effective Aeðilbald had eventually lost his touch. Onuist's staying power is a testament to rare savvy. No doubt instilling in his subjects a mix of respect, affection and outright terror, he was still king in Pictavia when Dumngual of Clyde Rock died.[6] Moll was just settling into his own kingdom, and may have taken heart from uncertainties still gripping the Mercians after the assassination of Aeðilbald. Then in 761 Onuist died in Pictavia. Moll's court, probably based primarily at York and other Deiran sites rather than at Bamburgh, doubtless breathed easier at the news.

Onuist's brother Bridei succeeded him, dying two years later in 763. His successor in turn was the obscure Ciniod son of Vuredech. There is no evidence to suggest that this king ever waged war beyond the frontiers of Pictavia. It must be admitted, however, that the Pictish evidentiary record for the second half of the eighth century is too poor to allow for great confidence that Ciniod was more peaceable or idle than his vigorous predecessors. At least his southern frontiers remained at peace, aided perhaps by Onuist's treaty of Clyde Rock in 756.

In Northumbria, Moll too proved unable or unwilling to test the mettle of his neighbours, probably as a result of ongoing domestic difficulties. On 6 August 761 he fought and won 'a severe battle' at Edwini's Cliff (*Ædwinesclif*), apparently below the three summits of Eildon Hill (*Eldunum*) rising above the Tweed at Melrose in the very heartland of Bernicia. Moll's obscure opponent, presumably a Bernician rival, was killed three days later.[7]

The victorious Deiran king's marriage in November 762 to Aeðilthryð, a woman of obscure background, may represent an attempt to dissipate unresolved antagonisms arising from the assassination of Oswulf and the difficult battle of Edwini's Cliff.[8] The royal wedding took place at Catterick (*Cateracta*) on the Deiran side of the Deiro-Bernician frontier. Did Moll have prior links with Catterick? If not, its selection – and the marriage itself – may represent a strategic Deiro-Bernician dynastic union by which the king hoped to heal rifts and encourage Northumbrian solidarity. His son too married at Catterick as king. Moll had now proven himself twice in the field in three years, and he began to mint coins.

---

[6] *Ann. Camb.* 760.2.
[7] *Chron. 802*, s. a. 761; *Chron. 766*, s. a. 761 records only the killing of Oswini. The name of the cliff is added by *Ang.-Sax. Chron. E*, s. a. 761.
[8] *Chron. 802*, s. a. 762.

THE BAD WINTER

Irish and Northumbrian sources note that the winter of 763–4 was particularly harsh. It brought heavy snows, and such relentless cold that the land lay under snow-cover well into the spring. A repeat of the 'Bad Winter', as it was remembered in the *Anglo-Saxon Chronicle*, would have brought hardship and misery even to twenty-first-century Britain and Ireland. The direct effects of the intense cold on people, animals and crops in 763–4 was only the beginning of the misery. Its preservation of heavy snows proved catastrophic across islands where the climate enabled farmers in many areas to graze livestock year-round, so that it was not at all customary to store winter feed. Where a cover of snow prevented or inhibited winter grazing, starvation of beasts and people could result. The lateness of the spring and the effects of run-off on the soil must also have disrupted normal agricultural routines in 764, delaying planting and reducing yields by shortening the growing season.

Indeed the 'Bad Winter' was followed by a famine lasting a year or more. Shortages continued, at least in Ireland, to the end of the 760s, not helped by instances of drought.[9] It is uncertain whether Pictavia suffered from these climatic hardships as Northumbria did. How many people and animals survived the winter cold, the snows and the spring flooding, only to perish of starvation in the ensuing famine, cannot be known. The levels of want and death among the population must have been high to merit mention in the chronicles. It has not been possible to afford the ordinary lives of ordinary people much attention in this book. It is only fitting that we spare a thought for them at this low ebb in their obscure history.

In Ireland, only three years earlier, 'a great snowfall' in February had been followed by a famine year.[10] Here, at least, the 'Bad Winter' afflicted an already weakened population. If matters were not bad enough, there came on the back of the 'Bad Winter' an outbreak 'in the whole of Ireland' of epidemic diarrhoeal disease ('bloody flux'), probably amoebic dysentery, which raged on for at least a decade, claiming even abbots and kings.[11] No doubt the sickness arose in no small part from contamination of food and water after two calamitous winters.

Were there political ramifications arising from all this misery? It was after the desperate year of want following the 'Bad Winter' that Moll

---

[9] *AU* 764.1, 764.4, 764.7, 765.9; *AT* 764.1, 764.5, 765.10; see also *Chron. 802*, s. a. 764.
[10] *AU* 760.1, 760.6; *AT* 760.2.
[11] *AU* 764.7, 764.10, 768.1, 770.1, 773.1, 773.4, 774.8; *AT* 764.5, 764.9.

found himself deposed as a result of obscure events at Finchale (*Wincanheale*), downriver from Durham on the Wear, on 30 October 765.[12] It cannot be ignored that this deposition took place in Bernicia, outside Moll's native Deira. The 'northern recension' of the *Anglo-Saxon Chronicle* records that he abandoned the kingship.[13] It seems that he preferred the cloister to the bloody fate of his predecessor, for Irish chronicles say that Moll *rí Saxan* was tonsured (*clericatus*). In the Durham *Liber vitae* he is commemorated as an abbot, not as a king.[14]

ÁED FIND: LIBERATOR OF DÁL RIATA?

If Moll fell afoul of a conspiracy outside his native province, an otherwise obscure 'battle in Fortriu between Áed and Ciniod' in 768 may mark a different sort of episode among the Picts.[15] Unlike Moll, who was overthrown and tonsured, it seems that Ciniod son of Vuredech emerged victorious (or at least intact) from this encounter. It is conventional to identify his foe as Áed Find, called *rex Dáil Riata* in his obit. He and his brother Fergus have already been encountered. Their father Eochaid was probably Eochu's son, the Cenél nGabráin king of Kintyre from *c.* 721 until his abdication in 731. Thanks to the efforts of Alpínid pseudo-historians, Áed's clash with Ciniod has conventionally been regarded as a pivotal moment in Scottish history, enabling Dál Riata to take the upper hand in its relations with the Picts.

It is rather more likely that Áed owed his position in Argyll to the efforts of Onuist son of Vurguist, enabling him to emerge after the 'smiting' of Dál Riata as its paramount prince. It is plausible that his brother was the same person as Vurguist, the father of the Pictish kings Constantín (789–820) and Onuist (820–34), whose names were eventually spuriously inserted into the Dalriadan king-list for reasons lost to us.[16] Analysis of the king-lists and Irish chronicles allows for the restoration of a better Dalriadan list, starting with Áed and Fergus, followed by Donncoirce *rex Dáil Riata*, who died in 792.[17] Crucially, this list includes

[12] *Chron. 802*, s. a. 765.

[13] *Ang.-Sax. Chron. E*, s. a. 759.

[14] *AT* 764.12; *Ann. Clon.* 759.7; *Lib. vit. eccl. Dunelm.*, fol. 17b.

[15] *AU* 768.7.

[16] Chadwick, *Early Scotland*, 129–32; Anderson, 'Dalriada', 109; Hudson, *Kings of Celtic Scotland*, 29–30. Broun, 'Pictish Kings 761–839', invalidates the king-list-based idea that Constantín and his family were Dalriadan Gaels.

[17] *AU* 792.4. This list has been constructed by Broun, 'Pictish Kings 761–839', 78–80.

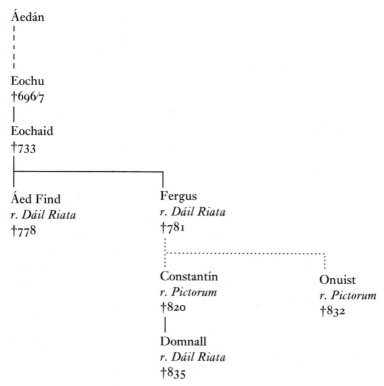

Table 12.1 Áed Find: some key relationships

a grandson of Vurguist in the ninth century, tending to confirm suspicions that Vurguist and Áed were brothers, or at least kin.

This dynasty's Dalriadan credentials notwithstanding, it was clearly fully engaged with Pictavia, testifying to the impact of the 'smiting', as well as to the earlier Pictish movements in Argyll. The dynasty had nothing to do with any conquest of the Picts, nor any union of Picts and Gaels. Thus, it is necessary to re-think the significance of Áed's battle in Fortriu in 768 and his family's burgeoning Pictish credentials over the next twenty years, culminating in Constantín's seizure of the Pictish kingship.

The most economical interpretation of the eighth-century evidence is arguably that Argyll, some twenty-seven years after its conquest, had become regarded, to all intents and purposes, as a province of the kingdom of Pictavia. Evidence surrounding Cóeti, 'bishop of Iona' c. 710, and the movements of Talorcan of Atholl c. 730, has indeed been understood in earlier chapters as suggesting that the realm of Atholl had spanned Drumalban into Argyll even before the 'smiting'. To that evidence we may now add the fact that, in the period after ours, Cenél nGabráin gave their name to Gowrie, while Cenél Loairn were associated with Moray. Did the 'smiting', therefore, involve some kind of partition of Argyll after 741?

It had certainly been the Waerteras of Fortriu who overcame the Lorn king in 736, but it was Onuist himself, a southern Pictish king, who had campaigned further south in Argyll that year. If Lorn was placed under Verturian domination thereafter, and Kintyre and Cowal under Atholl control, a context would be provided for understanding the later associations of Moray and Gowrie with these regions respectively, possibly reflecting actual 'accommodation' of Gaels from Argyll in Pictavia.[18]

Was Áed Find, then, Ciniod's Atholl colleague in 768, in a kingdom spanning Drumalban? The Dupplin Cross links his (possible) kinsman Constantín with Forteviot. The presence of such names as Vurguist, Onuist and Vuen among the attested members of the dynasty suggests that it linked itself quite closely with Onuist, and went on doing so long after 741.[19] He seems to have destroyed the leading members of the Atholl dynasty by 739 – men who had arguably been put in place there by the Verturian hegemons of the two previous generations. Did he replace them after 741 with Áed's Cenél nGabráin dynasty, charging the king to maintain as well his family's traditional ascendancy in Kintyre and Cowal?

We can but speculate about the details and significance of this episode. In any case, Áed, like Ciniod, survived it, and both kings returned to their respective kingdoms, reigning for a number of further years. On his death in 775, Ciniod was succeeded by Elphin son of Vurad, probably the same Elphin (erroneously) styled *rex Saxonum* in an obit in the *Annals of Ulster* in 780.[20] His father may have been Vurad (*Feroth*) son of Finnguine, slain by Onuist's retinue in 729.[21] His grandfather may have been Finnguine son of Deileroith, who fell in the Pictish army vanquished in Manau in 711.[22] If these identifications are correct, a reconciliation of this prominent (probably) Atholl family with Onuist after 729 might be envisaged.

---

[18] For a discussion of the later evidence, see Woolf, *From Pictland to Alba*, 341.
[19] The significance of Vuen relates to Onuist's family being named Éoganachta in *Éogan Már trá óenmac leis.*
[20] *AU* 775.1, 780.5; *Ann. Camb.* (Dumville) 776.1. Chadwick, *Early Scotland*, 19. Elphin is given a reign of three and a half years in the regnal list; probably this should be four and a half.
[21] *AU* 729.2.
[22] *AU* 711.3; *AT* 711.3; Clancy, 'Philosopher-King', 136–7.

Elphin's reign is obscure. Only one Irish chronicle, the *Annals of Ulster*, contains records from this period, and neither it nor the Northumbrian chronicles exhibit much interest in Pictavia after the death of Onuist. It is striking that Cinaed son of Alpín and his father shared the names of Ciniod and Elphin, successive kings of Picts three generations earlier. Were the Alpínids kinsmen to these kings?

Elphin died after a reign of some five years, during which Áed Find also died. What happened next to the kingship of Pictavia is complicated by disagreement between two sources. According to the Pictish king-list, which took shape in the ninth century, Elphin's successors were as follows:

> Drest son of Talorcan reigned one year [i.e. *c*. 780–1].
> Talorcan son of Drestan reigned four or five years [i.e. *c*. 781–5].
> Talorcan son of Onuist reigned two years and a half [i.e. *c*. 785–8].
> Conall son of Tadg reigned five years [i.e. *c*. 788–93].

The third of these kings was surely a son of Onuist son of Vurguist, and the first was probably a son of Onuist's brother Talorcan, slain at Mugdock. The *Annals of Ulster* do not correspond with this list, recording the death in 782 of *Dub Tholargg rex Pictorum citra Monoth*, 'Black Talorc, king of the Picts on this side of the Mounth', and the end of Conall's reign in 789.[23] The two texts can be made to agree fairly closely, however, by moving Onuist's son Talorcan to the beginning of the list, identifying him as the same person as Dub Talorc, and concluding from the phrase *citra Monoth* that he ruled jointly with the kings listed after him in the reconstructed list. Thus:

> Talorcan son of Onuist [i.e. Dub Talorc] reigned two years and a half [i.e. 780–2] on one side of the Mounth.
> Drest son of Talorcan reigned [jointly with him] one year [i.e. *c*. 780–1] on the other side of the Mounth.
> Talorcan son of Drestan reigned [initially jointly with Dub Talorc] four or five years [i.e. *c*. 781–5] on the other side of the Mounth.
> Conall son of Tadg reigned [alone?] five years [i.e. *c*. 785–9].

After *c*. 740 the information about northern Britain in the Irish chronicles seems to have come from southern Pictland, so that *citra* is likely to

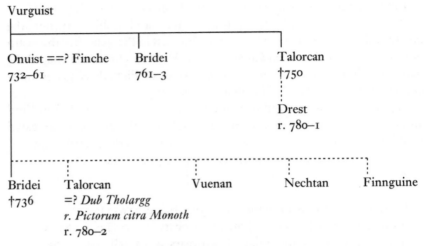

Vurguist

| Onuist ==? Finche | Bridei | Talorcan |
| 732–61 | 761–3 | †750 |

Drest
r. 780–1

Bridei	Talorcan	Vuenan	Nechtan	Finnguine
†736	=? *Dub Tholargg*			
	r. Pictorum citra Monoth			
	r. 780–2			

Table 12.2 Descendants of Vurguist (728–82)

indicate that Dub Talorc – Onuist's son Talorcan on this reconstruction – was a southerner like his father. In addition to his two successive colleagues Drest (his cousin) and Talorcan, he may have had a third, albeit subordinate colleague until 781 in the person of Áed Find's brother Fergus (or Vurguist?), who died in that year. Thereafter Fergus's kingship, associated with Dál Riata in the *Annals of Ulster*, was held by Donncoirce, who died in 792. With putative major kingdoms in Mag Gergind, Fortriu and Atholl, the last two with potential provinces in Argyll, we seem to have room in Pictland for three prominent kings at a time. After 724, three kings had competed for the kingship from apparent bases in Fortriu, Atholl and Mag Gergind, respectively. A similar situation could have emerged in the course of the 760s and 770s.

It seems, therefore, that, on or by Elphin's death in 780, Pictavia was partitioned along traditional cleavages, as had probably happened in 724. As on this earlier occasion, a joint reign was the order of the day. There is no particular reason to presume that the putative colleagues and cousins Dub Talorc and Drest were overtly hostile. Their putative third colleague Fergus too may have cultivated a family memory of strong links with Onuist after 741, if he was the same person as Vurguist, sire of Pictish kings.

Here at the very end of our period, then, exactly seven hundred years after the first Agricolan invasion of north-east Scotland, cleavages continued to have relevance which may have begun bedding down in the century after the battle of Mons Graupius. What had perhaps changed in the century since 685 was that it was becoming more normal to regard the northern and southern Pictish zones as halves of a coherent whole, divisible among heirs perhaps, but having a shared past shaped by ethnic solidarity. Pictavia would have been in line with the great kingdoms of Ireland, England and Scandinavia in the eighth century if it had developed a sense of nation and national kingship, but in fact remained sharply disunited in terms of its political community and consciousnesses of internal difference, and lacking much in the way of national institutions.

In 789, Conall son of Tadg was overcome in 'a battle between the Picts' (*bellum inter Pictos*) by Constantín son of Vurguist, apparently escaping or withdrawing into Argyll.[24] With this victory Constantín, possibly a nephew of Áed Find, established himself as king of Picts, the fifth man to reign in Pictavia in just nine years, though he and Conall may have been colleagues for years prior to their decisive clash. As in its previous experience of joint kingship after partition, Pictavia had succumbed to the domination of a new strongman. Like that earlier strongman Onuist, the new king maintained his position for over thirty years, dying peacefully in 820. The exquisite and suitably 'triumphalist' Dupplin Cross, with its inscribed panel beginning with the words CU[STA]NTIN FILIUS FIRCUS, was probably commissioned for Constantín to be placed on the slopes of the Gask Ridge overlooking Forteviot, in tandem perhaps with the Invermay cross.[25] The monuments may fix *c.* 800 as the foundation of the 'palace', *palacium Fothuirtabaicht*, where Cinaed son of Alpín died in 858, and where his brother is said to have promulgated laws (*Leges Áedo mac Echdach*) before 862.[26]

Further, like Onuist, and like Bridei son of Der-Ilei before that, Constantín was succeeded fairly seamlessly by his brother. So too was Cinaed. There are hints in the Pictish king-list, moreover, that seamless succession from brother to brother was characteristic of Pictish kingship in the sixth and seventh centuries. This element of Pictish succession has been appreciated for a very long time, but the matriliny debate has seen it neglected as a focus of study.[27]

---

[24] *AU* 789.11, 807.3; *AI* 807.2; *Ann. Clon.* 787.2 seems to date 'a great slaughter of Ulstermen by the Redshankes or Dalriada' to this year, but *AU* 790.6 shows that Dál n Araidi is correct.

[25] Forsyth, 'The Inscriptions on the Dupplin Cross', 240–3; Henderson and Henderson, *The Art of the Picts*, 190, 194.

[26] *Chron. Kings of Alba*, §§ 6–8.

[27] Skene, *Celtic Scotland*, vol. 1, 232–3. If -ech may be regarded as potentially a genitive ending, there is a possibility that Ciniod son of Vuredech and Elphin son of Vurad were brothers.

The partitions of Pictavia in the 720s and 780s may be instructive for understanding why sons of Pictish high kings seem rarely to have become high kings themselves. On those occasions the kingship seems not to have passed from brother to brother as a single legacy, but to have been partitioned, in passing from an older generation to a younger one. It also seems to have attracted the ambitious attentions of other Pictish kings somewhat outwith the ruling dynasty. Another joint kingship followed the reigns of the sons of Vurguist, Constantín and Onuist in 834. There are suggestions in the *Chronicle of the Kings of Alba* that yet another example followed the killing of Cinaed's son in 878.[28] It begins to look convincingly like a pattern, which may have had some antiquity by the eighth century when we can perceive it in our sources.

Again like Onuist, Constantín's name is commemorated in the Durham *Liber vitae*, where it followed immediately after that of the Frankish emperor Charlemagne in the source of that text.[29] Onuist had built on the achievements of the sons of Der-Ilei to break new ground in Pictish kingship, in particular testing its capacity to reach beyond Drumalban and the Forth. The later sons of Vurguist and, later still, the Alpínid dynasty seem to have broken newer ground still. These men took the kingship in such a strong grip that it was routinely inherited wholly, and by a succession of sons of prior kings. Did this new approach to royal succession replace an earlier custom favouring the partition of a dead king's legacy between joint heirs?

AELFWALD SON OF OSWULF AND THE SYNOD OF FINCHALE

The Northumbrian kings were having troubles of their own in this period. After the tonsuring of Moll in 765, Alchred son of Eanwini succeeded to the kingship. The *Chronicle of 802* says that he was 'sprung from the lineage of King Ida, as some say'. His genealogy, preserved in a collection compiled *c.* 796, gives Alchred descent from a son of Ida called Eadric.[30] As Moll had been a Deiran, it is perhaps predictable that his deposition brought a Bernician to power. In 768 Alchred married Osgifu,

---

[28] *Chron. Kings of Alba*, §§ 15–18; *AU* 878.2.

[29] *Lib. vit. eccl. Dunelm.*, fol. 12b.

[30] *Chron. 802*, s. a. 765; Dumville, 'The Anglian Collection of Royal Genealogies', 30, 32, 35, 39–40 (on the date). Interestingly, *Hist. Brit.*, § 61 names Ecgwulf's father as Eadric son of Ida, but this may be a mistake for Eadhelm, with Ocga having been skipped.

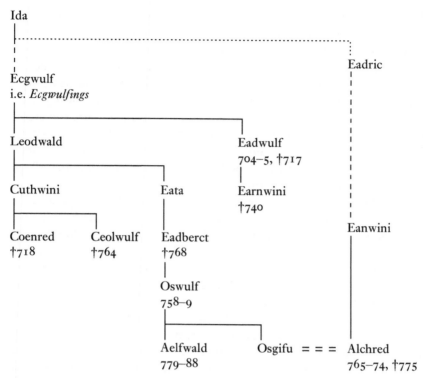

Table 12.3 Alchred son of Eanwini: some key relationships

evidently a daughter of the assassinated Ecgwulfing king Oswulf.[31] Was taking an Ecgwulfing bride a strategy whereby the king sought to consolidate his Bernician power-base?

In the next year either the church or the royal estate at Catterick 'was burned by the *tyrannus* Earnred, and by the judgement of God he himself miserably perished by fire'.[32] Catterick stood near the Deiro-Bernician frontier, vulnerable to attack in times of trouble between the two great districts. However, it may be significant that Moll and (after this episode) his son were married at Catterick. Was Earnred attacking it because of its associations with that dynasty? If so, we might conclude that Alchred's nine-year reign was quite unpleasant for those linked with Moll if they remained inside the kingdom. The evidence is too thin, however, to evaluate Earnred's crime.

In the last years of the eighth century, the Latin West entered the age of Charlemagne, sole ruler of the Franks from 771, who resurrected the

---

[31] *Chron. 802*, s. a. 768.
[32] *Chron. 802*, s. a. 769.

Roman Principate, after a fashion, in 800. Alchred and Osgifu reached out to him in 773, urging the great king by letter 'to spread the Christian faith among the peoples subject to you', and writing to the archbishop of Mainz, a West Saxon, seeking his 'help and care for our embassies' to the Carolingian court.[33] Onuist in the previous generation had looked far afield in his diplomatic efforts, but not, so far as we know, to the Continent. For many aristocrats, as well as for some clerics, the eighth century could be a mobile age as the more powerful kings in northern Britain situated themselves on the international stage. Such movements cannot, however, have helped the kingdoms involved in fending off the epidemic diseases of this period.

By 774, like his recent predecessors, Alchred had overstayed his welcome. His letter to Mainz less than twelve months earlier had thanked the archbishop for his concern 'about the disturbance in our churches and people'. While celebrating Easter at York on 3 April, the king was 'deprived of the fellowship of the royal household (*familia*) and the foremost men (*principes*)', and forced into exile 'by the design and consent of all his adherents'. Archbishop Ecgberct had died in 766, and the see of York was now held by Aelberct. One wonders what Alcuin, still a monk there at this time, made of this cashierment: in later life he wrote in positive terms about the reigns of Eadberct and his grandson Aelfwald, and he may not have thought much of these other kings of the period. The deposition happened outwith the king's native Bernicia, in an exact reversal of Moll's downfall at Finchale in 765. A sentence of anathema from his own retinue, men who had clearly become remarkably disaffected, was presumably a peaceable alternative to assassination, visited on the queen's father in 759. In 728 'the nobles and people of the Picts [had] turned their backs to Elphin'. Attested expulsions of earlier Pictish kings may have been similar in character.

With a party of companions, Alchred made his way from York to his royal stronghold at Bamburgh, whence he took ship north to Pictavia, finding refuge (and obscurity) in the court of Ciniod son of Vuredech.[34] His successor was Aeðilred son of Moll, a Deiran prince whose father had been deposed to make way for Alchred. He fared little better, reigning for just four years. In 778 he became implicated in the murders (or executions) of three royal lieutenants (*duces* or *heahgerefan*), having presumably uncovered (or anticipated) some conspiracy. A year later, with their blood on his hands, Aeðilred was 'expelled from his royal seat (*solium*), and

---

[33] Whitelock, ed., *English Historical Documents*, 832–4.
[34] *Chron. 802*, s. a. 774.

driven into exile', and so 'forced to undergo sad changes, and to experience much wretchedness'.[35] One chronicler, at least, was on his side – possibly demonstrating that he wrote with the knowledge of hindsight that Aeðilred was destined to be restored to the kingship.

In the meantime, Bernician predictably succeeded Deiran. The new king in 779 was Aelfwald son of Oswulf, whose grandfather Eadberct had maintained a tenacious grip on the kingship in stark contrast to any of his eighth-century successors. After twenty years in the wilderness, the Ecgwulfings were back in the saddle in Northumbria. Aelfwald's father had briefly held the kingship, and his sister Osgifu had become queen in 768 by marrying Alchred.

Aelfwald is the first Northumbrian king after his murdered father commemorated in the royal list on the Durham *Liber vitae*. Were the intervening reigns of Moll, Alchred and Aeðilred regarded as unwelcome – even illegitimate – at the church where its source was kept? The *Chronicle of 802* also implies that the restoration of Ecgwulfing power was regarded as a welcome event in the underlying contemporary chronicle, describing Aelfwald in partisan terms as 'a pious and upright king'.[36] Five years after his untimely death, Alcuin wrote to his successor that 'fornications, adulteries and incest' had 'poured over the land' in its wake.[37]

Not everyone in Northumbria shared such views of the king's uprightness. Aelfwald's reign had barely begun when, in December 780, his leading courtier (*patricius*) was burnt to death at Silton (*Seletun*) in Yorkshire by two lieutenants and their army.[38] It is significant, again, that this attack on a Bernician king's follower should have occurred in Deira. Eight years later, on 23 September 788, the king himself 'was miserably slain' near Hadrian's Wall. As if it was not difficult enough to face predictable Deiran hostility, Aelfwald had now run afoul of 'a conspiracy being formed by his leading courtier (*patricius*) Sicga', who later committed suicide. Does the fact that Aelfwald and his father were both murdered explain their commemorations in the *Liber vitae*?

The slain king was buried at Hexham in Bernicia, the fifth Northumbrian king in succession to be removed prematurely from power after only a handful of years in the kingship.[39] Aelfwald's father aside, slain in the first year of his reign, the average reign-length of these kings

[35] *Chron. 802*, s. a. 778, 779. These *duces* are *heahgerefan* in *Ang.-Sax. Chron. E*, s. a. 778.

[36] *Chron. 802*, s. a. 779.

[37] Whitelock, ed., *English Historical Documents*, 843.

[38] *Chron. 802*, s. a. 780; *Ang.-Sax. Chron. E*, s. a. 779.

[39] *Chron. 802*, s. a. 788; *Ang.-Sax. Chron. E*, s. a. 789.

was eighty-seven months – a little over seven years. It is probably unfair to belittle them because they did not enjoy the robust reigns of an Onuist or an Oswy, spanning a whole generation. Such kings were exceptional. Eighty-seven months in power is no mean span of time. American presidents serve only nine months more (if they win two terms). If it was difficult for any of them to feel really secure in their position, no doubt there were still long stretches of time during which they could forget their fear. It is a nice question how much this sad litany of human misery at the top in Northumbria – with all its rivalries, murders, intrigues, marriages, betrayals, exiles and suicides – may reflect the ordinary course of regional and local politics too, right down to the humblest levels of society.

In 773, Aelfwald's sister Osgifu and her husband had attempted to establish contact with Charlemagne. In 781, Aelfwald sent Alcuin from York as an ambassador to the Continent, and in 782 he was persuaded to join the Frankish court, where he became a vocal instrument of the mighty emperor and the most respected philosopher of his age. In 786, towards the premature end of Aelfwald's reign, 'legates from the apostolic see were sent to Britain by the lord Pope Hadrian'. The legates were two bishops, Theophylact of Todi near Perugia in central Italy, and his superior, George of Ostia (the harbour of Rome) and Amiens (on the Somme in northern Francia). They set about 'renewing among us,' states the *Chronicle of 802*, 'the ancient peace and catholic faith which St Gregory taught by blessed Augustine'.

Theophylact headed from Kent to Mercia, and eventually into British districts.[40] In 768 the last of the traditionalist British Churches had adopted the reformed Easter and perhaps other apostolicist reforms. The possibility has already been raised that North British Churches may have begun adopting it along with northern Irish Churches in the late seventh century. George, meanwhile, came north to York with Charlemagne's personal envoy. At the time Aelfwald 'was dwelling far to the north', presumably in his native Bernicia. At the urging of Eanbald, archbishop of York, the king convened a synod of 'the kings and bishops, chief men and primates of this country' at Finchale (*Pincanhala*) on the Wear on 2 September 787, a Sunday.[41]

Bishop George's report on the proceedings survives. Among other things, he ordered the bishops to stop participating in secular councils,

---

[40] *Chron. 802*, s. a. 786; *Ang.-Sax. Chron. E*, s. a. 785; Whitelock, ed., *English Historical Documents*, 836–40.

[41] *Chron. 802*, s. a. 787; *Ang.-Sax. Chron. E*, s. a. 788. The *P-* in *Pincanhala* is thought to be a scribal misreading of the Anglo-Saxon character Þ ('wynn').

and tantalisingly castigated the clergy for conspiring in killing kings. Oswulf had been the only Northumbrian king since the days of Bede to be assassinated, whose son was the very king who convened this synod. Moreover, Finchale was the very monastery where Oswulf's successor had been deposed. George's report also speaks of conspiratorial clerics having been 'cut off from divine and secular rights'. Had Aelfwald been punishing clergymen implicated in his father's murder?

The legate also made a point of condemning the raising up of kings 'begotten in adultery or incest'. Aelfwald had restored the Ecgwulfing dynasty to power – do George's remarks relate to Ecgwulfing aspersions cast on the parentage of the three intervening kings? The legation had Charlemagne's attention, and the Synod of Finchale may have given Aelfwald a sense of imperial, as well as papal, confirmation that his dynasty's royal claims were superior to those of others.[42] Just twelve months later, almost to the day, he was murdered. His killer Sicga was present at Finchale, and signatory to the capitularies promulgated there. Did Northumbria's bishops take them any more seriously than her princes?

Outwith the realm of high politics, the legate ordered the Northumbrians to stop scarring themselves with 'the injury of staining', inspired by 'the superstition of heathens'. This can only refer to tattooing, a habit long associated with the ethnonym *Picti*. Solinus in the third century had written that the Britons of *barbaricum* had 'shapes of various animals cunningly inscribed into their bodies', and in the early 630s, Isidore of Seville had linked tattooing with Pictish elites (*nobilitas*) in *Etymologiae*, his hugely influential encyclopaedia:

> Nor should we omit the Picts, whose name is taken from their
> bodies, because an artisan (*opifex*), with the tiny point of a pin and
> the juice squeezed from a native plant, tricks (*inludit*) them out
> with scars to serve as identifying marks, and their nobility are
> distinguished by their tattooed (*picti*) limbs.[43]

Were the Northumbrians emulating Pictish practices? George went on to outlaw other things done 'according to the fashion of the heathens whom,

---

[42] Kirby, *The Earliest English Kings*, 128.
[43] Solinus, *De mirab. mundi*, § 23; Isidore, *Etymologiae*, xix.23.7; Cowan, 'Myth and Identity', 117n is surely correct to infer that Isidore elsewhere confused *Picti* and *Scotti* when he wrote of the latter that they 'receive their name in their own language from their painted bodies, because they are marked by tattoos of various figures made with iron pricks and black pigment' (ix.2.103).

by the help of God, your fathers expelled by arms from the country'. These included styles of dress and subjecting horses to mutilations – slitting nostrils, fastening together ears and docking tails.[44] The legate sought to eradicate such traits by appealing to the Northumbrians' hostility towards the Britons. They are at least as likely, however, to have originated across the Forth. Along with other possible manifestations already noted, in such realms as art and royal power and prerogatives, do these traits reflect something of a shared Anglo-Pictish elite culture?

LINKS WITH IRELAND AND THE CONTINENT

Even before diplomats may have passed between the courts of Onuist and the Éoganacht kings of Cashel, a Pictish cleric was a bishop in Ireland. His appearance at a Church Council in Rome in 721 was recorded with the words *Fergustus episcopus Scotiae Pictus*, 'Vurguist the Pict, a bishop of Ireland'. The *Martyrology of Tallaght*, a ninth-century 'calendar' of saints probably based in part on a mid-eighth-century Iona calendar, names 'Fergus the Pict' (*Fergus cruthnech*), surely the same bishop, for commemoration.[45] In attendance at Rome alongside him was another bishop, 'Sedulius', described as *episcopus Britanniae de genere Scottorum*, 'a bishop of Britain of Gaelic stock', probably the Bishop Síadal (*Siatal epi*) commemorated in the same martyrology.[46] A Gael with his see in Britain, Síadal's description in Rome may simply have been a convoluted way of denoting an Argyll bishop; but he could equally have been Irishborn and, indeed, based anywhere in Britain. Two years prior to this Council, a monk with the conspicuous Pictish name Drestan died at the Irish monastery of Ardbraccan in Meath, outside Navan where the Blackwater meets the Boyne. The Irish chronicles call him 'Drostan of the Oratory' (*Dairtaige*). The outside possibility exists that he was St Drostan of Old Deer (*Deir*) in Aberdeenshire.[47]

The saint commemorated by the place-name of St Vigeans in Angus seems to be Féichín, abbot of the monastery of Fore, further up the Boyne from Ardbraccan, near Lough Lene in the Westmeath lake-lands. He perished in 664 or 665 of the same plague that claimed bishops of York

---

[44] Whitelock, ed., *English Historical Documents*, 836–40.

[45] *Mart. Tallaght*, 8 September; on the provenance of the text, see Ó Riain, *Anglo-Saxon Ireland*, 11–13.

[46] Haddan and Stubbs, eds., *Councils and Ecclesiastical Documents*, vol. 2, 7; *Mart. Tallaght*, 12 February; Clancy, 'Deer', forthcoming.

[47] *AU* 719.2; *AT* 719.2. Clancy, 'Deer', forthcoming.

and Canterbury.[48] The establishment of this cult in Pictavia, like the presence of Drestan at Ardbraccan, hints at links with the southern Uí Néill kingdom of Meath, dominated by Cland Cholmáin. Bede's Pictish source claimed that the Columban church of Durrow in southern Westmeath was founded before Iona – does this claim too reflect a link with Meath during the reigns of the sons of Der-Ilei? It is fascinating that Onuist, in the Éoganachta and Cenél Conaill, established links with fierce rivals of the southern Uí Néill dynasties. St Vigeans was clearly the site of a very significant Pictish monastery. Its magnificent corpus of sculpture is not thought to date as early as our period, but its foundation may well have taken place before 724.

Probably not uniquely among the eighth-century Hebridean monasteries, Iona retained its traditionally close contacts with Ireland in the second half of the eighth century. In the generations after the 'smiting' of Dál Riata, Abbot Sléibéne travelled to Ireland for the third promulgation of *Lex innocentium* on its sixtieth anniversary in 757, spearheaded by the Cland Cholmáin king Domnall son of Murchad. There was a fourth promulgation on its eightieth anniversary. Also in that year the retired king Níall Frossach died in Iona. Níall had abdicated the kingships of Cenél nÉogain and Ailech some years earlier. Four years after his death, the king of the Connachta in western Ireland, Artgal son of Cathal, followed the same path, dying at Iona in 791.[49] In this period of all periods, when the need for spiritual support was made particularly acute by climatic hardship and disease, we need not impugn the sincerity of such abdications.

The importance of Columba's monastery, two hundred years old in 763, as a focus of international activity cannot be denied. To characterise it as 'the Christian heart of Scotland' during this period, however, or 'the most spiritually significant centre in the country', is to place great faith in Iona's own conception of its place in the world.[50] The fact that it is so much better evidenced than Kingarth, Applecross and Lismore is not proof that these other Hebridean monasteries, with their different affiliations, were not also great centres. Pictish monasteries like Portmahomack, Cennrígmonaid and Abernethy might also have thrown their hats into the ring in any competition to identify 'the Christian heart of Scotland' at the end of our period. Moreover, the use of 'Scotland' in this period at all is not helpful, and Bernician monasteries like Whithorn,

---

[48] *AU* 665.3; *AT* 665.4; *CS* 665.3; *AI* 666.5.
[49] *AU* 778.4, 778.7, 782.2, 791.1.
[50] Ritchie, *Viking Scotland*, 18; Bannerman, 'The Scots of Dalriada', 14.

Melrose, Coldingham, Wearmouth-Jarrow and Lindisfarne can claim to have been influential centres affecting parts of what is now Scotland. The mere survival of the place-names at Kingarth, Applecross and Lismore, as compared with the disappearance of most Hebridean names known to Adomnán, may mark their significance.[51]

As a group, the principal Hebridean monasteries and their daughter houses must have played a key role in the maintenance of intellectual links between northern Britain and Ireland, and the transmission of texts, artistic aesthetics and expertise. The ecclesiastical and secular power centres of Atlantic Scotland after 741 may have continued to enjoy the even wider contacts of Adomnán's experience two generations earlier. He referred to ships arriving regularly from Gaul and implied that there was regular contact with Spain and Italy, in one instance during a discussion of the spread of virulent disease.[52] Thanks to the Gallo-Frankish bishop Arculf, who spent nine months visiting holy sites in the East, Adomnán was capable of describing Constantinople in De locis sanctis.[53] Such was the power of literate learning in seventh-century northern Britain, that a studious writer could picture vividly landscapes he had not beheld with his own eyes. In this text, Adomnán established his monastery's capacity to participate in Latin Christendom at the highest intellectual level, a feat repeated by another Ionan monk, Cú Chuimne, in his work on canon law a generation later.

There is little to indicate that Iona and St Columba had become less significant in Ireland than in the seventh century, even if they had become differently significant. Views on Iona's place in the world surely did not remain any more static between the abbacies of Adomnán and Sléibéne than between the compositions of De uirtutibus sancti Columbae and Vita Columbae. In the fifty years after Adomnán's death, both Cenél Conaill in Donegal and Cenél nGabráin in Argyll – Iona's most intimate political associates – had become decisively eclipsed. In addition the kings and Church of Fortriu had severed official ties with Iona. It would be surprising if these developments did not inspire adjustments in Iona's outlook.

Did the monastery grow increasingly reluctant to embrace the partisan politics that Cumméne Find, and to a lesser extent Adomnán, had embraced? Through repeated promulgations of Lex innocentium, the

---

[51] MacDonald, 'Iona's Style of Government', 178.
[52] Adomnán, V. s. Columbae, i.28, ii.46, iii.23.
[53] Adomnán, De loc. Sanct., iii.1. On Continental contacts, see also Fisher, Early Medieval Sculpture, 8.

abbots of Iona continued to affirm their commitment to the notion of an Uí Néill king of Ireland, but he would no longer be a Cenél Conaill king like Loingsech, the *rí Erenn* heading Adomnán's list of royal guarantors. The origins of the royal personages known to have come to Iona in the second half of the eighth century testify to a broadening of the monastery's horizons.

The Northumbrians retained robust links both with the Picts and the Continent in the second half of the eighth century. The papal legation at Finchale is only one example of their connections. Two Pictish kings were commemorated at one Bernician church. The royal court of Pictavia was the destination of (at least) two Northumbrian royal exiles in the decades after Onuist's death. Northumbrian participation in the Insular intellectual and artistic achievement of the Early Historic period, once called 'Hiberno-Saxon', is well attested and well known. The abandonment of this label by scholars reflects the extent to which the Picts in particular have asserted themselves in the consciousness of a scholarly community increasingly willing to look beyond texts in attempting to understand the Early Historic past. It is probably just as well – Pictland, at the ethnic crossroads of the Insular world with *Hibernenses* to one side and *Saxones* to the other, and with its powerful hegemons, may have been central to the 'Hiberno-Saxon' phenomenon.

It has been observed that study of the Mercian English 'depends to an astonishing degree upon information preserved by their neighbours, their enemies and those whom they conquered'.[54] So too the Picts, but it is not emphasised enough that both Irish and Anglo-Saxon chroniclers of Early Historic times consistently show far greater interest in the Picts and their goings-on than they ever do in one another's lands. If scholars had only the Irish chronicles to tell them about England in our period, or vice versa, they would be unable to tell anything like the story they can about the Picts. In lamenting the lack of indigenous written sources, and reliance on extraneous ones, scholars of the Picts have tended to miss this vital point about what is a remarkable weight of external evidence. Behind the phenomenon, as in the case of Mercia, lies the perceived significance of the Picts in the eyes of their neighbours in the seventh and eighth centuries and the extent of their Insular interlinkages.

The Irish and the Anglo-Saxons were interested in Pictavia, and informed about it, in Early Historic times because the kingdom mattered. The political and institutional achievements of the Pictish hegemons after 685, barely perceptible today, were no doubt partly responsible for

---

[54] Brooks, 'The Formation of the Mercian Kingdom', 159–60.

attracting attention. It is important to emphasise that achievement went beyond the kings of Picts. Evidence comes from the Northumbrian hagiographical poem *Miracula Nynie Episcopi*, penned towards the end of the eighth century. Here the poet, speaking of 'all their talents among far-flung nations', explains himself by remarking, not without embroidery, that the Picts have 'many monasteries . . . which flourish now with choicest choirs of monks, worshipping Christ truly and serving the monastic rule.'[55] The intellectual achievements of this vibrant monastic environment, which so impressed this Northumbrian poet, are today thinly attested in the extreme especially in the medium of the written word. At all costs, we must resist inclinations to regard such absences of evidence as evidence of absences.

Like the Gaels who influenced their nascent Church, Northumbrian clerics had become a common sight on the Continent by the middle of the eighth century. The first generation of such travellers included Benedict Biscop, the founder of Wearmouth-Jarrow, who made journeys to acquire writings and ecclesiastical accoutrements.[56] Wilfrid of York seems to have made similar acquisitions on his trips to the papal curia at Rome, and he brought relics back to Northumbria for the proliferation of saintly cults. The arrival of the relics of St Andrew at Cennrígmonaid, where the apostle's cult become the focus of Scotland's most important medieval church, probably depended ultimately on Wilfrid's relic-hunting.

By Bede's later years, Northumbrian clerics were becoming active as missionaries under the auspices of the Frankish Church, possibly (as Stephen maintains) due to pioneering work by Wilfrid. The most famous was Willibrord, patron saint of Utrecht in the Netherlands, who trained in Northumbria and Ireland before undertaking his mission to the Frisians of the Netherlands coast in the 690s.[57] Winfrith, his former pupil at Echternach, founded by Willibrord on the River Sûre in modern Luxembourg, assumed the Latinate name *Boniface* and was close to Charlemagne's grandfather Charles Martel, the power behind the Merovingian kingdom by 718. The first archbishop of Mainz on the Rhine, in 754 Boniface was murdered near Dokkum while evangelising among the Frisians, for which he was regarded as a martyr. His miserable fate did not prevent the archbishops of York from continuing to support missionary work, nor from mobilising their troubled kings and queens to throw their variable weight behind the proselytising movement.

[55] *Mir. Nynie Episc.*, 3.
[56] Bede, *Hist. Abbatum*, §§ 1–14; *V. s. Ceolfridi*, §§ 5–7, 9–10, 12, 15.
[57] Bede, *Hist. eccl.*, v.10.

Meanwhile 'Virgil', abbot of St Peter's monastery at Salzburg on the River Salzach, on the modern border between Germany and Austria, probably went there from Iona a year after the 'smiting' of Dál Riata and was bishop of Salzburg at his death in 784.[58]

FROM SEA-KINGS TO VIKINGS

Early Historic northern Britain was, then, part and parcel of a wider world, and the enjoyment of transmarine contacts was certainly nothing new. Scotland has never been isolated, even those parts of it that seem remote today. In the middle of the fourth century, its inhabitants had partaken in a Barbarian Conspiracy which shook the Roman provinces of Britannia and scandalised the Empire. As the eighth century was drawing to a close, a new barbarian conspiracy appeared in the form of piratical raiding by *gentiles*, 'heathens' in the form of Scandinavian vikings.[59] The story properly belongs to the next volume in this series, save for what the advent of the Viking Age may reveal about northern Britain in the preceding decades.

Is it post-viking hindsight which gives the second half of the eighth century some of its appearance as an ominous, troubled age in Insular sources? It was a time of sometimes desperate want and epidemic illness, sometimes arising together. Smallpox (*bolgach*) arose in Ireland in the 740s. Heavy snows in 748 resulted in predictable hardships, when 'the cattle were nearly destroyed in the whole of Ireland'.[60] The scenes were played out again in and after the Bad Winter with its accompanying wave of dysentery. Neither 'bloody flux' nor smallpox had yet abated when, in the summer of 777, the weather was so dismal that one Irish chronicler spoke of 'full winter in the summer'.[61] The intelligentsia of the age could not focus on global warming as the explanation of their ills, and focused on heaven for answers instead. But what was God trying to say?

For some, the vessels bearing vikings to Britain and Ireland a few years later were a part of God's message to the Insular world. They would have had a field day with the combined threats of climate change and international terrorism! In the sixth century, Gildas had envisioned the Picts and the Gaels as relentless sea-raiders who eventually made settlements in

---

[58] Clancy and Márkus, *Iona*, 17.
[59] *AU* 794.7.
[60] *AU* 742.9, 743.11, 748.3; *AT* 743.12, 748.3.
[61] *AU* 777.4, 777.9, 778.3, 779.3, 779.7. One wonders whether volcanic activity in Iceland may explain some of the climatic extremes experienced by Britain and Ireland in these decades.

northern Britain. If the Scandinavian incomers of the Viking Age could have read *De excidio Britanniae*, they might have found a certain poetic justice in their own raiding and eventual settlement.

Did the Early Historic Picts and Gaels retain any of the maritime savvy that Gildas envisaged in their ancestors? Living in an island community, Adomnán predictably has much to say about sailors and sea voyages. The Irish chronicles record shipwrecks which claimed the lives of Hebridean monks. It has been mentioned already that the great promontory fort at Burghead, probably the chief royal stronghold of the Verturian kings, was accessible by sea to large numbers of ships at a time. In 729, according to the *Annals of Tigernach*, 150 Pictish vessels were wrecked at Ros Cuissine, surely Troup Head on the Banffshire coast, midway between Banff and Fraserburgh. There was a Pictish coastal promontory fort here at Cullykhan, possibly occupied in 729. Only four kilometres inland from Troup Head, Cushnie probably preserves the Pictish British name of the district and its headland (*ros*).[62]

Such stray information provides an impression of busy Pictish and Hebridean sea-lanes in the eighth century, suggesting that 'sea-kings' were not confined to Argyll. The Bernician centre at Bamburgh was ideally situated for harbouring many vessels, the sea having retreated in recent centuries. The same was true of the important strongholds at Dunaverty and Dunollie in Argyll – and at Little Dunagoil in Bute – as well as the British citadel at Clyde Rock, and Iudeu in the midst (*in medio*) of the Firth of Forth, wherever it was. A putative promontory fort on the site of St Andrews Castle could be added to this list. Few princes across Early Historic northern Britain can have been strangers to journeys by sea in times of war or peace.

In 681 Bridei son of Beli led a devastating attack on Orkney, presumably a sea-borne operation in most respects. There is earlier evidence of sea-raiding and sea-borne campaigning, which must have been an unpleasant fact of life for most coastal communities in this period. One example in a season of trouble obliterated a (possibly Columban) monastic community on Eigg in the late spring of 619, apparently led by Donnán, one of Scotland's few historical martyrs.[63] Adomnán refers to raiding several times, even implicating a segment of Cenél nGabráin in sea-borne violence that included the 'persecution' of churches.[64] The

---

[62] *AT* 729.2. Watson, *Celtic Place-Names*, 507, interprets Cushnie, inland from Troup Head, as *cuisne*, frost. See also Anderson, *Early Sources*, vol. 1, 226.

[63] *AU* 617.1; *AT* 617.1; *CS* 617.1; *AI* 619.2.

[64] Adomnán, *V. s. Columbae*, ii.22.

early medieval island community at Inchmarnock has added its voice on the subject, in the form of the striking image of a raider etched on a slate – the so-called Hostage Stone. Sea-borne murder and mayhem, including the plundering of churches and women, was nothing new in the Hebrides and the Northern Isles, then, when its first Scandinavian practitioners arrived in the 790s.

The martyrs of Eigg (619)

St Donnán of Eigg was the focus of one of Atlantic Scotland's most significant native cults. The Chronicle of Ireland seems to have recorded the following: 'the burning (*combustio*) of Donnán of Eigg on 17 April with 150 martyrs (*cum .cl. martiribus*), and the devastation (*uastatio*) of Tory Island, and the burning (*loscadh*) of Connor'.[65] The recording of the date (17 April), like the use of the word *martires*, is suggestive of the early culting of Donnán and his community at Iona. It seems a good bet that their martyrdom had particular significance in that monastery, either because they had Ionan connections, or because of Iona's own anxieties about the possibility of being targeted by raiders. It is intriguing that, by the twelfth century, 'all the martyrs of the world' were commemorated on 17 April in Ireland.[66]

The attack on Eigg in 619 is associated in the chronicles with attacks on Tory Island and Antrim, suggesting that the Hebrides and the north coast of Ireland were afflicted by some great sea-borne conflagration. Conventional assumptions that the killers were pagans have taken too little account of *Vita Columbae*, where Adomnán describes Columba's excommunication of a band of Christians, 'persecutors of churches', led by descendants of Gabrán, whose operations extended north of Mull, and included sacking farms and attempting to kill Columba himself.[67] The actual events of 619 are utterly lost to hagiography. Instead, Scottish hagiographers produced variations on an admirably typical martyrdom tale: the foundation of Donnán's monastery offended a noblewoman; she persuaded local robbers to eradicate it; finding the monks at prayer in the oratory, the robbers were unable to kill them;

---

[65] *AU* 617.1 has in the primary hand *combustio martirum Ega*; this is glossed *combustio Donnain Ega hi .xu. kl. Mai cum .cl. martiribus* by hand H¹, reproducing exactly *AT* 617.1 and *CS* 617.1. *AI* 619.2 has *orguin Donnáin Ega hi .xu. Kl. Mai.*

[66] *Fél. Óengusso*, 114. The actual text of *Fél. Óengusso* at 17 April (*xv. cal. Maii*) reads the feast of Peter the Deacon, who advanced to victorious martyrdom, [and?] with his followers, a fair assembly, Donnán of chilly Eigg'.

[67] Adomnán, *V. s. Columbae*, ii.22, ii.24.

The martyrs of Eigg (619) (*continued*)

and Donnán, seeking martyrdom, willingly brought his community into the refectory where the deed could be done.[68]

The record of Donnán's death implies that the community of Eigg had 150 members in 619. If that number is reliable, it provides a basis for thinking about the size of the Iona community in our period. The record is also remarkable for being the only instance of the term *martir* in the Irish chronicles in the period 400–800, apart from the record of the martyrdom of the obscure Conall son of Moudan 'crowned with martyrdom (*martirio coronatus*)' in 727.[69] The chronicles occasionally record the killings of others whom we know were regarded (by Bede, for example) as martyrs, but it seems that they were not culted as *martires* at Iona.[70]

Adomnán's descriptions of voyages made by a prospective anchorite, Cormac ua Liatháin, are particularly important. One of these brings him to Orkney, some 400 kilometres from Iona. A voyage of the same distance eastwards from Orkney – a very different prospect – would take a vessel almost the whole way to Norway. Another voyage takes Cormac fourteen days' journey north of Iona into odd seas.[71] That such voyages could be envisioned is important, whether or not Cormac ever made them. Given heavy sea-traffic about the northern shores of Scotland, and stories of long voyages related by Adomnán, it is scarcely credible that Pictish and Gaelic sailors (and sea-raiders?) were unaware of Scandinavia before the Viking Age – and vice versa.

The advent of Norse raiding in the Northern Isles and the Hebrides (and beyond) marks a moment when Scandinavians began dominating the northern sea-lanes. Did they also create these lanes? Scandinavians may have found ways instead of taking control of an existing network of maritime relationships of warfare and exchange (including pillage and tribute-taking) which spanned the zone they came to dominate after 800. Intruding themselves into existing systems was their general way during the Viking Age. It can accordingly be argued that it was taking over the

---

[68] *Book of Leinster*, 1688 (ll. 51821–35); Anderson, *Early Sources*, 143–4. There are other versions of the story that differ little from it; for discussion, see Anderson, *Early Sources*, 144.

[69] *AU* 727.4.

[70] *AU* 806.8 makes no reference to *martires* despite referring to a massacre on Iona; however, the killing of Blathmac son of Fland is called a *martre* (*AU* 825.17; *CS* 825.9).

[71] Adomnán, *V. s. Columbae*, ii.42.

northern sea-lanes, rather than settlement, that drove Scandinavian activity in the Insular world for more than a generation after the onset of viking attacks.[72]

Orkney was 'annihilated' (*deletae sunt*) in 681, and the scene of further but obscure fighting in 709 or 710. In the intervening period, *Vita Columbae* placed a petty Orcadian king (*regulus*) at the sixth-century Verturian court, possibly inspired more by Adomnán's own experiences than by history.[73] Brutal Verturian assaults on communities in the north of Atlantic Scotland, aimed at subduing leaders and ensuring a steady flow of tribute, may not have been rare in the sixth and seventh centuries. Did the growing power of the Verturian kings after 671 tighten the noose still further around Orkney and its hinterland? If so, did such interference in this crucial kingdom create a situation that allowed Norse elements at its periphery to grab the upper hand in 'the Shetland corridor' by 800?

The matter may repay detailed research. Metalworking craftsmen in northern Britain had access to amber for inlays, evidenced by brooches unearthed in Ayrshire, Argyll, Perthshire and Stirlingshire. Alas, access to Baltic amber hardly proves direct contact with the Baltic. Similarly, the timber-laced fortification technique common among Pictish strongholds, unknown as yet from Atlantic contexts, was practised in Scandinavia. Yet it was also known elsewhere in temperate Europe, and cannot prove cultural interaction across the North Sea prior to the Viking Age.[74]

In 745, and again in 765, the community of Iona observed 'a horrible and wondrous sign in the stars at night'.[75] What can this refer to? Other portentous things seen in the sky in these decades included dragons (*dracones*) in 746, and in 749, most bizarrely of all, 'ships were seen in the air with their men over Clonmacnoise'.[76] Dragons and ships famously come together in the shape of Scandinavian long-ships. These 'portents' may have been conveniently recalled to mind after the first viking raids. It does seem, none the less, that the extraordinary weather of the 760s and 770s, and the famine and sickness arising from it, were being interpreted in theological terms by Insular thinkers.

Gildas interpreted plague as a divine warning that the sixth-century Britons should leave off their sins and return to God. Perhaps the Insular Churches were as nervous about the Bad Winter and the miserable years afterwards. The *Chronicle of 802* speaks of *poena*, punishment, in

---

[72] Woolf, *From Pictland to Alba*, 287–8.
[73] Adomnán, *V. s. Columbae*, ii.42.
[74] Ralston, *The Hill-Forts of Pictland*, 18–9.
[75] *AU* 745.1, 765.1; *AT* 745.1, 765.1.
[76] *AU* 746.2, 749.9; *AT* 746.3, 748.13.

reference to this event. The reformation of British Easter observances in 768 may not have been unrelated to fears of divine punishment. In 786, someone organised 'a great penance through all Ireland', clearly associated by its chronicler with the ominous events of the times.[77] The Synod of Finchale was convened in Northumbria a year later, and the presence of the papal legation may have soothed anxieties akin to those leading to the Great Penance of the Irish. Three and a half centuries earlier in Britain, according to Gildas, the gathering storm of sickness had been followed by a cloudburst, in the shape of shiploads of men borne over the North Sea. Towards the end of the eighth century another storm like it was gathering. The Great Penance had not been great enough. At Lindisfarne in 793, and at Iona in 795, the clouds burst and a hard rain fell.

---

[77] *AU* 786.3.

CHAPTER 13

Regime-craft in Early Historic Northern Britain

A mong historians, the last chapter in the story of Iron Age Scotland – its transformation into medieval Scotland – has commonly been regarded as a beginning. This book's position in its series is proof enough of that. This beginning is customarily dominated by Dál Riata – a custom rooted ultimately in nineteenth-century notions that Scottish history was the history of 'the Scottish race'. Survival rates of textual evidence, and the power of historical hindsight pertaining to Cinaed son of Alpín, have also influenced customary approaches. Models have included a Pictland little more than a plaything of Northumbrians, Alt Clut Britons and Dalriadan Gaels, or a Pictland that largely rejected Christianity, literacy and learning. After all, hindsight can encourage the nasty habit of making the eclipse of the Picts and the triumph of the Gaels seem inevitable, with causes becoming obvious in our period.

The foregoing chapters have taken a different view. The central theme of Scottish history in the Roman Iron Age and the Early Historic centuries, taken together, has been regarded as the forging of new peoples and nations, alongside the waning of what we have been calling 'fully civil' society and the replacement of 'farmer republics' by kings and kingdoms. The second of these themes is the focus of this final chapter of the book. As a result of the efforts of seven hegemons over 127 years – three Aeðilfrithings, three Waerteras and a Mearns man – the story has been dominated not by Dál Riata, but by the Northumbrian and Pictish kingdoms and peoples. The innovation will rankle those who would exclude the Northumbrians for their ethnic Englishness. It would certainly not have pleased, either, the commentator who wrote in 1927 that, 'for a people who played no very great part in the history of Europe, the Picts might very well be thought to have already received their due share of attention'.[1] Admittedly placing the Picts, from Caledonia to Pictland, at the heart of Scotland's story presupposes value in institutional, political and military history. The particular attentions of economic, legal and social historians are unlikely to be drawn to the Pictish achievement without a great deal more archaeological spade-work. The present writer looks forward to the day when such subjects can be done justice alongside those under examination in this book.

In broad terms the 'achievement' represented by Scotland's Early Historic regimes was, to quote one commentator, 'that overlordship [of] a far flung collection of people could become a reality . . . however nominal that authority might actually be in practice'.[2] The great hegemons of the seventh and eighth centuries dared to dream of such empires, perhaps, because of the achievements of earlier 'high lords of princes' like Urbgen, Aeðilfrith and Áedán, and no doubt others stretching back into the Roman Iron Age. Although not on the same order of magnitude, the achievement of the kings of Dál Riata in this vein of course deserves honourable mention. No doubt the kings of Alt Clut would deserve it too, if we knew more about their achievement. The greater regimes established in our period were a far cry from bureaucratic, highly centralised monarchy. They seem to have consisted primarily of unions of core territories – Mag Gergind, Atholl and Fortriu in Pictavia; Bernicia, Deira and the Solway basin in Northumbria; the Lorn and Clyde basins in Dál Riata and Alt Clut. In the margins any number of small, self-governing areas can have persisted, held in varying degrees of subjection, central places to their inhabitants, no doubt, but all but unnoticed in surviving texts. Some may have been preserves of Iron Age life, largely unaffected by the key social forces examined in this book, including Christianity. Some may be detectable through careful specialist study of material culture and place-names.

Yet the peoples of eighth-century northern Britain had come a long way from the days of Argentocoxos and his Flavian forebears. What the Picts achieved in the century after the battle of Dún Nechtain may be compared to the Mercian achievement after the complementary battle of the Trent six years before.[3] Established over roughly the same span of time, the polyethnic Mercian and Pictavian hegemonies were both eclipsed in the course of the ninth century. This parallel can be pushed further. The survival rate of Mercian texts is acutely poor relative to

---

[1] Fraser, 'The Question of the Picts', 172.
[2] Foster, 'Before Alba', 6.
[3] A point made by Woolf, 'Onuist', 36.

Northumbria and Wessex.[4] The usual suspects in the disappearance of Pictish texts include Protestant vandals and agents of Edward I. The case is strong that, in fact, 'the Pictish lacuna' had become a fact some time before even the Great Cause of the 1290s.[5] It might even be regarded as inevitable in an age predating the enduring archival practices of the central Middle Ages and later. Yet throughout this study we have seen that Pictish voices, however muffled, are not altogether silent – not least because Bede and Adomnán read and used Pictish texts.

SUPPORTING THE REGIME: HOUSES AND HIDES

How did great regimes actually 'work' in the seventh and eighth centuries? Important evidence is provided by the survey of Argyll, 'mixed up with' seventh-century genealogical material, recorded in *Míniugud senchasa fher nAlban*. As it stands, the survey is notoriously uneven in how it goes about defining Argyll peoples and their military obligations for service abroad. It begins with Islay, breaking the island down into a number of households (*tige*, literally 'houses') connected with particular place-names, and others pertaining explicitly to a particular kindred, Cenél nÓengusso, who are to provide an expeditionary force for sea-voyaging.[6] Such household units were fundamental to the social structures of all the Insular Early Historic peoples, and also to the administrative structures of their great regimes.

The *tech* seems to have been a special kind of household, however, for *Míniugud senchasa fher nAlban* distinguishes it from the actual farmstead (*treb*). It is best understood as broadly similar to the Anglo-Saxon hide (*hīd*), a 'household' unit known to Bede (*familia*) and Stephen (usually *mansio*), and distinct from the farmstead (*tūn*). Bede, like *Míniugud senchasa fher nAlban*, was aware of instances where entire kingdoms had been evaluated as consisting of a number of hides, as well as similar evaluations of estates and islands. The so-called *Tribal Hidage* records such an evaluation of the great kingdom of the Mercians and its satellites in the English midlands. The origins of the household unit were probably very ancient, and in early times it may have consisted simply of the nuclear family, the fundamental building-block of the kindred.

---

[4] Brooks, 'The Formation of the Mercian Kingdom', 159; Woolf, 'The Verturian Hegemony', 106, 111.

[5] Hughes, 'Writings of Early Scotland', 1–8, 15–20.

[6] *Mín. sench. fher nAlban*, §§ 32–4.

By the early eighth century, however, when Stephen could refer to the hide as a *tributarius*, a tributary unit, the Northumbrian hide (like the West Saxon one) had become a land unit, and a special one at that. In fact, it had probably become a particular area measurement which by then was recognised by law as 'the property qualification of a normal freeman'. What that qualification may have been is difficult to establish, but by Insular analogy it is likely to have been on the order of the medieval Scots 'ploughgate' of 104 acres, the notional area that could be ploughed annually by a full team of eight oxen.[7]

To judge from medieval evidence, the equivalent Pictish term for the hide-like household unit was probably taken into Scots as *davoch*, though *pett* seems to have been the favoured term for coining place-names.[8] The *pit-* place-names of Scotland are attached to sites almost exclusively boasting the best classes of soil in the northern and southern Pictish zones, usually inland from coastal areas, with drainage and slope favourable to cultivation.[9] Possession of such a unit of land was probably emblematic of free status. Possession of a full team of oxen capable of keeping the hide-like unit under cultivation was a linked emblem. Such notions are likely to have been much older than our period, since agriculture itself is unlikely to have experienced much change across the centuries that concern us in this book.

Individual farmsteads across the lowlands were seemingly fairly isolated little communities scattered across the country, or else members of similarly isolated clusters, where oats and (especially) barley predominated in fields cultivated by the 'cord-rig' method, producing narrower rigs than the medieval 'rig-and-furrow' method. The same cereals were cultivated in Argyll, where suitable land was abundant, but in much smaller patches than in the lowlands.[10] On the farmstead of a normal freeman and his wife, much of the necessary labour with hoe, spade and plough was probably done by slaves, or else by semi-free dependants with small farms of their own. Cultivation could be undertaken successfully on land that to modern eyes appears non-viable, the standard for success being self-sufficiency, rather than the production of surpluses for sale.

---

[7] The essential study is Charles-Edwards, 'Kinship, Status and the Origins of the Hide'; see also Campbell, *The Anglo-Saxons*, 58; Barrow, *Kingship and Unity*, 6, 19–20.

[8] Barrow, *Kingship and Unity*, 18; Whittington, 'Placenames and the Settlement Pattern', 105. As it stands the corpus of *pit-* place-names reflects a Gaelic-speaking milieu.

[9] Whittington, 'Placenames and the Settlement Pattern', 100–2.

[10] Harding, *The Iron Age in Northern Britain*, 11, 75–7, 103; Campbell, *Saints and Sea-Kings*, 22–3; Alcock, *Kings and Warriors*, 111.

House construction varied across both time and space in northern Britain in this period, with certain buildings possibly acting as byre-houses, with human occupation on a mezzanine floor above the live-stock. The Iron Age crannog or artificial island remained a feature of Early Historic architecture in some areas. Cattle were all-important, providing beef, dairy products, hides, bone and horn, as well as manure and, of course, heavy labour. On the whole, breeds seem to have been smaller than those reared in Scotland today. Swine, sheep and goats began to be raised domestically in the Neolithic epoch, but the last two are relatively scarce outwith what became the lowlands of Pictavia and Northumbria. By the earlier Bronze Age 'transhumance' had become a feature of stock-rearing, involving the movement of herds and flocks back and forth between rough summer pastures on hills or unploughable moors, and winter pastures on newly harvested hay- and corn-fields.

Comparatively sophisticated agricultural techniques and technologies in our period did not, however, signal an end to the customary exploitation of the natural environment extending back to Mesolithic bushcraft, revolving around hunting, fishing and gathering. Shellfish had long been a staple of coastal diets. Yet the striking hunting scenes depicted on Pictish monumental sculpture, where dogs and mounted men pursue red or roe deer, suggest that the hunt, in certain areas at least, may already have become something of an elite prerogative by the end of our period – a feature of medieval society. One wonders whether certain foreshores also become the preserves of the upper echelons of society, especially in Atlantic Scotland.

Free rights and privileges pertaining to land, movable property and nature's bounty had to be protected vigorously, and bearing arms, too, was probably emblematic of free status in the societies of northern Britain in our period. It is thus no coincidence that the household unit was intimately linked with military obligations everywhere in the early medieval West. Unfortunately, numerals were notoriously prone to mis-copying by scribes, but *Míniugud senchasa fher nAlban* (if its survey's numbers are remotely accurate) seems to preserve the theory that the household unit represented one warrior who might be called to arms. In practice, it was standard for later Anglo-Saxon kings and Frankish emperors to require a warrior's service for every five hide-like units, a much lighter burden of obligation than *Míniugud senchasa fher nAlban* envisions for Atlantic Scotland. Was Argyll 'on a permanent war footing' five times more intensive than the Frankish Empire? It seems much more likely that, in comparing the *Míniugud senchasa fher nAlban* survey with Anglo-Saxon and Frankish legal tracts, we are simply not comparing like with like.[11]

The survey assigns Cenél nGabráin 560 *tige*, Cenél nÓengusso 430, and Cenél Loairn 420.[12] By way of comparison, Bede assessed the Isle of Man at about 300 hides, a pool of normal freemen smaller than any of the Argyll kindreds, and the Isle of Thanet in Kent at 600, roughly on a par with Cenél nGabráin.[13] The whole 'three thirds of Dál Riata' emerge collectively as some fifty per cent more substantial than the inhabitants of Anglesey (960 hides), and marginally more than those of the Isle of Wight (1,200 hides), but only twenty per cent as substantial as the fertile kingdom of the South Saxons.[14] None of this seems far-fetched, considering the realities of terrain and climate. Had they appeared collectively as one of the peoples evaluated by the *Tribal Hidage*, the Argyll *cenéla* would have been just five per cent as substantial as Mercia itself, each *cenél* being a little more substantial than the smallest satellite peoples enumerated (300 hides each). Although it seems unlikely that Pictavia consisted of as many household units as Mercia, these ratios underline the point that the Argyll, Pictish and Northumbrian regimes were playing in different leagues in the power sweepstakes of Early Historic Britain.

By the middle of the seventh century, powerful men like Oswy were granting hides to monasteries, suggesting that the household unit was already conceivable by then, as it was by Stephen, as a *tributarius*, a unit of obligation, military or otherwise.[15] This development implies that, as lordly and royal status and prerogatives bedded down among the peoples of northern Britain, they shrewdly attached obligations to the rights and emblems of free status. Stated simply, obligations were attached to conditions of life – such things as access to resources and the bearing of arms – that people had, from time immemorial, been keen to seek and flaunt out of self interest. In the case of hides granted to monasteries or to individuals, the benefactor surely expected services in return for such grants, obligations that could presumably vary according to the benefactor's whim. Yet at all times there must also have been those who owed their possession of their hide or *tech* to normal inheritance, co-existing alongside those who enjoyed free status through the largesse of a benefactor.

[11] Aitchison, *The Picts and Scots at War*, 17–18, 21; see also Halsall, *Warfare and Society*, 93, 105.
[12] *Mín. sench. fher nAlban*, §§ 50–2.
[13] Bede, *Hist. eccl.*, ii.9; i.25.
[14] Bede, *Hist. eccl.*, ii.9; iv.16.
[15] John, *Land Tenure*, 30–1; Loyn, *The Governance of Anglo-Saxon England*, 36–8.

Although the genealogical matter in *Míniugud senchasa fher nAlban* appears to be securely seventh century in date, the survey of Argyll in this text is probably later. Its handling of the old Corcu Réti kingdom as a single unit associated solely with Cenél nGabráin is one hint that the survey post-dates *Cethri prímchenéla Dáil Riata*, composed after 706. Similarly, although sea-raiding was common in Atlantic Scotland throughout our period, explicit references to the fleets of Dál Riata (*classis Dál Riata*) and Fortriu (*loingius a Fortreanoibh*) – and for that matter to naval battles in Atlantic Scotland (a *bellum maritimum*) – are confined to the first third of the eighth century. It is striking that the survey takes detailed note of the internal politics of only one of the Argyll kindreds – Cenél Loairn – subdivided into their 'three thirds', with one-seventh of their expeditionary force 'from client peoples' (*airgialla*).[16] The text here may mean the Airgialla, a collection of small kingdoms south-west of Lough Neagh in northern Ireland. In either case, it is striking that a chronicle records of the battle of Ros Foichnae in 727, in which Cenél Loairn fought against Cenél nGabráin, that 'some *airgialla* fell' (*quidam ceciderunt dendibh Airgiallaib*).[17] Here again, the mention of *airgialla* in the *Míniugud senchasa fher nAlban* survey, like its particular interest in Cenél Loairn, point to the first third of the eighth century as the likeliest period of composition.

The previous chapters have argued for Verturian Pictish involvement in Argyll affairs for a generation or more prior to the *potestas* of Onuist son of Vurguist being extended across the whole district in the 730s. Does the *Míniugud senchasa fher nAlban* survey of Argyll represent a Pictish undertaking from this era of the 'smiting' of Dál Riata? Certainly the survey is remarkably even-handed: if it represented an enterprise undertaken by a Cenél Loairn or Cenél nGabráin king, we might have expected something similar to the *Tribal Hidage*'s assessment of the West Saxons at the gross figure of 100,000, thought to reflect a punitive burden imposed by conquering Mercians. The possibility that Onuist commissioned an assessment of Argyll and its military capacity before or after 741 therefore deserves consideration. After all, the compulsion of conquered peoples to provide the conqueror with military service was quite common in late Antiquity and the early Middle Ages.

Islay is called a *cét treb*, a 100-farm unit, in *Míniugud senchasa fher nAlban*, a concept also found in Wales (the *cantref*) and England, the Anglo-Saxon 'hundred' being a coherent block of farmsteads lumped

---

[16] *Mín. sench. fher nAlban*, §§ 39–48.
[17] *AU* 727.3.

together for (eventually) taxation, judicial and military recruitment purposes.[18] The concept implies the existence of a relatively central, if rudimentary, apparatus for defining such blocks and collecting renders and tribute from them, exploited by kings like Oswy, Selbach and Onuist to support their regimes, as well as to promulgate legal and other decisions, propaganda and ecclesiastical reform.

As a rule, Early Historic kings took renders from their own home districts – hospitality and military service from normal freemen and labour from others – rather than cattle-tribute, marking them as core territories with favoured status.[19] They would have spent most of their time in these core territories, frequenting the monasteries and the feasting halls of the mighty and providing elites and normal freemen with as much personal access as possible. No doubt lesser potentates behaved in a similar way at more regional and local levels. Personal visits beyond the core territories would have been noticeably infrequent. Crossing the Tees in Northumbria, and perhaps the Mounth or Drumalban in Pictavia, could be a risky prospect for a king and probably required careful planning. Other parts of his dominions were probably visited only in arms, emblematic of their subjugated status, signified also by regular payments of tribute in cattle.[20] In all cases, some rough knowledge of the number of farms and hide-like household units in a district would surely have been maintained, informing royal expectations of renders or tribute.

By the eighth century Northumbrian kings had established royal estates across their realm, seemingly with dependent satellite settlements where hide-holding tenants provided renders to support the occupant of the estate. Depending on variable circumstances, kings might have placed their kin in these estates, giving them a stake in the smooth operation of the socio-economic system – or they might have placed estates in the hands of local potentates for similar reasons. Perhaps Pictish, Dalriadan and Alt Clut kings too established royal estates. The satellite settlements were probably geared primarily towards fuelling the economies of prestige and kinship, stocking and re-stocking the feasting hall of the royal estate where the king or his deputy might hold court, dispense patronage and hospitality, or otherwise exert royal power and authority.[21]

---

[18] *Min. sench. fher nAlban*, § 32; Charles-Edwards, 'Kinship, Status and the Origins of the Hide', 18; Loyn, *The Governance of Anglo-Saxon England*, 140–1.

[19] Brooks, 'The Formation of the Mercian Kingdom', 159.

[20] Charles-Edwards, 'Early Medieval Kingships', 31–2.

[21] Charles-Edwards, 'Early Medieval Kingships', 28–33; Pelteret, *Slavery*, 35–7; Barrow, *Kingship and Unity*, 7–8; Woolf, 'Apartheid', 120–2. See also Woolf, *From Pictland to Alba*, 26.

It seems that it was usual to find a church attached to Anglo-Saxon royal estates.[22] Unlike Continental churches, Northumbrian ones seem largely to have been successful in avoiding the usual obligation to provide benefactors with military service (in the person of ecclesiastical tenants) in return for land grants. Bede famously complained to Ecgberct of York that Northumbrians were founding monasteries in order to obtain such an exemption.[23] One wonders to what extent the 100-farm unit already mentioned may have been exploited by the Church as a convenient unit of pastoral care in the age before the parish.

For some time it has been appreciated that the survey in *Míniugud senchasa fher nAlban* foreshadows to some extent the system of assessment, renders and taxation that had developed in Alba by the eleventh century, the details of which belong to another study. It has remained a matter of controversy whether this correspondence denotes the imposition of a Dalriadan system on the Picts, or else the legacy of a Pictish system developed during our period. In fact, notions of household units linked with free status, smaller farmsteads linked with dependent status, and blocks of farmsteads lumped together for administrative convenience seem to have been common to all Insular Early Historic societies. However it is explained, there can be little doubt that eleventh- and twelfth-century Alba, like eleventh-century England, retained a legacy of an administrative system that was bedding down during the lifetime of Bede.[24] The fundamental building-block of that system – the household unit emblematic of free status – was however much older, with prehistoric origins far earlier than the beginning of our period. Can prehistoric settlement archaeology detect those origins?

RUNNING THE REGIME

There is a whiff of bureaucracy about the survey in *Míniugud senchasa fher nAlban*. In 697, Bridei son of Der-Ilei was the sole Pictish secular guarantor of *Lex innocentium*. His brother, c. 715, enforced church reform on his personal authority. These are indications that the power enjoyed by the *reges Pictorum* was reminiscent of Anglo-Saxon, rather than Irish models. Like English kings, Pictish ones may have enjoyed considerable capacity to alienate land through grants to followers and churches. Like

---

[22] Campbell, *Anglo-Saxons*, 58–61.

[23] Bede, *Ep. ad Ecgbertum*, § 11; McClure and Collins, *Bede*, 350–1 (trans.); see also Halsall, *Warfare and Society*, 103.

[24] For a similar view, see Anderson, 'Dalriada', 126.

Northumbrian kings, they may have issued charters that do not survive, though administrative literacy is hardly necessary. When Adomnán wrote of seals on Mull *nostri iuris*, 'ours by right', did he have a document to back up that claim?[25] The kings of Pictavia did not mint coins like the *sceattas* struck at York as early as the reign of Aldfrith, or the impressive regal coinage of Eadberct. This non-adoption of coinage in Pictavia is remarkable, and may reflect a persistence of Iron Age economics, for in that epoch too coins were known but not produced in northern Britain. If stone discs and silver plaques bearing incised symbols had been inspired in Pictland by the striking of coins elsewhere, they would surely be more common than they are.[26]

The remarkable events in Argyll after 734 are eloquent testimony to the authority Onuist believed was his due. How did such authority function? He seems to have relied on the efforts of local potentates to execute his wishes. His brother and son led Pictish armies. It was probably common for Early Historic kings to rely on such deputies in exerting *potestas* outwith their home region. Oswy made use of his nephews and sons in this way in Deira and southern Pictland.

The creation and maintenance of such lieutenants was the key to running an Early Historic regime – men who could personify the king's presence as recognised bearers of his authority.[27] Bede and Stephen make many references to such lieutenants in Northumbria. They speak in particular of *praefecti*. Late Antique 'prefects' were governors of cities or districts, or military commanders (or both). Accordingly one *praefectus* in *Vita Wilfrithi*, who was 'second in rank to the king', like other *praefecti* led men to war.[28] Being second in rank to the king might have been formalised later in the eighth century by application of the title *patricius* to one of these lieutenants; 'leading courtier' has been the suggested translation in this book.[29] The translation of *praefectus* was *gerefa* in northern England (whence modern 'reeve'; Scots 'grieve'), the overseer of a district. In Pictish British the equivalent term was apparently *maer*, as it was in both Welsh and Gaelic, a borrowing of the same Latin term (*maior*) which denoted the chief official (literally 'greater man') of the Merovingian

---

[25] Adomnán, *V. s. Columbae*, i.41. See also Alcock, *Kings and Warriors*, 48; Forsyth, 'Literacy in Pictland', 42–3. Bede, *Ep. ad Ecgbertum*, § 12; McClure and Collins, *Bede*, 351 (trans.).

[26] *pace* Henderson and Henderson, *The Art of the Picts*, 88. See also Harding, *The Iron Age in Northern Britain*, 24–5.

[27] Foster, 'Before Alba', 2, 4–5; Campbell, *Saints and Sea-Kings*, 20.

[28] Stephen, *V. s. Wilfrithi*, § 50; Loyn, *The Governance of Anglo-Saxon England*, 47–8.

[29] Rollason, *Northumbria*, 181–2.

royal household (*maior domus*), who incidentally could also bear the title *patricius*. The proof lies in the name of the Mearns (Gaelic *An Mhaoirne*), 'the stewartry', which is British, rather than Gaelic, in origin.[30] That the homeland of Onuist should have been *the* stewartry in Pictish times implies that this district maintained some kind of special relationship with royal authority. Does the place-name further imply dynastic continuity in the kingship of Pictavia from Onuist and his family until the kingdom's demise?

In the eighth century, Northumbrian reeves and Pictish maers were probably governors like the *praefecti* of the late Empire, whose jurisdiction emanated from a royal estate, or possibly a power centre like a hill-fort, and might in some cases have embraced a whole district. They were probably charged with maintaining the king's peace in their stewartry. This responsibility ought to have involved them in protecting people, places and events which had been guaranteed royal protection, and intervening in disputes as an arbitrator, discouraging blood-feud. Yet influence at this time is likely to have stemmed from status and reputation – derived in no small part from being the king's man – rather than from profound coercive powers characteristic of state government.

Reeves and maers probably maintained a circuit around the royal estates within their stewartry, occasionally enjoying aristocratic hospitality as proxies of the king and occasionally playing host in turn. Royal business was probably conducted at open-air assembly-places in key strategic or symbolic locations, including hill-forts. Place-names thought to contain the term *comdál*, a meeting, are common in (and almost entirely confined to) the northern and southern Pictish zones, like other terms thought to have borne an administrative meaning by the time that Gaelic was replacing Pictish British.[31] In many cases, such assembly-places were probably very ancient bastions of the ancient fully civil nature of society, securing control over their proceedings being a key aspect of the rise of kingship in northern Britain from the middle of the Roman Iron Age.

In twelfth-century Alba (and clearly for some time before that), in addition to maers, there were great regional stewards with the title *mormaer*. The most natural translation of this term, which is Gaelic as we have it, is 'sea-maer', though the less likely 'great-maer' would be an exact parallel of the Anglo-Saxon 'high-reeve' (*heahgerefa*). As in the case of

---

[30] Watson, *Celtic Place-names*, 110–11; see also Barrow, *Kingship and Unity*, 16. Welsh *maeroni*, 'stewardship', is much closer to *An Mhaoirne* than Irish *maoracht* or Scottish Gaelic *maorsachd*. The surname Mair probably derives from this official.

[31] Barrow, '*Popular Courts*', 3–12; Driscoll, 'Christian Monumental Sculpture', 239.

the Mearns, one particular sea-stewartry seems to have retained its name in the Scottish landscape, namely in Morvern (Gaelic *A' Mhorbhairn*) on the Firth of Lorn.[32] Intriguingly, this district can be connected with Cenél nEchdach, the great Lorn kindred that flourished alongside the sons of Der-Ilei but eventually fell under pressure from Onuist. Can it really be a coincidence that Onuist's home region and one linked with the Argyll kindred he ruined were respectively *the* stewartry and *the* sea-stewartry of the kingdom of Alba? Or is the name of Morvern further evidence that Onuist was a decisive actor in shaping the political landscape inherited by his Alpínid successors a century later? Was Pictish royal *potestas* in Lorn and the old Corcu Réti kingdom after the 'smiting' of Dál Riata placed in the hands of sea-maers with regional stewartries? Such ultimate origins of the mormaer would help to explain how a maritime title came in time to be borne by Alba's great regional stewards, linked with such decidedly non-maritime stewartries as Angus and Moray.

Royal power centres in different parts of northern Britain have featured in the foregoing narrative. Identifying Pictish ones is particularly problematic. The royal *munitio* located by Adomnán near Inverness – possibly at Craig Phadraig – was probably on the royal circuit of the Verturian kings *c.* 700. Royal iconography on Pictish sculpture at Kinneddar, outside Lossiemouth, suggests that the church there received considerable royal patronage, perhaps reflecting links with Burghead eleven kilometres away. A prime candidate is the oft-mentioned and strategic stronghold at Dunnottar, surely the principal seat of Mag Gergind and the starting point of Onuist's rise to power. Moncrieffe Hill and Dundurn at opposite ends of Strathearn are also prime candidates, the former possibly being the principal seat of the kingdom of Atholl by 728, not far from the later power centre of Forteviot. Were the kings of Atholl inaugurated at Scone, taking *Amra Choluimb Chille*'s title 'great king of the Tay'? Neither must we forget the stronghold at Clatchard Craig above Newburgh, six kilometers further down the Tay from Abernethy: possibly one of the foremost power centres south of the Mounth, distinguished by six ramparts, the site was utterly quarried away between 1950 and 1980 at the behest of the Ministry of Transport.[33] Further south still Stirling suggests itself, with

---

[32] I owe this suggestion to Dauvit Broun; see Watson, *Celtic Place-Names*, 122–3, for the background (but a different etymology).
[33] Close-Brooks *et al.*, 'Excavations at Clatchard Craig', 148–9; Carver, *Surviving in Symbols*, 32.

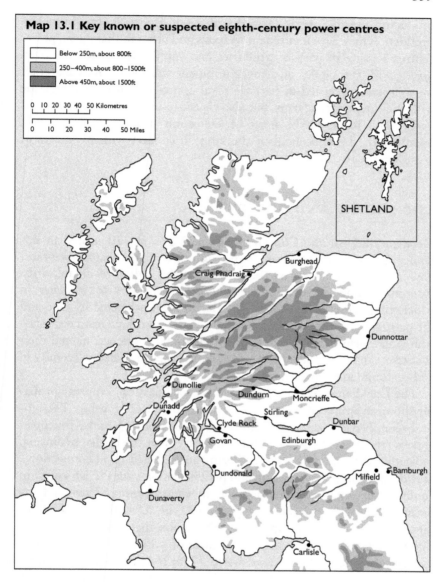

Map 13.1 Key known or suspected eighth-century power centres

the possibility that Clackmannan may have served as a royal inauguration site. A stronghold of our period has been identified on the Abbey Craig at Stirling, where the Victorian monument to William Wallace now stands.

Such power centres are likely also to have been hubs of such industrial activities as metalworking, boneworking and leatherworking, producing prestige items for redistribution, especially fine brooches. Production may have focused on weapons and other military gear, power centres serving in part as armouries and supply depots for the royal *cohors*, with stock-piles of arms, equipment and food.[34] Raw materials were probably accrued in part via royal estates out in the countryside with their dependent farms, but also via cattle-tribute from subject districts. The hands-on business of collection probably fell to select members of the household of the king, in concert with his maers or reeves on the royal estates.

THE REGIME AND THE CHURCH

Detailed study of the Church in our period is not attempted in this book.[35] What did it contribute to the running of Early Historic regimes? The clergy ought to have been enthusiastic about royal authority. Adomnán framed an idealised concept of kingship in *Vita Columbae*, in which kings were chosen by divine selection and protected by God and the patronage of saints. Ideal kings were also inaugurated in an ecclesiastical ritual, maintained a monopoly on legitimate violence, named their successors in life in consultation with churchmen and died peacefully in bed surrounded by loved ones.

The Davidian imagery of some Pictish ecclesiastical sculpture probably shows an appreciation at court for such a model of kingship. The biblical King David occurs on sculpture from St Andrews and Kinneddar, and also the Nigg cross-slab at the southern end of the Tarbat peninsula, indicating that the monastery at Portmahomack had royal connections. David was an imperial emblem, and his association with Pictish kingship confirms the imperial pretensions of the eighth-century kings of Picts outlined above.[36] Adomnán appreciated the Davidian possibilities inherent in Pictish kingship *c.* 700. The psalm that, according to *Vita Columbae*, Columba sang before the gates of a Pictish royal fortress is addressed explicitly to a king, exhorting him to 'gird your sword upon your side', and to 'ride forth victoriously in your majesty, on behalf of truth, humility and righteousness'. The psalmist also prayed that 'nations [might] fall beneath your feet' and might also 'praise you for ever and

---

[34] Nieke and Duncan, 'Dalriada', 13; Campbell, *Saints and Sea-Kings*, 25; Alcock, 'The Activities of Potentates', 25.

[35] I leave it for Clancy, *The Making of Scottish Christianity*.

[36] Charles-Edwards, 'The Continuation of Bede', 142–3.

ever', predicting that 'your sons will take the place of your fathers, and you will make them princes throughout the land'.[37] It was with Bridei son of Der-Ilei in mind that Adomnán placed this Davidian composition in the mouth of Columba, and in the ears of a ruler who shared the king's name. A generation later, Onuist was riding forth victoriously, that nations might fall beneath his feet.

There was a second king of Picts called Onuist son of Vurguist. One version of the Pictish king-list credits him with the foundation of St Andrews. Eighth-century records show this to be a mistake, for Cennrígmonaid, as St Andrews was known in Pictish times, was founded at least seventy years before the second Onuist became king. Túathalán, abbot of Cennrígmonaid, died in 747.[38] He need not have been its first or founding abbot, unless we place our reliance on the dubious twelfth-century foundation legend and identify the Mag Gergind king as *Hungus*. Cennrígmonaid may have been founded in the period of Ionan primacy instead, and the base of the ecclesiastical activity responsible for the *kil-* place-names of east Fife. Pictish sculpture from St Andrews includes the magnificent eighth-century 'sarcophagus' (actually a 'composite box-shrine') with its Davidian imagery, almost certainly a royal sepulchre. The sculptural corpus here is compelling evidence that the place was a key ecclesiastical centre in southern Pictavia by the end of the eighth century.

We do not know whether St Andrew was being culted at Cennrígmonaid as early as 747. There was an intriguing link between commemorations of St Peter and St Andrew in seventh-century Kent and Northumbria, two ecclesiastical provinces with strong Continental interlinkages. Both kingdoms were diphyletic – with two principal components – a church dedicated to St Peter standing in the senior ecclesiastical centre (Canterbury and York), and one dedicated to St Andrew in the junior episcopal seat in the other part of the realm (Rochester and Hexham). There are other examples of the pattern. Did Pictish ecclesiastical leaders seek to emulate it after the *correctio* of Naiton. The reformer built a new church dedicated to St Peter to mark this reformation – possibly at Rosemarkie, the probable episcopal seat of Curetán of Ross at the time of *Lex innocentium*. There was a medieval Petrine dedication there. A reasonable possibility thus emerges that a major church in southern Pictavia ought to have been dedicated to

---

[37] Adomnán, *V. s. Columbae*, i.37; Psalm 45 (*Vulg.* lxiv).

[38] *AU* 747.10; *AT* 747.11. For a discussion of the archaeology and layout of Cennrígmonaid, see Alcock, *Kings and Warriors*, 228–9.

St Andrew around this time to help identify it as the pre-eminent church south of the Mounth.[39]

Onuist was, at least, a southern king. The later of the two versions of the St Andrews foundation legend claims that three sons of *Hungus* donated Forteviot to St Andrew, in anxiety for their father's life while he was campaigning in Argyll, and their names – Éoganán (*Howonam*), Nechtan and Finnguine (*Phinguineghert*) – were certainly current among Alt Clut and Pictish royal dynasts in Onuist's period.[40] Whether or not plausible claims like this one, found in texts penned centuries after the fact, reflect reliable contemporary records involves scholars in problems with no easy solutions. It would be wonderful to be able to accept that a certain Finche was Onuist's wife as this text claims, for we know the name of no other Pictish queen.

If there were Andrean relics at Cennrígmonaid in the eighth century, they are likely to have come from Hexham, where Pictish interlinkages may be reflected in the spellings of Pictish names in the *Chronicle of 802*.[41] None the less, attention has been drawn to the fact that the Byzantine Roman emperor at Constantinople from 741 until 775 was the Iconoclast Constantine V. Pictish interest in the cult of St Andrew, patron saint of Constantinople, *c.* 747 could explain the appearance of the royal name Constantín in Pictavia in 789, as well as Byzantine and Coptic influences detected in Pictish and Ionan art.

Whether or not he built a new church at St Andrews, Onuist must have remained mindful of the state of the Pictish Church. After all, there was every likelihood that it would one day be his destination, as the Northumbrian Church accepted his Ecgwulfing colleagues Ceolwulf and Eadberct. The peripatetic movement of a royal court surely took the king to monasteries from time to time.[42] Like Oswy and Ecgfrith, the Verturian and Mag Gergind hegemons of eighth-century Pictavia would have selected particular churches within the realm – probably a mix of old and new – for special degrees of royal patronage. The eighth century probably marks a real high watermark for such patronage. It is likely that military and other pressures in the Viking Age resulted in significant shifts in patterns of patronage and endowment, including even the appropriation of Church lands.[43]

[39] Fraser, 'Rochester, Hexham and Cennrígmonaid'.
[40] Skene, *Chron. Picts and Scots*, 185.
[41] Woolf, 'Onuist', 37–8; *pace* Forsyth, 'Evidence of a Lost Pictish Source'.
[42] Charles-Edwards, 'Early Medieval Kingships', 28–9.
[43] Woolf, *From Pictland to Alba*, 316–20.

In Northumbria, small monastic estates were supported by the fruits of perhaps ten hides, while larger estates could reach as much as ten times that size, or even larger in rare cases. The estate of the monastery of Ely in East Anglia was 600 hides in size, dwarfing Ripon (thirty) and Whitby (ten) in Deiran Yorkshire.[44] Yet great opulence was on display at Ripon – Wilfrid's favourite monastery – while he was still in good royal graces. Churches clearly had other revenue streams than their dependent farms, including aristocratic and royal gifts, sometimes even originating in other realms. The fine monumental sculpture of Pictavia is our best surviving evidence that, by the middle decades of the eighth century, Pictish hegemons and lesser potentates were expending resources on church patronage. Bede famously reported that Naiton enlisted the help of Northumbrian builders to erect his new stone church dedicated to St Peter. Although Pictish ones have not survived, it was very probably the churches themselves, rather than the famous sculpture, that were the real objects of secular and ecclesiastical attention and investment in Early Historic times.[45]

The preferred medium for the execution of Pictish cross-slabs (and other monuments) was Old Red Sandstone, soft and susceptible to intricate carving. Access to it was probably privileged, with noble patrons also securing access to sculptors of some skill, apparently an offshoot of the same metalworking craft whose practitioners had a long history of elite patronage. It hardly takes a practised eye to notice that, in terms of opulence, the sculptors of seventh- and eighth-century Pictland were playing in quite a different league from the upper echelons of Frankish and Italian elites. The Italian legates Theophylact and George cannot have seen anything north of the Humber that the populations of Todi or Ostia would have thought magnificent. Within its own context, however, the monumental sculpture of northern Britain must have seemed quite splendid.

The sculptural evidence is by no means uncontroversial. Art-historical analysis of Pictish cross-slabs and sarcophagi, Argyll and Northumbrian high crosses and comparable sculpture in Clydesdale struggles to establish precise dating of individual pieces. Relative dating is more straightforward, as is identifying links with other media of expression in Insular art, like metalwork and manuscript illumination. Conventional dates tending to place Pictish sculpture mainly after our period are being

---

[44] Bede, *Hist. eccl.*, iii.24, iv.19, v.19.
[45] Driscoll, 'Political Discourse', 175; Henderson and Henderson, *The Art of the Picts*, 208–11; Fisher, *Early Medieval Sculpture*, 8–9.

challenged as art historians grow more convinced that sculpture did not lag much behind other media already in full flower at the end of the seventh century.

The distinctive Pictish cross-slabs consist of an often elaborate cross carved, usually in shallow relief, on one side of a dressed stone slab, usually accompanied by symbolic art and decoratively framed, with much the same look as certain 'carpet pages' in illuminated manuscripts. Two of the earlier surviving examples may be at Glamis on the Dean Water, which illustrate the form's decorative parallels with pan-Insular manuscript illumination and metalwork decoration – the Insular art style.[46] Metalworking may have been the proving ground upon which aspiring sculptors sought to catch a patron's eye. Various images, including ecclesiastical ones, may be carved on the back of a cross-slab, with similar accompaniments. The Glamis examples have rough hewn backs with simple incised carvings, features thought to support a relatively early date. Some sculptures bear inscriptions, and it has been argued that the enigmatic symbols, sported on so many examples, are inscriptions too.[47]

Here, as in the case of personal adornment and court poetry, patrons are likely to have taken a very active interest in what was conveyed in their names. It must have seemed to them that a cross-slab was a gift to posterity, and they are likely to have kept sculptors on a short leash. There is accordingly a conservative streak running through the form, including, of course, some continuity of skills and styles from the Roman Iron Age. Favoured images included hunting and martial scenes indicative of elite patronage, showing that Pictish aristocrats, like their peers elsewhere in Europe, regarded military equipment as the iconic symbol of their social station. They also included scenes from the life of David, indicative of royal patronage, and scenes from the lives of the Desert Fathers who popularised monasticism, indicative of monastic patronage. Representations of the Apostles are common, perhaps indicative of episcopal patronage.

A similar range of images occurs on the monumental sculpture of Atlantic Scotland, with some interesting differences. It is conventional to identify some techniques and aesthetics as 'Pictish', 'Irish' and so on, and it is clear that certain fashions became distinct to particular polities. The interlinkages in evidence across ethnic and political frontiers are

---

[46] Henderson and Henderson, *The Art of the Picts*, 35–7 (Glamis No. 2), 62, 70–1.

[47] For overviews of the inscriptions, see Forsyth, *Language in Pictland*, 31–6; Forsyth, 'Literacy in Pictland', 44–53, 55–6.

substantial, however. They speak of a highly mobile and adaptable class of craftsmen and artists, whose talents were employed by both secular elites and Churches in different parts of Britain and Ireland. The conventional notion of a great technical and artistic disjuncture, brought about by such reformations as those associated with the Synod of Whitby and Naiton's Council, has begun to give way as scholars recognise how similar and interlinked were Continental and Insular ('Celtic') Churches in the previous generations.

There is an association between the cross-slabs of Pictavia and the undressed standing symbol-stones. These latter monuments are most plausibly understood as markers of boundaries. The fact that some seem to have been set up at active cemeteries – which tended to be border phenomena too – works well with this idea.[48] The meaning of their incised symbols – each stone almost always bearing two plus a third very common one – is utterly lost, though there is no shortage of unprovable claims to have cracked the code. The symbol-stone phenomenon may have developed alongside new administrative ideas surrounding regime-craft. Some surviving examples probably stood in the landscape in our period. Four centuries later, they could still be used in charters as boundary markers.

Sculpture is our main evidence for Early Historic developments in the perceived needs of free, landed people for public and enduring forms of expression, in both rural and ecclesiastical spheres, affirming their relationships with the land and the Church.[49] The changes in outlook implied were not primarily religious in character, but socio-political. They arose from incentives to devote resources towards the erection of monuments and the endowment and enrichment of churches. They probably also speak of economic change, in the form of growing levels of elite revenue spent on such investment. They demonstrate, moreover, that church patronage could serve as a forum for ethnic expression, suggesting that the Church was actively engaged in encouraging such consciousness of difference.

The relationship between the churches and monasteries of Early Historic northern Britain and the aristocracy was thus something like the relationship between some modern universities and their wealthier alumni. Support and sustenance would have been offered with varying degrees of self-promotion, dutifulness and altruism, and with varying levels of expectation of reciprocal support and sustenance. We may seek

---

[48] Ashmore, 'Low Cairns', 352; Carver, *Surviving in Symbols*, 18–24; Henderson and Henderson, *The Art of the Picts*, 167–71.
[49] Driscoll, 'Political Discourse', 173–4.

to distinguish piety from self-promotion, but for Early Historic aristocrats and clergy, such distinctions were probably blurry and not at all
obvious. The mixture of ecclesiastical and secular iconography on the
cross-slabs is proof enough of that.

The kings whose careers have been sketched in this book struck balances between the violent necessities associated with maintaining and
extending their regimes, and the necessity to give succour to the
Church – an important element of regime-craft. The magnificent surviving collections of monumental sculpture at Meigle and St Vigeans, as
well as Iona and Govan, are rather later than our period. These particular monasteries may not have attracted top levels of patronage until the
Viking Age.

It seems that the eighth century marks the swan-song of the hill-fort
in northern Britain, after the revitalisation of the art of fortifying hill-
tops in the Roman Iron Age. As power-centres, hill-forts seem to have
given way in Pictavia to 'palaces' (*palacii*) some of which seem to have
been attached to major monasteries, possibly including sites now associated with rich sculptural remains. This shift in how royal – and perhaps
ecclesiastical – power was packaged and displayed marks a significant
social development. It helps to establish a logical terminus for the present
survey of societies in northern Britain which, before the eighth century,
retained plenty of echoes of their later Roman Iron Age past. The eighth
century is characterised by transitions that were incomplete in 789.

Northern Pictavia is much less liberally provided with surviving cross-
slabs than the southern Pictish zone. There are interesting links in the
sculptural evidence from Portmahomack and Kinneddar, suggesting that
they may have enjoyed the bulk of royal patronage to the relative impov-
erishment of other Verturian houses.[50] In the south, royal patronage was
perhaps more widely dispersed, though it is arresting that the Mearns is
something of a blank zone. As occurred in the Mercian hegemony in the
eighth century, Verturian and Mag Gergind hegemons may have made
their major ecclesiastical endowments in subject territories, rather than in
their heartlands.[51] Indeed, it is interesting that Lorn too is largely devoid
of extant monumental sculpture from this period. Iona, on the other
hand, retained robust patronage, despite the *correctio* of Naiton and the
'smiting' of Dál Riata. Some of that patronage was surely Pictish.

---

[50] See Henderson and Henderson, *The Art of the Picts*, 49, for the links.
[51] Woolf, 'The Verturian Hegemony', 110. The argument works even better once
Fortriu is recognised to lie in the north.

THE MANY BASKETS FOR IONA'S EGGS

It may have been a peculiar mark of Iona's politics in the eighth century that it cultivated links with many different regimes in Britain and Ireland. Far less well known today than Ségéne or Adomnán, Cilléne Droichtech, abbot from 726 until 752, presided over Columba's monastery during a key phase.[52] His community had been spurned by the Verturian regime c. 715, much as it had by Bamburgh fifty years before. In 727 the relics of Adomnán were taken to Ireland and his Lex innocentium renewed, probably to mark its thirtieth anniversary. Clearly Adomnán was now being venerated as a saint. The renewal of his Law indicates that Iona continued to attract great respect in Ireland, perhaps thanks to groundwork laid down by Adomnán. In the course of Cilléne's abbacy his community's traditional patrons in Donegal – the kin of St Columba – and in Kintyre were eclipsed or conquered. Did Iona fade into the background on the grand political stage?

The monastery seems to have lamented the defeat and exile of Elphin by Onuist in 728. Had he been a guarantor of the renewed Lex innocentium a year earlier? There is no hint in the chronicles that, when the Law was renewed again in 757, its sixtieth anniversary, by Cilléne's successor Sléibéne, Onuist was among its guarantors. It is difficult to draw firm conclusions about this, however, for the first Pictish promulgation went unrecorded here.[53]

The Northumbrian Chronicle of 766, unlike the Chronicle of 802, uses Gaelic orthography (Oengus) in rendering the king's name. Its view of Onuist as 'a despotic butcher' was probably Gaelic – or possibly Verturian – in provenance.[54] If so, the statement reinforces the conclusion that there was no loosening of Onuist's grip on Argyll 'right up to the end' of his reign. Did Iona share this view of Onuist? Alliance between his son Bridei, Donngal of Lorn and Cenél Conaill in the early 730s may have been negotiated in part with Ionan brokerage. Yet Onuist's relationship with Cathal son of Finnguine in Munster, precocious enemy of the southern Uí Néill, probably did his relationship with Iona little good.

Even if Onuist's political outlook was out of step with Cilléne's monastery, the possibility remains that some Pictish nobles, not least in

---

[52] AU 752.1, 752.8; AT 752.1, 752.10. Cilléne mac Congaile and Cilléne droctigh were presumably the same person.

[53] AU 757.9; AT 757.9.

[54] Woolf, 'Onuist', 37; see also Forsyth, 'Evidence of a Lost Pictish Source', 23–7, whose subsequent conclusions are here challenged by Woolf.

Fortriu, continued to patronise Iona in this period. Substantial patrons, Pictish or otherwise, the eighth-century *familia Iae* certainly had, as Iona's surviving monumental sculpture so clearly attests. The great free-standing crosses, the earliest examples of which may have been created there, may even be Pictish work of the age of Onuist and Cilléne.[55] The details of Onuist's rise to power – with their hints of 'spin' – got into Iona's chronicle somehow.

Cilléne and his monks may have been less intricately involved in high politics than their seventh-century predecessors. They none the less remained active and influential in the broad and non-partisan issue of protecting non-combatants, as well as in philosophical thought. It seems to have been in these ways that Cilléne sought to exploit and maintain the historic international renown and credibility of Iona. Among Insular churches, Canterbury alone, with its papal backing, can have rivalled Columba's monastery in such respects. Internationalism may have been largely a legacy of Adomnán. He envisioned a broad audience for *Vita Columbae*, composed a universalist Law and travelled extensively in Britain and Ireland, even to destinations outside his *paruchia*.

Despite having become, by Pictish reckoning, a Pictish monastery, Iona's ongoing position within Gaeldom is clear from the affinities expressed in its contributions to the Insular art phenomenon. With Cilléne's blessing, one of his monks, Cú Chuimne 'the wise' (*sapiens*), formed half the scholarly duo which composed the formidable work of legal scholarship known as *Collectio canonum Hibernensis*.[56] The ninth-century monastic thinkers known as *Céli Dé*, 'clients of God', also drew substantially on Ionan thought in formulating their teachings, the origins of which traditionally lie with Máel Ruain of Tallaght, who died in 792.[57] The *Hibernensis* was an achievement of international and enduring significance, sixty-seven books of canons drawing on extensive expertise in patristic, Irish and international legal writing, including British and Anglo-Saxon works. Its impact on Latin Christendom was far greater than the admirably idealistic *Lex innocentium*. Its systematic organisation of canons by topic (rather than chronologically) may have been unprecedented. In that respect, the *Hibernensis* mirrored Irish consensual legal tradition, codified by theme. It gave the text such transparent utility to canon lawyers that copies very quickly began to reach England and Francia, where they influenced the development and presentation of canon law for centuries to come.

---

[55] Fisher, *Early Medieval Sculpture*, 15–16; Campbell, *Saints and Sea-Kings*, 40–1.
[56] *AU* 747.5; *AT* 747.6 note the death of Cú Chuimne.
[57] *AU* 792.1 notes the death of Máel Ruain.

If Iona avoided political intimacy for much of the eighth century, the monastery may have paid a very high price for that. It was sacked for the first time by Scandinavian raiders in 795, the second in 802 and the third in 806 at a cost, in the last instance, of sixty-eight lives.[58] The nearest secular powers capable of protecting the brethren and the relics of their saints from this kind of brutal harm were now very far away from their little Hebridean island. Cellach son of Congall, under whose abbatial leadership the crisis arose, seems to have decided that the status quo was no option. In the wake of the third raid, building was begun on a new Columban centre at Kells on the Blackwater in Meath, in the southern Uí Néill kingdom of Brega. On its completion seven years later, Cellach demitted office. Faced with repeated pillaging of his monastery, Cellach naturally looked to Meath for support.[59] Back in the 750s, Sléibéne had promulgated Adomnán's Law alongside a king of Meath. His successor Suibne was followed in 772 by Bresal son of Ségéne, who promulgated the Law again in 778, a year after its eightieth anniversary, alongside another king of Meath, the son of Sléibéne's royal collaborator twenty years before.[60]

Cellach did not, however, place all of Iona's eggs in Meath's basket. He also looked to Pictavia. It was during the reign of Constantín son of Vurguist, according to the Pictish king-list, that the great Columban church at Dunkeld was built on the edge of modern Atholl.[61] *Chronicon Scotorum* records that Cellach's successor Diarmait took the shrine (*sgrín*) of Columba to northern Britain in 818. A series of Pictish promulgations of Adomnán's Law in eighth-century Pictavia is therefore likely, linked with those recorded in Ireland. The chronicles record a second sojourn of Diarmait and the relics of Columba in northern Britain from 829 to 831.[62] By then, Iona had suffered a fourth terrible attack, in which Blathmac son of Fland and others had been butchered, later to be reckoned martyrs.[63] A century after the reign of Naiton, the Columban *familia* east of Drumalban had been reinvigorated by the plantation of the saint's relics at the heart of the old kingdom of Atholl, perhaps not far from where Columba himself had once stood before 'the great king of the Tay'.

---

[58] *AU* 794.7, 802.9, 806.8; *CS* 806.3; *AI* 795.2.
[59] *AU* 801.4, 807.4, 814.9; *CS* 807.2.
[60] *AU* 772.5, 778.4. Sléibéne seems to have demitted office by 766; *AU* 766.6, 767.5; *AI* 767.2.
[61] Anderson, *Kings and Kingship*, 266 *et seq.*
[62] *AU* 829.3, 831.1; *CS* 818.4, 829.2, 831.1.
[63] *AU* 825.17; *CS* 825.9.

While Diarmait was busily reorienting the Columban *familia*, in part through negotiations with Pictish and Irish kings, he was also shaping its future in another way. The architects, exponents and followers of Céli Dé thought had turned in part to Iona for ideas. Diarmait himself and the martyr Blathmac were two of the Ionan figures whom these 'spiritual shock troops of their society' particularly admired.[64] *The Monastery of Tallaght*, composed within a few years of Diarmait's death, preserves anecdotes from their lives as object-lessons in monastic wisdom.[65] The concept of Céli Dé monasticism revolved around eremitical asceticism – the life of the hermit – and hermits associated with Iona could be found at places like Eigg during Cilléne's abbacy.[66] Their interest in asceticism may have been less about reform than is often believed. Céli Dé philosophy was primarily concerned with establishing a hierarchy within monasticism, which distinguished between 'paramonastics', ordinary dutiful monks and nuns, and an extraordinary spiritual nobility, in direct clientage to God.[67]

In perhaps the most famous passage in *Agricola*, Tacitus had a Calidonian leader say of Roman aggression that, 'where they make a desert, they call it peace'. Six hundred years later, deserts and peace had taken on very different connotations in the monasteries of northern Britain. *Vita Columbae*'s handling of the desire to seek 'a desert in the ocean' (*desertus in ociano*) suggests that, as late as Adomnán's abbacy, hermitude had not been much encouraged at Iona.[68] Fifty years after Adomnán's death, the monastery had a leader in Cilléne who was also a hermit (*anchorita*). Was his leadership central to the blossoming of 'eremitical theory' at Iona, on which Máel Ruain and later Céli Dé thinkers would draw? 'Anchorites' were widespread in northern Britain in the eighth century. His Northumbrian hagiographers, including Bede, celebrated that aspect of the life of St Cuthbert, and in 756 the Northumbrian *anchorita* Balthere died, probably in East Lothian, where he was later venerated as St Baldred.[69]

Iona's international connections are evident from the products of its scriptorium, most of which were probably destroyed or lost in repeated Scandinavian attacks. A product of great interest in this book has been

[64] O'Loughlin, *Celtic Theology*, 137.

[65] For example, *Mon. Tallaght*, §§ 52, 65–71, 80. See Clancy, 'Iona, Scotland, and the Céli Dé', 115–17.

[66] *AU* 752.2; *AT* 752.3. On Eigg, see Macdonald, 'Two Major Early Monasteries', 57–60.

[67] Wagner, 'Ritual Impurity'; see also Woolf, *From Pictland to Alba*, 314–15.

[68] Tacitus, *Agric.*, § 30; Adomnán, *V. s. Columbae*, i.6.

[69] *Chron. 802*, s. a. 756; Coates, 'The Role of Bishops', 181; Rollason, *Northumbria*, 136–9.

the Iona Chronicle. No such text survives today. Its discovery, imbedded in the medieval Irish chronicle tradition, arguably represents the single most important contribution by historians in fifty years to the study of Early Historic Scotland. The surviving records based on it show that this text was compiled in the first instance *c.* 643, arguably as part of the same programme which saw the composition of *De uirtutibus sancti Columbae.* At that stage, the chronicle seems to have contained a king-list of the Corcu Réti kings from Domangart Réti down to Domnall Brecc, killed in 643. There were also records of their key military encounters and, of course, a list of the abbots of Iona. There were also lists of the abbots of Lismore in the Firth of Lorn and Bangor on Belfast Lough. The careers of Columba and his contemporaries were treated at fifty years' remove, creating problems of interpretation that have shaped the relevant chapters of this book.

A second phase of compilation followed *c.* 670, possibly under the direction of Cumméne Find. He had been a *scriptor* at Iona *c.* 643, but was abbot by the 660s. The chronicle seems to have been kept more or less contemporary thereafter until *c.* 741, when its information all but petered out, though it continued as a thinner record for some time afterwards. It seems to have done so indirectly, presumably via some Columban house in Ireland. From this same point the character of the record from northern Britain changes noticeably in the Irish chronicles. Northumbria and Clyde Rock virtually vanish, as do Argyll and Atlantic Scotland, in sharp contrast to the record preceding *c.* 740. Yet a thin record of Pictish events (apart from royal deaths) persists, and links between Armagh and Dunkeld (the deaths of two abbots of this monastery are recorded) have been shown to be the likeliest conduit for bringing this information into the Irish chronicle record. The description of Dub Talorc as *rex Pictorum citra Monoth* in 782, 'king of the Picts on this side of the Mounth', therefore probably locates his kingdom in the southern Pictish zone like Dunkeld.[70]

In the second phase, the chronicle seems to have been expanded to include information on three segments of the descendants of Áedán son of Gabrán, two of which had shared in the Corcu Réti kingship since 643. The protracted struggle of the third segment against Cenél nGartnait – a kindred which itself claimed descent from Gabrán – was also recorded. For the first time, the chronicle also shows interest in Pictland, starting in the middle of the 660s. Attention increased during and after the reign of Bridei son of Beli, about which time a Pictish king-list was copied into the chronicle back to the time of Columba.

[70] Evans, 'Irish chronicles'; Broun, 'Dunkeld', 99–102.

Interest in Cenél Comgaill waned in this phase of the chronicle, and seems mainly to have been excited when the kindred vied seriously for the Corcu Réti kingship. Similarly, it now became interested in Cenél nEchdach, alone among the Cenél Loairn kindreds, in the person of Ferchar Fota and his descendants, who established themselves as paramount kings at this time. Little interest in Cenél nÓengusso or the Uí Chóelbad can be detected, the latter having featured prominently in the earlier phase. The list of Iona abbots was continued and occasionally fleshed out with details. Interest in the abbots of Lismore appears to have resumed only when the kings of Lorn were dominant in Argyll, with records of the deaths of Iarnlaigh in 700 or 701, Colmán son of Findbarr in 704 and Crónán ua Eoain in 718. There was no attempt to insert the names of Lismore abbots from the sixty-three years between the deaths of Eochaid in 637 and Iarnlaigh.[71] Similarly, the deaths of only two bishops of Kingarth in the Firth of Clyde are recorded, those of Daniel in 659 or 660 and Iolán in 688, during whose episcopates kings of Cowal (in whose kingdom Kingarth lay) were prominent.[72] These patterns are surely indicative of relationships, acknowledged at Iona, between the kings of Cowal and the church of Kingarth, and between the kings of Lorn and the church of Lismore.

The events surrounding Onuist's rise to power and his conquest of Argyll are uncommonly extensive, and may have come to Iona as a package from a Pictish scriptorium. Were Onuist's activities in Argyll responsible for the petering out of the Iona Chronicle? It seems less likely that Iona feared attack than that dispossession of the principal kindreds of Dál Riata since Adomnán's death ushered in a period of relative indifference to Argyll politics. There appear to be five more Lismore obits in the second half of the eighth century, as well as two more Kingarth ones, along with the Dalriadan royal obits of this period which may relate to a realm spanning Drumalban.[73] Does the significance of Lismore in this latest phase of the Iona Chronicle confirm the suggestion above that Lorn contin-

---

[71] *AI* 701.1, 707.1, 730.1 provides a plausibly complete list of abbots of Lismore Mo-Chutu in Waterford in this period (see Macdonald, 'Two Major Early Monasteries', 49, whose optimism about recovering Lismore obits seems justified). Thus, Iarnlaigh (*AU* 700.3), Colmán (*AU* 703.3; *AT* 703.3) and Crónán (*AU* 718.4; *AT* 718.5), omitted from *AI*, are likely to have been abbots at Lismore Mo-Luóc.

[72] *AU* 660.1, 689.1; *AT* 660.2, 689.2.

[73] For Kingarth, see *AU* 737.1 (Rónán), 776.6 (Máel Manach), 790.1 (Nóe). For Lismore, *AI* 730.1, 752.3 (*cf. AU* 753.2; *AT* 753.2), 760.1, 768.1 (*cf. AU* 768.3), 774.2 (*cf. AU* 774.5), 778.2, 783.3 (*cf. AU* 783.2), 814.1–2 provides a plausibly complete list of abbots of Lismore Mo-Chutu in this period. Thus, Mac Luiged (*AT* 751.1), Findchú (*AU* 757.4; *AT* 757.4), Conait (*AU* 760.7; *AT* 760.3), Éogan (*AU* 776.10) and Orach (*AU* 781.3), omitted from *AI*, are likely to have been abbots at Lismore Mo-Luóc.

ued after 741 to be a seat of power in Argyll, perhaps in the hands of a mormaer based in Morvern? In that event, does the Kingarth evidence suggest the existence of second, southern sea-steward – possibly even the partition of post-'smiting' Argyll contemplated in an earlier chapter?

MANAGING HEARTS AND MINDS

Iona's particular interest in Onuist prior to 741 reveals something of his power and influence. It is, of course, impossible to know how nominal his *potestas* may have been in different parts of Pictavia. Early Historic regimes in northern Britain, like early medieval regimes generally, were unlike modern governments, experiencing little pressure to show interest in areas that seemed to lack strategic or economic importance. Conversely, in their desire to establish a controlling interest in areas that seemed crucial, they inevitably faced stiff competition for a piece of the action from regional and local potentates, as well as from the Church. When push came to shove in these areas, not all parties will always have preferred carrots to sticks. Sometimes points and examples could only be made by the spilling of blood, before consensual politics, reinvigorated, could resume. Violence in the name of blood-feud remained as endemic as ever between potentates, between their retinues, between lesser aristocrats and between kindreds of normal freemen.

We must presume that kings none the less strove as best they could to give their regimes the appearance of peace. The fact that both Northumbria and Pictavia were polyethnic is particularly notable. It remained a defining characteristic of the medieval Scottish kingdom. At their hearts, Early Historic regimes were ideas shared by select collections of warrior and clerical elites. From conception, the ideas spread, in no small part through military means, chiefly perhaps among the *cohortes* and households of its leading men and women.

In the cases of Pictavia and Northumbria, these ideas are unlikely to have been conceived much earlier than the mid- to late seventh century. By the end of the eighth century, the idea of Pictavia had probably come to encompass the Northern Isles. Here the cultural background of the population was significantly different from that of Fortriu, not to mention regions further south. The most recent survey of northern Britain's Early Historic archaeology omits the Northern Isles on the basis of their distinctiveness. Yet the artistic achievement of their inhabitants lies comfortably in that branch of the Insular art style so often called 'Pictish'.[74]

---

[74] Alcock, *Kings and Warriors*, 4.

The idea of Pictavia had also come to encompass the Gaels of Atlantic Scotland, allowing for considerable doubt that the mere fact of composition in Gaelic must preclude a text from being 'Pictish' in provenance, at least in the wider sense. The central immutable fact about Pictavia, long appreciated, is that it was not a monoculture. Further south in Britain, Mercian and West Saxon hegemons were forging polyethnic kingdoms inspired by common ideas, albeit preserving distinctions between Anglo-Saxon and British units. The Northumbrian kingdom was probably more similar than is conventionally supposed.[75] In such a context the 'smiting' of Argyll royal kindreds and the putative assimilation of willing elite families to the idea of Pictavia is not extravagant. It could even be thought fairly unremarkable for the period were it not for subsequent events, and the place afforded to Dalriadan identity in the new idea which supplanted Pictavia in the tenth century.

The circumstances surrounding that development lie outwith our scope. It is unnecessary to seek to anticipate them here. Grooming the Picts (or for that matter Northumbrian independence) for their inevitable disappearance, and grooming the Gaels for their inevitable triumph, are unnecessary and distorting pastimes. The curse of such hindsight has made it too easy to overlook the words of the Northumbrian hagiographical poet who, in the last decades of the eighth century, made casual reference to 'all their talents among far-flung peoples' in reference to the Picts. The comment sits comfortably alongside their artistic achievement at the heart of Insular art, and the political and other achievements, however shadowy, of their first four great hegemons as outlined above. As such, it seems an appropriate note on which to close our discussion of their remarkable journey from Caledonia to Pictland.

---

[75] Rollason, *Northumbria*, 57–64, surveys the evidence pessimistically.

Postscript
Remote from the Roman Nation

At the time of the *correctio* over which he presided, Naiton son of Der-Ilei implied in a letter that he and his people might find it difficult following papal directives, being 'remote from the Roman language and nation' (*longe a Romanorum loquella et natione segregati*).[1] The phrase is extraordinary and has attracted comment.

Our witness is Bede. He tells us himself, at another point in *Historia ecclesiastica*, that the Picts were not at all remote from the Latin language (*lingua Latinorum*). On the contrary, in his generation it was 'in general use' among all the peoples of Britain, symbolising their Christian unity.[2] There can be no question of reading into Naiton's words that the Pictish Church was illiterate, or that christianisation had barely begun in eighth-century Pictland. Moreover, Pictavia marched at the Forth with Northumbria, and in spatial terms was hardly any more remote (from anywhere) than its neighbour!

It can only be that Naiton was not speaking in spatial terms. Our rich Northumbrian evidence reveals that the ecclesiastical province that produced Bede did not at all regard itself as remote from the *Romanorum natio*. It exhibited an uncommon proximity in conceptual terms, even by the standards of the day. Naiton too was surely speaking in conceptual terms. Was he making the point that adherence to reformed observances brought the Picts no nearer to Rome than had hitherto been the case? Do his words thus provide a fleeting glimpse of a world-view at odds with others current in Britain and Ireland at the time? Is Bede's use of *Romanorum*, which unlike *Latinorum* explicitly links the language with Rome, a clue?

---

[1] Bede, *Hist. eccl.*, v.21.
[2] Bede, *Hist. eccl.*, i.1.

Among the Irish – and increasingly among the Anglo-Saxons too by Naiton's time – elements of the intelligentsia were assiduously engaging with and contributing to the literate culture of the Latin Church in our period. The Codex Amiatinus and Lindisfarne Gospels are the most famous Northumbrian relics reflecting this phenomenon.[3] More than that, Irish and Anglo-Saxon clerics, like Columbanus and Willibrord, were making names for themselves as energetic *peregrini*, interacting with kings, bishops and the pope himself. By the time of Naiton's reformation, Irish and Anglo-Saxon pilgrims and missionaries were attracting attention across the Latin West. They occur frequently in Continental texts and documents from the seventh century onwards. Their ancestors had never been Roman provincials in all the long years of the Empire, but by 724 their best and brightest had become as *au fait* in the intellectual legacies of that Empire as anyone in Western Europe.

One strives in vain to find Picts of similar inclination in these sources, and Naiton's assertion of Pictish remoteness from the *Romani* and their talk is consistent with this intriguing pattern. Students of the Picts have perhaps become so accustomed to silent sources that they have been little fascinated by this remarkable lack of engagement with the Latin West. Are we being presented with an elite mentality sharply different from Irish and Anglo-Saxon thinking?

There can be no denying the Picts' Continental contacts. Some images on Pictish sculpture (such as centaurs and griffins) and other art suggest links – perhaps not direct – with late Antique art, including Byzantine Roman art. Hints of a tendency for Pictish kingdoms to be partitioned when they were inherited by a new generation recall the Merovingian model. Frankish models may also lie behind the recumbent 'grave covers' of Pictland, as well as the highly repetitive nomenclature of Pictish kings, a feature long recognised, and quite out of keeping with the naming practices of Gaelic and Anglo-Saxon elites. A coin dating from Naiton's reign and struck in the Low Countries has been unearthed at Portmahomack. None of this need preclude, however, the possibility that remoteness from Rome was something fundamental to the idea (but not the reality) of Pictishness that had emerged by 724.[4]

After all, the Roman world-view that created the idea of *Picti*, now embraced by the Picts themselves, made them savage and persistent enemies of Rome, as any Pictish monk could read for himself, not least in Gildas's *De excidio Britanniae*. Moreover, by 698 the southern frontier of

---

[3] Rollason, *Northumbria*, 143–53.
[4] Carver, 'Iona of the East', 23.

Pictavia was probably formed by the Antonine Wall, at least in part. By and large, the Irish approach to this world-view was to react against it. Was the Pictish approach different? Was Naiton giving voice to a mentality that embraced literary notions of Pictish savagery and hostility towards Rome?

One epigrapher has remarked that 'one of the most striking things about Pictland is the marked preference there for non-Roman script'.[5] Quite apart from its frequent use, the ogham script imported from Ireland was routinely used in Pictavia for formal inscriptions. This tendency is quite out of keeping with Irish practice, and cannot be explained simply as gaelicisation, nor as a function of Gaelic settlement. Does the contrast in preference in this formal register for public expression – Roman script in Ireland and non-Roman in Pictavia – not mirror levels of conscious (non-)engagement with Latin culture already noted? The even greater appeal of the distinctly non-Roman native symbolic 'script' to the Pictish elites who patronised inscribed monuments is a further case in point. Picts were quite capable of highly formal monumental inscriptions in the Latin tradition: the Tarbat inscription in particular demonstrates that. More often than not, however, it seems that they chose to express themselves monumentally in other ways. The issue here is identity, not ability.

Other evidence is similarly consistent with this possibility that consciousness of difference from the *Romanorum natio* lay at the heart of Pictish ethnic identity by the eighth century. The Pictish Church experienced many foreign influences, but it has long been appreciated that the primary influence was Irish. Is it a coincidence that the Irish shared the Picts' origins in *barbaricum*? Warnings have already been sounded that the engine driving this trend is likely to have been Pictish fashion and inclination. The papal legation of 786–7 complained about tattooing and other aspects of elite culture in Northumbria explicitly regarded as native influences rooted in pre-Christian barbarism. The Irish too developed a robust attachment to their vernacular register alongside their absorption of Latin Christian culture: it was publicly expressed by its literati through vernacular literature, rather than through monumental epigraphy.

Respect for *romanitas* across *barbaricum* in late Antiquity and afterwards lived in 'fundamental tension' with the desire to preserve ancient heritage, at least as such things were perceived.[6] A similar tension surely occurred in Pictavia. A case can be made that the Pictish establishment

---

[5] Forsyth, 'Literacy in Pictland', 54; see also Forsyth, 'The Inscriptions on the Dupplin Cross', 237.
[6] Wormald, '*Lex Scripta*', 123.

was inclined to stress its (perceived) cultural heritage as part of the consciousness of difference that underpinned Pictish ethnicity. It was arguably joining in a wider pan-British phenomenon, which saw the final obsolescence of Insular Romance culture and Roman identity in the bedding-down of post-Roman Britishness.[7] There is strong potential for 'antiquarian revivalism' in such a movement, looking back with an Early Historic perspective on the (largely imagined) Iron Age, in order to help shape new consciousnesses.

Thus, after seven centuries and so much change, we come full circle on the subject of relations and interlinkages between the inhabitants of northern Britain and the Eternal City. Eighth-century Pictish rhetoric and ethnicity notwithstanding, remoteness from the Romans was seldom achieved between the Flavian conquest and the flourishing of Northumbria and Pictavia. The northern reaches of Britain were penetrated by Roman soldiers, sailors and others during the Roman Iron Age, almost certainly more times than is recorded in our thin textual record. In the fifth, sixth and seventh centuries, the Roman religion was flowering among the Picts, the Northumbrians, the North Britons and the Argyll Gaels. The St Ninian's Isle treasure shows that fine tableware of Mediterranean manufacture was still in demand in northern Britain twenty generations after Roman wares began gracing the tables – if tables they had – of Caledonian aristocrats. Far from the Mediterranean basin, northern Britain none the less wrote its own chapter in the story of the transformation of the Roman world in the late Antique and early medieval centuries as we saw in Part One.

The danger of taking an 'overly synchronic view' of our lengthy period must be acknowledged, of course.[8] Yet nowhere do scholars of the early Middle Ages proceed on the basis that late Antiquity was irrelevant to their subject. Scotland need be no different. If Pictish ethnicity in the eighth century included an element of conscious rejection of (what was perceived to be) *romanitas*, the explanation must lie in perceptions of the Roman Iron Age past. What did they know about it? No doubt Gildas and other writers of his ilk had an important part to play in conjuring up lurid images of the history of Romano-Pictish relations. Real antagonism between Rome and the peoples of Caledonia in the fourth century is also suggested by aspects of the archaeological record. That period of crisis and transformation need not have been entirely expunged from the folk memory three hundred years later.

[7]   Woolf, 'Britons', 373–9.
[8]   Forsyth, *Language in Pictland*, 16.

The modern-day nationalist might take a certain comfort in precocious nativism among eighth-century Pictish elites. She or he might also forget that Picts who followed Naiton's lead regarding *romanitas* were engaged in collective denial of cultural and historical realities that were rather different. Amnesia is as important as memory in identities, then and now. In this Part of the book, we have seen that all the indications are that the clergy of Pictavia were conversant in the literate culture of the Latin Church, and its establishment at least passably so in the art of early medieval Christian regime-craft. Other Roman legacies in northern Britain have been discussed. The journey from Caledonia to Pictavia was a long and complex one, characterised by change, anything but linear. The evaluation and adaptation of Roman and Continental cultural ideas and influences, in the pursuit of native needs and interests, may have been the only constant.

Timeline

286–93 Rebellion of Marcus Carausius
305   Flavius Constantius invades northern Britain
306   Death of Constantius at Eboracum
367   *Barbarica conspiratio* overruns Britannia
368–9   Theodosius repels barbarians
383   Magnus Maximus rebels
c. 384 Maximus fights *Picti* and *Scotti*
c. 400 Flavius Stilicho fights a Pictish war?
400–50 'Latinus Stone' and 'Cat Stane' erected
450–93 Patrick writes to the warriors of Coroticos at Clyde Rock
542   Onset of 'plague of Justinian' at Constantinople
563   Foundation of Í (Iona)
570   Conall son of Comgall on campaign in the Hebrides
573   Battle of Arthuret
576   Áedán son of Gabrán becomes king of Kintyre
578   Áedán wins battle of Teloch, securing kingship of Corcu Réti
580   Urbgen son of Cinmarch becomes king of Rheged?
581   Death of Uinniau
582   Death of Galam Cennaleph – 'the great king of the Tay'?
582/3   Áedán's raid on Orkney
584/5   Áedán wins battle of Manau
590   Fíachnae Lurgan ('Longshanks') becomes king of Ulster
c. 591 Columbanus leaves Bangor for Francia
c. 592 Áedán meets Áed son of Ainmere at Druimm Cete; Aeðilfrith
        son of Aeðilric becomes king of Bernicia
594   Death of Mo-Luóc of Lismore
597   Death of Columba; foundation of Gregorian mission to
        Anglo-Saxons
603   Aeðilfrith defeats Áedán at Degsastan
c. 604 Aeðilfrith subjugates Deira
609   Death of Áedán
615   Aeðilfrith wins battle of Chester
616   Aeðilfrith slain at battle of the River Idle; Oswald arrives in
        Argyll; Eanfrith arrives in Pictland
617   Battle of Fidnach; kingship of the Corcu Réti passes from
        Eochaid Buide to Connad Cerr?
619   Martyrdom of Donnán of Eigg
624   Domnall Brecc in Meath
625   Death of Uineus, abbot of Nér; Ségéne becomes abbot of Iona
        on death of Virgno; Bamburgh attacked by Fíachnae
        Longshanks?

627   Run son of Urbgen attends baptism of Edwini of Deira?
628   Fíachnae Longshanks slain
629   Connad Cerr wins battle of Ard Corand; Connad becomes
        king of Ulster?
631   Connad slain at Fid Euin
633   Catguollaun defeats Edwini at Hatfield
634   Oswald victorious at Hexham; foundation of Lindisfarne
636   Domnall Brecc defeated in Calathros
637   Death of Gartnait son of Vuid
639   Battle of Moira; Ferchar son of Connad becomes king of
        Corcu Réti?; Oswald captures Deira?
640   Domnall Brecc defeated at Glend Mureson; Edinburgh
        besieged, possibly by Oswald; Ségéne receives papal letter on
        subject of Easter and Pelagianism
642   Oswald slain at Maserfelth
643   Oswy fights Britons (i.e. Rheged?); Domnall Brecc slain by
        forces of Eugein son of Beli in Strathcarron
c. 643 Cumméne Find writes *De uirtutibus sancti Columbae*
650   Death of Ferchar of Cowal, last certain Cenél Comgaill king of
        the Corcu Réti
651   Oswy subjugates Deira after murder of Oswini; death of Aidan
        of Lindisfarne
652   Death of Ségéne of Iona
654   Donnchad son of Conaing slain in Strathyre by forces of
        Talorcan son of Anfrith
655   'Restitution of Iudeu'; Penda slain by forces of Oswy at battle
        of Maes Gai (*Winwaed*)
656   Cumméne Find becomes abbot of Iona; Oswy plunders Britons
657   Death of Guret ('son of Guryan'?)
664   Synod of Whitby; York supplants Lindisfarne as principal
        church in Northumbria
664/5   Death of Féichín (St Vigean) of Fore
668/9   Death of Cumméne Find; death of Itarnan/Ethernan
        (Taranan?)
669   Wilfrid confirmed in see of York by Theodore of Canterbury
669/70 Cenél nGartnait return to Skye from Ireland
670   Death of Oswy
671   Ecgfrith and Beornhaeth win battle of the Two Rivers;
        beginning of reign of Bridei son of Beli
672   Domangart son of Domnall slain; Ecgfrith defeats Wulfhere
        son of Penda; Applecross founded

673	Council of Hertford
675	Picts drown in ?Loch Awe
677	Cenél nEchdach defeated by British forces
678	Adomnán becomes abbot of Iona; death of Nechtan of Nér; Wilfrid expelled from York
679	Ecgfrith defeated by forces of Aeðilred son of Penda at the River Trent
680	Wilfrid imprisoned at Dunbar; Dunnottar besieged, probably by Bridei
681	Orkney ravaged by Bridei; British invasion of Mag Line; Theodore creates see of Abercorn
682	Dunadd besieged (by Britons?); Dundurn besieged (by Bridei?)
684	Berctred son of Beornhaeth attacks Brega; Cuthbert becomes bishop of Hexham
685	Bridei defeats Ecgfrith at battle of Dún Nechtain; Dargart son of Finnguine slain
687	Cano son of Gartnait slain; Wilfrid restored to communion in Northumbria; Cuthbert becomes bishop of Lindisfarne
688	Adomnán visits Northumbria
689	Ceolfrith becomes abbot of Wearmouth-Jarrow
690	Death of Theodore of Canterbury; Dalriadan attack on north-east Ireland
c. 690	Kingarth reforms Easter calculation?
692	Bede becomes deacon; death of Bridei son of Beli
693	Death of Dumngual son of Eugein, king of Clyde Rock
696/7	*Lex innocentium* promulgated; Tarain son of Enfidaig expelled from Pictavia; death of Ferchar Fota
697	Osthryð daughter of Oswy murdered in Mercia
698	Berctfrith slain in battle against Picts; Verturian suzerainty reaches Forth?
c. 700	Adomnán writes *Vita sancti Columbae*
701/2	Cenél Cathboth 'slaughtered'; Selbach son of Ferchar destroys Dunollie
c. 702	Council of Austerfield
703	Bede becomes priest
704	Death of Aldfrith
705	Bamburgh besieged; Eadwulf toppled by supporters of Osred; British massacre of Dalriadan forces; death of Adomnán
707	Death of Bridei son of Der-Ilei
707/8	Donnchad assumes principate of Iona
709	A battle in Orkney (against Verturian domination?)

710   Naiton's sons slain in Cowal
711   Berctfrith defeats Picts in Manau; Dalriadan victory over Britons
712   Selbach invades Kintyre
713   Death of Dorbbéne, probable scribe of Schaffhausen *Vita Columbae*; death of Aelffled; *Vita Wilfrithi* written by this date; Naiton binds Talorcan of Atholl
714   Selbach rebuilds Dunollie
715   Pictish *correctio*?
716   Osred killed; Acca expelled from Hexham?; revision of *Vita Wilfrithi*; Easter reformed at Iona; Aeðilbald becomes king of Mercians
717   Expulsion of Ionans from Pictavia; death of Donnchad; headship of Iona re-united; death of Eadwulf son of Ecgwulf; Dál Riata defeats Britons
718   Death of Coenred son of Cuthwini
719   Selbach defeats his brother Ainbcellach at Finglen; death of Drostan *Dairtaige* at Ardbraccan
721   *Fergustus episcopus Scotiae Pictus* in Rome
723   Selbach abdicates
724   Naiton abdicates
726   Cilléne Droichtech becomes abbot of Iona
727   Selbach fights Cenél nGabráin; *Lex innocentium* renewed for first time
728   Onuist defeats Elphin at Moncrieffe and *Castellum Credi*
729   Death of Osric son of Aldfrith; Onuist defeats Drest at Monid Carno and Druimm Derg Blathuug; Naiton restored
c. 729   Anglo-Pictish peace treaty concluded
730   Death of Selbach
731   Bede completes *Historia ecclesiastica gentis Anglorum*; Donngal and Bridei son of Onuist attack Kintyre; Ceolwulf briefly removed from power; Acca expelled from Hexham
732   Death of Naiton
733   Donngal supports Cenél Conaill against Cenél nÉogain (with Bridei?); Donngal captures Bridei at Tory Island; Muiredach becomes king of Lorn
734   *Potestas* of Onuist in Argyll; Talorcan of Atholl captured at Dunollie; Talorc son of Congus drowned by Picts; Donngal escapes wounded to Ireland
735   Ecgberct son of Eata receives metropolitan rank from Rome
736   Onuist devastates Argyll and captures Dunadd; Muiredach defeated by Talorcan in Calathros

737	Cathal son of Finnguine at Terryglass; second abdication of Ceolwulf
740	Northumbria at war with Picts and Mercians
741	'The smiting of Dál Riata'
742	'Virgil' of Iona goes to Salzburg
744	War between Picts and Britons
750	Talorcan defeated and slain at Mugdock; battle of Circhind; Eadberct conquers Ayrshire; bishop of Lindisfarne arrested
752	Death of Cilléne Droichtech
754	Martyrdom of Winfrith Boniface near Dokkum
756	Treaty of Clyde Rock between Onuist, Eadberct and Dumngual; death of Balthere
757	Murder of Aeðilbald; *Lex innocentium* renewed for second time
758	Eadberct abdicates
759	Assassination of Oswulf son of Eadberct
761	Death of Onuist; Moll wins battle of Edwini's Cliff
762	Moll marries Aeðilthryð at Catterick
763	Death of Bridei son of Vurguist
763–4	Bad Winter
765	Moll deposed and tonsured
766	Death of Ecgberct of York
768	Battle in Fortriu between Ciniod and Áed; Alchred marries Osgifu; last British Churches reform Easter
769	Burning of Catterick
773	Alchred and Osgifu pursue links with Charlemagne
774	Alchred deposed and expelled, going to Pictavia
775	Death of Ciniod
778	Death of Áed Find; three *duces* executed in Northumbria; *Lex innocentium* renewed for third time
779	Aeðilred son of Moll deposed and expelled
780	Death of Elphin son of Vurad; death of Aelberct of York
781	Death of Fergus; death of Drest son of Talorcan
782	Death of Dub Talorc (of Fortriu?); Alcuin joins Carolingian court
785	Death of Talorcan son of Drestan
786	Papal legation to Britain; Great Penance in Ireland
787	Synod of Finchale
788	Aelfwald slain 'near the wall'
789	Constantín son of Vurguist defeats Conall son of Tadg
793	Viking assault on Lindisfarne
795	Viking assault on Iona

Guide to Further Reading

1. GENERAL SURVEYS

On their own, the centuries examined in this book have never been surveyed together; rather, they have formed parts of broader or narrower surveys. The most important and influential of these for the Early Historic period – Skene's *Celtic Scotland* (1876–80), Duncan's *Scotland: the Making of the Kingdom* (1975) and Smyth's *Warlords and Holy Men* (1984) – are recommended and described in Alex Woolf's Guide to Further Reading in the next volume of this series. Skene and Duncan both sought to encapsulate a century of scholarship and their surveys will always stand as landmarks. This book is riddled with ideas from them, but students must tread carefully because of the scholarly revolution outlined in the Introduction. With the narrative framework in a state of flux, the initiative in surveying our period has since been taken by archaeologists. Ian Armit's *Celtic Scotland* (1997), David Breeze's *Roman Scotland* (1996) and Sally Foster's *Picts, Gaels and Scots* (2nd edition, 2004), all published by Historic Scotland and comprehensively illustrated, together span our period. These short but significant surveys consider mainly social and cultural themes well suited to archaeological examination, largely ignored in the great prior surveys. More recently Leslie Alcock's *Kings and Warriors, Craftsmen and Priests* (2003) and Dennis Harding's *The Iron Age in Northern Britain* (2004) have considered archaeological themes spanning our period, encapsulating the wisdom of two exceptional careers devoted to understanding the material culture. Two general surveys of Scottish place-names, with ramifications for understanding our period, also merit mention here. However, the achievements of William Watson's *History of the Celtic Place-Names of Scotland* (1926) and Bill Nicolaisen's *Scottish Place-*

Names (1976) are currently being re-examined by place-names scholars like Simon Taylor and Richard Cox, whose works only sometimes touch upon our period. Finally, *After Rome* (2003), edited by Thomas Charles-Edwards, wonderfully contextualises northern Britain in our period within broader Insular political, social and cultural trends.

2. THE SOURCES

Our principal narrative sources have been Adomnán's *Vita sancti Columbae* and Bede's *Historia ecclesiastica gentis Anglorum*. Students should consult the excellent modern editions with translations facing the original Latin text: *Adomnán's Life of Columba*, edited by Alan and Marjorie Anderson (2nd edition, 1991), and *Bede's Ecclesiastical History of the English People*, edited by Bertram Colgrave and R. A. B. Mynors (2nd printing, 1991). The exercise serves to remind us that people did not write in modern accessible English in our period, and the extent to which students and specialists alike find themselves somewhat at the mercy of modern editors and translators. Good accessible translations do exist: the best are Penguin Classics's *Life of St Columba* (1995), translated by Richard Sharpe, with wonderful notes and commentary; and Oxford World's Classics's *Ecclesiastical History of the English People* (1999), containing Colgrave's translation with notes and commentary by Judith McClure and Roger Collins. At a pinch translations of both texts may be consulted online, scanned from out-of-copyright printed works, but the quality of these versions can vary enormously and they are often difficult to read and provided with unorthodox book and chapter numbers.

The most important additional source for the narrative historian is Irish chronicle material: the principal texts are those recommended and described in Alex Woolf's volume, which provides URLs to very useful online editions. Use of these chronicles throughout this book has been influenced by the Glasgow doctoral dissertation of Nicholas Evans, 'The Textual Development of the Principal Irish Chronicles in the Tenth and Eleventh Centuries' (2003), particularly its conclusions relating to the AD dating of chronicle records.

Other published sources used in this book can be found in the Bibliography. As regards their study, the revolution outlined in the Introduction has mainly been prosecuted through scholarly articles. One of the chief standard-bearers has been David Dumville, some of whose most important contributions are collected and reprinted in *Histories and*

Pseudo-Histories of the Insular Middle Ages (1990). Another study in a similar vein, which includes a provocative analysis of Bede's historical and hagiographical works, is Walter Goffart's *The Narrators of Barbarian History* (1988). The chief contributor with a Scottish focus has been Dauvit Broun, with key examples to be found in such edited collections of essays as Sally Foster's *The St Andrews Sarcophagus* (1998), on Pictish and Dalriadan king-lists; and Ted Cowan's and Andrew McDonald's *Alba* (2000), on *De situ Albanie*. His *Scottish Independence and the Idea of Britain from the Picts to Alexander III* (2007) marks something of a culmination of Broun's source-work over some twenty years, largely focused on later centuries than ours. Alan Anderson's magisterial work in collecting valuable sources in *Scottish Annals from English Chroniclers* (1908) and *Early Sources of Scottish History* (1922) can still be read with profit, along with Marjorie Anderson's astute analyses of them in *Kings and Kingship in Early Scotland* (1973); but past scholarship like this must always be examined with one eye on more recent movements.

3. ROMAN IRON AGE SCOTLAND

The study of Roman Iron Age Scotland has taken an exciting turn of late, thanks to such works as David Woolliscroft's and Birgitta Hoffmann's *Rome's First Frontier* (2006) and Fraser Hunter's *Beyond the Edge of the Empire* (2007). Both works, in very different ways, challenge paradigms that have been growing up since the radio-carbon revolution convulsed archaeology in the middle of last century. Such landmark works as David Breeze's *The Northern Frontiers of Roman Britain* (1982) and *Roman Scotland* (1996), Bill Hanson's and Gordon Maxwell's *Rome's North West Frontier* (2nd edition, 1986) and Hanson's *Agricola and the Conquest of the North* (1987), represent recent contributions to that paradigm. Stated simply, Woolliscroft, Hoffmann and Hunter reject the 'Roman interlude' way of understanding this period, interpreting their evidence as indicating that Rome was far from an insignificant factor in developments. In part their work reflects movements in 'frontier studies', such as those found in John Barrett *et al.*'s *Barbarians and Romans in North-West Europe* (1989), and also in 'romanisation studies', such as Martin Millett's *The Romanization of Britain* (1990). It also reflects a growing interest in the native peoples of Roman Iron Age Scotland, a field conventionally infatuated with the country's fascinating Roman remains. Woolliscroft and Hoffmann offer radical reinterpretations of Flavian evidence, while Hunter's published lecture explores the significance of Roman material on native sites. At present it is difficult to predict how the field will respond to these provocative studies, and the exciting burgeoning of dialogue and debate between 'romanists' and 'nativists'.

More general works of significance, particularly as regards contextualising northern Britain in its wider world, include Leo Rivet's and Colin Smith's *The Place-Names of Roman Britain* (1981) on linguistic and textual themes; Richard Hingley's 'Society in Scotland from 700 BC to AD 200' in the journal *Proceedings of the Society of Antiquaries of Scotland* (1992), on the study of native society; Tony Birley's *Septimius Severus* (3rd edition, 1999) on the principate of Severus; and Barbara Levick's *Vespasian* (1999) on the principate of Vespasian.

4. CHRISTIANISATION, APOSTLES AND THE EARLY CHURCH

The great leap forward in Columban studies was taken in Máire Herbert's *Iona, Kells, and Derry* (1988), which comprehensively reassessed the textual evidence. Ninianic studies had to wait some years before Thomas Clancy's 'The Real St Ninian', in the journal *Innes Review* (2001), offered something comparable. Adventurous archaeological approaches to christianisation in Charles Thomas's *Christianity in Roman Britain* (1981) and Ian Smith's essay on 'The origins and development of Christianity in North Britain and southern Pictland' in John Blair's and Carol Pyrah's *Church Archaeology* (1996), were undertaken without the benefit of such revisionist textual scholarship, but remain of interest. Fascinating contributions have been made by place-name scholars, particularly Simon Taylor, who criticises and develops earlier studies in essays in Barbara Crawford's *Scotland in Dark Age Britain* (1996), in the journal *Records of the Scottish Church History Society* (1998), and in Dauvit Broun's and Thomas Clancy's *Spes Scotorum* (1999). Broader studies like Guy Halsall's *Early Medieval Cemeteries* (1995), Richard Fletcher's *The Barbarian Conversion* (1997) and Carole Cusack's *Conversion Among the Germanic Peoples* (1998) are indispensable for contextualising Scotland's patchy textual, place-name and archaeological evidence. As regards the early Church, Thomas Clancy's forthcoming book *The Making of Scottish Christianity* is eagerly anticipated. In the meantime, a useful but difficult book for students is Colmán Etchingham's *Church Organisation in Ireland* (1999), which reflects the collapse of the 'Celtic Church' paradigm.

5. NORTHUMBRIA AND THE NORTH BRITONS

The Roman to post-Roman transition still awaits its historian. Simon Esmonde Cleary's *The Ending of Roman Britain* (1989), reviewing and re-interpreting the archaeological evidence, remains the most indispensable general study. Another, Ken Dark's *Civitas to Kingdom* (1994), offers some radical challenges to many of Esmonde Cleary's ideas, but has failed to find much support. Bryan Ward-Perkins's even more general *The Fall of Rome and the End of Civilization* (2005), challenges tendencies to remove barbarian violence from the equation. Still more contextualising may be achieved through such collections of essays as Walter Pohl's and Helmut Reimitz's *Strategies of Distinction* (1998) and Andrew Gillett's *On Barbarian Identity* (2002), exploring ethnic transitions from late Antiquity to the early Middle Ages across Europe. Guy Halsall's *Warfare and Society in the Barbarian West* (2003) is a fine example of comparative scholarship relating to developments in key aspects of early medieval society.

As regards the early Northumbrian and North British kingdoms, much to be recommended as starting places are James Campbell's *The Anglo-Saxons* (1982), which is both erudite and well illustrated, David Kirby's *The Earliest English Kings* (2nd edition, 2000) and Barbara Yorke's *Kings and Kingdoms of Early Anglo-Saxon England* (1990). More unorthodox and provocative is Nick Higham's *The Convert Kings* (1997), one of several relevant books by a very prolific scholar. Higham's work may be fairly described as idiosyncratic, but often very stimulating too. John Koch's *The Gododdin of Aneirin* (1997) can make the same claim: its treatment of early Welsh poetry and North British history has been very controversial, but also a spur to scholarship. Unfortunately, it is a very difficult book for many students; more student-friendly is Chris Lowe's *Angels, Fools and Tyrants* (1999), which admirably studies Northumbrians and North Britons side by side and is very well illustrated. More advanced students will want to consult several essays in Steve Bassett's *The Origins of Anglo-Saxon Kingdoms* (1989), particularly that of David Dumville; Alan Macquarrie's 'The Kings of Strathclyde', in Sandy Grant's and Keith Stringer's *Medieval Scotland* (1993), though the principal source of the essay is sometimes misunderstood; Alex Woolf's 'Caedualla *Rex Brettonum* and the Passing of the Old North', in the journal *Northern History* (2004); and Katherine Forsyth's '*Hic Memoria Perpetua*', in Sally Foster's and Morag Cross's *Able Minds and Practised Hands* (2005), which reviews the early Christian monuments of the North British zone.

6. ĐÁL RIATA

The revolution outlined in the Introduction has done something of a hatchet job on the scholarship of John Bannerman relating to the Argyll Gaels, culminating in *Studies in the History of Dalriada* (1974). That influential collection none the less remains a landmark publication steeped in profound learning, one of the last great expressions of the scholarship behind the old framework. With caution, it can still be read with great profit. However, David Dumville's analyses of *Cethri prím-chenéla Dáil Riata* in the journal *Scottish Gaelic Studies* (2000) and *Míniugud senchasa fher nAlban* in Colm Ó Baoill's and Nancy McGuire's *Rannsachadh na Gàidhlig 2000* (2002) have highlighted key weaknesses in Bannerman's work. The present writer has challenged other aspects in the journals *Northern Studies* (2004), *Innes Review* (2005) and *Early Medieval Europe* (2007), and in Wilson McLeod's (and others') *Cànan & Cultar* (2006), regarding the political and ethnic constitution of Dál Riata and the evidence furnished by *Vita Columbae*. What has been at particular issue has, in brief, been Bannerman's inclination to regard the Argyll Gaels as a single Dalriadan people, ruled by a single dynasty and a single Church. Still more earth-shattering has been Ewan Campbell's 'Were the Scots Irish?', in the journal *Antiquity* (2001), which highlights the problems of accepting at face value the notion that the origins of Scottish Gaeldom lay in Ireland. Less controversial works to be recommended include Ian Fisher's masterly *Early Medieval Sculpture in the West Highlands and Islands* (2001) and Alan Lane's and Ewan Campbell's *Dunadd* (2000), the report of a model archaeological investigation which sought to understand earlier excavations, as well as those undertaken anew by the authors.

7. THE PICTS

If Bannerman's *Dalriada* has fared badly in the course of the scholarly revolution, so too has Isabel Henderson's *The Picts* (1967). In this case, Henderson herself has been part of the process, her *The Art of the Picts* (2004), written with George Henderson, departing in a number of key ways from her book of thirty-seven years before. In this underlying acceptance of Pictish studies as a living field in a state of transition, as well as in its learning, its wonderful illustrations and its robust ideas, this book is much to be recommended as an instant classic. David Henry's collection of essays, *The Worm, the Germ, and the Thorn* (1997), is a fitting tribute to Henderson, with a number of valuable studies relating to the Picts. Another valuable edited collection is Sally Foster's *St Andrews Sarcophagus* (1998), which blends close studies of that fascinating artefact with explorations of broader themes, including indispensable studies by Dauvit Broun and Steve Driscoll. Key challenges to conventional ideas include Katherine Forsyth's *Language in Pictland* (1997), which has emboldened scholars to accept the Britishness of the Pictish tongue; Alex Woolf's 'Pictish Matriliny Reconsidered', in the journal *Innes Review* (1998), which endorses and develops Smyth's rejection of matriliny; Katherine Forsyth's 'Literacy in Pictland', in Huw Pryce's *Literacy in Medieval Celtic Societies* (1998), challenging notions that the Picts were less literate than other Insular peoples; and, most important of all, Alex Woolf's 'Dún Nechtain, Fortriu and the Geography of the Picts', in the journal *Scottish Historical Review* (2006), which shows that Fortriu was incorrectly located in the southern Pictish zone by Skene.

Bibliography

PRIMARY AND MEDIEVAL SOURCES

Adomnán, *Cáin Adomnáin*; M. Ní Dhonnchadha, 'The Law of Adomnán: a translation',
in T. O'Loughlin, ed., *Adomnán at Birr, AD 697: Essays in Commemoration of the Law
of the Innocents* (Dublin, 2001), 53–68.

'Adomnán', *Canones Adomnani*; L. Bieler, ed., *The Irish Penitentials* (Dublin, 1963),
176–80.

Adomnán, *De locis sanctis*; D. Meehan, ed., *Adamnan's De Locis Sanctis* (Dublin, 1983).

Adomnán, *Vita sancti Columbae*; A. O. Anderson and M. O. Anderson, eds, *Adomnán's
Life of Columba*.

Ammianus Marcellinus, *Res gestae*; J. C. Rolfe, ed., *Ammianus Marcellinus*, vol. III
(London and Cambridge, MA, 1972).

Amra Choluimb Chille; T. O. Clancy and G. Márkus, eds, *Iona* (Edinburgh, 1995),
104–14.

'Aneirin', *E Gododin*. 'A-text'; I. Williams, ed., *Canu Aneirin* (Cardiff, 1938).

'Aneirin', *E Gododin*. 'B-text'; I. Williams, ed., *Canu Aneirin*.

Anglo-Saxon Chronicle E; S. Irvine, ed., *The Anglo-Saxon Chronicle: a Collaborative
Edition*, vol. 7: MS. E (Cambridge, 2004).

Annales Cambriae; E. Faral, ed., *Légende Arthurienne* (Paris, 1929), 44–50.

Annals of Clonmacnoise; D. Murphy, ed., *The Annals of Clonmacnoise* (Llanerch, 1993).

Annals of Inisfallen; S. Mac Airt, ed., *The Annals of Inisfallen* (Dublin, 1977).

Annals of Tigernach; W. Stokes, ed., *The Annals of Tigernach*, vol. 1 (Llanerch, 1993).

Annals of Ulster; S. Mac Airt and G. Mac Niocaill, eds, *The Annals of Ulster (to A.D.
1131)* (Dublin, 1983).

Augustine of Hippo, *De Civitate Dei*; H. Bettenson, trans., *St Augustine: Concerning the
City of God against the Pagans* (London, 1972).

Beccán mac Luigdech, *Fo réir Choluimb*; Clancy and Márkus, *Iona*, 136–42.

Beccán mac Luigdech, *To-fed andes*; Clancy and Márkus, *Iona*, 146–50.

Bede, *Epistola ad Ecgbertum*; C. Plummer, ed., *Venerabilis Baedae* (Oxford, 1896),
405–23.

Bede, *Historia abbatum*; Plummer, ed., *Venerabilis Baedae*, 364–87.

Bede, *Historia ecclesiastica gentis Anglorum*; B. Colgrave and R. A. B Mynors, eds, *Bede's
Ecclesiastical History* (Oxford, 1991).

Bede, *Vita sancti Cuthberti*; Colgrave, ed., *Two* Lives *of Saint Cuthbert* (Cambridge, 1940).

Book of Leinster; A. O'Sullivan, ed., *The Book of Leinster*, vol. 6 (Dublin, 1983).

Bower, W. *Scotichronicon*; D. E. R. Watt, gen. ed., *Scotichronicon*, vol. 2 (J. and W. MacQueen, eds) (Aberdeen, 1989).

Bríathra Flainn Fína maic Ossu; C. A. Ireland, ed., *Old Irish Wisdom Attributed to Aldfrith of Northumbria: an edition of* Bríathra Flainn Fína maic Ossu (Tempe AZ, 1999).

Bromwich, R., ed., *Trioedd Ynys Prydein: the Welsh Triads*, 2nd edn (Cardiff, 1978).

Cassius Dio, *Roman History*; E. Cary, ed., *Dio's Roman History*, vol. IX (London and Cambridge MA, 1927).

Cethri prímchenéla Dáil Riata; D. N. Dumville, *Cethri prímchenéla*, *Scottish Gaelic Studies* (2000), 175–83.

Chronicle of 452; T. Mommsen, ed., *Chronica Minora* (Berlin, 1892), 646–62.

Chronicle of 766; Colgrave and Mynors, eds, *Bede's Ecclesiastical History*, 572–76.

Chronicle of 802; T. Arnold, ed., *Symeonis Monachi Opera Omnia*, vol. II (Rolls: Edinburgh, 1885).

Chronicle of the Kings of Alba; M. O. Anderson, *Kings and Kingship* (Edinburgh and London, 1973), 149–53.

Chronicon Scotorum; W. M. Hennessy, ed., *Chronicum Scotorum: a Chronicle of Irish Affairs from the Earliest Times to A.D. 1135* (London, 1866).

Columbanus, *Epistula* I; G. S. M. Walker, ed., *Sancti Columbani Opera* (Dublin, 1957), 2–12.

Columbanus, *Regula Coenobialis*; Walker, ed., *Sancti Columbani Opera*, 142–68.

Columbanus, *Regula Monachorum*; Walker, ed., *Sancti Columbani Opera*, 122–42.

De Situ Albanie; Anderson, *Kings and Kingship*, 240–3.

Éogan Már trá óenmac leis; M. A. O'Brien, ed., *Corpus Genealogiarum Hiberniae* (Dublin, 1976), MS Rawlinson B 502, fol. 148a.

Félire Óengusso; W. Stokes, ed., *Félire Óengusso Céli Dé – The Martyrology of Oengus the Culdee* (London, 1905).

Fó sén dia ngaib Óengus Albain; K. Meyer, ed., *Bruchstücke der älteren Lyrik Irlands* (Berlin, 1919), 6–7.

Fordun, John of. *Chronica gentis Scotorum*; W. F. Skene, ed., *Johannis de Fordun: Chronica gentis Scotorum*, Historians of Scotland 1 (Edinburgh, 1871–2).

Genelach Dáil Araidi; M. E. Dobbs, ed., 'The History of the Descendants of Ir', *Zeitschrift für celtische Philologie* 14 (1923), 44–144, at 62–72.

Gildas, *De excidio Britanniae*; M. Winterbottom, ed., *Gildas: The Ruin of Britain and other Documents* (London and Chichester, 1978), 87–142.

Gildas, *Praefatio Gildae de Poenitentia*; Bieler, ed., *Irish Penitentials*, 60–4.

Gveleys y dull o Bentir a doyn; Williams, ed., *Canu Aneirin*, 'A-text', ll. 966–71, 'B-text', ll. 972–77.

Haddan, A. W. and W. Stubbs, eds, *Councils and Ecclesiastical Documents Relating to Great Britain and Ireland*, vol. 2 (Oxford, 1873).

Harleian MS. 3859; P. C. Bartrum, ed., *Early Welsh Genealogical Tracts* (Cardiff, 1966), 9–13.

Hartmann, L. M., ed., *Gregorii I Papae Registrum Epistolarum*, vol. 2, Monumenta Germaniae Historica, Epistolarum 2 (Berlin 1899).

Herodian, *History*; C. R. Whitaker, ed., *Herodian*, vol. I (London, 1969).

Historia Augusta vita Hadriani; J. P. Callu, ed., *Histoire Auguste* (Paris, 1992), vol. 1, 18–48.

Historia Augusta vita Pii; Callu, ed., *Histoire Auguste*, vol. 1, 76–88.

Historia Brittonum; Faral, ed., *Légende Arthurienne*, 4–62.

Iniu feras Bruide cath; J. N. Radner, ed., *Fragmentary Annals* (Dublin, 1978), § 165.

Is uar in gáeth dar Ile; Stokes, ed., *Annals of Tigernach*, vol. 1, 178.

Isidore, *Etymologiae*; S. A. Barney *et al.*, trans., *The* Etymologies *of Isidore of Seville* (Cambridge, 2006).

Jonas, *Vita sancti Columbani*; B. Krusch, ed., *Passiones* (Hannover, 1902), 65–108.

Julius Caesar, *De bello Gallico*; H. J. Edwards, ed., *Caesar: the Gallic War* (London and New York, 1917).

Liber vitae ecclesiae Dunelmensis; Stevenson, ed., *Liber Vitae Ecclesiae Dunelmensis*, Surtees Society (Edinburgh, 1841).

Lifris, *Vita sancti Cadoci*; A. W. Wade-Evans, ed., *Vita Sanctorum Britanniae et Genealogiae* (Cardiff, 1944), 24–141.

Martyrology of Tallaght; R. I. Best and H. J. Lawlor, eds, *The Martyrology of Tallaght* (London, 1931).

Míniugud senchasa Síl Chuind; O'Brien, ed., *Corpus Genealogiarum Hiberniae*, MS Rawlinson B 502, fols 139b–40a.

Míniugud senchasa fher nAlban; D. N. Dumville, 'Ireland and North Britain' (Aberdeen, 2002), 201–3.

Miracula Nynie Episcopi; K. Strecker, ed., *Monumenta Germanica Historica: poetae Latini aevi Carolini IV* (Berlin, 1923), 943–61.

Monastery of Tallaght; E. J. Gwynn and W. J. Purton, eds, 'The Monastery of Tallaght', *Proceedings of the Royal Irish Academy* 29, Section C (1911–12), 115–79.

Mór do ingantu do-gní; M., Herbert and P. Ó Riain, eds, *Betha Adamnáin: the Irish Life of Adamnán*, Irish Texts Society (London, 1988), § 14.

Ní Dhonnchadha, M. 'The Guarantor List of Cáin Adomnáin, 697', *Peritia* 1 (1982), 178–215.

Panegyrici Latini; C. E. V. Nixon, B. S. Rodgers and R. A. B. Mynors, eds, *In Praise of Later Roman Emperors: the* Panegyrici Latini (Oxford, 1994).

Patricius, *Confessio*; A. B. E. Hood, ed., *St Patrick* (London and Chichester, 1978) 23–34.

Patricius, *Epistola*; Hood, ed., *St Patrick*, 35–8.

Pausanias, *Description of Greece*; W. H. S. Jones, ed., *Pausanias* (London and Cambridge, 1935), vol. IV.

Penitentialis Vinniani; Bieler, ed., *Irish Penitentials*, 74–94.

Prophecy of Berchán; B. T. Hudson, ed., *Prophecy of Berchán: Irish and Scottish High-kings of the Early Middle Ages* (London and Westport, CT, 1996).

Prosper, *Chronicle*; Mommsen, ed., *Chronica Minora*, 385–485.

Senchas Dáil Fiatach; O'Brien, ed., *Corpus Genealogiarum Hiberniae*, MS Book of Leinster, fol. 330b–d.

Solinus, *De mirabilis mundi*; M. A. Agnant, ed., *Polyhistor* (Paris, 1847).

Stephen, *Vita sancti Wilfrithi*; B. Colgrave, ed., *The Life of Bishop Wilfrid* (Cambridge, 1927).

Synodus Episcoporum; Bieler, ed., *Irish Penitentials*, 54–9.

Tacitus, *Agricola*; R. M. Ogilvie and I. Richmond, eds, *Cornelii Taciti: De Vita Agricolae* (Oxford, 1967).

Tacitus, *Annales*; J. Jackson, ed., *Tacitus: the Annals*, vol. III (London and Cambridge, MA, 1951).

Tacitus, *Historiae*; C. H. Moore, ed., *Tacitus: the Histories*, vol. I (London and New York, 1925).

'Taliesin', *Ardwyre Reget*; I. Williams, ed., *The Poems of Taliesin* (Dublin, 1968), VII.

'Taliesin', *Ar vn blyned*; Williams, ed., *The Poems of Taliesin*, V.

'Taliesin', *Arwyre gwyr Katraeth*; Williams, ed., *The Poems of Taliesin*, II.

'Taliesin', *E bore duw Sadwrn kat uawr a uu*; Williams, ed., *The Poems of Taliesin*, VI.

'Taliesin', *Eg gorffowys*; Williams, ed., *The Poems of Taliesin*, IV.

'Taliesin', *Eg gwrhyt gogyueirch yn trafferth*; Williams, ed., *The Poems of Taliesin*, VIII.

'Taliesin', *Eneit Owein ap Vryen*; Williams, ed., *The Poems of Taliesin*, X.

'Taliesin', *Lleuuyd echassaf*; Williams, ed., *The Poems of Taliesin*, IX.

'Taliesin', *Uryen Yrechwyd*; Williams, ed., *The Poems of Taliesin*, III.

Vita sanctissimi Ceolfridi Abbatis; Plummer, ed. *Venerabilis Baedae*, 388–404.

Vita sancti Cuthberti auctore anonymo; B. Colgrave, ed., *The Two Lives of Saint Cuthbert* (Cambridge, 1940).

Vita sancti Servani; A. Macquarrie, ed., '*Vita Sancti Servani*', *Innes Review* (1993).

Whitelock, D., ed., *English Historical Documents c. 500–1042*, 2nd edn (London and New York, 1979).

MODERN SCHOLARSHIP

Abels, R., 'The Council of Whitby: a study in early Anglo-Saxon politics', *Journal of British Studies* 23 (1983), 1–25.

Aitchison, N., *The Picts and the Scots at War* (Stroud, 2003).

Alcock, L., 'The Activities of Potentates in Celtic Britain: a positivist approach', in S. I. Driscoll and M. R. Nieke, eds, *Power and Politics* (Edinburgh, 1988), 22–39.

Alcock, L., *Kings and Warriors, Craftsmen and Priests in Northern Britain AD 550–850* (Edinburgh, 2003).

Anderson, A. O., ed., *Early Sources of Scottish History 500–1286*, vol. 1 (Edinburgh, 1922).

Anderson, A. O., *Prospects of the Advancement of Knowledge in Early Scottish History* (Dundee, 1940).

Anderson, A. O. and M. O. Anderson, eds, *Adomnán's Life of Columba* (Oxford, 1991).

Anderson, M. O., *Kings and Kingship in Early Scotland* (Edinburgh and London, 1973).

Anderson, M. O., 'Dalriada and the Creation of the Kingdom of the Scots', in D. Whitelock *et al.*, eds, *Ireland in Early Medieval Europe: Studies in Memory of Kathleen Hughes* (Cambridge, 1982), 106–32.

'The Anglo-British Cemetery at Bamburgh', interview in *The Heroic Age* 4 (2001), http://www.heroicage.org/issues/4/Bamburgh.html (last verified 18 June 2007).

Armit, I., *Celtic Scotland* (London, 1997).

Ashmore, P. J., 'Low cairns, long cists and symbol stones', *Proceedings of the Society of Antiquaries of Scotland* 110 (1978–80), 346–55.

Bannerman, J., *Studies in the History of Dalriada* (Edinburgh and London, 1974).

Bannerman, J., 'The Scots of Dalriada', in P. McNeill and R. Nicholson, eds, *Historical Atlas* (St Andrews, 1975), 13–15.

Barmann, B. C., 'The Mount Athos Epitome of Cassius Dio's Roman History', *Phoenix* 25 (1971), 58–67.

Barnes, T. D., *Constantine and Eusebius* (Cambridge, MA and London, 1981).

Barrett, J. C. *et al.*, eds, *Barbarians and Romans in North-West Europe from the Later Republic to Late Antiquity* (BAR International Series 471, 1989).

Barrow, G. W. S., 'Popular courts in Early Medieval Scotland: some suggested place-name evidence', *Scottish Studies* 25 (1981), 1–24 [also *Scottish Studies* 27 (1983), 67–8].

Barrow, G. W. S., 'The childhood of Scottish Christianity: a note on some place-name Evidence', *Scottish Studies* 27 (1983), 1–15.

Barrow, G. W. S., 'Religion in Scotland on the eve of Christianity', in K. Borchardt and E. Bünz, eds, *Forschungen zur Reichs-, Papst- und Landesgeschichte* (Stuttgart, 1998), 25–31.

Barrow, G. W. S., *Kingship and Unity: Scotland 1000–1306*, 2nd edn (Edinburgh, 2003).

Bassett, S., ed., *The Origins of Anglo-Saxon Kingdoms* (London and New York, 1989).

Bieler, L., ed., *The Irish Penitentials* (Dublin, 1963).

Birley, A. R., *Septimius Severus: the African Emperor*, 3rd edn (London, 1999).

Birley, A. R., 'The Anavionenses', in N. J. Higham, ed., *Archaeology of the Roman Empire: a Tribute to the Life and Works of Professor Barri Jones* (Oxford, 2001), 15–24.

Bloch, M., *Feudal Society* (L. A. Manyon, trans.) (London and New York, 1989).

Bourke, C., 'Cillíne Pontifex', *Innes Review* 49 (1998), 77–80.

Bowlus, C. R., 'Ethnogenesis: the tyranny of a concept', in A. Gillett, ed., *On Barbarian Identity* (Turnhout, 2002), 241–56.

Brather, S., 'Ethnic identities as constructions of archaeology: the case of the *Alamanni*', in Gillett, ed., *On Barbarian Identity*, 149–75.

Breeze, D. J., *The Northern Frontiers of Roman Britain* (London, 1982).

Breeze, D. J., *Roman Scotland: Frontier Country* (London, 1996).

Breeze, D. J., *The Antonine Wall* (Edinburgh, 2006).

Brooks, N., 'The creation and early structure of the kingdom of Kent', in S. Bassett, ed., *The Origins of Anglo-Saxon Kingdoms* (London and New York, 1989), 55–74.

Brooks, N., 'The Formation of the Mercian Kingdom', in Bassett, ed., *Origins of Anglo-Saxon Kingdoms*, 159–70.

Brooks, N., *The Early History of the Church of Canterbury: Christ Church from 597 to 1066* (London and New York, 1996).

Brooks, N., *Bede and the English* (Jarrow Lecture, 1999).

Broun, D., 'Pictish Kings 761–839: integration with Dál Riata or separate development?', in S. M. Foster, ed., *St Andrews Sarcophagus* (Dublin, 1998), 71–83.

Broun, D., 'Dunkeld and the Origin of Scottish Indentity', in Broun and Clancy (eds), *Spes Scotorum*, 95–111.

Broun, D., *The Irish Identity of the Kingdom of the Scots in the Twelfth and Thirteenth Centuries* (Woodbridge, 1999).

Broun, D., 'The seven kingdoms in *De Situ Albanie*: a record of Pictish political geography or imaginary map of ancient Alba?', in E. J. Cowan and R. A. McDonald, eds, *Alba* (East Linton, 2000), 24–42.

Broun, D., *Scottish Independence and the Idea of Britain from the Picts to Alexander III* (Edinburgh, 2007).

Broun, D. and T. O. Clancy, eds, *Spes Scotorum, Hope of Scots: Saint Columba, Iona and Scotland* (Edinburgh, 1999).

Burt, J. R. F., 'Long-cist cemeteries in Fife', in D. Henry, ed., *The Worm, the Germ, and the Thorn* (Balgavies, 1997), 64–6.

Byrne, F. J., *Irish Kings and High-Kings* 2nd edn (Dublin, 2001).

Calise, J. M. P., *Pictish Sourcebook: Documents of Medieval Legend and Dark Age History* (Westport, CT and London, 2002).

Callu, J.-P., ed., *Histoire Auguste*, vol. 1 (Paris, 1992).

Campbell, D. B., 'The Roman siege of Burnswark', *Britannia* 34 (2003), 19–33.

Campbell, E., *Saints and Sea-Kings: the First Kingdom of the Scots* (Edinburgh, 1999).

Campbell, E., 'Were the Scots Irish?', *Antiquity* 75 (2001), 285–92.

Campbell, J., *Bede's Reges and Principes* (Jarrow Lecture, 1979).

Campbell, J. *et al.*, *The Anglo-Saxons* (London, 1982).

Campbell, J., *Essays in Anglo-Saxon History* (London and Ronceverte, 1986).

Carver, M., 'Conversion and politics on the eastern seaboard of Britain; some archaeological indicators', in B. E. Crawford, ed., *Conversion and Christianity* (St Andrews, 1998), 11–40.

Carver, M., *Surviving in Symbols: a Visit to the Pictish Nation* (Edinburgh, 1999).

Carver, M., 'An Iona of the East: the early-medieval monastery at Portmahomack, Tarbat Ness', *Medieval Archaeology* 48 (2004), 1–30.

Carver, M., 'Sculpture in action: contexts for stone carving on the Tarbat peninsula, Easter Ross', in S. M. Foster and M. Cross, eds, *Able Minds and Practised Hands* (Leeds, 2005), 13–36.

Carver, M. O. H. *et al.*, Bulletins and Reports of the Tarbat Discovery Programme, 1995–2006, URL: http://www.york.ac.uk/depts/arch/staff/sites/tarbat/.

Chadwick, H. M., *Early Scotland: the Picts, the Scots and the Welsh of Southern Scotland* (Cambridge, 1949).

Chadwick, N. K., 'St Ninian: a preliminary study of sources', in *Transactions and Journal of Proceedings of the Dumfriesshire and Galloway Natural History and Antiquarian Society*, Third Series, 27 (1950), 9–53.

Chalmers, G., *Caledonia*, vol. 1, 2nd edn (Paisley, 1887).

Charles-Edwards, T. M., 'Kinship, status and the origins of the hide', *Past and Present* 56 (1972), 3–33.

Charles-Edwards, T. M., 'The authenticity of the *Gododdin*: an historian's view', in R. Bromwich and R. B. Jones, eds, *Astudiaethau ar yr Hengerdd/ Studies in Old Welsh Poetry* (Cardiff, 1978), 44–71.

Charles-Edwards, T., 'Early medieval kingships in the British Isles', in Bassett, ed., *Origins of Anglo-Saxon Kingdoms*, 28–39.

Charles-Edwards, T. M., 'Irish warfare before 1100', in T. Bartlett and K. Jeffery, eds, *A Military History of Ireland* (Cambridge, 1996), 26–51.

Charles-Edwards, T. M., ' "The continuation of Bede", *s. a.* 750: high-kings, kings of Tara and "Bretwaldas" ', in A. P. Smyth, ed., *Seanchas: Studies in Early and Medieval Irish Archaeology, History and Literature in Honour of Francis J. Byrne* (Dublin, 1999), 137–45.

Charles-Edwards, T. M., *Early Christian Ireland* (Cambridge, 2000).

Charles-Edwards, T. M., ed., *After Rome* (Oxford, 2003).

Charles-Edwards, T. M., 'Nations and kingdoms: a view from above', in Charles-Edwards, ed., *After Rome*, 23–58.

Charles-Edwards, T. M., 'Conversion to Christianity', in Charles-Edwards, ed., *After Rome*, 103–39.

Clancy, T. O., 'Annat in Scotland and the origins of the parish', *Innes Review* 46 (1995), 91–115.

Clancy, T. O., 'Iona, Scotland, and the Céli Dé', in B. E. Crawford, ed., *Scotland in Dark Age Britain* (St Andrews, 1996), 111–30.

Clancy, T. O., ed., *The Triumph Tree: Scotland's Earliest Poetry AD 550–1350* (Edinburgh, 1998).

Clancy, T. O., 'The Real St Ninian', *Innes Review* 52 (2001), 1–28.

Clancy, T. O., 'Philosopher-king: Nechtan mac Der-Ilei', *Scottish Historical Review* 83 (2004), 125–49.

Clancy, T. O., 'Deer and the early Church in the north-east', in K. Forsyth, ed., *This Splendid Little Book: Studies in the Book of Deer* (Dublin, forthcoming).

Clancy, T. O., *The Making of Scottish Christianity: a History to 1215* (Edinburgh, forthcoming).

Clancy, T. O. and G. Márkus, eds, *Iona: the Earliest Poetry of a Celtic Monastery* (Edinburgh, 1995).

Close-Brooks, J. *et al.*, 'Excavations at Clatchard Craig, Fife', *Proceedings of the Society of Antiquaries of Scotland* 116 (1986), 117–84.

Coates, S., 'The role of Bishops in the early Anglo-Saxon Church: a reassessment', *History* 81 (1996), 177–96.

Colgrave, B., ed., *The Life of Bishop Wilfrid by Eddius Stephanus* (Cambridge, 1927).

Colgrave, B., ed., *Two Lives of Saint Cuthbert* (Cambridge, 1940).

Colgrave, B. and R. A. B. Mynors, eds, *Bede's Ecclesiastical History of the English People* (Oxford, 1991).

Collingwood, R. G. and R. P. Wright, eds, *The Roman Inscriptions of Britain*, vol. 1 (Oxford, 1965).

Collis, J., *The Celts: Origins, Myths and Inventions* (Stroud, 2003).

Cowan, E. J., 'Myth and identity in early medieval Scotland', *Scottish Historical Review* 63.2 (1984), 111–35.

Cowan, E. J. and R. A. McDonald, eds, *Alba: Celtic Scotland in the Middle Ages* (East Linton, 2000).

Crawford, B. E., ed., *Scotland in Dark Age Europe* (St Andrews, 1994).

Crawford, B. E., ed., *Scotland in Dark Age Britain* (St Andrews, 1996).

Crawford, B. E., ed., *Conversion and Christianity in the North Sea World* (St Andrews, 1998).

Cruickshank, G. D. R., 'The battle of Dunnichen and the Aberlemno battle-scene', in Cowan and McDonald, eds, *Alba*, 69–87.

Cusack, C. M., *Conversion among the Germanic Peoples* (London and New York, 1998), paperback version entitled *The Rise of Christianity in Northern Europe, 300–1000*.

Dark, K. R., *Civitas to Kingdom: British Political Continuity 300–800* (London and New York, 1994).

Davies, J. R., *The Book of Llandaf and the Norman Church in Wales* (Woodbridge, 2003).

Davies, J. R., *The Cult of St Constantine and the Ecclesiastical History of Strathclyde*, Govan Lecture, Series 6 (Glasgow, 2008).

Davies, S., *Welsh Military Institutions, 633–1283* (Cardiff, 2004).

de Jong, M., 'Monastic prisoners or opting out? Political coercion and honour in the Frankish kingdoms', in M. de Jong *et al.*, eds, *Topographies of Power in the Early Middle Ages* (Leiden, 2001), 291–328.

Devine, T. M., *The Scottish Nation 1700–2000* (London, 1999).

Dobbs, M., 'Cé: the Pictish name of a district in eastern Scotland', *Scottish Gaelic Studies* 6 (1949), 137–8.

Driscoll, S. T., 'Political discourse and the growth of Christian ceremonialism in Pictland: the place of the St Andrews sarcophagus', in S. M. Foster, ed., *The St Andrews Sarcophagus* (Dublin, 1998), 168–78.

Driscoll, S. T., 'Christian monumental sculpture and ethnic expression in early Scotland', in W. O. Frazer and A. Tyrrell, eds, *Social Identity in Early Medieval Britain* (London and New York, 2000), 233–52.

Driscoll, S. and K. Forsyth, 'The Late Iron Age and Early Historic Period', *Scottish Archaeological Journal* 26 (2004), 4–11.

Driscoll, S. T. and M. R. Nieke, eds, *Power and Politics in Early Medieval Britain and Ireland* (Edinburgh, 1988).

Driscoll, S. T. *et al.*, eds, *Pictish Studies for the Twenty-First Century* (forthcoming).

Dumville, D., 'Some aspects of the chronology of the *Historia Brittonum*', *Bulletin of the Board of Celtic Studies* 25 (1972–4), 439–45.

Dumville, D., '"Nennius" and the *Historia Brittonum*', *Studia Celtica* 10/11 (1975–6), 78–95.

Dumville, D., 'The Anglian collection of Royal Genealogies and Regnal Lists', *Anglo-Saxon England* 5 (1976), 23–50.

Dumville, D., 'On the North British section of the *Historia Brittonum*', *Welsh History Review* 8 (1976–7), 345–54.

Dumville, D., 'Sub-Roman Britain: history and legend', *History* 62 (1977), 173–92.

Dumville, D., 'Kingship, genealogies and regnal lists', in P. H. Sawyer and I. N. Wood, eds, *Early Medieval Kingship* (Leeds, 1977), 72–104.

Dumville, D., 'The Welsh Latin Annals', *Studia Celtica* 12/13 (1977–8), 461–7.

Dumville, D. N., 'Gildas and Uinniau', in M. Lapidge and D. Dumville, eds, *Gildas* (Woodbridge, 1984), 207–14.

Dumville, D., 'The historical value of the *Historia Brittonum*', *Arthurian Literature* 6 (1986), 1–26.

Dumville, D. N., 'Early Welsh poetry: problems of historicity', in B. F. Roberts, ed., *Early Welsh Poetry: Studies in the Book of Aneirin* (Aberystwyth, 1988), 1–16.

Dumville, D., 'The origins of Northumbria: some aspects of the British background', in Bassett, ed., *The Origins of Anglo-Saxon Kingdoms*, 213–22.

Dumville, D., '*Cath Fedo Euin*', *Scottish Gaelic Studies* 17 (1996), 114–27.

Dumville, D. N., *The Churches of North Britain in the First Viking-Age* (Whithorn Lecture, 1997).

Dumville, D. N., 'The Chronicle of the Kings of Alba', in S. Taylor, ed., *Kings, Clerics and Chronicles* (Dublin, 2000), 73–86.

Dumville, D. N., '*Cethri prímchenéla Dáil Riata*', *Scottish Gaelic Studies* 20 (2000), 170–91.

Dumville, D. N., 'Ireland and north Britain in the earlier Middle Ages: contexts for *Míniugud Senchasa Fher nAlban*', in C. Ó Baoill and N. R. McGuire, eds, *Rannsachadh na Gàidhlig 2000* (Aberdeen, 2002), 185–211.

Dumville, D. N., *Annales Cambriae, A.D. 682–954: texts A–C in Parallel* (Cambridge, 2002).

Dumville, D. N. *et al.*, *Saint Patrick* (Woodbridge, 1993).

Duncan, A. A. M., *Scotland: the Making of the Kingdom*, Edinburgh History of Scotland I (Edinburgh, 1975).

Duncan, A. A. M., 'Bede, Iona, and the Picts', in R. H. C. Davis and J. M. Wallace-
Hadrill, eds, *The Writing of History in the Middle Ages* (Oxford, 1981), 1–42.

Duncan, A. A. M., *The Kingship of the Scots 842–1292: Succession and Independence*
(Edinburgh, 2002).

Enright, M. J., 'Royal succession and abbatial prerogative in Adomnán's Vita
Columbae', *Peritia* 4 (1985), 83–103.

Esmonde Cleary, A. S., *The Ending of Roman Britain* (London, 1989).

Etchingham, C., *Church Organisation in Ireland A.D. 650 to 1000* (Maynooth, 1999).

Etchingham, C. and C. Swift., 'English and Pictish terms for brooch in an 8th-century
Irish law tract', *Medieval Archaeology* 48 (2004), 31–49.

Evans, N. J., 'The textual development of the principal Irish chronicles in the tenth and
eleventh centuries', unpublished Ph.D. dissertation (University of Glasgow, 2003).

Evans, N., 'Irish Chronicles as sources for the history of Northern Britain, AD
660–800', *The Journal of Celtic Studies* (2005).

Evans, N., 'Ideology, literacy and matriliny: approaches to medieval texts on the Pictish
past', in S. T. Driscoll *et al.*, eds, *Pictish Studies* (forthcoming).

Faral, E., ed., *La Légende Arthurienne: études et documents*, vol. 3 (Paris, 1929).

Field, P. J. C., 'Gildas and the City of the Legions', *The Heroic Age* 1 (1999),
http://www.mun.ca/mst/heroicage/issues/1/hagcl.htm (last verified 16 June 2007).

Fisher, I., *Early Medieval Sculpture in the West Highlands and Islands* (Edinburgh, 2001).

Fletcher, R., *The Barbarian Conversion from Paganism to Christianity* (New York, 1997).

Foley, W. T., *Images of Sanctity in Eddius Stephanus' Life of Bishop Wilfrid, an Early
English Saint's Life* (Lampeter, 1992).

Forsyth, K., 'The inscriptions on the Dupplin Cross', in C. Bourke, ed., *From the Isles
of the North: Early Medieval Art in Ireland and Britain* (Belfast, 1995), 237–44.

Forsyth, K., *Language in Pictland: the Case Against 'non-Indo-European Pictish'*
(Utrecht, 1997).

Forsyth, K., 'Literacy in Pictland', in H. Pryce, ed., *Literacy in Medieval Celtic Societies*
(Cambridge, 1998), 39–61.

Forsyth, K., 'Evidence of a lost Pictish source in the *Historia Regum Anglorum* of
Symeon of Durham', in Taylor, ed., *Kings, Clerics and Chronicles*, 19–32.

Forsyth, K., '*Hic Memoria Perpetua*: the early inscribed stones of southern Scotland in
context', in S. M. Foster and M. Cross, eds, *Able Minds and Practised Hands* (Leeds,
2005), 113–34.

Foster, S. M., 'Before Alba: Pictish and Dál Riata power centres from the fifth to the
late ninth centuries AD', in S. Foster, A. Macinnes and R. MacInnes, eds, *Scottish
Power Centres* (Glasgow, 1998), 1–31.

Foster, S. M., ed., *The St Andrews Sarcophagus: a Pictish Masterpiece and its
International Connections* (Dublin, 1998).

Foster, S. M., *Picts, Gaels and Scots: Early Historic Scotland*, 2nd edn (London, 2004).

Foster, S., A. Macinnes and R. MacInnes, eds, *Scottish Power Centres from the Early
Middle Ages to the Twentieth Century* (Glasgow, 1998).

Foster, S. M. and M. Cross, eds, *Able Minds and Practised Hands: Scotland's Early
medieval Sculpture in the 21st Century*, Society for Medieval Archaeology Monograph
23 (Leeds, 2005).

Fraser, J., 'The question of the Picts', *Scottish Gaelic Studies* 2 (1927), 172–201.

Fraser, J. E., 'Northumbrian Whithorn and the making of St Ninian', *Innes Review* 53
(2002), 40–59.

Fraser, J. E., *The Battle of Dunnichen 685* (Stroud, 2002).

Fraser, J. E., 'Adomnán, Cumméne Ailbe, and the Picts', *Peritia* 17–18 (2003–4), 183–98.

Fraser, J. E., 'The Iona Chronicle, the descendants of Áedán mac Gabráin, and the "Principal Kindreds of Dál Riata"', *Northern Studies* 38 (2004), 77–96.

Fraser, J. E., *The Roman Conquest of Scotland: the Battle of Mons Graupius AD 84* (Stroud, 2005).

Fraser, J. E., 'Strangers on the Clyde: Cenél Comgaill, Clyde Rock and the bishops of Kingarth', *Innes Review* 56 (2005), 102–20.

Fraser, J. E., '*Dux Reuda* and the Corcu Réti', in W. McLeod *et al.*, eds, *Cànan & Cultar/Language & Culture: Rannsachadh na Gàidhlig 3* (Edinburgh, 2006), 1–9.

Fraser, J. E., 'St Columba and the convention at Druimm Cete: peace and politics at seventh-century Iona', *Early Medieval Europe* 15.3 (2007), 315–34.

Fraser, J. E., 'Picts in the west in the 670s? Some thoughts on AU 673.3 and AU 676.3', *Journal of Scottish Name Studies* 1 (2007), 144–8.

Fraser, J. E., 'Bede, the Firth of Forth and the location of *Urbs Iudeu*', *Scottish Historical Review* 86.1 (2008), forthcoming.

Fraser, J. E., 'Rochester, Hexham and Cennrígmonaid: the movements of St Andrew in Britain, 604–747', in S. Boardman *et al.*, eds, *Saints Cults in the Celtic World* (Woodbridge, forthcoming).

Fraser, J. E., 'From ancient Scythia to *The Problem of the Picts*: thoughts on the quest for Pictish origins', in S. T. Driscoll *et al.*, eds, *Pictish Studies for the Twenty-First Century* (Leiden, forthcoming).

Fraser, J. E., '"All the northern part of Britain": the metropolitan episcopate of Wilfrid of York, 669–78', in S. Turner and D. A. Petts, eds, *Early Medieval Northumbria: Kingdoms and Communities, ad 450–1100* (Turnhout, forthcoming).

Fraser, J. E., 'Adomnán and the morality of war', in R. Aist *et al.*, eds, *Adomnán of Iona: Theologian – Lawmaker – Peacemaker* (Dublin, forthcoming).

Fraser, J. E., 'The early Middle Ages *c*. 500–1093', in J. Crang *et al.*, eds, *A Military History of Scotland* (Edinburgh, forthcoming).

Frazer, W. O. and A. Tyrrell, eds, *Social Identity in Early Medieval Britain* (London and New York, 2000).

Frere, S., *Britannia: a History of Roman Britain* 3rd edn (London, 1987).

Geary, P. J., 'Ethnic identity as a situational construct in the early Middle Ages', *Mitteilungen der Anthropologischen Gesellschaft in Wien* 113 (1983), 15–26.

Gibbs, M., 'The decrees of Agatho and the Gregorian plan for York', *Speculum* 48 (1973), 213–46.

Gillett, A., ed., *On Barbarian Identity: Critical Approaches to Ethnicity in the Early Middle Ages* (Turnhout, 2002).

Gillett, A., 'Was ethnicity politicized in the earliest medieval kingdoms?', in A. Gillett ed., *On Barbarian Identity*, 85–121.

Goldsworthy, A. K., *The Roman Army at War 100 BC–AD 200* (Oxford, 1996).

Goffart, W., *The Narrators of Barbarian History (A.D. 550–800): Jordanes, Gregory of Tours, Bede, and Paul the Deacon* (Princeton, 1988).

Goffart, W., 'Two notes on Germanic antiquity today', *Traditio* 50 (1995), 9–30.

Goffart, W., 'Does the distant past impinge on the invasion age Germans?', in Gillett, ed., *On Barbarian Identity*, 21–37.

Graham, A., 'Giudi', *Antiquity* 33 (1959), 63–5.

Grant, L., 'United parishes of Ardchattan and Muckairn', in D. J. Withrington and
I. R. Grant, eds, *The Statistical Account of Scotland 1791–1799, edited by Sir John
Sinclair*, vol. viii (East Ardsley, 1983).

Gruffydd, R. G., 'From Gododdin to Gwynedd: reflections on the story of Cunedda',
Studia Celtica 24–5 (1989–90), 1–14.

Halsall, G., *Early Medieval Cemeteries: an Introduction to Burial Archaeology in the post-
Roman West* (Glasgow, 1995).

Halsall, G., ed., *Violence and Society in the Early Medieval West* (Woodbridge, 1998).

Halsall, G., 'Violence and society in the early Medieval West: an introductory survey',
in Halsall, ed., *Violence and Society in the Early Medieval West*, 1–45.

Halsall, G., *Warfare and Society in the Barbarian West, 450–900* (London and New York,
2003).

Hanson, W. S., *Agricola and the Conquest of the North* (London, 1987).

Hanson, W. S. and G. S. Maxwell, *Rome's North West Frontier: the Antonine Wall*, 2nd
edn (Edinburgh, 1986).

Harding, D. W., *The Iron Age in Northern Britain: Celts and Romans, Natives and
Invaders* (London and New York, 2004).

Harris, A., *Byzantium, Britain and the West: the archaeology of cultural identity AD
400–650* (Stroud, 2003).

Heather, P., 'State formation in Europe in the first millennium A.D.', in B. E. Crawford,
ed., *Scotland in Dark Age Europe* (St Andrews, 1994), 47–70.

Heather, P. J., 'Disappearing and reappearing tribes', in W. Pohl and H. Reimitz, eds,
Strategies of Distinction (Leiden, 1998), 95–111.

Henderson, I., *The Picts* (London, 1967).

Henderson, G. and I. Henderson, *The Art of the Picts: Sculpture and Metalwork in Early
Medieval Scotland* (London, 2004).

Henry, D., ed., *The Worm, the Germ, and the Thorn: Pictish and Related Studies presented
to Isabel Henderson* (Balgavies, 1997).

Herbert, M., *Iona, Kells, and Derry: the History and Hagiography of the Monastic* familia
of Columba (Oxford, 1988).

Herbert, M., 'The legacy of Columba', in T. M. Devine and J. F. McMillan, eds,
Celebrating Columba: Irish–Scottish connections 597–1997 (Edinburgh, 1999),
1–14.

Higham, N. J., *The Convert Kings: Power and Religious Affiliation in early Anglo-Saxon
England* (Manchester and New York, 1997).

Hind, J. G. F., 'The "Genounian" part of Britain', *Britannia* 8 (1977), 229–34.

Hind, J. G. F., 'Caledonia and its occupation under the Flavians', *Proceedings of the
Society of Antiquaries of Scotland* 113 (1983), 373–8.

Hines, J., 'Society, community and identity', in Charles-Edwards, ed., *After Rome*,
61–101.

Hingley, R., 'Society in Scotland from 700 BC to AD 200', *Proceedings of the Society of
Antiquaries of Scotland* 122 (1992), 7–53.

Hobley, A. S., 'The numismatic evidence for the post-Agricolan abandonment of the
Roman frontier in northern Scotland', *Britannia* 20 (1989), 69–74.

Hood, A. B. E., ed., *St Patrick: his Writings and Muirchu's Life* (London and Chichester,
1978).

Hudson, B. T., *Kings of Celtic Scotland* (Westport, CT and London, 1994).

Hughes, K., *Early Christianity in Pictland* (Jarrow Lecture, 1970).

Hughes, K., 'The Welsh Latin Chronicles: *Annales Cambriae* and related texts', *Proceedings of the British Academy* 59 (1973), 233–58.

Hughes, K., 'Where are the writings of early Scotland?', in D. Dumville, ed., *Celtic Britain in the Early Middle Ages: Studies in Scottish and Welsh sources* (Woodbridge, 1980), 1–12.

Hummer, H. J., 'The fluidity of Barbarian identity: the ethnogenesis of Alemanni and Suebi, AD 200–500', *Early Medieval Europe* 7.1 (1998), 1–27.

Hunter, F., 'New light on Iron Age massive armlets', *Proceedings of the Society of Antiquaries of Scotland* 136 (2006), 135–60.

Hunter, F., *Beyond the Edge of the Empire: Caledonians, Picts and Romans*, Groam House Lecture (Rosemarkie, 2007).

Hunter Blair, P., 'The origins of Northumbria', *Archaeologia Aeliana* 25 (1947), 1–51.

Hunter Blair, P., 'The Bernicians and their northern frontier', in N. K. Chadwick, ed., *Studies in Early British History* (Cambridge, 1954), 137–72.

Innes, C., *Scotland in the Middle Ages* (Edinburgh, 1860).

Jackson, K., 'Two early Scottish names', *Scottish Historical Review* 33 (1954), 14–18.

Jackson, K., 'The Britons in southern Scotland', *Antiquity* 29 (1955), 77–88.

Jackson, K., 'The Pictish language', in F. T. Wainwright, ed., *The Problem of the Picts* (Edinburgh, 1955), 129–66.

Jackson, K. H., 'Edinburgh and the Anglian occupation of Lothian', in P. Clemoes, ed., *The Anglo-Saxons: Studies in Some Aspects of the History and Culture presented to Bruce Dickins* (London, 1959), 35–42.

Jackson, K., 'On the Northern British section of Nennius', in N. Chadwick, ed., *Celt and Saxon: Studies in the Early British border* (Cambridge, 1963), 20–62.

Jackson, K., 'Bede's *Urbs Giudi*: Stirling or Cramond?', *Cambridge Medieval Celtic Studies* 2 (1981), 1–7.

James, E., 'The origins of Barbarian kingdoms: the Continental evidence', in Bassett, ed., *Origins of Anglo-Saxon Kingdoms*, 40–52.

John, E., *Land Tenure in Early England: a Discussion of Some Problems*, 2nd edn (Leicester, 1964).

John, E., 'The social and political problems of the Early English Church', *Agricultural History Review* 18 (1970); Supplement: Land, Church and People: essays presented to Professor H. P. R. Finberg, 39–63.

Jones, S., *The Archaeology of Ethnicity: Constructing Identities in the Past and Present* (London and New York, 1997).

Jones, W. H. S., ed., *Pausanias: Description of Greece*, vol. IV (London and Cambridge, 1935).

Keeley, L. H., *War Before Civilization* (Oxford, 1996).

Kelly, F., *A Guide to Early Irish Law* (Dublin, 1988).

Kirby, D. P., 'Bede and the Pictish Church', *Innes Review* 24 (1973), 6–25.

Kirby, D. P., 'Northumbria in the time of Wilfrid', in D. P. Kirby, ed., *Saint Wilfrid at Hexham* (Newcastle, 1974), 1–34.

Kirby, D. P., 'Bede, Eddius Stephanus and the "Life of Wilfrid"', *English Historical Review* 98 (1983), 101–14.

Kirby, D. P., *The Earliest English Kings*, 2nd edn (London and New York, 2000).

Koch, J. T., *The Gododdin of Aneirin: Text and Context from Dark-age North Britain* (Cardiff and Andover, MA, 1997).

Krusch, B., ed., *Passiones Vitaeque Sanctorum aevi Merovingici*, Monumenta Germaniae Historica, Scriptorum Rerum Merovingicarum IV (Hannover, 1902).

Kulikowski, M., 'Nation versus army: a necessary contrast?', in Gillett, ed., *On Barbarian Identity*, 69–84.

Lamb, R., 'Pictland, Northumbria and the Carolingian empire', in Crawford, ed., *Conversion and Christianity*, 41–56.

Lane A. and E. Campbell, *Dunadd: an Early Dalriadic Capital* (Oxford, 2000).

Lapidge, M. and D. Dumville, eds, *Gildas: New Approaches* (Woodbridge, 1984).

Lethbridge, T. C., *The Painted Men* (London, 1954).

Levick, B., *Vespasian* (London and New York, 1999).

Lewis, C. T. and C. Short, *A Latin Dictionary* (Oxford, 1900).

Lowe, C., *Angels, Fools and Tyrants: Britons and Anglo-Saxons in Southern Scotland AD 450–750* (Edinburgh, 1999).

Loyn, H. R., *The Governance of Anglo-Saxon England 500–1087* (London, 1984).

MacDonald, A., 'Two major early monasteries of Scottish Dalriata: Lismore and Eigg', *Scottish Archaeological Forum* 5 (1973), 47–70.

MacDonald, A. D. S., 'Iona's style of government among the Picts and Scots: the toponymic evidence of Adomnán's Life of Columba', *Peritia* 4 (1985), 174–86.

Mac Eoin, G. S., 'On the Irish legend of the origin of the Picts', *Studia Hibernica* 4 (1962), 138–54.

Macinnes, L., 'Brochs and the Roman occupation of lowland Scotland', *Proceedings of the Society of Antiquaries of Scotland* 114 (1984), 235–49.

Macinnes, L., 'Baubles, bangles and beads: trade and exchange in Roman Scotland', in Barrett *et al.*, eds, *Barbarians and Romans*, 108–16.

Mac Lean, D., 'Maelrubai, Applecross and the late Pictish contribution west of Druimalban', in Henry, ed., *The Worm, the Germ, and the Thorn*, 173–87.

Mac Lean, D., 'The Northumbrian perspective', in Foster, ed., *The St Andrews Sarcophagus*, 179–201.

Macquarrie, A., 'The kings of Strathclyde, c. 400–1018', in A. Grant and K. J. Stringer, eds, *Medieval Scotland: Crown, Lordship and Community* (Edinburgh, 1993), 1–19.

Macquarrie, A., '*Vita Sancti Servani*: the Life of St Serf', *Innes Review* 44 (1993), 122–52.

Macquarrie, A., *The Saints of Scotland: Essays in Scottish Church History AD 450–1093* (Edinburgh, 1997).

MacQueen, J., *St Nynia*, 2nd edn (Edinburgh, 1990).

Márkus, G., 'Iona: monks, pastors and missionaries', in Broun and Clancy, eds, *Spes Scotorum*, 115–38.

Maxwell, G. S., 'Settlement in southern Pictland: a new overview', in A. Small, ed., *The Picts* (Dundee, 1987), 31–44.

McClure, J. and R. Collins, eds, *Bede: The Ecclesiastical History of the English People. The Greater Chronicle. Bede's Letter to Egbert* (Oxford, 1999).

McNeill, P. and R. Nicholson, eds, *An Historical Atlas of Scotland c. 400–c. 1600* (St Andrews, 1975).

Meckler, M., 'Colum Cille's Ordination of Aedán mac Gabráin', *Innes Review* 41 (1990), 139–50.

Meckler, M., 'The *Annals of Ulster* and the date of the meeting at Druim Cett', *Peritia* 11 (1997), 44–52.

Millar, F., *A Study of Cassius Dio* (Oxford, 1964).

Miller, M., 'Stilicho's Pictish war', *Britannia* 6 (1975), 141–5.

Miller, M., 'Eanfrith's Pictish son', *Northern History* 14 (1978), 47–66.

Miller, W. I., *Bloodtaking and Peacemaking: Feud, Law and Society in Saga Iceland* (Chicago and London, 1990).

Millett, M., *The Romanization of Britain: an Essay in Archaeological Interpretation* (Cambridge, 1990).

Moisl, H., 'The Bernician royal dynasty and the Irish in the seventh century', *Peritia* 2 (1983), 103–26.

Mommsen, T., ed., *Chronica Minora saec. IV. V. VI. VII.*, Monumenta Germaniae Historica, Auctorum Antiquissimorum 9 (Berlin, 1892).

Murray, A. C., '*Post vocantur Merohingii*: Fredegar, Merovech, and "sacral kingship" ', in Murray, ed., *After Rome's Fall*, 121–52.

Murray, A. C., ed., *After Rome's Fall: Narrators and Sources of Early Medieval History* (Toronto, 1998).

Murray, A. C., 'Reinhard Wenskus on "ethnogenesis", ethnicity, and the origin of the Franks', in Gillett, ed., *On Barbarian Identity*, 39–68.

Nelson, J. L., 'Queens as Jezebels: the careers of Brunhild and Balthild in Merovingian history', in D. Baker, ed., *Medieval Women* (Oxford, 1978), 31–77.

Nelson, J. L., 'Violence in the Carolingian world and the ritualization of ninth-century warfare', in Halsall, ed., *Violence and Society in the Early Medieval West*, 90–107.

Newton, M., *Gaelic in Scottish History and Culture* (Belfast, 1997).

Nicolaisen, W. F. H., *Scottish Place-Names: their Study and Significance* (London, 1976).

Nieke, M. R. and H. B. Duncan, 'Dalriada: the establishment and maintenance of an Early Historic kingdom in northern Britain', in Driscoll and Nieke, eds, *Power and Politics*, 6–21.

O'Brien, M. A., ed., *Corpus Genealogiarum Hiberniae*, vol. 1 (Dublin, 1976).

O'Loughlin, T., *Celtic Theology: Humanity, World and God in Early Irish Writings* (London and New York, 2000).

Ó Riain, P., 'St Finnbarr: a study in a cult', *Journal of the Cork Historical and Archaeological Society* 82 (1977), 63–82.

Ó Riain, P., *Anglo-Saxon Ireland: the Evidence of the Martyrology of Tallaght* (Cambridge, 1993).

Pelteret, D. A. E., *Slavery in Early Mediaeval England* (Woodbridge, 1995).

Piggott, S., 'The archaeological background', in Wainwright, ed., *The Problem of the Picts*, 54–65.

Plummer, C., ed., *Venerabilis Baedae Opera Historica*, vol. 1 (Oxford, 1896).

Pohl, W., 'Telling the difference: signs of ethnic identity', in Pohl and Reimitz, eds, *Strategies of Distinction*, 17–69.

Pohl, W., 'Ethnicity, theory, and tradition: a response', in Gillett, ed., *On Barbarian Identity*, 221–39.

Pohl, W. and H. Reimitz, eds, *Strategies of Distinction: the Construction of Ethnic Communities, 300–800* (Leiden, 1998).

Poole, R. L., 'The chronology of Bede's *Historia Ecclesiastica* and the Councils of 679–680', *Journal of Theological Studies* 20 (1918), 24–40.

Poole, R. L., 'St Wilfrid and the see of Ripon', *English Historical Review* 34 (1919), 1–24.

Proudfoot, E., 'The Hallow Hill and the origins of Christianity in eastern Scotland', in Crawford, ed., *Conversion and Christianity*, 57–73.

Radner, J. N., ed., *Fragmentary Annals of Ireland* (Dublin, 1978).

Ralston, I., *The Hill-Forts of Pictland Since 'The Problem of the Picts'* (Groam House Lecture, 2004).

Ralston, I., *Celtic Fortifications* (Stroud, 2006).

Reed, N., 'The Scottish campaigns of Septimius Severus', *Proceedings of the Society of Antiquaries of Scotland* 107 (1975–6), 97–102, at 98.

Reynolds, S., 'Our forefathers? Tribes, peoples, and nations in the historiography of the age of migrations', in A. C. Murray, ed., *After Rome's Fall* (Toronto, 1998), 17–36.

Richardson, P. and M. Kirby, 'Lockerbie Academy, Dumfries & Galloway', CFA Archaeology News (2006) http://www.cfaarchaeology.co.uk/news/news_lockerbie.html (last verified 18 June 2007).

Richmond, I. A., 'Roman and native in the fourth century A.D., and after', in I. A. Richmond, ed., *Roman and Native in Northern Britain* (London, 1958), 112–30.

Ritchie, A., *Viking Scotland* (London, 1993).

Rivet, A. L. F., 'The Brittones Anavionenses', *Britannia* 13 (1982), 321–2.

Rivet, A. L. F. and C. Smith, *The Place-Names of Roman Britain* (London, 1981).

Rollason, D., *Northumbria, 500–1100: Creation and Destruction of a Kingdom* (Cambridge, 2003).

Ross, A., 'Pictish matriliny?', *Northern Studies* 34 (1999), 11–22.

Salway, P., *Roman Britain*, Oxford History of England 1A (Oxford, 1981).

Sawyer, P. H. and I. N. Wood, eds, *Early Medieval Kingship* (Leeds, 1977).

Sellar, W. D. H., 'Warlords, holy men and matrilineal succession', *Innes Review* 36 (1985), 29–43.

Sharpe, R., 'Gildas as a father of the Church', in Lapidge and Dumville, eds, *Gildas*, 193–205.

Sharpe, R., *Adomnán of Iona: Life of St Columba* (London, 1995).

Sharpe, R., 'The thriving of Dalriada', in S. Taylor, ed., *Kings, Clerics and Chronicles* (Dublin, 2000), 47–61.

Skene, W. F., 'Notice of the early ecclesiastical settlements at St Andrews', *Proceedings of the Society of Antiquaries of Scotland* 4 (1860–2), 300–21.

Skene, W. F., 'Notice of the site of the battle of Ardderyd or Arderyth', *Proceedings of the Society of Antiquaries of Scotland* 6 (1864–6), 91–8.

Skene, W. F., ed., *Chronicles of the Picts, Chronicles of the Scots, and Other Early Memorials of Scottish History* (Edinburgh, 1867).

Skene, W. F., *Celtic Scotland: a History of Ancient Alban*, vol. 1: History and Ethnology, 2nd edn (Edinburgh, 1886).

Skene, W. F., *Celtic Scotland: a History of Ancient Alban*, vol. 2: Church and Culture, 2nd edn (Edinburgh, 1887).

Small, A., ed., *The Picts: a New Look at Old Problems* (Dundee, 1987).

Smith, I., 'The origins and development of Christianity in north Britain and southern Pictland', within 'The archaeology of the early Christian Church in Scotland and Man AD 400–1200', in J. Blair and C. Pyrah, eds, *Church Archaeology: Research Directions for the Future* (York, 1996), 19–37.

Smyth, A. P., *Warlords and Holy Men: Scotland AD 80–1000* (London, 1984).

Snyder, C., 'The age of Arthur: some historical and archaeological background', *The Heroic Age* 1 (1999), http://www.mun.ca/mst/heroicage/issues/1/haage.htm (last verified 16 June 2007).

Taylor, S., 'Place-names and the early Church in eastern Scotland', in Crawford, ed., *Scotland in Dark Age Britain*, 93–110.

Taylor, S., 'Place-names and the early Church in Scotland', *Records of the Scottish Church History Society* 28 (1998), 1–22.

Taylor, S., 'Seventh-century Iona abbots in Scottish place-names', in Broun and Clancy, eds, *Spes Scotorum*, 35–70.

Taylor, S., ed., *Kings, Clerics and Chronicles in Scotland 500–1297: Essays in Honour of Marjorie Ogilvie Anderson on the Occasion of her Ninetieth Birthday* (Dublin, 2000).

Thomas, A. C., 'The evidence from North Britain', in M. W. Barley and R. P. C. Hanson, eds, *Christianity in Britain, 300–700* (Leicester, 1968), 93–121.

Thomas, C., *Christianity in Roman Britain to AD 500* (London, 1981).

Tomlin, R., 'The date of the "Barbarian Conspiracy"', *Britannia* 5 (1974), 303–9.

Veitch, K., 'The Columban Church in northern Britain, 664–717: a reassessment', *Proceedings of the Society of Antiquaries of Scotland* 127 (1997), 627–47.

Wagner, S. M., 'Ritual impurity and the Céli Dé: sin, theology, and practice in the eighth and ninth centuries', unpublished Ph.D. thesis (University of Edinburgh, 2006).

Wainwright, F. T., ed., *The Problem of the Picts* (Edinburgh, 1955).

Wainwright, F. T., 'The Picts and the problem', in Wainwright, ed., *Problem of the Picts*, 1–53.

Walker, G. S. M., ed., *Sancti Columbani Opera* (Dublin, 1957).

Wallace-Hadrill, J. M., *Bede's Ecclesiastical History of the English People: a Historical Commentary* (Oxford, 1988).

Ward-Perkins, B., *The Fall of Rome and the End of Civilization* (Oxford, 2005).

Watson, W. J., *The History of the Celtic Place-Names of Scotland* (Edinburgh and London, 1926; reprinted Dublin, 1986).

Watson, W. J., *Scottish Place-Name Papers* (London, 2002).

Webb, J. F. and D. H. Farmer, *The Age of Bede* (London, 1983).

Wenskus, R., *Stammesbildung und Verfassung: Das Werden der frühmittelalterlichen gentes* (Cologne, 1961).

Whitaker, C. R., 'Supplying the system: frontiers and beyond', in Barrett *et al.*, eds, *Barbarians and Romans*, 64–80.

Whittington, G., 'Placenames and the settlement pattern of Dark-Age Scotland', *Proceedings of the Society of Antiquaries of Scotland* 106 (1974-5), 99-110.

Williams, I., ed., *Canu Aneirin* (Cardiff, 1938).

Williams, I., ed., *The Poems of Taliesin* (Dublin, 1968).

Wolfram, H., *History of the Goths* (T. J. Dunlap, trans.) (Berkeley, 1988).

Wood, I., 'Kings, kingdoms and consent', in Sawyer and Wood, eds, *Early Medieval Kingship*, 6–29.

Wood, I., 'The end of Roman Britain: Continental evidence and parallels', in Lapidge and Dumville, eds, *Gildas*, 1–25.

Wood, I., *The Merovingian Kingdoms 450–751* (London and New York, 1994).

Wood, I., 'Northumbrians and the Franks in the age of Wilfrid', *Northern History* 31 (1995), 10–21.

Woolf, A., 'Pictish matriliny reconsidered', *Innes Review* 49 (1998), 147–67.

Woolf, A., 'The Verturian hegemony: a mirror in the north', in M. P. Brown and C. A. Farr eds, *Mercia: an Anglo-Saxon Kingdom in Europe* (London and New York, 2001), 106–11.

Woolf, A., 'The Britons: from Romans to barbarians', in H.-W. Goetz *et al.*, eds, *Regna and Gentes: the Relationship between late Antique and early Medieval peoples and Kingdoms in the Transformation of the Roman World* (Leiden, 2003), 345–80.

Woolf, A., 'Caedualla *Rex Brettonum* and the passing of the old north', *Northern History* 41 (2004), 5–24.

Woolf, A. 'Onuist son of Uurguist: *tyrannus carnifex* or a David for the Picts?', in
    D. Hill and M. Worthington, eds, *Æthelbald and Offa: two Eighth-century Kings of
    Mercia*, BAR British Series 383 (Oxford, 2005), 35–42.

Woolf, A., 'AU 729.2 and the last years of Nechtan mac Der-Ilei', *Scottish Historical
    Review* 85 (2006), 131–4.

Woolf, A., 'Dún Nechtain, Fortriu and the geography of the Picts', *Scottish Historical
    Review* 85 (2006), 182–201.

Woolf, A., 'Apartheid and economics in Anglo-Saxon England', in N. J. Higham, ed.,
    The Britons in Anglo-Saxon England (Woodbridge, 2007), 115–29.

Woolf, A., *From Pictland to Alba (789–1070)* (Edinburgh, 2007).

Woolf, A., 'Ancient kindred? Dál Riata and the Cruithin', unpublished conference
    paper.

Woolf, A., 'Early Historic Scotland', *A Short History of Scotland* (Edinburgh,
    forthcoming).

Woolliscroft, D. J. and B. Hoffmann, *Rome's First Frontier: the Flavian Occupation of
    Northern Scotland* (Stroud, 2006).

Wormald, P., '*Lex Scripta* and *Verbum Regis*: legislation and Germanic kingship, from
    Euric to Cnut', in Sawyer and Wood, eds, *Early Medieval Kingship*, 105–38.

Wright, R. P., 'Carpow and Caracalla', *Britannia* 5 (1974), 289–92.

Yeoman, P. A., 'Pilgrims to St Ethernan: the archaeology of an early saint of the Picts
    and Scots', in Crawford, ed., *Conversion and Christianity*, 75–91.

Yorke, B., *Kings and Kingdoms of Early Anglo-Saxon England* (London and New York,
    1990).

Ziegler, M., 'Artúr mac Aedan of Dalriada', *The Heroic Age* 1 (1999),
    http://www.mun.ca/mst/heroicage/issues/1/haaad.htm (last verified 16 June
    2007).

Ziegler, M., 'The politics of exile in early Northumbria', *The Heroic Age* 2 (1999),
    http://www.mun.ca/mst/heroicage/issues/2/ha2pen.htm (last verified 16 June
    2007).

Index